A People & A Nation

A HISTORY OF THE UNITED STATES

Volume I: To 1877

Eleventh Edition

Jane Kamensky
Harvard University

Carol Sheriff
College of William and Mary

David W. Blight
Yale University

Howard P. Chudacoff
Brown University

Fredrik Logevall
Harvard University

Beth Bailey
University of Kansas

Mary Beth Norton
Cornell University

CENGAGE

Australia • Brazil • Mexico • Singapore • United Kingdom • United States

Territorial Growth of the United States

CANADA

Lake Superior

MINNESOTA
1858

WISCONSIN
1848

Lake Michigan

Lake Huron

MICHIGAN
1837

Lake Ontario

Lake Erie

NEW YORK

St. Lawrence R.

MAINE
1820

VT.
1791

N.H.

MASS.

CONN.

R.I.

IOWA
1846

ILLINOIS
1818

INDIANA
1816

OHIO
1803

PENNSYLVANIA

NEW
JERSEY

MASON-DIXON LINE 1790

DELAWARE

MARYLAND

THIRTEEN COLONIES

MISSOURI
1821

KENTUCKY
1792

WEST
VIRGINIA
1863

VIRGINIA

THE ORIGINAL

THE ORIGINAL UNITED STATES
(By Treaty with Britain, 1783)

MISSOURI
COMPROMISE
LINE
36°30'N

2000

TENNESSEE
1796

NORTH
CAROLINA

ATLANTIC
OCEAN

ARKANSAS
1836

Mississippi R.

MISSISSIPPI
1817

ALABAMA
1819

SOUTH
CAROLINA

GEORGIA

LOUISIANA
1812

(Seized from Spain,
1810, 1813)

1820 Date of states admission to the Union

● Geographic center of population by decade

0   150   300 Km.

0   150   300 Mi.

FLORIDA
(By Treaty with
Spain, 1819)

FLORIDA
1845

Gulf of Mexico

BAHAMAS

CUBA

HAITI

DOMINICAN
REPUBLIC

PUERTO RICO
(Acquired from
Spain, 1898)

VIRGIN IS.
(Acquired from
Denmark, 1916–1917)

19°N

68°W

PUERTO RICO

VIRGIN
ISLANDS

18°N

0   25   50 Km.

0   25   50 Mi.

67°W

66°W

65°W

N

ALASKA
(U.S.)

GREENLAND
(DENMARK)

ICELAND

CANADA

UNI
KING

IRELAND

UNITED STATES

40°N

Bermuda
(U.K.)

ATLANTIC OCEAN

PORTUGAL

SP

Azores
(Port.)

MOROC

Midway Is.
(U.S.)

WESTERN
SAHARA
(MOROCCO)

Hawaiian Is.
(U.S.)

BAHAMAS

DOMINICAN REP.

MEXICO

CUBA

Virgin Is.
(U.S.)

20°N

MAURITANIA

JAMAICA

HAITI

Puerto Rico
(U.S.)

ST. KITTS AND NEVIS

ANTIGUA AND BARBUDA

CAPE
VERDE

SENEGAL

BELIZE

HONDURAS

DOMINICA

BARBADOS

GAMBIA

PACIFIC OCEAN

GUATEMALA

NICARAGUA

ST. LUCIA

GRENADA

ST. VINCENT AND
THE GRENADINES

GUINEA-BISSAU

GUINEA

EL SALVADOR

SIERRA
LEONE

IVOR
COAS

COSTA RICA

TRINIDAD AND TOBAGO

LIBERIA

GHA

PANAMA

VENEZUELA

GUYANA

FR. GUIANA
(FRANCE)

EQUATO

COLOMBIA

SURINAM

SÃO TOMÉ AN

Equator

Galapagos Is.
(Ecuador)

ECUADOR

0°

SAMOA

PERU

BRAZIL

French Polynesia
(France)

BOLIVIA

20°S

TONGA

PARAGUAY

Easter Is.
(Chile)

CHILE

URUGUAY

ARGENTINA

40°S

0   1,000   2,000 Km.

0   1,000   2,000 Mi.

Falkland Is.
(U.K.)

160°W   140°W   120°W   100°W   80°W   60°W   40°W   20°W

60°S

80°S

A People & A Nation, **Eleventh Edition, Volume I: To 1877**
Jane Kamensky /Carol Sheriff/David W. Blight/ Howard P. Chudacoff/ Fredrik Logevall/ Beth Bailey/Mary Beth Norton

Product Manager: Joseph Potvin

Senior Content Developer: Kate MacLean

Associate Content Developer: Claire Branman

Product Assistant: Alexandra Shore

Senior Marketing Manager: Valerie Hartman

Senior Content Project Manager: Carol Newman

Manufacturing Planner: Julio Esperas

IP Analyst: Alexandra Ricciardi

IP Project Manager: Betsy Hathaway

Production Service/Compositor: MPS Limited

Senior Art Director: Cate Rickard Barr

Text and Cover Designer: tani hasegawa, TT EYE.

Cover Image: *The Sargent Family,* 1800. Granger, NY—All rights reserved

For product information and technology assistance, contact us at **Cengage Customer & Sales Support, 1-800-354-9706**

For permission to use material from this text or product, submit all requests online at **www.cengage.com/permissions.** Further permissions questions can be emailed to **permissionrequest@cengage.com.**

Library of Congress Control Number: 2017955520

Student Edition:
ISBN: 978-1-337-40272-9

Loose-leaf Edition:
ISBN: 978-1-337-40490-7

Cengage
20 Channel Center Street
Boston, MA 02210
USA

Cengage is a leading provider of customized learning solutions with employees residing in nearly 40 different countries and sales in more than 125 countries around the world. Find your local representative at **www.cengage.com.**

Cengage products are represented in Canada by Nelson Education, Ltd.

To learn more about Cengage platforms and services, visit **www.cengage.com.**

To register or access your online learning solution or purchase materials for your course, visit **www.cengagebrain.com.**

Printed at CLDPC, USA, 02-19

TIC OCEAN

PACIFIC OCEAN

NORWAY
SWEDEN
FINLAND
ESTONIA
LATVIA
LITHUANIA
BELARUS
DEN.
GERMANY POLAND
CZ.
AUS.
SLK.
UKRAINE
SLN. CR.
HUNG.
MOLDOVA
B. H. SE.
ROMANIA
ITALY
Z.
BULGARIA
MO. MAC.
ALBANIA
GREECE
MALTA
TUNISIA
CYPRUS
LEBANON
ISRAEL
TURKEY
ARMENIA
SYRIA
IRAQ
JORDAN
KUWAIT
SAUDI
ARABIA
BAHRAIN
QATAR
UNITED
ARAB EMIRATES
OMAN

RUSSIA

KAZAKHSTAN

GEORGIA

UZBEKISTAN

AZERBAIJAN
TURKMENISTAN
KYRGYZSTAN
TAJIKISTAN
AFGHANISTAN
IRAN
PAKISTAN

MONGOLIA

N. KOREA
S. KOREA
JAPAN

PEOPLE'S REPUBLIC OF CHINA

NEPAL
BHUTAN
BANGLADESH
INDIA
MYANMAR
(BURMA)
LAOS
THAILAND
VIETNAM
CAMBODIA
(KAMPUCHEA)

Taiwan

Mariana
Islands
(U.S.)
Guam
(U.S.)

Wake I.
(U.S.)

MARSHALL
ISLANDS

RIA
LIBYA
EGYPT

NIGER
CHAD
SUDAN
ERITREA
YEMEN
DJIBOUTI
ETHIOPIA

BENIN
NIGERIA
CAMEROON
CENTRAL
AFRICAN REP.
UGANDA
KENYA
SOMALIA

SRI LANKA
MALDIVES
SINGAPORE
PHILIPPINES
BRUNEI
DARUSSALAM
MALAYSIA
PALAU

FEDERATED STATES
OF MICRONESIA

KIRIBATI

NEA
GABON
PE
F CONGO
RWANDA
DEM. REP.
OF CONGO
BURUNDI
TANZANIA
SEYCHELLES

INDIAN OCEAN

INDONESIA
TIMOR LESTE
PAPUA
NEW
GUINEA
SOLOMON IS.

NAURU

TUVALU

ANGOLA
ZAMBIA
MALAWI
COMOROS
MADAGASCAR
MAURITIUS

VANUATU

FIJI

NAMIBIA
ZIMBABWE
BOTSWANA
MOZAMBIQUE
SWAZILAND
SOUTH
AFRICA
LESOTHO

New Caledonia
(France)

AUSTRALIA

ABBREVIATIONS

AUS.	AUSTRIA
BEL.	BELGIUM
B. H.	BOSNIA AND HERZEGOVINA
CR.	CROATIA
CZ.	CZECH REPUBLIC
DEN.	DENMARK
HUNG.	HUNGARY
K.	KOSOVO
LUX.	LUXEMBOURG
MAC.	MACEDONIA
MO.	MONTENEGRO
NETH.	NETHERLANDS
SE.	SERBIA
SLK.	SLOVAKIA
SLN.	SLOVENIA
SWITZ.	SWITZERLAND

NEW
ZEALAND

20°E   40°E   60°E   80°E   100°E   120°E   140°E   160°E

NTARCTICA

BRIEF CONTENTS

CONTENTS

1 Three Old Worlds Create a New, 1492–1600   2

2 Europeans Colonize North America, 1600–1650   32

3 North America in the Atlantic World, 1650–1720   60

4 Becoming America? 1720–1760   88

5 The Ends of Empire, 1754–1774   118

6 American Revolutions, 1775–1783   146

7 Forging a Nation, 1783–1800   174

8 Defining the Nation, 1801–1823   208

9   The Rise of the South, 1815–1860   240

10   The Restless North, 1815–1860   272

11   The Contested West, 1815–1860   306

12   Politics and the Fate of the Union, 1824–1859   336

13 Transforming Fire: The Civil War, 1860–1865   370

14 Reconstruction: An Unfinished Revolution, 1865–1877 410

Appendix A-1

Index I-1

FEATURES

MAPS

FIGURES

TABLES

LINKS TO THE WORLD

LEGACY FOR A PEOPLE AND A NATION

VISUALIZING THE PAST

With this eleventh edition, *A People and A Nation* consolidates the last edition's broad structural changes, fine-tuning the streamlining and chapter combinations that made the text easier to assign over the course of an average academic semester. In this edition the authors introduced new interpretations, updated content to reflect recent research, and thought hard about what new features might engage our readers. This edition also more fully embraces the possibilities offered by digital platforms, as you will learn about in the MindTap description that follows later in this introduction.

A People and A Nation represents our continuing rediscovery of America's history—our evolving understandings of the people and the forces that have shaped the nation and our stories of the struggles, triumphs, and tragedies of America's past.

Key Themes in A People and A Nation

Published originally in 1982, A People and A Nation was the first U.S. history survey textbook to move beyond a political history to tell the story of the nation's people—the story of all its people—as well. That commitment remains. Our text encompasses the diversity of America's people and the changing texture of their everyday lives. The country's political narrative is here, too, as in previous editions. But as historical questions have evolved over the years and new authors have joined the textbook team, we have asked new questions about "a people" and "a nation." In our recent editions, we remind students that the "A People" and "A Nation" that appear in the book's title are neither timeless nor stable. European colonists and the land's indigenous inhabitants did not belong to this "nation" or work to create it, and Americans have struggled over the shape and meaning of their nation since its very beginning. The people about whom we write thought of themselves in various ways, and in ways that changed over time. Thus we emphasize not only the ongoing diversity of the nation's people, but their struggles, through time, over who belongs to that "people" and on what terms.

In *A People and A Nation,* the authors emphasize the changing global and transnational contexts within which the American colonies and the United States have acted. We pay attention to the economy, discussing the ways that an evolving market economy shaped the nation and the possibilities for its different peoples. We show how the meaning of identity—gender, race, class, sexuality, as well as region, religion, and family status—changes over time, and we find the nation's history in the mobility and contact and collision of its peoples. We discuss the role of the state and the expanding role and reach of the federal government; we pay attention to region and emphasize historical contests between federal power and local authority. We trace America's expansion and rise to unprecedented world power and examine its consequences. And we focus on the meaning of democracy and equality in American history, most particularly in tales of Americans' struggles for equal rights and social justice.

In *A People and A Nation*, we continue to challenge readers to think about the meaning of American history, not just to memorize facts. More than anything else, we want students to understand that the history of the American nation was not foreordained. Ours is a story of contingency. As, over time, people lived their day-to-day lives, made what choices they could, and fought for things they believed in, they helped to shape the future. What happened was not inevitable. Throughout the course of history, people faced difficult decisions, and those decisions mattered.

What's New in This Edition

Planning for the eleventh edition began at an authors' meeting near Cengage headquarters in Boston. Authors' meetings are always lively, and we discussed everything from recent scholarship and emerging trends in both U.S. and global history to the possibilities offered by digital platforms and the needs of the students who would be reading our work.

This edition continues to build on *A People and A Nation*'s hallmark themes, giving increased attention to the global perspective on American history that has characterized the book since its first edition. From the "Atlantic world" context of European colonies in North and South America to the discussion of international terrorism, the authors have incorporated the most recent globally oriented scholarship throughout the volume. We have stressed the incorporation of different peoples into the United States through territorial acquisition as well as through immigration. At the same time, we have integrated the discussion of such diversity into our narrative so as not to artificially isolate any group from the mainstream.

We have continued the practice of placing three probing questions at the end of each chapter's introduction to inspire and guide students' reading of the pages that follow. Additionally, focus questions and key terms have been added to this edition. The focus questions appear beneath each section title within every chapter to further support students in their reading and comprehension of the material. Key terms appear near the first mention of a term and are placed throughout each chapter.

Chapter-level Changes for the Eleventh Edition

For this edition, the authors reexamined every sentence, interpretation, map, chart, illustration, and caption, refined the narrative, presented new examples, updated bibliographies, and incorporated the best new scholarship. What follows here is a description of chapter-level changes for the eleventh edition:

1. **Chapter 2: Europeans Colonize North America, 1600–1650**
   - New chapter-opening vignette on an episode of interracial violence in 1630 New England

2. **Chapter 3: North America in the Atlantic World, 1650–1720**
   - New *Legacy for a People and a Nation* feature: "Fictions of Salem: Witch-Hunting in the American Grain"

3. **Chapter 4: Becoming America? 1720–1760**
   - Increased attention to Canadian maritime provinces in King George's War

4. **Chapter 5: The Ends of Empire, 1754–1774**
   - New information on Caribbean colonies' response to the Stamp Act and other imperial tax laws from rare pamphlets published in Barbados
   - New primary source material about the Stamp Act repeal and Boston Massacre trials
   - The *Legacy for a People and a Nation* feature, "Women's Political Action," has been updated to reflect the 2016 presidential election

5. **Chapter 6: American Revolutions, 1775–1783**
   - Increased attention to the Spanish empire and the war in the Gulf of Mexico
   - More attention is given to African American soldiers in the American Revolution
   - New *Visualizing the Past* feature: "A British View of the Colonial Army"

6. **Chapter 8: Defining the Nation, 1801–1823**
   - New *Legacy for a People and a Nation* feature: "The Star-Spangled Banner"

7. **Chapter 9: The Rise of the South, 1815–1860**
   - New section on slavery and capitalism
   - New material on the domestic slave trade
   - Additional information on slave religion
   - Additions to discussion of "planter paternalism"
   - Updated *Legacy for a People and a Nation* feature on reparations

8. **Chapter 11: The Contested West, 1815–1860**
   - New topic ("The Mexican-United States Border") for *Legacy for A People and a Nation* feature

9. **Chapter 12: Politics and the Fate of the Union, 1824–1859**
   - Includes additional information about states' rights under nullification
   - Features a revised map for the Mexican War
   - Added material on Fremont, California, and the coming of the Mexican War

- New scholarship on the underground railroad in New York
- Increased attention to voter turnout in the Jackson era
- The *Legacy for a People and a Nation* feature on coalition politics has been updated

10. **Chapter 13: Transforming Fire: The Civil War, 1860–1865**
    - Chapter-opening vignette has been revised
    - Clarified discussion of secession crisis
    - Added discussion of Native Americans fighting in the Civil War
    - New discussion of the importance of the "Union Cause" to Northerners

11. **Chapter 14: Reconstruction: An Unfinished Revolution, 1865–1877**
    - Revised discussion of Radical Republican vision of Reconstruction
    - New scholarship on the military occupation of the South
    - New scholarship on the movement West
    - Revised discussion of railroad growth and expansion
    - Updated *Legacy for a People and a Nation* feature on the Lost Cause

Format for Each Chapter

Opening Vignette

Each chapter opens with a brief story about a person, place, or event and includes an image related to the story. The stories highlight specific events with historical significance while bringing attention to the larger themes in U.S. History during that period.

Focus Questions

Each chapter section is accompanied by a set of focus questions that guide students in absorbing and interpreting the information in the section that follows. This is a new pedagogical feature added in this edition to help students retain the information they are learning as they move through the book.

Chapter Features: *Legacies, Links to the World*, and *Visualizing the Past*

The following three features— *Legacy for* A People and a Nation, *Links to the World*, and *Visualizing the Past*—are included in each chapter of *A People and A Nation*, eleventh edition:. These features all illustrate key themes of the text and give students alternative ways to experience historical content.

Legacy for A People and A Nation features appear toward the end of each chapter and offer compelling and timely answers to students who question the relevance of historical study by exploring the historical roots of contemporary topics. New *Legacies* in this edition include "Fictions of Salem: Witch-Hunting in the American Grain," "The Star-Spangled Banner," and "The Mexican-United States Border."

Links to the World features examine ties between America (and Americans) and the rest of the world. These brief essays detail the often little-known connections between developments here and abroad, vividly demonstrating that the geographical region that is now the United States has never been isolated from other peoples and countries. Essay topics range broadly over economic, political, social, technological, medical, and cultural history, and the feature appears near relevant discussions in each chapter. This edition includes new *Links* on anthropologist Margaret Mead and on Sputnik and American education. Each *Link* feature highlights global interconnections with unusual and lively examples that will both intrigue and inform students.

Visualizing the Past features offer striking images along with brief discussions intended to help students analyze the images as historical sources and to understand how visual materials can reveal aspects of America's story that otherwise might remain unknown. New to this edition is "A British View of the Colonial Army" in Chapter 6.

Summary

The core text of each chapter ends with a brief summary that helps students synthesize what they have just read and directs students to see long-term trends and recurring themes that appear across chapters.

Suggested Readings

A list of secondary sources appears at the end of each chapter for students and instructors who want to dig deeper into the content of the chapter.

Key Terms

Within each chapter, terms are boldfaced for students' attention with brief definitions appearing on the same page. Terms highlighted include concepts, laws, treaties, movements and organizations, legal cases, and battles.

MindTap for *A People and A Nation*

- MindTap 2-semester Instant Access Code: ISBN 9781337402750

- MindTap 2-semester Printed Access Card: ISBN - 9781337402767

- MindTap 1-semester Instant Access Code: ISBN 9781337404686

- MindTap 1-semester Printed Access Card: ISBN 9781337404693

MindTap for *A People and A Nation* is a flexible online learning platform that provides students with an immersive learning experience to build and foster critical thinking skills. Through a carefully designed chapter-based learning path, MindTap allows students to easily identify learning objectives; draw connections and improve writing skills by 1) completing unit-level essay assignments; 2) reading short, manageable sections from the ebook: 3) and testing their content knowledge with map-based critical thinking questions.

MindTap allows instructors to customize their content, providing tools that seamlessly integrate YouTube clips, outside websites, and personal content directly into the learning path. Instructors can assign additional primary source content through the Instructor Resource Center and Questia primary- and secondary-source databases that house thousands of peer-reviewed journals, newspapers, magazines, and full-length books.

The additional content available in MindTap mirrors and complements the authors' narrative, but also includes primary-source content and assessments not found in the printed text. To learn more, ask your Cengage sales representative to demo it for you—or go to www.Cengage .com/MindTap.

Supplements for *A People and A Nation*

- **Instructor's Companion Website.** The Instructor's Companion Website, accessed through the Instructor Resource Center (login.cengage.com), houses all of the supplemental materials you can use for your course. This includes a Test Bank, Instructor's Manual, and PowerPoint Lecture Presentations. The Test Bank, offered in Microsoft® Word® and Cognero® formats, contains multiple-choice, true-or-false, and essay questions for each chapter. Cognero® is a flexible, online system that allows you to author, edit, and manage test bank content for *A People and a Nation*, 11e. Create multiple test versions instantly and deliver through your LMS from your classroom, or wherever you may be, with no special installs or downloads required. The Instructor's Resource Manual includes chapter summaries, and outlines, learning objectives, suggested lecture topics, discussion questions class activities, and suggestions for additional films to watch. Finally, the PowerPoint Lectures are ADA-compliant slides collate the key takeaways from the chapter in concise visual formats perfect for in-class presentations or for student review.

- **Cengagebrain.com.** Save your students time and money. Direct them to www.cengagebrain.com for a choice in formats and savings and a better chance to succeed in your class. Cengagebrain.com, Cengage's online store, is a single destination for more than 10,000 new textbooks, eTextbooks, eChapters, study tools, and audio supplements. Students have the freedom to purchase à la carte exactly what they need when they need it. Students can save 50 percent on the electronic textbook and can purchase an individual eChapter for as little as $1.99.

- *Doing History: Research and Writing in the Digital Age,* 2e ISBN: 9781133587880 Prepared by Michael J. Galgano, J. Chris Arndt, and Raymond M. Hyser of

James Madison University. Whether you're starting down the path as a history major or simply looking for a straightforward, systematic guide to writing a successful paper, this text's "soup to nuts" approach to researching and writing about history addresses every step of the process: locating your sources, gathering information, writing and citing according to various style guides, and avoiding plagiarism.

■ *Writing for College History,* 1e ISBN: 9780618306039 Prepared by Robert M. Frakes of Clarion University. This brief handbook for survey courses in American, western, and world history guides students through the various types of writing assignments they may encounter in a history class. Providing examples of student writing and candid assessments of student work, this text focuses on the rules and conventions of writing for the college history course

■ *The Modern Researcher,* 6e ISBN: 9780495318705 Prepared by Jacques Barzun and Henry F. Graff of Columbia University. This classic introduction to the techniques of research and the art of expression thoroughly covers every aspect of research, from the selection of a topic through the gathering of materials, analysis, writing, revision, and publication of findings. They present the process not as a set of rules but through actual cases that put the subtleties of research in a useful context. Part One covers the principles and methods of research; Part Two covers writing, speaking, and getting one's work published.

■ *Reader Program.* Cengage publishes a number of readers. Some contain exclusively primary sources, others are devoted to essays and secondary sources, and still others provide a combination of primary and secondary sources. All of these readers are designed to guide students through the process of historical inquiry. Visit www.cengage.com/history for a complete list of readers.

■ *Custom Options.* Nobody knows your students like you, so why not give them a text that is tailor-fit to their needs? Cengage offers custom solutions for your course—whether it's making a small modification to *A People and a Nation,* 11e, to match your syllabus or combining multiple sources to create something truly unique. Contact your Cengage representative to explore custom solutions for your course.

Acknowledgments

The authors would like to thank Timothy Cole, David Farber, Mark Guerci, Anna Daileader Sheriff, and Benjamin Daileader Sheriff for their assistance with the preparation of this edition.

We also want to thank the many instructors who have adopted *APAN* over the years. We have been very grateful for the comments from the historian reviewers who read drafts of our chapters. Their suggestions, corrections, and pleas helped guide us through this revision. We could not include all of their recommendations, but the book is better for our having heeded most of their advice. We heartily thank:

Dawn Cioffoletti, *Florida Gulf Coast University*
Charles Cox, *Bridgewater State College*
Mary Daggett, *San Jacinto College - Central*
Jesse Esparza, *Texas Southern University*
Miriam Forman-Brunell, *University of Missouri, Kansas City*
Amy Forss, *Metropolitan Community College – South*
Devethia Guillory, *Lonestar College - North Harris*
Gordon Harvey, *Jacksonville State University*
Kathleen Gorman, *Minnesota State University, Mankato*
Jennifer Gross, *Jacksonville State University*
Donna Hoffa, *Wayne County Community College*
Richard Hughes, *Illinois State University*
Lesley Kauffman, *San Jacinto College – Central*
Karen Kossie-Chernyshev, *Texas Southern University*
Mary Hovanec, *Cuyahoga Community College*
Yu Shen, *Indiana University - Southeast*
Michael Swope, *Wayne County Community College*
Nancy Young, *University of Houston*

The authors thank the helpful Cengage people who designed, edited, produced, and nourished this book. Many thanks to Joseph Potvin, product manager; Kate MacLean, senior content developer; Claire Branman, associate content developer; Pembroke Herbert, photo researcher; Charlotte Miller, art editor; and Carol Newman, senior content project manager.

J. K.
C. S.
D. B.
H. C.
F. L.
B. B.
M. B. N.

Jane Kamensky

Born in New York City, Jane Kamensky earned her BA (1985) and PhD (1993) from Yale University. She is now Professor of History at Harvard University and the Pforzheimer Foundation Director of the Schlesinger Library on the History of Women in America. She is the author of *A Revolution in Color: The World of John Singleton Copley* (2016), winner of the New York Historical Society's Barbara and David Zalaznick Book Prize in American History and the Annibel Jenkins Biography Prize of the American Society for Eighteenth-Century Studies; *The Exchange Artist: A Tale of High-Flying Speculation and America's First Banking Collapse* (2008), a finalist for the 2009 George Washington Book Prize; *Governing the Tongue: The Politics of Speech in Early New England* (1997); and *The Colonial Mosaic: American Women, 1600–1760* (1995); and the coeditor of *The Oxford Handbook of the American Revolution* (2012). With Jill Lepore, she is the coauthor of the historical novel *Blindspot* (2008), a *New York Times* editor's choice and *Boston Globe* bestseller. In 1999, she and Lepore also cofounded *Common-place* (www.common-place.org), which remains a leading online journal of early American history and life. Jane has also served on the editorial boards of the *American Historical Review*, the *Journal of American History*, and the *Journal of the Early Republic*; as well as on the Council of the American Antiquarian Society, the Executive Board of the Organization of American Historians, and as a Commissioner of the Smithsonian's National Portrait Gallery. Called on frequently as an advisor to public history projects, she has appeared on PBS, C-SPAN, the History Channel, and NPR, among other media outlets. Jane, who was awarded two university-wide teaching prizes in her previous position at Brandeis, has won numerous major grants and fellowships to support her scholarship.

Carol Sheriff

Born in Washington, D.C., and raised in Bethesda, Maryland, Carol Sheriff received her BA from Wesleyan University (1985) and her PhD from Yale University (1993). Since 1993, she has taught history at the College of William and Mary, where she has won the Thomas Jefferson Teaching Award; the Alumni Teaching Fellowship Award; the University Professorship for Teaching Excellence; The Class of 2013 Distinguished Professorship for Excellence in Scholarship, Teaching, and Service; and the Arts and Sciences Award for Teaching Excellence. Her publications include *The Artificial River: The Erie Canal and the Paradox of Progress* (1996), which won the Dixon Ryan Fox Award from the New York State Historical Association and the Award for Excellence in Research from the New York State Archives, and *A People at War: Civilians and Soldiers in America's Civil War, 1854–1877* (with Scott Reynolds Nelson, 2007). In 2012, she won the John T. Hubbell Prize from *Civil War History* for her article on the state-commissioned Virginia history textbooks of the 1950s, and the controversies their portrayals of the Civil War era provoked in ensuing decades. Carol has written sections of a teaching manual for the New York State history curriculum, given presentations at Teaching American History grant projects, consulted on an exhibit for the Rochester Museum and Science Center, and appeared in The History Channel's Modern Marvels show on the Erie Canal. She worked on several public-history projects marking the sesquicentennial of the Civil War, and is involved in public and scholarly projects to commemorate the Erie Canal's bicentennial. At William and Mary, she teaches the U.S. history survey as well as upper-level classes on the Early Republic, the Civil War Era, and the American West.

David W. Blight

Born in Flint, Michigan, David W. Blight received his BA from Michigan State University (1971) and his PhD from the University of Wisconsin (1985). He is now professor of history and director of the Gilder Lehrman Center for the Study of Slavery, Resistance, and Abolition at Yale University. For the first seven years of his career, David was a public high school teacher in Flint. He has written *Frederick Douglass's Civil War* (1989) and *Race and Reunion: The Civil War in American Memory, 1863–1915* (2000), which received eight awards, including the Bancroft Prize, the Frederick Douglass Prize, the Abraham Lincoln Prize, and four prizes awarded by the Organization of American Historians. His most recent books are a biography of Frederick Douglass (forthcoming in 2018); *American Oracle: The Civil War in the Civil Rights Era* (2011) and *A Slave No More: The Emancipation of John Washington and Wallace Turnage* (2007), which won three book prizes. His edited works include *When This Cruel War Is Over: The Civil War Letters of Charles Harvey Brewster* (1992), *Narrative of the Life of Frederick Douglass* (1993), W. E. B. Du Bois, *The Souls of Black Folk* (with Robert Gooding Williams, 1997), *Union and Emancipation* (with Brooks Simpson, 1997), and *Caleb Bingham, The Columbian Orator* (1997). David's essays have appeared in the *Journal of American History* and *Civil War History*, among others. A consultant to several documentary films, David appeared in the 1998 PBS series, *Africans in America*. David also teaches summer seminars for secondary school teachers, as well as for park rangers and historians of the National Park Service. He has served on the Executive Board of the Organization of American Historians, and in 2012, he was elected to the American Academy of Arts and Sciences. In 2013–2014 David was Pitt Professor of American History and Institutions at the University of Cambridge in the United Kingdom.

Howard P. Chudacoff

Howard P. Chudacoff, the George L. Littlefield Professor of American History and Professor of Urban Studies at Brown University, was born in Omaha, Nebraska. He earned his AB (1965) and PhD (1969) from the University of Chicago. He has written *Mobile Americans* (1972), *How Old Are You?* (1989), *The Age of the Bachelor* (1999), *The Evolution of American Urban Society* (with Judith Smith, 2004), and *Children at Play: An American History* (2007) and *Changing the Playbook: How Power, Profit, and Politics Transformed College Sports* (2015). He has also coedited (with Peter Baldwin) *Major Problems in American Urban History* (2004). His articles have appeared in such journals as the *Journal of Family History, Reviews in American History*, and *Journal of American History*. At Brown University, Howard has cochaired the American Civilization Program and chaired the Department of History, and served as Brown's faculty representative to the NCAA. He has also served on the board of directors of the Urban History Association and the editorial board of *The National Journal of Play*. The National Endowment for the Humanities, Ford Foundation, and Rockefeller Foundation have given him awards to advance his scholarship.

Fredrik Logevall

A native of Stockholm, Sweden, Fredrik Logevall is Laurence D. Belfer Professor of International Affairs at Harvard University, where he holds appointments in the Department of History and the Kennedy School of Government. He received his BA from Simon Fraser University (1986) and his PhD from Yale University (1993). His most recent book is *Embers of War: The Fall of an Empire and the Making of America's Vietnam* (2012), which won the Pulitzer Prize in History and the Francis Parkman Prize, and which was named a best book of the year by the *Washington Post* and the *Christian Science Monitor*. His other publications include *Choosing War* (1999), which won three prizes, including the Warren F. Kuehl Book Prize from the Society for Historians of American Foreign Relations (SHAFR); *America's Cold War: The Politics of Insecurity* (with Campbell Craig; 2009); *The Origins of the Vietnam War* (2001); *Terrorism and 9/11: A Reader* (2002); and, as coeditor, *The First Vietnam War: Colonial Conflict and Cold War Crisis* (2007); and *Nixon and the World: American Foreign Relations, 1969–1977* (2008). Fred is a past recipient of the Stuart L. Bernath article, book, and lecture prizes from SHAFR, and a past member of the Cornell University Press faculty board. He serves on numerous editorial advisory boards. A past president of SHAFR, Fred is a member of the Society of American Historians and the Council of Foreign Relations.

Beth Bailey

Born in Atlanta, Georgia, Beth Bailey received her BA from Northwestern University (1979) and her PhD from the University of Chicago (1986). She is now Foundation Distinguished Professor of History and director of the Center for Military, War, and Society Studies at the University of Kansas. Beth served as the coordinating author for the tenth and eleventh editions of *A People and A Nation*. She is the author of *America's Army: Making the All-Volunteer Force* (2009), which won the Army Historical Foundation's Distinguished Writing Award; *The Columbia Companion to America in the 1960s* (with David Farber, 2001); *Sex in the Heartland* (1999); *The First Strange Place: The Alchemy of Race and Sex in WWII Hawaii* (with David Farber, 1992); and *From Front Porch to Back Seat: Courtship in 20th Century America* (1988). She also co-edited *Understanding the U.S. Wars in Iraq and Afghanistan* (2015); *America in the Seventies* (2004); and the reader *A History of Our Time* (multiple editions). Beth has lectured in Australia, Indonesia, France, Germany, the Netherlands, Great Britain, Japan, Saudi Arabia, Lebanon, and China. She is a trustee for the Society of Military History and was appointed by the Secretary of the Army to the Department of the Army Historical Advisory Committee. Beth has received several major grants or fellowships in support of her research. She teaches courses on the history of gender and sexuality and on U.S. Military, War, and Society.

Mary Beth Norton

Born in Ann Arbor, Michigan, Mary Beth Norton received her BA from the University of Michigan (1964) and her PhD from Harvard University (1969). She is the Mary Donlon Alger Professor of American History at Cornell University. Her dissertation won the Allan Nevins Prize. She has written *The British-Americans* (1972); *Liberty's Daughters* (1980, 1996); *Founding Mothers & Fathers* (1996), which was one of three finalists for the 1997 Pulitzer Prize in History; and *In the Devil's Snare* (2002), one of five finalists for the 2003 *L.A. Times* Book Prize in History and won the English-Speaking Union's Ambassador Book Award in American Studies for 2003. Her most recent book is *Separated by Their Sex* (2011). She has coedited three volumes on American women's history. She was also general editor of the *American Historical Association's Guide to Historical Literature* (1995). Her articles have appeared in such journals as the *American Historical Review, William and Mary Quarterly*, and *Journal of Women's History*. Mary Beth has served as president of the American Historical Association and the Berkshire Conference of Women Historians, as vice president for research of the American Historical Association, and as a presidential appointee to the National Council on the Humanities. She has appeared on Book TV, the History and Discovery Channels, PBS, and NBC as a commentator on Early American history, and she has lectured frequently to high school teachers. She has received four honorary degrees and is an elected member of both the American Academy of Arts and Sciences and the American Philosophical Society. She has held fellowships from the National Endowment for the Humanities; the Guggenheim, Rockefeller, and Starr Foundations; and the Henry E. Huntington Library. In 2005–2006, she was the Pitt Professor of American History and Institutions at the University of Cambridge and Newnham College.

A People & A Nation

Three Old Worlds Create a New, 1492–1600

ycpolínhq̃ mexuca

A generation after Columbus crossed the Atlantic, a Spanish soldier named Hernán Cortés traded words with the ruler of the Aztec empire. Motecuhzoma II was among the most powerful men in the Americas (as Europeans had recently named their "new" world). Thousands of loyal courtiers accompanied him to the gates of Tenochtitlán, the capital, one of the largest cities in the world. Cortés, his Spanish troops, and their Native allies approached on horseback, flying the flag of Charles V, the king of Spain and Holy Roman Emperor, one of the most powerful men in the "old" world. The conquistador and the Aztec ruler bowed to each other, and spoke. "Montezuma bade him welcome," recalled Bernal Díaz del Castillo, a soldier on the expedition. "There is nothing to fear," Cortés told his host. "We have come to your house in Mexico as friends."

This mixture of ceremony, half-truths, and outright lies was among the first exchanges between two great civilizations from two sides of a great ocean. It was not an easy conversation to have. Motecuhzoma spoke Nahuatl and had never heard Spanish; Cortés spoke Spanish and knew no Nahuatl. (The Spanish could not even pronounce the Aztec emperor's name, garbling "Motecuhzoma" as "Montezuma.") But in fact the conversation between Cortés and Motecuhzoma was not a dialogue but a three-way exchange. As Bernal Díaz explains, Cortés addressed the Aztec emperor "through the mouth of Doña Marina."

Who was Doña Marina? Born at the eastern edge of Motecuhzoma's dominion around the year 1500, she grew up at the margins of Aztec and Maya territories, worlds in motion and often at war. Her parents were Nahuatl-speaking nobles. The name they gave her is lost to history. As a child,

◀ Perched on a throne and wearing elaborate plumes in his hat, Cortès accepts the surrender of the Cuauthemoc in August 1521. Seated behind him in traditional dress, Doña Marina translates the negotiation, with gestures that exactly mirror his. The image, from a mural created by Tlaxcalan artists in the 1550s, shows the complex role of the interpreter in the meeting of worlds. AKG Images

Chronology

13,000–10,000 BCE	■ Paleo-Indians migrate from Siberia to western North America, some by boat and some across the Beringia land bridge
7000 BCE	■ Cultivation of food crops begins in America
ca. 2000 BCE	■ Olmec civilization appears
ca. 300–600 CE	■ Height of influence of Teotihuacán
ca. 600–900 CE	■ Classic Mayan civilization
1000 CE	■ Ancient Pueblos build settlements in modern states of Arizona and New Mexico
	■ Bantu-speaking peoples spread across much of southern Africa
1001	■ Norse establish settlement in "Vinland"
1050–1250	■ Height of influence of Cahokia
	■ Prevalence of Mississippian culture in modern midwestern and southeastern United States
14th century	■ Aztec rise to power
Early 15th century	■ Portuguese establish trading posts in North Africa
1450s–80s	■ Portuguese colonize islands in the Mediterranean Atlantic
1477	■ Marco Polo's *Travels* describes China
1492	■ Columbus reaches Bahamas
1494	■ Treaty of Tordesillas divides land claims in Africa, India, and South America between Spain and Portugal
1497	■ Cabot reaches North America
1499	■ Amerigo Vespucci explores South American coast
1513	■ Ponce de León explores Florida
1518–30	■ Smallpox epidemic devastates indigenous populations of West Indies and Central and South America
1519	■ Cortés invades Mexico
1521	■ Aztec Empire falls to Spaniards
1524	■ Verrazzano sails along Atlantic coast of North America
1534–35	■ Cartier explores St. Lawrence River
1539–42	■ De Soto explores southeastern North America
1540–42	■ Coronado explores southwestern North America
1587–90	■ Raleigh's Roanoke colony vanishes
1588	■ Harriot publishes *A Briefe and True Report of the New Found Land of Virginia*
	■ English defeat of the Spanish Armada

she was either stolen from her family or given by them to indigenous slave traders. She wound up in the Gulf Coast town of Tabasco, in the household of a Maya cacique. There, in addition to her native Nahuatl, she learned Yucatec, the local strain of the Mayan language. She spoke both tongues well when she encountered the Spanish, who brought yet a third civilization into her changing world in the spring of 1519.

The leaders of Tabasco showered Cortés with tribute, offerings they hoped would persuade the Spanish to continue west, into the heart of their enemies' territory. In addition to gold and cloth, the caciques gave the invaders twenty Native women. The young bilingual slave was one of them. The invaders baptized her under the Christian name "Marina."

Marina learned Spanish quickly, and her fluency in this third language greatly increased her value to the would-be conquerors. As Cortés and his troops progressed inland, Marina's way with words proved as vital to the success of the expedition as any other weapon they carried. Díaz called her "a person of the greatest importance." Cortés, reluctant to share credit for his triumphs, rarely mentioned her in his letters. But she bore him a son, Martín. Sometime before her death in 1527 or 1528, Marina married another Spanish officer.

A speaker of Nahuatl, Yucatec, and Spanish; the mother of one of the first *mestizo* or mixed-race children; the wife of a conquistador: Marina was a young woman in whom worlds met and mingled. The Spanish signaled their respect by addressing her as "Doña," meaning lady. Nahuatl speakers rendered *Marina* as *Malintzin*, using the suffix *–tzin* to denote her high status. Spaniards stumbled over the Nahuatl *Malintzin* and often called her *La Malinche*: a triple name, from a double mistranslation.

The legacy of Doña Marina/Malintzin/La Malinche remains as ambiguous as her name. Her fluency helped the invaders to triumph—a catastrophe for the Aztecs and other indigenous peoples. Their descendants consider Doña Marina their foremother and their betrayer, at once a victim and a perpetrator of the Spanish conquest. Today in Mexico, the word *malanchista* is a grave insult, equivalent to "collaborator" or even "traitor." Though she lived for less than thirty years, nearly half a millennium ago, Marina continues to embody the ambiguities of colonial American history, in which power was shifting and contested, and much was lost in translation.

Experience an interactive version of this story in MindTap®.

What happens when worlds collide? For thousands of years before 1492, human societies in the Americas developed in complex relation to each other, yet in isolation from the rest of the world. The era that began in the Christian fifteenth century brought that long-standing isolation to an end. As Europeans sought treasure and trade, peoples from two sides of the globe came into regular contact for the first time. Their interactions involved curiosity and confusion, trade and theft, enslavement and endurance. All were profoundly changed.

By the time Doña Marina held Cortés's words in her mouth, the age of European expansion and colonization was already under way. Over the next 350 years, Europeans would spread their influence across the globe. The history of the tiny colonies that became the United States must be seen in this broad context of European exploration and exploitation, of Native resistance, and of African enslavement and survival. Even as Europeans slowly achieved dominance, their fates continued to be shaped by the strategies of Americans and Africans. In the Americas of the fifteenth and sixteenth centuries, three old worlds came together to produce a new.

The continents that European sailors reached in the late fifteenth century had their own histories, internal struggles that the intruders sometimes exploited and often ignored. The indigenous residents of what came to be called *the Americas* were the world's most skillful plant breeders; they developed crops more nutritious and productive than those grown in Europe, Asia, or Africa. They had invented systems of writing and mathematics, and created more accurate calendars than those used on the other side of the Atlantic. In the Americas, as in Europe, societies rose and fell as leaders succeeded or failed to expand their power. But the arrival of Europeans altered the Americans' struggles with one another, just as the colonization of the Americas repeatedly reshaped the European balance of powers.

After 1400, European nations not only warred on their own continent but also tried to acquire valuable colonies and trading posts elsewhere in the world. Initially interested primarily in Asia and Africa, Europeans eventually focused mostly on the Americas. Their designs changed the course of history on four continents.

"In the beginning, all the world was America," wrote the English philosopher John Locke at the end of the seventeenth century. But in fact, America wasn't "America" until Europeans renamed the ancient homelands of hundreds of nations after one of their own explorers. The continent was not innocent, empty, and waiting, as Locke implied, but densely peopled and engaged in its own complex history. The collision of old and new worlds changed that history. New opportunities for some meant new risks for others. Every conquest contained a defeat. Every new place name was layered upon an older history. And a great deal was lost in translation.

■ *What were the key characteristics of the three worlds that met in the Americas?*

■ *What impacts did their encounter have on each of them?*

■ *What were the crucial initial developments in that encounter?*

1-1 American Societies

▶ **How were the Americas settled?**

▶ **How did the first Americans—the Paleo-Indians—adapt to their environment?**

▶ **How did Native peoples who began to domesticate and cultivate food crops develop socially and culturally?**

Human beings originated on the continent of Africa, where hominid remains about 3 million years old have been found in what is now Ethiopia. Over many millennia, the growing population slowly dispersed to the other continents. Because the climate was then far colder than it is now, much of the earth's water was concentrated in huge rivers of ice called glaciers. Sea levels were accordingly lower, and landmasses covered a larger proportion of the earth's surface than they do today. Scholars long believed that the Clovis people, Siberians who were among the earliest inhabitants of the Americas, crossed a land bridge known as Beringia (at the site of the Bering Strait) approximately twelve thousand to fourteen thousand years ago. Yet striking new archaeological discoveries in both North and South America suggest that parts of the Americas may have been settled significantly earlier, perhaps by seafarers. Some geneticists now theorize that three successive waves of migrants began at least thirty thousand years ago. About 12,500 years ago, when the climate warmed and sea levels rose, Americans were separated from the peoples living on the connected continents of Asia, Africa, and Europe.

1-1a Ancient America

The first Americans, now called **Paleo-Indians**, were nomadic hunters of game and gatherers of plants. They spread throughout North and South America, probably moving as bands composed of extended families. By about 11,500 years ago, the Paleo-Indians were making fine stone projectile points, which they attached to spears and used to kill and butcher bison (buffalo), woolly mammoths, and other large mammals. As the Ice Age ended and the human population increased, the large American mammals except the bison disappeared. Scholars disagree about whether overhunting or the change in climate caused

Paleo-Indians The earliest peoples of the Americas.

their extinction. In either case, deprived of their primary source of meat, Paleo-Indians found new ways to survive.

By approximately nine thousand years ago, the residents of what is now central Mexico began to cultivate food crops, especially maize (corn), squash, beans, avocados, and peppers. In the Andes Mountains of South America, people started to grow potatoes. As knowledge of agricultural techniques improved and spread through the Americas, vegetables and maize proved a more reliable source of food than hunting and gathering. Except in the harshest climates, most Paleo-Indians started to stay longer in one place, so that they could tend fields regularly. Some established permanent settlements; others moved several times a year among fixed sites. They used controlled burning to clear forests, which created cultivable lands by killing trees and fertilizing the soil with ashes, and also opened meadows that attracted deer and other wildlife. Although they traded such items as shells, flint, salt, and copper, no society became dependent on another group for items vital to its survival.

Wherever agriculture dominated the economy, complex civilizations flourished. Such societies, assured of steady supplies of grains and vegetables, no longer had to devote all their energies to procuring sufficient food. Instead, they were able to accumulate wealth, trade with other groups, produce ornamental objects, and create rituals and ceremonies to cement and transmit their cultures. In North America, the successful cultivation of nutritious crops, especially maize, beans, and squash, seems to have led to the growth and development of all the major civilizations: first the large city-states of Mesoamerica (modern Mexico and Guatemala) and then the urban clusters known collectively as the Mississippian culture and located in the present-day United States. Each of these societies reached its height of population and influence only after achieving success in agriculture. Each later declined and collapsed after reaching the limits of its food supply, with dire political and military consequences.

1-1b Mesoamerican Civilizations

Archaeologists and historians know little about the first major Mesoamerican civilization, the Olmecs, who about four thousand years ago lived near the Gulf of Mexico in cities dominated by temple pyramids. The Mayas and Teotihuacán, which developed approximately two thousand years later, are better recorded. Teotihuacán, founded in the Valley of Mexico about 300 BCE (Before the Common Era), eventually became one of the largest urban areas in the world, housing perhaps 100,000 people in the fifth century CE (Common Era). Teotihuacán's commercial network extended hundreds of miles in all directions; many peoples prized its obsidian (a green volcanic glass), used to make fine knives and mirrors. Pilgrims traveled long distances to visit Teotihuacán's immense pyramids and the great temple of Quetzalcoatl—the feathered serpent, primary god of central Mexico.

On the Yucatan Peninsula, in today's eastern Mexico, the Mayas built urban centers boasting tall pyramids and temples. They studied astronomy and created an elaborate writing system. Their city-states, though, engaged in near-constant battle with one another, much as Europeans did at the same time. Warfare and an inadequate food supply caused the collapse of the most powerful cities by 900 CE, thus ending the classic era of Mayan civilization. When the Spaniards arrived 600 years later, only a few remnants of the once-mighty society remained, in places like the town where Doña Marina was enslaved.

1-1c Pueblos and Mississippians

Ancient Native societies in what is now the United States learned to grow maize, squash, and beans from Mesoamericans, but the nature of the relationship among the various cultures remains unknown. (No Mesoamerican artifacts have been found north of the Rio Grande, but some items resembling Mississippian objects have been excavated in northern Mexico, suggesting the presence of trade routes.) The Hohokam, Mogollon, and ancient Pueblo peoples of the modern states of Arizona and New Mexico subsisted by combining hunting and gathering with agriculture in an arid region. Hohokam villagers constructed extensive irrigation systems, occasionally relocating settlements when water supplies failed. Between 900 and 1150 CE in Chaco Canyon, the Pueblos built fourteen "Great Houses," multistory stone structures averaging two hundred rooms. The canyon, at the juncture of perhaps four hundred miles of roads, served as a major regional trading and processing center for turquoise, used then as now to create beautiful ornamental objects. Yet the sparse and unpredictable rainfall eventually caused the Chacoans to migrate to other sites.

At almost the same time, the unrelated Mississippian culture flourished in what is now the midwestern and southeastern United States. Relying largely on maize, squash, nuts, pumpkins, and venison for food, the Mississippians lived in substantial settlements organized hierarchically. The largest of their urban centers was the **City of the Sun** (now called **Cahokia**), which was located near modern St. Louis. Located on rich farmland near the confluence of the Illinois, Missouri, and Mississippi rivers, Cahokia, like Teotihuacán and Chaco Canyon, served as a focal point for both culture and trade. At its peak (in the eleventh and twelfth centuries CE), the City of the Sun covered more than five square miles and had a population of about twenty thousand: small by Mesoamerican standards but larger than any other northern community—indeed, larger than London in the same era.

Although the Cahokians never invented a writing system, these sun-worshippers developed an accurate calendar, evidenced by their creation of a woodhenge—a large circle of tall timber posts aligned with the solstices and the equinox. The tallest of the city's 120 pyramids, today called Monks Mound, covered sixteen acres at its base and stood 100 feet high at its topmost level. It remains the largest earthwork ever built in the Americas. It sat at the northern end of the Grand Plaza, surrounded by seventeen other mounds, some used for burials. Yet following 1250 CE, the city was abandoned, several decades after a disastrous earthquake. Archaeologists

Nursing-mother-effigy bottle, Cahokia Culture, Mississippian Period, 1200–1400 (ceramic), American School / St. Louis Museum of Science & Natural History, Missouri, US/Photo © The Detroit Institute of Arts/The Bridgeman Art Library

▲ Archaeologists discovered this effigy bottle near Cahokia in present-day Illinois. The statue, which was made c1200–1400 CE, depicts a woman sitting cross-legged and nursing an infant.

believe that climate change and the degradation of the environment, caused by overpopulation and the destruction of nearby forests, contributed to the city's collapse. Afterwards, warfare increased as large-scale population movements destabilized the region.

1-1d Aztecs

Far to the South, the Aztecs (also called Mexicas) migrated into the Valley of Mexico during the twelfth century CE. The ruins of Mayan Teotihuacán, deserted for at least two hundred years, awed and mystified the migrants. Their chronicles record that their primary deity, Huitzilopochtli—a war god represented by an eagle—directed them to establish their capital on an island where they saw an eagle eating a serpent, the symbol of Quetzalcoatl. That island city became Tenochtitlán, the nerve center of a rigidly stratified society composed of warriors, merchants, priests, common people, and slaves.

The Aztecs conquered their neighbors, demanding tribute in textiles, gold, foodstuffs, and human beings who could be sacrificed to Huitzilopochtli. The war god's taste for blood was not easily quenched. In the Aztec year Ten Rabbit (the Christian 1502), at the coronation of Motecuhzoma II, thousands of people were sacrificed by having their still-beating hearts torn from their bodies.

City of the Sun (Cahokia) Area located near modern St. Louis, Missouri, where about twenty thousand people inhabited a metropolitan area.

▲ Even today, many centuries after the peak of its ceremonial and economic power, the central mound of the Cahokia settlement, known as the Monk's Mound, still dominates the flat landscape around it, as this 2010 photo shows.

The Aztecs believed they lived in the age of the Fifth Sun. Four times previously, they wrote, the earth and all the people who lived on it had been destroyed. They predicted their own world would end in earthquakes and hunger. In the Aztec year Thirteen Flint, volcanoes erupted, sickness and hunger spread, wild beasts attacked children, and an eclipse of the sun darkened the sky. Did some priest wonder whether the Fifth Sun was approaching its end? In time, the Aztecs learned that Europeans knew the year Thirteen Flint as 1492.

1-2 North America in 1492

▶ What factors contributed to the diversity of indigenous peoples in North America?

▶ What role did gender play in the development and organization of indigenous societies?

▶ What role did warfare play in pre-Columbian American society?

Over the centuries, the Americans who lived north of Mexico adapted their once-similar ways of life to very different climates and terrains, thus creating the diverse culture areas (ways of subsistence) that the Europeans encountered when they arrived (see Map 1.1). Scholars often delineate such culture areas by language group (such as Algonquian or Iroquoian), because neighboring indigenous nations commonly spoke related languages. Societies that lived in environments not well suited to agriculture—because of inadequate rainfall or poor soil, for example—followed a nomadic lifestyle. Within the area of the present-day United States, these groups included the Paiutes and Shoshones, who inhabited the Great Basin (now Nevada and Utah). Because of the difficulty of finding sufficient food, such hunter-gatherer bands were small, usually composed of one or more related families. The men hunted small animals, and women gathered seeds and berries. Where large game was more plentiful and food supplies therefore more certain, as in present-day central and western Canada and the Great Plains, bands of hunters were somewhat larger.

In more favorable environments, larger indigenous groups combined agriculture with gathering, hunting, and fishing. Those who lived near the seacoasts, like the Chinooks of present-day Washington and Oregon, consumed fish and shellfish in addition to growing crops and gathering seeds and berries. Residents of the interior (for example, the Arikaras of the Missouri River valley) hunted large animals while also cultivating maize, squash, and beans. The peoples of what is now eastern Canada and the northeastern United States also combined hunting, fishing, and agriculture. They used controlled fires both to open land for cultivation and to assist in hunting.

Extensive trade routes linked distant peoples. For instance, hoe and spade blades manufactured from stone mined in modern southern Illinois have been found as far northeast as Lake Erie and as far west as the Plains. Commercial and

Map 1.1 Native Cultures of North America

The Native peoples of the North American continent effectively used the resources of the regions in which they lived. As this map shows, coastal groups relied on fishing, residents of fertile areas engaged in agriculture, and other peoples employed hunting (often combined with gathering) as a primary mode of subsistence.

other interactions among disparate groups speaking different languages were aided by the universally understood symbol of friendship—the calumet, a feathered tobacco pipe offered to strangers at initial encounters. Across the continent, Native groups sought alliances and waged war against their enemies when diplomacy failed. Their histories, though not written, were complex and dynamic, long before Europeans arrived.

1-2a Gendered Division of Labor

Societies that relied primarily on hunting large animals, such as deer and buffalo, assigned that task to men, allotting food preparation and clothing production to women. Before such nomadic bands acquired horses from the Spaniards, women—occasionally assisted by dogs—also carried

the family's belongings whenever the band relocated. Such a sexual division of labor was universal among hunting peoples, regardless of location. Agricultural societies assigned work in divergent ways. The Pueblo peoples, who lived in sixty or seventy autonomous villages and spoke five different languages, defined agricultural labor as men's work. In the east, large clusters of peoples speaking Algonquian, Iroquoian, and Muskogean languages allocated most agricultural chores to women, although men cleared the land. French colonizers often commented on Native gender roles that were very different from their own. "Men leave the arrangement of the household to the women, without interfering with them; they cut, and decide, and give away as they please, without making the husband angry," noted Father Paul le Juene of the Algonquian peoples he missionized along the shores of the St. Lawrence River. In the six nations of the Haudenosaunee (whom French called "Iroquois"), women held positions of political and cultural authority. This too Europeans found striking. "Amongst the Huron nations," wrote Father Pierre de Charlevoix, "the women name the counselors, and often chuse persons of their own sex." Indeed, he said, "the women have the chief authority amongst all the nations of the Huron language," excepting the Oneida. In general, he thought, they handled this surprising power ably.

Everywhere in North America, women cared for young children, while older youths learned adult skills from their same-sex parent. Children had a great deal of freedom. Young people commonly chose their own marital partners, and in most societies couples could easily divorce if they no longer wished to live together. In contrast to the earlier Mississippian cultures, populations in these societies remained at a level sustainable by existing food supplies, largely because of low birth rates. Infants and toddlers nursed until the age of two or even longer, and taboos prevented couples from having sexual intercourse during that period.

1-2b Social Organization

The southwestern and eastern agricultural peoples had similar social organizations. They lived in villages, sometimes with a thousand or more inhabitants. The Pueblos resided in multistory buildings constructed on terraces along the sides of cliffs or other easily defended sites. Northern Iroquois villages (in modern New York State) were composed of large, rectangular, bark-covered structures, or longhouses; the name Haudenosaunee means "People of the Longhouse." In the present-day southeastern United States, Muskogeans and southern Algonquians lived in large houses made of thatch. Most of the eastern villages were surrounded by wooden palisades and ditches to fend off attackers.

In all the agricultural societies, each dwelling housed an extended family defined matrilineally (through a female line of descent). Mothers, their married daughters, and their daughters' husbands and children all lived together. Matrilineal descent did not imply matriarchy, or the wielding of power by women, but rather served as a means of reckoning kinship. Matrilineal ties also linked extended families into clans. The nomadic bands of the Prairies and Great Plains, by contrast,

▲ Jacques Le Moyne, an artist accompanying the French settlement in Florida in the 1560s (see Section 1-9b, p. 28), produced some of the first European images of North American peoples. His depiction of Native agricultural practices shows the gendered division of labor: men breaking up the ground with fishbone hoes before women drop seeds into the holes. But Le Moyne's version of the scene cannot be accepted uncritically: unable to abandon a European view of proper farming methods, he erroneously drew plowed furrows in the soil.

Collection of Mary Beth Norton

were most often related patrilineally (through the male line). They lacked settled villages and defended themselves from attack primarily by moving to safer locations when necessary.

1-2c War and Politics

The defensive design of Native villages points to the significance of warfare in pre-Columbian America. Long before Europeans arrived, residents of the continent fought one another for control of prime hunting and fishing territories, fertile agricultural lands, or sources of essential items, such as salt (for preserving meat) and flint (for making knives and arrowheads). Native warriors protected by wooden armor battled while standing in ranks facing each other, the better to employ their clubs and throwing spears, which were effective only at close quarters. They began to shoot arrows from behind trees only when they confronted European guns, which rendered their armor useless. People captured in such wars were sometimes enslaved and dishonored by losing their previous names and identities, but slavery was not a primary source of labor in pre-Columbian America.

Indigenous political structures varied considerably. Among Pueblos, the village council, composed of ten to thirty men, was the highest political authority; no larger organization connected multiple villages. Nomadic hunters also lacked formal links among separate bands. The Iroquois, by contrast, had an elaborate political hierarchy incorporating villages into nations and nations into a confederation. A council of representatives from each nation made crucial decisions of war and peace for the entire confederacy. In all the North American cultures, civil and war leaders divided political power and wielded authority only so long as they retained the confidence of the people. Autocratic rulers held sway only in southeastern chiefdoms descended from the Mississippians. Women more often assumed leadership roles among agricultural peoples, especially those in which females were the primary cultivators. Female sachems (rulers) led Algonquian villages in what is now Massachusetts, but women never became heads of hunting bands. Iroquois women did not become chiefs, yet clan matrons exercised political power, including the power to start and stop wars.

1-2d Religion

The continent's Native peoples were polytheistic, worshipping a multitude of gods, sometimes under one chief creator. The major deities of agricultural peoples like the Pueblos and Muskogeans were associated with cultivation, and their main festivals centered on planting and harvest. The most important gods of hunters like those living on the Great Plains were associated with animals, and their festivals were related to hunting.

A wide variety of cultures, comprising more than 10 million people, inhabited America north of Mexico when Europeans arrived. The hierarchical kingdoms of Mesoamerica bore little resemblance to the nomadic hunting societies of the Great Plains or to the agriculturalists of the Northeast or Southwest. The diverse inhabitants of North America spoke well over one thousand distinct languages. They are "Americans" only in retrospect, grouped under the name the Europeans assigned to the continent. They did not consider themselves one people, just as the inhabitants of England, France, Spain, and the Netherlands did not imagine themselves as "Europeans." Nor did they think of uniting to repel the invaders who washed up on their shores beginning in 1492.

1-3 African Societies

▶ How did the environment affect the development of societies in Africa?

▶ What was the influence of Islamic culture on African societies?

▶ What roles did gender play in the organization of African societies?

Fifteenth-century Africa, like fifteenth-century America, housed a variety of cultures adapted to different terrains and climates (see Map 1.2). Many of these cultures were of great antiquity. Like the ancient cultures of North America, the diverse peoples of Africa were dynamic and changing, with complex histories of their own.

In the north, along the Mediterranean Sea, lived the Berbers, who were Muslims—followers of the Islamic religion founded by the prophet Mohammed in the seventh century CE. On the east coast of Africa, Muslim city-states engaged in far-ranging trade with India, the Moluccas (part of modern Indonesia), and China. In these ports, sustained contact and intermarriage among Arabs and Africans created the Swahili language and culture. Through the East African city-states passed the Spice Route, the conduit of waterborne commerce between the eastern Mediterranean and East Asia; the rest followed the long land route across Central Asia known as the Silk Road.

South of the Mediterranean coast in the African interior lie the great Saharan and Libyan deserts, vast nearly waterless expanses crisscrossed by trade routes passing through oases. The introduction of the camel in the fifth century CE made long-distance travel possible, and as Islam expanded after the ninth century, commerce controlled by Muslim merchants helped to spread similar religious and cultural ideas throughout the region. Below the deserts, much of the continent is divided between tropical rain forests (along the coasts) and grassy plains (in the interior). People speaking a variety of languages and pursuing different subsistence strategies lived in a wide belt south of the deserts. South of the Gulf of Guinea, the grassy landscape came to be dominated by Bantu-speaking peoples, who left their homeland in modern Nigeria about two thousand years ago and slowly migrated south and east across the continent.

1-3a West Africa (Guinea)

The inhabitants of West Africa's tropical forests and savanna grasslands supported themselves with fishing, cattle herding, and agriculture for at least ten thousand years before Europeans set foot there in the fifteenth century. The northern region of West Africa, or Upper Guinea, was heavily influenced by

Map 1.2 Africa and Its Peoples, ca. 1400

On the African continent resided many different peoples in a variety of ecological settings and political units. Even before Europeans began to explore Africa's coastlines, its northern regions were linked to the Mediterranean (and thus to Europe) by a network of trade routes.

Major climatic zones of Africa
- Wet equatorial
- Woodland savannah
- Dry savannah with long dry season (6–9 months)
- Sahel or subdesert
- Desert
- Mediterranean
- Highland (climate moderated by altitude)
- Trans-Saharan trade routes
- Traditional Arab spice routes
- Spread of Bantu-speakers, by ca. 1000
- TEDA Major language
- *BERBERS* Selected peoples

the Islamic culture of the Mediterranean. By the eleventh century CE, many of the region's inhabitants had become Muslims. Trade via camel caravans between Upper Guinea and the Muslim Mediterranean connected sub-Saharan Africa to Europe and West Asia. Africans sold ivory, gold, and slaves to northern merchants to obtain salt, dates, silk, and cotton cloth.

Upper Guinea runs from Cape Verde in the northeast to Cape Palmas in the southwest. The people of its northernmost region, the so-called Rice Coast (present-day Gambia,

Senegal, and Guinea), fished and cultivated rice in coastal swamplands. The Grain Coast, to the south, was thinly populated and not readily accessible from the sea because it had only one good harbor (modern Freetown, Sierra Leone). Its inhabitants concentrated on farming and raising livestock.

In Lower Guinea, south and east of Cape Palmas, most Africans were farmers who practiced traditional religions, rather than Islam. Believing that spirits inhabited particular places, they invested those places with special significance. Like

▲ This brass depiction of a hunting scene with a man and animals was employed by the Akan peoples of the modern Ivory Coast to weigh gold. An otherwise mundane object required for domestic and foreign trade thus was decorative as well as useful, providing for today's viewers a sense of ancient African life.

RMN-Grand Palais/Art Resource, NY

the agricultural peoples of the Americas, they developed rituals intended to ensure good harvests. Throughout the region, villages composed of kin groups were linked into hierarchical kingdoms. At the time of initial European contact, decentralized political and social authority characterized the region.

1-3b Complementary Gender Roles

In the societies of West Africa, as in those of the Americas, men and women pursued different tasks. In general, both sexes shared agricultural duties. Men also hunted, managed livestock, and did most of the fishing. Women were responsible for child care, food preparation, manufacture, and trade. They managed the extensive local and regional networks through which families, villages, and small kingdoms exchanged goods.

Despite their different economies and the rivalries among states, the peoples of Lower Guinea had similar social systems organized on the basis of what anthropologists have called the dual-sex principle. Each sex handled its own affairs: male political and religious leaders governed men, and females ruled women. In the Dahomean kingdom, for example, every male official had his female counterpart; in the thirty Akan states on the Gold Coast, chiefs inherited their status through the female line, and each male chief had a female assistant who supervised other women. Many West African societies practiced polygyny (one man's having several wives, each of whom lived separately with her children). Thus, few adults lived permanently in marital households, but the dual-sex system ensured that their actions were subject to scrutiny by elders of their own sex.

Throughout Guinea, both women and men served as heads of the cults and secret societies that directed the spiritual life of the villages. Young women were initiated into the Sandé cult, young men into Poro. Neither cult was allowed to reveal its secrets to the opposite sex. Unlike some of their Native American contemporaries, West African women rarely held formal power over men.

1-3c Slavery in Guinea

Africans, like North America's Native peoples, created various forms of slavery long before contact with Europeans. Enslavement was sometimes used to punish criminals, but more often slaves were enemy captives or people who voluntarily enslaved themselves or their children to pay debts.

West African law recognized both individual and communal landownership, but men seeking to accumulate wealth needed access to laborers—wives, children, or slaves—who could work the land. People enslaved for life composed essential elements of the economy. Slaveholders had a right to the products of the men and women they held in bondage, although the degree to which slaves were exploited varied greatly, and slave status did not always descend to the next generation. Some slaves were held as chattel; others could engage in trade, retaining a portion of their profits; and still others achieved prominent political or military positions. All, however, found it difficult to overcome the social stigma of enslavement, and could be traded or sold at the will of their owners.

West Africans, then, were agricultural peoples, skilled at tending livestock, hunting, fishing, and manufacturing cloth from plant fibers and animal skins. They were accustomed to a relatively egalitarian relationship between the sexes, especially within the context of religion. Carried as captives to the Americas, they became essential to transplanted European societies that used their labor but had little respect for their cultures.

1-4 European Societies

▶ **What were the similarities in the everyday lives of Europeans across the continent?**

▶ **What roles did gender play in the social and cultural development of European society?**

▶ **What developments drove Europeans to engage in the exploration of the wider world?**

In the fifteenth century, Europeans, too, were agricultural peoples. Split into numerous small, warring peoples, the continent of Europe was divided linguistically, politically, and economically. Yet the daily lives of ordinary men and women exhibited many similarities. In most European societies, a few families wielded autocratic power over the rest. English society in particular was organized as a series of interlocking hierarchies; that is, each person (except those at the very top or bottom) was superior to some, inferior to others. At the base of such hierarchies were people held in various forms of bondage. Although Europeans were not subjected to perpetual slavery, Christian doctrine permitted the enslavement of "heathens" (non-Christians), and some Europeans' freedom was restricted by such conditions as serfdom, which tied them to particular plots of land if not to specific owners. In short, Europe's kingdoms resembled those of Africa or Mesoamerica but differed greatly from the more egalitarian societies found in America north of Mexico (see Map 1.3).

Map 1.3 Europe in 1453

The Europeans who ventured out into the Atlantic came from countries on the northwestern edge of the continent, which was divided into numerous competing nations.

Spread of Roman Christendom

- In 1000 CE
- Added 1000–1200
- Lost 1000–1200 (Regained 1200–1500)
- Added 1200–1500
- Lost 1200–1500
- English holdings, 1360
- Boundary of the Holy Roman Empire

KHANATE OF THE KAZAN

KHANATE OF THE GOLDEN HORDE

KHANATE OF THE ASTRAKHAN

KHANATE OF THE CRIMEA

GRAND PRINCIPALITY OF MOSCOW
• Moscow

Don R.

Volga R.

Tigris R.

Euphrates R.

NOVGOROD

ESTONIA

PRUSSIA
• Riga

GRAND PRINCIPALITY OF LITHUANIA

Dnieper R.

• Kiev

MOLDAVIA

WALLACHIA

Black Sea

Cyprus

OTTOMAN EMPIRE

Constantinople •

• Athens

Rhodes

Crete

30°E

40°E

50°N

50°E

NORWAY
• Oslo

SWEDEN
• Stockholm

Baltic Sea

PRUSSIA
Königsberg •
Danzig •

• Copenhagen

DENMARK

Hamburg •

Elbe R.

• Frankfurt

HOLY ROMAN EMPIRE

BOHEMIA

Warsaw •

POLAND

Budapest •
HUNGARY

SERBIA

MONTENEGRO

BOSNIA

ALBANIA

AUSTRIA

Vienna •

STYRIA

TYROL

Rhine R.

SWITZERLAND

FRANCHE-COMTÉ

LUXEMBOURG

FLANDERS

CHAMPAGNE

BURGUNDY

• Paris

• Orléans

BRITTANY

ENGLAND
• London

WALES

SCOTLAND

IRELAND
• Dublin

North Sea

N

ATLANTIC OCEAN

FRANCE

Lyons •

AQUITAINE

NAVARRE

Ebro R.

PORTUGAL
• Lisbon

KINGDOM OF CASTILE AND LEÓN
• Toledo

KINGDOM OF ARAGON
Barcelona •

• Granada
GRANADA

MOROCCO

ALGIERS

TUNIS

Corsica

Sardinia

Sicily

Malta

Mediterranean Sea

KINGDOM OF NAPLES
Naples •

Rome •

PAPAL STATES

VENETIAN REPUBLIC

Adriatic Sea

Venice •

FLORENCE

GENOA

MILAN

SAVOY

ALPS

Po R.

Rhône R.

Avignon •

Marseilles •

Danube R.

20°E

10°E

0°

10°W

40°N

Rome

300 Mi.

300 Km.

150

150

0

0

1-4a Gender, Work, Politics, and Religion

Most Europeans, like most Africans and Americans, lived in small villages. Only a few cities dotted the landscape, most of them seaports or political capitals. European farmers, called peasants, owned or leased separate plots of land, but they worked the fields communally. Men did most of the field-work; women helped out chiefly at planting and harvest. In some regions men concentrated on herding livestock while women cared for children, prepared and preserved food, milked cows, and kept poultry. A woman married to a city artisan or storekeeper might assist her husband in business. Because Europeans kept domesticated animals (pigs, goats, sheep, and cattle) for meat, hunting had little economic importance in their cultures, and served instead primarily as a sport for male aristocrats.

Unlike in Africa or the Americas, men dominated all areas of public life in Europe. A few women—notably Queen Elizabeth I of England—achieved status or power by right of birth, but the vast majority were excluded from positions of authority. European women also generally held inferior social, religious, and economic positions, yet they wielded power in their own households over children and servants. In contrast to the freedom children enjoyed in Native American families, European children were tightly controlled and subjected to harsh discipline.

Christianity was the dominant European religion. In the West, authority rested in the Catholic Church, based in Rome and led by the pope, who then as now directed a wholly male and officially celibate clergy. Although Europeans were, until the sixteenth century, nominally Catholic, many adhered to local belief systems that the church deemed heretical but failed to extinguish. Kings allied themselves with the church when it suited them, but often acted independently. Yet even so, the Christian nations of Europe from the twelfth century on publicly united in a goal of driving non-Christians (especially Muslims) not only from the European continent but also from the holy city of Jerusalem, which caused the series of wars known as the Crusades. Nevertheless, in the fifteenth century, Muslims dominated the commerce and geography of the Mediterranean world, especially after they conquered Constantinople (capital of the Christian Byzantine empire) in 1453. Few would have predicted that Christian Europeans would ever challenge that dominance.

1-4b Effects of Plague and Warfare

When the fifteenth century began, European nations were slowly recovering from the devastating epidemic known as the Black Death, which first struck in 1346. This plague seems to have arrived in Europe from China, traveling with long-distance traders along the Silk Road. The disease then recurred with particular severity in the 1360s and 1370s. Although no precise figures are available and the impact of the Black Death varied from region to region, the best estimate is that fully one-third of Europe's people died during those terrible years. A precipitous economic decline followed—in some regions more than half of the workers had died—as did severe social, political, and religious disruption because of the deaths of clergymen and other leading figures.

As plague ravaged the population, England and France waged the Hundred Years' War (1337–1453), which began after English monarchs claimed the French throne. The war interrupted overland trade routes connecting England and Antwerp (in modern Belgium) to Venice, and thence to India and China. England, on the periphery of the Mediterranean commercial core, exported wool and cloth to Antwerp in exchange for spices and silks from the East. Needing a new way to reach their northern trading partners, eastern Mediterranean merchants forged a maritime route to Antwerp. Using a triangular, or lateen, sail (rather than then-standard square rigging) improved the maneuverability of ships, enabling vessels to sail north around the European coast. Maritime navigation also improved through the acquisition of a Chinese invention, the compass, and the perfection of instruments like the astrolabe and the quadrant, which allowed sailors to gauge their latitude by measuring the relationship of the sun, moon, or certain stars to the horizon.

Everyday scenes, illuminated page from Book of Hours of King Don Manuel I, manuscript, Portugal 16th Century./DE AGOSTINI EDITORE/ Bridgeman Images

▲ Daily life in early sixteenth-century Portugal, as illustrated in a manuscript prayer book. At top a prosperous family shares a meal being served by an enslaved African. Other scenes show male laborers clearing land and hunting birds (left) and chopping wood (right), while at bottom a woman plants seeds in a prepared bed and in the top background female servants work in the kitchen.

1-4c Political and Technological Change

After the Hundred Years' War, European monarchs forcefully consolidated their previously diffuse political power and raised new revenues by increasing the taxes they levied on an already hard-pressed peasantry. The long military struggle led to new pride in national identity, which began to eclipse prevailing regional and dynastic loyalties. In England, Henry VII in 1485 founded the Tudor dynasty and began uniting a divided land. In France, the successors of Charles VII made the kingdom more cohesive. Most successful of all were Ferdinand of Aragón and Isabella of Castile, who married in 1469, founding a strongly Catholic and increasingly unified Spain. In 1492, they defeated the Muslims who had lived in Spain and Portugal for centuries, and expelled all Jews and Muslims from their domain.

The fifteenth century also brought technological change to Europe. **Movable type** and the **printing press**, invented in Germany in the 1450s, made information more accessible over wider distances. Printing stimulated Europeans' curiosity about fabled lands across the seas, lands they could now read about in books. The most important such works were Ptolemy's *Geography*, a description of the known world written in ancient times, first published in 1475; and Marco Polo's *Travels*, published in 1477. The *Travels* recounted the Venetian merchant's adventures in thirteenth-century China and intriguingly described that nation as bordered on the east by an ocean. Polo's account circulated widely among educated elites, first in manuscript and later in print. The book led many Europeans to believe they could reach China in oceangoing vessels instead of relying on the Silk Road or the Spice Route overland across East Africa. A transoceanic route, if it existed, would allow northern Europeans to circumvent the Muslim and Venetian merchants who had long controlled their access to Asian goods.

1-4d Motives for Exploration

Technological advances and the growing strength of newly powerful national rulers catalyzed the European explorations of the fifteenth and sixteenth centuries. Each country craved easy access to African and Asian goods—silk, dyes, perfumes, jewels, sugar, gold, and especially spices. Pepper, cloves, cinnamon, and nutmeg were desirable not only for seasoning food but also because they were believed to have medicinal and magical properties. Their allure stemmed largely from their rarity, their extraordinary cost, and their mysterious origins. They passed through so many hands en route to London or Seville that no European knew exactly where they came from. (Nutmeg, for example, grew only on nine tiny islands in the Moluccas, now eastern Indonesia.) Avoiding intermediaries in Venice and Constantinople, and acquiring such valuable products directly, would improve a nation's balance of trade and its standing relative to other countries, in addition to supplying its wealthy leaders with coveted luxury items that bolstered their power.

A concern for spreading Christianity around the world supplemented these economic motives. The linking of material and spiritual goals may seem contradictory, but fifteenth-century Europeans saw no necessary conflict between the two. Explorers and colonizers—especially Roman Catholics—sought to convert "heathen" peoples to Christianity. At the same time, they hoped to increase their nation's wealth by establishing direct trade with Africa, China, India, and the Moluccas.

1-5 Early European Explorations

▶ **What navigational tools and techniques enabled Europeans to engage in exploration?**

▶ **What were the consequences of early European exploration?**

To establish that trade, European mariners first had to explore the oceans. Seafarers needed not just the maneuverable vessels and navigational aids increasingly used in the fourteenth century but also knowledge of the sea, its currents, and especially its winds, which powered their ships. Where would Atlantic breezes carry their square-rigged ships, which, even with the addition of a triangular sail, needed to run before the wind (that is, to have the wind directly behind the vessel)?

1-5a Sailing the Mediterranean Atlantic

Europeans honed new navigation techniques in the region called the Mediterranean Atlantic, the expanse of ocean located south and west of Spain and bounded by the islands of the Azores (on the west) and the Canaries (on the south), with the Madeiras in their midst (see Map 1.4). Europeans reached all three sets of islands during the fourteenth century—first the Canaries in the 1330s, then the Madeiras and the Azores. The Canaries proved a popular destination for mariners from Iberia, the peninsula that includes Spain and Portugal. Sailing to the Canaries from Europe was easy, because strong winds known as the Northeast Trades blow southward along the Iberian and African coastlines. The voyage took about a week, and the volcanic peaks on the islands made them easy to spot.

The problem was getting back. The Iberian sailor attempting to return home faced a major obstacle: the winds that had brought him so quickly to the Canaries now blew directly at him. Confronted by contrary winds, mariners had traditionally waited for the wind to change, but the Northeast Trades blew steadily. So they developed a new method: sailing "around the wind." That meant sailing as directly against the wind as was possible without being forced to change course. In the Mediterranean Atlantic, a mariner would head northwest into the open ocean, until—weeks later—he reached the winds that would carry him home, the so-called Westerlies.

movable type Type in which each character is cast on a separate piece of metal.

printing press A machine that transfers lettering or images by contact with various forms of inked surface onto paper or similar material fed into it in various ways.

Map 1.4 Atlantic Winds and Islands

European mariners had to explore the oceans before they could find new lands. The first realm they discovered was that of Atlantic winds and islands.

Those winds blow (we now know) northward along the coast of North America before heading east toward Europe.

This solution must at first have seemed to defy common sense, but it became the key to successful exploration of both the Atlantic and the Pacific oceans. Once a sailor understood the winds and their allied currents, he no longer feared leaving Europe without being able to return.

1-5b Islands of the Mediterranean Atlantic

During the fifteenth century, armed with knowledge of the winds and currents of the Mediterranean Atlantic, Iberian seamen regularly visited the three island groups, which they could reach in two weeks or less. The uninhabited Azores were soon settled by Portuguese migrants, who raised wheat for sale in Europe and sold livestock to passing sailors. The Madeiras also had no Native peoples, and by the 1450s Portuguese colonists were employing slaves (probably Jews and Muslims from Iberia) to grow sugar for export to the mainland. By the 1470s, Madeira had developed a colonial **plantation** economy. For the first time in world history, a region was settled explicitly to cultivate a valuable crop—sugar—to be sold elsewhere. Moreover, because the work involved in large-scale plantation agriculture was so back-breaking, only a supply of enslaved laborers (who could not opt to quit) could ensure the system's continued success.

The Canaries did have indigenous residents—the Guanche people, who began trading animal skins and dyes with their European visitors. After 1402, the French, Portuguese, and Spanish began sporadically attacking the islands. The Guanches resisted vigorously, even though they were weakened by their susceptibility to alien European diseases. One by one, the seven islands fell to Europeans who then carried off Guanches as slaves to the Madeiras or Iberia. Spain conquered the last island in 1496 and subsequently converted the land into sugar plantations. Collectively, the Canaries and Madeira became known as the Wine Islands because much of their sugar production was used to fortify sweet wines.

1-5c Portuguese Trading Posts in Africa

While some European rulers and traders concentrated on exploiting the islands of the Mediterranean Atlantic, others used them as stepping-stones to Africa. In 1415, Portugal seized control of Ceuta, a Muslim city in North Africa (see Map 1.2). Prince Henry the Navigator, son of King John I of Portugal, knew that vast wealth awaited the first European nation to tap the riches of Africa and Asia directly. Repeatedly, he dispatched ships southward along the African coast, attempting to discover an oceanic route to Asia. But not until after Prince Henry's death did Bartholomew Dias round the southern tip of Africa (1488) and Vasco da Gama finally reach India (1498).

plantation A large-scale agricultural enterprise growing commercial crops and often employing coerced or slave labor.

At Malabar, da Gama located the richest source of peppercorns in the world.

Long before that, Portugal reaped the benefits of its seafarers' voyages. Although West African states successfully resisted European penetration of the interior, they allowed the Portuguese to establish coastal trading posts. Charging the traders rent and levying duties on goods they imported, the African kingdoms benefited considerably from easier access to European manufactures. The Portuguese gained, too, for they no longer had to rely on trans-Saharan camel caravans. Their vessels earned immense profits by swiftly transporting African gold, ivory, and slaves to Europe. By bargaining with African masters to purchase their slaves and then carrying those bondspeople to Iberia, the Portuguese introduced black slavery into Europe.

1-5d Lessons of Early Colonization

An island off the African coast, previously uninhabited, proved critical to Portuguese success. In the 1480s, the Portuguese colonized São Tomé, located in the Gulf of Guinea (see Map 1.2). By that time, Madeira had reached the limit of its capacity to produce sugar. The soil of São Tomé proved ideal for raising that valuable crop, and plantation agriculture there expanded rapidly. Planters imported large numbers of slaves from the mainland to work in the cane fields, thus creating the first economy based primarily on the bondage of black Africans.

By the 1490s, even before Christopher Columbus set sail to the west, Europeans had learned three key lessons of colonization in the Mediterranean Atlantic. First, they had learned how to transplant their crops and livestock successfully to exotic locations. Second, they had discovered that the Native peoples of those lands could be either conquered (like the Guanches) or exploited (like the Africans). Third, they had developed a viable model of plantation slavery and a system for supplying nearly unlimited quantities of such workers. The stage was set for a pivotal moment in world history.

1-6 Voyages of Columbus, Cabot, and Their Successors

▶ **What was the relationship between explorers and European monarchs?**

▶ **What knowledge of the wider world did European explorers gain?**

Christopher Columbus was well schooled in the lessons of the Mediterranean Atlantic. Born in 1451 in the Italian city-state of Genoa, this largely self-educated son of a wool merchant was by the 1490s an experienced sailor and mapmaker. Like many

Christopher Columbus Genoese explorer who claimed the island of San Salvador in the Bahamas and other places in the Caribbean and Central America for the king and queen of Spain.

mariners of the day, he was drawn to Portugal and its islands, especially Madeira, where he commanded a merchant vessel. At least once he sailed to the Portuguese outpost on Africa's Gold Coast. There he became obsessed with gold, and there he came to understand the economic potential of the slave trade.

Like all accomplished seafarers, Columbus knew the world was round. But he differed from other cartographers in his estimate of the earth's size: he thought that China lay only three thousand miles from Europe's southern coast. Thus, he argued, it would be easier to reach Asia by sailing west than by making the difficult voyage around the southern tip of Africa. Experts scoffed at this crackpot notion, accurately predicting that the two continents lay twelve thousand miles apart. When Columbus in 1484 asked the Portuguese rulers to back his plan to sail west to Asia, they rejected what appeared to be a crazy scheme.

1-6a Columbus's Voyage

Jealous of rival Portugal's successes in Africa, Spain's Ferdinand and Isabella were more receptive to Columbus's ideas. Urged on by some Spanish noblemen and a group of Italian merchants residing in Castile, the monarchs agreed to finance most of the risky voyage—Columbus himself would have to pay a quarter of the costs. They hoped the profits would pay for a new expedition to conquer Muslim-held Jerusalem. And so, on August 3, 1492, Columbus set sail from the Spanish port of Palos in command of three ships—the *Pinta*, the *Niña*, and the *Santa Maria*.

The first part of the journey was familiar, for the ships steered down the Northeast Trades to the Canary Islands. There Columbus refitted his ships, adding triangular sails to make them more maneuverable. On September 6, the flotilla weighed anchor and headed into the unknown ocean. The sailors were anxious about the winds, the waves, and the distance. To stave off panic, Columbus lied, underreporting the number of nautical miles the convoy covered each day. He kept two sets of logbooks, an early chronicler remembered, "one false and the other true."

Just over a month later, the vessels found land approximately where Columbus thought Cipangu (Japan) was located (see Map 1.5). On October 12, he and his men anchored off an island in the present-day Bahamas, called Guanahaní by its inhabitants. The admiral and members of his crew went ashore with guns drawn. Planting a flag bearing a Christian cross and the initials of Ferdinand and Isabella, Columbus claimed the territory for Spain and renamed Guanahaní San Salvador. (Because Columbus's description of his landfall can be variously interpreted, several different places today claim to be his landing site.) Later, he went on to explore the islands now known as Cuba and Hispaniola, which the Native Taíno people called Colba and Bohío. Because he thought he had reached the East Indies (the Spice Islands), Columbus referred to the inhabitants of the region as "Indians," a mistake that continues to reverberate even today. The Taínos thought the Europeans had come from the sky, and wherever Columbus

Map 1.5 European Explorations in America

In the century following Columbus's voyages, European adventurers explored the coasts and parts of the interior of North and South America.

went crowds of curious Taínos gathered to meet and exchange gifts with him.

1-6b Columbus's Observations

Three themes predominate in Columbus's log, the major source of information on this first recorded encounter between Europe and what would come to be called the Americas. First, he was eager to exploit the region's natural resources. He insistently asked the Taínos where he could find gold, pearls, and spices. Each time, his informants replied (via signs) that such products could be obtained on other islands or on the mainland. Eventually, he came to mistrust such answers, noting, "I am beginning to believe . . . they will tell me anything I want to hear."

Second, Columbus was amazed by the strange and beautiful plants and animals he encountered. "Here the fishes are so unlike ours that it is amazing . . . . The colors are so bright that anyone would marvel," he noted. "The song of the little birds might make a man wish never to leave here." Yet Columbus's interest was not only aesthetic.

"I believe that there are many plants and trees here that could be worth a lot in Spain for use as dyes, spices, and medicines," he observed, adding that he was carrying home to Europe "a sample of everything I can," so that experts could examine them.

Included in his cargo of curiosities were some of the islands' human residents, whom Columbus also evaluated as resources to answer European needs. The Taínos were, he said, handsome, gentle, and friendly, though they told him of the fierce Caniba (today called Caribs) who lived on other islands, raided their villages, and ate their captives (hence today's word *cannibal*). Although Columbus feared and distrusted the Caribs, he saw the Taínos as likely converts to Catholicism, remarking that "if devout religious persons knew the Indian language well, all these people would soon become Christians." In his mind, conversion was the ally of enslavement. The islanders "ought to make good and skilled servants," Columbus declared. It would be easy to "subject everyone and make them do what you wished."

Naming America

In 1507, German cartographer Martin Waldseemüller created the first map to label the newly discovered landmass on the western side of the Atlantic as "America." He named the continent after Amerigo Vespucci, the Italian explorer who realized he had reached a "new world" rather than islands off the coast of Asia. Waldseemüller's map appeared in a short book called *Cosmographiae Introductio*, or *Introduction to Cosmography*—the study of the known world. The globe he illustrated was both familiar and new. The sun revolved around the earth, as scholars had believed for a millennium. Yet the voyages of Columbus, Vespucci, and others had reconfigured the earth.

When the twelve sheets of Waldseemüller's map are put together, the image stretches nearly five by eight feet. One of the largest printed maps ever then produced, it includes an astonishing level of detail.

CRITICAL THINKING

- What symbols indicate European territorial claims in America and Africa?
- Why might Africa be shown as the center of the known world?

◀ *Waldseemüller map*

Library of Congress Geography and Map Division Washington, D.C. [G3200 1507 .W3]

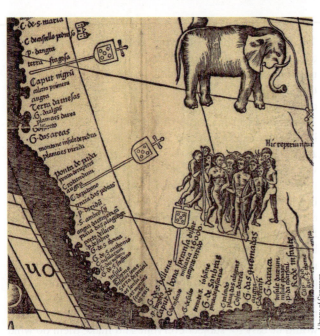

▲ *African peoples*

Library of Congress

▲ *America*

Library of Congress

The records of the first encounter between Europeans and Americans revealed themes that would be of enormous significance for centuries to come. Europeans marveled at the new world, and they wanted to extract profits by exploiting American resources, including plants, animals, and people alike. Later explorers would follow Columbus's tendency to divide Native peoples into "good" (Taínos) and "bad" (Caribs).

Columbus made three more voyages, exploring most of the major Caribbean islands and sailing along the coasts of Central and South America. Until the day he died, in 1506 at the age of fifty-five, he believed he had reached Asia.

Others knew better. The Florentine merchant Amerigo Vespucci, who explored the South American coast in 1499, was the first to promote the idea that a new continent had been discovered. In 1502 or 1503, versions of Vespucci's letters were printed in Florence under the title *Mundus Novus*—"new world." By then, Spain, Portugal, and Pope Alexander VI had signed the Treaty of Tordesillas (1494), confirming Portugal's dominance in Africa—and later Brazil—in exchange for Spanish preeminence in the rest of the Western Hemisphere.

1-6c Norse and Other Northern Voyagers

Five hundred years before Columbus, about the year 1001, a **Norse** expedition under Leif Ericsson sailed to North America across the Davis Strait, which separated Greenland from Baffin Island (located northeast of Hudson Bay; see Map 1.1) by just 200 nautical miles. They settled at a site they named "**Vinland**," but attacks by local residents forced them to abandon it after just a few years. In the 1960s, archaeologists determined that the Norse had established an outpost at what is now L'Anse aux Meadows, Newfoundland. Vinland was probably located farther south.

Later European explorers knew nothing of the earlier Norse voyages, but some historians argue that during the fifteenth century, whalers and fishermen from the Basque country (modern southern France and northern Spain) located rich fishing grounds off Newfoundland but kept the information secret. Whether or not fishermen crossed the entire Atlantic, they thoroughly explored its northern reaches, sailing regularly between Europe, England, Ireland, and Iceland. The mariners who explored the region of North America that was to become the United States and Canada built on their knowledge.

The winds that the northern sailors confronted posed problems on their outbound rather than on their homeward journeys. The same Westerlies that carried Columbus back to Europe blew in the faces of northerners looking west. But mariners soon learned that the strongest winds shifted southward during the winter. By departing from northern ports in the spring, they could make adequate headway if they steered northward. Thus, whereas the first landfall of most sailors to the south was somewhere in the Caribbean, those taking the northern route usually reached North America along the coast of today's Maine or Canada.

1-6d John Cabot's Explorations

The European generally credited with "discovering" mainland North America is Zuan Cabboto, known today as **John Cabot**. Cabot brought to Europe the first formal knowledge of the northern continental coastline and claimed the land for England. Like Columbus, Cabot was a master mariner from the Italian city-state of Genoa; the two men probably knew each other. Calculating that England—which traded with Asia only through a long series of intermediaries—would be eager to sponsor exploratory voyages, he gained financial backing from King Henry VII. He set sail from Bristol in May 1497 in the *Mathew*, reaching North America about a month later. After exploring the coast of modern Newfoundland for a month, Cabot rode the Westerlies back to England, arriving just fifteen days after he left North America.

The voyages of Columbus, Cabot, and their successors brought the Eastern and Western Hemispheres together. Portuguese explorer Pedro Álvares Cabral reached Brazil in 1500; John Cabot's son Sebastian followed his father to North America in 1507; France financed Giovanni da Verrazzano in 1524 and Jacques Cartier in 1534; and in 1609 and 1610, Henry Hudson explored the North American coast for the Dutch West India Company (see Map 1.5). All were searching primarily for the legendary "Northwest Passage" through the Americas, hoping to find an easy water route to the riches of Asia. (Nonexistent in early modern days, the Northwest passage may soon become a reality because of global warming.) But in a sign of what was to come, Verrazzano observed, "the [American] countryside is, in fact, full of promise and deserves to be developed for itself."

1-7 Spanish Exploration and Conquest

▶ **Why did Spaniards conquer parts of the Americas?**

▶ **What was the Spanish method of colonization in the Americas?**

▶ **What was the impact of the Spanish discovery and control of silver deposits in the Americas?**

Only in the areas that Spain explored and claimed did colonization begin immediately. On his second voyage in 1493, Columbus brought to Hispaniola seventeen ships loaded with twelve hundred men, along with seeds,

Norse Also known as Vikings, they were members of a warrior culture from Scandinavia.

Vinland The site of the first known attempt at European settlement in the Americas.

John Cabot Italian explorer who established English claims to the "New World."

plants, livestock, chickens, and dogs—as well as microbes, rats, and weeds. The settlement he named Isabela (in the modern Dominican Republic) and its successors became the staging area for the Spanish invasion of America, an often brutal and highly centralized conquest. On the islands of Cuba and Hispaniola, the Europeans and the animals they imported learned to adapt to the new environment. When the Spaniards moved on to explore the mainland, they rode island-bred horses and ate island-bred cattle and hogs.

1-7a Cortés and Other Explorers

At first, Spanish explorers fanned out around the Caribbean basin. In 1513, Juan Ponce de León reached Florida, and Vasco Núñez de Balboa crossed the Isthmus of Panama to the Pacific Ocean, followed by Pánfilo de Narváez and others who traced the coast of the Gulf of Mexico. In the 1530s and 1540s, **conquistadors** traveled farther, exploring many regions claimed by the Spanish monarchs: Francisco Vásquez de Coronado journeyed through the southwestern portion of what is now the United States at approximately the same time that Hernán de Soto explored the Southeast. Juan Rodríguez Cabrillo sailed along the California coast. Francisco Pizarro, who ventured into western South America, acquired the richest silver mines in the world by conquering the Incas. But the most important conquistador was Hernán Cortés, a Spanish notary who first arrived in the Caribbean in 1506. In 1519, he led a force of roughly six hundred men from Cuba to the Mexican mainland to search for rumored wealthy cities.

1-7b Capture of Tenochtitlán

As he traveled on horseback toward the Aztec capital, Cortés, speaking through Doña Marina and other interpreters, recruited peoples whom the Aztecs had long subjugated. The Spaniards' huge domesticated beasts and noisy weapons awed their new allies. Yet the Spaniards, too, were awed. Years later, Bernal Díaz del Castillo recalled his first sight of Tenochtitlán, built on islands in Lake Texcoco: "We were amazed and said that it was like the enchantments … on account of the great towers and cues [temples] and buildings rising from the water, and all built of masonry." Soldiers wondered "whether the things that we saw were not a dream."

The Spaniards came to Tenochtitlán not only with horses and guns but also with smallpox, transmitting an epidemic that had begun on Hispaniola. The disease peaked in 1520, fatally weakening Tenochtitlán's defenders. "It spread over the people as great destruction," an Aztec later remembered. "There was great havoc. Very many died of it." Largely as a consequence, Tenochtitlán surrendered

conquistadors Spanish conquerors or adventurers in the Americas.

encomienda Spanish system which awarded Native peoples' labor to wealthy colonists.

in 1521, and the Spaniards built Mexico City on its site. Cortés and his men seized a fabulous treasure of gold and silver. Thus, less than three decades after Columbus's first voyage, the Spanish monarchs—who treated the American territories as their personal possessions—controlled the richest, most extensive empire Europe had known since ancient Rome.

1-7c Spanish Colonization

Spain established the model of colonization that other countries later imitated, a model with three major elements. First, the Crown tried to maintain tight control over the colonies, imposing a hierarchical government that allowed little autonomy to remote jurisdictions. That control included, for example, carefully vetting prospective emigrants and limiting their number. Settlers were then required to live in towns under the authorities' watchful eyes, and to import all their manufactured goods from Spain. Roman Catholic priests dispatched to the new territories attempted to ensure the colonists' conformity with orthodox religious views.

Second, men comprised most of the first colonists. Although some Spanish women later immigrated to America, the men took primarily indigenous—and, later, African—women as their wives or concubines, a development more often than not encouraged by colonial administrators. They thereby began creating the racially mixed population that characterizes much of Latin America to the present day.

Third, the colonies' wealth was based on the exploitation of both the Native population and slaves imported from Africa. Spaniards took over the role once assumed by Native leaders who had exacted labor and tribute from their subjects. Cortés established the **encomienda system**, which granted indigenous villages to individual conquistadors as a reward for their services, thus legalizing slavery in all but name.

In 1542, after stinging criticism from a colonial priest, Bartolomé de las Casas, the Spanish monarch formulated a new code of laws to reform the system, forbidding the conquerors from enslaving Native peoples while still allowing them to collect money and goods from tributary villages. In response to the restrictions and to the declining indigenous populations, the *encomenderos*, familiar with slavery in Spain, began to import kidnapped Africans in order to increase the labor force under their direct control. They employed Native peoples and Africans primarily in gold and silver mines, on sugar plantations, and on huge horse, cattle, and sheep ranches. African slavery was far more common on the larger Caribbean islands than on the mainland.

Many demoralized residents of Mesoamerica accepted the Christian religion brought to New Spain by Franciscan and Dominican friars—men who had joined religious orders bound by vows of poverty and celibacy. The friars devoted their energies to persuading indigenous peoples to

Snark/Art Resource, NY

▲ An image from the Codex Azcatitlan, an account of the Aztec (Mexica) people's history from their arrival in the Valley of Mexico through the conquest by Cortés. Printed European-style in the late sixteenth century—that is, about seven decades after the conquest— the codex nonetheless presents a Native viewpoint on the cataclysmic events. Here Cortés and his men are preceded by Malinche, his interpreter and mistress, and followed by their Native allies bearing food supplies. Also in the crowd is Cortés's black slave.

move into towns and to build Roman Catholic churches. Spaniards leveled existing cities, constructing cathedrals and monasteries on sites once occupied by Aztec, Incan, and Mayan temples. In such towns, Native peoples were exposed to European customs and religious rituals designed to assimilate Catholic and pagan beliefs. Friars deliberately juxtaposed the cult of the Virgin Mary with that of the corn goddess, and Native peoples adeptly melded aspects of their traditional worldview with Christianity, in a process anthropologists call *syncretism*. Thousands of indigenous men and women residing in Spanish territory embraced Catholicism, at least partly because it was the religion of their new rulers and they were accustomed to obedience.

1-7d Gold, Silver, and Spain's Decline

The New World's rich deposits of gold and silver, initially a boon, ultimately brought about the decline of Spain as a

major power. China, a huge country with silver coinage, insatiably demanded Spanish silver, gobbling up an estimated half of the total output of New World mines while paying twice the price current in Europe. In the 1570s, the Spanish began to dispatch silver-laden galleons annually from Acapulco (on Mexico's west coast) across the Pacific Ocean to trade at their new settlement at Manila, in the Philippines. This gave Spaniards easy access to luxury Chinese goods such as silk and Asian spices.

But the influx of wealth led to rapid inflation, which caused Spanish products to be overpriced in international markets and imported goods to become cheaper in Spain. The once-profitable Spanish textile industry collapsed. The seemingly endless income from American colonies also emboldened Spanish monarchs to spend lavishly on wars against the Dutch and the English. Several times in the late sixteenth and early seventeenth centuries, the monarchs repudiated the state debt, wreaking havoc on the nation's finances. When the South American gold and silver mines started to give out in the mid-seventeenth century, Spain's economy crumbled, and the nation lost much of its international importance.

1-8 The Columbian Exchange

▶ **What was the Columbian Exchange?**

▶ **What were the consequences of the Columbian Exchange for the peoples on both sides of the Atlantic?**

A broad mutual transfer of diseases, plants, and animals (called the **Columbian Exchange** by historian Alfred Crosby; see Map 1.6) resulted directly from the European voyages of the fifteenth and sixteenth centuries and from Spanish colonization. Separated for millennia, the

Columbian Exchange The widespread exchange, both deliberate and accidental, of animals, plants, germs, and peoples between Europe, Africa, and the Americas.

Eastern and Western Hemispheres had developed widely different life forms. Many large mammals, such as cattle and horses, were native to the connected continents of Europe, Asia, and Africa, while the Americas contained no domesticated beasts larger than dogs and llamas. The vegetable crops of the Americas—particularly maize, beans, squash, cassava, and potatoes—were more nutritious and produced higher yields than Europe's and Africa's wheat, millet, and rye. In time, Native peoples learned to raise and consume European livestock, and Europeans and Africans became accustomed to planting and eating American crops. (About three-fifths of all crops cultivated in the world today were first grown in the Americas.) The diets of ordinary people in all three parts of the globe were consequently vastly enriched. Partly as a result, the world's population doubled over the next three hundred years. The pressure of increased population in Europe propelled further waves of settler colonists westward, keeping the exchange in motion.

1-8a Smallpox and Other Diseases

Diseases carried west from Europe and Africa had a devastating impact on the Americas. Native peoples fell victim to microbes that had long infested the other continents and had

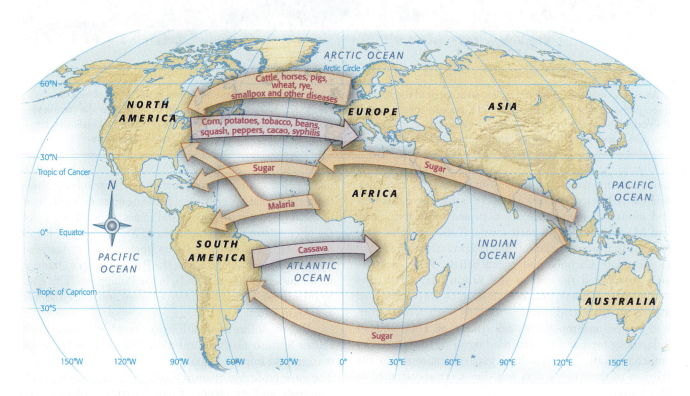

Map 1.6 Major Items in the Columbian Exchange

As European adventurers traversed the world in the fifteenth and sixteenth centuries, they initiated the "Columbian Exchange" of plants, animals, and diseases. These events changed the lives of the peoples of the world forever, bringing new foods and new pestilence to both sides of the Atlantic.

repeatedly killed hundreds of thousands but had also often left survivors with some measure of immunity. It was not only their isolation that made the indigenous populations of the Americas vulnerable, however. Non-biological processes, especially contacts forged through slave-trading and other forms of long-distance commerce, exacerbated the power of microbes and furthered the dramatic depopulation trend. When Columbus landed on Hispaniola in 1492, approximately half a million people resided there. Fifty years later, that island had fewer than two thousand Native inhabitants. Within thirty years of the first landfall at Guanahaní, not one Taíno survived in the Bahamas.

Although measles, typhus, influenza, malaria, and other illnesses severely afflicted the Native peoples, the greatest of the new infectious killers was smallpox, spread primarily by direct human contact. Epidemics recurred at twenty- or thirty-year intervals, when bouts often appeared in quick succession, so that weakened survivors of one wave would be felled by a second or third. Large numbers of deaths further disrupted societies already undergoing severe strains caused by colonization, rendering Native peoples more vulnerable to droughts, crop failures, and European invaders.

Even far to the north, where smaller American populations encountered only a few Europeans, disease ravaged the countryside. A great epidemic, probably viral hepatitis, swept through the villages along the coast north of Cape Cod from 1616 to 1618. Again, the mortality rate may have been as high as 90 percent. An English traveler several years later commented that the people had "died on heapes, as they lay in their houses." Bones and skulls covered the ruins of villages. Just a few years after this dramatic depopulation of the area, English colonists were able to establish settlements virtually unopposed. Disease made a powerful if accidental ally.

The Americans, though, seem to have taken an unintended revenge. They probably gave the Europeans syphilis, a virulent sexually transmitted disease. The first recorded European case of the ailment occurred in 1493 in Spain, shortly after Columbus's return from the Caribbean. Although less likely than smallpox to cause immediate death, syphilis was dangerous and debilitating. Carried by soldiers, sailors, and prostitutes, it spread quickly through Europe and Asia, reaching China by 1505.

1-8b Sugar, Horses, and Tobacco

The exchange of three commodities had significant impacts on Europe and the Americas. Sugar, first domesticated in the East Indies, was being grown on the islands of the Mediterranean Atlantic by 1450. The ravenous European demand for sugar—a medicine that quickly became a luxury foodstuff—led Columbus to take Canary Island sugar canes to Hispaniola on his 1493 voyage. By the 1520s, plantations in the Greater Antilles worked by African slaves regularly shipped cargoes of sugar to Spain. Half

▲ A male effigy dating from 200–800 CE, found in a burial site in Nayarit, Mexico. The lesions covering the figurine suggest that the person it represents is suffering from syphilis, which, untreated, produces these characteristic markings on the body in its later stages. Such evidence as this pre-Columbian effigy has now convinced most scholars that syphilis originated in the Americas—a hypothesis in dispute for many years.

a century later, the Portuguese colony in Brazil (founded 1532) was producing sugar for the European market on an even larger scale. After 1640, sugar cultivation became the crucial component of English and French colonization in the Caribbean.

Horses—which, like sugar, were brought to America by Columbus in 1493—fell into the hands of Native peoples in North America during the seventeenth century. Through trade and theft, horses spread among the peoples of the Great Plains, reaching most areas by 1750. Lakotas, Comanches, and Crows, among others, came to use horses for transportation and hunting, calculated their wealth in number of horses owned, and waged war primarily on horseback. Some groups that previously had cultivated crops abandoned agriculture. Because of the acquisition of horses, a mode of subsistence that had been based on hunting several different animals, in combination with gathering and agriculture, became one focused almost wholly on hunting buffalo.

In America, Europeans encountered tobacco, which at first they believed to have beneficial medicinal effects. Smoking and chewing the "Indian weed" became a fad in Europe in the sixteenth century. Despite the efforts of

The Pierpont Morgan Library/Art Resource, NY

▲ The mysterious illustrated text known as the Drake Manuscript and formally titled *Histoire Naturelle des Indies* (*Natural History of the Indies*) contains many depictions of the culture of the indigenous people of Spanish America in the 1580s. This delightful scene shows the end of a successful courtship: the woman's father sits under a tree while giving his blessing to the young couple. The future husband has proved his prowess as a hunter (note the rabbit in his hand) and the future wife her ability as a cook (she is grinding corn). Both are well dressed, and the pot boiling in the house in the background suggests a prosperous future for the happy pair.

such skeptics as King James I of England, who in 1604 pronounced smoking "loathsome to the eye, hatefull to the Nose, harmfull to the brain, [and] dangerous to the Lungs," tobacco's popularity soared. By the early seventeenth century, Englishmen could smoke the leaves at as many as seven thousand tobacco "houses" in London alone. At that point, the supply of the noxious weed came entirely from the colonies of New Spain.

The European and African invasion of the Americas therefore had a significant biological component, for the invaders carried plants and animals with them in both directions. Some creatures, such as livestock, they brought intentionally. Others, including rats (which infested their ships), weeds, and diseases, arrived unexpectedly. And the same process occurred in reverse. When Europeans returned home, they deliberately took crops including maize, potatoes, and tobacco, along with that unanticipated stowaway, syphilis.

1-9 Europeans in North America

▶ What kinds of economic exchanges occurred between Native peoples and Europeans?

▶ How did exploration and engagement with the American continent and its peoples affect the relationship between Spain and England?

▶ Why did early English attempts at colonization fail?

Europeans were initially more interested in exploiting North America's natural resources than in establishing colonies there. John Cabot had reported that fish were extraordinarily plentiful near Newfoundland, so Europeans rushed to take advantage of abundant codfish, which were in great demand as an inexpensive source of protein.

Maize

Mesoamericans believed that maize was a gift from Quetzalcoatl, the plumed serpent god. Cherokees told of an old woman whose blood produced the prized stalks after her grandson buried her body in a cleared, sunny field. For the Abenakis, the crop began when a beautiful maiden ordered a youth to drag her by the hair through a burned-over field. The long hair of the Cherokee grandmother and the Abenaki maiden turned into corn silk, the flower on the stalks that Europeans called "Indian" corn. Both tales' symbolic association of corn and women intriguingly supports archaeologists' recent suggestion that—in eastern North America

at least—female plant breeders substantially improved the productivity of maize.

Maize was a major part of the ancient American diet, sacred to the Native peoples who grew it. Ground into meal, dried maize was cooked as a mush or shaped into baked flat cakes, the forerunners of modern tortillas. Native peoples also heated the dried kernels of some varieties until they popped open, just as is done today. Although the European invaders of North and South America initially disdained maize, they soon learned it could be cultivated in a wide variety of conditions—from sea level to elevations of twelve thousand feet, from regions with abundant rainfall to lands with very little rainfall. Corn was also highly productive, yielding almost twice as many calories per acre as wheat. So Europeans, too, came to rely on corn, growing it not only in their American settlements but also in their homelands.

Maize cultivation spread to Asia and Africa. Today, China is second only to the United States in corn production. In Africa, corn is grown more widely than any other crop. Still, the United States produces over 40 percent of the world's corn, almost half of it in the three states of Illinois, Iowa, and Nebraska. Heavily subsidized by the federal government, corn is the nation's largest crop. More than half of American corn is consumed by livestock. Much of the rest is processed into syrup, which sweetens carbonated beverages and candies and has been linked to the spread of obesity and Type II diabetes in the modern United States. Corn is ubiquitous: an ingredient in light beer, toothpaste, and gasolines. It is used in the manufacture of tires, wallpaper, cat litter, and aspirin. Remarkably, of the ten thousand products in a modern American grocery store, about one-fourth rely to some extent on corn.

Today, this crop bequeathed to the world by ancient American plant breeders provides one-fifth of all the calories consumed by the earth's peoples. The gift of Quetzalcoatl has linked the globe.

CRITICAL THINKING

■ The dramatic ways Europeans changed the "New World" when they arrived are well known. But the currents of change ran in the reverse direction as well. This article describes the importance of maize or corn in the Americas as well as Europe. What other ideas or products that originated in the Americas made an impact on Europe?

◀ Painted by the Englishman John White, who accompanied an expedition to the new Virginia plantation in 1585 and was later named governor of that colony, this watercolor shows three stages of the cultivation of maize in the village of Secotan. "Rype corne" appears at the top right, with "greene corne" below it, beside orderly rows of "corne newly sprong." In all three fields, the crop is carefully fenced. White's painting was a study for a printed engraving, sold to satisfy the many English readers curious about American lifeways.

French, Spanish, Basque, and Portuguese sailors regularly fished North American waters throughout the sixteenth century; Verrazzano and Cartier, in 1524 and 1534, respectively, each encountered vessels already fishing along the American coast. In the early 1570s, after Spain opened its markets to English shipping, the English (who previously had fished near Iceland for home consumption only) eagerly joined the Newfoundland fishery, thereafter selling salt cod to Spain in exchange for valuable Asian goods. The English soon became dominant in the region, which by the end of the sixteenth century was the focal point of a European commerce more valuable than that with the Gulf of Mexico.

1-9a Trade Among Native Peoples and Europeans

Fishermen quickly realized they could increase their profits by exchanging cloth and metal goods, such as pots and knives, for Native trappers' beaver pelts, used to make fashionable hats in Europe. Initially, Europeans traded from ships sailing along the coast, but later they set up outposts on the mainland to centralize and control the traffic in furs. Such outposts were inhabited chiefly by male adventurers, who aimed to send as many pelts as possible home to Europe.

The Europeans' demand for furs, especially beaver, was matched by Native peoples' desire for European goods that could make their lives easier and establish their superiority over their neighbors. Some Native groups began to concentrate so completely on trapping for the European market that they abandoned their traditional economies and became partially dependent on others for food. The intensive trade in pelts also had serious ecological consequences. In some regions, the beaver were wiped out. The disappearance of their dams led to soil erosion, which increased when European settlers cleared forests for farmland in later decades.

1-9b Contest Between Spain and England

English merchants and political leaders watched enviously as Spain was enriched by its valuable American possessions. In the mid-sixteenth century, English "sea dogs" like John Hawkins and Sir Francis Drake began to raid Spanish treasure fleets sailing home from the Caribbean. Their actions caused friction between the two countries and helped foment a war that in 1588 culminated in the defeat of a huge Spanish invasion force—the Armada—off the English coast. As part of the contest with Spain, English leaders started to think about planting colonies in the Western Hemisphere, thereby gaining better access to valuable trade goods while preventing their enemy from dominating the Americas. By the late sixteenth century, world maps labeled not only "America" but also vast territories designated "New Spain" and "New France." The glaring absence of a region called "New

England" would have been a sore spot for Queen Elizabeth I and her courtiers.

Encouraging the queen to fund increased exploration across the Atlantic was Richard Hakluyt, an English clergyman who became fascinated by tales of exploratory voyages while he was a student in the 1560s. He translated and published numerous accounts of discoveries around the globe, insisting on England's preeminent claim to the North American continent. In *Divers Voyages* (1582) and especially *Principall Navigations* (1589), he argued for the benefits of English colonization, contending that "there is none, that of right may be more bolde in this enterprice than the Englishmen."

The first English colonial planners saw Spain's possessions as a model and a challenge. They hoped to reproduce Spanish successes by dispatching to America men who would exploit the Native peoples for their own and their nation's benefit. A group that included Sir Walter Raleigh began to promote a scheme to establish outposts that could trade with Native groups and serve as bases for attacks on Spain's new world possessions. Approving the idea, Queen Elizabeth authorized Raleigh to colonize North America.

1-9c Roanoke

After two preliminary expeditions, in 1587 Raleigh sent 118 colonists to the territory that tens of thousands of Native peoples called Ossomocomuck. Raleigh renamed it Virginia, after Elizabeth, the "Virgin Queen." The group, which included a small number of women and children, established a settlement on Roanoke Island, in what is now North Carolina. Their powerful neighbors included Secotans, Weapemeocs, and Chowanocs: Algonquian-speakers who had recently suffered war and drought. In this unstable environment, Native translators—kidnapped and taken to England on earlier voyages—once again played vital roles in colonial diplomacy. Negotiation was crucial, since the small band of settlers depended heavily on Native assistance; the ships scheduled to resupply them were delayed for two years by England's war with Spain. When resupply ships finally reached the tiny village in August 1590, the colonists had vanished, leaving only the word *Croatoan* (the name of a nearby island as well as one of the area's powerful Native groups) carved on a tree. Tree-ring studies show that the North Carolina coast experienced a severe drought between 1587 and 1589, which would have created a subsistence crisis for the settlers and could have led them to abandon the Roanoke site. Recent examination of a sixteenth-century watercolor map using modern imaging techniques reveals an inland fort to which the settlers may have retreated in a desperate attempt to survive.

England's first effort at planting a permanent settlement on the North American coast failed, as had earlier ventures

*A chiefe Heroroans wyfe of Pomeioc.
and her daughter of the age of. 8. or.
.10. yeares .*

▲ John White identified his subjects as the wife and daughter of the chief of Pomeioc, a village near Roanoke. Note the woman's elaborate tattoos and the fact that the daughter carries an Elizabethan doll, obviously given to her by one of the Englishmen.

by Portugal on Cape Breton Island (early 1520s), Spain in modern Georgia (mid 1520s), and France in South Carolina and northern Florida (1560s). All three enterprises collapsed because of the hostility of neighboring peoples and colonists' inability to be self-sustaining in foodstuffs. The Portuguese, the Spanish, the first French settlers, and the English failed to maintain friendly relations with indigenous peoples, and Spanish soldiers destroyed the Florida French colony in 1565 (see Section 2-1, "Spanish, French, and Dutch North America").

1-9d Harriot's *Briefe and True Report*

The reasons for such failings become clear in Thomas Harriot's *A Briefe and True Report of the New Found Land of Virginia*, published in 1588 to publicize Raleigh's colony. Harriot, a noted scientist who sailed with the second of the preliminary voyages to Roanoke, described the animals, plants, and people of the region. His account reveals that, although the explorers depended on nearby villagers for most of their food, they needlessly antagonized their neighbors by killing some of them for what Harriot admitted were unjustifiable reasons.

Harriot advised later colonizers to deal more humanely with Native peoples. But his book also reveals why that advice would rarely be followed. *A Briefe and True Report* examined the possibilities for economic development in America. Harriot stressed three points: the availability of valuable commodities, the potential profitability of exotic American products, and the relative ease of manipulating the Native population. Should the Americans attempt to repel the invaders, Harriot asserted, England's disciplined soldiers and superior weaponry would deliver easy victory.

Harriot's *Briefe and True Report* depicted for his English readers a bountiful land full of opportunities for quick profit. The Native people residing there would, he thought, "in a short time be brought to civilitie" through conversion or conquest—if they did not die from disease, the ravages of which he witnessed. If Thomas Harriot anticipated key elements of the story, the fate of Roanoke demonstrates that his prediction was far off the mark. European dominance of North America would be difficult to achieve. Indeed, it never was fully achieved, in the sense Harriot and his compatriots intended.

Summary

The process of initial contact among Europeans, Africans, and Americans began in the fourteenth century, when Portuguese sailors first explored the Mediterranean Atlantic and the West African coast. Those seamen established commercial ties that brought African slaves first to Iberia and then to the islands the Europeans conquered and settled. The Mediterranean Atlantic and its island sugar plantations nurtured the ambitions of mariners who, like Christopher Columbus, ventured into previously unknown waters—those who sailed to India and Brazil as well as to the Caribbean and the North American coast. When Columbus reached the Americas, he thought he had found Asia. Later explorers knew better but, except for the Spanish, regarded the Americas primarily as a barrier that prevented them from reaching their long-sought goal of an oceanic route to the riches of China and the Moluccas. Ordinary European fishermen were the first to realize that the northern coasts had valuable products to offer: fish and furs, both much in demand in their homelands.

Revitalizing Native Languages

If knowledge is power, then language is power. Words make us human, and languages carry the DNA of cultures. From one generation to the next, humans use language as a tool to maintain the distinct identities of individuals and groups. Like peoples, languages evolve. And like all living things, they are fragile. Their lives depend upon the regular nourishment that new speakers provide.

On the eve of European contact, the indigenous peoples of the Americas spoke a dizzying variety of languages. Continental North America was home to the speakers of as many as 1,200 distinct tongues, grouped into over a dozen major language families. (For comparison, linguists sort the languages of Europe into just four main families.)

Over the last five centuries, many of those languages— a crucial part of the biodiversity of humankind—have been silenced by the violence of colonialism, by dispersal and disease, by informal pressures to assimilate to increasingly dominant European cultures, and in some cases by formal campaigns to suppress their usage.

Today an estimated 139 native languages are spoken in the United States; the fluent speakers of perhaps 70 of these tongues are elderly, leaving those languages at risk.

Since the 1970s, however, a native language revitalization movement has grown in strength and visibility across the United States. From Hawai'i to the Florida everglades, cultural survival activists have created immersion schools and nests, language camps, computer programs, even video games to preserve and transmit indigenous languages. Such efforts have trained many fluent speakers of languages once endangered, such as Hawaiian, for example: in 1984, there were fewer than thirty fluent speakers of O-lelo Hawai'i under the age of twelve. Today, there are tens of thousands.

One of the most extraordinary language reclamation programs instructs students in Wôpanâak, the Algonquian-family language of the Wampanoag nation of Massachusetts. Founded in 1993 by Jessie "Little Doe" Baird (Mashpee) and the late Helen Manning, the Wôpanâak Language Reclamation Project (WLRP)

faced especially formidable obstacles: although Wôpanâak was the first indigenous American language to be expressed in alphabetic characters, its last speakers had died in the mid-nineteenth century. Using a range of documents—including sermons and scripture printed in Wôpanâak in the seventeenth century by English missionaries, and colonial land records using the language well into the eighteenth—the WLRP has created a dictionary of over 11,000 words, as well as first- and second-language curricula, an apprenticeship program, and immersion camps. A young Mashpee girl fluent in Wôpanâak and English is the language's first native speaker in seven generations.

CRITICAL THINKING

- Why are the efforts to reclaim or preserve indigenous languages important to the survival of indigenous peoples and their cultures in the modern world?
- How can new respect for indigenous cultures translate to an effort to right some of the social and economic wrongs of centuries?

The Aztecs predicted that their Fifth Sun would end in earthquakes and hunger. Hunger they surely experienced after Cortés's invasion, and even if there were no earthquakes, their great temples tumbled to the ground, as the Spaniards used their stones (and indigenous laborers) to construct cathedrals honoring their God and his son, Jesus. The conquerors coerced Native peoples and, later, relied on enslaved African workers to till the fields, mine the precious metals, and herd the livestock that earned immense profits for themselves and their mother country.

The first contacts of old world and new devastated the Western Hemisphere's Native inhabitants. European diseases killed millions; European livestock, along with a wide range

of other imported animals and plants, forever modified the American environment. Flourishing civilizations were markedly altered in just a few decades. Europe, too, was changed: American foodstuffs like corn and potatoes improved nutrition throughout the continent, and American gold and silver first enriched, then ruined, the Spanish economy.

A century after Columbus landed, many fewer people resided in North America than had lived there in 1491. And the people who did live there—Native, African, and European peoples—together made a world that was indeed new, a world engaged in the unprecedented process of combining religions, economies, ways of life, and political systems that had developed separately for millennia.

Suggestions for Further Reading

David Abulafia, *The Discovery of Mankind: Atlantic Encounters in the Age of Columbus* (2008)

Alfred W. Crosby, *The Columbian Exchange: Biological and Cultural Consequences of 1492* (1972)

John H. Elliott, *Empires of the Atlantic World: Britain and Spain in America, 1492–1830* (2006)

Elizabeth A. Fenn, *Encounters at the Heart of the World: A History of the Mandan People* (2014)

Alison Games, *The Web of Empire: English Cosmopolitans in an Age of Expansion, 1560–1660* (2008)

Paul Kelton, *Epidemics and Enslavement: Biological Catastrophe in the Native Southeast, 1492-1715* (2007)

Peter C. Mancall, *Hakluyt's Promise: An Elizabethan's Obsession for an English America* (2007)

Charles C. Mann, *1491: New Revelations of the Americas Before Columbus* (2005); *1493: Uncovering the New World Columbus Created* (2011)

Daniel K. Richter, *Before the Revolution: America's Ancient Pasts* (2011)

John K. Thornton, *Africa and Africans in the Making of the Atlantic World, 1400–1680* (1992)

MINDTAP From Cengage

MindTap® is a fully online personalized learning experience built upon Cengage Learning content. MindTap® combines student learning tools—readings, multimedia, activities, and assessments—into a singular Learning Path that guides students through the course and helps students develop the critical thinking, analysis, and communication skills that are essential to academic and professional success.

Europeans Colonize North America, 1600–1650

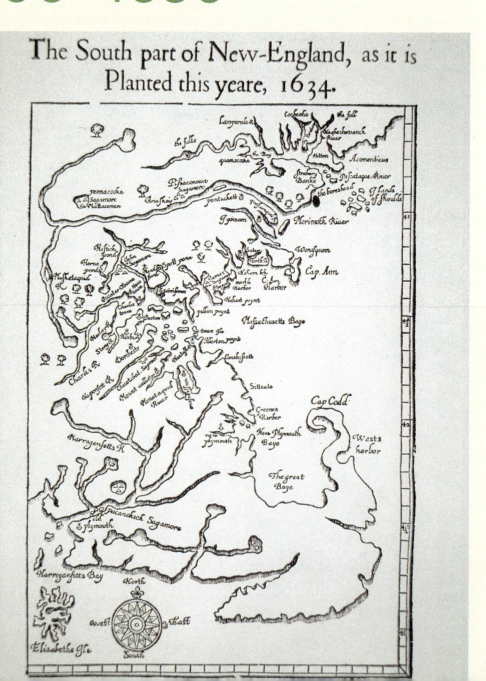

The South part of New-England, as it is Planted this yeare, 1634.

The timber of the country grows straight and tall, some trees being twenty, some thirty foot high, before they spread forth their branches," wrote the aptly-named William Wood in 1634. Printed in London, Wood's *New England's Prospect* was at once a travelogue and a recruitment brochure for England's new plantations. A rhyming verse inventoried the region's forests: proud stands of chestnut and walnut, oak and cypress, maple and hawthorn, elm and alder, and especially those "sky-towering pines," which made peerless masts.

Having set sail from a land largely deforested centuries before, English travelers marveled at New England's trees, a "commodity" Wood deemed second only to the region's waterways. In the 1620s and 1630s, soon after staking their claims to the Nauset territory they called Cape Cod, the Wampanoag lands they rechristened Plymouth, and the Massachusett harbors they renamed Salem and Boston, the transplants began to fell the forests. They built houses to shelter their fledgling villagers, churches to honor their God, and ships to sustain their way of life.

Theirs was a maritime culture. They had crossed a great ocean to plant their "new" world on its western shores. They huddled along that coastline, and along rivers that flowed toward it, for generations. They depended on the sea for food, for trade, for people, and for power. Shipbuilding was one of the region's first industries, and long remained one of the most important.

The *Desire* was one of the first large ships fashioned in New England. Holding 120 tons of cargo, it would have had two masts and a length of about 90 feet, making it only a little smaller than the

◄ William Wood's "The South Part of New-England," which appeared in his book *New England's Prospect* (London, 1634), was the first printed map of the region by an Englishman who had settled there. English place names and icons indicating churches dot the map, illustrating the colonists' desire to remake the territory in the image of their homeland. But Wood also records many Native place names—including those of particular Algonquian leaders or sagamores—reminding the viewer of the power of local Native groups and their proximity to English settlement. He is careful, too, to indicate the stands of trees crucial to the region's maritime economy.

Chronology

1558	■ Elizabeth I becomes queen of England
1565	■ Founding of St. Augustine (Florida), oldest permanent European settlement in present-day United States
1598	■ Oñate conquers Pueblos in New Mexico for Spain
1603	■ James I becomes king of England
1607	■ Jamestown founded, first permanent English settlement in North America
1608	■ Quebec founded by the French
1610	■ Santa Fe, New Mexico, founded by the Spanish
1614	■ Fort Orange (Albany, New York) founded by the Dutch
1619	■ Virginia House of Burgesses established, first representative assembly in the English colonies
1620	■ Plymouth colony founded, first permanent English settlement in New England
1622	■ Powhatan Confederacy rebels against Virginia
1624	■ Dutch settle on Manhattan Island (New Amsterdam) ■ James I revokes Virginia Company's charter
1625	■ Charles I becomes king of England
1627	■ English colonize Barbados
1630	■ Massachusetts Bay colony founded ■ Providence Island founded
1630s–1640s	■ "Sugar revolution" in the West Indies
1634	■ Maryland founded
1636	■ Roger Williams expelled from Massachusetts Bay, founds Providence, Rhode Island ■ Connecticut founded
1636–1638	■ Pequot War in New England
1638	■ Anne Hutchinson expelled from Massachusetts Bay
1642	■ Montreal founded by the French
1646	■ Treaty ends hostilities between Virginia and Powhatan Confederacy

Mayflower that famously landed on Plymouth Rock in 1620. Loath to waste anything, the craftsmen who built the *Desire* fitted it out with equipment salvaged from the wreck of the English barque *Warwick*, which had run aground at Natasket, just beyond Boston Harbor. The *Desire* inherited the *Warwick*'s rigging, its ironwork, and its mounted guns. It was a merchant vessel, but commerce and conquest were never very far apart. The same ships that brought families of New England settlers who considered themselves religious refugees also carried muskets, bandoliers, swords, and pikes by the dozen.

Experience an interactive version of this story in MindTap®.

By the time the *Desire* was built, in the fall of 1636, the colonization of New England had been revealed for the violent enterprise that tracts like Wood's *New England Prospect* did much to disguise. Tensions with the Pequots, who controlled trade in much of present-day Connecticut, ran high, and English settlers began to talk of war. The following May, English soldiers and Narragansett warriors allied to rain devastation on Pequot country. Many of the survivors were taken captive. Pequot women and "maid children" should be "disposed aboute in the townes," the Massachusetts governor wrote, describing human spoils of war, distributed as slaves. Captive men and boys were deemed more dangerous; they were to be transported to the English plantations of the West Indies, which were just beginning to experiment with the cultivation of sugar, a labor-intensive crop.

The *Desire* headed south that June, likely its maiden voyage, its new-cut timbers still smelling sharply of pine. No bill of lading survives, so we do not know everything Captain William Pierce crammed into the ship's hold. His cargo likely included salted fish and imported rum, which Governor John Winthrop called "the only commodities for those parts." We do know that among the goods Pierce meant to peddle in Bermuda were seventeen Pequot captives, all but two of them boys.

Pierce, an experienced mariner, had crossed the Atlantic several times already. But on this trip, he missed his mark, fetching up in the English settlement known as Providence Island, off the coast of present-day Nicaragua. He spent the summer and fall trading there, and in some of the other islands dotting those crystal blue waters, before returning north.

In January, the *Desire* sailed back into Boston Harbor, its hold stuffed with the fruits of the Indies trade. Pierce unloaded cotton, tobacco, and salt, along with an unspecified number of "negroes": men and women first taken from Africa by Spanish slave traders, then stolen from Spanish ships by English privateers, and now peddled for sale in the cold new world of New England. Though never the predominant labor system in New England, chattel slavery would continue to be a crucial part of the region's economy and culture, fueling its vital trade with the West Indies for nearly two centuries.

By the time the *Desire* plied the waters of the Caribbean, Spain no longer predominated in the Americas. France, the Netherlands, and England all had permanent colonies in North America by the 1640s. Like the conquistadors, French and Dutch merchants (on the mainland) and planters (in the Caribbean) hoped to make a quick profit and then perhaps return to their homelands. As Thomas Harriot had made clear in the 1580s, English colonists were just as interested in profiting from North America. But they pursued profit in a different way.

Most of the new world's English colonists—including those who settled in New England—came to America intending to stay. They were settlers, whose every success in claiming land and creating community meant the permanent displacement of Native populations. Along the northeast Atlantic coast, settler-colonists arrived in family groups, sometimes accompanied by friends and relatives. They re-created the European agricultural economy and family life to an extent impossible in colonies where single men predominated, as they did in the English colonies of the Chesapeake region and the Caribbean, which focused on the large-scale production of cash crops for export.

Wherever they settled, the English, like other Europeans, prospered only where they learned to adapt to the alien environment. Settlers had to learn to grow such unfamiliar American crops as maize and squash. They also had to develop extensive trading relationships with Native peoples and with other English and European colonies. Needing laborers for their fields, they first used English **indentured servants**. But even in New England, they experimented with enslaving Native peoples and soon began to import Africans to hold in bondage. The early history of England's America is best understood not as an isolated story of English settlement but rather as a series of complex negotiations among European, African, and American peoples.

- *Why did different groups come to the Americas? Which people came by choice, and which were forced to migrate?*

- *How did different Native peoples react to the colonists' presence?*

- *In what ways did the English colonies in North America and the Caribbean differ, and in what ways were they alike?*

2-1 Spanish, French, and Dutch North America

▶ **How did the Spaniards and the French interact with Native American populations?**

▶ **What economic developments emerged in the early European settlements in North America?**

▶ **Why did European powers come into conflict with one another in North America?**

Spaniards established the first permanent European settlement within the boundaries of the modern United States, but others had initially attempted that feat. Twice in the 1560s Huguenots (French Protestants), who were seeking to escape persecution, planted colonies on the south Atlantic coast. A passing ship rescued the starving survivors of the first colony, located in present-day South Carolina. The second, near modern Jacksonville, Florida, was destroyed in 1565 by a Spanish expedition under the command of Pedro Menéndez de Avilés. To ensure Spanish domination of the strategically important region (located near sea-lanes used by

indentured servants Young men and women, usually unemployed and poor, who were given free passage to America, plus basic needs such as food, shelter, and clothing, in exchange for labor after their arrival, usually for four to seven years.

Spanish treasure ships), Menéndez set up a fortified outpost named St. Augustine—now the oldest continuously inhabited European settlement in the United States.

The local Guale and Timucua nations initially allied themselves with the powerful newcomers and welcomed Franciscan friars into their villages. The relationship did not remain peaceful for long, though, because the Guale and Timucua nations resisted the imposition of Spanish authority. Still, the Franciscans offered these indigenous peoples spiritual solace for the diseases and troubles besetting them after the Europeans' invasion, and eventually gained numerous converts at missions that stretched westward across Florida and northward into the islands along the Atlantic coast.

2-1a New Mexico

More than thirty years after the founding of St. Augustine, conquistadors ventured anew into the present-day United States. In 1598, drawn northward by rumors of rich cities, Juan de Oñate, a Mexican-born adventurer whose *mestiza* wife descended from both Cortés and Motecuhzoma, led about five hundred soldiers and settlers to New Mexico. At first, the Pueblo peoples greeted the newcomers cordially. But when the Spaniards began to use torture, murder, and rape to extort supplies from the villagers, the residents of Acoma killed several soldiers, among them Oñate's nephew. The invaders responded ferociously, killing more than eight hundred people and capturing the remainder. All captives above the age of twelve were enslaved for twenty years, and men older than twenty-five had one foot amputated. Not surprisingly, the other Pueblo villages surrendered.

Yet Oñate's bloody victory proved illusory, for New Mexico held little wealth, and it was too far from the Pacific to assist in protecting Spanish sea-lanes. Officials considered abandoning the isolated colony, which lay 800 miles north of the nearest Spanish settlement. But for defensive purposes, the authorities decided to maintain a small military outpost and a few Christian missions in the area, with the capital at Santa Fe (founded 1610) (see Map 3.2, Section 3-2c). As in regions to the south, Spanish leaders were granted *encomiendas,* giving them control over the labor of Pueblo villagers. In the absence of mines or fertile agricultural lands, however, such grants yielded small profit. After most of the Spanish departed, their horses remained, transforming the lives of the indigenous inhabitants.

2-1b Quebec and Montreal

The French turned their attention to the area that Jacques Cartier had explored in the 1530s. Several times they tried to establish permanent bases along Canada's Atlantic coast but failed until 1605, when they founded Port Royal. Then in 1608, Samuel de Champlain set up a trading post at an interior site that the local Iroquois called Stadacona. Champlain renamed it Quebec. He had chosen well: Quebec was the most defensible spot in the entire St. Lawrence River valley, a stronghold that controlled access to the heartland of the continent. In 1642, the French established a second post, Montreal, at the falls of the St. Lawrence (and thus at the end of navigation by oceangoing vessels), a place the Iroquois knew as Hochelaga.

The new posts quickly took over the lucrative trade in beaver pelts (see Table 2.1). The colony's leaders granted

Table 2.1 The Founding of Permanent European Colonies in North America, 1565–1640

Colony	Founder(s)	Date	Basis of Economy
Florida	Pedro Menéndez de Avilés	1565	Farming
New Mexico	Juan de Oñate	1598	Livestock
Virginia	Virginia Co.	1607	Tobacco
New France	France	1608	Fur trading
Bermuda	English sailors	1609	Tobacco, ship-building
New Netherland	Dutch West India Co.	1614	Fur trading
Plymouth	Separatists	1620	Farming, fishing
Maine	Sir Ferdinando Gorges	1622	Fishing
St. Kitts, Barbados, et al.	European immigrants	1624	Sugar
Massachusetts Bay	Massachusetts Bay Company	1630	Farming, fishing, fur trading
Maryland	Cecilius Calvert	1634	Tobacco
Rhode Island	Roger Williams	1636	Farming
Connecticut	Thomas Hooker	1636	Farming, fur trading
New Haven	Massachusetts migrants	1638	Farming
New Hampshire	Massachusetts migrants	1638	Farming, fishing

Acoma Pueblo

Today, as in the late sixteenth century when it was besieged and eventually captured by the Spanish, the Acoma Pueblo sits high atop an isolated mesa. The Ancient Pueblo selected the location, 365 feet above the valley floor, because they could easily defend it. Building the complex was a massive undertaking. Over forty tons of sandstone had to be cut from the surrounding cliffs and pulled up the mesa to make each of the pueblo's hundreds of rooms. Roofing Acoma and the other dwellings in Chaco Canyon consumed some 200,000 trees. Much of the labor was likely provided by other Native groups enslaved by the Ancient Pueblos. The buildings for which they gave their labor and their lives endured; some structures dating to the eleventh century still stand in the middle of the village.

In addition to making construction difficult, situating the city so high above the plains created problems with water supply. To this day there is no source of water in the village. Acoma's residents had to carry water up a steep set of stairs cut into the mesa's side (today there is an almost equally steep road). The women of Acoma were and are accomplished potters. Some pots, like the one shown here, were designed with a low center of gravity.

CRITICAL THINKING

- How would that design help women to reach the top of the mesa with much-needed water?
- How would they carry such pots?

Kevin Fleming/Corbis/VCG/Getty Images

▲ Acoma Pueblo today. The village is now used primarily for ritual purposes; few people reside there permanently, because all water must be trucked in.

Richard A. Cooke III/Getty Images

▲ A pot designed for carrying water to the top of the mesa.

Map 2.1 European Settlements and Native American Tribes in Eastern North America, 1650

The few European settlements established in the East before 1650 were widely scattered, hugging the shores of the Atlantic Ocean and the banks of its major rivers. By contrast, America's Native inhabitants controlled the vast interior expanse of the continent, and Spaniards had begun to move into the West.

land along the river to wealthy *seigneurs* (nobles), who then imported tenants to work their farms. Only a few Europeans resided in New France; most were men, some of whom married Native women. A small number of Frenchmen brought their wives and took up agriculture. Even so, more than twenty-five years after its founding, Quebec had just sixty-four resident families, along with traders and soldiers. Northern New France never grew much beyond the confines of the river valley between Quebec and Montreal (see Map 2.1). Thus, it differed significantly from New Spain, characterized by scattered cities and direct supervision of indigenous laborers.

2-1c Jesuit Missions in New France

French missionaries of the Society of Jesus (Jesuits), a Roman Catholic order dedicated to converting nonbelievers to Christianity, also came to New France. First arriving in Quebec in 1625, the Jesuits, whom the Huron, Iroquois, and Abenaki peoples called Black Robes, tried to persuade indigenous peoples to live near French settlements and to adopt European agricultural methods. When that effort failed, the Jesuits concluded that they could introduce their new charges to Catholicism without insisting that they fundamentally alter their traditional ways of life. Accordingly, the Black Robes learned indigenous languages and traveled to remote regions of the interior, where they lived in twos and threes among hundreds of potential converts. Fluent linguists and careful observers, the Jesuits wrote in great detail about the ways of the Huron, Iroquois, and Abenaki men and women whose souls they attempted to "harvest" for the Christian God.

Jesuits used various strategies to gain the confidence of influential men and to undermine the authority of traditional religious leaders. Trained in rhetoric, Jesuits won admirers with their eloquence. Immune to smallpox (for all had survived the disease already), the Black Robes said epidemics were God's punishment for sin, their arguments aided by the ineffectiveness of traditional remedies against the new pestilence. Drawing on European science, Jesuits predicted solar and lunar eclipses. They further amazed villagers by communicating with each other over long distances through marks on paper. Native peoples' desire to harness the extraordinary power of literacy was one of the factors that made them receptive to the missionaries.

Jesuits slowly gained thousands of converts, some of whom moved to reserves set aside for Christian Native peoples. Catholicism offered women in particular the inspiring role model of the Virgin Mary, personified in Montreal and Quebec by Ursuline nuns who ministered to indigenous women and children. Many male and female converts followed Catholic teachings with fervor, casting off native customs allowing premarital sex and easy divorce, which Catholic doctrine prohibited. In the late 1670s, one convert, a young Mohawk named Kateri Tekakwitha, inspired thousands with her celibacy and other ascetic devotional practices. Known as "the Lily of the Mohawks," her grave was said to be the site of miracles. In October 2012, the Roman Catholic Church made her the first Native American saint.

If they embraced some Christian doctrine, most Native converts resisted Jesuits' attempts to foster strict European child-rearing methods, instead retaining their more relaxed practices. Jesuits, unlike Franciscans in New Mexico, recognized that such aspects of Native cultures could be compatible with Christian beliefs. Their efforts to attract converts were further aided by their lack of interest in labor tribute or land acquisition.

2-1d New Netherland

Jesuit missionaries faced little competition from other Europeans for Native people's souls, but French fur traders had to confront a direct challenge to their economic designs. In 1614,

only five years after Henry Hudson explored the river that now bears his name, his sponsor, the Dutch West India Company, established an outpost (Fort Orange) at the site of present-day Albany, New York. Like the French, the Dutch sought beaver pelts, and their presence so close to Quebec threatened France's interests in the region. The Netherlands, the world's dominant commercial power, aimed primarily at trade rather than at colonization. Thus **New Netherland**, like New France, remained small, confined largely to a river valley offering easy access to its settlements. The colony's southern anchor was **New Amsterdam**, founded in 1624 on an island at the mouth of the Hudson River that the Lenape called Manahatta.

New Netherland was a small outpost of a vast commercial empire that extended to Africa, Brazil, and modern-day Indonesia. Autocratic directors-general ruled the colony for the Dutch West India Company. With no elected assembly, settlers felt little loyalty to their nominal leaders. Few migrants arrived. Even an offer in 1629 of large land grants, or patroonships, to people who would bring fifty settlers to the province failed to attract many takers. (Only one such tract—Rensselaerswyck, near Albany—was ever fully developed.) As late as the mid-1660s, New Netherland had only about five thousand European inhabitants. Some were Swedes and Finns who resided in the former colony of New Sweden (founded in 1638 on the Delaware River; see Map 2.1), which the Dutch seized in 1655.

The Native American allies of New France and New Netherland clashed in part because of fur-trade rivalries. In the 1640s the Iroquois, who traded chiefly with the Dutch and lived in modern upstate New York, went to war against the Huron, who traded primarily with the French and lived in present-day Ontario. The Iroquois wanted to become the major supplier of pelts to Europeans and wanted to ensure the security of their hunting territories. They achieved both goals by using guns supplied by the Dutch to virtually exterminate the Huron, whose population had been decimated by smallpox. The Iroquois thus established themselves as a major force in the region, one that Europeans could ignore only at their peril.

2-2 England's America

▶ **What factors contributed to the migration of English men and women to the North American colonies?**

▶ **What religious changes emerged in European society because of the Reformation?**

▶ **How did the Reformation reshape English society and government?**

The failure of Sir Walter Raleigh's Roanoke colony ended English efforts to settle in North America for nearly two decades. When the English decided in 1606 to try once more, they again planned colonies that imitated the Spanish model. Yet greater success came when

New Netherland Dutch colony in America.

New Amsterdam Dutch seaport that would become New York City.

they abandoned that model. Unlike Spain, France, or the Netherlands, England eventually sent large numbers of men and women to set up agriculturally based colonies on the mainland. Two major developments prompted approximately two hundred thousand ordinary English men and women to move to North America in the seventeenth century and led their government to encourage their emigration.

2-2a Social and Economic Change

The first development was the onset of dramatic social and economic change. In the 150-year period after 1530, largely as a result of the importation of nutritious American crops, which raised the caloric intake of ordinary Europeans, England's population doubled. All those additional people needed food, clothing, and other goods. The competition for goods led to inflation, and the increased number of workers caused a fall in real wages. In these new circumstances, some people—especially those whose sizable landholdings could produce food and clothing fibers for the growing population—grew richer. Others, particularly landless laborers and those with small amounts of land, fell into poverty. When landowners raised rents, took control of lands that peasants had long used in common (enclosure), or combined smallholdings into large units, they displaced their tenants. Geographical as well as social mobility increased. England's cities swelled to bursting. Approximately seventy-five thousand people lived in London in 1550. A century later, nearly four hundred thousand people packed its narrow alleys and cramped buildings.

As "masterless men"—the landless and homeless—crowded the streets and highways, wealthy English people reacted with alarm. Obsessed with maintaining order, officials came to believe England was overcrowded. They hoped that colonies in North America would siphon off England's "surplus population," easing social strains at home. Many ordinary people decided they could improve their circumstances by migrating from a small, land-scarce, apparently overpopulated island to a boundless, land-rich, apparently empty new world. Among those tempted to emigrate were men like William Rudyerd: the younger sons of gentlemen, excluded from inheriting land by the practice of primogeniture, which reserved all real estate for the eldest son. Such economic considerations were rendered even more significant in light of the second development: a major change in English religious practice.

2-2b English Reformation

The sixteenth century witnessed a religious transformation that eventually led large numbers of English dissenters to leave their homeland. In 1533 Henry VIII, wanting a male heir and infatuated with Anne Boleyn, asked the pope to annul his nearly twenty-year marriage to the Spanish-born Catherine of Aragón. When the pope refused, Henry broke with the Roman Catholic Church. He founded the Church of England and—with Parliament's concurrence—proclaimed himself its head.

At first, the Church of England differed little from Catholicism. Under Henry's daughter, Elizabeth I (child of his second marriage, to Anne Boleyn), though, currents of religious belief that had originated on the European continent early in the sixteenth century dramatically affected England's recently established church.

These currents constituted the **Protestant Reformation**, led by **Martin Luther**, a German monk, and **Jean Calvin**, a French cleric and lawyer. Challenging the Catholic doctrine that priests were intermediaries between laypeople and God, Luther and Calvin insisted that people could interpret the Bible for themselves. That notion stimulated the spread of literacy: to understand and interpret the Bible, people had to learn how to read. Both Luther and Calvin rejected Catholic rituals, denying the need for elaborate ceremony and church hierarchy. They also asserted that the key to salvation was faith in God, rather than—as Catholic teaching had it—a combination of faith and good works. Calvin went further, stressing God's omnipotence and emphasizing the need for people to submit totally to God's will.

2-2c Puritans, Separatists, and Presbyterians

Elizabeth I tolerated diverse forms of Christianity as long as her subjects acknowledged her authority as head of the Church of England. During her long reign (1558–1603), Calvin's ideas gained influence in England, Wales, and especially Scotland. (In Ireland, also part of her realm, Catholicism remained dominant.) The Scottish church eventually adopted Presbyterianism, an organizational structure that dispensed with bishops and placed religious authority in bodies of clerics and laymen called presbyteries. By the late sixteenth century, though, many Calvinists—including those called Puritans (a nickname used to insult those who wanted to purify the church), or Separatists (because they wanted to leave it entirely)—believed that reformers in England and Scotland had not gone far enough. Henry had simplified the church hierarchy, and the Scots had altered it; Puritans and Separatists wanted to abolish it altogether. Henry and the Scots had subordinated the church to the interests of the state; the dissenters wanted a church free from political interference. The established churches of England and Scotland, like the Catholic Church or the official Protestant churches of continental European countries, continued to encompass all residents of the realm. Calvinists in England and Scotland wanted to confine church membership to those God had chosen for salvation.

Paradoxically, though, dissenters insisted that people could not know for certain if they were "saved." Mere mortals could not comprehend or affect their predestination to heaven or hell. Thus, pious Calvinists confronted serious dilemmas: if the saved (or "elect") could not be identified with certainty, how could proper churches be constituted? And if you were predestined and could not alter fate, why attend church or respect civil law? Calvinists dealt with the

Protestant Reformation Split of Christian reformers from Roman Catholic church; triggered by Martin Luther.

Martin Luther (1483–1546) German theologian who critiqued the practices of the Catholic church, including the authority of the pope.

Jean Calvin (1509–1554) French Protestant theologian who believed in the "predestination" of individuals for either heaven or hell, regardless of their behavior.

Table 2.2 Tudor and Stuart Monarchs of England, 1509–1649

Monarch	Reign	Relation to Predecessor
Henry VIII	1509–1547	Son
Edward VI	1547–1553	Son
Mary I	1553–1558	Half-sister
Elizabeth I	1558–1603	Half-sister
James I	1603–1625	Cousin
Charles I	1625–1649	Son

first dilemma by admitting that their judgments about church membership only approximated God's unknowable decisions. They resolved the second by reasoning that God gave the elect the ability to accept salvation and to lead a moral life. Though good works would not earn you a place in heaven, pious behavior might signal that you belonged there.

2-2d Stuart Monarchs

Elizabeth I's Stuart successors, her cousin James I (1603–1625) and his son Charles I (1625–1649), exhibited less tolerance for Calvinists (see Table 2.2). As Scots, they also had little respect for the traditions of representative government that had developed in England. The wealthy landowners who sat in Parliament had grown accustomed to wielding considerable influence over government policies, especially taxation. But James I, taking a position later endorsed by his son, publicly declared his belief in the divine right of kings. The Stuarts insisted that a monarch's power came directly from God and that his subjects had a duty to obey him. They likened the king's absolute authority to a father's authority over his children.

Both James I and Charles I believed their authority included the power to enforce religious conformity. Because Calvinists—and remaining Catholics in England and Scotland—challenged many of the most important precepts of the Church of England, the Stuart monarchs authorized the removal of dissenting clergymen from their pulpits. In the 1620s and 1630s, some Puritans, Separatists, Presbyterians, and Catholics decided to move to America, where they hoped to practice their diverse religious beliefs unhindered by the Stuarts or their bishops. Some fled hurriedly to avoid arrest and imprisonment.

2-3 The Founding of Virginia

▶ How did the early settlers of Jamestown interact with local Native American populations?

▶ How did the competing viewpoints of one another impact the relationship between the English and Native American populations?

▶ What impact did the Virginia Company have on the Jamestown settlement?

The impetus for England's first permanent colony in the Western Hemisphere was both religious and economic. The newly militant English Protestants were eager to combat "popery" both at home and in the Americas. They concurred with the English writer Richard Hakluyt, who remarked that if Spaniards, "in their superstition," had "don so great thinges in so shorte space," surely the adherents of "our true and sincere Religion" could achieve even more remarkable results.

Accordingly, in 1606, a group of merchants and wealthy gentry—some of them aligned with religious reformers—obtained a royal charter for the Virginia Company, organized as a **joint-stock company**. Such forerunners of modern corporations, initially created to finance trading voyages, pooled the resources of many small investors through stock sales. Yet the joint-stock company ultimately proved to be a poor vehicle for establishing colonies, which required significant continuing investments of capital. The lack of immediate returns generated tension between stockholders and colonists. Although investors in the Virginia Company anticipated great profits, neither settlement the company established—one in Maine that collapsed within a year and Jamestown—ever earned much.

2-3a Jamestown and Tsenacommacah

In 1607, the Virginia Company dispatched 108 men and boys to a region near Chesapeake Bay called Tsenacommacah by its Native inhabitants. That May, the colonists established the palisaded settlement called **Jamestown** on a swampy peninsula in a river they also named for their monarch. Ill equipped for survival in the unfamiliar environment, the colonists attempted to maintain traditional English hierarchies, but soon fell victim to dissension and disease. Familiar with Spanish experience, the gentlemen and soldiers at Jamestown expected to rely on local Native peoples for food and tribute, yet the residents of Tsenacommacah refused to cooperate. Moreover, the settlers had the bad luck to arrive in the midst of a severe drought (now known to be the worst in the region for 1,700 years). The lack of rainfall made it difficult to cultivate crops and polluted their drinking water. The arrival of hundreds more colonists over the next several years only added to the pressure on scarce resources.

The powerful weroance (chief) of Tsenacommacah, Powhatan, had inherited rule over six Algonquian villages and later gained control of some twenty-five others (see Map 2.1). Late in 1607, Powhatan tentatively agreed to an alliance negotiated by Captain **John Smith**, one of the English colony's leaders. In exchange for foodstuffs, Powhatan hoped to acquire guns, hatchets, and swords, which would give him a technological advantage over his enemies. Each side in the alliance wanted to subordinate the other, but neither succeeded.

The fragile relationship soon foundered on mutual mistrust. The weroance

joint-stock company Business partnership that amasses capital through sales of stock to investors.

Jamestown First enduring English colony, established in 1607.

John Smith (1580–1631) English soldier and adventurer who become one of the early leaders of Jamestown.

relocated his primary village in early 1609 to a place the new-comers could not access easily. Without Powhatan's assistance, Jamestown experienced a "starving time" (winter 1609–1610). Hundreds perished and at least one survivor resorted to digging up corpses for food. When spring came, barely 60 of the 500 colonists who had come to Jamestown remained alive. They packed up to leave on a newly arrived ship, but en route up the James River encountered ships carrying a new governor, male and female settlers, and added supplies, so they returned to Jamestown.

Sporadic skirmishes ensued as the standoff with the Powhatans continued. To gain the upper hand, the settlers in 1613 kidnapped Powhatan's daughter, Pocahontas, and held her hostage. In captivity, she converted to Christianity and married a colonist, John Rolfe. Their union initiated a period of peace between the English and her people. Funded by the Virginia Company, she and Rolfe sailed to England to promote interest in the colony. Pocahontas died at Gravesend in 1616, probably of dysentery, leaving an infant son who returned to Virginia as a young adult.

Although their royal charter nominally laid claim to a much wider territory, the Jamestown settlers saw their "Virginia" as essentially corresponding to Tsenacommacah. Powhatan's dominion was bounded on the north by the Potomac, on the south by the Great Dismal Swamp, and on the west by the fall line—the beginning of the upland Piedmont. Beyond those boundaries lay the Powhatans' enemies and (especially in the west) lands the Powhatans feared to enter. English people relied on the Powhatans as guides and interpreters, traveling along rivers and precontact paths in order to trade with the Powhatans' partners.

2-3b Algonquian and English Cultural Differences

In Tsenacommacah and elsewhere on the North American coast, English settlers and Algonquians focused on their cultural differences—not their similarities—although both groups held deep religious beliefs, subsisted primarily through agriculture, accepted social and political hierarchy, and observed well-defined gender roles. From the outset, English men regarded Native men as lazy because they did not cultivate crops and spent much of their time hunting (a sport, not work, in English eyes). Native men thought English men effeminate because they did the "woman's work" of cultivation. In the same vein, the English believed Algonquian women were oppressed because they did heavy field labor.

Algonquian and English hierarchies differed. English political and military leaders tended to rule autocratically, whereas Algonquian leaders (even Powhatan) had more limited authority. Accustomed to the powerful kings of Europe, the English overestimated the ability of chiefs to make treaties that would bind their people.

Furthermore, Algonquian and English concepts of property differed. Most Algonquian villages held their land communally. Land could not be bought or sold outright, although certain rights to use it (for example, for hunting or fishing)

▲ During her visit to London, the Powhatan princess—called "Pocahontas" or Matoaka in her childhood and Rebecca as an adult—sat for a portrait by Simon Van de Passe, a young Dutch artist. This image, based on de Passe's engraving, was completed by an anonymous painter roughly a century later. Both the seventeenth-century original and the eighteenth-century copy depict Pocahontas wearing pearl earrings and an elaborate cloak topped by a gorgeous lace ruff. The ostrich fan she holds symbolizes royalty, but her hat is of a type more commonly worn by Puritan men. Van de Passe did not "Europeanize" Pocahontas's features in the image he drew from life in the 1610s, but the later artist did, lightening her skin and hair, and making her cheekbones less prominent.

could be transferred. Once, most English villagers, too, had used land in common, but enclosures in the previous century had made them accustomed to individual farms and to buying and selling land. The English also refused to accept the validity of Native peoples' claims to traditional hunting territories, insisting that only land intensively cultivated or "improved" could be regarded as owned or occupied. As one colonist put it, "salvadge peoples" who "rambled" over a region without farming it could claim no "title or propertye" in the land. Ownership of such "unclaimed" property, the English believed, lay with the English monarchy, whose flag John Cabot had planted in North America in 1497.

Above all, where native belief systems tended readily to absorb new ideas, the English settlers believed unwaveringly in the superiority of their own civilization. If they often anticipated living peacefully alongside indigenous peoples, they always assumed that they would dictate the terms of such coexistence. Like Thomas Harriot at Roanoke, they expected Native peoples to adopt English customs and to convert to Christianity. They showed little respect for the Native Americans when they believed English interests

National Portrait Gallery, Smithsonian Institution/Art Resource, NY

were at stake, as was demonstrated by developments in Virginia once the settlers found the salable commodity they sought.

2-3c Tobacco Cultivation

That commodity was tobacco, the American crop introduced to Europe by the Spanish. In 1611, John Rolfe planted seeds of a variety from the Spanish Caribbean, which was considered superior to the strain Virginia Algonquians grew. Nine years later, Virginians exported forty thousand pounds of cured leaves; by the late 1620s, annual shipments had jumped to 1.5 million pounds. The great tobacco boom had begun, fueled by high prices and high profits for planters who responded to escalating demand from Europe and Africa. The price later fell almost as sharply as it had risen, fluctuating wildly from year to year in response to a glutted market and growing international competition. Nevertheless, tobacco made Virginia prosper.

The spread of tobacco cultivation altered life for everyone. Farming tobacco required abundant land because the crop quickly drained soil of nutrients. Planters soon learned that a field could produce only about three good crops before it had to lie fallow for several years to regain its fertility. As eager applicants asked the Virginia Company for land grants on both sides of the James River, small English settlements began to expand rapidly. Lulled into a false sense of security by years of peace with their Powhatan neighbors, Virginians established farms along the riverbanks at some distance from one another—a settlement pattern convenient for tobacco cultivation but dangerous for defense.

2-3d Opechancanough's Rebellion

Opechancanough, Powhatan's brother and successor, watched the English colonists' expansion and witnessed their attempts to convert Native peoples to Christianity. Recognizing the danger, the war leader launched coordinated attacks along the James River on March 22, 1622. By the end of the day, 347 English men, women, and children (about one-quarter of the colony) lay dead. Only a timely warning from two Christian converts saved Jamestown from destruction.

▲ A comparison of the portrait of Sir Walter Raleigh and his son (left), with that of an Algonquian man drawn by John White, from Raleigh's Roanoke expedition (right), shows a dramatic difference in standard dress styles that, for many, must have symbolized the apparent cultural gap between Europeans and Americans. Yet the fact that both men (and the young boy) were portrayed in similar stances, with "arms akimbo," demonstrated that all were high-status individuals. In Europe, only aristocrats were represented in such a domineering pose.

UniversalImagesGroup/Getty Images

The Trustees of the British Museum/Art Resource, NY

Virginia reeled from the blow but did not collapse. Reinforced by new shipments of migrants and arms from England, the settlers repeatedly attacked Opechancanough's villages. A peace treaty was signed in 1632, but in April 1644 the elderly Opechancanough assaulted the invaders one last time, though he must have known he could not prevail. In 1646, survivors of the Powhatan Confederacy formally subordinated themselves to England. Although they continued to live in the region, their efforts to resist the spread of European settlement ended.

2-3e End of Virginia Company

The 1622 assault that failed to obliterate the colony did succeed in destroying its corporate parent. The Virginia Company never made any profits from the enterprise, for internal corruption and heavy costs offset all its earnings. But before its demise, the company developed two policies that set key precedents. First, to attract settlers, its leaders in 1617 established the "headright" system. Every new arrival paying his or her own way was promised fifty acres; those who financed the passage of others received similar headrights for each person. To ordinary English farmers, many of whom owned little or no land, the headright system offered a powerful incentive to move to Virginia. To wealthy gentry, it promised even more: the possibility of establishing vast agricultural enterprises worked by large numbers of laborers. Two years later, the company introduced a second reform, authorizing the landowning men of the major Virginia settlements to elect representatives to an assembly called the **House of Burgesses**. English landholders had long been accustomed to electing members of Parliament and controlling their own local governments; they expected the same privilege in the nation's colonies.

When James I revoked the charter in 1624, transforming Virginia into a royal colony, he continued the company's headright policy. Because he distrusted legislative bodies, the king abolished the assembly. But Virginians protested so vigorously that by 1629 the House of Burgesses was functioning again. Only two decades after the first permanent English settlement was planted in North America, the colonists successfully insisted on governing themselves at the local level. Already, the political structure of England's American possessions differed from those of the Spanish, Dutch, and French colonies—all of which were ruled autocratically.

2-4 Life in the Chesapeake

▶ How did English settlers in the Chesapeake fulfill their demand for labor?

▶ What were the conditions of indentured servitude in the Chesapeake?

▶ What were the main features of social and political development in the Chesapeake?

House of Burgesses This first elected representative legislature in North America began meeting in 1619.

By the 1630s, tobacco was firmly established as the staple crop and chief source of revenue in Virginia.

It quickly became just as important in the second English colony planted on Chesapeake Bay: Maryland, given by Charles I to George Calvert, first Lord Baltimore, as a personal possession (proprietorship), which was colonized in 1634. (Because Virginia and Maryland both border Chesapeake Bay—see Map 2.1—they often are referred to collectively as "the Chesapeake.") Members of the Calvert family intended the colony as a haven for their persecuted fellow Catholics. Cecilius Calvert, second Lord Baltimore, became the first colonizer to offer freedom of religion to all Christian settlers; he understood that protecting the Protestant majority could also ensure Catholics' rights. Maryland's Act of Religious Toleration codified his policy in 1649.

In everything but religion, the two Chesapeake colonies resembled each other. In Maryland as in Virginia, tobacco planters spread out along the riverbanks, establishing isolated farms. The region's deep, wide rivers offered dependable water transportation in an age of few and inadequate roads. Each farm or group of farms had its own wharf, where oceangoing vessels could load or discharge cargo. Consequently, Virginia and Maryland had few towns, for their residents did not need commercial centers in order to buy and sell goods.

2-4a Demand for Laborers

Planting, cultivation, harvesting, and curing tobacco were repetitious, time-consuming, and labor-intensive tasks. Clearing land for new fields also demanded heavy labor. Above all else, successful Chesapeake farms required workers. But where and how could they be found? Neighboring Powhatans, their numbers reduced by war and disease, could not supply such needs. Nor were enslaved Africans widely available: traders could more easily and profitably sell slaves to Caribbean planters. By 1650, only about seven hundred blacks lived in Virginia and Maryland—roughly 3 percent of the population. Most were enslaved, but a few were or became free. Northampton County's Anthony Johnson, called "Antonio a Negro" when first sold to the English at Jamestown in 1621, earned his freedom in 1635. Two decades later, he and his wife had saved enough to purchase 250 acres of land. Like many of his fellow colonists, Johnson frequently landed in court. But the judges never threatened his freedom. Accused by a local grandee of idleness, Johnson replied, "I know myne owne ground and I will worke when I please and play when I please." While the practice of slavery constrained the lives of all Africans in the Chesapeake, their status in these early years was often quite fluid.

At first, Chesapeake tobacco farmers looked primarily to England to supply their labor needs. The headright system (which Maryland also adopted) allowed a tobacco planter anywhere in the region to obtain both land and labor by importing workers from England. Good management would make the process self-perpetuating: a farmer could use his profits to pay for the passage of more workers, thereby gaining title to more land, and even movement into the ranks of the emerging planter gentry.

Because men did the agricultural work in European societies, colonists assumed that field laborers—at least white field laborers—should be men. Such laborers, along with a few women, immigrated to America as indentured servants, paying their passage by contracting to work for periods ranging from four to seven years. Indentured servants accounted for 75 to 85 percent of the approximately 130,000 English immigrants to Virginia and Maryland during the seventeenth century.

Males between the ages of fifteen and twenty-four composed roughly three-quarters of the servants; only one immigrant in five or six was female. Most of these young men came from farming or laboring families, and many originated in regions of England experiencing severe social disruption. Often they came from the middling ranks of society—what their contemporaries called the "common sort." Most had not yet established themselves in their homeland.

2-4b Conditions of Servitude

From a distance at least, the Chesapeake seemed to offer such people chances for advancement unavailable in England. Servants who fulfilled the terms of their indenture earned "freedom dues" consisting of clothes, tools, livestock, casks of corn and tobacco, and sometimes even land. Yet immigrants' lives were difficult. Servants typically worked six days a week, ten to fourteen hours a day, in a disease-riddled semitropical climate. Malaria—unknown in England—was rampant, as were typhoid and dysentery. As Richard Freethorne, a young servant from Jamestown, explained to his parents back in England, "the nature of the country, is such that it causeth much sickness." Freethorne was also starving. "I have eaten more in [one] day at home than I have allowed me here for a week," he reported. "[I]f you love or respect me as your child," he begged, "release me from this bondage and save my life."

Servants like Freethorne faced severe penalties for running away. But the laws offered them some protection. Their masters were supposed to supply them with sufficient food, clothing, and shelter, and they were not to be beaten excessively. Cruelly treated servants could turn to the courts for assistance, sometimes winning verdicts that transferred them to more humane masters or released them from their indentures.

Servants and their owners alike contended with epidemic disease. Immigrants first had to survive the process the colonists called "seasoning," a bout with disease (probably malaria) that usually occurred during their first Chesapeake summer. About 40 percent of male servants did not survive long enough to become freedmen. Young men of twenty-two who successfully weathered their seasoning could expect to live only another twenty years.

But for those who survived, the opportunities for advancement were real. Until the last decades of the seventeenth century, former servants often became independent farmers ("freeholders"), living a modest but comfortable existence. Some assumed positions of political prominence, such

as justice of the peace or militia officer. But in the 1670s, tobacco prices entered a fifty-year period of stagnation and decline. Good land grew increasingly scarce and expensive. In 1681, Maryland dropped its requirement that servants receive land as part of their freedom dues, forcing large numbers of freed servants to live for years as wage laborers or tenant farmers. By 1700, the Chesapeake was no longer the land of opportunity it once had been.

2-4c Standard of Living

Life in the early Chesapeake was hard for everyone, regardless of sex or status. The imbalanced sex ratio (see Figure 2.1), the incidence of servitude, and the high rates of mortality combined to produce small and fragile households. Schooling was haphazard at best; whether Chesapeake-born children learned to read or write depended largely on whether their parents were literate and took the time to teach them.

Farmers (and sometimes their wives) toiled in the fields alongside servants. Because hogs could forage for themselves, Chesapeake households subsisted mainly on pork and corn, a filling but not nutritious diet. Families supplemented this monotonous fare with fish, shellfish, and wildfowl, in addition to the vegetables they grew in small gardens. The near impossibility of preserving food for safe winter consumption magnified the health problems caused by epidemic disease.

Few households had many material possessions beyond farm implements, bedding, and basic cooking and eating utensils. Chairs, tables, candles, knives, and forks were luxury items. Most people rose and went to bed with the sun, sat on crude benches or chests, and held plates or bowls in their hands while eating with spoons. Their ramshackle houses commonly had just one or two rooms. Chesapeake colonists devoted their income to buying livestock and purchasing more laborers instead of improving their standard of living. Rather than making clothing or tools, families imported necessary manufactured goods from England.

2-4d Chesapeake Politics

Throughout the seventeenth century, immigrants composed a majority of the Chesapeake population. Most of the members of Virginia's House of Burgesses and Maryland's House of Delegates (established in 1635) were immigrants; they also dominated the governor's council, which simultaneously served as each colony's highest court, part of the legislature, and executive adviser to the governor. A cohesive, native-born ruling elite emerged only in the early eighteenth century.

In the seventeenth-century Chesapeake, most property-owning white males could vote, and such freeholders chose as their legislators (burgesses) the local elites who seemed to be their natural leaders. But because most such men were immigrants lacking strong ties to one another or to the region, the assemblies remained unstable and often contentious.

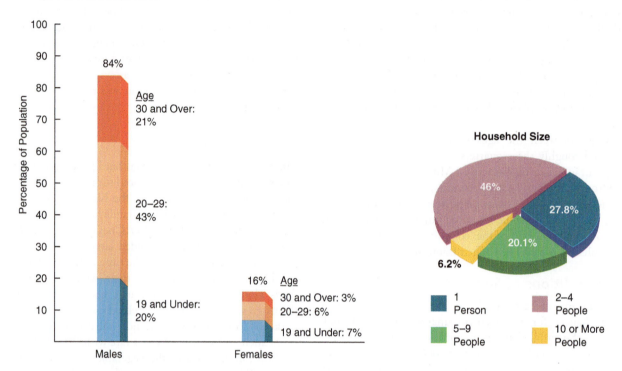

Figure 2.1 Population of Virginia, 1625

The only detailed censuses taken in the English mainland North American colonies during the seventeenth century were prepared in Virginia in 1624, with more detail added in 1625. The colony's population then totaled 1,218 people, arranged in 309 "households" and living in 278 dwellings. (Some houses contained more than one family.) The bar graph on the left shows the age and gender distribution of the 765 individuals for whom full information was recorded; in the pie chart on the right we see the variation in the sizes of the 309 households. The approximately 42 percent of the residents of the colony who were servants were concentrated in 30 percent of the households. At the time of these censuses, less than 2 percent of Virginia's inhabitants were of African descent.

Data from *Wells, Peter S.* The Population of the British Colonies in America Before 1776.

2-5 The Founding of New England

▶ How did the demographic patterns and religious experience of settlers in New England differ from those of the Chesapeake?

▶ To what extent did religion shape the founding and development of settlements in New England?

▶ How did the relationship between New England settlers and Native American peoples evolve over time?

The mingled economic and religious motives that lured English people to the Chesapeake also drew men and women to New England, the region the English called North Virginia until Captain John Smith renamed it in 1616 (see Map 2.2). But because Puritans organized the New England colonies, and because of environmental factors, the northern settlements developed very differently from their southern counterparts. The divergence became apparent even as the would-be colonists left England.

2-5a Contrasting Regional Religious Patterns

Hoping to exert control over a migration that appeared disorderly (and which included dissenters seeking to flee the authority of the Church of England), royal bureaucrats in late 1634 ordered port officials in London to collect information on all travelers departing for the colonies. The resulting records for the year 1635 are a treasure trove for historians. They document the departure of fifty-three vessels—twenty to Virginia, seventeen to New England, eight to Barbados, five to St. Christopher, two to Bermuda, and one to Providence Island. Almost five thousand people sailed on those ships—two thousand bound for Virginia, about twelve hundred for New England, and the rest for island destinations. Nearly three-fifths of the passengers were between fifteen and twenty-four years old, reflecting the predominance of

Map 2.2 New England Colonies, 1650

The most densely settled region of the mainland was New England, where English settlements and the villages of the region's indigenous Algonquian-speaking peoples existed side by side.

young male servants among migrants to most colonies in British America.

But among those bound for New England, such youths constituted less than one-third of the total; nearly 40 percent were older, and another third were younger. Whereas women made up just 14 percent of those headed to Virginia, they composed almost 40 percent of the passengers to New England. New England migrants often traveled in family groups. They also brought more goods and livestock with them, and tended to travel with others from the same towns. More than half the passengers aboard one vessel came from York; on another, nearly half came from Buckinghamshire. In short, people migrated to New England with their close associates. This must have made their lives in North America more comfortable and less lonely than those of their southern counterparts.

2-5b Contrasting Regional Demographic Patterns

Puritan congregations quickly became key institutions in colonial New England. Anglican worship had less impact on the early development of the Chesapeake colonies, where

spread-out settlement patterns made it difficult to organize a church. Catholic and Anglican bishops in England paid little attention to their coreligionists in America, and Chesapeake congregations languished in the absence of sufficient numbers of ordained clergymen. (In 1665, only ten of Virginia's fifty Church of England parishes had resident clerics.) Not until the 1690s did the Church of England plant deeper roots in Virginia; by then, it had also replaced Catholicism as the established church in Maryland.

In both New England and the Chesapeake, religion affected the lives of pious Calvinists who were expected to reassess the state of their souls regularly. Many devoted themselves to self-examination and Bible study, and families often prayed together under the guidance of the husband and father. Yet because even the most pious could never be certain they were among the elect, anxiety about their spiritual state troubled devout Calvinists. This anxiety lent a special intensity to their religious beliefs and to their concern with proper behavior—their own and that of others.

2-5c Separatists

Separatists who thought the Church of England too corrupt to be salvaged became the first religious dissenters to move to New England. In 1609, a Separatist congregation relocated to Leiden, in the Netherlands, where they found the freedom of worship denied them in Stuart England. But they soon found the Netherlands too permissive; the nation that tolerated them also tolerated religions and behaviors they abhorred. Hoping to isolate themselves from worldly temptations, these people, known today as Pilgrims, received permission from the Virginia Company to colonize the northern part of its territory.

In September 1620, more than one hundred people, only thirty of them Separatists, set sail from England on the old and crowded *Mayflower*. Like a few English families that had settled along the coast of Newfoundland during the previous decade, the Pilgrims expected to support their colony through profits from codfishery. In November, they landed on Cape Cod, farther north than they had intended. Given the lateness of the season, they decided to stay put. They moved across Massachusetts Bay to a fine harbor (named Plymouth by John Smith, who had visited it in 1614) and into the empty dwellings of a Pautuxet village whose inhabitants had died in the epidemic of 1616–1618.

2-5d Pilgrims and Pokanokets

Even before they landed, the Pilgrims had to surmount their first challenge—from the "strangers," or non-Separatists, who sailed with them to America. Because they landed outside the jurisdiction of the Virginia Company, some of the strangers questioned the authority of the colony's leaders. In response, the **Mayflower Compact**, signed in November 1620 on shipboard, established a "Civil Body Politic" as a temporary substitute for a charter. The male settlers elected

Mayflower Compact Agreement signed by Mayflower passengers to establish order in their new settlement.

a governor and initially made all decisions for the colony at town meetings. Later, after more towns had been founded and the population increased, Plymouth colony, like Virginia and Maryland, created an assembly to which the landowning male settlers elected representatives.

Like the Jamestown settlers before them, the residents of Plymouth were poorly prepared to subsist in the new environment. Only half of the *Mayflower*'s passengers lived to see the spring. That the others survived owed much to the Pokanokets (a branch of the Wampanoags) who controlled the area. As many as two hundred thousand Algonquian-speaking peoples had lived in the region before contact. But Pokanoket villages had suffered terrible losses in the recent epidemic. To protect themselves from the powerful Narragansetts of the southern New England coast, the Pokanokets allied themselves with the newcomers. In the spring of 1621, their leader or sachem, Massasoit, agreed to a treaty, and during the colony's first years the Pokanokets supplied the settlers with essential foodstuffs. The colonists also relied on Tisquantum (or Squanto), a Pautuxet who served as a conduit between Native peoples and Europeans, as Cortés's Doña Marina had in Mexico. Captured by fishermen in the early 1610s and taken to Europe, Tisquantum had learned to speak English. On his return, he discovered that the epidemic had wiped out his village. Caught between worlds, Tisquantum became the settlers' interpreter and a major source of information about the environment.

2-5e Massachusetts Bay Company

Before the 1620s ended, another group of Puritan dissenters, who hoped to reform the Church of England from within rather than to abandon it, launched the colonial enterprise that would come to dominate New England. (They would later come to be known as Congregationalists, for their insistence on a local level of church governance.) Charles I, who became king in 1625, was more hostile to Puritans than his father had been. Under his leadership, the Church of England drove dissenting clergymen from their pulpits, forcing congregations to worship secretly. Some Congregationalist merchants, concerned about their long-term prospects in England, dispatched a group of colonists to Cape Ann (north of Cape Cod) in 1628. The following year, the merchants obtained a royal charter, constituting themselves as the Massachusetts Bay Company.

The new joint-stock company quickly attracted the attention of Puritans who were increasingly convinced that they no longer would be able to practice their religion freely in their homeland. They remained committed to the goal of reforming the Church of England but concluded that they should pursue that aim in America. In a dramatic move, the Congregationalist merchants decided to transfer the Massachusetts Bay Company's headquarters to New England. The settlers would then be answerable to no one in the mother country and would be able to handle their affairs—secular and religious—as they pleased. Like the Plymouth settlers, they expected to profit from the codfishery; they also planned to export timber products.

2-5f Governor John Winthrop

In October 1629, the Massachusetts Bay Company elected John Winthrop, a member of the lesser English gentry, as its governor. Winthrop organized the initial segment of the Puritan migration to America. In 1630, more than one thousand English men and women moved to Massachusetts—most of them to Boston. By 1643, nearly twenty thousand more had followed.

Winthrop and his company were eager to avoid the failures that beset previous English settlements. Caught up in the currents of European utopian thought that over-swept England in the sixteenth and seventeenth centuries, the colony's backers envisioned a utopia across the ocean—a new Jerusalem. Some time before the colonists embarked, Winthrop set down his expectations for the new colony in an essay called "Christian Charitie."

"Christian Charitie" stressed the communal nature of the colonists' endeavor. God, Winthrop explained, "hath so disposed of the condition of mankind as in all times some must be rich, some poor, some high and eminent in power and dignity, others mean and in subjection." But differences in status did not imply differences in worth.

John Winthrop, c. 1630-91 (oil on canvas)/AMERICAN ANTIQUARIAN SOCIETY/American Antiquarian Society, Worcester, Massachusetts, USA/Bridgeman Images

▲ This unsigned likeness of John Winthrop is believed to be of English origin, painted in the seventeenth century by a follower of Anthony van Dyck, the leading portraitist of the day. Born in 1588, Winthrop would have seen such stiff lace collars, known as ruffs, during his youth under the reign of Queen Elizabeth I. A generation later, van Dyck and his imitators used them as a kind of Elizabethan masquerade, a style of costume popular among fashionable sitters.

Turkeys

As they neared the end of their first year in North America, the Plymouth colonists held a traditional English feast to celebrate the harvest. Famously, they invited Massasoit's Pokanokets to join them, and just as famously, they probably consumed the bird known even then as the "wild turkey." But why was this bird, originally from America and still commonly eaten by Americans at Thanksgiving, given the name of a region of the then-Ottoman Empire? The Native peoples of the Americas had named the fowl in their own languages; Aztecs, for example, called a male bird *huexoloti* and a female *totolin*, while some northeastern Native peoples termed both *nehm*.

When Columbus returned from his first voyage, the birds were among the items he carried to Spain. The Iberian Peninsula had long served as a focal point for Mediterranean commerce, and Spanish mariners sailed frequently to ports in the Middle East. Before long, one of those Spanish vessels took some *huexoloti* and *totolin* to the Ottoman Empire. There, farmers already familiar with distant Asian relatives of the bird began to improve the breed. Within a few decades, they succeeded in producing a plumper and tamer version of the American fowl. By the 1540s, that bird had arrived in England, and by the end of the century "turkeys" were widely consumed for food throughout the British Isles.

Accordingly, when Thomas Harriot in his 1588 *Briefe and True Report* mentioned the wild North American version of the birds, he termed them "Turkie cockes and Turkie hennes." He failed to give the names local Native peoples used because— unlike the many other new plants and animals he encountered—these birds were already familiar to him and his reading audience.

The settlers at Jamestown and Plymouth recognized the birds they saw in their new homelands as relatives of the fowls they had consumed in England. But they regarded the wild American birds as inferior to English ones. Swift and hungry foragers, they ravaged young crops and were viewed primarily as pests. (Of course, any colonist fortunate enough to shoot one of them could have a tasty meal.) So the settlers in both Virginia and New England soon imported English turkeys, which they raised for meat along with chickens and pigs.

The origin of the "turkeys" most likely consumed at the so-called First Thanksgiving remains a mystery. Were they the wild American birds or the tame Ottoman-English variety? No matter; that they were termed "turkeys" linked these fowls of American origin to the Mediterranean, Europe, and the Middle East as a prime example of animals in the Columbian Exchange.

CRITICAL THINKING

■ Using the colonists' preference for "English" turkeys over "American" turkeys as an example, describe the ideological underpinnings of English colonization. Did English colonizers always presume their own superiority?

■ Have you encountered evidence of exceptions to this pattern?

A turkey-cock, brought to Jahangir from Goa in 1612, from the Wantage Album, Mughal, c.1612 (gouache on paper)/Mansur (Ustad Mansur) (fl.c.1590-1630)/Victoria & Albert Museum, London, UK/Bridgeman Images

◀ Turkeys from the Americas quickly traveled around the world, as is illustrated by this Mughal painting from the Islamic empire in India. The local artist Ustad Mansur painted a "turkey-cock" brought to the emperor Jahangir in 1612 from Goa—a Portuguese enclave on the west coast of the Indian subcontinent. Presumably the turkey had been transported from the Iberian Peninsula to that European outpost, whence the fowl made its way to Jahangir's court—where it was immortalized by an artist to whom it was an unusual sight.

On the contrary, God had planned the world so that "every man might have need of others, and from hence they might be all knit more nearly together in the bond of brotherly affection." In New England, Winthrop warned, "we shall be as a city upon a hill, the eyes of all people are upon us." If the Puritans failed to carry out their "special commission" from God, "the Lord will surely break out in wrath against us," and the colony would become "a story and a by-word through the world."

Almost unknown in its day, Winthrop's essay became famous two centuries later. In 1838, one of his descendants published it for the first time, under its now-familiar title, "A Model of Christian Charity," recasting the discourse as a sermon preached en route to New England, and as a parable about uniquely American virtues.

Many modern-day politicians—most famously Ronald Reagan—have quoted Winthrop's speech to underline what they see as the exceptional destiny of the United States. But Winthrop of course could not have imagined an American nation. Rather, he envisioned a biblical commonwealth in which each person worked for the good of the whole. As in seventeenth-century England, this ideal society would be characterized by clear hierarchies of status and power. But Winthrop hoped its members would live according to the precepts of Christian love. Of course, such an ideal was beyond human reach. Early Massachusetts and its Caribbean counterpart, Providence Island, had their share of bitter quarrels and unchristian behavior. Remarkably, though, in New England the ideal persisted for generations.

2-5g Covenant Ideal

The Puritans expressed their communal ideal chiefly in the doctrine of the covenant. They believed God had made a covenant—that is, an agreement or contract—with them when they were chosen for the special mission to America. In turn, they covenanted with one another, promising to work together toward their goals. The founders of churches, towns, and even colonies in Anglo-America often drafted formal documents setting forth the principles on which their institutions would be based. The Pilgrims' Mayflower Compact was a covenant, as was the Fundamental Orders of Connecticut (1639), which laid down the basic law for the settlements established along the Connecticut River valley.

The leaders of Massachusetts Bay likewise transformed their original joint-stock company charter into the basis for a covenanted community. Under pressure from landowning male settlers, they gradually changed the General Court—officially the company's small governing body—into a colonial legislature. They also granted the status of freeman, or voting member, to all property-owning adult male church members. Less than two decades after the first large group of Puritans arrived in Massachusetts Bay, the colony had a functioning system of self-government composed of a governor and a two-house legislature.

2-5h New England Towns

The colony's method of distributing land helped to further its communal ideal. Unlike Virginia and Maryland, where individual planters acquired headrights and sited their farms separately, in Massachusetts groups of men—often from the same English village—applied together to the General Court for grants of land on which to establish towns (novel governance units that did not exist in England). Understandably, the grantees copied the villages whence they had come. First, they laid out lots for houses and a church. Then they gave each family parcels of land scattered around the town center—a pasture here, a woodlot there, an arable field elsewhere—reserving the best and largest plots for the most distinguished residents, including the minister. The "lower sort" received smaller and less desirable allotments. Still, every man and even a few single women obtained land, which sharply differentiated these villages from their English counterparts. When migrants began to move beyond the territorial limits of Massachusetts Bay into Connecticut (1636), New Haven (1638), and New Hampshire (1638), the same pattern of town formation persisted.

Town centers developed quickly, evolving in three distinct ways. Some, chiefly isolated agricultural settlements in the interior, tried to sustain Winthrop's vision of harmonious community life based on diversified family farms. A second group, the coastal towns like Boston and Salem, became bustling seaports, serving as focal points for trade and places of entry for thousands of new immigrants. The third category, commercialized agricultural towns, grew up in the Connecticut River valley, where easy water transportation made it possible for farmers to sell surplus goods readily. In Springfield, Massachusetts, for example, the merchant-entrepreneur William Pynchon and his son John began as fur traders and ended as large landowners with thousands of acres. Even in New England, then, the entrepreneurial spirit characteristic of the Chesapeake found expression. Yet the plans to profit from exports did not materialize quickly or easily; the new settlements lacked both the infrastructure necessary to support such enterprises and a climate conducive to staple crops.

2-5i Pequot War and Its Aftermath

Migration into the Connecticut valley ended the Puritans' relative freedom from clashes with nearby Pequots and Mohegans. The first English people in the valley moved there from Massachusetts Bay under the direction of their minister, Thomas Hooker. Although their new settlements were remote from other English towns, the wide river promised ready access to the ocean. The site had just one problem: it fell within the territory controlled by the powerful Pequot nation.

The Pequots' dominance stemmed from their role as intermediaries in the trade between New England Algonquians and the Dutch in New Netherland. The arrival of English settlers ended the Pequots' monopoly over regional trading networks. Clashes between Pequots and English colonists began even before the establishment of settlements in the Connecticut valley, but their founding tipped the balance toward war, and resulted in a series of exceptionally violent clashes that came to be known as the **Pequot War**. The Pequots tried unsuccessfully to enlist local Mohegan, Niantic, and Narragansett groups in resisting English expansion. After two English traders were killed in 1636 (not by Pequots), the English raided a Pequot village. In return, Pequots raided Wethersfield, Connecticut, in April 1637, killing nine and capturing two. That May, Englishmen and their Narragansett allies burned the main Pequot town on the Mystic River, slaughtering at least four hundred men, women, and children. John Underhill, one of the leaders of the English raid, said it was terrible "to see so many soules … gasping on the ground so thicke in some places, that you could hardly passe along." Nonetheless, he insisted, the colonists had "sufficient light from the word of God for our proceedings," since "Scripture declareth women and children must perish with their parents." By September 1638, when the violence abated, most survivors of the slaughter were enslaved, some in New England and more in the cane fields of the Caribbean.

For the next four decades, the Native peoples of New England accommodated themselves to the European invasion. They traded with the newcomers and sometimes worked for them, but for the most part they resisted acculturation or incorporation into English society. Native Americans continued to use traditional farming methods, which did not employ plows or fences, and women rather than men remained the chief cultivators. The one European practice they consistently adopted was keeping livestock, for domesticated animals provided excellent sources of meat once the English had turned traditional hunting territories into farms and wild game had disappeared.

2-5j Missionary Activities

Although the official seal of the Massachusetts Bay colony featured a Native figure crying, "Come over and help us," only a few Massachusetts clerics, most notably John Eliot and Thomas Mayhew, seriously undertook missionary work among the Algonquian. Eliot believed that Native people could not be properly Christianized unless they were also "civilized." He insisted that converts live in towns, farm the land in English fashion, take English names, wear European-style clothing and shoes, cut their hair, and discard a wide range of their own customs. Because Eliot demanded cultural transformation from his adherents, he met with little success. At the peak of Eliot's efforts, only eleven hundred Native people (out of many thousands) lived in the fourteen "Praying Towns" he established, and just 10 percent of the town residents had been formally baptized.

Eliot's failure to win converts contrasted sharply with the successful missions in New France. Puritan services lacked Catholicism's beautiful ceremonies and special appeal for women, and Calvinists could not promise believers a heavenly afterlife. Yet on the island of Martha's Vineyard, Thomas Mayhew showed that it was possible to convert substantial numbers of Native peoples to Calvinist Christianity. He

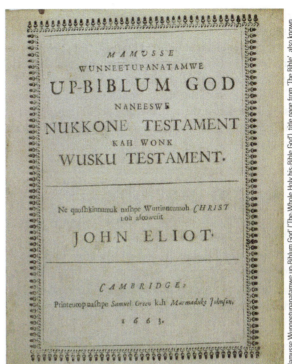

'Mamusse Wunneetupanatamwe up-Biblum God' ('The-Whole Holy his-Bible God'), title page from 'The Bible', also known as the 'Eliot Indian Bible', translated into the Massachuset language by the Reverend John Eliot (1604-90), published by Samuel Green and Marmaduke Johnson, 1663 (engraving)/American School, (17th century)/MASSACHUSETTS HISTORICAL SOCIETY/© Massachusetts Historical Society, Boston, MA, USA/Bridgeman Images

▲ The first Bible printed in the English colonies in North America was this translation into the Algonquian dialect spoken by the Native peoples of Massachusetts. The Puritan minister John Eliot arranged for its translation and publication as part of his efforts to convert the Native peoples to Christianity. He did not succeed in gaining many adherents, but today this Bible is serving as a vocabulary source for Wampanoag activists who are revitalizing their language, Wôpanâak, the knowledge of which had been lost by the nineteenth century.

allowed Wampanoag Christians there to lead traditional lives, and he trained men of their own community to minister to them.

What attracted Native peoples to such religious ideas? Many must have turned to European religion to cope with the dramatic changes the intruders had wrought. The combination of disease, alcohol, new trading patterns, and loss of territory disrupted customary ways of life to an unprecedented extent. Shamans had little success restoring traditional ways. Many Native people must have concluded that the Europeans' own ideas could provide the key to survival in the new circumstances.

John Winthrop's description of a great smallpox epidemic that swept through southern New England in the early 1630s reveals the relationship among smallpox, conversion to Christianity, and English land claims. "A great mortality among the Indians," he noted in his journal in 1633.

Pequot War a series of violent clashes (c. 1636–1638) between English colonists and their Native allies and Pequot groups struggling to hang onto their lands in the Connecticut Valley.

"Divers of them, in their sickness, confessed that the Englishmen's God was a good God; and that if they recovered, they would serve him." Most did not recover: in January 1634, an English scout reported that smallpox had spread "as far as any Indian plantation was known to the west." By July, most of the Native peoples within a 300-mile radius of Boston had died of the disease. Winthrop noted with satisfaction, "the Lord hath cleared our title to what we possess."

2-6 Life in New England

▶ How did family life in New England differ from that in the Chesapeake?

▶ What were the characteristics of the New England economy and labor?

▶ What were the consequences of the institution of a Puritan legal code and behavioral expectations?

New England's colonizers adopted modes of life different from those of both their Algonquian neighbors and their Chesapeake counterparts. Algonquian bands usually moved four or five times each year to take full advantage of their environment. In spring, women planted the fields, but once crops were established, the plants did not need regular attention for several months. Villages then divided into small groups, women gathering wild foods and men hunting and fishing. The villagers returned to their fields for harvest, then separated again for fall hunting. Finally, the people wintered together in a sheltered spot before returning to the fields to resume the cycle the following spring.

Unlike the mobile Algonquians, English people lived year-round in the same location. And unlike residents of the Chesapeake, New Englanders constructed sturdy dwellings intended to last. (Some survive to this day.) Household furnishings and house sizes resembled those in the Chesapeake, but without a cash-crop monoculture, New Englanders' diets were more varied. They replowed the same fields, believing it was less arduous to employ manure as fertilizer than to clear new fields every few years. Furthermore, they fenced their croplands to prevent them from being overrun by the cattle, sheep, and hogs that were their chief sources of meat. Animal crowding more than human crowding caused New Englanders to spread out across the countryside; their livestock constantly needed more pasturage.

2-6a New England Families

Because Puritans often moved to America in family groups, the age range in early New England was wide; and because many more women migrated to New England than to the tobacco colonies, the population could immediately begin to reproduce itself. New England was also healthier than

Cradle, from Barnstable or Yarmouth, Massachusetts, 1665-85 (red oak & white pine)/American School, (17th century)/ HISTORIC NEW ENGLAND/Historic New England, Boston, Massachusetts, USA/Bridgeman Images

▲ Cradles like this one, made by a joiner living in the English plantations on Cape Cod in the third quarter of the seventeenth century, would have seen a lot of use in New England, where an even ratio of male to female settlers, early marriages, and relatively long life expectancies meant that large families—of five or more surviving children—quickly became the norm.

the Chesapeake and even the mother country. Adult male migrants to the Chesapeake lost about a decade from their English life expectancy of fifty to fifty-five years; their Massachusetts counterparts gained five or more years.

Where Chesapeake population patterns gave rise to families that were few in number, small in size, and transitory, New England's demographics made families there numerous, large, and long-lived. More even sex ratios allowed most to marry. Immigrant women married young (at age twenty, on the average); and marriages lasted longer and produced more children, who were more likely to live to maturity. New England women could anticipate raising five to seven healthy children.

The presence of so many children, combined with Puritans' stress on the importance of reading the Bible, led to widespread concern for the education of youth in New England. That people lived in towns meant small schools could be established; girls and boys were taught basic reading by their parents or a school "dame," and boys could then proceed to learn writing and eventually arithmetic and Latin.

Further, New England in effect invented grandparents. In England people rarely lived long enough to know their

Unidentified Artist, American, New England, 17th Century, Elizabeth Eggington, 1664, Oil on canvas, 36 1/4 x 29 3/4 in (92.1 x 75.6 cm). Wadsworth Atheneum Museum of Art, Hartford, CT. Gift of Mrs. Walter H. Clark. Endowed by her daughter, Mrs. Thomas L. Archibald, 1956.93. Photo: Allen Phillips/Wadsworth Atheneum.

▲ Elizabeth Eggington was eight years old when an unknown artist recorded her likeness in 1664. Among the earliest known paintings from New England, it shows the girl's high status. Her sumptuous clothing, edged with costly lace and decorated with red, yellow, and green ribbons, reveals the Puritans' surprising love of ornament. There is a picture within the picture: Elizabeth sports a tiny miniature portrait tied to her collar. Miniatures commemorated dead or absent loved ones. Elizabeth's portrait, too, may have been a mourning picture; the girl died soon after, or possibly before, the artist painted her.

children's children. And whereas early Chesapeake parents commonly died before their children married, New England parents exercised a good deal of control over their adult offspring. Young men could not marry without acreage to cultivate, and they depended on their fathers for that land. Daughters, too, needed a dowry of household goods supplied by their parents. These needs sometimes led to conflict between the generations.

2-6b Labor in a New Land

The large number of young people in New England also shaped the region's labor force. Where Chesapeake planters—who had small families and large cash-crop farms—relied chiefly on bound workers, New England settlers—who farmed smaller lots with larger families—shaped a different economy to fit their different society. Early New England farms produced chiefly for subsistence and local sale; the region's climate generally did not support the production of staple crops intended for large-scale

sale overseas. On the large estates of the Connecticut River valley, where the microclimate allowed farmers to grow tobacco, landless male tenants served as hired hands. In eastern New England villages, poorer sons and daughters were often "put out" or apprenticed in the households of richer neighboring families. But family labor was the norm. Sons took up the callings of their fathers and daughters, their mothers.

The prevalence of family labor should not blind us to the presence of slavery in New England. As the 1638 voyage of the *Desire* to sell captive Pequots in the Caribbean, and Africans in Massachusetts demonstrates, Puritan principles did not rule out chattel slavery. John Winthrop himself kept a Narragansett man and his wife as slaves; upon his death, he bequeathed them to one of his sons. Another early Boston settler, Samuel Maverick, purchased three of the people Pierce brought to Massachusetts, two women and one man. Maverick, who wanted from this purchase "to have a breed of Negroes," compelled his enslaved man to rape one of the women. One of Maverick's houseguests heard her scream during the assault.

Like cotton, tobacco, and salt, African men, women, and children were Atlantic commodities, bought and sold in Boston and other ports around the ocean's rim. Pierce's human cargo numbered among the first Africans trafficked in New England. By mid-century, roughly four hundred people of African descent lived in the region, the great majority enslaved. Their number increased slowly but steadily, hovering around two in every hundred New Englanders for most of the colonial era, with higher concentrations in seaports like Boston and, later, Newport, Rhode Island. In 1650, the scale of New England's black population, and the legal status of those forced migrants, closely resembled that of the Chesapeake.

2-6c Impact of Religion

Puritanism gave New England a distinctive culture. Puritans controlled the governments of Massachusetts Bay, Plymouth, Connecticut, and the other early northern colonies. In Massachusetts Bay and New Haven, church membership was a prerequisite for voting in colony elections. All the early English colonies, north and south, taxed residents to build churches and pay ministers' salaries, but only in New England were provisions of criminal codes based on the Old Testament. Massachusetts's first bodies of law (1641 and 1648) drew heavily from scripture; New Haven, Plymouth, New Hampshire, and Connecticut later copied them. All New Englanders were required to attend religious services, whether or not they were church members. Their leaders also believed the state was obliged to support and protect the one true church—theirs.

Puritan legal codes dwelled heavily on moral conduct. Children who dishonored their parents broke the Fifth Commandment and thus risked execution, though only one young man, Salem's John Porter, Jr., was ever prosecuted for this offense. (He was not convicted.) Laws forbade drunkenness, card playing, dancing, or even cursing—yet the frequency of such offenses demonstrates that New Englanders regularly engaged in these banned activities. Couples who had sex before marriage (as revealed by the birth of a baby less than nine months after their wedding) faced fines and public humiliation. Nonetheless, roughly one bride in ten was pregnant. Sodomy, usually defined as sex between men, was punishable by death. Yet only two men were executed for the crime in the seventeenth century; though not accepted, "sodomitical" conduct was often overlooked. "Considering their Actions," J. W., one of New England's many critics, quipped in 1682, "their Laws look like but Scarecrows."

It is easy to think of the Puritans as killjoys and hypocrites, as many people did at the time. (They had "God in their mouths, but the Devil in their hearts and actions," J. W. said.) But New England's social conservatism stemmed from its radical views on the nature of true religion and the relationship of true religion to just government. A central irony of Puritan dissent—and a central dilemma of the early New England colonies—was that their godly experiment tended to attract people more radical than the colonies' leaders. Although they came to America seeking freedom to worship as they pleased, New England preachers and magistrates saw no contradiction in refusing to grant that freedom to those who held different religious beliefs.

2-6d Roger Williams

Roger Williams, a young minister trained at Cambridge, England, migrated to Massachusetts in 1631 trailing a reputation as "a godly and zealous preacher." Zealous he was. The Bay Colony, he believed, had gone too far in some areas, and not far enough in others. Williams preached that the Massachusetts Bay Company had no right to land already occupied by Native peoples, that church and state should be entirely separate, and that Puritans should not impose their ideas on others. The bond between God and the faithful was intimate and individual, Williams said; policing it was not the role of government.

For years, the colony's leaders tried without success to wean Williams from his "dangerous opinions," which began to "infect" many others. Called before the General Court in October 1635, he refused to retract his claim that the colony's churches were "full of Antichristian pol[l]ution," among other statements. Fearful that his beliefs tended to anarchy, the magistrates banished him from the colony. When soldiers came to escort him to a ship back to England, they discovered that he had already fled.

Williams trekked through the hard winter

Roger Williams A minister who advocated complete separation of church and state and religious tolerance.

Anne Hutchinson Dissenter who was feared not only for her theology but also because she challenged gender roles; banished from Massachusetts in 1638.

of 1636 to the head of Narragansett Bay, where he founded the town of Providence on land he obtained from the Narragansetts and Wampanoags. Providence and other towns in what became Rhode Island adopted a policy of tolerating all faiths, including Judaism. In the following years, the tiny colony founded by Williams became a haven for other dissenters whose ideas threatened New England orthodoxy. Some Puritans called it "Rogue's Island."

2-6e Anne Hutchinson

No sooner was Williams banished than Mistress **Anne Hutchinson** presented another sustained challenge to Massachusetts leaders. The daughter of an English clergyman—the title *Mistress* signaled her high status—Hutchinson was a skilled medical practitioner popular with the women of Boston. She greatly admired John Cotton, a minister who emphasized the covenant of grace, or God's free gift of salvation to unworthy human beings. (By contrast, most Puritan clerics stressed the need for believers to engage in good works in preparation to receive God's grace.) After spreading her ideas when women gathered during childbirths, Hutchinson began holding meetings in her home to discuss Cotton's sermons. Proclaiming that the faithful could communicate directly with God, she questioned the importance of the institutional church and its ministers. Such ideas—along with Hutchinson's model of female authority—posed a dangerous threat to Puritan orthodoxy.

In November 1637, officials charged her with maligning the colony's ministers. During her trial, Hutchinson cleverly matched wits with her learned adversaries, including Winthrop himself. But after two days of holding her own in debate, she boldly declared that God had spoken to her directly. That assertion assured her banishment. The clergy also excommunicated her—thus in their view, consigning her to hell. "You have stepped out of your place," one preacher told her, "you have rather been a Husband than a Wife and a preacher than a Hearer; and a Magistrate than a Subject." Civil authorities were concerned enough about the revolutionary potential of Hutchinson's ideas that they disarmed scores of her male supporters and exiled Hutchinson, her family, and some of her followers to Rhode Island in 1638.

2-7 The Caribbean

▶ **In what ways was the Caribbean at the center of the "Americas" in the seventeenth century?**

▶ **How did sugar cultivation develop in the Caribbean?**

New England and the Chesapeake often dominate histories of colonial America. Projecting backward in time from the establishment of the United States, we find in those regions of the North American mainland seedbeds of the American nation: the passion for self-government revealed in the Mayflower Compact and the House of Burgesses, the family culture of the Puritans, the tolerance of Rhode Island and Maryland. But if we look forward from the seventeenth century instead of backward from 1776, or if we imagine ourselves in the counting houses of London rather than the meetinghouses of Boston, New England and the Chesapeake recede in importance, and the Caribbean looms large (see Map 2.3). In many respects, the island colonies of the West Indies lay at the center, rather than the margins, of what Europeans meant by "America."

France, the Netherlands, and England collided repeatedly in the Caribbean. The Spanish concentrated their colonization efforts on the Greater Antilles—Cuba, Hispaniola, Jamaica, and Puerto Rico. The tiny islands Spain ignored attracted other European powers seeking bases from which to attack Spanish ships loaded with American gold and silver. In the late sixteenth century, as England and Spain warred continually, treasure seized by privateers in the Spanish West Indies added between £100,000 and £200,000 per year to England's treasury.

England was the first northern European nation to establish a permanent foothold in the smaller Caribbean islands (the Lesser Antilles), colonizing St. Christopher (St. Kitts) in 1624, then later other islands, such as Barbados (1627), Providence (1630), and Antigua (1632).

France defeated the Caribs to colonize Guadeloupe and Martinique, and the Dutch gained control of tiny St. Eustatius (strategically located near St. Christopher). In addition to indigenous resistance, tropical diseases, and devastating hurricanes, Europeans in the West Indies worried about conflicts with one another. Like Providence Island, many colonies changed hands during the seventeenth century. For example, the English drove the Spanish out of Jamaica in 1655, and the French soon thereafter took over half of Hispaniola, creating the colony of St. Domingue (modern Haiti).

2-7a Sugar Cultivation

At first, most English planters in the West Indies grew fiber crops including cotton and flax (for linen), dye plants such as indigo, food crops like cacao, and tobacco. But beginning in the 1630s, what historians call a "sugar revolution" remade the West Indies and changed the center of gravity in England's America.

Europeans loved sugar, which offered sweetness and calories. The crop greatly enriched those who grew and processed it for international markets. Entering Europe in

Map 2.3 Caribbean Colonies ca. 1700

English, Spanish, French, Dutch, and other European powers fought for territory in the Caribbean basin throughout the colonial period. At stake were prized shipping routes and the high value of the cash crops produced on the islands, especially sugar, which brought in far more revenue than any other colonial product. Sugar demanded a huge labor force, and so the Caribbean was also the center of the transatlantic slave trade. Many of the enslaved people in mainland British North America were first brought in chains to Jamaica or Barbados.

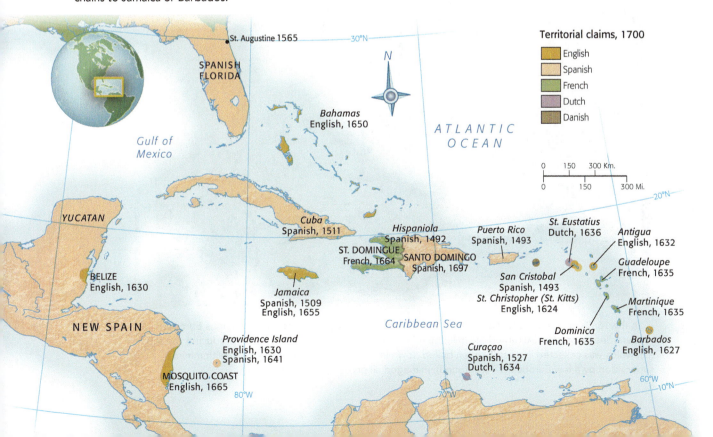

substantial quantities at approximately the same time as coffee and tea—stimulating, addictive, and bitter Asian drinks—sugar quickly became crucial to the European diet. By 1700, the English were consuming four pounds of sugar per person each year—a figure that would more than quadruple by the end of the century.

Until Columbus, Europe's sugar came primarily from the wine islands of the Mediterranean Atlantic and from São Tomé, the Portuguese colony located off West Africa's Slave Coast. The first sugar grown in the West Indies reached Spain in 1517. By the 1530s, some thirty-four sugar mills operated on the island of Hispaniola alone. (Columbus's son Diego owned the largest one.) These were factory-like complexes, with grinding mills, boiling houses, refineries, warehouses, and round-the-clock workforces. Sugar cane had to be processed within two days of being harvested, or the juice would dry, so producers rushed their cane to be crushed, boiled down, and finally refined into brown and white sugars. The work was backbreaking, even lethal. The Spanish population of Hispaniola was relatively small, and warfare and disease had virtually wiped out the indigenous Taíno. The island's sugar was processed by large numbers of enslaved Africans—perhaps 25,000 of them by 1550. "[A]s a result of the sugar factories," one chronicler noted in 1546, Hispaniola had become "an image of Ethiopia itself."

By 1600, Brazil had come to dominate the West Indies sugar trade. Connections between Portuguese planters in the northeastern province of Pernambuco and the Portuguese merchants who controlled the slaving forts of Angola gave Brazilian sugar growers a competitive advantage. Eager to seize that advantage for themselves, the Dutch conquered both ends of this supply chain in the 1630s.

The English colonizers of Barbados discovered in the early 1640s that the island's soil and climate were ideal for cultivating sugar cane. Several of them had visited Dutch Brazil, and Dutch capital, technology, and slaving routes would prove crucial to Barbados's sugar revolution. In the 1640s and 1650s, Barbadian tobacco growers and other small farmers sold out to sugar planters, who used the profits from their crop to amass enormous landholdings. The sugar planters staffed their fields and furnaces with large gangs of bound laborers—African slaves, English and Irish servants, Portuguese convicts—any man who could be bought and worked for six or eight years, until sugar used him up.

But as the Atlantic trade in Africans grew cheaper and more efficient, race-based slavery came to prevail. By the last quarter of the seventeenth century, 175 large planters, each of whom owned more than 100 acres and 60 slaves, controlled the economy of Barbados. So much of the island's arable land was devoted to sugarcane that the planters had to

© RMN-Grand Palais/Art Resource, NY

▲ In the 1660s, a French book illustrated the various phases of sugar processing for curious European readers. Teams of oxen (A) turned the mill, the rollers of which crushed the canes (C), producing the sap (D), which was collected in a vat (E), then boiled down into molasses (K). African slaves, with minimal supervision by a few Europeans (foreground), managed all phases of the process.

▲ First printed in 1657, Richard Ligon's map of Barbados depicts the colony in the midst of its transition to a sugar-growing monoculture. English plantations line the island's Leeward Coast. At the top left corner of the map, a planter on horseback fires his musket at two enslaved Africans attempting to escape. Ligon had seen such cruelty first-hand, and he wrote about it in his *True and Exact History of Barbados*.

import their food; farmers and fishermen on the mainland grew rich shipping grain, cod, and beef to the Caribbean. Barbados, like West Indies more broadly, had become a slave society. The island's English population fell from 30,000 in the 1640s to less than 20,000 in 1680, while the number of the enslaved rose from 6,000 to more than 46,000. Guadeloupe, Jamaica, St. Kitts, and Antigua witnessed similar transitions.

Life for servants and slaves in the West Indies was vicious and short. In Barbados, the English traveler Richard Ligon observed in 1647, "I have seen an overseer beat a servant with a cane about the head till the blood has followed for a fault that is not truly worth the speaking of." The planter aristocracy had learned that such brutality paid. By 1680, Barbados had become the most valuable colony in British America, the jewel in the empire's crown. Sugar exports from that small island alone were worth more than all of the exports from the rest of British America—*combined*.

Summary

By the middle of the seventeenth century, Europeans had come to North America and the Caribbean to stay, a fact that signaled major changes for the peoples of both hemispheres. These newcomers had indelibly altered not only their own lives but also those of Native peoples. Europeans killed Native peoples with their weapons and diseases and had varying success in converting them to Christianity. Indigenous peoples taught Europeans to eat new foods, speak new languages, and to recognize—however reluctantly—the persistence of other cultural patterns. The prosperity and even survival of many of the European colonies depended on the cultivation of American crops (maize and tobacco) and an Asian crop (sugar), thus attesting to the importance of post-Columbian ecological exchange.

Political rivalries once confined to Europe spread around the globe, as England, Spain, Portugal, France, and the Netherlands vied for control of the peoples and resources of Asia, Africa, and the Americas. In South America, Spaniards reaped the benefits of their gold and silver mines, while French colonists earned their primary profits from the fur trade (in Canada) and cultivating sugar (in the Caribbean). Sugar also enriched the Portuguese in Brazil and the English in Barbados. The Dutch concentrated on commerce, trading in furs in North America and sugar in the West Indies.

To a greater extent than their European counterparts, the English transferred the society and politics of

"Modern" Families

Since the late twentieth century, "family values" has been a catchphrase in American politics. Organizations such as Focus on the Family and the American Family Association (both founded by Christian evangelicals in 1977) lobby Washington to protect so-called traditional families from what they see as the modern plagues of premarital sex, fatherless households, and easy divorce. But not much about the "traditional" American family is in fact traditional. In many ways, the families created by seventeenth-century English migrants to the Chesapeake look remarkably modern.

English women were scarce in early Virginia and Maryland. In the first decades of colonization, men outnumbered women by as much as six to one; by mid-century, there were still as many as three male settlers for every female. Young women who made the journey typically migrated as servants, owing five to seven years of labor after they docked. By law, they could not marry during that time; masters did not want to lose working hands to pregnancy. Roughly one in five servant women became pregnant while under indenture nonetheless. Many did so shortly after their contracts ended. In parts of Maryland, one woman in three was pregnant when she married, more than double the rate in most English parishes. Servant women were often punished for bearing an illegitimate child. But marriage itself could be informally contracted. With few ministers around to solemnize their vows, some couples simply declared themselves wed—or, on occasion, divorced.

Both more valuable and more vulnerable than they would have been in England, women in the Chesapeake had their pick of husbands. But indenture delayed marriage, and the region's high rates of endemic disease meant that families easily formed were also easily broken. Only one marriage in three lasted as long as a decade before a spouse died—typically the man. Widows remarried quickly, often within a few months of a husband's death. Men planned for this eventuality, giving their wives an unusual degree of control over their property and their children.

What did early Chesapeake families look like, then? With two or three children, they were smaller than American families in the post–World War II era. Households formed when parents remarried and combined the remnants of previous families included a motley array of blood kin and step-kin. Children routinely grew up with orphaned cousins, half-siblings, and stepparents. One Baltimore County boy had three different stepfathers within a decade.

As the region's demography slowly stabilized, these decidedly modern households of English descent began to police family boundaries more zealously—especially as people of African descent were brought in chains to the Chesapeake. Those boundaries, too, were modern innovations, not time-honored traditions. Then as now, new worlds made extraordinary demands on families, and tradition was a luxury few could afford.

CRITICAL THINKING

- When sex ratios were imbalanced in colonial America, family life was much more fluid. As the ratio of men to women, and with it the number of marriages, began to stabilize, English colonists began to police familial boundaries more closely. Similarly, modern groups like Focus on the Family and the American Family Association police modern families in an effort to prevent the erosion of what they deem traditional family values. Are the motivations of both efforts similar?
- Why or why not?

their homeland to a new environment. Their sheer numbers, coupled with their hunger for vast quantities of land on which to grow crops and raise livestock, brought them into conflict with their indigenous neighbors. New England and the Chesapeake differed in the structure of their populations, the nature of their economies, their settlement patterns, and their religious culture. Yet they resembled each other in the conflicts their expansion engendered, and in their tentative experiments with the use of slave labor. In years to come, both regions would become embroiled in increasingly fierce rivalries besetting the European powers.

Suggestions for Further Reading

Richard S. Dunn, *Sugar and Slaves: The Rise of the Planter Class in the English West Indies, 1624–1713* (1972)

Alison Games, *Migration and the Origins of the English Atlantic World* (1999)

David D. Hall, *A Reforming People: Puritanism and the Transformation of Public Life in New England* (2011)

Jane Kamensky, *Governing the Tongue: The Politics of Speech in Early New England* (1997)

Karen O. Kupperman, *The Jamestown Project* (2007)

Mary Beth Norton, *Founding Mothers & Fathers: Gendered Power and the Forming of American Society* (1996)

Stephan Palmié and Francisco Scarano, eds., *The Caribbean: A History of the Region and Its Peoples* (2011)

Christopher L. Tomlins, *Freedom Bound: Law, Labor, and Civic Identity in Colonizing English America, 1580–1865* (2010)

Wendy Warren, *New England Bound: Slavery and Colonization in Early America* (2016)

David J. Weber, *The Spanish Frontier in North America* (1992)

North America in the Atlantic World, 1650–1720

Their journey began in Mohawk country, where western New York met eastern Iroquoia. As European settlements in the region grew in size and power, each of the four men had sought a new birth under the Christian God. Tejonihokarawa, from the Wolf Clan, became Hendrick. Sagayenkwaraton, whose Mohawk name meant Vanishing Smoke, would be called Brant. Onigoheriago was baptized John. Etowaucum, a Mohican, took the name Nicholas. They may have found solace in their adopted faith; they also found in the English new allies against old enemies.

Now, in a season of war—part of England's decades-long struggle to wrest the heart of North America from the French—those allies tapped the four Christian Native Americans for a diplomatic mission. Peter Schuyler, a fur trader of Dutch descent who had become a leading citizen of English Albany, directed the operation. His cousin, who knew Mohawk, would serve as interpreter. A British army officer advised the Native emissaries on delicate matters of protocol.

Hendrick, Brant, John, Nicholas, and their retinue traveled overland from Albany to Boston, the capital of another English colony. At Boston's Long Wharf, they boarded one of the vessels that regularly sailed the Atlantic, carrying English manufactures to New England and returning east loaded with timbers, fish, and furs. Six weeks later, after what they called "a long and tedious Voyage," the delegation landed "on the other side of the Great Water." From Portsmouth, coaches took them to London, a city housing three-quarters of a million people—more than twice as many as lived in all of mainland British America.

In the teeming metropolis, the go-betweens were groomed for their task. A theater company's costumers fitted them out "in black under clothes after the English manner." Scarlet cloaks trimmed

◀ Images of the "Indian Kings" circulated widely during and after their visit to London. Queen Anne commissioned these formal state portraits, painted by the Dutch artist John Verelst. Their likenesses were also reproduced in formats ranging from mezzotint engravings to woodcuts on ballads and broadsides affordable by the masses of people who followed their story. Etow Oh Koam, King of the River Nations, 1710 (oil on canvas)/Verelst, Johannes or Jan (b.1648-fl.1719)/Private Collection/Bridgeman Images/Sa Ga Yeath Qua Pieth Ton, King of the Maquas, 1710 (oil on canvas)/Verelst, Johannes or Jan (b.1648-fl.1719)/Private Collection/Bridgeman Images/No Nee Yeath Tan no Ton, King of the Generath, 1710 (oil on canvas)/Verelst, Johannes or Jan (b.1648-fl.1719)/Private Collection/Bridgeman Images/Tac Yec Neen Ho Gar Ton, Emperor of the Six Nations, 1710 (oil on canvas)/Verelst, Johannes or Jan (b.1648-fl.1719)/Private Collection/Bridgeman Images

Chronology

1642–46	■ English Civil War
1649	■ Charles I executed
1651	■ First Navigation Act passed to regulate colonial trade
1660	■ Stuarts (Charles II) restored to throne
1663	■ Carolina chartered
1664	■ English conquer New Netherland; New York founded
	■ New Jersey established
1670	■ Marquette, Jolliet, and La Salle explore the Great Lakes and Mississippi valley for France
1672	■ England's Royal African Company chartered; becomes largest single slave-trading enterprise
1675–76	■ Bacon's Rebellion disrupts Virginia government; Jamestown destroyed
1675–78	■ King Philip's War devastates New England
1680–1700	■ Pueblo revolt temporarily drives Spaniards from New Mexico
1681	■ Pennsylvania chartered
1685	■ Charles II dies; James II becomes king of England, Ireland, and Scotland
1686–88	■ Dominion of New England established, superseding charters of colonies from Maine to New Jersey
1688–89	■ James II deposed in Glorious Revolution; William and Mary ascend English throne
1689	■ Glorious Revolution in America; Massachusetts, New York, and Maryland overthrow royal governors
1688–99	■ King William's War fought on northern New England frontier
1691	■ New Massachusetts charter issued
1692	■ Witchcraft crisis in Salem; nineteen people hanged
	■ Earthquake ravages Port Royal, Jamaica
1696	■ Board of Trade and Plantations established to coordinate English colonial administration
	■ Vice-admiralty courts established in America
1701	■ Iroquois Confederacy adopts neutrality policy toward France and England
1702–13	■ Queen Anne's War fought by French and English
1707	■ Act of Union unites Scotland and England as Great Britain
1710	■ Four "Indian Kings" visit London
1711–13	■ Tuscarora War (North Carolina) leads to capture or migration of most Tuscaroras
1715	■ Yamasee War nearly destroys South Carolina

in gold replaced their blankets. Their feet were encased in soft yellow slippers and their long hair tucked beneath turbans. They were given grand new titles to match their elaborate costumes: not even lesser sachems at home among the nations of the Iroquois Confederacy, in London the four men became "Indian Kings."

Finally, on the morning of April 19, 1710, they arrived at St. James Palace. Queen Anne—ruler of Scotland and England, newly unified as Great Britain—received the American ambassadors with "more than ordinary solemnity," one observer noted. The diplomats presented the "Great Queen" with gifts of wampum, pledged their help against "her Enemies the *French*," and asked her to commit more men and materiel to prosecute the war at the western edges of her dominion.

The Four Indian Kings stayed in London for two weeks, making a royal progress. They sat for state portraits that would hang in Kensington Palace. They dined with dukes and admirals; they met with American merchants and British officials; they visited inmates in the madhouse and paupers in the workhouse; they watched plays and cockfights. Crowds trailed them everywhere, and thousands more read about them in the newspapers, which reported that the visitors loved "*English* Beef before all other Victuals" and preferred English ales to "the best *French* wines." Before they left, the Four Kings sailed down the Thames to Greenwich, where they toured the dockyards that made the ships that were knitting together the Crown's growing blue-water empire.

Experience an interactive version of this story in MindTap®.

Hendrick, Brant, John, and Nicholas were far from the first Native Americans to cross the Atlantic. Encounters between new world peoples and the courts of Europe had begun in 1493, when Columbus brought half a dozen Taíno back from his first voyage "so that they can learn to speak," as he put it. In 1616, Pocahontas sailed from Jamestown to St. James, where she was greeted as Lady Rebecca.

But the Four Indian Kings came as tributaries from a *new* new world. In the near-century between Pocahontas's Atlantic crossing and theirs, England's tentative plantations overseas had become a coherent international network: an empire. North America, like England itself, was embedded in a worldwide matrix of trade and warfare. The web woven by oceangoing vessels—once composed of only a few strands spun by Columbus and his successors—now crisscrossed the globe, carrying European goods to America and Africa, Africans to the Americas, Caribbean sugar to New England and Europe, and New England fish and timber (and occasionally Native American slaves) to the Caribbean. Formerly tiny outposts, the North American colonies expanded their territorial claims and diversified their economies after the mid-seventeenth century. Mohawk country was closer to the British metropolis than ever before.

Three developments shaped life in the mainland English colonies between 1650 and 1720: escalating conflicts with Native peoples and with other European colonies in North America; the expansion of slavery, especially in the southern coastal regions and the Caribbean; and changes in the colonies' relationships with England.

The explosive growth of the slave trade significantly altered the Anglo-American economy. Carrying human cargoes paid off handsomely, as many mariners and ship owners learned. Planters who could afford to buy slaves also reaped huge profits. At first involving primarily Native peoples and already enslaved Africans from the Caribbean, the trade soon came to focus on men and women kidnapped in Africa and brought directly to the Americas. The arrival of large numbers of captive West African peoples expanded agricultural productivity, fueled the international trading system, and dramatically reshaped every facet of colonial society.

The burgeoning North American economy attracted new attention from English administrators. Especially after the Stuarts were restored to the throne in 1660 (having lost it for a time because of the English Civil War), London bureaucrats attempted to supervise the American settlements more effectively to ensure that the mother country benefited from their economic growth. By the early eighteenth century, following three decades of upheaval, a new stability characterized colonial political institutions.

Neither English colonists nor London officials could ignore other peoples living on the North American continent. As English settlements expanded, they came into conflict not only with powerful American Indian nations but also with the Dutch, the Spanish, and especially the French. By 1720, war—between Europeans and Native Americans, among Europeans, and among the Native allies of different colonial powers—had become an all-too-familiar feature of American life. No longer isolated from one another or from Europe, the people and products of the North American colonies had become integral to the world trading system and inextricably enmeshed in its conflicts.

- *What were the consequences of the transatlantic slave trade in North America and Africa?*

- *How did English policy toward the colonies change from 1650 to 1720?*

- *What were the causes and results of heightened friction between Europeans and Native peoples?*

3-1 The Growth of Anglo-American Settlements

▶ **How did the English Civil War, and then the Restoration, affect the development of the colonies?**

▶ **What forms of government did settlers establish in the Restoration colonies?**

▶ **How did colonists interact with Native American populations in the Restoration colonies?**

Between 1642 and 1646, civil war between supporters of King Charles I and the Puritan-dominated Parliament engulfed England. Parliament triumphed, leading to the execution of the king in 1649 and interim rule by the parliamentary army's leader, Oliver Cromwell, during the so-called Commonwealth period. But after Cromwell's death late in 1658, Parliament agreed to restore the monarchy if Charles I's son and heir agreed to restrictions on his authority. Charles II did so, and the Stuarts were returned to the throne in 1660 (see Table 3.1).

The Restoration, as the period following the coronation of Charles II was known, transformed the king's realm, including England's overseas plantations. After two decades of Puritan plainness, the restored Stuart monarchy reveled in pomp and splendor. The king's jeweled coronation suit was said to cost £30,000. But Charles also lavished funds beyond the grandeur of his court. Royal patronage buoyed literature, art, philosophy, and science. The intellectual life of England faced outward, from a small island to an expanding world. The money for the government's growing expenditures was to come from overseas commerce as well. More than his predecessors, Charles II and his ministers saw trade as the wellspring of England's greatness. Merchants won new charters for trading ventures around the world. Increasingly, England's America lay at the heart of a grand commercial design.

The new king rewarded nobles and others who had supported him during the Civil War with vast tracts of land in North America and the West Indies. The colonies thereby established made up six of the thirteen provinces that eventually would form the United States—New York, New Jersey, Pennsylvania (including Delaware), and North and South Carolina (see Map 3.1)—as well as Jamaica, the richest of the thirteen colonies that would remain loyal to the Crown. Collectively, these became known as the Restoration colonies, because they were created by the restored Stuart monarchy.

3-1a New York

In 1664, Charles II deeded the region between the Connecticut and Delaware rivers, including the Hudson Valley and Long Island, to his younger brother James, the duke of York. That the Dutch had settled there mattered little; the English and the Dutch were engaged in sporadic warfare, and the English were also attacking other Dutch colonies. In August, James's warships anchored off Manhattan Island, demanding New Netherland's surrender. The colony complied without resistance. Although in 1672 the Netherlands briefly retook the colony, the Dutch permanently ceded it in 1674.

In New Netherland, James acquired a heterogeneous possession, which he renamed after himself, as New York (see Table 3.2). In 1664, a significant minority of English people (mostly Puritan New Englanders on Long Island) already lived there, along with the Dutch and sizable numbers of Algonquians, Mohawks, Mohicans, Iroquois, Africans, Germans, Scandinavians, and a smattering of other Europeans. The Dutch West India Company had imported slaves into the colony; at the time of the English conquest, almost one-fifth of Manhattan's approximately fifteen hundred inhabitants were of African descent. Slaves then made up a higher proportion of New York's urban population than of the Chesapeake's rural people.

James's representatives moved cautiously in their efforts to establish English authority over this diverse population. The Duke's Laws, a legal code proclaimed in 1665, applied solely to the English settlements on Long Island, only later extended to the rest of the colony. James's

Table 3.1 Restored Stuart Monarchs of England, 1660–1714

Monarch	Reign	Relation to Predecessor
Charles II	1660–1685	Son
James II	1685–1688	Brother
Mary	1688–1694	Daughter
William	1688–1702	Son-in-law
Anne	1702–1714	Sister, Sister-in-law

Table 3.2 The Founding of English Colonies in North America and the West Indies, 1661–1681

Colony	Founder(s)	Date	Basis of Economy
Jamaica	Oliver Cromwell Charles II	1655/1661	Cacao, indigo, beef, sugar
New York (formerly New Netherland)	James, Duke of York	1664	Farming, fur trading
New Jersey	Sir George Carteret John Berkeley (Lord Berkeley)	1664	Farming
North Carolina	Carolina proprietors	1665	Tobacco, forest products
South Carolina	Carolina proprietors	1670	Rice, indigo
Pennsylvania (incl. Delaware)	William Penn	1681	Farming

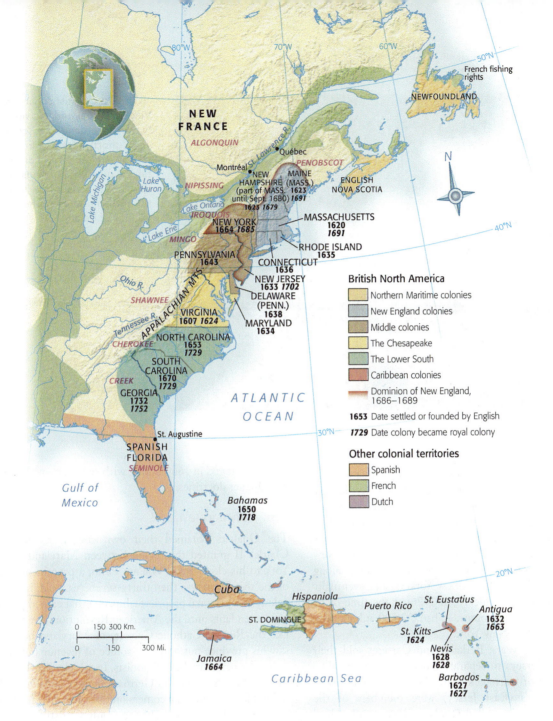

Map 3.1 The Anglo-American Colonies in the Early Eighteenth Century

By the early eighteenth century, the English colonies nominally dominated the Atlantic coastline of North America. But their formal boundary lines are deceiving. The western reaches of each colony were still largely unfamiliar to Europeans. Much of the land was still inhabited and controlled by Native Americans.

policies initially preserved Dutch forms of local government, confirmed Dutch land titles, and allowed Dutch residents to maintain customary legal practices. Each town was permitted to decide which church (Dutch Reformed, Congregational, or Anglican) to support with its taxes. Like other Stuarts, James distrusted legislative bodies, and not until 1683 did he agree to the colonists' requests for an elected legislature. Before then, an autocratic royal governor ruled New York.

The duke did not promote migration, so the colony's population grew slowly, barely reaching eighteen thousand by the time of the first English census in 1698. Until the second decade of the eighteenth century, Manhattan remained a commercial backwater within the orbit of Boston.

3-1b New Jersey

The English conquest brought so little change to New York primarily because the duke of York in 1664 regranted the land between the Hudson and Delaware rivers—East and West Jersey—to his friends Sir George Carteret and John Berkeley (Lord Berkeley). That grant left the duke's own

NIEUW AMSTERDAM ofte nue nieuw IORX opt TEYLANT MAN

◀ The Dutch artist Johannes Vingboons painted this view of New Amsterdam/New York in 1665, shortly after the English takeover. Note the windmill, the tall government buildings, and the small row houses, which made the settlement resemble European villages of its day.

The New York Public Library/Art Resource, NY

colony hemmed in between Connecticut to the east and the Jerseys to the west and south, depriving it of much fertile land. Meanwhile, the Jersey proprietors acted rapidly to attract settlers, promising generous land grants, limited freedom of religion, and—without authorization from the Crown—a representative assembly. Large numbers of Puritan New Englanders migrated southward to the Jerseys, along with some Barbadians, Dutch New Yorkers, and eventually Scots. New Jersey grew quickly; in 1726, at the time of its first census as a united colony, it had 32,500 inhabitants, only 8,000 fewer than New York.

Within twenty years, Berkeley and Carteret sold their interests in the Jerseys to separate groups of investors. The purchasers of all of Carteret's share (West Jersey) and portions of Berkeley's (East Jersey) were members of the Society of Friends, also called **Quakers**. That small radical sect rejected earthly and religious hierarchies. With no formally trained clergy, Quakers allowed both men and women to speak in meetings and become "public Friends" who traveled to preach God's word. Quakers proselytized throughout the Atlantic world in the 1650s, recruiting followers in all of England's colonies from a base in Barbados. The authorities did not welcome the Quakers' radical egalitarianism, and Friends encountered persecution everywhere. Mary Dyer—a follower of Anne Hutchinson in the 1630s—became a Quaker, returned to Boston as a missionary,

and was hanged in 1660 (along with several men) for preaching Quaker doctrines.

3-1c Pennsylvania

The Quakers obtained their own colony in 1681, when Charles II granted the region between Maryland and New York to his close friend **William Penn**, a prominent member of the sect. Penn was then thirty-seven years old; he held the colony as a personal proprietorship, one that earned profits for his descendants until the American Revolution. Even so, Penn, like the Roman Catholic Calverts of Maryland before him, saw his province not only as a source of revenue but also as a haven for persecuted coreligionists. In widely distributed promotional tracts printed in German, French, and Dutch, Penn offered fertile land to all comers on liberal terms. He promised to tolerate all religions—although only Christian men could vote—and to establish a representative assembly. He also guaranteed such legal protections as the right to bail and trial by jury, prized and ancient rights known then and after throughout England's American realm as "English liberties."

Penn's activities and the Quakers' attraction to his lands gave rise to a migration whose magnitude equaled the Puritan exodus to New England in the 1630s. By mid-1683, more than three thousand people—among them Welsh, Irish, Dutch, and Germans—had moved to Pennsylvania. By 1688, the population had quadrupled, to twelve thousand. (It took Virginia more than three decades to grow as large.) Philadelphia, sited on the Delaware River and planned as the major city in the province, drew merchants and artisans from throughout the English-speaking world. From mainland and Caribbean colonies alike came Quakers with well-established trading connections. Pennsylvania's plentiful and fertile lands soon enabled its residents to export surplus flour and other foodstuffs to the

Quakers Properly known as the Society of Friends, Quakers embraced egalitarianism and rejected traditional religious hierarchies. They believed that the Holy Spirit or the "inner light" could inspire every soul.

William Penn The first proprietor of the last unallocated tract of American territory at the king's disposal, which would become Pennsylvania.

William Penn, later the proprietor of Pennsylvania, as he looked during his youth in Ireland. In numerous pamphlets printed in the late seventeenth century, Penn spread the word about his new colony to thousands of readers in England and its other colonial possessions.

West Indies. Practically overnight, Philadelphia acquired more than two thousand citizens and began to challenge Boston's commercial dominance on the mainland.

A pacifist with egalitarian principles, Penn attempted to treat Native Americans fairly. He learned the language of the Delawares (or Lenapes), from whom he purchased land to sell to European settlers. Penn also established strict regulations for trade and forbade the sale of alcohol to Native peoples. His policies attracted Native peoples who moved to Pennsylvania near the end of the seventeenth century to escape repeated clashes with English colonists in Maryland, Virginia, and North Carolina. Tuscaroras migrated northward, and Shawnees and Miamis moved eastward from the Ohio valley. Yet the same toleration that attracted Native Americans also brought non-Quaker Europeans who disregarded Native American claims to the soil. The Scots-Irish (Irish Protestants), Germans, and Swiss who settled in Pennsylvania in the early eighteenth century clashed repeatedly over land with the Delaware, Shawnee, and other Native groups who had recently migrated there.

3-1d Carolina

The southernmost proprietary colony, granted by Charles II in 1663, stretched from the southern boundary of Virginia to Spanish Florida. The area had great strategic importance: a successful English settlement there would prevent Spaniards from pushing farther north. The fertile, semitropical land also held forth the promise of producing such exotic and valuable commodities as figs, olives, wines, and silk. The proprietors named their new province Carolina in honor of Charles (whose Latin name was Carolus). The "Fundamental Constitutions of Carolina," which they asked the political philosopher John Locke to draft for them, set forth an elaborate plan for a colony governed by landholding aristocrats and characterized by a carefully structured distribution of political and economic power.

But Carolina failed to follow the course the proprietors laid out. Instead, it quickly developed two distinct population centers, which in 1729 split into separate colonies under direct royal rule. Virginia planters settled the Albemarle region that became North Carolina. They established a society much like their own, with an economy based on exporting tobacco and such forest products as pitch, tar, and timber. Because North Carolina lacked a satisfactory harbor, planters there relied on Virginia's ports and merchants to conduct their trade. The other population center, which eventually formed the core of South Carolina, developed at Charles Town, founded in 1670 near the juncture of the Ashley and Cooper rivers. Many of its early residents migrated from Barbados, where land was increasingly consolidated under a small number of large holders as the sugar revolution advanced.

Carolina settlers raised corn and herds of cattle, which they sold to Caribbean planters to feed their growing enslaved workforces. Like other colonists before them, they also depended on trade with nearby Native peoples to supply commodities they could sell elsewhere. In Carolina, those items were deerskins, sent to Europe, and enslaved Native Americans, who were shipped to Caribbean islands and northern colonies. Nearby Native American nations hunted deer with increasing intensity and readily sold captured enemies to the English settlers. During the first decade of the eighteenth century, South Carolina exported over fifty thousand skins annually. Before 1715, Carolinians additionally exported an estimated thirty thousand to fifty thousand Native American slaves.

3-1e Jamaica

Like Carolina, Jamaica absorbed numerous migrants from Barbados in the late seventeenth century. First colonized by Spain in 1494, the enormous island—at nearly 4,500 square miles, it is the third largest in the Caribbean, twenty-six times the size of Barbados—was still thinly settled when English troops seized it in 1655, as part of Oliver Cromwell's Western Design. Intended as a base from which to plunder Spanish treasure ships, the English garrison fared poorly at first. After the Restoration, however, powerful merchants in London convinced Charles II there was money to be made by converting it to a royal colony. In 1664, the king appointed Sir Thomas Modyford, a wealthy Barbadian

William Penn (1664-1718) in Armour, aged 22, 1666 (oil on canvas)/English School, (17th century)/PHILADELPHIA HISTORY MUSEUM AT THE ATWATER KENT/© Philadelphia History Museum at the Atwater Kent,/Bridgeman Images planter, to govern Jamaica. Modyford, who brought nearly a thousand experienced planters with him from Barbados, treated the fledgling colony as a personal fiefdom, awarding key offices to his family and generous tracts of land to his friends. He summoned an assembly only once before the Crown ended his tenure in 1671. In those early years, Jamaica was a haven for privateers, transported convicts, and smugglers.

But for all its anarchic tendencies, the colony soon began to grow and even flourish after a fashion. A census taken in 1673 put the island's population at about 17,000, more than ten times what it had been when the English captured it. More than half the inhabitants—over 9,500—were enslaved Africans, forced to grow crops including cacao, indigo, and, increasingly, sugar. As the sugar revolution took hold in Jamaica, the number of the slaves soared. By 1713 the island's enslaved population reached 55,000, more than eight times the number of white settlers. The enslaved rebelled frequently; six organized revolts rocked the colony before 1693. In the mid-eighteenth century, as sugar and slavery exploded in tandem, Jamaica's slave rebellions escalated into full-scale wars.

Jamaica proved as profitable as it was volatile, however. Nowhere was the combustible mixture more visible than in the city of Port Royal. Located on a finger of sand reaching into the Caribbean, Port Royal was a provincial English boomtown. By 1680, it had nearly three thousand inhabitants, including one in six of the island's white settlers. In all of English America, only Boston housed more people. But Port Royal was no Boston. Here wealthy planters, privateers, and the merchants who fenced their loot lived in opulent brick houses standing four stories high, while their slaves—a third of the town's population—crowded into huts. "The Merchants and Gentry live here to the Hight of Splendor, in full ease and plenty," reported one traveler in 1688. Taverns and brothels lined the wharves. Dueling and brawling were common. Those who thought of Port Royal as a new world Sodom—as many did—saw divine justice in the cataclysm that struck in June 1692, when an earthquake buried the city and hundreds of its inhabitants beneath the sea. The news reached Boston by the beginning of August, and London shortly afterwards. "Was there not in this American Island a short representation of the great Day of Tryal?" wrote one English clergyman who saw in Port Royal's fate an intimation judgment day.

An island of extremes unvarnished by piety, Jamaica was easy to scorn. In a pamphlet published in London in 1698 and frequently reprinted, the Grub Street hack Ned Ward called it the "Dunghill of the Universe, the Refuse of the whole Creation … The Place where *Pandora* fill'd her Box." Yet Port Royal, no less than Boston, and Jamaica, no less than Pennsylvania, epitomized British America. The island slowly recovered from the heavy blows of the late seventeenth century to achieve matchless prosperity by the mid-eighteenth. On the eve of the American Revolution, Jamaica was the most valuable British colony, if not the economic capital of the Anglo-Atlantic world.

3-1f Chesapeake

The English Civil War retarded the development of the earlier English settlements. In the Chesapeake, struggles between supporters of the king and Parliament caused military clashes in Maryland and political upheavals in Virginia in the 1640s. But once the war ended and immigration resumed, the colonies again expanded. Settlers on Virginia's eastern shore and along that colony's southern border raised grain, livestock, and flax, which they sold to English and Dutch merchants. Tobacco growers imported increasing numbers of English indentured servants to work their farms, which had begun to develop into plantations. Freed from concerns about Native American attacks by the defeat of the Powhatan Confederacy in 1646, they—especially recent immigrants—eagerly sought to enlarge their landholdings.

Although they still depended primarily on English laborers, Chesapeake tobacco planters continued to acquire small numbers of enslaved workers. At first, almost all of them were people whom historian Ira Berlin has termed "Atlantic creoles": widely traveled people (sometimes of mixed race) who came from other European settlements in the Atlantic world, primarily from Iberian outposts. Not all the Atlantic creoles who came to the Chesapeake were enslaved; some were free or indentured. With their arrival, the Chesapeake became what Berlin calls a "society with slaves," or one in which slavery does not dominate the economy but coexists with other labor systems.

3-1g New England

Migration to New England essentially ceased when the Civil War began in 1642. While English Puritans were first challenging the king and then governing England as a commonwealth, they had little incentive to leave their homeland, and few emigrated after the Restoration. Yet the Puritan colonies' population continued to grow dramatically by natural increase. By the 1670s, New England's population had more than tripled to reach approximately seventy thousand. Such rapid expansion placed pressure on available land. Colonial settlement spread far into the interior of Massachusetts and Connecticut, and many members of the third and fourth generations migrated—north to New Hampshire or Maine, southwest to New York or New Jersey—to find sufficient farmland for themselves and their children. Others abandoned agriculture and learned such skills as blacksmithing or carpentry to support themselves in the growing towns. By 1680, some 4,500 people lived in Boston, which was becoming a genuine city, if not the utopian "city on a hill" that John Winthrop had imagined.

New Englanders who remained in the small, yet densely populated older communities experienced a range of social tensions. Far from being "knit together . . . as one man," as Winthrop had urged in "Christian Charitie," New England

▲ Map from A *New Description of Carolina*, by John Ogilby, 1671 (with south at the top). Ogilby's tract, illustrated by a map drawn from information supplied by John Lederer, a German Indian trader, was intended to attract settlers to the new Carolina colony. He filled his text with information supplied by the Lords Proprietors, stressing the colony's pleasant climate, abundant resources, and friendly Native peoples, a message underscored by the peaceful scenes in the corner cartouches.

towns were intensely fractious. Men and women frequently took to the courts, suing their neighbors for slander, debt, and other offenses. After 1650, accusations of witchcraft—roughly 100 in all before 1690—landed suspects in courtrooms across Massachusetts, Connecticut, and New Hampshire. (Though most seventeenth-century people believed witches existed, those suspected were subjected to very few formal trials in other regions.) Most suspects were middle-aged women who had angered their neighbors. Daily interactions in these close-knit communities, where the same families lived nearby for decades, fostered long-standing quarrels that led some colonists to believe their neighbors had used occult means to cause misfortunes ranging from infant death to crop failure. Legal codes influenced by the Old Testament made witchcraft a capital offense in New England, yet judges and juries remained skeptical of such charges. Few of those accused of witchcraft were convicted, and fewer still were executed.

3-1h Colonial Political Structures

That New England courts halted questionable witchcraft prosecutions suggests the maturity of colonial institutions.

By the last quarter of the seventeenth century, almost all the Anglo-American colonies had well-established governments and courts. In New England, property-holding men or the legislature elected the governors; in other regions, the king or the proprietor appointed such leaders. A council, either elected or appointed, advised the governor on matters of policy and served as the upper house of the legislature. Each colony had a judiciary with local justices of the peace, county courts, and, usually, an appeals court composed of the councilors.

Local political institutions also developed. In New England, elected selectmen initially governed the towns, but by the end of the seventeenth century, town meetings—held at least annually and attended by most free adult male residents—handled matters of local concern. In the Chesapeake and the Carolinas, appointed magistrates ran local governments. At first, the same was true in Pennsylvania, but by the early eighteenth century, elected county officials began to take over some government functions. And in New York, local elections were the rule even before the establishment of the colonial assembly in 1683.

The Pine Tree Shilling

The early settlers of Massachusetts shipped most of the coins they had brought with them back across the Atlantic, to pay for goods imported from England and Europe. The resulting trade deficit meant that money was always in short supply. Colonists made do by conducting local and regional trade with a variety of tokens, including musket balls and wampum, the clamshell beads Algonquian and Iroquois peoples prized for ceremonial exchanges. But in the 1640s, the value of wampum collapsed, just as Bostonians entered Caribbean trade.

Long-distance commerce demanded a circulating medium whose value held stable across space and time. That meant coins made from precious metal, whose weight governed their worth. Trade brought silver coins to New England from the Spanish mines at Potosí, but they were often shaved or debased—worth less than their face value. So in 1652, Massachusetts began to mint its own higher-quality coins. Mint master John Hull, a staunch Puritan, designed them without a human face, since the Bible's commandments forbade the worship of graven images. For the king's profile, he substituted a tall pine tree: the only figure to grace these New England shillings.

When Charles II was restored to the throne, he began to question colonial laws that departed from English norms. In 1665, his royal commissioners directed Massachusetts to close its mint, since "Coyning is a Royal prerogative." By minting money, Boston was acting like a city-state; the Crown would have it behave like a colony. Yet Massachusetts kept producing silver shillings until the colony's charter was revoked in the late 1680s.

CRITICAL THINKING

- What did the pine tree signify in Atlantic commerce?
- How did the colonists identify themselves on the shilling?

▲ Pine Tree Shilling front

▲ Pine Tree Shilling back

3-2 A Decade of Imperial Crises: The 1670s

▶ Why did conflict emerge between European powers and Native American peoples in the 1670s?

▶ What impact did warfare and violence have on Native American populations?

▶ How did conflict over land shape the societies of New England and Virginia?

As the Restoration colonies were extending the range of English settlement, the first English colonies and French and Spanish settlements in North America faced crises caused primarily by their changing relationships with America's indigenous peoples. Between 1670 and 1680, New France, New Mexico, New England, and Virginia experienced bitter conflicts as their interests collided with those of America's original inhabitants. All the early colonies changed irrevocably as a result.

3-2a New France and the Iroquois

In the mid-1670s Louis de Buade de Frontenac, the governor-general of Canada, decided to expand New France's reach into the south and west, hoping to establish a trade route to Mexico and to gain direct control of the valuable fur trade. Accordingly, he encouraged the explorations of Father Jacques Marquette, Louis Jolliet, and René-Robert Cavelier de La Salle in the Great Lakes and Mississippi Valley regions. Frontenac's goal, however, brought him into conflict with the powerful Iroquois Confederacy, then composed of five nations—the Mohawks, Oneidas, Onondagas, Cayugas, and Senecas. (In 1722, the Tuscaroras became the sixth.)

Under the terms of a unique defensive alliance forged in the sixteenth century, a representative council made decisions about war and peace for the entire Iroquois Confederacy, although no nation could be forced to comply with a council directive against its will. Before the arrival of Europeans, the Iroquois waged wars primarily to acquire captives. Contact with foreign traders brought ravaging disease as early as 1633, devastating traditional structures of authority in Iroquoia, and intensifying the need for captives. The Europeans' presence also created an economic motive for warfare: the desire to dominate the fur trade and to gain unimpeded access to imported goods. In the 1640s, bloody conflict between the Senecas and the French-allied Hurons soon touched off a series of broader conflicts now known as the **Beaver Wars**, in which the nations of the Iroquois confederacy fought for control of the lucrative peltry trade. Between 1643 and 1647, western Iroquois battled Hurons in engagements that claimed large numbers of warriors and civilians on both sides. Firearms provided as trade goods by colonial powers made the conflicts far deadlier than traditional warfare. "So far as I can divine," wrote a Jesuit priest captured in one such engagement, "it is the design of the Iroquois to capture all the

Courtesy Palace of the Governors Photo Archives (NMHM/DCA), 11409

▲ Don Diego de Vargas, leader of the expedition to reconquer the Pueblo peoples in 1692. This is the only known portrait of him; today it hangs in the Palace of the Governors in the New Mexico History Museum.

Hurons, . . . to put the chiefs and a great part of the nation to death, and with the rest to form one nation and one country." By the 1650s, the Iroquois league had indeed consolidated its power, and replenished its population with war captives.

In the mid-1670s, as Iroquois dominance grew, the French intervened, seeking to preserve their own trade channels with

Beaver Wars A series of conflicts over trade in the 1640s between the Huron (and other Native peoples) and Iroquois.

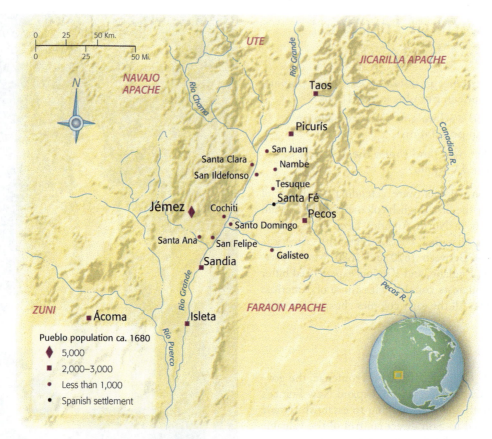

Map 3.2 New Mexico, ca. 1680

In 1680, the lone Spanish settlement at Santa Fe was surrounded and vastly outnumbered by the many Pueblo villages nearby. *Source: Adapted from Apache, Navaho, and Spaniard, by Jack D. Forbes. Copyright © 1960 by the University of Oklahoma Press. Reprinted by permission of the University of Oklahoma Press.*

the western Native peoples. Over the next twenty years, the French launched repeated attacks on Iroquois villages. Although in 1677 New Yorkers and the Iroquois established a formal alliance known as the Covenant Chain, the English offered little beyond weapons to their trading partners. Without much aid, the Confederacy held its own and even expanded its reach, enabling it in 1701 to negotiate neutrality treaties with France and other Native groups. For the next half-century, Iroquois nations maintained their power through trade and skillful diplomacy rather than warfare. The mission of the "Indian Kings" to London belonged to this diplomatic tradition.

3-2b Pueblo Peoples and Spaniards

In New Mexico, too, events of the 1670s led to a crisis with long-term consequences. After years under Spanish domination, the Pueblo peoples had added Christianity to their religious beliefs while retaining traditional rituals, engaging in syncretic practices as Meso-americans had done. But as decades passed, Franciscans adopted increasingly brutal and violent tactics, attempting to erase all traces of the native religion. Priests and secular colonists who held *encomiendas* placed heavy labor demands on the people, who were also suffering from Apache raids and food shortages. In 1680, the Pueblos revolted under the leadership of **Popé**, a respected shaman, successfully driving the Spaniards from New Mexico (see Map 3.2). Even though Spain managed to restore its authority by 1700, imperial officials had learned their lesson. After the rebellion, Spanish governors stressed cooperation with the Pueblos, relying on their labor but no longer attempting to violate their cultural integrity. The Pueblo revolt constituted the most successful and longest-sustained indigenous resistance movement in colonial North America.

Spanish military outposts (*presidios*) and Franciscan missions offered some protection to Pueblos, but other Native peoples' desire to obtain horses and guns from the European colonizers led to endemic violence throughout the region. Navajos, Apaches, and Utes attacked each other and the Pueblos, gaining captives and hides to trade to the Spanish. Captured Native American men might be sent to Mexican silver mines, whereas Spaniards often retained women and children as domestic laborers. When Comanches migrated west from the

Popé Leader of the Pueblo Revolt against the Spanish in 1680.

Great Plains in the late seventeenth century, Utes allied with them, and after the Pueblo revolt that alliance dominated New Mexico's northern borderlands for several decades.

In the more densely settled English colonies, hostilities developed in the decade of the 1670s, not over religion (as in New Mexico) or trade (as in New France), but over land. Put simply, the rapidly expanding Anglo-American population wanted to seize more of it. In both New England and Virginia, settlers began to encroach on territories that had belonged for centuries to Native Americans.

3-2c King Philip's War

By the early 1670s, the growing settlements in southern New England surrounded Wampanoag ancestral lands on Narragansett Bay. The local chief, Metacom—whom the English called "King Philip"—was troubled by the impact of European culture on his land and people. Philip led his warriors in attacks on nearby communities in June 1675. Other Algonquian peoples, among them Nipmucks and Narragansetts, soon joined Metacom's forces. That fall, the allied Native American nations attacked settlements in the northern Connecticut River valley; the war spread to Maine when the Abenakis entered the conflict. In 1676, Metacom's Native allies devastated villages like Lancaster, and even attacked Plymouth and Providence; Abenaki assaults forced the abandonment of most settlements in Maine. Altogether, the Native alliance wholly or partially destroyed twenty-seven of ninety-two English towns and attacked forty others, pushing the colonizers back toward the coast.

The tide turned in the summer of 1676. As the Native American coalition in southern New England ran short of food and ammunition, colonists began to use indigenous Christian converts as guides and scouts. On June 12, the Mohawks—ancient Iroquois enemies of New England Algonquians—devastated a major Wampanoag encampment while most of the warriors were away attacking an English town. King Philip was shot to death near Plymouth that August; the settlers' captain, Benjamin Church, had his body quartered and decapitated. They mounted the sachem's head on a tall pole, much as the English staked the heads of traitors on London Bridge. After Philip's death, the southern alliance crumbled. But fighting on the Maine frontier continued for another two years. There the English colonists never defeated the Abenakis; both sides, their resources depleted, simply agreed to end the conflict in 1678.

After the war, hundreds of Wampanoags, Nipmucks, Narragansetts, and Abenakis were captured and sold into slavery; many more died of starvation and disease. New Englanders had broken the power of the southern coastal tribes. Thereafter the southern Native peoples lived in smaller clusters, subordinated to the colonists and often working as servants or sailors. Only on the island of Martha's Vineyard did Christian Wampanoags (who had not participated in the war) substantially preserve their autonomy.

The settlers paid a terrible price for their victory: an estimated one-tenth of New England's able-bodied adult male population was killed or wounded. Proportional to population, **King Philip's War**—which the Native peoples called Metacom's

Rebellion—was the most lethal conflict in American history on a per capita basis. The colonists' heavy losses caused many Puritans to wonder if God had turned against them. New Englanders did not fully rebuild abandoned interior towns for another three decades, and not until the American Revolution did the region's per capita income return to pre-1675 levels.

3-2d Bacon's Rebellion

Conflict over land simultaneously wracked Virginia. In the early 1670s, ex-servants unable to acquire land greedily eyed the territory reserved by treaty for Virginia's Native peoples. Governor William Berkeley, the leader of an entrenched coterie of large eastern landowners, resisted starting a war to further the aims of backcountry settlers who challenged his authority. Dissatisfied colonists then rallied behind the leadership of a recent immigrant, the gentleman Nathaniel Bacon. Like other new arrivals, Bacon had found that all the desirable land in settled eastern areas had already been claimed. Using as a pretext the July 1675 killing of an indentured servant by some members of the Doeg tribe, Bacon and his followers attacked not only the Doegs but also the more powerful Susquehannocks. In retaliation, Susquehannock bands raided outlying farms early in 1676.

Berkeley and Bacon soon clashed. The governor outlawed Bacon and his men; the rebels then held Berkeley hostage, forcing him to authorize their attacks on the Native peoples. During the chaotic summer of 1676, Bacon alternately waged war on Native villages and battled the governor. In September, Bacon's forces attacked Jamestown, burning the capital to the ground. But when Bacon died of dysentery the following month, the rebellion began to collapse. Even so, the rebels had made their point. Berkeley was recalled to England, and a new treaty signed in 1677 opened much of the disputed territory to settlement. The end of **Bacon's Rebellion** thus pushed most of Virginia's Native peoples farther west, beyond the Appalachians. And elite Virginians would increasingly rely on laborers forbidden by law to become free and demand land of their own.

3-3 The Atlantic Trading System

▶ What factors contributed to the emergence of African slave labor in the British colonies?

▶ How did the Atlantic trading system operate?

▶ What role did the slave trade play in the Atlantic trading system?

▶ What impact did the slave trade have on West African people and their governments?

King Philip's War Devastating war between several allied Native American nations and New England settlers.

Bacon's Rebellion Uprising that resulted from many conflicts, among them an increasing land shortage and settlers' desires for Native American lands.

In the 1670s and 1680s, the prosperity of the Chesapeake rested on tobacco, and successful tobacco cultivation depended, as it always had, on an ample labor supply. But ever fewer English men and women proved willing to indenture themselves for long terms of service in Maryland and Virginia. Population pressures had eased in England, and the founding of the Restoration colonies, along with the boom in Caribbean sugar, gave migrants many American destinations to choose from. Furthermore, fluctuating tobacco prices in Europe and the growing scarcity of land made the Chesapeake less appealing to potential settlers. That posed a problem for wealthy Chesapeake planters. Where could they obtain the workers they needed? They found the answer in the Caribbean sugar islands, where Dutch, French, English, and Spanish planters were accustomed to purchasing African slaves.

3-3a Why African Slavery?

Slavery had been practiced in Europe and in Islamic lands for centuries. European Christians—both Catholics and Protestants—believed that the Bible justified enslaving heathen peoples, especially those of exotic origin. Muslims, too, thought infidels could be enslaved, and they imported tens of thousands of black Africans into slavery in North Africa and the Middle East. Some Christians argued that holding those they termed "heathens"—people with beliefs other than Christianity, Judaism, or Islam—in bondage would lead to their conversion. Others believed that any heathen taken prisoner in wartime could be justly enslaved. Consequently, when Portuguese mariners reached the sub-Saharan coast and encountered African societies holding slaves, they purchased men and women along with gold and other items. From the 1440s on, Portugal imported large numbers of slaves into the Iberian Peninsula; by 1500, enslaved Africans composed about one-tenth of the population of Lisbon and Seville, the chief cities of Portugal and Spain. In 1555, a few of them were taken to England. Others followed, and residents of London and Bristol soon became accustomed to seeing enslaved black people on the streets.

Iberians exported African slavery to their American possessions, New Spain and Brazil. Because the Catholic Church prevented the formal enslavement of Native peoples in those domains, and because free laborers saw no reason to work voluntarily in mines or on sugar plantations when they could earn better wages under easier conditions elsewhere, enslaved Africans (who had no choice) quickly became mainstays of the Caribbean and Brazilian economies. European planters throughout the West Indies began purchasing slaves soon after they settled in the Caribbean. The first enslaved Africans in the Americas were imported from Angola, Portugal's major early trading partner, and the

View of the Southwell Frigate Trading on the Coast of Africa, c.1760 (pen & ink and wash)/Pocock, Nicholas (1741-1821)/BRISTOL MUSEUMS GALLERIES & ARCHIVES/© Bristol Museum and Art Gallery, UK/Bridgeman Images

▲ Nicholas Pocock made this engraving of the frigate *Southwell*, a former privateer from Bristol, England, turned into a slave-trading vessel, about 1760. The images at the bottom show the ship's company trading for slaves on the coast of West Africa.

Portuguese word *Negro*—for "black"—came into use as a common descriptor.

English people had few moral qualms about enslaving other humans. Slavery was sanctioned in the Bible, and it was widely practiced by their contemporaries. Until the eighteenth century, few questioned the decision to hold Africans and their descendants—or captive Native peoples—in perpetual bondage. Yet colonists did not inherit the law and culture of slavery fully formed. Instead, they fashioned the institution of chattel slavery and its supporting concepts of "race" to suit their economic and social needs.

The 1670 Virginia law that first tried to define which people could be enslaved notably failed to employ the racial terminology that would later become common-place. Instead, awkwardly seeking to single out imported Africans without mentioning them, the statute declared, "all servants not being christians imported into this colony by shipping shall be slaves for their lives." Such phrasing reveals that Anglo-American settlers had not yet fully developed the meaning of *race* or the category of *slave*. They did so in tandem over decades, through their experience with slavery itself.

3-3b Atlantic Slave Trade

The planters of the North American mainland could not have obtained the people they wanted to enslave without the rapid development of an Atlantic trading system, the linchpin of which was the traffic in enslaved human beings. Although this elaborate Atlantic economic system has been called the triangular trade, people and products did not move across the ocean in easily diagrammed patterns. Instead, their movements created a complicated web of exchange that inextricably tied together the peoples of the four continents bordering the Atlantic (see Map 3.3).

Though enslavement was ancient, the oceanic slave trade belonged to the Atlantic world that began with Columbus. The expanding network of commerce between Europe and its colonies was fueled by the sale and transport of slaves, the exchange of commodities produced by slave labor, and the need to feed and clothe the escalating number of bound laborers. Previously oriented around the Mediterranean and Asia, Europe's economy tilted toward the Atlantic. By the late seventeenth century, commerce in slaves and slave-made commodities and goods to clothe and feed slaves had become the basis of the European economic system.

Map 3.3 Atlantic Trade Routes

By the late seventeenth century, an elaborate trade network linked the countries and colonies bordering the Atlantic Ocean. The most valuable commodities exchanged were enslaved people and the products of slave labor.

The various elements of the trade had different relationships to one another and to the wider web of exchange. Chesapeake tobacco and Caribbean and Brazilian sugar were in great demand in Europe, so planters often shipped those products directly to their home countries. The profits paid for the African laborers who grew their crops and for European manufactured goods. The African coastal rulers who ran the entrepôts where European slavers acquired their human cargoes took payment in European manufactures and East Indian textiles; they had little need for most North American products. Europeans purchased slaves from Africa for resale in their colonies and acquired sugar and tobacco from the Americas, in exchange dispatching their manufactures everywhere.

European nations fought bitterly to control the lucrative Atlantic trade. The Portuguese dominated at first, but were supplanted by the Dutch in the 1630s. Between 1652 and 1674, England and the Netherlands fought three wars—conflicts over naval supremacy that largely centered on the slave trade. The Dutch lost out to the English, who controlled the trade through the Royal African Company, chartered by Charles II in 1672. Holding a monopoly on all English trade with sub-Saharan Africa, the company became the largest single business in the Atlantic slave trade. The company built and maintained seventeen forts and trading posts, dispatched to West Africa hundreds of ships carrying English goods, and transported thousands of slaves every year to the Caribbean colonies. Some of its agents made fortunes, yet even before the company's monopoly expired in 1712, many individual English and North American traders had illegally entered the market for slaves. By the early eighteenth century, such independent traders carried most of the Africans imported into the colonies. In the fifty years beginning in 1676, British and American ships transported an estimated 689,600 captured Africans, more than 177,000 of them in vessels owned by the Royal African Company. From the founding of the Royal African Company until long after its demise, British slaving voyages dwarfed the trafficking controlled by France, Portugal, and the Netherlands, combined.

3-3c West Africa and the Slave Trade

Most of the enslaved people carried to North America originated in West Africa. Some came from the regions Europeans called the Rice Coast and the Grain Coast, but even more had resided in the Gold Coast, the Slave Coast, and the Bight of Biafra (modern Nigeria) and Angola (see Map 1.2, Section 1-3a). Certain coastal rulers—for instance, the Adja kings of the Slave Coast—served as intermediaries, allowing the establishment of permanent slave-trading posts in their territories and supplying resident Europeans with slaves to fill ships that stopped regularly at coastal forts. Such rulers controlled Europeans' access to enslaved laborers and simultaneously controlled inland Africans' access to desirable trade goods, such as textiles, iron bars, alcohol, tobacco, guns, and cowry shells from the Maldive Islands (in the Indian Ocean),

which were widely used as currency. At least 10 percent of all slaves exported to the Americas passed through Whydah (or Ouidah), Dahomey's major slave-trading port. Portugal, England, and France established forts there.

As the scale of the trade grew, slaving forts became more extensive and elaborate. From simple storerooms housing captured men, women, and children along with trade goods, the coastal forts expanded into full-blown prisons, where shackled captives might be kept for months. Despite thicker walls and a steady provision of "short irons" to bind wrists and "long irons" to shackle ankles, desperate prisoners regularly escaped. In July 1682, one official reported, a group of fourteen captives, including one woman, "undermined the prison walls" and slipped past a guard in the middle of the night.

The slave trade had varying consequences for the nations of West Africa. The trade's centralizing tendencies helped to create such powerful eighteenth-century kingdoms as Dahomey and Asante (formed from the Akan States). Traffic in slaves destroyed smaller polities and disrupted traditional economic patterns. Goods once sent north toward the Mediterranean were redirected to the Atlantic, and local

▲ By the middle of the eighteenth century, American tobacco had become closely associated with African slavery. An English woodcut advertising Virginia tobacco and distilled spirits depicted a pipe-smoking English man watching Africans hoe tobacco in the hot Virginia sun.

Tobacco label featuring Virginia planter and distillery (woodcut)/English School, (18th century)/VIRGINIA HISTORICAL SOCIETY/Virginia Historical Society, Richmond, Virginia, USA/Bridgeman Images

In the fifteenth century, Portuguese explorers renamed the town of Elmina—a trading village on the coast of present-day Ghana—after the gold they exported from the site. (*El mina* means "the mine.") The construction of the massive fort or "castle" depicted in this watercolor began in 1482. At first, its primary purpose was to protect the precious metal trade along what Europeans called Africa's Gold Coast. But during the seventeenth century, enslaved Africans became the primary exports of ports like Elmina, which the Dutch acquired in 1637. Captive men, women, and children were held in the fortress's dungeons before beginning the long voyage to the Americas. The fort's export gate, facing the sea, came to be known as the Door of No Return.

Atlas Blaeu van der Hem

manufactures declined in the face of European competition. Agricultural production intensified, especially in rice-growing areas, because of the need to supply hundreds of slave ships with foodstuffs for transatlantic voyages. Because prisoners of war constituted the bulk of the exported slaves, the most active traders were also the most successful in battle. Some nations initiated conflicts specifically to acquire valuable captives. For example, the state of Benin sold captive enemies to the Portuguese in the late fifteenth century, did not do so at the height of its power in the sixteenth and seventeenth centuries, and renewed the sale of prisoners in the eighteenth century, when its waning power led to conflicts with neighboring states.

Rulers in parts of Upper Guinea, especially modern Gambia and Senegal, largely resisted involvement with the trade; the few slave vessels that departed from that area were much more likely than others to experience onboard rebellions. Despite planters' preference for male slaves, women predominated in cargoes originating in the Bight of Biafra. In such regions as the Gold Coast, the trade had a significant impact on the sex ratio of the remaining population. There a relative shortage of men increased work demands on women, encouraged polygyny, and opened new opportunities to women and their children.

3-3d New England and the Caribbean

New England had a complex relationship to the trading system. The region produced only one item England wanted: tall trees to serve as masts for sailing vessels. To buy English manufactures, New Englanders therefore needed to earn profits elsewhere. The Caribbean colonies lacked precisely the items that New England could produce in abundance: cheap food (primarily corn and salted fish) to feed the burgeoning slave population, and wood for barrels to hold sugar and molasses. The sale of foodstuffs and wood products to Caribbean sugar planters provided New England farmers and merchants with a major source of income. By the late 1640s, decades before the Chesapeake

economy became dependent on *production* by slaves, New England's commerce rested on *consumption* by slaves and their owners. Pennsylvania, New York, and New Jersey later participated in the lucrative West Indian trade as well.

Shopkeepers in the interior of the northern and middle colonies bartered with farmers for grains, livestock, and barrel staves, then traded those items to merchants located in port towns. Such merchants dispatched ships to the Caribbean, where they sailed from island to island, exchanging their cargoes for molasses, sugar, fruit, dyestuffs, and slaves. Once they had a full load, the ships returned to Boston, Newport, New York, or Philadelphia to sell their cargoes (which often included enslaved people). Americans began to distill molasses into rum, a crucial aspect of the only part of the trade that could accurately be termed triangular. Rhode Islanders took rum to Africa to trade for slaves, whom they carried to Caribbean islands to exchange for molasses, which they carried north to produce more rum.

3-3e Slaving Voyages

Tying the system together was the voyage commonly called the **middle passage**, which brought Africans to the Americas. Slaving ships were specially outfitted for the trade, with platforms built between decks to double the surface area to hold human cargo. In its contract with the *Barbados Merchant* for a slaving voyage in 1706, for example, the Royal African Company directed the owners to provide "platforms for ye Negroes, Shackles, bolts, firewood," and beans, as well as "a sword & fire lock, Muskett and ammunition for each of ye ships Comp[any]." Foodstores were priced "per 100 Negroes." Brought aboard in small groups, drawn from many inland nations, speaking diverse languages, an average of 300 men, women, and children comprised what slave merchants called

middle passage The brutal and often fatal journey of enslaved Africans across the Atlantic.

▲ A Procession in Benin, 1668. A contemporary European engraving shows a royal procession leaving the city of Benin, capital of the prosperous West African kingdom. During the seventeenth century, the power of Benin's rulers scared off would-be challengers, and so the kingdom did not engage in frequent warfare. In the fifteenth and eighteenth centuries, by contrast, when the kingdom was weaker, it did capture and sell its enemies.

a "full complement" of human merchandise, though voyages transporting 400 or 500 Africans were not uncommon, and cargoes exceeding 600 were not unheard of.

On shipboard, men were shackled in pairs in the hold except for periods of exercise on deck. During the day, women and children were usually allowed to move around, and made to work at such tasks as food preparation and cleaning. At night, men and women were confined to separate quarters. The best evidence of the captives' reaction to their plight comes from secondhand accounts of their behavior, since few ever had the chance to record their experiences. Many resisted enslavement by refusing to eat, jumping overboard, or joining in revolts, which rarely succeeded. Their communal singing and drumming, reported by numerous observers, must have simultaneously lifted their spirits and forged a sense of solidarity. But conditions on board were hellish, as captains packed as many people as possible into holds that were hot, crowded, and reeking with smells from vomit and the "necessary tubs."

The traumatic voyage unsurprisingly brought heavy fatalities to captives and crew alike. An average of 10 to 20 percent of the newly enslaved died en route; on unusually long or disease-ridden voyages, mortality rates could run much higher. Another 20 percent or so died either before the ships left Africa or shortly after their arrival in the Americas. Merchants tallied lost lives in pounds sterling.

Sailors also died at high rates—one in four or five—chiefly through exposure to such diseases as yellow fever and malaria, which were endemic to Africa. Just 10 percent of the men sent to run the Royal African Company's forts in Lower Guinea lived to return home to England. Sailors signed on to slaving voyages reluctantly; indeed, many had to be coerced or tricked. Slave merchants were notoriously greedy and captains notoriously brutal. Some crew members were themselves slaves or freedmen. Unfortunately, the sailors, often the subject of abuse, in turn frequently abused the African captives in their charge. Yet at the same time, through intimate contact with the enslaved, they learned the value of freedom, and sailors became well known throughout the Atlantic world for their fierce attachment to personal independence.

3-4 Slavery in North America and the Caribbean

▶ What were the primary features of "slave societies" in Britain's American colonies?

▶ What were the similarities and differences among African slave labor in the Chesapeake, the Carolinas, and Northern colonies?

Exotic Beverages

American and European demand for tea (from China), coffee (at first from Arabia), chocolate (from Mesoamerica), and rum (distilled from sugar, which also sweetened the bitter taste of the other three) helped to reshape the world economy after the mid-seventeenth century. One historian has estimated that approximately two-thirds of the people who migrated across the Atlantic before 1776 were involved in one way or another, primarily as slaves, in the production of tobacco, calico, and these four drinks for the world market. As they moved from luxury to necessity, the exotic beverages had a profound impact on custom and culture.

Each beverage had its own pattern of consumption. Chocolate, brought to Spain from Mexico and enjoyed there for a century before spreading throughout Europe, became the preferred drink of aristocrats, who took it hot, at intimate gatherings in palaces and mansions. Coffee, by contrast, became the preeminent morning beverage of English and colonial businessmen, who praised it for keeping drinkers sober and focused. Coffee was served in new public coffeehouses, patronized chiefly by men, where politics and business were the topics of conversation. The English called them "penny universities"; government leaders thought coffeehouses were nurseries of subversion. The first coffeehouse opened in London in the 1660s; Boston had several by the 1690s. By the mid-eighteenth century, though, tea had supplanted coffee as the preferred hot, caffeinated beverage in England and America. It was consumed in the afternoon in private homes at tea tables presided over by women. Where tea embodied genteel status and polite conversation, rum was the drink of the masses. Distilled from sugar, this inexpensive, potent spirit was enthusiastically imbibed by free working people everywhere in the Atlantic world.

The American colonies played a vital role in the production, distribution, and consumption of each of these beverages. Chocolate originated in America, and cacao plantations in the tropics multiplied in size and number to meet the rising demand. Coffee and tea (particularly the latter) were as avidly consumed in the colonies as in England. By the eighteenth century, coffee was grown increasingly in the Caribbean and South America. And rum involved Americans in every phase of its production and consumption. The sugar grown on French and English Caribbean plantations was transported to the mainland in barrels and ships made from North American wood. There the syrup was turned into rum at 140 distilleries. The Americans themselves drank a substantial share of the distilleries' output—an estimated four gallons per person each year. Much of the rest they transported to Africa, where the rum purchased more slaves to produce more sugar to make still more rum, beginning the cycle again.

CRITICAL THINKING

- Tea, chocolate, coffee, and rum were all integral parts of the Columbian Exchange between the Americas and Europe. How did these luxury commodities affect Africans, Euro-American colonists, and continental Europeans?
- What evidence might document their impact on the Native peoples of the Americas?

England: The Coffee House Mob, frontispiece to Part IV of Vulgus Britannicus, or the British Hudibras (London, 1710)/PICTURES FROM HISTORY/Bridgeman Images

◄ This print entitled "The Coffee House Mob," the frontispiece *Vulgus Britannicus, or the British Hudibras* (1710), illustrates the culture of debate and dispute associated with coffee drinking in the Anglophone world. A wide variety of written and printed materials—books, newspapers, and letters—is visible, the range of public (and published) opinion perhaps fueling the heated debates that unfold among the coffee drinkers. Most of the customers are well-dressed men, though a young boy imbibes in the foreground, and a woman serves from the counter.

▶ **How did Africans and their descendants shape their lives in slavery and the character of "slave societies"?**

Barbados, America's first "slave society" (an economy wholly dependent on enslavement) spawned many others. As the island's population expanded and large planters consolidated their landholdings, about 40 percent of the early English residents dispersed to other colonies. The migrants carried their laws, commercial contacts, and slaveholding practices with them; the Barbados slave code of 1661, for example, served as the model for later statutes in Jamaica, Antigua, Virginia, and South Carolina. Moreover, a large proportion of the first Africans imported into North America came via Barbados. In addition to the many Barbadians who settled in Carolina, others moved to the southern regions of Virginia (where they specialized in selling foodstuffs and livestock to their former island home), New Jersey, and New England, where they already had slave-trading partners.

3-4a African Enslavement in the Chesapeake

Newly arrived Africans in the Chesapeake tended to be assigned to outlying parts of plantations (called quarters), at least until they learned some English and the routines of American tobacco cultivation. The crop that originated in the Americas was also grown in various locations in West Africa, so Chesapeake planters could well have drawn on their laborers' expertise. Such Africans—the vast majority of them men—lived in groups of ten to fifteen housed together in one or two buildings and supervised by an Anglo-American overseer. Each man was expected to cultivate about two acres of tobacco a year. Their lives must have been filled with toil and loneliness, for few spoke the same language, and all were expected to work for their owners six days a week. On Sundays, planters allowed them a day off. Many used that time to cultivate their own gardens or to hunt or fish to supplement their meager diet. Only rarely could they form families because of the scarcity of women.

Enslaved workers usually cost about two and a half times as much as indentured servants, but they could repay the greater investment with a lifetime of service, assuming they survived—which large numbers did not. Planters with enough money could take the chance and acquire slaves, accumulate greater wealth, and establish large plantations worked by tens, if not hundreds, of slaves. The less affluent could not even afford to purchase indentured servants, whose price rose because of scarcity. As time passed, the gap between rich and poor planters steadily widened. The introduction of large numbers of Africans into the Chesapeake accordingly had a significant impact on the structure of Anglo-American society.

So many Africans were imported into Virginia and Maryland so rapidly that, as early as 1690, those colonies contained more slaves than English indentured servants. By 1710, people of African descent comprised one-fifth of the region's population. Even so, and despite sizable continuing imports, a decade later American-born slaves already outnumbered their African-born counterparts in the Chesapeake, and the American-born proportion of the enslaved population continued to increase thereafter.

3-4b African Enslavement in South Carolina

Africans came with their owners from Barbados to South Carolina in 1670, totaling one-quarter to one-third of the colony's early population. The Barbadian slave owners quickly discovered that African-born slaves had a variety of skills well suited to the semitropical environment of South Carolina. African-style dugout canoes became the chief means of transportation in the colony, which was crisscrossed by rivers and bordered by large islands. Fishing nets copied from African models proved more efficient than those of English origin. Baskets that enslaved laborers wove and gourds they hollowed out came into general use as containers for food and drink. Africans also adapted their traditional techniques of cattle herding for use in America. Because meat and hides initially numbered among the colony's chief exports, Africans contributed significantly to South Carolina's prosperity.

In 1693, as slavery was taking firm root in South Carolina, officials in Spanish Florida began offering freedom to runaways who would convert to Catholicism. Over the years, hundreds of South Carolina fugitives took advantage of the offer, although not all won their liberty. Many settled in a town founded for them near St. Augustine, Gracia Real de Santa Teresa de Mose, headed by a former slave, Francisco Menendez.

After 1700, South Carolinians started to import slaves directly from Africa. From about 1710 until midcentury, the African-born constituted a majority of the enslaved population in the colony, and by 1750, enslaved men and women comprised a majority of its residents. The similarity of the South Carolinian and West African environments, coupled with the substantial African-born population, ensured the survival of more aspects of West African culture than elsewhere on the North American mainland. Only in South Carolina did enslaved parents continue to give their children African names; only there did a dialect develop that combined English words with terms from Wolof, Bambara, and other African languages. (Known as Gullah, it has survived to the present day in isolated coastal areas.) African skills remained useful, so techniques lost in other regions when the migrant generation died were instead passed down to the migrants' children. And in South Carolina, African women became the primary petty traders, dominating the markets of Charles Town as they did those of Guinea.

3-4c Rice and Indigo

The importation of Africans coincided with the successful introduction of rice in South Carolina. English people knew nothing about growing and processing rice, but captives taken

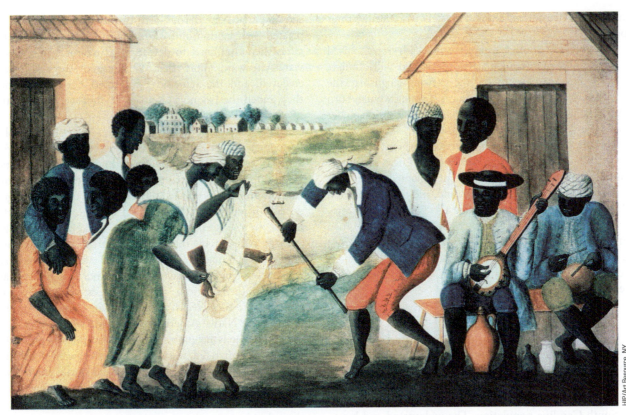

HIP/Art Resource, NY

▲ This watercolor, entitled "The Old Plantation" (c. 1785), has been attributed to John Rose, a slaveholder in the Beaufort district of South Carolina. It depicts a group of ten enslaved people, young and old, male and female, playing music and dancing without ostensible European presence. Many details in the scene, from the banjo-like instrument known in Yoruba as a molo, to the small drum, to the stick dance, to the styles of headdress worn by the women, demonstrate the survival of African culture ways amidst the devastating institution of chattel slavery.

from Africa's Rice Coast had spent their lives working with the crop. Productive rice-growing techniques known in West Africa, especially cultivation in inland swamps and tidal rivers, both of which involved substantial water-control projects,

HIP/Art Resource, NY

▲ This 1761 engraving illustrates an indigo manufactory in French Guyana, on the northern coast of South America. Raw plants were fermented and distilled in a series of descending tanks until they yielded the deep blue dyestuff that cloth-dyers, painters, and others greatly prized.

were widely adopted and combined with European technologies. Enslaved men dug ditches and prepared fields for planting, but as in West Africa, women were responsible for sowing and weeding the crop. Because English grindstones damaged rice kernels, South Carolinians continued to employ the West African system of pounding rice by hand to remove the hulls and bran; planters assigned men as well as women to that task.

On rice plantations, which were far larger than Chesapeake tobacco quarters, every field worker was expected to cultivate three to four acres of rice a year. Most of those field workers were female because many enslaved men were assigned to jobs like blacksmithing or carpentry. To cut expenses, planters also expected slaves to grow part of their own food. By the early eighteenth century, a "task" system of predefined work assignments prevailed. After enslaved people had finished their set tasks for the day, they could rest or work their own garden plots or undertake other projects. Experienced laborers could often complete their tasks by early afternoon; after that, as on Sundays, their masters had no legitimate claim on their time. One scholar has suggested that the **task system**, which gave slaves more autonomy than gang labor, resulted from negotiations between slaves

task system Labor system in which each slave had a daily or weekly quota of tasks to complete.

familiar with rice cultivation and masters who needed their expertise.

Developers of South Carolina's second cash crop also used the task system and drew on slaves' specialized skills. Indigo, the only source of blue dye for the growing English textile industry, was much prized. Eliza Lucas, a young woman born in Antigua, began to experiment with indigo cultivation on her father's Carolina plantations during the early 1740s. Drawing on the knowledge of slaves and overseers whom the family brought with them from the West Indies, Lucas developed planting and processing techniques later adopted throughout the colony. Indigo grew on high ground, and rice was planted in low-lying regions; rice and indigo also had different growing seasons. Thus, the two crops complemented each other. South Carolina indigo never matched the quality of that from the Caribbean, but the crop was so valuable that Parliament paid Carolinians a bounty on every pound exported to Great Britain.

3-4d Enslavement of Indigenous Peoples in North and South Carolina

Among the enslaved people in both Carolinas were indigenous captives who had been retained rather than exported. In 1708, enslaved Native peoples comprised as much as 14 percent of the South Carolina population. The widespread and lucrative traffic in indigenous slaves significantly affected South Carolina's relationship with its indigenous neighbors. Native Americans knew they could always find a ready market for captive enemies in Charles Town, so they took that means of ridding themselves of real or potential rivals. Yet the Westos and other indigenous nations in the region soon learned that Carolinians could not be trusted. As Anglo-American settlers and traders shifted their priorities, first one set of Native allies, then another, found themselves the enslaved rather than the enslavers.

The trade in Native American slaves began when the Westos (originally known as the Eries) migrated south from the Great Lakes region in the mid-1650s, after the Beaver Wars. Expert in the use of European firearms, the Westos began raiding Spain's lightly defended Florida missions and selling the resulting indigenous captives to Virginians. The Carolina proprietors took for themselves a monopoly of trade with the Westos, which infuriated settlers shut out of the profitable commerce in slaves and deerskins. Carolina planters secretly financed attacks on the Westos, essentially wiping them out by 1682. Southeastern Native peoples reacted to such slave raids—continued by other Native peoples after the defeat of the Westos—by trying to protect themselves either through subordination to the English or Spanish, or by coalescing into new, larger political units, such as those known later as Creeks, Chickasaws, or Cherokees.

At first, the Carolinians did not engage directly in conflicts with neighboring Native peoples. But in 1711 the Tuscaroras, an Iroquoian people, attacked a Swiss-German settlement at New Bern, North Carolina, which had expropriated their lands. South Carolinians and their indigenous allies then combined to defeat the Tuscaroras in a bloody war. Afterward, more than a thousand Tuscaroras were enslaved, and the remainder migrated northward, where they joined the Iroquois Confederacy but were not allotted a seat on the council.

Four years later, the Yamasees, who had helped Carolina to conquer the Tuscaroras, turned on their onetime English allies. In what seems to have been long-planned retaliation for multiple abuses by traders as well as threats to their own lands, the Yamasees enlisted the Creeks and other Muskogean peoples in coordinated attacks on outlying English settlements. In the spring and summer of 1715, English and African refugees by the hundreds streamed into Charles Town. The Yamasee-Creek offensive was thwarted only when reinforcements arrived from the north, colonists hastily armed their African slaves, and Cherokees joined the fight against the Creeks. After the war, Carolina's involvement in the Native American slave trade ceased, because all their indigenous neighbors moved away for self-protection: the Creeks migrated west, the Yamasees went south, and the Tuscaroras and other groups moved north. In the war's aftermath, the Native peoples of the Carolinas were able to rebuild their strength, for they were no longer subjected to slavers' raids.

3-4e Enslavement in the North

Atlantic creoles from the Caribbean and Native peoples from the Carolinas and Florida, along with members of local tribes who had been sentenced to slavery for crime or debt, composed the diverse group of enslaved laborers in the northern mainland colonies. The involvement of northerners in the web of commerce surrounding the slave trade ensured that many people of African descent lived in America north of Virginia and that "Spanish Indians" became an identifiable component of the New England population. Some slaves resided in urban areas, especially New York, which in 1700 had a larger black population than any other mainland city. Women tended to work as domestic servants, men as unskilled laborers on the docks. At the end of the seventeenth century, three-quarters of wealthy Philadelphia households included one or two slaves.

Yet even in the North most enslaved men and women worked in the countryside. Dutch farmers in the Hudson Valley and northern New Jersey were especially likely to rely on enslaved African field hands, as were large landowners in the Narragansett region of Rhode Island. Some slaves toiled in new rural enterprises, such as ironworks, working alongside hired laborers and indentured servants at forges and foundries. Slavery made its most dramatic contribution to the northern economy at one remove, through the West Indies provision trade. But although relatively few northern colonists owned slaves, some individual northern slaveholders benefited directly from the institution and had good reason to want to preserve it.

3-4f Slave Resistance

As slavery became an integral part of the North American and Caribbean landscapes, so too did slaves' resistance to their bondage. Most commonly, resistance took the form of work slowdown or escape, but occasionally enslaved people planned rebellions. Seven times before 1713, the English Caribbean experienced major revolts involving at least fifty slaves and causing the deaths of both whites and blacks. In 1675 and 1692, Barbados authorities thwarted plots shortly before they were to be implemented, afterward executing more than sixty convicted conspirators. Jamaica, where a mountainous terrain offered ideal hideouts for runaways, experienced frequent slave mutinies. A 1685 uprising beginning in the northern part of the island lasted nearly a year, and involved more than 250 slaves, before colonial authorities suppressed the rebels with horrific punishments.

The first slave revolt in the mainland English colonies took place in New York in 1712, at a time when enslaved people constituted about 15 percent of the city's population. The rebels, primarily recent arrivals from the Akan States of the Gold Coast, set a fire and then ambushed those who tried to put it out, killing eight and wounding another twelve. Some rebels committed suicide to avoid capture; of those caught and tried, eighteen were tortured and executed. Their decapitated bodies were left to rot outdoors as a warning to others.

The Granger Collection, NYC

▲ This advertisement for a sale of slaves of African descent appeared in the *New York Journal* in 1768. The expertise of two of the people described would have appealed to urban buyers: a cooper would have been useful to a barrelmaker or shipper, and the seamstress might have attracted attention from dressmakers. The other men, women, and girls mentioned could have been purchased by people who wanted house servants or laborers.

3-5 Forging and Testing the Bonds of Empire

▶ What was mercantilism and how did English mercantilist policies affect the colonies?

▶ How and why did the English seek to exercise more political authority and control over the North American colonies?

▶ What internal and external issues threatened to destabilize Britain's American colonies?

English officials seeking new sources of revenue decided to tap into the profits of the expanding Atlantic trading system in slaves and the products of slave labor. Caribbean sugar had the greatest value, but other colonial commodities also had considerable potential. Parliament and the Stuart monarchs accordingly drafted laws designed to harness the proceeds of the trade for the primary benefit of the mother country.

3-5a Colonies into Empire

Like other European nations, England based its commercial policy on a series of assumptions about the operations of the world's economic system, collectively called *mercantilism*. The theory viewed the economic world as a collection of countries whose governments competed for shares of a finite amount of wealth. What one nation gained, another lost. Each nation sought to become as economically self-sufficient as possible while maintaining a favorable balance of trade with other countries by exporting more than it imported. Colonies played an important role, supplying the mother country with valuable raw materials and serving as a market for the parent country's manufactured goods.

Parliament's Navigation Acts—passed between 1651 and 1673—established three main principles that accorded with mercantilist theory. First, only English or colonial merchants and ships could legally trade in the colonies. Second, certain valuable American products could be sold only in the mother country or in other English colonies. At first, these "enumerated" commodities included wool, sugar, tobacco, indigo, ginger, and dyes; later acts added rice, naval stores (masts, spars, pitch, tar, and turpentine), copper, and furs to the list. Third, all foreign goods destined for sale in the colonies had to be shipped through England, paying English import duties. Some years later, new laws established a fourth principle: the colonies could not export items (such as wool clothing, hats, or iron) that competed with English manufactures.

These laws adversely affected some colonies, like those in the Chesapeake, because planters there could not seek foreign markets for their staple crops. The statutes initially helped the sugar producers of the English Caribbean by driving Brazilian sugar out of the home market, but later prevented those English planters from selling their sugar elsewhere. In some places, the impact was minimal or even positive. Builders and owners of ships benefited from the monopoly on American trade given to English and colonial merchants; the laws stimulated the creation of a lucrative shipbuilding industry in New England. And the northern and middle colonies produced many unenumerated goods—for example, fish, flour, meat and livestock, and barrel staves. Such products could be traded directly to the French, Spanish, or Dutch Caribbean islands as long as they were carried in English or American ships.

3-5b Mercantilism and Navigation Acts

English authorities soon learned that it was easier to write mercantilist legislation than to enforce it. The many harbors of the American coast provided ready havens for smugglers, and colonial officials often looked the other way when illegally imported goods were offered for sale. In Dutch Caribbean ports like St. Eustatius, American merchants could easily exchange enumerated goods for foreign items on which no duty had been paid. Because American juries tended to favor local smugglers over customs officers (a colonial customs service was instituted in 1671), Parliament in 1696 established several American vice-admiralty courts, which operated without juries and adjudicated violations of the Navigation Acts.

The Navigation Acts imposed regulations on Americans' international trade, but by the early 1680s mainland governments and their residents had become accustomed to a considerable degree of political autonomy. Local rule was most firmly established in New England, where Massachusetts, Plymouth, Connecticut, and Rhode Island operated essentially as independent entities, subject neither to the direct authority of the king nor to a proprietor. Virginia was a royal colony and New Hampshire (1679) and New York (1685) gained that status, but all other mainland settlements were proprietorships, over which the Crown exercised little control. Everywhere in the English colonies, free adult men who owned more than a minimum amount of property expected to have a voice in their governments, especially in decisions concerning taxation.

After James II became king in 1685, such expectations clashed with those of the monarch. The new king and his successors sought to bring order to the apparently chaotic state of colonial administration by tightening the reins of government and by reducing the colonies' political autonomy. English officials targeted New England, which they saw as a hotbed of smuggling. Moreover, Puritans refused to allow freedom of religion to non-Congregationalists and insisted on maintaining laws incompatible with English practice. New England thus seemed an appropriate place to exert English authority with greater vigor. The charters of all the colonies from New Jersey to Maine were revoked, and a royal Dominion of New England was established in 1686. (For the boundaries of the Dominion, see Map 3.1, Section 3-1.) Sir Edmund Andros, the Dominion's governor, had immense power: Parliament dissolved all the assemblies, and Andros needed only the consent of an appointed council to make laws and levy taxes.

3-5c Glorious Revolution in America

New Englanders had endured Andros's autocratic rule for more than two years when they learned that James II's hold on power was crumbling. The king had angered his subjects by levying taxes without parliamentary approval and by announcing his conversion to Catholicism. In April 1689, Boston's leaders jailed Andros and his associates. The following month, they received definite news of the bloodless coup known as the Glorious Revolution, in which James had been replaced on the throne in late 1688 by his daughter Mary and her husband, the Dutch prince William of Orange.

The Glorious Revolution affirmed the supremacy of Protestantism and Parliament. The new king and queen acceded to Parliament's Declaration of Rights "vindicating and asserting their ancient rights and liberties" as Englishmen. Codified as a Bill of Rights in 1689, this revolutionary document confirmed citizens' entitlement to free elections, fair trials, and petition, and specified that no monarch could ignore acts of Parliament on key issues of taxation and defense. The English Declaration inaugurated a century of heated rhetoric on rights in England, in the colonies, and on the continent. In 1776, the American Declaration of Independence would borrow heavily from Parliament's 1689 Declaration of Rights.

Across the mainland colonies, the Glorious Revolution emboldened people for revolt. In Maryland, the Protestant Association overturned the government of the Catholic proprietor, and in New York a militia officer of German origin, Jacob Leisler, assumed control of the government. Bostonians, Marylanders, and New Yorkers alike allied themselves with the supporters of William and Mary. They saw themselves as defending English liberties by carrying out the colonial phase of the revolt against Stuart absolutism.

But like James II, William and Mary believed England should exercise tighter control over its unruly American possessions. Consequently, only the Maryland rebellion received royal sanction, primarily because of its anti-Catholic thrust. In New York, Leisler was hanged for treason. Massachusetts (incorporating the formerly independent Plymouth) became a royal colony with an appointed governor. The province retained its town meeting system and continued to elect its council, but the new 1691 charter eliminated the traditional religious test for voting and office holding. A parish of the Church of England appeared in the heart of Boston. The "**city upon a hill**," as John Winthrop had envisioned it, had fallen.

3-5d King William's War

A war with the French and their Algonquian allies compounded New England's difficulties. After King Louis XIV of France allied himself with the deposed James II, England declared war on France in 1689. (This war is today known as the Nine Years' War, but the colonists called it King William's War.) Even before war broke out in Europe, Anglo-Americans and Abenakis clashed over settlements in Maine that colonists had reoccupied after the 1678 truce. Abenaki attacks wholly or partially destroyed a number of towns, including Schenectady, New York, and Falmouth (now Portland) and York, Maine. Expeditions organized by the colonies against Montreal and Quebec in 1690 failed miserably, and throughout the rest of the conflict New England found itself on the defensive. The Peace of Ryswick (1697) formally ended the war in Europe but failed to bring much respite to North America's northern frontiers. New Englanders understandably feared a repetition of the devastation of King Philip's War.

3-5e The 1692 Witchcraft Crisis

For eight months in 1692, witchcraft accusations spread like wildfire through the rural communities of Essex County, Massachusetts, a heavily populated area directly threatened by the Native American attacks to the north. Earlier incidents in which personal disputes occasionally led to witchcraft charges bore little relationship to the witch fears that convulsed the region beginning that February. Before the outbreak ended, fourteen women and five men were hanged, one man was pressed to death with heavy stones, fifty-four people confessed to being witches, and more than 140 suspects were jailed, some for many months. The worst phase of the crisis concluded when the governor dissolved the special court established to try the accused. During the final trials, which took place in regular courts, judges and juries discounted so-called spectral evidence, offered by witnesses who claimed to be afflicted by specters of witches. Almost all the defendants were acquitted, and the governor quickly reprieved the few found guilty. If frontier warfare and political turmoil had created an environment where witch fears could become epidemic, the imposition of a new imperial order on the colony helped to cure the plague.

3-5f New Imperial Measures

In 1696, England created the fifteen-member Board of Trade and Plantations, which thereafter served as the chief organ of government concerned with the American colonies. The board gathered information, reviewed Crown appointments in America, scrutinized legislation passed by colonial assemblies, supervised trade policies, and advised successive ministries on colonial issues. Still, the Board of Trade did not have any direct powers of enforcement. It also shared jurisdiction over American affairs with the customs service, the navy, and a cabinet minister. Although the Board of Trade improved the quality of colonial administration, supervision of the American provinces remained decentralized and haphazard.

Lax enforcement surely made it easier for the English colonies to accommodate themselves to the new imperial order. Most colonists resented English "placemen" who arrived in America determined to implement the policies of king and Parliament, but they adjusted to their demands and to the trade restrictions imposed by the Navigation Acts. They fought another of Europe's wars—the War of the Spanish Succession, called Queen Anne's War in the colonies—from 1702 to 1713. The "Four Indian Kings" journeyed to London to seek greater Crown support for an offensive against the French on the northern front of Queen Anne's War.

Colonists who allied themselves with the royal government received patronage in the form of offices and land grants and composed "court parties" that supported English officials. Others, who were either less fortunate in their friends or more zealous in defense of colonial autonomy, made up the opposition, or "country" interest. By the end of the first quarter of the eighteenth century, most men in both groups had been born in America, along the western margins of Britain's emerging empire.

Summary

The period from 1650 to 1720 established economic and political patterns that would structure subsequent changes in mainland colonial society. England's first attempt to regulate colonial trade, the Navigation Act of 1651, was quickly followed by others. By 1720, essential elements of the imperial administrative structure that would govern the English colonies until 1775 had been put in place.

In 1650, just two isolated centers of English settlement, New England and the Chesapeake, existed along the seaboard, along with the tiny Dutch colony of New Netherland. In 1720, nearly the entire East Coast of North America was in English hands, and Native American control east of the Appalachian Mountains had largely been broken by the outcomes of King Philip's War, Bacon's Rebellion, the Yamasee war, the Tuscarora war, and Queen Anne's War. To the west of the mountains, though, Iroquois power reigned supreme. What had been an immigrant population was now mostly American-born, except for the many African-born people in South Carolina and the Chesapeake; economies originally based on trade in fur and skins had become far more complex and more closely linked with the mother country; and a wide variety of political structures had

"city upon a hill" John Winthrop's biblical phrase describing the Puritan settlement of Massachusetts Bay in 1630 as a model for the world.

Fictions of Salem: Witch-Hunting in the American Grain

Like a nightmare that evaporates upon waking, Salem's witchcraft crisis ended as quickly as it began. Prisoners who outlasted the ordeal trudged home from the fetid village jail. The most tormented of the bewitched accusers went on to marry and live seemingly normal lives, beyond the glare of written records. Some of those responsible came to regret their roles in what was soon widely acknowledged as a grave miscarriage of justice. In early 1697, Judge Samuel Sewall, an educated Bostonian who had served on the special court that arraigned the suspects, publicly lamented his share of "the Blame and Shame of it." Sewall may have cleared his conscience, but Salem did not recover its reputation. The trials had inflicted a lasting, "smutty deformity," wrote the merchant Joshua Scottow, who worried that "New-England will be called, new Witch-land," the sweet smell of its pine forests replaced by the stink of hemlock and brimstone.

History has proved Scottow right. In the centuries since the Salem trials, spirals of false accusation, imprisonment, destruction, and regret have often evoked comparisons to 1692. After an alleged and almost certainly imaginary slave conspiracy in New York City resulted in thirty-four gruesome executions in 1741,

one observer said that the "bloody Tragedy" put him "in mind of our New England Witchcraft in the year 1692," already two generations gone but not forgotten.

It wasn't until the nineteenth century that writers began to make art of Salem's witch panic, which was dramatized in stories, plays, paintings, and novels. Many of these fictions contrasted the rational temperament of the young United States with the supposedly bygone superstitions of the Puritans, who were both beloved and mocked for their stern, ancient faith, so quaintly out of step with a polity that had largely ceased to believe in witches. But in a country that readily fastened on new enemies—immigrants, bankers, laborers, enslaved and emancipated African Americans—it was not quite so easy to remain smug about 1692. As the poet Emily Dickinson wrote, "Witchcraft was hung, in History, / But History and I / Find all the Witchcraft that we need / Around us, every Day—."

The most enduring allegory of Salem was created in 1953, at the height of the anti-communist hysteria fueled by Wisconsin Senator Joseph McCarthy. That year, McCarthy began using a senate subcommittee to root out suspected subversives in the entertainment industry, the government, and finally the military.

Playwright Arthur Miller never referred to McCarthy's purges in *The Crucible*, which he both painstakingly researched and freely adapted from the historical record. "This play is not history," Miller insisted. Instead of a truth of the past, Miller hoped the reader would discover in his fiction of Salem "the essential nature of one of the strangest and most awful chapters in human history."

More than sixty years after its first Broadway run, and more than three centuries after the events it so memorably depicts, *The Crucible* has become iconic. Two feature-length versions have been filmed, and it remains one of the most produced plays in high schools and colleges across the United States. In 2016, it was revived on Broadway to rave reviews. Ben Brantley, critic for the *New York Times*, said the play "feels perfectly timed in this presidential election year, when politicians traffic in fears of outsiders and otherness."

CRITICAL THINKING

- The legacy of the Salem witchcraft trials reverberates throughout American history in historical moments like the McCarthy era of the twentieth century. Ben Brantley, critic for the *New York Times*, implied a more recent comparison can be seen in the election of 2016. What merit do you see in Brantley's criticism?

---

been reshaped into a more uniform pattern. Yet at the same time the adoption of large-scale slavery in the Chesapeake, the Carolinas, and the West Indies differentiated their societies from those of the colonies to the north. They had become true slave societies, heavily reliant on a system of perpetual servitude, not societies with slaves, in which a relatively small number of enslaved people mingled with indentured servants and free wage laborers.

Yet the economies of the northern colonies, much like their southern counterparts, rested on profits derived from the Atlantic trading system, the key element of which was traffic in enslaved humans. New England sold corn, salt fish, and wood products to the West Indies. Slaves subsisted on these foodstuffs, and Caribbean planters shipped their sugar

and molasses in barrels made from staves crafted by northern farmers. Pennsylvania and New York, too, found in the Caribbean islands a ready market for their livestock, grains, and flour. The rapid growth of Atlantic slavery drove all the English colonial economies in these years. The colonies of the West Indies, especially Barbados and Jamaica, were the economic engine of the empire. In 1720, their exports to Britain—chiefly 705,000 tons of sugar—were worth more than double what the combined mainland colonies produced.

Spanish settlements in America north of Mexico remained largely centered on Florida missions and on New Mexican presidios and missions during these years. The French had explored the Mississippi valley, but had not yet planted many settlements in the Great Lakes or the west.

Both nations' colonists depended on indigenous people's labor and goodwill. The Spanish could not fully control their indigenous allies, and the French did not even try. Yet the extensive Spanish and French presence to the south and west of the English settlements meant that future conflicts among the European powers in North America were nearly inevitable.

Suggestions for Further Reading

David Eltis and David Richardson, *Atlas of the Transatlantic Slave Trade* (2010)

Eric Hinderaker, *The Two Hendricks: Untangling a Mohawk Mystery* (2010)

Malcolm Gaskill, *Between Two Worlds: How the English Became Americans* (2014)

Andrew Knaut, *The Pueblo Revolt of 1680* (1995)

Jill Lepore, *The Name of War: King Philip's War and the Origins of American Identity* (1998)

Edmund S. Morgan, *American Slavery, American Freedom: The Ordeal of Colonial Virginia* (1975)

Mary Beth Norton, *In the Devil's Snare: The Salem Witchcraft Crisis of 1692* (2002)

Daniel K. Richter, *The Ordeal of the Longhouse: The Peoples of the Iroquois League in the Era of European Colonization* (1992)

Brett Rushforth, *Bonds of Alliance: Indigenous and Atlantic Slaveries in New France* (2012)

Stephanie E. Smallwood, *Saltwater Slavery: A Middle Passage from Africa to American Diaspora* (2007)

Owen Stanwood, *The Empire Reformed: English America in the Age of the Glorious Revolution* (2011)

MINDTAP
From Cengage

MindTap® is a fully online personalized learning experience built upon Cengage Learning content. MindTap® combines student learning tools—readings, multimedia, activities, and assessments—into a singular Learning Path that guides students through the course and helps students develop the critical thinking, analysis, and communication skills that are essential to academic and professional success.

Becoming America?
1720–1760

Dr. Alexander Hamilton was a learned man. The son of a theologian, he studied medicine at the University of Edinburgh, which boasted the best medical school in the world. But if Edinburgh was crowded with genius, it was hardly brimming with opportunity. So many Scots left "to range about to all parts of the world," Hamilton wrote, because his country offered "cold comfort … nothing is to be got." Like thousands of other émigrés, the doctor sought a stage on which his talents might loom larger and fetch more. In 1739, he lit out for the colonies, settling in Annapolis, where his older brother preached.

Maryland's capital offered plenty of work to a university-trained physician, and Dr. Hamilton quickly established himself among the town's elite. But like many migrants to the Chesapeake, he sickened in the climate. By 1744, he was suffering from "an Incessant cough." He thought travel might improve his health. Late that May, he and an enslaved man named Dromo set off to tour the countryside from Maryland to Maine. Their four-month journey wound through eight colonies, scores of villages, numerous towns, and the burgeoning cities of Philadelphia, New York, Newport, and Boston. An avid reader of polite literature, including the new books called *novels* then flooding British presses, the doctor recorded his impressions of this strange new world in a journal to which he gave the Latin title *Itinerarium*.

The diversity of the colonists astonished Hamilton, who had known in Scotland a far narrower range of humanity. In one Philadelphia tavern, he dined "with a very mixed company of different nations and religions. There were Scots, English, Dutch, Germans, and Irish; there

◀ Dr. Hamilton said he had "a foolish Sort of a Genius for drawing." In this sketch, "Mr. Neilson's Battle with the Royalist Club," he shows the raucous civic life of Annapolis in the late 1740s. To illustrate American roughness, Hamilton used a British model: the engravings of London's William Hogarth, which were popular throughout the English-speaking world. John Work Garrett Collections of the Milton Eisenhower Library of Johns Hopkins University.

Chronology

1690	■ Locke's Essay *Concerning Human Understanding* published, a key example of Enlightenment thought
1718	■ New Orleans founded in French Louisiana
1721–22	■ Smallpox epidemic in Boston leads to first widespread adoption of inoculation in America
1732	■ Founding of Georgia
1733	■ Printer John Peter Zenger tried for and acquitted of "seditious libel" in New York
1737	■ "Walking Purchase" of Delaware and Shawnee lands in Pennsylvania
1739	■ Stono Rebellion (South Carolina) ■ George Whitefield arrives in America; Great Awakening broadens
1739–48	■ King George's War affects American economies
1740s	■ Black population of the Chesapeake begins to grow by natural increase
1741	■ New York City "conspiracy" reflects whites' continuing fears of slave revolts
1745	■ Fall of Louisbourg to New England troops; returned to France in 1748 Treaty of Aix-la-Chapelle
1751	■ Franklin's *Experiments and Observations on Electricity* published, important American contribution to Enlightenment science
1760–75	■ Peak of eighteenth-century European and African migration to English colonies

were Roman Catholicks, Church [of England] men, Presbyterians, Quakers, Newlightmen, Methodists, Seventh day men, Moravians, Anabaptists, and one Jew," all talking politics, while a "knott of Quakers" debated the price of flour. He met rich planters from Jamaica, Antigua, and Barbados. He saw Africans everywhere, Mohawks now and again. In Boston, he watched "a parade of Indian chiefs" decked out in fine linens. Their leader, the Mohawk sachem Hendrick Theyanoguin, urged the assembled Native people to "brighten the chain with the English, our friends, and take up the hatchet against the French, our enemies."

Hamilton called Hendrick a "bold, intrepid fellow." Why did so many of these provincials act bold when they should be humble? In Scotland, a better man commanded deference from his inferiors. Here, there was little respect on offer. He and Dromo watched "a boxing match between a master and his servant," who had called the master a "shitten elf." On Long Island he met a shoemaker who had "laid aside his awls and leather" to practice medicine; the self-taught physician now cobbled "bodies" instead of "soals." These "infant countrys of America" bred "aggrandized upstarts," Hamilton wrote. About the "different ranks of men in polite nations" they knew little, and cared less.

But for all their "nastiness, impudence, and rusticity," there was a strange worldliness about "the American provinces." Farmers' wives wore fine imported cloth, and tradesmen talked philosophy. Hamilton viewed botanical engravings in rural Maryland and a plaster copy of the Venus de Medici in Boston. He purchased Montaigne's essays and Henry Fielding's latest novel in Philadelphia, and heard Italian concerti played on German flutes in an Albany tavern. He drank tea in every hamlet, coffee in every town, and rum at every crossroads. Always, there was talk of international politics, especially "the dreaded French war"—King George's War—that once again drew the raw edges of the empire into the maelstrom of European rivalries.

Experience an interactive version of this story in MindTap®.

r. Hamilton encountered a mobile and fast-changing world on his tour of Britain's American provinces. What he saw there changed him in turn. The boorish multitude convinced him that authority rested "upon the Strong and brawny Shoulders of that gyant called popular opinion." The many—"the vulgar," he called them—were ultimately more powerful than the great.

As many European travelers to North America in the eighteenth century noticed, they did things differently in the colonies. People didn't stay within their stations. Property was held more widely, and opinions voiced more readily, in more languages, than anywhere in Europe. After 1720, a massive migration of European and African peoples changed the North American landscape. Ethnic diversity became especially pronounced in the cities where Hamilton drank and disputed. The British colonies south of New England drew by far the largest number of newcomers, many to the fertile countryside. Their arrival altered political balances and introduced new religious sects. Unwilling immigrants (slaves and transported convicts) likewise clustered in the middle and southern colonies. The rough equality Hamilton witnessed among whites was everywhere built upon the bondage of Africans and their descendants.

This polyglot population, with its distinctive customs and mores, hardly resembled the places from which its peoples had been drawn. But in some ways, the America Hamilton encountered was more British than ever. A flood of European and especially British goods allowed genteel and middling folks to style themselves in the image of fashionable Britons. Educated colonists participated in transatlantic intellectual life; Hamilton found Enlightenment ideas wherever he traveled. Yet most colonists, whether free or enslaved, worked with their hands daily from dawn to dark. The social and economic distance among different ranks of Anglo-Americans had widened noticeably. Workhouses sprang up alongside coffeehouses—just as in London.

In 1720, much of eastern North America remained under Native peoples' control. Four decades later, indigenous peoples still dominated the interior of the continent, yet their lives had been indelibly altered by the expansion of European settlements. France extended its reach from the St. Lawrence to the Gulf of Mexico. Spanish outposts spread both east and west from a New Mexican heartland. The British colonies, the largest and most prosperous on the continent, stretched from the Atlantic coast to the Appalachian Mountains, where they threatened French and indigenous claims. North America's resources were worth fighting for, and Europe's balance of power was always precarious. As European conflicts crossed the Atlantic once again during the 1740s (see Table 4.1), many colonists in British North America defended King George II's empire against other nations jockeying for control of the continent.

■ *What were the effects of demographic, geographic, and economic changes on Europeans, Africans, and American Indian nations alike?*

■ *What were the key elements of eighteenth-century provincial cultures?*

■ *In what ways was North America becoming less like Britain at midcentury? In what ways were colonists more British than before?*

4-1 Geographic Expansion and Ethnic Diversity

▶ **What patterns of settlement did forced and voluntary migrants create in French, British, and Spanish American territories?**

▶ **How did the socioeconomic demographic makeup of the British North American colonies shift over the course of the eighteenth century?**

▶ **How did colonists relate to peoples already present in French, British, and Spanish settlements, and to one another?**

Europe's North American possessions expanded both geographically and demographically during the middle decades of the eighteenth century. The most striking development was the dramatic population growth of the British mainland colonies. In 1700, only about 250,000 European Americans and African Americans resided in the colonies. Thirty years later, that number had more than doubled; by 1775, it would reach 2.5 million.

Migration from Scotland, Ireland, England, Germany, and especially Africa accounted for a considerable share of the growth. Between 1700 and 1780, an estimated 350,000 European immigrants and roughly 280,000 forced migrants from Africa came to Britain's mainland colonies. But even more of the gain stemmed from natural increase. Once the difficult early decades of settlement had passed, the population of Britain's mainland colonies doubled approximately every twenty-five years. Such a rate of growth, unparalleled in human history until very recent times, had a variety of causes, chief among them women's youthful age at first marriage (early twenties for Euro-Americans, late teens for African Americans). Because married women became pregnant every two to three years, they normally bore five to ten children. Since the colonies, especially those north of Virginia, were relatively healthful places to live, a large proportion of children who survived infancy reached maturity and began families of their own. The result was a young, rapidly growing population; about half the people in Anglo America were under sixteen years old in 1775. (By contrast, about one-fifth of the U.S. population today is under sixteen.)

4-1a Spanish and French Territorial Expansion

The rapidly expanding population of mainland British North America was sandwiched between the Atlantic coast (on the east) and Appalachian Mountains (on the west). Older settlements in New England had come to feel crowded. By contrast, Spanish and French territories expanded across much of North America while their populations increased only modestly. At the end of the eighteenth century, Texas had but three thousand Spanish residents and California less than one thousand; the largest Spanish colony, New Mexico, included twenty thousand or so settlers. The total European population of the mainland French colonies increased from approximately fifteen thousand in 1700 to about seventy thousand in the 1760s, but those colonists clustered in a few widely scattered locations. If the population of most French and Spanish settlements remained small, their geographic expansion had far-reaching effects on Native peoples.

Still seeking the rewards that had motivated their American designs for centuries—an inland waterway to the Pacific, fat veins of gold and silver, an advantage over their European rivals—the French by water and the Spanish by land ventured separately into the Mississippi valley in the early eighteenth century. There they encountered powerful American Indian nations like the Quapaws, Osages, and Caddos. A few Europeans—priests, soldiers, farmers, traders, ranchers—found themselves surrounded by Native peoples who wanted access to manufactured goods, and who accordingly sought friendly relations with the newcomers. The Spanish and French invaders of these territories had to accommodate themselves to Native peoples' diplomatic and cultural practices in order to achieve their objectives. French officials, for example, often complained of being forced to endure lengthy calumet ceremonies; Spaniards, unaccustomed to involving women in diplomacy, had to accede to Texas Native peoples' use of female representatives. The European nations established neighboring outposts in the lower Mississippi region in 1716—the French at Natchitoches (west of the Mississippi), the Spaniards at nearby Los Adaes (see Map 4.1). France had already founded a settlement on Biloxi Bay (in the modern state of Mississippi) in 1699, and later strengthened its presence near the Gulf of Mexico by establishing New Orleans in 1718, a move the Spanish could not counter because the overland distance from Santa Fe was too great.

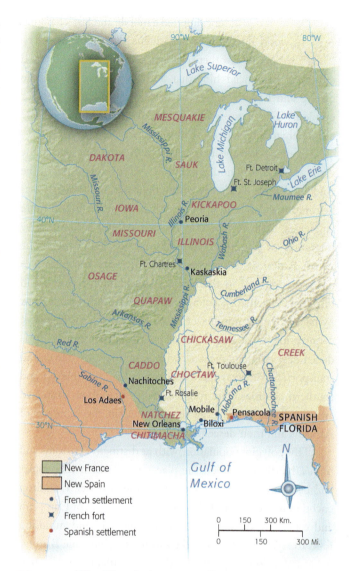

Map 4.1 The North American Interior, ca. 1720

By 1720, French forts and settlements dotted the Mississippi River and its tributaries in the interior of North America. Two isolated Spanish outposts were situated near the Gulf of Mexico.

Instead, Spaniards focused their attention first on Texas (for instance, establishing San Antonio in 1718), and later on the region they called Alta (upper) California. After learning that Russians who hunted sea otters along the Pacific coast were planning to colonize the region, they sent expeditions north from their missions in Baja California. From a base at San Diego, where the Franciscan Junipero Serra set up the first mission in Alta California in 1769, they traveled north by land and sea to Monterey Bay. There, in 1770, they formally claimed Alta California for Spain. Over the next decades, they established presidios and missions along the coast from modern San Francisco south to San Diego. In those centers, Franciscan friars from Spain and a few settlers from Mexico lived amid thousands of Native peoples who had converted to Christianity.

4-1b France and the Mississippi

French settlements north of New Orleans served as the glue of empire. *Coureurs de bois* (literally, "forest runners") used the rivers and lakes of the American interior to carry goods between Quebec and the new Louisiana territory. At such sites as Michilimackinac (at the junction of Lakes Michigan and Huron) and Kaskaskia (in present-day Illinois), Native peoples traded furs and hides for guns, ammunition, and other valuable items. The Osages were so eager to acquire firearms that they became, in effect, commercial hunters; witnesses reported that their women were sometimes so fully occupied processing hides that older men prepared the communities' meals. The population of the largest French settlements in the region, known collectively as *le pays de Illinois* ("the Illinois country"), never totaled much above three thousand. Located along the Mississippi south of modern St. Louis, the settlements produced wheat for export to New Orleans.

French expansion reshaped native alliances far from the Mississippi. For example, the equestrian Comanches of the Plains, able to trade with the French through Native American intermediaries, no longer needed Spanish goods—or their previous allies, the Utes. Deprived of such powerful partners, the Utes negotiated peace with New Mexico in 1752. Once commonly enslaved by Spaniards, Utes instead became the enslavers of Paiutes and other nonequestrian peoples living to the north and west of the colony. They exchanged hides and slaves—mostly young women—for horses and metal goods. That commercial relationship endured until the end of Spanish rule in the region.

In French officials' minds, Louisiana's paramount goals were protection of the valuable Caribbean islands and prevention of Spanish and British expansion. They accordingly did not focus their attention on the colony's economic development. But the profit-seeking farmers and Native traders from Canada who settled there soon demanded that the French government supply them with slaves. In 1719 officials acquiesced, dispatching more than six thousand Africans, mostly from Senegal, over the next decade. But Louisiana's residents failed to develop a successful plantation economy. They did raise some tobacco and indigo, which, along with skins and hides obtained from Native peoples, composed the colony's major exports for most of the eighteenth century. Some enslaved Africans were carried north to the Illinois country, as farm laborers and domestic servants. They made up nearly 40 percent of the region's population in the 1730s.

Louisiana's expansion angered the Natchez, whose lands the French had usurped. In 1729, the Natchez, assisted by newly arrived slaves, attacked northern reaches of the colony,

▲ A Russian artist in 1816 painted this view of Ohlone/Costanoan men dancing in front of Mission Delores and Spanish spectators. Today the building shown at the left still stands in the middle of the city of San Francisco. The scene conveys a sense of the religious syncretism characteristic of the missions, as native customs combined with the friars' Catholicism to create a fertile blend of spiritual beliefs.

Map 4.2 Major Origins and Destinations of Africans Enslaved in the Americas

Enslaved Africans were drawn from many regions of western Africa (with some coming from the interior of the continent) and were shipped as captives to areas throughout the Americas.

killing more than 10 percent of its settlers. The French struck back, slaughtering the Natchez and their enslaved allies, but Louisiana remained a fragile and neglected colony as long as French rule continued.

4-1c Involuntary Migrants from Africa

Across the Americas, slavery took hold more firmly during the eighteenth century. In all, more Africans than Europeans came to the Americas, the overwhelming majority of them as slaves and about half between 1700 and 1800. Most Africans were transported to Brazil or the Caribbean, primarily in British or Portuguese vessels. The estimated 280,000 people imported before 1780 into the region that became the United States amounted to less than 3 percent of the approximately 12.3 million enslaved people brought to the Americas during the existence of slavery. Rice, indigo, tobacco, and sugar plantations all expanded rapidly in these years, steadily increasing the demand for slaves. In the slaveholding societies of South America and the Caribbean, a surplus of enslaved males over females and appallingly high mortality rates meant that only a continuing influx of new captives could maintain and expand the workforce. On the North American mainland, only South Carolina, where malaria-carrying mosquitoes in the swamps made rice cultivation especially unhealthful,

relied on an inflow of Africans to sustain and expand its labor force.

The involuntary migrants came from many different ethnic groups and regions of Africa (see Map 4.2). More than 40 percent embarked from West Central Africa (modern Congo and Angola), nearly 20 percent from the Bight of Benin (modern Togo, Benin, and southwestern Nigeria), about 13 percent from the Bight of Biafra (today's Cameroon, Gabon, and southeastern Nigeria), and approximately 9 percent from the Gold Coast (modern Ghana and neighboring countries). Smaller numbers of enslaved migrants came from East Africa, the Windward Coast, and the Rice Coast (modern Senegal, Gambia, and Sierra Leone).

Standard slave-trading practice, in which a vessel loaded its human cargo at one port and sold it in another, meant that people from the same broad area (enemies as well as allies) tended to arrive in the Americas together. That tendency was heightened by planter partiality for particular ethnic groups. Virginians, for example, favored Igbos from the Bight of Biafra, whereas South Carolinians and Georgians selected Senegambians and people from West Central Africa. Louisiana planters first chose slaves from the Bight of Benin but later bought many from West Central Africa. Rice planters' desire to purchase

Senegambians, who cultivated rice in their homeland, is easily explained, but historians disagree about the reasons underlying the other preferences.

Thousands, possibly tens of thousands, of these enslaved Africans were Muslims. Some were literate in Arabic, and some came from noble families. Job Ben Solomon, for example, arrived in Maryland in 1732. A slave trader from Senegal, he had been captured by raiders while selling slaves in Gambia. A letter he wrote in Arabic so impressed his owners that they liberated him the next year. Abd al-Rahman, brought to Louisiana in 1788, was less fortunate. Known to his master as "Prince" because of his aristocratic origins, he was not freed until 1829.

Despite the hundreds of thousands of Africans brought to the eighteenth-century mainland, American-born people of African descent came to dominate the mainland's enslaved population numerically because of high levels of natural increase, especially after 1740. Although about 40 percent of the Africans were male, women and children together composed a majority of slave imports; planters valued girls and women for their reproductive as well as productive capacities. All of the colonies passed laws to ensure that the children of enslaved women were born into slavery. This meant that a planter who owned adult female slaves could engineer the steady growth of his labor force without additional major purchases of workers. The slaveholder Thomas Jefferson later observed, "I consider a woman who brings a child every two years more profitable than the best man of the farm. What she produces is an addition to the capital, while his labors disappear in mere consumption."

In the Chesapeake, the number of people held in bondage grew rapidly as imported African people joined an enslaved population that had begun to sustain itself through natural increase. The work routines involved in cultivating tobacco, coupled with a roughly equal sex ratio, reduced slave mortality and increased fertility. Even in unhealthful South Carolina, where substantial imports continued, American-born slaves outnumbered the African-born as early as 1750.

4-1d Newcomers from Europe

In addition to the new Africans, a roughly equal number of Europeans—about 350,000—moved to mainland British North America between 1700 and 1780, most of them after 1730. Late in the seventeenth century, English officials decided to recruit German and French Protestants for their overseas plantations in order to prevent further large-scale emigration from England itself. Influenced by mercantilist thought, they had come to regard a large, industrious population at home as an asset. Thus, they discouraged emigration, except for the deportation of such "undesirables" as vagabonds and Jacobite rebels (supporters of the deposed Stuart monarchs). They offered foreign Protestants free lands and religious toleration, even financing the passage of some. After 1740, they relaxed citizenship (naturalization) requirements,

National Gallery of Art, Washington, D.C. Gift of Edgar William and Bernice Chrysler Garbisch

▲ In December 1729, probably in New York's Hudson Valley, an unknown artist portrayed J. M. Stolle, son of a Palatine immigrant who came to North America from Germany in 1709. The young man's fancy clothing and the column and balustrade in the background suggest that the artist wanted to convey an image of the family's economic success, though whether that image was accurate is unknown.

demanding only the payment of a small fee, seven years' residence, Protestantism, and an oath of allegiance to the British Crown. Such policies created an ethnic diversity unknown outside Britain's American colonies.

Early arrivals wrote home, urging others to come; those contacts created chains of migration from particular regions. The most successful migrants came well prepared, having learned from their American correspondents that land and resources were abundant, especially in the inland areas known as the backcountry, but that they would need capital to take full advantage of the new opportunities. People who arrived penniless did less well; approximately 40 percent of the newcomers fell into that category, for they immigrated as bound laborers of some sort.

Worst off among European emigrés were the roughly fifty thousand migrants who arrived as convicted felons sentenced to transportation for two to fourteen years instead of execution. Typically unskilled and perhaps one-third female, they were dispatched most often to Maryland, where they labored in the tobacco fields, or as ironworkers or household servants. Little is known about the ultimate fate of most, but some who committed further crimes in the colonies became notorious on both sides of the Atlantic.

Slaves' Symbolic Resistance

Although revolts and escapes have been the focus of many studies of enslaved Africans' resistance to bondage, archaeological finds from the mid-eighteenth century such as those illustrated here reveal important aspects of slaves' personal lives and other forms of resistance. The set of objects found in Annapolis constitutes a *minkisi*, or West African spiritual bundle. Africans and African Americans placed such groupings of objects, each with a symbolic meaning (for example, bent nails reflected the power of fire), under hearths or sills to direct the spirits who entered houses through doors or chimneys. The *minkisi's* primary purpose was to protect the enslaved from the power of their masters—for example, by preventing the breakup of a family. The statue of a man was uncovered in an enslaved blacksmith's quarters. It too reflects resistance, but of a different sort: the quiet rebellion of a talented craftsman who used his master's iron and his own time and skill to create a remarkable object.

CRITICAL THINKING

■ How can such material evidence compliment the written records of enslaved people's lives, which were typically written by their owners?

▲ *This iron figure, a product of skilled artisanship, was discovered during the excavation of an enslaved blacksmith's quarters.*

▲ A minkisi *from the eighteenth century found under the floor of the Charles Carroll house in Annapolis, Maryland.*

4-1e Scots-Irish, Scots, and Germans

One of the largest groups of immigrants—about 143,000—came from Ireland or Scotland, largely in family units. About 66,000 Scots-Irish, descendants of Presbyterian Scots who had settled in the north of Ireland during the seventeenth century, joined some 35,000 people who came directly to America from Scotland (see Figure 4.1). Another 42,000, both Protestants and Catholics, migrated from southern Ireland. High rents, poor harvests, and religious discrimination (in Ireland) combined to push people from lands their families had long occupied. Many of the Irish migrants had worked as linen weavers in their homeland, but linen prices declined significantly in the late 1710s. Because the flax used for linen weaving was imported from Pennsylvania, and Irish flaxseed was exported to the same place, vessels regularly sailed between Ireland and Pennsylvania. By the 1720s, the migration route was well established, fueled by positive reports of the prospects for advancement in North America.

Irish immigrants usually landed in Philadelphia, Pennsylvania or New Castle, Delaware. Many moved into the Pennsylvania backcountry along the Susquehanna River, where the colonial government created a county named Donegal for them. Later migrants traveled farther west and south, to the backcountry of Maryland, Virginia, and the Carolinas. Frequently unable to afford any acreage, they squatted on land belonging to Native communities, land speculators, or colonial governments. In the frontier setting, they gained a reputation for lawlessness, hard drinking, and ferocious fighting among themselves and with neighboring Delaware and Shawnee villagers.

Migrants from Germany and German-speaking areas of Switzerland numbered about 85,000, most of them leaving the Rhineland between 1730 and 1755. They, too, usually came in family groups and landed in Philadelphia. Like the English indentured servants of the previous century, many paid for their passage by contracting to work as servants for a specified period. Germans tended to settle together when they could; they composed up to half of the population of some counties. Many Germans moved west into Pennsylvania and then south into the backcountry of Maryland and Virginia. Others landed in Charles Town and settled in the Carolina interior. The Germans belonged to a wide variety of Protestant sects—primarily Lutheran, German Reformed, and Moravian—and added to the already substantial religious diversity of Pennsylvania. Late in the century, they and their descendants comprised one-third of Pennsylvania's residents. Benjamin Franklin, for one, feared as early as 1751 that they would "Germanize" Pennsylvania.

The years between 1760 and 1775 witnessed the colonial period's most concentrated immigration to Britain's American colonies. Tough economic times in Germany and the British Isles led many to seek a better life in America;

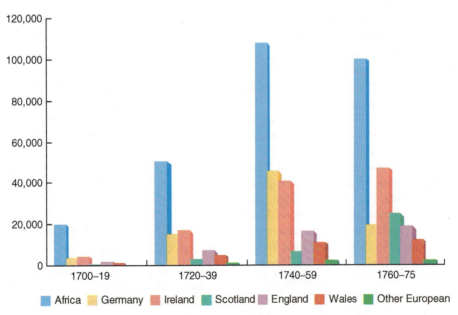

Figure 4.1 **Atlantic Origins of Migrants to Thirteen Mainland Colonies of British North America, 1700–1775**

Immigrants from Ireland, Scotland, and Germany significantly outnumbered those from England throughout the eighteenth century. But as this figure shows, forced migrants from Africa comprised by far the largest number of new arrivals in the mainland British colonies. In the Caribbean colonies, the pattern was yet more pronounced. *Data for European numbers: Aaron Fogelman, "Migrations to the Thirteen British North American Colonies, 1700–1775: New Estimates," The Journal of Interdisciplinary History, vol. 22, no. 4 (Spring 1992), pp. 691–709. Data for African numbers: The Trans-Atlantic Slave Trade Database, available online at: http://www .slavevoyages.org. Accessed August 1, 2012.*

simultaneously, the slave trade burgeoned. In those fifteen years alone, more than 125,000 free migrants and 100,000 enslaved people arrived—nearly 10 percent of the entire population of mainland British North America in 1775. Late-arriving free immigrants had little choice but to crowd into the cities or move to the edges of settlement; land elsewhere was occupied (see Map 4.3). In the peripheries they became the tenants of, or bought property from, land speculators who had purchased giant tracts in the (usually vain) hope of making a fortune.

4-1f Maintaining Ethnic and Religious Identities

The migration patterns of the eighteenth century made British North America one of the most diverse places on earth. Even in New England, the most homogeneous region of the mainland provinces, nearly a third of inhabitants had non-English origins by 1760. In the mid-Atlantic, non-English Europeans predominated; less than half of New York's inhabitants, and less than a third of Pennsylvania's, were of English descent. Farther south, settlers of English origin remained a minority. By 1760, Irish and Scots-Irish migrants comprised roughly 15 percent of the region's population; Africans and their descendants accounted for more than half.

How readily migrants assimilated into Anglo-American culture depended on patterns of settlement, the size of the group, and the strength of the migrants' ties to their common culture. For example, in the late seventeenth century, the French Protestants (**Huguenots**) who migrated to Charles Town or New York City were unable to sustain either their language or their religious practices for more than two generations. Yet the Huguenots who created rural communities in the Hudson valley remained recognizably French and Calvinist for a century. By contrast, small groups of colonial Jews maintained a distinct identity regardless of where they settled. In places like New York City, Newport, Savannah, and Kingston, Jamaica, they established synagogues and worked actively to preserve their faith and culture.

Larger groups of migrants (Germans, Irish, and Scots) found it easier to sustain European ways. Some ethnic groups dominated certain localities. Near Frederick, Maryland, a visitor would have heard more German than English; in Anson and Cumberland counties, North Carolina, the same visitor might have thought she was in Scotland. Many New Yorkers continued to speak Dutch. In Coney Island, Dr. Hamilton and an enslaved man Dromo met a Dutch-speaking African woman, with whom Dromo conversed in a kind of pidgin. "Dis de way to York?" he asked. "Yaw, dat is Yarikee… Yaw, mynheer," she replied.

Where migrants from different countries settled in the same region, ethnic antagonisms often surfaced. One German clergyman in Pennsylvania, for example, claimed that "it is very seldom that German and English blood is happily united in wedlock." Anglo-American

Huguenots French Calvinist dissenters from that country's dominant Catholicism.

Map 4.3 Non-English Ethnic Groups in the British Colonies, ca. 1775

Non-African immigrants arriving in the years after 1720 were pushed to the peripheries of settlement, as is shown by these maps. Scottish, Scots-Irish, French, and German newcomers had to move to the frontiers. The Dutch remained where they had originally settled in the seventeenth century. Africans were concentrated in coastal plantation regions.

elites fostered such antagonisms in order to fracture opposition and maintain their political and economic power, and they frequently subverted the colonies' generous naturalization laws, depriving even long-resident immigrants of a voice in government. The elites probably would have preferred to ignore the British colonies' growing racial and ethnic diversity, but ultimately they could not do so. In the political crises of the 1770s, they needed the support of non-English Americans.

4-2 Economic Growth and Development in British America

▶ How did the coastal trade and the internal economy of the British North American economy develop in the eighteenth century?

▶ What role did overseas trade play in the British North American colonial economy?

▶ What was the impact of the growth of the colonial economy in the eighteenth century?

Despite the vagaries of international markets, the dramatic increase in the population of British America caused colonial economies to grow. A comparison with French and Spanish America is instructive. The population and economy of New Spain's northern Borderlands stagnated, for the isolated settlements produced few items for export. French Canada exported large quantities of furs and fish, but the government's monopoly on trade ensured that most of the profits ended up in the home country. The Louisiana colony required substantial government subsidies just to survive. Of France's American possessions, only the Caribbean islands flourished economically, largely on the profits of sugar and slaves.

4-2a Commerce and Manufacturing

In British North America, by contrast, the rising population generated ever-greater demand for goods and services, leading to the development of small-scale colonial manufacturing and a complex network of internal trade. Colonists built roads, bridges, mills, and stores to serve new settlements. A lively coastal trade developed; by the late 1760s, more than half of the vessels leaving Boston harbor sailed to other mainland colonies. Such ships not only collected goods for export and distributed imports but also sold items made locally. The colonies no longer wholly depended on European manufactured goods. For the first time, the American population created sufficient demand to support local manufacturing.

Iron making became British America's largest industry. Ironworks in the Chesapeake and the middle colonies required sizable investments and substantial workforces—usually indentured servants, convicts, and slaves—to dig the ore, chop trees for charcoal, and smelt and refine the ore into iron bars. Because the work was dirty, dangerous, and difficult, convicts and servants often tried to flee, but iron making offered enslaved men new avenues to learn valuable skills and accumulate property when they were compensated for doing

more than their assigned tasks. By 1775, Anglo America's iron production surpassed England's.

Foreign trade nevertheless dominated the colonial economy. Settlers' prosperity depended heavily on overseas demand for American tobacco, rice, indigo, salted fish, and timber products. The sale of such items earned the colonists the credit they needed to buy English and European goods. Between 1700 and 1775, colonists' purchases of British manufactures grew fivefold, from 5 percent to 25 percent of Britain's total exports. The English politician Edmund Burke told Parliament that in 1772, the "Export trade to the colonies alone" approached what "the whole trade of England" had been in 1700. But whenever British demand for American products slowed, the colonists' income dropped, along with their ability to buy imports. Colonial merchants were particularly vulnerable to economic downswings, and bankruptcies were common.

4-2b Wealth and Poverty

Despite fluctuations, the American economy grew during the eighteenth century. That growth in turn produced better standards of living for all property-owning colonists. Early in the century, as the price of British manufactures fell in relation to colonists' incomes, more households began to acquire amenities such as chairs and earthenware dishes. Diet also improved as trading networks brought access to more varied foodstuffs. After 1750, luxury items could be found in the homes of the wealthy, and the "middling sort" began to purchase imported English ceramics. Even the poorest property owners had more and better household goods. The differences lay not so much in *what* items people owned, but rather in the quality and quantity of those possessions.

The benefits of economic growth were unevenly distributed: wealthy Americans improved their position relative to other colonists. The American-born elite families who dominated the colonies' political, economic, and social life by 1750 had begun the century with sufficient capital to take advantage of the changes caused by population growth. They were the urban merchants who exported staples and imported luxury goods, the large landowners who rented small farms to immigrant tenants, the slave traders who supplied planters with forced migrants from Africa and the Caribbean, and the rum distillers who processed the sugar grown and refined by slaves in the West Indies. The rise of this group of moneyed families helped to make the social and economic structure of mid-eighteenth-century America more stratified than before. New arrivals had less opportunity for advancement than their predecessors. Even so, few free settlers in rural areas (where about 95 percent of the colonists lived) appear to have been truly poor. By 1750, at least two-thirds of rural householders owned their own land.

4-2c City Life

Nowhere was the maturation of the colonial economy more evident than in the port cities of British North America. By 1760, Boston (with a population holding steady around

15,600), New York (18,000), and fast-growing Philadelphia (nearly 24,000) had become provincial British cities on the scale of Bristol and Liverpool. Life in these cities differed considerably from that on northern farms, southern plantations, or southwestern ranches. City dwellers purchased their food and wood. They lived by the clock rather than the sun, and men's jobs frequently took them away from their households.

Early American cities also saw growing extremes of wealth and poverty. By the last quarter of the eighteenth century, some of the largest merchant families—such as the Hancocks and the Apthorps in Boston or the Allens and the Drinkers in Philadelphia—had amassed trading fortunes their forebears could not have imagined. Yet roughly one-fifth of Philadelphia's workforce was enslaved, and blacks composed nearly 15 percent of the population of New York City. White or black, the families of urban laborers lived on the edge of destitution. As applicants for assistance overwhelmed traditional poor-relief systems, cities began to build workhouses or almshouses to shelter growing numbers of the poor, elderly, and infirm. Between 1758 and 1775, more than 1,800 people—two-thirds of them women and children—were admitted to Boston's almshouse. "Mary Pilsbery came into the house Wednesday May 5, 1762 and brought with her Only the Cloaths on her Back," reads one entry in the town's poor relief records. Three days later, Pilsbery was dead.

City people were in many ways more cosmopolitan than their rural counterparts. Even some of the poorest among them—common sailors, prostitutes—had extensive contact with worlds far beyond their homes. By 1760, most substantial towns had at least one weekly newspaper, and some had two or three. The press offered the latest "advices from London" (usually two to three months old) and news from other colonies, as well as local reports. Newspapers were available (and often read aloud) at taverns and coffee-houses, so people who could not afford or even read them could learn the news. Contact with the outside world, however, had its drawbacks. Sailors sometimes brought deadly diseases into port. Boston, New York, Philadelphia, and New Orleans endured epidemics of smallpox and yellow fever, which Europeans and Africans in the countryside largely escaped.

4-2d Regional Economies

Within this overall picture, broad regional patterns emerged, heightened by **King George's War**, the western front of the War of the Austrian Succession (1739–1748). New England's economy rested on trade with the Caribbean: northern forests supplied the timber for building the ships and the barrels that carried salt fish to feed the slaves on island sugar plantations. The outbreak of war created strong demand for ships and sailors, thus invigorating the economy, but when the shipbuilding boom ended, the economy stagnated.

By contrast, the war and its aftermath brought prosperity to the middle colonies and the Chesapeake, where fertile soil and a long growing season produced an abundance of grain, much of which likewise was shipped to the Caribbean. After 1748, when a series of poor harvests in Europe caused flour prices to rise sharply, Philadelphia and New York took the lead in the foodstuffs trade. Some Chesapeake planters converted tobacco fields to wheat and corn. Tobacco remained the largest single export from the mainland colonies, yet the beginnings of grain cultivation caused a significant change in Chesapeake settlement patterns by encouraging the development of port towns (like Baltimore) where merchants and shipbuilders established businesses to handle the new trade.

South Carolina's staple crop, rice, shaped its distinctive economic pattern. The colony's rice and indigo fields—like cane fields in the Caribbean—were periodically devastated by Atlantic hurricanes, causing hardship and bankruptcies. Yet after 1730, when Parliament removed rice from the list of products enumerated by the Navigation Acts, South Carolinians prospered by trading directly with Europe. The outbreak of war disrupted that trade. The colony entered a depression that did not end until the 1760s brought renewed European demand. Overall, though, South Carolina experienced more rapid economic growth than did Britain's other mainland colonies. By the time of the Revolution, its freeholders had the highest average wealth in continental Anglo America, though the wealth of Barbadian and Jamaican planters dwarfed even theirs.

Closely linked to South Carolina was the newest British settlement, Georgia, chartered in 1732 as a haven for English debtors released from prison. Its founder, James Oglethorpe, envisioned Georgia as a garrison province peopled by sturdy farmers who would defend the southern flank of English settlement against Spanish Florida. To ensure that all adult men in the colony could serve as its armed protectors, Georgia's charter prohibited slavery. But Carolina rice planters won the removal of the restriction in 1751. Thereafter, they essentially invaded Georgia, which—despite remaining politically independent and becoming a royal colony in 1752—developed into a rice-planting slave society.

King George's War initially helped New England and hurt South Carolina and Georgia, but in the long run those effects reversed. In the Chesapeake and the middle colonies, the war ushered in a long period of prosperity. Such variations highlight the mainland colonies' disparate experiences within the British empire, and their economic distance from each other. Despite an increasing coastal trade, each province's fortunes depended less on neighboring colonies than on the shifting markets of Europe and the Caribbean. Had it not been for an unprecedented crisis in the British imperial system (discussed in Chapter 5), it is unlikely they could have been persuaded to join in a common endeavor.

King George's War Also known as the War of Austrian Succession; started out as a conflict between Britain and Spain, but then escalated when France sided with Spain.

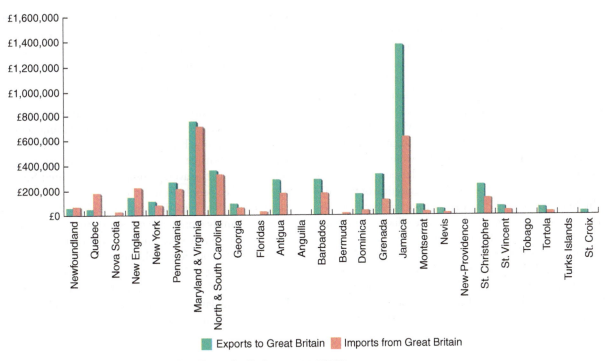

Figure 4.2 Trade Revenue from the British Colonies in 1769

As this figure shows, the different regions of the British mainland colonies had distinct trading patterns with Britain. New England imported more than it exported; much of its export trade was with the Caribbean. The exports of the Chesapeake colonies (especially tobacco) and the Carolinas (rice and indigo) were more significant, but the value of sugar from Jamaica dwarfed the produce of all the other British colonies. *Data from David MacPherson,* Annals of Commerce, Manufactures, Fisheries and Navigation, with Brief Notices of the Arts and Sciences Connected with them, Containing the Commercial Transactions of the British Empire and Other Countries *(1805), volume III, p. 495.*

4-3 "Oeconomical" Households: Families, Production, and Reproduction

▶ **How did European settlement in British North America affect Native American families?**

▶ **What were the meanings and functions of the family to eighteenth-century European settlers?**

▶ **How did enslaved African Americans resist and ameliorate their bondage through family roles?**

Throughout the colonial era and well into the nineteenth century, the household was the basic unit of economic production, and economic production was the overriding concern of American families. Indeed, the Greek word *oikos*, meaning "household," is also the root of the English word *economy*. Seventeenth-century English writers often used the term *oeconomie* to discuss household and family matters. People living together as families, commonly under the direction of a marital pair, everywhere constituted the chief mechanisms for both production and consumption. Yet family forms and structures varied widely in the mainland colonies.

4-3a Native American and Mixed-Race Families

As Europeans consolidated their hold on North America, Native peoples had to adapt to novel circumstances. Ethnic groups reduced in numbers by disease and warfare recombined into new units; for example, the Catawbas emerged in the 1730s in the western Carolinas from the coalescence of earlier peoples including Yamasees and Guales. Likewise, European **secular** and religious authorities reshaped Native family forms. Whereas many Native societies had permitted easy divorce, European missionaries frowned on such practices; societies that had allowed polygynous marriages (including New England Algonquians) redefined such relationships, designating one wife "legitimate" and others "concubines."

Once Europeans established dominance in any region, it became difficult for Native communities to pursue traditional modes of subsistence. That led to unusual family structures as well as to a variety of economic strategies. In New England, Algonquian husbands and wives often could not live together, for adults supported themselves by working separately (perhaps wives as domestic servants, husbands as sailors). Some Native women married African American

secular Not specifically relating to religion or to a religious body.

men, unions encouraged by sexual imbalances in both populations. And in New Mexico, detribalized Navajos, Pueblos, Paiutes, and Apaches employed as servants by Spanish settlers clustered in the small towns of the Borderlands. Known collectively as *genizaros*, they lost contact with indigenous cultures, instead living on the fringes of Hispanic society.

Wherever the population contained relatively few European women, sexual liaisons (both within and outside marriage) occurred between European men and Native women. The resulting mixed-race people, whom Spanish colonists called *mestizos* and French settlers labeled *métis,* often served as go-betweens, navigating the intersection of two cultures. In New France and the Anglo-American backcountry, such families frequently resided in Native villages, and many children of these unions became Native American leaders. For example, Peter Chartier, son of a Shawnee mother and a French father, led a pro-French Shawnee band in western Pennsylvania in the 1740s. By contrast, in the Spanish Borderlands, the offspring of Europeans and *genizaros* were considered inferior. Often denied the privilege of legal marriage, they bore generations of "illegitimate" children of various racial mixtures, giving rise in Latino society to a wide range of labels describing degrees of skin color with a precision unknown in English or French America.

4-3b European American Families

Eighteenth-century Anglo-Americans referred to all the people who occupied one household (including servants or slaves) as a family. European men or their widows headed households considerably larger than American families today; in 1790, the average home in the United States contained 5.7 free people. Few such households included grandparents or other extended kin. Bound by ties of blood or servitude, family members worked together to produce goods for consumption or sale. The head of the household represented it to the outside world, voting in elections, managing the finances, and holding legal authority over the rest of the family—his wife, his children, and his servants or slaves. In the eyes of the law, wives were *femes covert*, their personhood "covered" by their husbands.

Album/Art Resource, NY

▲ People in eighteenth-century Spain were fascinated by the topic of *mestizaje*: race mixing or, pejoratively, miscegenation. Such curiosity created a market for so-called *casta* paintings, which illustrated different sorts of multiracial households, focusing on the gradations of color in people's skin. This anonymous painting, one of a series (it's labeled *Escena de mestizaje n° 13,* or thirteenth miscegenation scene) illustrates the children of parents from different Mesoamerican groups, the Arvarraso and the Barsino.

In English, French, and Spanish America, the vast majority of European families supported themselves through farming and raising livestock. The production of cash crops such as indigo in Louisiana and South Carolina, or tobacco in the Chesapeake, required different kinds of labor from subsistence farming in New England or cattle ranching in New Mexico and Texas. But regardless of the scale and the crop, household tasks were allocated by sex. The master, his sons, and his male servants or slaves performed one set of chores; the mistress, her daughters, and her female servants or slaves, a different set.

The mistress took responsibility for what Anglo-Americans called "indoor affairs." She and her female helpers prepared food, cleaned the house, and washed and often made clothing. Preparing food involved planting and cultivating a "kitchen" garden, harvesting and preserving vegetables, salting and smoking meat, drying apples and pressing cider, milking cows and making butter and cheese, not to mention cooking and baking. Women's work—often performed while pregnant, nursing, or sometimes both—was unremitting. Mary Cooper, a farm wife from Long Island, wrote in her diary in 1769, "This day is forty years sinc I left my father's house and come here, and here have I seene little els but harde labour and sorrow."

The head of the household and his male helpers, responsible for "outdoor affairs," also had heavy workloads. They planted and cultivated fields, built fences, chopped wood, harvested and marketed crops, tended livestock, and butchered cattle and hogs. So extensive was the work involved in maintaining a farm household that no married couple could do it alone. If they had no children to help them, they hired servants or purchased slaves.

4-3c African American Families

Most African American families lived as components of European American households. More than 95 percent of colonial African Americans were held in bondage. Although many lived on farms with only one or two other enslaved people, others lived and worked in a largely black setting. In South Carolina, a majority of the population was of African descent; in Georgia, about half; and in the Chesapeake, 40 percent. Portions of the Carolina low country were nearly 90 percent African American by 1790.

The setting in which African Americans lived determined the shape of their families, yet wherever possible slaves established family structures in which youngsters carried relatives' names or—in South Carolina—followed African naming patterns. In the North, the scarcity of other blacks made it difficult for enslaved men and women to form households. In the Chesapeake, men and women who regarded themselves

London Coffee House.

▲ This 1830 lithograph of "The Old London Coffee House" in eighteenth-century Philadelphia shows a slave auction taking place on its porch. That such a scene could have occurred in front of such a prominent and popular meeting place serves as a reminder of the ubiquity of slavery in the colonies, north as well as south.

as married (slaves could not legally wed) frequently lived in different quarters or even on different plantations. Children generally resided with their mother, seeing their father only on Sundays. The natural increase of the population created wide American-born kinship networks among Chesapeake slaves. On large Carolina and Georgia rice plantations, enslaved couples usually lived together with their children, and could accumulate property by working for themselves after they had completed their daily "tasks." Everywhere, slave family ties were forged against the threat of sale that separated husbands from wives and parents from children.

4-3d Forms of Resistance

Because all the British colonies permitted slavery, bondspeople had few options for escaping servitude other than fleeing to Florida, where the Spanish offered protection. Some recently arrived Africans stole boats to try to return home or ran off in groups to frontier regions, to join Native communities or establish independent communities. Others made their way to cities like Philadelphia, where they might melt into small populations of free black laborers and artisans. Masters paid for advertisements in Philadelphia newspapers to reclaim runaways thought to be working as blacksmiths, tanners, barbers, brick makers, ironworkers, and sailors. The revenue from runaway ads underwrote the printing of many newspapers.

Among American-born slaves, family ties strongly affected the decision to steal oneself by running away. South Carolina planters soon learned, as one wrote, that slaves "love their families dearly and none runs away from the other," so many owners sought to keep families together for practical reasons. Most escaped slaves advertised in the newspapers were young men; it was harder for women with children to flee.

Although colonial slaves rarely rebelled collectively, they resisted enslavement in other ways. Enslaved men and women rejected owners' attempts to commandeer their labor on Sundays without compensation. Extended-kin groups protested excessive punishment of relatives and sought to live near one another. The links that developed among African American families who had lived on the same plantation for several generations helped to ameliorate the uncertainties of existence under slavery. If parents and children were separated by sale, other relatives could help with child rearing. Among African Americans, just as among Native Americans, the extended family thus served a more crucial function than it did among European Americans.

Most slave families managed to carve out a small measure of autonomy, especially in their working and spiritual lives, and particularly in the Lower South. Enslaved Muslims often preserved their Islamic faith, a pattern evident in Louisiana and Georgia. Some African Americans maintained traditional beliefs, and others converted to Christianity (often retaining some African elements), finding comfort in the Bible's promise that all would be free and equal in heaven. Slaves in South Carolina and Georgia jealously guarded their customary ability to control their own time after completing their

"tasks." On Chesapeake tobacco plantations, enslaved people planted their own gardens, trapped, and fished to supplement the minimal diet their owners supplied. Late in the century, some Chesapeake planters with a surplus of laborers began to hire slaves out to others, often allowing some enslaved men and women to keep a small part of their earnings. Such wages could buy desired goods or provide a legacy for children.

4-4 Provincial Cultures

▶ **What kinds of cultural exchanges and rituals emerged in eighteenth-century British North America?**

▶ **What value did colonists find in the expansion of consumption activities in the eighteenth century?**

▶ **How did "genteel culture" differ from "everyday culture" in eighteenth-century British North America?**

In addition to serving as the basic unit of economic production and social reproduction, the early American household was a nursery of culture, a term with many, sometimes competing definitions. When anthropologists speak of culture, they typically mean the customs and rituals that define a community—its folkways, in other words. Where folkways belong to the many, learned or "high" culture—art, literature, philosophy, and science—may be the realm of the few, especially in a premodern society, where learning was hardly democratic. Yet folkways interact with the life of the mind, and cultures are always plural. This was particularly the case in eighteenth-century North America, with its dizzying diversity of peoples and its growing social stratification. There were then (and are now) many American cultures. In some respects, these cultures grew more British as the disparate colonies became more fully integrated provinces of empire. But in other ways, as Dr. Hamilton learned on his progress along the eastern seaboard, the ragged outer margins of the British realm fashioned very distinctive cultures indeed.

4-4a Oral Cultures

Most people in North America were illiterate. Those who could read—a small proportion in French and Spanish America, about two-thirds of Anglo-Americans—often could not write. Parents, older siblings, or widows who needed extra income taught youngsters to read; middling boys and genteel girls might then learn to write in private schools. Few Americans other than some Anglican missionaries in the South tried to instruct enslaved children; indeed, masters feared literate slaves, who could forge documents in order to pass as free. And only the most zealous Indian converts learned European literacy skills.

Thus, the everyday cultures of colonial North America were primarily oral and—at least through the first half of the eighteenth century—intensely local. Face-to-face conversation was the chief means of communication. Information tended to travel slowly, within relatively confined regions. Different locales developed divergent traditions, and racial and ethnic variations heightened those differences. Household and public rituals served as the chief means through which the colonists forged cultural identities and navigated the boundaries among them.

4-4b Rituals on the "Middle Ground"

Particularly important rituals developed on what the historian Richard White has termed the "middle ground"—the psychological and geographical space in which Native peoples and Europeans encountered each other, especially but not only in the upper Midwest. Most of those cultural encounters occurred in the context of trade or warfare.

When Europeans sought to trade with Native peoples, they encountered indigenous systems of exchange that stressed gift giving rather than buying and selling. Successful bargaining required French and English traders to present Native individuals with gifts (cloth, rum, gunpowder, and other goods) before negotiating with them for pelts and skins. Eventually, those gifts would be reciprocated. Only then could formal trading proceed.

Intercultural rituals also developed to deal with crime. Both Native peoples and Europeans believed that murder required a compensatory act, but they differed over what the act should be. Europeans sought primarily to identify and punish perpetrators. To Native peoples, such "eye for an eye" revenge was just one of many remedies, including capturing a Native person from an enemy group or a colonist to take the dead person's place, or "covering the dead" by providing the family of the deceased with compensatory goods. The French and the Algonquians evolved elaborate rituals for handling frontier murders that encompassed elements of both societies' traditions.

4-4c Civic Rituals

Ceremonial occasions reinforced identities within as well as boundaries between cultures. New England governments proclaimed days of thanksgiving (for good harvests, military victories, and other "providences") and days of fasting and prayer (to lament war, drought, or epidemic). Everyone was expected to participate in the church rituals held on such occasions. Because able-bodied men between the ages of sixteen and sixty were required to serve in local militias—the only military forces in the colonies—monthly musters also brought townsfolk together.

In the Chesapeake, widely spaced farms meant that communities came together less frequently. Ritual life centered on court and election days. When the county court met, men came to file lawsuits, appear as witnesses, or serve as jurors. Attendance at court functioned as a method of civic education; men watched the proceedings to learn what their neighbors expected of them. Elections served a similar purpose, for property-holding men voted in public. An election official, often flanked by the candidates for office, called each man forward to declare his preference. The gentleman for whom the ballot was cast would then thank the voter. Later, the candidates repaired to nearby taverns, where they plied supporters with rum, a custom called "treating."

Everywhere in colonial North America, the punishment of criminals served to remind the community of proper behavioral standards. Public hangings and whippings, along with orders to sit in the stocks, expressed a community's outrage and restored harmony to its ranks. Judges often devised shaming penalties that mirrored a particular crime. In San Antonio, Texas, for example, one cattle thief was led through the town's streets "with the entrails hanging from his neck." When a New Mexico man assaulted his father-in-law, he was directed not merely to pay medical expenses but also to kneel before him and beg forgiveness publicly.

4-4d Rituals of Consumption

By 1770, Anglo-Americans spent roughly one-quarter of their household budgets on consumer goods, chiefly of British manufacture. Since similar imports flooded shop counters from Maine to Georgia, such purchases established cultural links among the various residents of North America, creating what historians have termed "an empire of goods." The governor of New York scarcely exaggerated when he reported, in 1774, "more than Eleven Twelfths of the Inhabitants of this province ... are cloathed in British Manufactures." Their houses were likewise furnished with Britain's bounty, from the plates on their tables to the very paint on their walls.

Seventeenth-century settlers had acquired necessities by bartering with neighbors or ordering products from a home-country merchant. By the middle of the eighteenth century, specialized shops proliferated in colonial towns and cities. In 1770, Boston had more than five hundred stores, offering a vast selection of cloth wares, exotic groceries, tobacco, ceramics, and metalwork. Most small towns had one or two retail establishments. Colonists would take time to "go shopping," a novel and pleasurable leisure activity in Anglo America as in Britain. Buyers confronted a dazzling array of possibilities and fashioned their identities by choosing among them. Some historians have termed this shift a "consumer revolution."

The purchase of an object—for example, a teapot, a mirror, or some beautiful imported fabric—initiated a complex series of consumption rituals. Consumers would deploy their purchases: hanging the mirror prominently on a wall, displaying the teapot on a sideboard, sewing the fabric into a special piece of clothing. Colonists proudly showed off their acquisitions (and thus their status and taste). Moralists fretted about encroaching luxury. "If we are now *poorer* than we were thirty Years ago, we are at the same Time *finer*," proclaimed a Boston pamphleteer in 1753. "Our Beds, our Tables and our Bodies are covered" with cloth "from foreign Countries." (Instead, he proposed, the poor should be put to work weaving linen.)

A prosperous man might hire an artist to paint his family using imported objects and wearing fine clothing, thereby creating a pictorial record to be admired and passed down as

Mrs. James Smith (Elizabeth Murray), 1769 (oil on canvas)/Copley, John Singleton (1738-1815)/MUSEUM OF FINE ARTS, BOSTON/ Museum of Fine Arts, Boston, Massachusetts, USA/Bridgeman Images

▲ Elizabeth Murray, the subject of this 1769 painting by John Singleton Copley, was the widow of James Smith, a wealthy rum distiller. She commissioned this likeness after her husband's death. Her fashionable dress and pose would seem to mark her as a lady of leisure, yet before, during, and after her marriage this Scottish immigrant ran a successful dry goods shop in Boston. She thus simultaneously catered to and participated in the new culture of consumption.

a kind of cultural inheritance. In the early eighteenth century, most portraitists active in the colonies were itinerants from Britain. But by midcentury, a small number of American-born painters were gaining prominence. Benjamin West, born in rural Pennsylvania, attracted ever-wealthier patrons in Lancaster and Philadelphia before embarking for Europe in 1760. John Singleton Copley, the son of a Boston tobacco-seller, became the leading artist in the colonies, making a good living by taking likenesses of merchant families grown rich in Atlantic trade. His reputation (and his art) preceded him to London in 1774.

Poor and rural people also participated in the new trends, taking obvious pleasure even in inexpensive purchases. Backcountry storekeepers accepted bartered goods from customers who lacked cash. One Virginia woman traded hens and chickens for a pewter dish; another swapped yards of handwoven cloth for a necklace. Slaves exchanged cotton they grew in their free time for ribbons and hats they must have worn with pride. Some also purchased mirrors so they could see themselves bedecked in their acquisitions.

4-4e Tea and Madeira

Tea drinking, a consumption ritual largely controlled by women, played an important role throughout Anglo America. Households with aspirations to genteel status purchased the items necessary for the proper consumption of tea: pots and cups, strainers and sugar tongs, even special tables. Tea provided a focal point for socializing and, because of its cost, served as a crucial marker of cosmopolitan status. Tea drinking bridged the miles between the East Indies (tea), the West Indies (sugar), and North America, uniting the edges of Britain's empire.

Gentlewomen regularly entertained male and female friends at afternoon tea parties. Even poor households consumed tea, although they could not afford the fancy equipment used by their better-off neighbors. In Connecticut, Dr. Hamilton met a "wild and rustic" family living in a log cabin whose meager possessions included a teapot. Some Mohawk people adopted the custom, much to the surprise of a traveler from Sweden, who observed them drinking tea in the late 1740s.

Madeira wine, imported from the Portuguese islands by merchants with extensive transatlantic familial connections, also connoted gentility. By 1770, Madeira had become a favored drink of the elite. Serving the wine required specialized accoutrements and elaborate ceremony; purchasing it involved considerable expense. In 1784, one Philadelphia merchant's spending on Madeira and other exotic liquors equaled the combined annual budgets of two artisan families.

4-4f Polite and Learned Culture

Colonists who acquired such wealth through trade, agriculture, or manufacturing spent their money ostentatiously, drinking and dressing fashionably, traveling in horse-drawn carriages, and throwing lavish parties. They built large brick homes of the neoclassical style newly fashionable in England, with columns, symmetrical floor plans, and an array of specialized rooms. The grandest houses in the colonies—William Byrd's Westover and Landon Carter's Sabine Hall, both in Virginia; or Thomas Hancock's mansion overlooking Boston Common—would barely have qualified as outbuildings of England's great country houses. Yet they were far more elaborate than the homes of earlier settlers.

Sufficiently well-off to enjoy "leisure" time (a first for North America), genteel Euro-Americans cultivated polite manners, adopting stylized forms of address and paying attention to "proper" comportment. In the late 1740s, a young George Washington, son of an aspiring Virginia planter, copied into his school exercise book a list of 110 "Rules of Civility and Decent Behaviour" taken from an English courtesy manual. Politeness had to be learned, and earned.

Although the effects of accumulated wealth were most pronounced in British America, elite families in New Mexico, Louisiana, and Quebec also fashioned genteel cultures that distinguished them from the "lesser sort." One historian has termed these processes "the refinement of America."

▲ This British conversation piece, "A Family of Three at Tea," painted by Richard Collins (c. 1727), depicts a genteel husband, wife, and daughter at the tea table, surrounded by the specialized imported silver and porcelain that accompanied the drinking of tea among the elite. Tea-drinking was often associated with women, family, and home; it was considered feminine and domestic where coffee was masculine and public. The dog in the scene, known then as now as a Cavalier King Charles spaniel, might have identified the family with Tory politics.

Refined gentlemen prided themselves not only on their possessions, but also on their education and on their intellectual connections to Europe. Many had been tutored by private teachers; some even attended college in Europe or America. (Harvard, the first colonial college, founded in 1636, was joined by William and Mary in 1693, Yale in 1701, and later by several others, including Princeton in 1747.) In the seventeenth century, only aspiring clergymen attended college, where they studied ancient languages and theology. But in the eighteenth century, college curricula broadened to include mathematics, the natural sciences, law, and medicine. By the 1740s, aspiring colonial gentlemen regularly traveled to London and Edinburgh to complete their educations in law or medicine, and to Italy to become connoisseurs of art and antiquities.

American women were largely excluded from advanced education, with the exception of female religious who joined nunneries in Canada or Louisiana and engaged in sustained study within convent walls. Instead, genteel daughters

perfected womanly accomplishments like French (rather than Latin), needlework, and musicianship. Even relatively educated women including John Adams's wife Abigail and Benjamin Franklin's sister Jane—women who regularly read books and wrote letters—bemoaned their scant learning and poor spelling.

Yet women, like their brothers, sons, and husbands, took part in a burgeoning world of print in Anglo America. There were more than a thousand private libraries in seventeenth-century Virginia, some of them encompassing hundreds of volumes. In Boston, the Mather family's collection numbered several thousand titles by 1700. More than half of free white Marylanders owned books by the middle of the eighteenth century. Booksellers in cities and towns offered a wide selection of titles imported from England and an increasing number printed in the colonies. The number of newspapers grew rapidly as well. In 1720, only three journals were published in Anglo America. By 1770, there were thirty-one, printed in every colony from Massachusetts to Georgia. Those who

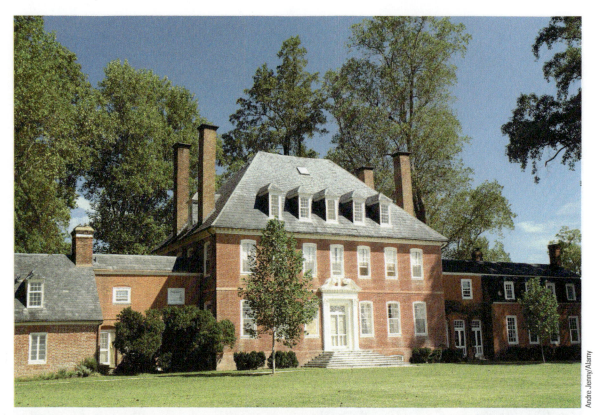

Andre Jenny/Alamy

▲ Built in 1730, William Byrd's grand home, which he called Westover, reflects the genteel aspirations of a new generation of British Americans. Byrd, one of Virginia's wealthiest planters, had spent time in London, and he designed his James River plantation according to the most current English tastes, with an emphasis on symmetry and a highly theatrical entrance. Byrd's diaries reveal the uneasy combination of cosmopolitan refinement and slave-holding barbarism that marked the daily lives of elites in the southern colonies.

could not afford to buy newspapers perused them in coffee-houses, and those who could not afford to buy books might read them in new civic institutions called libraries. Benjamin Franklin, a candle-maker's son who made his living as a printer, founded the Library Company of Philadelphia, the first subscription library in North America, in 1731. Works of fiction made up a large percentage of social library collections and numbered among the most highly circulated titles. One Philadelphia library served a nearly equal number of male and female readers.

4-4g The Enlightenment

Spreading through travel and print and polite conversation, the intellectual currents known as the **Enlightenment** deeply affected American provincials. Around 1650, some European thinkers began to analyze nature in order to determine the laws governing the universe. They conducted experiments to discover general principles underlying phenomena like the motions of planets, the behavior of falling objects, and the characteristics of light. Enlightenment philosophers sought knowledge through reason, taking particular delight in challenging previously unquestioned assumptions. **John Locke's** *Essay Concerning Human Understanding* (1690), for example, disputed the notion that human beings are born already imprinted with innate ideas. All knowledge, Locke asserted, derives from one's observations of the external world. Belief in witchcraft and astrology, among other occult phenomena, thus came under attack in this new empirical order.

The Enlightenment supplied educated Europeans and Americans with a common vocabulary and world-view, one that insisted the enlightened eighteenth century was better, and wiser, than ages past. It joined them in a shared effort to make sense of God's creation. American naturalists like John and William Bartram supplied European scientists with information about new world plants and animals for newly formulated universal classification systems. So, too, Americans interested in astronomy took part in an international project to learn about the solar system by studying a rare occurrence, the transit of Venus across the face of the sun in 1769. A prime example of America's participation in the Enlightenment

Enlightenment Intellectual revolution in eighteenth-century Europe and America that elevated reason, science, and logic.

John Locke British philosopher and major Enlightenment thinker; known for his emphasis on the power of human reasoning.

was **Benjamin Franklin**, who retired from his successful printing business in 1748 when he was just forty-two, thereafter devoting himself to scientific experimentation and public service. His *Experiments and Observations on Electricity* (1751) established the terminology and basic theory of electricity still used today.

Enlightenment rationalism affected politics as well as science. Locke's *Two Treatises of Government* (1691) and other works by French and Scottish philosophers challenged previous concepts of a divinely sanctioned, hierarchical political order originating in the power of fathers over families. Men created governments and so could alter them, Locke declared—a philosophy that aligned with the life experience of many who lived under the locally-created governments in the colonies. A ruler who broke the social contract and failed to protect people's rights could legitimately be ousted by peaceful—or even violent—means. A proper political order could prevent the rise of tyrants; God's natural laws governed even monarchs. The rough and tumble political philosophy Dr. Hamilton found on his 1744 journey through the colonies offers evidence of a vernacular enlightenment bubbling up from the lower orders as well as trickling in from Europe.

4-5 A Changing Religious Culture

▶ How did eighteenth-century religious revivals affect the practice of religion?

▶ How did the eighteenth-century religious revivals contribute to new ideas and practices within society?

Religious observance was perhaps the most pervasive facet of eighteenth-century provincial culture. In New England's Congregational (Puritan) churches, church leaders assigned seating to reflect standing in the community. By the mid-eighteenth century, wealthy men and their wives sat in privately owned pews; children, servants, slaves, and the less fortunate still sat in sex-segregated fashion in the rear, sides, or balcony of the church. Seating in Virginia's Church of England parishes also mirrored the local status hierarchy. In Quebec City, formal processions of men into the parish church celebrated Catholic feast days; each participant's rank determined his place in the procession. By contrast, Quaker meetinghouses in Pennsylvania and elsewhere used an egalitarian but sex-segregated seating system. The varying rituals surrounding colonial churches symbolized believers' place in society and the values of the community.

While such aspects of Anglo-American religious practice reflected traditions of long standing, the religious culture of the colonies began to change significantly in the mid-eighteenth century. From the mid-1730s through the 1760s, waves of revivalism—today known collectively as the First **Great Awakening**—swept over British America, especially New England (1735–1745) and Virginia (1750s–1760s). In the colonies as in Europe, orthodox Calvinists sought to combat Enlightenment rationalism, which denied innate human depravity. Simultaneously, the uncertainty accompanying King George's War made colonists receptive to **evangelists'** messages. Moreover, many recent immigrants and residents of the backcountry had no strong religious affiliation, thus presenting evangelists with numerous potential converts.

America's revivals began in New England. In the mid-1730s, the Reverend Jonathan Edwards, a noted preacher and theologian, observed a remarkable reaction among the youthful members of his church in Northampton, Massachusetts, to sermons based squarely on Calvinist principles. Sinners could attain salvation, Edwards preached, only by recognizing their depraved nature and surrendering completely to God's will. Moved by this message, parishioners of both sexes experienced an intensely emotional release from sin, which came to be seen as a moment of conversion, a new birth.

4-5a George Whitefield

Such ecstatic conversions remained isolated until 1739, when **George Whitefield**, an Anglican clergyman already renowned for leading mass revivals in Britain, crossed the Atlantic. For fifteen months, he toured the British colonies, concentrating his efforts in the major cities: Boston, Newport, New York, Philadelphia, Charles Town, and Savannah. One historian has termed Whitefield "the first modern celebrity" because of his skillful self-promotion. Everywhere he traveled, his fame preceded him. Readers snapped up books by and about him, and newspapers advertised his upcoming appearances and hawked portrait engravings of his famous face. Thousands of free and enslaved folk turned out to listen—and to experience conversion. Whitefield's preaching tour, the first such ever undertaken, created new interconnections among far-flung colonies.

Established clerics initially welcomed Whitefield and the American-born itinerant evangelist preachers who imitated him. Soon, however, many clergymen began to realize that, although "revived" religion filled their churches, it challenged their approach to doctrine and practice. They disliked the emotional style of the revivalists, whose itinerancy also disrupted normal patterns of church attendance. Particularly troublesome to the orthodox were the dozens of female exhorters who took to streets and

Benjamin Franklin American thinker, printer, and politician who embodied the experimental spirit of the Enlightenment.

Great Awakening Protestant revival movement that emphasized each person's urgent need for salvation by God.

evangelists Preachers or ministers, often traveling beyond a fixed congregation, who enthusiastically promote the Christian gospels to gain new converts.

George Whitefield English preacher who toured the colonies and played a major role in the Great Awakening on both sides of the Atlantic.

Smallpox Inoculation

Smallpox, the world's greatest killer of human beings, repeatedly ravaged the population of North America. Thus, when the vessel *Seahorse* arrived in Boston from the Caribbean in April 1721 carrying smallpox-infected passengers, New Englanders feared the worst. The authorities quarantined the ship, but smallpox escaped into the city, and soon dozens caught the dread disease.

The Reverend Cotton Mather, a member of London's Royal Society (chartered during the Restoration to promote Enlightenment approaches to science), had read in its journal several years earlier two accounts by physicians—one in Constantinople and one in Smyrna—of a medical technique unknown to Europeans but widely employed in North Africa and the Middle East. Called inoculation, it involved scraping material from the pustules (or poxes) of an infected person and inserting it into a small cut on the arm of a healthy individual. With luck, that person would experience a mild case of smallpox, followed by lifetime immunity from the disease. Mather's interest in inoculation was further piqued by his slave, Onesimus, a North African who had been inoculated as a youth and who described the procedure in detail. "How many Lives might be saved by it, if it were practised?" Mather wondered in his diary that May, as the epidemic spread.[1]

The next month, Mather wrote up what he called "a little Treatise on the *Small-pox*." His strategy blended science and religion: "first awakening Sentiments of *Piety*," then "exhibiting the best Medicines and Methods," and "finally, adding the new Discovery": inoculation. But when Mather circulated the manuscript, the city's doctors ridiculed his ideas. "They rave, they rail, they blaspheme; they talk not only like Ideots but also like *Franticks*," he wrote. He feared, not least, for his own children. Mather won only one major convert, Zabdiel Boylston, a physician and apothecary, who wanted to publish Mather's arguments. The two men inoculated their own children and about two hundred others, despite bitter opposition, including an attempt to firebomb Mather's house. But by late fall, as the epidemic abated, Bostonians could clearly see the results: of those inoculated, just 3 percent had died, a fraction of the 15 percent mortality experienced by those who took the disease "in the natural way."[2] Even Mather's most vocal opponents were convinced, thereafter supporting inoculation as a remedy for the disease. Mather wrote reports for the Royal Society, and following their publication even Britain's royal family was inoculated.

In the twentieth century, global campaigns for vaccination—a modern cousin of inoculation—eliminated smallpox worldwide. Yet in twenty-first-century America, childhood vaccination has become newly controversial, as New Age religion battles Enlightenment science some three centuries after Mather's time.

CRITICAL THINKING

- Aside from general fear of the disease, what other factors may have contributed to the colonists' aversion to adopt inoculation, a common practice in non-Western parts of the world?

[1] *Mather Diary*, II: 621

[2] Ibid, quotations at II: 627–38, 632

An Historical
ACCOUNT
OF THE
SMALL-POX
INOCULATED
IN
NEW ENGLAND,
Upon all Sorts of Perfons, *Whites, Blacks,* and of all Ages and Conftitutions.

With fome Account of the Nature of the Infection in the NATURAL and INOCULATED Way, and their different Effects on HUMAN BODIES.

With fome fhort DIRECTIONS to the UNEXPERIENCED in this Method of Practice.

Humbly dedicated to her Royal Highnefs the Princefs of WALES, by *Zabdiel Boylfton*, Phyfician.

LONDON:
Printed for S. CHANDLER, *at the* Crofs-Keys *in the* Poultry. M. DCC. XXVI.

'Account of the Small Pox innoculated in New England', pamphlet published in London (ink on paper)/English School, (18th century)/PETER NEWARK'S PICTURES/Private Collection/Bridgeman Images

◄ Several years after he and Cotton Mather combated a Boston smallpox epidemic by employing inoculation, Zabdiel Boylston published this pamphlet in London to spread the news of their success. The dedication to the Princess of Wales was designed to indicate the royal family's support of the procedure.

pulpits, proclaiming their right (even duty) to expound God's word.

4-5b Impact of the Awakening

Opposition to the Awakening mounted rapidly, causing congregations to splinter. "Old Lights"—orthodox clerics and their followers—engaged in bitter disputes with "New Light" evangelicals. Already characterized by numerous sects, American Protestantism fragmented further as Congregationalists and Presbyterians split into factions, and as new evangelical groups—Methodists and Baptists—gained adherents. After 1771, Methodists sent "circuit riders" (preachers on horseback) to the far reaches of settlement, where they achieved widespread success in converting frontier dwellers. Paradoxically, the proliferation of distinct denominations eventually fostered a willingness to tolerate religious pluralism. Where no sect could monopolize orthodoxy, denominations had to coexist if they were to exist at all.

The Awakening challenged traditional modes of thought. Itinerants offered a spiritual variant of the choices colonists found in the world of goods. Revivalists' emphasis on emotion over learning undermined received wisdom about society and politics as well as religion. Some New Lights began to defend the rights of groups and individuals to dissent from a community consensus, thereby challenging one of the fundamental tenets of colonial political life.

4-5c Virginia Baptists

The egalitarian themes of the Awakening tended to attract ordinary folk and repel the elite. Nowhere was this trend more evident than in Virginia, where taxes supported the established Church of England, and the plantation gentry dominated society. By the 1760s, Baptists had gained a secure foothold in Virginia; inevitably, their beliefs and behavior clashed with the refined lifestyle of the genteel.

Strikingly, almost all Virginia Baptist congregations included both free and enslaved members, and some congregations had African American majorities. Church rules applied equally to all members; interracial sexual relationships, divorce, and adultery were proscribed for all. In addition, congregations forbade masters' breaking up slave couples through sale. Yet it is easy to overstate the racial egalitarianism

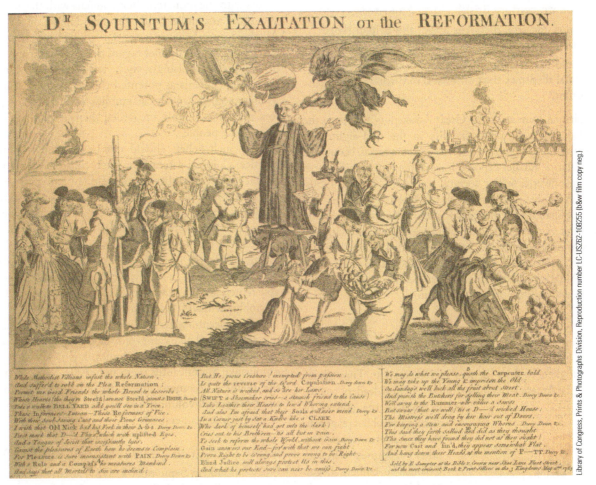

▲ This cartoon, printed in London in 1763, mocks George Whitefield, who was cross-eyed, as "Dr. Squintum." The satirist sets him on a stool, preaching outdoors, as he often did. An imp or small devil feeds words into his ear, while Fame—depicted as part woman, part serpent—listens through an ear-trumpet, and barks Whitefield's words to the crowd. Under the preacher's stool, the Devil snatches up gold coins.

of Virginia evangelicals and the attractiveness of the new sects to black members. Masters censured for abusing their slaves were quickly readmitted to church fellowship. Even later in the century, African Americans continued to make up a minuscule proportion of southern evangelicals—roughly 1 percent of the total.

The revivals of the mid-eighteenth century were not a dress rehearsal for Revolution. Still, the Great Awakening had important social and political consequences. In some ways, the evangelicals were profoundly conservative, preaching an old-style theology of original sin and divine revelation that ran counter to the Enlightenment's emphasis on human perfectibility and reason. In other respects, the revivalists were recognizably modern, using the techniques of Atlantic commerce, and calling into question habitual modes of behavior in the secular as well as the religious realm.

4-6 Stability and Crisis at Midcentury

▶ **What internal crises challenged the peoples of eighteenth-century British North America?**

▶ **How did imperial disputes affect the British North American colonists?**

▶ **How did Native American peoples respond to imperial disputes that emerged in British North America?**

The spiritual foment of the Great Awakening points to the unsettled nature of provincial life in the mid-eighteenth century. A number of other crises—ethnic, racial, economic, and military—further exposed lines of fracture within North America's diverse settler society. In the 1740s and 1750s, Britain expanded its claims to North American territory and to the obligations of provincials within the empire. At the same time, Anglo-American colonists—as veterans, citizens, and consumers—felt more strongly entitled to the liberties of British subjects. And Britain and France alike came to see North America as increasingly central to their economic, diplomatic, and military strategies in Europe.

4-6a Colonial Political Orders

Men from genteel families dominated the political structures in each province, for voters (free male property holders) tended to defer to their "betters" on election days. Throughout the Anglo-American colonies, these political leaders sought to increase the powers of elected assemblies relative to the powers of governors and other appointed officials. Colonial assemblies began to claim privileges associated with the British House of Commons, such as the

John Peter Zenger New York printer whose trial in the 1730s challenged prevailing restrictions on the press.

Glorious Revolution Overthrow of James II in favor of William and Mary in 1688.

rights to initiate tax legislation and to control the militia. The assemblies also developed ways of influencing Crown appointees, especially by threatening to withhold their salaries. In some colonies (Virginia and South Carolina, for example), members of the assembly presented a united front to royal officials, while in others (such as New York), provincials fought among themselves. To win hotly contested elections, New York's leaders began to appeal directly to "the people," competing openly for votes. Yet in 1735, the colony's government imprisoned a newspaper editor, **John Peter Zenger**, who had too vigorously criticized its actions. Defending Zenger against the charge of "seditious libel," his lawyer argued that the truth could not be defamatory, thus helping to establish a free-press principle later found in American law.

Assemblymen saw themselves as thwarting encroachments on colonists' British liberties—for example, by preventing governors from imposing oppressive taxes. By midcentury, they often compared the structure of their governments to Britain's mixed polity, which reputedly balanced monarchy, aristocracy, and democracy in ways admired since the days of ancient Greece and Rome. Drawing rough analogies, political leaders equated their royally-appointed governors with the monarch, their councils with the aristocracy, and their assemblies with Britain's House of Commons. All three were believed essential to good government, but Anglo-Americans did not regard them with the same degree of approval. Increasingly, they viewed governors and their appointed councils as potential threats to colonial liberties. Many colonists saw the assemblies as the people's protectors, and the assemblies regarded themselves as representatives of the people.

Yet such beliefs should not be equated with modern practice. Colonial assemblies, often controlled by dominant families whose members were reelected by voters year after year, rarely responded to the concerns of poorer constituents. Although settlements continually expanded, assemblies failed to reapportion themselves, which led to grievances among backcountry dwellers, especially those from non-English ethnic groups. In the ideal, the assembly was the representative defender of liberty. In reality, the most ardently defended and ably represented were wealthy male colonists, particularly the assembly members themselves.

At midcentury, the political structures that had stabilized in a period of relative calm confronted a series of crises. None affected all the mainland colonies, but no colony escaped untouched. Significantly, these upheavals demonstrated that the political accommodations forged in the aftermath of the **Glorious Revolution** had become inadequate to govern Britain's American empire.

4-6b Slave Rebellions and Internal Disorder

Early on Sunday, September 9, 1739, about twenty enslaved men, most likely Catholics from the Kongo region of West Africa, gathered near the Stono River south of Charles Town. September fell in the midst of South Carolina's rice harvest (and thus at a time of great pressure for male Africans), and September 8 was, to Catholics, the birthday of the Virgin Mary, venerated by Kongolese converts with special fervor. Seizing guns and ammunition, the rebels killed storekeepers and nearby planter families. Joined by other enslaved people, they then headed toward Florida in hopes of finding refuge. By midday, however, slaveholders in the district had sounded the alarm. That afternoon a troop of militia attacked the fugitives, who numbered about a hundred, killing some and dispersing the rest. The colony quickly captured and executed the survivors, but rumors about escaped renegades haunted the colony for years.

News of the **Stono Rebellion** reverberated far beyond South Carolina. The press frequently reported on slave uprisings in the West Indies—in Danish St. John's in 1733, in Antigua in 1736, and in Jamaica throughout the 1720s and

1730s, for examples—but on the mainland, where slaves did not so vastly outnumber their masters, such an organized revolt was remarkable, and terrifying. Throughout British America, laws governing the behavior of African Americans were stiffened after Stono. The most striking response came in New York City, which had witnessed the first mainland slave revolt in 1712. The news from the South, coupled with fears of Spain generated by the outbreak of King George's War, set off a reign of terror in Manhattan in 1741. Colonial authorities suspected a biracial gang of illicit traders of conspiring to foment a slave uprising under the guidance of a Spanish priest. Thirty blacks and four whites were executed—gruesomely—for participating in the alleged plot. The Stono Rebellion and the New York "conspiracy" not only exposed and confirmed Anglo-Americans' deepest fears about the dangers of slaveholding but also revealed the assemblies' inability to prevent serious internal disorder.

4-6c European Rivalries in North America

In addition to their internal divisions, Britain's mainland colonies were surrounded by hostile, or potentially hostile, neighbors: Native peoples everywhere, the Spanish in Florida and along the Gulf coast, the French along the great inland system of rivers and lakes that stretched from the St. Lawrence to the Mississippi. Despite the fevered imagination of New Yorkers during the 1741 "conspiracy," the Spanish posed little direct threat. The French were another matter. Their long chain of forts and trading settlements made them the dominant colonial power in the continent's interior. In none of the three Anglo-French wars fought between 1689 and 1748 was Britain able to shake France's hold on the American frontier (see Table 4.1; see also Map 5.1, Section 5-1).

4-6d The Fall of Louisbourg

In the North American theater of King George's War, hostilities largely played out along the northern border between British and French America. Built after Queen Anne's War, the massive French fortress at Louisbourg, on Cape Breton Island, quickly became the largest French town on the continent, with more than 4,000 settlers and some 1,500 soldiers. Privateers based in the fortified port regularly menaced New England merchants and fisherman. In 1744, William Shirley, the royal governor of Massachusetts, hatched a scheme to advance Britain's war aims—and boost New England's prosperity—by seizing the fort for the Crown. New Hampshire, Connecticut, and Rhode Island raised significant sums of money and smaller numbers of recruits; some 3,000 Massachusetts men comprised three-quarters of the expedition force.

Many thought Shirley's plan to conquer Louisbourg foolhardy. As Benjamin Franklin wrote to his brother John in Boston, "Fortified towns are hard nuts to crack; and your teeth are not accustomed to it." But New England merchants, sailors, and militiamen prosecuted the empire's errand with gusto

Title Page of "A Journal of the Proceedings in the Detection of Conspiracy," 1741 (litho)/American School, (18th century)/NEW YORK HISTORICAL SOCIETY/© Collection of the New-York Historical Society, USA/Bridgeman Images

▲ Daniel Horsmanden played a leading role in the prosecution of alleged conspirators who so terrified white inhabitants of New York City in 1741. He expected many buyers for his *Journal of the Proceedings in the Detection of the Conspiracy*, an exacting and often sensationalist account of the trials that had resulted in the execution of thirty-four people, thirteen of whom were burned at the stake. But by 1744, public opinion had begun to turn against the trials, which some compared to the Salem witchcraft hysteria. Horsmanden was mocked in the newspapers, and in 1748 the *Journal's* printer slashed its price, noting, "as he has been a considerable Loser by printing that Book, he proposes to sell 'em very cheap."

Table 4.1 The Colonial Wars, 1689–1763

American Name	European Name	Dates	Participants	American Sites	Dispute
King William's War	Nine Years' War	1689–97	England, Holland versus France, Spain	New England, New York, Canada	French power
Queen Anne's War	War of Spanish Succession	1702–13	England, Holland, Austria versus France, Spain	Florida, New England	Throne of Spain
King George's War	War of Austrian Succession	1739–48	England, Holland, Austria versus France, Spain, Prussia	West Indies, New England, Canada	Throne of Austria
French and Indian War	Seven Years' War	1756–63	England versus France, Spain	Ohio country, Canada	Possession of Ohio country

Siege of the French fortress of Louisbourg in 1745 by British vessels and New England colonials (colour litho)/English School, (18th century)/PETER NEWARK'S PICTURES/Private Collection/Bridgeman Images

▲ This anonymous painting depicts the siege of the French fortress at Louisbourg by British and provincial troops in 1745, in the middle of King George's War. The British capture of the fortress—sometimes called the Gibraltar of America—was considered a major strategic victory, because Louisbourg guarded access to the valuable North Atlantic fisheries to the east and the St. Lawrence waterway to the west.

that amazed their allies and their enemies alike. In June 1745, after a two-month-long siege, Louisbourg fell to ragtag regiments of colonial soldiers. As news of the victory trickled south, bells pealed in celebration from Boston to Philadelphia. In London, too, the New Englanders' surprising triumph was greeted with astonishment. But when the war ended in 1748, Britain returned the fortress to France in exchange for concessions in India and the Low Countries, the imperial priorities of the moment. As its wartime shipping boom went bust, Massachusetts was left with staggering debt and hundreds of new widows and orphans, as well as needy soldiers crippled in the futile fight.

4-6e The Ohio Country

By the time King George's War ended, the crucible of North America's imperial rivalries could be found farther south, in lands west of the Appalachians and east of the Mississippi that came to be known as the Ohio Country. The trouble started in the 1730s, as Anglo-American traders pushed west from the Carolinas and Virginia, challenging French power beyond the Appalachians. French officials' fear of British incursions increased when the Delawares and Shawnees ceded large tracts of land to Pennsylvania. In 1737, two sons of William Penn and their Iroquois allies persuaded the Delawares to sell off as much land as a man could walk in a day and a half. Then the Pennsylvania negotiators rigged the deal, sending trained runners down prepared trails to multiply the acreage. Delawares derided the deceitful Walking Purchase as "ye Running Walk." This betrayal by the English and the Iroquois rankled for decades, and other fraudulent land cessions followed. On isolated farms in Delaware territory, backcountry squatters—mostly Scots-Irish and Germans—had coexisted peacefully with their Native neighbors, sometimes even paying rent to Indian leaders who owned the acres on which they farmed. But the agreements reached by the Penn family and the Iroquois ignored the claims of both the local Native communities and the squatters, all of whom were told to move. Disgruntled Delawares and Shawnees migrated west, where they joined other displaced eastern Native peoples who nursed similar grievances.

Claimed by both Virginia and Pennsylvania, the region to which they migrated was coveted by wealthy Virginians. In 1745, a group of land speculators organized as the Ohio Company of Virginia received a grant of nearly a third of a million acres from the House of Burgesses. The company's agents quickly established trading posts that aimed to dominate the crucial area where the Allegheny and Monongahela rivers join to form the Ohio (see Map 5.1, Section 5-1). But that region was also strategically vital to the French, because the Ohio River offered direct access by water to French posts along the Mississippi. By the early 1750s, Pennsylvania fur traders, Ohio Company representatives, the French military, Scots-Irish and German squatters, Iroquois, Delawares, and Shawnees all jostled for position in the region.

4-6f Iroquois Neutrality

Maintaining the policy of neutrality they developed in 1701, the Iroquois Confederacy skillfully manipulated the European rivals and consolidated their control over the vast regions northwest of Virginia and south of the Great Lakes. During Queen Anne's War and again in King George's War, they refused to commit warriors exclusively to either side, and so were showered with gifts by both. Ongoing conflict with Cherokees and Catawbas in the South gave young Iroquois warriors combat experience and allowed them to replace population losses by acquiring new captives. They also cultivated peaceful relationships with Pennsylvania and Virginia; their role in treaties like the Walking Purchase furthered Iroquois domination of the Shawnees and

Lapowinsa (oil on canvas)/Hesselius, Gustavus (1682–1755)/PHILADELPHIA HISTORY MUSEUM AT THE ATWATER KENT/© Philadelphia History Museum at the Atwater Kent./Bridgeman Images

▲ The Swedish-born portraitist Gustav Hesselius painted this half-length canvas depicting the Delaware leader Lapowinsa in 1735. Hesselius did not Europeanize the headman, whose weary, tattooed face and steady gaze confronts the viewer directly. The squirrel-skin pouch hanging from his neck would have held tobacco. Two years after this portrait was made, Lapowinsa was among the negotiators who agreed to the fraudulent "Walking Purchase" ceding Delaware lands to William Penn's sons and their Iroquois allies.

Delawares. And they forged friendly ties with Algonquians of the Great Lakes region, thwarting potential assaults from those allies of the French and making themselves indispensable go-betweens for commerce and communication between the Atlantic coast and the West. But even the Iroquois could not fully control the Ohio Country as clashes there escalated in the early 1750s. Later that decade, in a distinct reversal of previous patterns of imperial rivalry, conflict would spread from the Ohio Country to Europe, and then around the globe.

When he traveled the colonies in 1744, Dr. Hamilton described "America," but he never once referred to the people who lived there as *Americans*. Nor did colonial settlers much use that term to identify themselves at the time. But after King George's War, and especially after the French and Indian War, the most convulsive of the century's Anglo-French wars, Britain's subjects in mainland North America began increasingly to imagine themselves as a group with shared and distinct

"Self-Made Men"

American culture celebrates the "self-made man" (always someone explicitly *male*) of humble origins who gains wealth or prominence through extraordinary effort and talent. Those most commonly cited include such successful nineteenth-century businessmen as Andrew Carnegie (once a poor immigrant from Scotland) and John D. Rockefeller (born on a hardscrabble farm in upstate New York).

The first exemplars of this tradition lived in the eighteenth century. Benjamin Franklin's *Autobiography* chronicled his method for achieving success after beginning life as the seventeenth child of a Boston candle-maker. From such humble origins Franklin became a wealthy, influential man active in science, politics, education, and diplomacy. Yet Franklin's tale is rivaled by that of a slave who became one of the eighteenth century's leading antislavery activists. He acquired literacy, purchased his freedom, married a wealthy Englishwoman, and published

a popular autobiography that predated Franklin's in print. His first master called him Gustavus Vassa, the name he primarily used. But when publishing his *Interesting Narrative* in 1789, he called himself Olaudah Equiano.

In that *Narrative*, Equiano said he was born in Africa in 1745, kidnapped at the age of eleven, and transported to Barbados and then to Virginia, where a British naval officer purchased him. For years, scholars and students have relied on that account for its insights into the experience of the middle passage. But evidence recently uncovered by Vincent Carretta, although confirming the accuracy of much of Equiano's autobiography, shows that Equiano twice identified his birthplace as Carolina and was three to five years younger than he claimed. Why would Equiano reinvent his origins and alter his age? Carretta speculates that the *Narrative* gained part of its credibility from Equiano's African birth and that admitting his real age would have

raised questions about the account of his early life by revealing his youth at the time of the reputed kidnapping.

Equiano, or Vassa, thus truly "made himself," just as Benjamin Franklin and many others have done. (Franklin tended to omit, rather than alter, inconvenient parts of his personal history—for example, his illegitimate son and his ownership of slaves.) Equiano used information undoubtedly gleaned from acquaintances who *had* experienced the middle passage to craft an accurate depiction of the horrors of the slave trade. In the process, he became one of the first Americans to explicitly remake himself.

CRITICAL THINKING

- Does knowing that Equiano and Franklin altered or even fabricated some details about their lives change their import as self-made men in the lexicon of American culture?
- Does it make their autobiographies any less compelling or impressive? Why or why not?

---

concerns. In addition to calling themselves "His Majesty's subjects in America," colonial writers began occasionally to refer to "Americans," "American colonists," or "continentals." These newly labeled Americans were not yet a people, and they were certainly not a nation. They continued to pledge their allegiance to Britain. But the more these overseas Britons came to prize their liberties as the king's subjects, the more some of them began to wonder whether Parliament and the Crown fully understood their needs and, indeed, their rights.

Summary

The decades before 1760 transformed North America. French and Spanish settlements expanded their geographic reach dramatically, and newcomers from Germany, Scotland, Ireland, and Africa brought their languages, customs, and religions with them to the British colonies. European immigrants settled throughout Anglo America but were concentrated in the growing cities and in the backcountry. By contrast, most enslaved migrants from Africa lived and worked within one hundred miles of the Atlantic coast. In many areas of the colonial South, 50 to 90 percent of the population was of African origin. In the West Indies, the enslaved black majority was far larger.

The economic life of Europe's mainland North American colonies proceeded simultaneously on local and transatlantic levels. On the farms, plantations, and ranches on which most colonists resided, daily, weekly, monthly, and yearly rounds of chores dominated people's lives, providing goods consumed by households and sold in markets. Simultaneously, an intricate international trade network affected colonial economies. The bitter wars fought by European nations during the eighteenth century inevitably involved the colonists, creating new opportunities for overseas sales and disrupting their traditional markets. Those fortunate few who—through skill, control of essential resources, or luck—reaped the profits of international commerce comprised the wealthy class of merchants and landowners who dominated colonial political, intellectual, and social life. At the other end of the economic scale, poor colonists, especially city dwellers, struggled to make ends meet.

A century and a half after European peoples first settled in North America, the colonies mixed diverse European, American, and African traditions into a novel cultural blend that owed much to Europe but just as much, if not more, to North America itself. Interacting regularly with peoples of African and American origin—and with Europeans from nations other than their own—colonists developed new methods of accommodating intercultural differences. Yet at the same time, they continued to identify themselves as French, Spanish, or British rather than as Americans. That did not change in the West Indies, Canada, Louisiana, or in the Spanish territory, but in the 1760s some Anglo-Americans began to realize that their interests did not necessarily coincide with those of Great Britain or its monarch.

Suggestions for Further Reading

Richard R. Beeman, *The Varieties of Political Experience in Eighteenth-Century America* (2004)

Catherine A. Brekus, *Sarah Osborn's World: The Rise of Evangelical Christianity in Early America* (2013)

Richard Bushman, *The Refinement of America: Persons, Houses, Cities* (1992)

Kathleen DuVal, *The Native Ground: Indians and Colonists in the Heart of the Continent* (2006)

Rebecca Anne Goetz, *The Baptism of Early Virginia: How Christianity Created Race* (2012)

Ellen Hartigan-O'Connor, *The Ties That Buy: Women and Commerce in Revolutionary America* (2009)

Rhys Isaac, *The Transformation of Virginia, 1740–1790* (1982)

Jill Lepore, *New York Burning: Liberty, Slavery, and Conspiracy in Eighteenth-Century Manhattan* (2005)

Paul W. Mapp, *The Elusive West and the Contest for Empire, 1713–1763* (2011)

David Waldstreicher, *Runaway America: Benjamin Franklin, Slavery, and the American Revolution* (2004)

MINDTAP
From Cengage

MindTap® is a fully online personalized learning experience built upon Cengage Learning content. MindTap® combines student learning tools—readings, multimedia, activities, and assessments—into a singular Learning Path that guides students through the course and helps students develop the critical thinking, analysis, and communication skills that are essential to academic and professional success.

The Ends of Empire, 1754–1774

A spectacular victory demanded a stirring celebration, and the British capture of Quebec from the French in September 1759 was indeed a spectacular victory. When news of this latest British triumph reached Boston, in October, town fathers proclaimed a "Day of general Rejoicing." Church bells started ringing at dawn and pealed through the day. Preachers thundered praise from the pulpits. Troops paraded down King Street, pausing to blast "Rejoicing Fires" from their muskets. Ninety cannons sounded at the fort called Castle William, after William of Orange; guns mounted on the batteries in nearby Charlestown and on the decks of warships in the harbor echoed the salute.

As night fell, public buildings blazed with candlelight. The hills surrounding the town glowed with "large bonfires formed in a pyramidal manner." An "abundance of extraordinary Fire-Works were play'd off in almost every Street," the *Boston Gazette* reported, "the greatest Quantity of Sky-Rockets ever seen on any Occasion." In the seaport's lanes and alleys, "Persons of all Ranks" joined in the revelry. At the Concert Hall on Hanover Street (named after the dynasty whose rule of Britain had begun with George I, in 1714), His Excellency Thomas Pownall, the royally appointed governor, heard a musical tribute. Then he and his council and members of both houses of the provincial assembly headed to the Town House, a brick building topped by golden statues of the English lion and the Scottish unicorn. Together the politicians toasted the wisdom of the king and the health of the royal family.

Experience an interactive version of this story in MindTap®.

◄ Images of the death of British General James Wolfe at the Battle of Quebec were popular in Britain and America. Pennsylvania-born Benjamin West painted the most celebrated of them in London in 1770. It features an idealized Mohawk warrior, a kilted Scottish Highlander, and a colonial Ranger as well as English officers: a harmonious fantasy of Britain's empire. George III commissioned a copy for himself in 1771. World History Archive/Image Asset Management Ltd/Alamy Stock Photo

Chronology

1754	■ Albany Congress fails to forge colonial unity
	■ George Washington defeated at Fort Necessity, Pennsylvania
1755	■ Braddock's army routed in Pennsylvania
1756	■ Britain declares war on France; Seven Years' War officially begins
1759	■ British take Quebec, ending a military *annus mirabilis*—a "year of wonders"—for the British
1760	■ American phase of war ends with British capture of Montreal
	■ George III becomes king
1763	■ Treaty of Paris ends Seven Years' War
	■ Pontiac's allies attack forts and settlements in American West
	■ Proclamation of 1763 attempts to close land west of Appalachians to settlement
1764	■ Sugar Act lays new duties on molasses, tightens existing customs regulations
	■ Currency Act outlaws colonial paper money
1765	■ Stamp Act requires stamps on all printed materials in colonies
	■ Sons of Liberty forms in resistance to the Stamp Act
1765–66	■ Hudson River land riots pit tenants and squatters against large landlords
	■ Regulator movement begins in North Carolina

1766	■ Parliament repeals Stamp Act
	■ Declaratory Act insists that Parliament can tax the colonies
1767	■ Townshend Acts lay duties on trade within the empire, send new officials to America
1767–69	■ Regulator movement in South Carolina tries to establish order in backcountry
1768–70	■ Townshend duties resisted; boycotts and protests divide merchants and urban artisans
1770	■ Townshend duties repealed except for tea tax
	■ Five colonial rioters killed by British regulars; patriots call this the Boston Massacre
1771	■ North Carolina regulators defeated by eastern militia; six executed for treason
1772	■ Boston Committee of Correspondence formed
1773	■ Tea Act aids East India Company; spurs protest in Boston
1774	■ Coercive Acts punish Boston and Massachusetts
	■ Quebec Act reforms government of Quebec
	■ "Lord Dunmore's War" between Shawnees and backcountry settlers in Virginia
	■ First Continental Congress convenes in Philadelphia, adopts Articles of Association
1774–75	■ Provincial conventions replace collapsing colonial governments

Boston's "Rejoicing" was "the greatest ever known … an universal Joy," the *Gazette* declared. As word of Britain's stunning victory in the long conflict that would come to be known as the Seven Years' War spread through the colonies in the waning days of 1759, similar festivities took place across Anglo America. In Flushing, New York, proud British subjects raised their glasses to "the paternal Tenderness of our Most Gracious Sovereign for these infant Colonies." In Philadelphia, a writer in the *Pennsylvania Gazette* joked, dour Quakers feared that the incessant bonfires would "put out the Sun." One Albany correspondent predicted—correctly—that the rest of Canada would quickly follow Quebec, and "hope[d] soon to hear all this Country is to be English."

The celebratory mood would not last. Within months, the war in North America would be over, and the wartime business boom in the port towns would go bust. By the end of the 1760s, many of those who had toasted the health of George II in 1759 would come to suspect that his grandson George III had turned tyrant, bent upon reducing his colonies to slavery. From Nova Scotia to Antigua, protestors against the Crown's new taxes—taxes designed to pay for costly British victories like the one at Quebec—would flood the streets. Of course, the inhabitants of Anglo America knew none of this in the fall of 1759. Proud subjects living on the western edge of His Majesty's empire, they had little reason to anticipate that "this country" would ever be anything but British.

The American Revolution required a thorough transformation in consciousness: a shift of political allegiance from Britain to a polity that was called, at first, the United Colonies. "The Revolution was effected before the war commenced,"

John Adams later wrote. The true Revolution was not the war, he said, but a fundamental change "in the minds and hearts of the people." Between 1760 and 1775, huge numbers of ordinary Americans transferred their obligations and affections from their mother country to their sister colonies. Yet Adams spoke of a singular Revolution, when in fact there were many. Rich and poor, free and enslaved, indigenous and European, urban and rural, mainland and Caribbean, even male and female Americans experienced the era's upheavals differently.

In the long history of British settlement in the Western Hemisphere, considerable tension had occasionally flared up between individual provinces and the mother country. But except for the crisis following the Glorious Revolution in 1689, such tension had rarely endured or expanded. The primary divisions affecting Britain's American colonies had been internal rather than external. In the 1750s, however, a series of events began to draw colonists' attention from local matters to their relations with Great Britain. It started with the conflict in which Britain captured Quebec: the **Seven Years' War**.

Britain's overwhelming victory in that war dramatically altered the balance of power in North America and in Europe. France was ousted from the continent and Spain was ejected from Florida, shifts with major consequences for the indigenous peoples of the interior and for the residents of the British colonies. Native peoples, who had become expert at playing European powers against one another, found one of their major diplomatic tools blunted. Anglo-Americans no longer had to fear the French on their northern and western borders or the Spanish in the Southeast. Had France controlled the interior in 1776, some historians contend, the colonies along the coast would never have dared to break with Britain.

The British victory in 1763 also transformed Great Britain's colonial policy. Britain's massive war-related debt—the price of the country's victory—needed to be paid. Parliament saw the colonies as the chief beneficiaries of British success, and for the first time imposed revenue-raising taxes on the North American territories, in addition to the customs duties that had long regulated trade. That decision exposed differences in the political thinking of Britons in mainland America and Britons in the home islands and the West Indies—differences long obscured by a shared political vocabulary centered on English liberties.

During the 1760s and early 1770s, a broad coalition of Anglo American women and men resisted the new tax levies and attempts by British officials to tighten their control over provincial governments. The colonies' elected leaders grew ever more suspicious of Britain's motives. They laid aside old antagonisms to coordinate responses to the new measures, and they slowly began to reorient their political thinking. As late as the summer of 1774, though, most continued to seek a solution within the framework of the empire.

■ *What were the causes and consequences of the Seven Years' War?*

■ *What British policies did Americans protest, and what theories and strategies did they develop to support those protests?*

■ *Why did the Tea Act of 1773 dramatically heighten tensions between the mainland colonies and Great Britain?*

5-1 From the Ohio Country to Global War

▶ **How did the imperial conflicts of the 1750s and 1760s, and the resulting influx of European settlers into the Ohio Country and other areas, affect the lives and strategies of Native American peoples?**

▶ **Why did the Albany Plan of Union fail?**

In the early 1750s, the Six Nations of the Iroquois Confederacy—despite their considerable diversity—were far more politically integrated than Britain's North American colonies. British officials drafted plans to better coordinate what one writer called "the Interior Government" of their American territories. It was not only the fractiousness of the colonial legislatures, or even the rampant evasion of the Navigation Acts that worried these imperial reformers. Their concerns were also strategic; the disunity of the colonies made it hard to construct an effective bulwark against the French, who were once again on the march in the continent's interior. The unchecked incursions of backcountry traders and squatters had alienated Native allies vital to the British colonies' defense (see Map 5.1). In the summer of 1753, as the French erected a chain of forts in the Ohio Country, the Mohawk leader Hendrick Theyanoguin declared the Covenant Chain binding his people to the English broken. "So brother you are not to expect to hear of me any more," he told New York's governor, "and Brother we desire to hear no more of you." When news of the Iroquois alliance breakdown and the French buildup reached London,

Seven Years' War Major French-English conflict that was the first worldwide war.

Map 5.1 European Settlements and Native Peoples, 1754

By 1754, Europeans had expanded the limits of the English colonies to the eastern slopes of the Appalachian Mountains. Few independent Indian nations still existed in the East, but beyond the mountains they controlled the countryside. Only a few widely scattered English and French forts maintained the Europeans' presence there.

▲ This engraving, labeled "The brave old Hendrick, the Great Sachem or Chief of the Mohawk Indians . . . now in Alliance with & Subject to the King of Great Britain," was sold in London in late 1755, just after the war chief Hendrick Theyanoguin died fighting for the British at the Battle of Lake George. Though he holds a hatchet and a wampum belt, Hendrick wears a fine English-style coat edged with braid, and elegant ruffled linens. This costume matches the finery Alexander Hamilton described when he saw Hendrick parade through the streets of Boston a decade before (see Chapter 4 introduction).

the Board of Trade directed the colonies to assemble in conference and bury the hatchet.

5-1a Albany Congress

In response to the board's instructions, twenty-five delegates from the seven northern and middle colonies and more than two hundred Native individuals from the Six Nations gathered in Albany, New York, in June 1754. The colonists had two goals: to forge a stronger alliance with the Iroquois and to coordinate plans for intercolonial defense. They failed on both counts. Hendrick's Mohawks renewed their support for the British, but the other Iroquois nations reaffirmed the neutrality policy that had served them well for half a century. The colonists, too, remained divided. Connecticut land speculators battled the Pennsylvania proprietors; New England commissioners refused funds to defend western New York; New York's delegates fought even among themselves.

Before they dispersed in July, the delegates endorsed the Plan of Union crafted by Pennsylvania's Benjamin Franklin, then postmaster general of British America. Franklin's plan called for an unprecedented level of cooperation among the disparate provinces. It proposed the creation of an elected intercolonial legislature with the power to tax and outlined strategies for a common defense. The plan met with quick and universal rejection in the provincial legislatures, which wanted to safeguard their autonomy more than their citizens. Virginia, which had much to lose in the Ohio Country, had declined to attend the Albany Congress and refused even to consider the plan. Other assemblies failed to vote on it. Franklin despaired that the colonies would ever find the common ground they so clearly needed. "[I]f ever there be an Union," he told a correspondent in London, "it must be form'd at home by the Ministry and Parliament." (By "home," this would-be architect of colonial cooperation meant London.) The British ministry agreed, preferring to create a commander in chief for North America rather than an intercolonial legislature.

While the Albany Congress deliberated, the war for which the delegates struggled to prepare had already begun. In the fall of 1753, Governor Robert Dinwiddie of Virginia dispatched a small militia detachment to build a palisade at the forks of the Ohio River—a backstop against the French advance. Reinforcements quickly followed. When a substantial French force arrived at the forks the following April, the first contingent of Virginia militia surrendered,

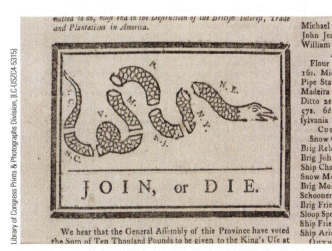

▲ Benjamin Franklin published this cartoon, labeled "Join, or Die," in his newspaper, *The Pennsylvania Gazette*, in May 1754. The woodcut depicts the British provinces from South Carolina to New England as segments of a snake that had perished because of its violent division. The cartoon promoted Franklin's Plan of Union, which would have created an intercolonial legislature. Though the Albany Congress endorsed the plan, it was roundly rejected by the legislatures of those colonies that considered it.

abandoning the site, and the French began to construct the larger and more elaborate Fort Duquesne. Upon learning of the confrontation, the inexperienced young major who commanded the Virginia reinforcements pressed onward instead of awaiting further instructions. He soon engaged a French detachment. Hoping to start a war that would force the British to defend the Ohio Country against the French, Tanaghrisson, the leader of the major's Ohio Native scouts, murdered the French commander and allowed his warriors to slay the wounded French soldiers. Pursuing French troops then trapped the Virginians and their Native allies in the crudely built Fort Necessity at Great Meadows, Pennsylvania. After a day-long battle during which more than one-third of his men were killed or wounded, the Virginia militia commander, twenty-two-year-old Major George Washington, surrendered on July 3, 1754.

5-1b Seven Years' War

Tanaghrisson's plan to set the British against the French succeeded beyond anything he could have dreamed. His attack, and Washington's blunder, ignited what became the first global war. The fighting at the forks of the Ohio helped to reignite a long-simmering conflict between Austria and Prussia. European nations scrambled for allies. Eventually England, Hanover, and Prussia lined up against France, Austria, and Russia, which were joined by Sweden, Saxony, and, later, Spain. Fighting spread from the American interior to the Caribbean, Europe, Africa, and Asia. That the conflict eventually embroiled combatants around the world attests to the growing importance of European nations' overseas empires, and to the increasing centrality of North America to their struggles for dominance.

The war began disastrously for the British. In February 1755, Major General Edward Braddock arrived in Virginia, followed by two regiments of British soldiers, or "regulars." His orders assigned him the command of all British forces from Nova Scotia to South Carolina. That July, French and Native warriors attacked Braddock's troops as they prepared for a renewed assault on Fort Duquesne. Braddock was killed and his forces decimated. It was a shocking defeat—a rout. Convinced that the British could not protect them, many Ohio Native peoples joined the French. The Pennsylvania frontier bore the brunt of repeated attacks by Delaware warriors for two more years; over a thousand residents of the backcountry—nearly 4 percent of the population in some counties—were captured or killed. Settlers felt betrayed because the Native warriors attacking them had once been (as one observer noted) "familiars at their houses [who] eat drank cursed and swore together" with their Euro American neighbors.

In 1756, after news of the debacle reached London, Britain declared war on France, thus formally beginning what came to be known as the Seven Years' War. Even before then, Britain, poised for renewed conflict with old enemies, took a fateful step. New Englanders lobbied London, insisting that France would try to retake Nova Scotia, where most of the population was descended from seventeenth-century French settlers who had intermarried with local M'ikmaqs. Afraid that the settlers, known as Acadians (after the province's name, Acadie), would abandon their long-standing posture of neutrality, British commanders in 1755 forced about seven thousand of them from their homeland—the first large-scale modern deportation, now called ethnic cleansing. Ships crammed with Acadians and outfitted with irons, in the manner of slaving vessels, sailed to each of the mainland colonies, where the refugees encountered hostility and discrimination. "About a thousand of them arrived in Boston, just in the beginning of the winter, crowded almost to death," recalled Thomas Hutchinson, soon to become lieutenant governor of Massachusetts. Dispersed to widely scattered communities, many of the transported families were separated, some forever. After the Peace of Paris in 1763, the survivors relocated. Some returned to Canada, others traveled to France or its Caribbean colonies, and many eventually settled in Louisiana, where they became known as Cajuns (derived from *Acadian*).

Despite such brutal precautions, one calamity followed another for three years after Braddock's defeat. British officers met with scant success coercing the colonies to supply men and materiel to the army. William Pitt, the Member of Parliament placed in charge of the Crown's war effort in 1757, changed tactics. Pitt agreed to reimburse the colonies for their wartime expenditures. He placed recruitment in local hands, thereby gaining greater American support for the war. Large numbers of colonial militiamen served, not always happily, alongside equally large numbers of red-coated regulars from Britain. Even so, Virginia's burgesses appropriated more funds to defend against slave insurrections than to fight the French and their Native allies.

The actions of Anglo-American merchants added to the tension. During the war, firms in Boston, Philadelphia, and New York continued trading with the French West Indies. Seeking markets for their fish, flour, timber, and other products, they bribed customs officers to look the other way while cargoes nominally bound for such neutral ports as Dutch St. Eustatius or Spanish Monte Cristi (on Hispaniola) actually ended up in the French Caribbean. Colonial merchants acquired valuable French sugar in exchange. British officials failed to stop the illicit commerce, some of which was conducted under the guise of exchanging prisoners of war using flags of truce. North American merchants in fact supplied not only the French Caribbean but also France itself with vital materiel during the war.

Pitt's strategy turned the tide. In July 1758, British forces recaptured the fortress at Louisbourg—returned to the French just a decade before—thus severing the major French supply artery down the St. Lawrence River. That fall, the Delawares and Shawnees accepted British peace overtures, and the French abandoned Fort Duquesne. Then, in a stunning attack in September 1759, General James Wolfe's forces defeated the French on the Plains of Abraham and took Quebec. The capture of Quebec, which

The taking of Belle Isle, 1761, by Commodore Keppel and Col. Hodgson/Serres, Dominic (1722-93)/CHRISTIES IMAGES/Private Collection/Bridgeman Images

▲ This image, by the preeminent British seascape painter Dominic Seres, shows the British capture in 1761 of Belle Isle, a French island off the coast of Brittany. The victory was hard fought; French forces repulsed an earlier attack, and withstood a British siege for six weeks. British forces held the island until the end of the Seven Years' War, when it was returned to the French in exchange for Minorca, which France had taken from Britain early in the conflict. Such images and the battles they commemorate remind us of the importance of island fortresses in an age of naval war.

followed British victories in the Caribbean and eastern India, was hailed as the culmination of an *annus mirabilis*—a year of wonders—for the British. "[O]ur bells are worn threadbare with ringing for victories," wrote one English politician. Many colonists could have said the same. A year later, the British captured Montreal, the last French stronghold on the continent. The North American phase of the Seven Years' War had ended.

In the **Treaty of Paris** (1763), France surrendered to Britain its major North American holdings (excepting New Orleans), as well as several Caribbean islands, its slaving prisons in Senegambia, and all of its possessions in India. Spain, an ally of France toward the end of the war, granted parts of Florida to the victors. France, meanwhile, ceded western Louisiana to Spain, in compensation for its ally's losses elsewhere. No longer would the English seacoast colonies have to worry about the threat posed by France's extensive North American territories (see Map 5.2).

Britain's triumph stimulated some provincial Britons to think expansively. Men like Benjamin Franklin, who had long touted the colonies' wealth and dynamism, predicted a glorious new future for North America—a future that included not just geographical expansion but also economic and demographic growth. Some such thinkers would lead the resistance

to British measures in the years after 1763. For ultimately, the winners as well as the losers would be made to pay for this first worldwide war.

5-2 1763: A Turning Point

▶ How did the French and Indian War contribute to instability in the North American interior?

▶ How did British American colonists interpret the political ideas of representation and power?

▶ What did British American colonists dislike about the Sugar Act and Currency Act?

Britain's great victory had a wide-ranging impact on North America, felt first by the indigenous peoples of the interior. With France excluded from the eastern half of the continent and Spanish territory confined west of the Mississippi, the Native Americans' time-tested diplomatic strategy of playing European nations against one another became obsolete. The consequences were immediate and devastating.

Treaty of Paris Treaty by which France ceded most of its North American provinces to Great Britain and some smaller territories to Spain.

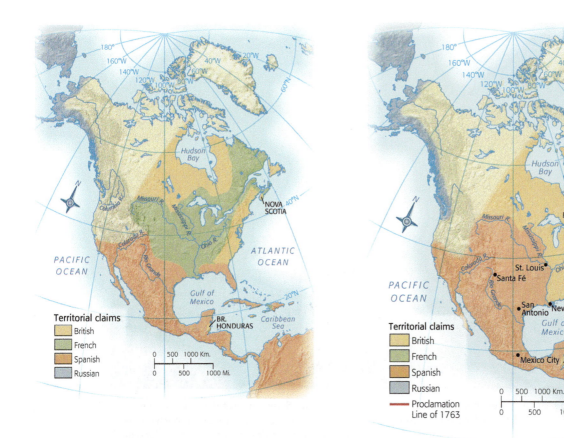

Map 5.2 European Claims in North America

The dramatic results of the British victory in the Seven Years' (French and Indian) War are vividly demonstrated in these maps, which depict the abandonment of French claims to the mainland after the Treaty of Paris in 1763.

Even before the Treaty of Paris, southern Native peoples had to adjust to new circumstances. After Britain gained the upper hand in the American theater of war in 1758, the Creeks and Cherokees lost their ability to force concessions by threatening to turn to France or Spain. In desperation, and in retaliation for British atrocities, Cherokees attacked the Carolina and Virginia frontiers in 1760. Though initially victorious, the Native warriors were defeated the following year by a force made up of British regulars and colonial militia. Late in 1761, the two sides concluded a treaty under which the Cherokees allowed the construction of British forts in their territories and opened a large tract to European settlement.

5-2a Neolin and Pontiac

In the Ohio Country, the Ottawas, Chippewas, and Potawatomis reacted angrily when Great Britain, no longer facing French competition, raised the price of trade goods and ended traditional gift-giving practices. As settlers surged into the Monongahela and Susquehanna valleys, a shaman named Neolin (also known as the Delaware Prophet) urged Native peoples to oppose European incursions on their lands and cultures. For the first time since King Philip in 1675, an influential Native leader called for the unity of all tribes in the face of an

Anglo-American threat. Contending that Native peoples were destroying themselves through dependence on European goods (especially alcohol), Neolin advocated resistance, both peaceful and armed. If Native peoples west of the mountains united against the invaders, he declared, the Master of Life would once again look kindly upon his people. Ironically, Neolin's call for a revival of native traditions itself revealed European influence; his reference to a single powerful deity bore traces of his people's encounter with Christianity.

Pontiac, war chief of an Ottawa village near Detroit, became the leader of a rebellion based on Neolin's precepts. In spring 1763, Pontiac forged an alliance among Hurons, Chippewas, Potawatomis, Delawares, Shawnees, and Mingoes (Pennsylvania Iroquois). Pontiac's forces besieged Fort Detroit while war parties attacked other British outposts in the Great Lakes. Detroit withstood the siege, but by late June, the other forts west of Niagara and north of Fort Pitt (the renamed Fort Duquesne) had fallen to Pontiac's warriors. Native forces then raided the Virginia and Pennsylvania frontiers throughout the summer, killing at least two thousand settlers. Native raiders carried off many enslaved African Americans, raising fears of a Native-black alliance. Still, those who had rallied to Pontiac's cause failed to take Niagara, Fort Pitt, or Detroit. In August, colonial militiamen soundly defeated a combined Native force at Bushy Run, Pennsylvania. Pontiac broke off the siege of Detroit in late October. A treaty ending the war was finally negotiated three years later.

The warfare on the Pennsylvania frontier in 1755–1757 and 1763 ended what had once been a uniquely peaceful relationship between European settlers and Native peoples in that province. For nearly eighty years, the many peoples who lived in "Penn's Woods" had avoided major conflicts with each other. But first the Native attacks and then the settlers' responses—especially the massacre of several defenseless Conestoga families in December 1763 by Scots-Irish vigilantes known as the Paxton Boys—inaugurated violence that would become endemic in the region. In fact, one historian has argued, such acts of violence toward Native peoples helped the disparate European settlers of the Pennsylvania backcountry forge a common American identity in the years ahead.

5-2b Proclamation of 1763

Pontiac's war demonstrated that the huge territory Britain acquired from France would prove a curse as well as a blessing. London officials had no experience managing such a vast territory, particularly one inhabited by restive peoples: the remaining French settlers along the St. Lawrence, the many Native communities, as well as growing numbers of eastern settlers and speculators. In October, George III's ministry issued the **Proclamation of 1763**, which designated the headwaters of rivers flowing into the Atlantic from the Appalachians as the western boundary for colonial settlement (see Map 5.1 and Map 5.2). The crown expected the proclamation line to prevent clashes by forbidding colonists to move onto Native American lands until further treaties had been negotiated. Instead, it infuriated two groups of colonists: settlers who had already squatted west of the line (among them many Scots-Irish immigrants), and investors in land speculation companies from Pennsylvania and Virginia.

In the years after 1763, the speculators (who included George Washington, Thomas Jefferson, Patrick Henry, and Benjamin Franklin) lobbied vigorously to have their claims validated by colonial governments and London administrators. At a treaty conference in 1768 at Fort Stanwix, New York, they negotiated with Iroquois representatives to push the boundary line farther west and south, opening modern-day Kentucky to British settlement. Still claiming to speak for the Delawares and the Shawnees (who used Kentucky as their hunting grounds), the Iroquois agreed to the deal, which brought them valuable trade goods and did not affect their own territories. Yet even though the Virginia land companies eventually gained the support of the House of Burgesses, they never made any headway where it really mattered—in London—because administrators there realized that significant western expansion would require funds they did not have.

5-2c George III

In the Seven Years' War, Britain captured immense territory at immense cost. The country's hard-won hegemony, in Europe as well as in North America, was both isolating and expensive. The British national debt doubled during the war, to £137 million.

The Granger Collection

▲ Benjamin West, the first well-known American artist, was living in London when he painted the picture that served as the basis of this engraving. It illustrates a treaty conference at the end of Pontiac's Rebellion. Colonel Henry Bouquet negotiates with a Shawnee leader who holds an elaborate wampum belt. West drew from his own life in Pennsylvania for many of the details of native dress, but he also incorporated poses from ancient works he had seen in Italy.

Having tightened their belts to finance an overseas conflict, Britons in the home islands anticipated a peace dividend, not further austerity in the service of faraway colonies. From the perspective of London, America's imperial crisis was Britain's American problem, and solutions were hard to come by.

The challenge of paying the war debt, and of finding the money to defend the newly acquired territories, bedeviled young George III, who succeeded his grandfather, George II, in 1760. The twenty-two-year-old monarch, an intelligent, passionate man with a mediocre education, proved to be a poor leader of his government. During the crucial years between 1763 and 1770, as the rift between Britain and the American colonies widened, the king replaced cabinet ministers with bewildering rapidity. Although determined to assert the power of the monarchy, George III stubbornly regarded adherence to the status quo as the hallmark of patriotism. His lack of flexibility in the face of changing conditions would have enormous consequences.

Proclamation of 1763
England's attempt to end clashes over Native American lands by preventing westward movement by colonists.

Like many imperial reformers, the man the king selected as prime minister in 1763, George Grenville, believed the colonies should be more firmly administered. Grenville confronted a financial crisis. Before the war, annual government expenditures had totaled no more than £8 million; now the interest on the national debt came to £5 million per year. Grenville's ministry had to find new sources of funds, and the British people were already heavily taxed. Because the colonists had benefited greatly from wartime outlays, Grenville concluded, Anglo-Americans should shoulder a larger share of the cost of running the expanded empire.

5-2d Theories of Representation

Grenville did not doubt Great Britain's right to levy taxes on the colonies. Like his countrymen, he believed that government's legitimacy derived ultimately from the consent of the people. But he defined consent differently than many colonists did. Grenville and many of his English contemporaries believed that Parliament—king, lords, and commons acting together—by definition represented all British subjects, wherever they resided and whether or not they could vote. Many who lived in the North American provinces, by contrast, had come to believe that their interests could be represented only by men who lived nearby, and for whom they (or their property-holding neighbors) actually voted.

Britons in England, Scotland, and Ireland saw Parliament as collectively representing the entire nation. When voters elected a member of the House of Commons, they did not imagine that he would advance the specific interests of their specific district, nor that they would have any special claim on that member's vote. Indeed, members of Parliament did not even have to live near their constituents. According to this theory, called *virtual representation*, each member of Parliament worked for the entire British nation, and all Britons—including colonists—were represented in Parliament. Their consent to its laws could thus be presumed.

In the colonies, however, members of the lower houses of the assemblies were viewed as *actually* representing the regions that had elected them. Voters cast their ballots for those they believed would advance the particular interests of a given district and province. Before Grenville proposed to tax the colonists, no conflict had exposed the contradiction between the two notions. But events of the 1760s revealed the incompatibility of these two understandings of representation.

5-2e Real Whigs

The same events threw into sharp relief Americans' attitudes toward political power. The colonists had grown accustomed to a faraway central government that affected their daily lives very little. Consequently, they believed a good government was one that left them alone, a view in keeping with the theories of British writers known as the Real Whigs or Commonwealth thinkers. Drawing on a tradition of dissent that reached back to the English Civil War, the Real Whigs stressed the dangers posed by a powerful government, particularly one headed by a monarch. Some of them even favored republicanism, which proposed to eliminate monarchs and vest political power more directly in the people. Real Whig writers warned people to guard against government's attempts to threaten their liberty and seize their property. Political power was always to be feared, wrote John Trenchard and Thomas Gordon in essays entitled *Cato's Letters* (published in London in 1720–1723 and reprinted many times thereafter in the colonies).

Britain's efforts to tighten the reins of government and to raise revenues from the colonies in the 1760s and early 1770s convinced many colonists that Real Whig logic applied to their circumstances. Excessive and unjust taxation, they believed, could destroy their freedoms. By 1775, a large number of mainland colonists would come to see the actions of Grenville and his successors as tyrannical. In the mid-1760s, however, colonial leaders did not accuse Parliament of conspiring to oppress them. Rather, they questioned the wisdom of the particular laws Grenville proposed.

5-2f Sugar and Currency Acts

Parliament passed the first such measures, the Sugar Act and the Currency Act, in 1764. The **Sugar Act** (also known as the Revenue Act) revised existing customs regulations and laid new duties on some imports into the colonies. North American colonists differed sharply with those in the West Indies over its key provisions, revealing a division of interests between Britain's thirteen provinces on the mainland and the equal number located in the Caribbean. As the imperial crisis unfolded, that division would become a chasm. Influential Caribbean sugar planters lobbied for the Sugar Act, which protected their commerce against cheaper smuggled sugar products from the French islands. The act also established a vice-admiralty court at Halifax, Nova Scotia, to adjudicate violations of the law. Although the Sugar Act resembled the earlier Navigation Acts, which the colonies considered legitimate, it was explicitly designed to raise revenue, not to channel American trade through Britain.

The Currency Act effectively outlawed most colonial paper money, something the Crown had tried to do for decades. British merchants had long complained that Americans paid their debts in local currencies of indeterminate value. The Currency Act forced them to pay their debts in pounds and pence—real money, as the British saw it. But Americans imported more than they exported, and so could accumulate little sterling; colonists complained that the act deprived them of a vital medium of exchange.

The Sugar Act and the Currency Act were imposed on an economy already reeling from depression. A business boom accompanied the Seven Years' War, but the brief spell of prosperity ended abruptly in 1760, when fighting moved overseas. Urban merchants found fewer buyers for imported goods, and the loss of the military's demand for everything from food to horseshoes hurt farmers and city dwellers alike. The bottom dropped out of the European tobacco market,

Sugar Act Act passed by British Parliament in 1764 that sought to raise revenues by taxing colonial imports, notably sugar products like molasses and rum.

threatening the livelihood of Chesapeake planters. Sailors were thrown out of work, and artisans found fewer customers. In such circumstances, the prospect of new import duties and inadequate supplies of currency panicked merchants.

Individual essayists and incensed colonial governments protested the new policies. But lacking any precedent for a campaign against acts of Parliament, colonists in 1764 took only hesitant and uncoordinated steps. Eight provincial legislatures sent separate petitions to Parliament requesting the Sugar Act's repeal. They argued that its commercial restrictions would hurt Britain as well as the colonies and insisted that they had not consented to its passage. The protests had no effect. The law remained in force, and Grenville proceeded with another new revenue plan.

5-3 The Stamp Act Crisis

▶ Why did many British colonists perceive the Stamp Act as a threat?

▶ How did North American colonial argumentation against parliament's power to tax them develop amid the Stamp Act Crisis?

▶ What were the competing goals and methods of demonstrators who protested the Stamp Act?

The **Stamp Act** (1765), Grenville's most important proposal, was modeled on a law that had been in effect in Britain for almost a century. It touched nearly every colonist by requiring tax stamps on printed materials, but it placed the heaviest burden on members of the colonial elite, who used printed matter more intensively than did ordinary folk. Anyone who purchased a newspaper or pamphlet, made a will, transferred land, earned a diploma, bought playing cards, applied for a license, accepted a government post, or took a loan would have to buy a stamp. Adding injury to insult, the act also required that scarce coin be used to purchase tax stamps. Never before had a revenue measure of such scope been proposed for the colonies. The Stamp Act broke with the colonial tradition of self-imposed taxation. Violators were to be tried by vice-admiralty courts, in which judges alone rendered decisions, leading Americans to fear for their right to trial by jury. And since the revenues would pay for British peacekeepers in North America, the tax also mobilized long-established fears of a standing army.

5-3a James Otis's *Rights of the British Colonies*

The most important colonial pamphlet protesting the Sugar Act and the proposed Stamp Act was *The Rights of the British Colonies Asserted and Proved*, by James Otis Jr., a brilliant young Massachusetts attorney. Otis starkly exposed the dilemma that confounded the colonists for the next decade. How could they oppose particular acts of Parliament without fundamentally questioning Parliament's authority? On the one hand, he asserted, colonists were "entitled to all the natural, essential, inherent, and inseparable rights" of Britons, including the

▲ This page from the Halifax Nova Scotia *Gazette* in November 1765 shows printers' fury at the Stamp Act. The new law stipulated that newspapers had to be printed on stamped paper; the official seal or stamp appears in red. The printer has created a crude illustration of a devil, who appears to spear the detested stamp with a pitchfork. Below the stamp, he has printed, "Devils clear the way for STAMPS."

right not to be taxed without their consent. This logic followed colonial notions of representation. But Otis also conceded that "the power of parliament is uncontrollable but by themselves … Let the parliament lay what burthens they please on us, we must … submit and patiently bear them." Here Otis accepted the prevailing theory of British government: Parliament was the supreme authority in the empire. To resolve the dilemma, Otis proposed colonial representation in Parliament, an idea that was never taken seriously on either side of the Atlantic.

Like many Enlightenment thinkers, Otis reasoned from natural rights. He argued that the colonists and "their brethren of Great-Britain" were "children of the same Creator," born into "a state of equality and perfect freedom." But like very few writers of his day, Otis extended this natural rights logic to the enslaved. "The Colonists are by the law of nature free born, as indeed are all men, white or black," he wrote. Slavery debased everyone connected with it; the institution threatened "to reduce both Europe and America to the ignorance and barbarity of the darkest ages." It was common, in the 1760s, for colonists to protest that Britain's tyranny enslaved them. To receive the stamps "is Death—is worse than Death—it is slavery!" proclaimed Pennsylvania's John Dickinson. James Otis went further. Not only did unfair taxes reduce people to slavery; chattel slavery itself was the basest tyranny. He warned: "It is a clear truth, that those who every day barter away other mens liberty, will soon care little for their own." Slowly, in small corners of the colonies and in England, the era's talk of liberty would begin to erode the intellectual foundations of human bondage.

Stamp Act Obliged colonists to purchase and use special stamped (watermarked) paper for newspapers, customs documents, various licenses, college diplomas, and legal forms used for recovering debts, buying land, and making wills.

When Otis published his pamphlet, the Stamp Act was rumored, but not yet passed. When Americans first learned of the act's adoption, in the spring of 1765, they reacted indecisively. Few colonists—even appointed government officials—publicly favored the law. But colonial petitions had failed to prevent its passage, and further lobbying appeared futile. Perhaps Otis was correct: Americans had to pay the tax, reluctantly but loyally. Acting on that assumption, colonial agents in London sought the appointment of their American friends as stamp distributors so that the law would at least be enforced equitably.

5-3b Patrick Henry and the Virginia Stamp Act Resolves

Not all colonists resigned themselves to paying the new tax. A young attorney serving his first term in Virginia's House of Burgesses was appalled by his fellow legislators' complacency. The son of a prosperous Scots immigrant, Patrick Henry had little formal education. But his oratorical skills made him a formidable advocate.

Near the end of the legislative session, when many burgesses had already departed for home, Henry introduced seven proposals against the Stamp Act. The few burgesses remaining adopted five of Henry's resolutions by a bare majority. Although they repealed the most radical of the five the next day, their action had far-reaching effects. Some newspapers printed Henry's original resolutions as if the House had passed them all, even though one was rescinded and two others were never even debated or voted on.

The four propositions adopted by the burgesses echoed Otis's arguments about taxation, asserting that colonists had never forfeited the rights of British subjects. The other three resolutions went much further. The repealed resolution claimed for the burgesses "the only exclusive right" to tax Virginians. The final two (never considered) asserted that Virginians need not obey tax laws passed by other legislative bodies—namely, Parliament.

5-3c Continuing Loyalty to Britain

The burgesses' decision to accept only some of Henry's resolutions anticipated the position most mainland colonists would adopt throughout the following decade. Though willing to fight for their liberties as Britons within the empire, they did not seek independence. The Maryland lawyer Daniel Dulany, whose *Considerations on the Propriety of Imposing Taxes on the British Colonies* was the most widely read pamphlet of 1765, expressed the consensus: "The colonies are dependent upon Great Britain, and the supreme authority vested in the king, lords, and commons, may justly be exercised to secure, or preserve their dependence." But, warned Dulany, a condition of "dependence and inferiority" was very different from one of "absolute vassalage and slavery."

Over the next decade, colonial leaders searched for a formula that would let them control their internal affairs, especially taxation, while retaining the many benefits of British rule. But British officials could not compromise on the issue of parliamentary power. Even the harshest British critics of the ministries during the 1760s and 1770s questioned only specific policies, not the principles on which they rested.

In effect, the American rebels wanted British leaders to revise their fundamental understanding of how government worked. That was simply too much to expect.

The effectiveness of Americans' opposition to the Stamp Act rested on more than ideological arguments over parliamentary power. The battle was waged on the streets as well as on the page. The decisive and inventive actions of some colonists during the summer and fall of 1765 gave the resistance its primary force.

5-3d Anti–Stamp Act Demonstrations

In August, the Loyal Nine, a Boston artisans' social club, organized a protest against the Stamp Act. Hoping to show that people of all ranks opposed the act, they approached the leaders of the city's rival laborers' associations, groups of unskilled workers and poor tradesmen based in Boston's North End and South End neighborhoods.

Early on August 14, the demonstrators hung an effigy of Andrew Oliver, the province's stamp distributor, from a tree on Boston Common. The crowds viewing the straw man swelled throughout the day. At dusk, a large group led by about fifty well-dressed tradesmen paraded the effigy around the city and through the Town House, the seat of government. Demonstrators then built a bonfire near Oliver's house and fed the effigy to the flames: a kind of proxy murder. They also broke most of Oliver's windows and threw stones at officials who tried to disperse them. Two days later, Oliver publicly renounced the duties of his office. One Bostonian jubilantly wrote, "I believe people never was more Universally pleased."

Twelve days later, another crowd action—aimed this time at Oliver's brother-in-law, Lieutenant Governor Thomas Hutchinson—drew no praise from Boston's respectable citizens. On the night of August 26, a mob destroyed Hutchinson's elegant townhouse. The lieutenant governor reported that by the next morning, nothing was left of his mansion "but the bare walls and floors." His fine imported furniture was broken to bits, his trees and garden ruined, his valuable library lost. But Hutchinson took some comfort in the fact that the leaders of the resistance "never intended matters should go this length and the people in general express the utmost detestation of this unparalleled outrage."

5-3e Americans' Divergent Interests

The differences between the two Boston crowds of August 1765 exposed divisions that would characterize subsequent protests. Few colonists sided with Britain during the 1760s, but various colonial insurgents had divergent goals. Skilled craftsmen as well as merchants, lawyers, and other educated elites preferred orderly demonstrations centered on political issues. For the city's laborers, by contrast, economic grievances were often paramount. Certainly, their "hellish Fury" as they wrecked Hutchinson's house suggests resentment of his ostentatious display of wealth.

Colonists, like other Britons, had a long tradition of crowd action in which disfranchised people—including women—took to the streets to redress economic grievances. But the Stamp Act controversy for the first time drew ordinary folk into transatlantic politics. Matters that previously had been of

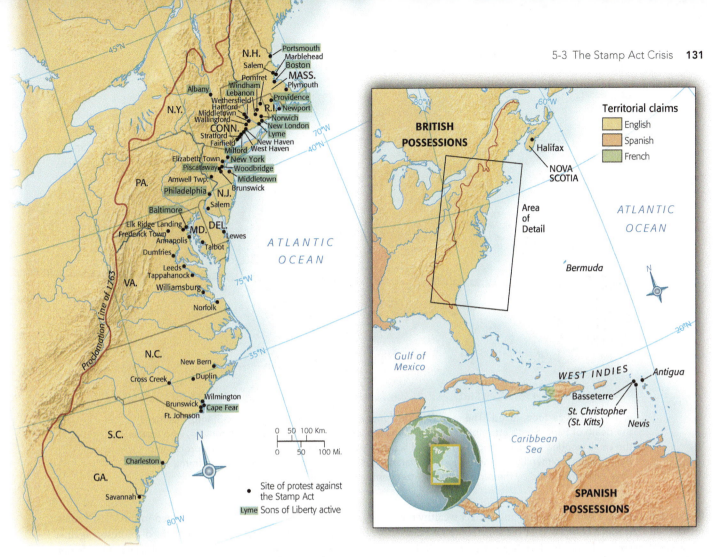

Map 5.3 **Colonial Resistance to the Stamp Act**

All of the towns and islands labeled on this map witnessed crowd actions protesting the Stamp Act of 1765; British colonies outside the eventual United States joined in the nearly universal opposition to the hated measure.

concern only to an elite few were now discussed in every tavern and coffeehouse. As Benjamin Franklin's daughter told her father, then serving as a colonial agent in London, "nothing else is talked of, the Dutch [Germans] talk of the stompt act the Negroes of the tamp, in short every body has something to say."

Anti–Stamp Act demonstrations took place from Nova Scotia to the West Indies (see Map 5.3). But though the act placed the heaviest tax burden on the Caribbean colonies—levying double or triple duty on large island land transfers, for example—protests there were muted. As on the mainland, West Indian pamphleteers argued for the local imposition of taxes and against their virtual representation in Parliament. But only the Leeward Islands—those most dependent on mainland American merchants for their food—actively resisted the act. Like their counterparts in Massachusetts, rioters in St. Kitts and Nevis burned effigies, torched stamps, and attacked officials' houses. In Montserrat and Antigua, stamp collectors were shunned and the tax largely ignored.

But Jamaica and Barbados, the largest, most populous, and richest islands, complied with the tax. Since the wealthiest sugar planters were sojourners more than settlers, they had strong personal ties to Britain. They also depended on mercantilist legislation to favor their sugar exports over the cheaper French

product. Finally, they relied upon British military might to protect them from the enslaved workforces whose labor made them both obscenely rich and acutely vulnerable. Slaveholders who comprised a tiny ruling minority amidst an enormous enslaved African population saw British troops as a bulwark of liberty, not a threat to it. In such circumstances, abstract principle seemed less important than self-interest. "The Privilege of being taxed by our immediate Representatives, is indeed a most valuable one," supposed one pamphleteer in Barbados. But that privilege was enjoyed by "a very small, not a tenth Part of the People." American provincials were not among those lucky few, yet they were "connected with the Mother Country in point of Interest," and thus well enough represented. The planters grumbled, but they paid the tax. Over three-quarters of the revenues collected during the Stamp Act's brief life came from the West Indies. Jamaica alone paid more stamp duty than the rest of the empire combined.

On the mainland, street protests were so successful that by November 1, when the law was scheduled to take effect, not one stamp distributor was willing to enforce the act. But the entry of unskilled workers, slaves, and women into the realm of imperial politics both aided and troubled the elite men who wanted to mount effective opposition to British measures.

▲ This British cartoon, called "The repeal, or the funeral procession of Miss Americ-Stamp," satirizes the death of Parliament's attempt to tax the colonies via stamped paper. George Grenville, who carries the small wooden coffin holding the repealed act, looks crestfallen, as do the politicians processing behind him. The merchants who owned the warehouses full of goods at the right of the frame would have been overjoyed by the repeal and the attendant boost to transatlantic trade.

Crowd action clearly had a stunning impact. Yet wealthy men recognized that mobs composed of the formerly powerless—whose goals were rarely identical to their own—posed a threat in their own right. What would happen, they wondered, if the "hellish Fury" of the crowd turned against them?

5-3f Sons of Liberty

Elites attempted to channel resistance into acceptable forms by creating an intercolonial association, the **Sons of Liberty**. New Yorkers organized the first such group in early November 1765, and groups emerged rapidly in other coastal cities, eventually coordinating their actions. By early 1766, the Sons of Liberty, composed of merchants, lawyers, and prosperous tradesmen, linked protest leaders from Charleston, South Carolina, to Portsmouth, New Hampshire. The central role of taverns in the exchange of news and opinions makes it unsurprising that a considerable number of members owned taverns.

The Sons of Liberty could influence events but not control them. In Charleston (formerly Charles Town) in October 1765, a crowd shouting, "Liberty Liberty and stamp'd paper" forced the resignation of the South Carolina stamp distributor. The subsequent victory celebration—the largest demonstration the city had ever known—featured a British flag emblazoned with the word "Liberty." But the Charleston Sons of Liberty were horrified when in January 1766 local slaves paraded through the streets similarly proclaiming, "Liberty!" Freedom from slavery was the last thing elite slave owners had in mind, but the language of liberty could easily slip its channels.

Sons of Liberty Groups formed in many colonial port cities to resist the Stamp Act.

No Sons of Liberty chapters emerged in the West Indies. Indeed, mainland Sons groups organized protests against Caribbean colonists as well as British officials. The *Boston Gazette* called on merchants to boycott "the SLAVISH Islands of Barbados and Antigua—Poor, mean spirited, Cowardly, Dastardly Creoles." The sugar islands should receive no "Fresh or Salt Provisions from any Son of LIBERTY on the Continent." Such starvation tactics may only have deepened the rift between continental and Caribbean British Americans.

5-3g Opposition and Repeal

During the fall and winter of 1765–1766, opponents of the Stamp Act pursued several different strategies. Colonial legislatures petitioned Parliament to repeal the hated law, and courts closed because they could not obtain the stamps now required for all legal documents. In October, nine mainland colonies sent delegates to New York to attend a general congress, the first since the Albany Congress of 1754. The Stamp Act Congress met to draft a remonstrance stressing the law's adverse economic effects. At the same time, the Sons of Liberty held mass meetings, rallying public support for the resistance movement. Finally, American merchants organized nonimportation associations to pressure British exporters by refusing to buy their goods. By the 1760s, one-quarter of all British exports went to the colonies, and colonial merchants reasoned that London merchants whose sales suffered from their boycotts would lobby for repeal. Because times were bad and fewer customers were buying imported goods anyway, a general moratorium on future purchases would also help colonial merchants reduce their bloated inventories.

Writing and Stationery Supplies

In the seventeenth century, colonists stressed the importance of teaching children to read the Bible; writing was not seen as nearly so necessary, and many who could read never learned to write. Yet as the eighteenth century progressed, and especially during the era of the American Revolution, writing skills acquired heightened significance. Family members parted by the war needed to communicate with each other, and new opportunities arose for merchants who could deal with distant correspondents. Such experiences led Americans to place increased emphasis on teaching youngsters to write as well as to read.

Most books were either imported from England or printed in the colonies (and later the new United States), but writing drew on a wide range of items from around the world. Paper was either imported from Britain or manufactured at an increasing number of American paper mills; more than thirty were built between 1750 and 1780. The quill pens (goose feathers) that Americans used as writing implements often originated in Germany or Holland. The feathers would be heated to remove fat and to harden their points before they were shipped by the thousands across the Atlantic. Penknives, needed to sharpen blunt quills, and inkpots (typically made of brass, glass, or pewter), largely came from Britain. But the Americans could not write readily without additional items obtained from international trade.

For example, to absorb ink properly, paper needed to be treated with pounce, a powder made from a combination of gum sandarac (a tree resin from North Africa) and pumice, a powdered volcanic glass. Lacking envelopes, eighteenth-century writers folded their sheets of paper, addressed them on the outside, and sealed them with wax made in Holland or Britain from a combination of lac (a resinous secretion of insects, still used today for shellac) from India and cinnabar, a red quartz-like crystal, from Spain. Ink was compounded from a set of diverse ingredients: oak galls from Aleppo (in Syria), gum arabic (sap from acacia trees) from Sudan, and alum and copperas (derived from different stones) from Britain. Most ink was shipped from Britain in powdered form; in America, another key ingredient, urine, would be added to blend the alum with the other substances to create the liquid ink. (Printers' shops famously reeked of piss.) Merchants who sold such supplies sometimes touted the virtues of the "Best Dutch Sealing Wax" or "Aleppo ink" they stocked.

When colonial elites drafted petitions to remonstrate against the Stamp Act that taxed their printed materials, the implements they employed connected them to a long commercial chain stretching to Great Britain, the European continent, North Africa, and the Middle East.

CRITICAL THINKING

- For their writing materials, American colonists depended on many products they obtained through international trade. How else was their literary culture dependent upon international imports?

Desk and Bookcase, c. 1762 (mahogany, white cedar, yellow poplar, yellow pine, silvered glass & gilded brass)/American School, (18th century)/PHILADELPHIA MUSEUM OF ART/Philadelphia Museum of Art, Pennsylvania, PA, USA/Bridgeman Images

◄ This writing desk, made in Pennsylvania in the mid-to-late eighteenth century, would have been owned by a well-to-do family from the mid-Atlantic states. The pigeonholes would hold incoming and outgoing letters; the many drawers could store paper, ink, seals and sealing wax, and other supplies. The new importance of writing thus produced a perceived need for novel types of furniture.

In March 1766, Parliament repealed the Stamp Act. The nonimportation agreements had indeed created allies for the colonies among wealthy London merchants. But boycotts, petitions, and crowd actions were less important in winning repeal than was the appointment of a new prime minister, chosen by George III for reasons unrelated to colonial politics. Lord Rockingham, who replaced Grenville in the summer of 1765, had opposed the Stamp Act, not because he believed Parliament lacked authority to tax the colonies, but because he thought the law needlessly divisive. Although Rockingham championed repeal, he linked it to passage of a **Declaratory Act**, which asserted Parliament's authority to tax and legislate for Britain's American possessions "in all cases whatsoever."

That spring, crown officials of the provinces waited anxiously as rumors of repeal swirled. "Thinking Men know not which will bring most danger, a Repeal or a Confirmation," Massachusetts Governor Francis Bernard wrote. Upholding the act would "make the People mad with desperation." But repeal, he worried, would make the rebels "insolent with Success."

Bernard's concerns proved prophetic. News of the repeal reached New England in late April, and the Sons of Liberty quickly dispatched messengers to carry the welcome tidings throughout the mainland colonies. They organized celebrations commemorating the glorious event and Americans' loyalty to Britain. Their goal achieved, the Sons of Liberty dissolved. Few colonists yet saw the ominous implications of the Declaratory Act.

5-4 Resistance to the Townshend Acts

▶ **How did the Townshend Acts differ from earlier parliamentary acts?**

▶ **How did individual colonies and colonists begin to join forces in protesting the Townshend Acts?**

In the summer of 1766, another change in the ministry in London revealed how fragile the colonists' victory had been. The new prime minister, William Pitt, had fostered cooperation between the colonies and Britain during the Seven Years' War. But Pitt fell ill, and Charles Townshend became the dominant force in the ministry. An ally of Grenville and a supporter of colonial taxation, Townshend decided to try again to obtain badly needed funds from Britain's American possessions (see Table 5.1).

The duties Townshend proposed in 1767 would be levied on trade goods like paper, glass, and tea, extending the existing Navigation Acts. But the Townshend duties differed from previous customs levies in two ways. First, they applied to items imported into the colonies from Britain, rather than

Declaratory Act Affirmed parliamentary power to legislate its colonies "in all cases whatsoever."

Table 5.1 British Ministries and Their American Policies

Head of Ministry	Major Acts
George Grenville	Sugar Act (1764)
	Currency Act (1764)
	Stamp Act (1765)
Lord Rockingham	Stamp Act repealed (1766)
	Declaratory Act (1766)
William Pitt/Charles Townshend	Townshend Acts (1767)
Lord North	Townshend duties (except for tea tax) repealed (1770)
	Tea Act (1773)
	Coercive Acts (1774)
	Quebec Act (1774)

to those from foreign countries. Accordingly, they violated mercantilist theory. Second, the revenues would be used to pay some provincial officials. Assemblies would no longer be able to threaten to withhold salaries in order to win those officials' cooperation. Townshend's scheme also established an American Board of Customs Commissioners and created vice-admiralty courts at Boston, Philadelphia, and Charleston. Those moves angered merchants, whose profits would be threatened by more vigorous enforcement of the Navigation Acts. Significantly, Townshend exempted the West Indies from key provisions of the new duties, a divide-and-conquer tactic revealing that Parliament had learned from the Stamp Act protests.

5-4a John Dickinson's *Letters*

The passage of the Townshend Acts drew a quick response. One series of essays in particular, *Letters from a Farmer in Pennsylvania*, by the prominent lawyer John Dickinson, expressed a broad consensus. All but four mainland newspapers reprinted Dickinson's essays; in pamphlet form, they went through seven American editions. Dickinson contended that Parliament could regulate colonial trade but could not use that power to raise revenue. By distinguishing between regulation and taxation—or "external" and "internal" taxes—Dickinson avoided the sticky issue of Parliament's authority. But his argument created an equally knotty problem, suggesting the colonies should assess Parliament's motives in passing any law pertaining to trade before deciding whether to obey it.

The Massachusetts assembly responded to the Townshend Acts by drafting a letter to the other colonial legislatures, suggesting a joint protest petition. What ultimately united the mainland colonies, however, was less the letter itself than the ministry's reaction to it. When Lord Hillsborough, recently named to the new post of secretary of state for America, learned of the Massachusetts circular letter, he ordered the colony's governor, Francis Bernard, to demand that the assembly recall it. He also directed other governors to prevent their assemblies from discussing the letter. Hillsborough's order gave colonial assemblies an incentive to join forces. In late 1768, the Massachusetts legislature rejected Bernard's recall order by a vote of 92 to 17. Bernard dissolved the assembly in response, and other governors followed suit when their legislatures debated the Massachusetts circular letter.

5-4b Rituals of Resistance

The number of votes cast against recalling the circular letter—92—assumed ritual significance in the resistance movement. The number 45 already had symbolic meaning because **John Wilkes**, a radical Londoner sympathetic to the American cause, had been jailed for publishing a pamphlet entitled *The North Briton*, No. 45. In Boston, the silversmith Paul Revere made a punchbowl weighing 45 ounces that held 45 gills (half-cups) and was engraved with the names of the "glorious 92" opposition legislators; James Otis, John Adams, and others publicly drank 45 toasts from it. In Charleston, tradesmen decorated a tree with 45 lights and set off 45 rockets. They adjourned to a tavern where 45 tables were set with 45 bowls of wine, 45 bowls of punch, and 92 glasses.

Such rituals served important political functions. Just as pamphlets by Otis, Dulany, Dickinson, and others acquainted literate colonists with the philosophical issues raised by British actions, so public rituals enlisted common people in the argument. Boston's Sons of Liberty invited hundreds of city residents to dine with them each August 14 to commemorate the first Stamp Act demonstration. Songs supporting the American cause also helped to spread the word.

The Sons of Liberty and other resistance leaders made a deliberate effort to involve ordinary folk in the campaign against the Townshend duties. They urged colonists of all ranks and both sexes to sign agreements not to purchase or consume British products. The consumer revolution that had previously linked colonists culturally and economically now linked them politically as well, supplying them with a ready method of displaying their allegiance. As "A Tradesman" wrote in a Philadelphia paper in 1770, it was essential "for the Good of the Whole, to strengthen the Hands of the Patriotic Majority, by agreeing not to purchase British Goods."

5-4c Daughters of Liberty

As the primary purchasers of textiles and household goods, women played a central role in the nonconsumption movement. More than three hundred Boston matrons publicly promised not to buy or drink tea, "Sickness excepted." The women of Wilmington, North Carolina, burned their tea after walking through town in a solemn procession. Throughout the colonies, women exchanged recipes for tea substitutes or drank coffee instead. The best known of the protests, the so-called Edenton Ladies Tea Party, had little to do with tea. It was a meeting of prominent North Carolina women who pledged formally to work for the public good and to support resistance to British measures.

Women also encouraged home manufacturing. In many towns, young women calling themselves Daughters of Liberty met to spin in public squares to encourage colonists to end the colonies' dependence on British cloth by wearing homespun. These symbolic displays of patriotism—publicized by newspapers and broadsides—served the same purpose as the male rituals involving the numbers 45 and 92. When young ladies from well-to-do families sat outdoors at spinning wheels all day, eating only American food, drinking local herbal tea, and listening to patriotic sermons, they served as political instructors. Many women took great satisfaction in their newfound role. When a satirist hinted that women discussed only "such triffling subjects as Dress, Scandal and Detraction" during their spinning bees, three Boston women replied angrily, "Inferior in abusive sarcasm, in personal invective, in low wit, we glory to be, but inferior in veracity, sincerity, love of virtue, of liberty and of our country, we would not willingly be to any."

5-4d Divided Opinion over Boycotts

Colonists were by no means united in support of nonimportation and nonconsumption. The Stamp Act boycotts had helped to revive a depressed economy by creating a demand for local products and reducing merchants' inventories. But by 1768 and 1769, merchants were again enjoying boom times and had no financial incentive to support a boycott. Many signed the agreements reluctantly and violated them flagrantly. In contrast, artisans supported nonimportation enthusiastically, recognizing that the absence of British goods would increase demand for their own manufactures. Tradesmen formed the core of the crowds that picketed importers' stores, publicized offending merchants' names in the press, and sometimes destroyed their property.

Such tactics were effective: colonial imports from England dropped dramatically in 1769, especially in New York, New England, and Pennsylvania. But the pressure exerted by the rebels also aroused heated opposition. Even some Americans who supported resistance to British measures began to question the use of violence to enforce the boycott. In addition, the threat to private property inherent in the campaign frightened wealthier men and women. Political activism by ordinary colonists challenged the ruling elite's domination, just as its members had feared in 1765.

Colonists were relieved when news arrived in April 1770 that the Townshend duties had been repealed, with the exception of the tax on tea. A new prime minister, Lord North, persuaded Parliament that duties on trade within the empire

John Wilkes British Whig politician and frequent opponent of King George III who became a hero to American colonists.

In 1775, an English cartoonist satirized American women's involvement in the resistance movement by depicting the women of Edenton, North Carolina, as grotesque, flirtatious figures who neglected their responsibilities as mothers when they dared to enter the political arena. In the background, he showed them discarding their tea.

Library of Congress Prints and Photographs Division Washington, D.C. [LC-US262-12711]

were ill advised. Although some argued that nonimportation should continue until the tea tax was rolled back, merchants quickly resumed importing.

5-5 Confrontations in Boston

▶ What were the origins of the "Boston Massacre"?

▶ How did patriot organizers use the "Boston Massacre" as evidence of the oppression of American colonists?

▶ How did the emergence of Committees of Correspondence alter the resistance movement?

On the very day Lord North proposed repeal of the Townshend duties—news the colonists would learn weeks later—a confrontation between Boston civilians and British soldiers led to five Americans' deaths. The seeds of the event that patriots labeled the "**Boston Massacre**" were planted years before, when Parliament decided to base the American Board of Customs Commissioners in Boston.

Mobs had targeted the customs officials from the day they arrived in November 1767. In June 1768, their seizure of the patriot leader John Hancock's sloop *Liberty* on suspicion of smuggling caused a riot. The riot in turn helped to convince

Boston Massacre Confrontation between colonists and British troops in which five colonists were shot and killed.

the ministry that troops were needed to maintain order in the unruly port. That October, two regiments of British regulars—about 700 men—marched up Long Wharf toward the Common, "with muskets charged, bayonets fixed, colours flying, [and] drums beating," the *Boston Evening Post* reported. These "lobster-backs," as Bostonians called the red-coated soldiers, served as constant visible reminders of the oppressive potential of British power. Patrols roamed the streets at all hours, questioning and sometimes harassing passersby. Parents feared for the safety of their daughters, whom soldiers subjected to coarse sexual insults. But the greatest potential for violence lay in the uneasy relationship between the troops and Boston laborers. Many redcoats sought employment in their off-duty hours, competing for unskilled jobs with the city's workingmen. Members of the two groups brawled repeatedly in taverns and on the streets.

5-5a Boston Massacre

On the evening of March 5, 1770, a crowd of laborers began throwing hard-packed snowballs at troops guarding the Customs House. Goaded beyond endurance, the sentries ignored their orders and fired on the crowd, killing four and wounding eight, one of whom died a few days later. Reportedly, the first to fall was Crispus Attucks, a sailor of mixed Nipmuck and African ancestry. Rebel leaders idealized Attucks and the other dead rioters as martyrs for liberty, holding a solemn funeral and later commemorating March 5 with patriotic orations. Paul Revere's engraving entitled "The Bloody

Massacre Perpetrated in King Street," which Revere pirated from a rival image by Henry Pelham) was part of a hugely effective propaganda campaign by the rebels. "The prints exhibited in our houses have added wings to fancy; and in the fervour of our zeal, reason is in hazard of being lost," warned Samuel Quincy, the colony's solicitor general, who prosecuted the officer in charge at the time of the massacre.

As the trials unfolded that fall, cool reason carried the day. John Adams and Josiah Quincy Jr., both unwavering patriots, acted as the soldiers' defense attorneys. Almost all the accused were acquitted, and the two men convicted were released after being branded on the thumb.

5-5b A British Plot?

The outcome of the soldiers' trials persuaded London officials not to retaliate against Boston. For more than two years after the massacre, the imperial crisis seemed to quiet. But the most outspoken newspapers, including the *Boston Gazette* (which British officials called the "Weekly Dung Barge"), continued to accuse Great Britain of scheming to oppress Americans. After the Stamp Act's repeal, the protest leaders had praised Parliament; following repeal of the Townshend duties, they warned of impending tyranny. What had seemed to be a single ill-chosen stamp tax now appeared part of a coordinated plot against American liberties. Essayists pointed to the stationing of troops in Boston, and the growing number of vice-admiralty courts as evidence of plans to enslave the colonists. Indeed, patriot writers played repeatedly on the word *enslavement*—though they rarely questioned the institution of race-based chattel slavery, as James Otis had done in 1764.

Still, almost no one advocated American independence. Although some colonists were becoming convinced that they should seek freedom from parliamentary authority, they continued to trumpet their British liberties and to acknowledge their allegiance to George III. But they began to envision a system that would enable them to be ruled by their own elected legislatures while remaining subordinate to the king. Of course, any such scheme violated Britons' conception of the nature of government, which accepted Parliament's sole, undivided sovereignty. Furthermore, in the British mind, Parliament encompassed the king as well as lords and commons; separating the monarch from the legislature was impossible.

Then, in the fall of 1772, the North ministry began to implement the Townshend Act that provided for governors and judges to be paid from customs revenues. In early November, voters at a Boston town meeting established a **Committee of Correspondence** to publicize the decision by exchanging letters with other Massachusetts towns.

Committee of Correspondence Local committees established throughout colonies to coordinate anti-British actions.

▲ Offering visual support for the patriots' version of events, Henry Pelham rushed this drawing into print in April 1770. Entitled "The Fruits of Arbitrary Power," the engraving depicted British soldiers firing on an unresisting crowd, instead of the aggressive mob described at the soldiers' trials. Pelham anticipated economic as well as political success from the image, and was furious when Paul Revere copied his drawing and beat him to market.

▲ Shortly after the Boston Massacre, Paul Revere pirated this illustration of the confrontation near the Customs House from Pelham's version, adding inflammatory details such as a gun firing from a nearby building, which he labeled "Butcher's Hall." He replaced Pelham's quotation from Psalms with a sensationalized doggerel verse about the events of March 5, 1770. Both engravings call the chaotic events a "Bloody Massacre."

Phillis Wheatley, Enslaved Poet in the Cradle of Liberty

In July 1761, the *Phillis* docked at Boston's Long Wharf after a long voyage during which nearly a quarter of its human cargo died. The captain placed an advertisement in the papers hawking "prime young SLAVES, from the Windward Coast." One of the least valuable among them was a little girl still missing her two front teeth. A merchant named John Wheatley purchased her as a gift for his wife, naming the child after the boat that brought her from Africa.

Phillis Wheatley grew up in a genteel house on King Street, part of a prosperous family that included at least one other slave. The Wheatleys, influenced by the ideas of the Great Awakening, recognized her talents and educated her beyond the station of nearly all slaves and, indeed, of most white girls and women. At a young age, she began to write poetry. In 1770, several months after the Boston Massacre took place just steps from the Wheatley mansion, Phillis's elegy on the death of George Whitefield made her famous on both sides of the Atlantic. In 1773, as the crisis over tea engrossed Boston, a volume of her poems was published in London.

Wheatley's *Poems on Various Subjects* included an "elegant engraved likeness of the Author." In an era when books seldom featured portraits of female authors and almost never bore the likenesses of people of African descent, Wheatley's image—probably based on a painting by the black Boston artist Scipio Moorhead—is a striking exception.

CRITICAL THINKING

- What attributes does the portrait give the poet?
- How do the title page and the frontispiece depict her race, age, gender, and genius?

▲ Wheatley frontispiece

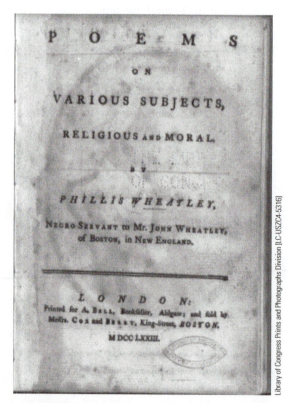

▲ Wheatley title page

Heading the committee was Samuel Adams, who had proposed its formation.

5-5c Samuel Adams and Committees of Correspondence

Aged fifty-one in 1772, Samuel Adams was about a decade older than other leaders of American resistance, including his distant cousin John. The Harvard-educated son of a wealthy maltster, he had been a Boston tax collector, a clerk of the Massachusetts assembly, and one of the Sons of Liberty. Adams drew a sharp contrast between a corrupt, vice-riddled Britain and the simple, liberty-loving folk of the mainland colonies. His Committee of Correspondence undertook the task of creating consensus among the residents of Massachusetts.

Such committees, which were eventually established throughout the colonies, opened a new chapter in the American resistance. Until 1772, the protest movement was confined almost entirely to the mainland, largely to the seacoast, and primarily to major cities and towns (see Map 5.3). An experienced political organizer, Adams sought to involve more colonists in the struggle. Accordingly, the Boston town meeting directed the Committee of Correspondence to send copies of its report to other towns in the province.

The statement prepared by the Boston Committee declared, "All persons born in the British American Colonies" had natural rights to life, liberty, and property. The idea that "a British house of Commons, should have a right, at pleasure, to give and grant the property of the colonists" was "irreconcilable" with "natural law and Justice" and with "the British Constitution." Their grievances included taxation without representation, the increased presence of troops and customs officers on American soil, the expanded jurisdiction of vice-admiralty courts, and the nature of the instructions given to American governors by their superiors in London. The document exhibited none of the hesitation that had characterized colonial claims in the mid-1760s. No longer were resistance leaders—at least in Boston—preoccupied with defining the limits of parliamentary authority. No longer did they mention the necessity of obedience to Parliament. They placed colonial rights first, loyalty to Britain a distant second.

The responses to the committee's pamphlet confirmed this shift in thinking. Some towns disagreed with Boston's assessment, but most aligned themselves with the city. The town of Holden declared, "the People of New England have never given the People of Britain any Right of Jurisdiction over us." Pownallborough warned, "Allegiance is a relative Term and like Kingdoms and commonwealths is local and has its bounds."

5-6 Tea and Turmoil

▶ **How did Parliament respond to Boston's reaction against the Tea Act?**

The tea tax was the only Townshend duty still in effect by 1773. In the years after 1770, some Americans had continued to boycott English tea, while many resumed drinking it. Tea figured prominently in both the colonists' diet and their cultures, so observing the boycott required them not only to forgo a favorite beverage but also to alter their everyday rituals. Tea thus retained an explosively symbolic character even after the boycott began to disintegrate.

5-6a Reactions to the Tea Act

In May 1773, Parliament passed an act designed to save the East India Company from bankruptcy. The company, which held a monopoly on British trade with the East Indies, was vital to the British economy and to the

prosperity of many British politicians who invested in its stock. According to the **Tea Act**, tea would be sold in America only by agents of the East India Company. This would enable the company to avoid intermediaries in Britain and the colonies, and thus to price its tea competitively with that sold by smugglers. The net result would be cheaper tea for American consumers. But since the less expensive tea would still be taxed under the Townshend law, resistance leaders interpreted the new measure as another attempt to make them admit Parliament's right to tax them. Others saw the Tea Act as the first step in creating an East India Company monopoly on colonial trade. Residents of the four cities designated to receive the first shipments of tea accordingly prepared to respond to this perceived new threat to their freedom.

A tea ship sent to New York City never arrived. In Philadelphia, Pennsylvania's governor persuaded the captain to sail back to Britain. Tea bound for Charleston was unloaded and stored there; some was destroyed, and the rest was later sold by the new state government. The only confrontation occurred in Boston.

The first of three tea ships, the *Dartmouth*, entered Boston harbor on November 28. Customs laws required cargo to be landed and the appropriate duty paid by its owners within twenty days of a ship's arrival; otherwise, customs officers would seize the cargo. After a series of mass meetings, Bostonians voted to post guards on the wharf to prevent the tea from being unloaded. Hutchinson refused to permit the vessels to leave the harbor. On December 16, a day before the cargo was to be confiscated, more than five thousand people crowded into Old South Church. The meeting, chaired by Samuel Adams, made a final attempt to convince Hutchinson to return the tea to England. (The merchants who had consigned the tea had long since refused to do so.) But the governor remained adamant. In the early evening Adams reportedly announced "that they had now done all they could for the Salvation of their Country." Cries rang out from the crowd: "Boston harbor a tea-pot tonight! The Mohawks are come!" Within a few minutes, about sixty men—merchants and doctors as well as Boston artisans and country farmers—crudely disguised as Native men assembled at the wharf. Moving quickly, they boarded the three ships and dumped their cargo into the harbor. By 9:00 P.M., 342 chests of tea worth approximately £10,000 floated in splinters. John Adams praised the crowd's action. "There is a Dignity, a Majesty, a Sublimity in this last Effort of the Patriots, that I greatly admire," he wrote in his diary. "This Destruction of the Tea is so bold, so daring, so firm, intrepid and inflexible, and it must have so important Consequences, and so lasting, that I cant but consider it as an Epocha in History." He also recognized the violence of the moment, noting that "Many Persons wish, that as many dead Carcasses were floating in the Harbour, as there are Chests of Tea."

Tea Act England's attempt to bail out the East India Company that heightened tensions between the British and the colonies.

5-6b Coercive, or Intolerable Acts and the Quebec Act

The North administration reacted with outrage when it learned of the events in Boston. In March 1774, Parliament adopted the first of four laws that colonists referred to as the **Coercive, or Intolerable, Acts.** It ordered the port of Boston closed until the tea was paid for, prohibiting all but coastal trade in food and firewood. Later that spring, Parliament passed three other punitive measures. The Massachusetts Government Act altered the province's charter, substituting an appointed council for the elected one, increasing the governor's powers, and forbidding most town meetings. The Justice Act allowed a person accused of committing murder in the course of suppressing a riot or enforcing the laws to be tried outside the colony where the incident had occurred. Finally, the Quartering Act permitted military officers to commandeer privately owned buildings to house their troops. The Coercive Acts punished not only Boston but also Massachusetts as a whole, alerting other colonies to the possibility that their residents, too, might face retaliation if they opposed British authority.

Parliament next turned its attention to much-needed reforms in the government of Quebec. The Quebec Act became linked with the Coercive Acts in the minds of the colonial insurgents. Intended to ease strains that had arisen since the British conquest of the formerly French colony, the Quebec Act granted greater religious freedom to Catholics, alarming Protestant colonists who equated the Church of Rome with despotism. In an attempt to provide northern Indians with some protection against Anglo-American settlement, the act also annexed to Quebec the area west of the Appalachians, east of the Mississippi River, and north of the Ohio River. That region, still with few European inhabitants, was thus removed from the jurisdiction of the seacoast colonies. The wealthy speculators who hoped to develop the Ohio Country to attract additional settlers would now have to deal with officials in Quebec.

Members of Parliament who supported the punitive legislation believed they had finally solved the American problem. But resistance leaders saw the Coercive Acts and the Quebec Act as proof of what they had long feared: that Britain had embarked on a deliberate plan to oppress them. If the port of Boston could be closed, why not the ports of Philadelphia or New York? If the royal charter of Massachusetts could be changed, why not the charter of South Carolina? If certain suspects could be tried in distant locations, why not any violator of any law? If troops could be forcibly quartered in private houses, did that not portend the occupation of all America? If the Catholic Church could receive protection in Quebec, why not everywhere? It seemed as though the plot against American rights and liberties had at last been laid bare.

The Boston Committee of Correspondence urged all colonies to join an immediate boycott of British goods. But other provinces hesitated to take such a drastic step. In the West Indies, even opponents of Parliament's evolving American policy thought the "Boston firebrands" had gone too far and hoped the Coercive Acts might restore order. Rhode Island, Virginia, and Pennsylvania each suggested convening another intercolonial congress like the one that had followed the Stamp Act. Few people wanted to take hasty action; even the most ardent patriots remained loyal Britons and hoped for reconciliation. So the colonies agreed to send delegates to Philadelphia in September to attend a Continental Congress.

5-7 The Unsettled Backcountry

▶ **What disputes emerged between elites and common folk during the imperial crisis?**

▶ **How did these internal struggles develop during the imperial crisis?**

In the same years that residents of British North America wrestled over deepening divisions between the colonies and the mother country, they confronted divisions *within* colonial society. For a century, historians have debated the relative importance of struggles over home rule—the imperial crisis—and battles over who should rule at home—social crises within the colonies—to the coming of the Revolution. Rifts between elites and common folk were visible everywhere in the mainland and island colonies: between merchants and the laboring poor in the cities, between tenants and landlords in the backcountry, between slaves and planters in the South and the Caribbean. Along the western edges of British settlement in the 1760s and 1770s, these internal struggles sometimes verged on civil war.

5-7a Land Riots in the North

By midcentury, most of the fertile land east of the Appalachians had been purchased—sometimes fraudulently—or occupied—often illegally. Conflicts over land grew in number and frequency. As early as 1746, some New Jersey farmers clashed violently with agents of the East Jersey proprietors, who claimed the farmers' land and demanded annual payments for the use of the property. Similar violence occurred in the 1760s in the region that later became Vermont.

The most serious land riots took place along the Hudson River in 1765–1766. Late in the seventeenth century, the governor of New York had granted huge tracts in the lower Hudson Valley to prominent families. The proprietors in turn divided these estates into small farms, which they rented to

Coercive, or Intolerable, Acts A series of restrictive laws comprised of the Boston Port Bill, the Massachusetts Government Act, the Justice Act, the Quartering Act, plus the subsequent Quebec Act. Intended by the British Parliament to primarily punish Massachusetts, the acts instead pushed most colonies to the brink of rebellion.

poor Dutch and German migrants who saw tenancy as a step on the road to independent freeholder status. But in the eighteenth century, newcomers from New England and Europe resisted this tenancy system. Many squatted on vacant portions of great estates, rejecting attempts to evict them. In the mid-1760s, the Philipse family sued farmers who had lived on Philipse land for two decades. The courts upheld the landlords' claim, ordering the squatters to make way for tenants with valid leases. A diverse group of farmers rebelled, terrorizing proprietors and loyal tenants, freeing their friends from jail, and on one occasion battling a county sheriff and his posse. The rebellion lasted nearly a year, ending only when British troops captured its leaders.

Such clashes increased in intensity and frequency after the Seven Years' War. Ignoring the Proclamation of 1763, pronouncements by colonial governors, and the threat of Native attacks, land-hungry folk—many of them recent immigrants from Ireland or soldiers who demobilized after the war—swarmed into the Ohio River valley. Sometimes, they purchased property from opportunists with grants of dubious origin; often, they simply claimed land, squatting in hopes that their titles would eventually be honored. Britain's 1771 decision to abandon (and raze) Fort Pitt rendered the Proclamation of 1763 unenforceable, and thus removed the final restraints on settlement in the region. By the mid-1770s, thousands of new homesteads dotted the backcountry from western Pennsylvania south through Virginia and eastern Kentucky into western North Carolina. Their presence provoked confrontations with eastern landowners and Native peoples alike.

5-7b "Regulators" in the South

The Regulator movements of the late 1760s and early 1770s pitted backcountry farmers in the Carolinas against wealthy eastern planters who controlled the colonial governments. In South Carolina, Scots-Irish settlers protested their lack of an adequate voice in colonial political affairs. For months, they policed the countryside in vigilante bands known as Regulators, complaining of lax and biased law enforcement. North Carolina Regulators objected primarily to heavy taxation by the colonial legislature. In 1769, they seated men who held their views in the provincial assembly. The backcountry legislators proposed more equitable tax policies and greater freedom from the established Anglican Church. But their grievances were soon sidelined by battles over the Townshend duties. In September 1770, the Regulators took vigilante action, dragging a justice from the Rowan County Courthouse and then ransacking his home. In form, the crowd's action echoed the destruction of Thomas Hutchinson's Boston mansion in 1765. But in content, the farmers' grievances were very different, focused on local inequality rather than imperial tyranny. The following spring, insurrection became war. Several thousand Regulators fought and lost a battle with eastern militiamen at Alamance in May 1771. A month later, six of the insurgents were hanged for treason.

5-7c Renewed Warfare with Native Peoples

In addition to distrusting their wealthy eastern rulers, few of the backcountry folk viewed the region's Native peoples positively. (Rare exceptions were the Moravian missionaries who settled with their Native converts in small frontier communities in the upper Ohio Valley.) The frontier dwellers had little interest in the small-scale trade that had once helped to sustain an uneasy peace in the region; they wanted only land on which to grow crops and pasture their livestock.

In 1774 Virginia, headed by a new royally appointed governor, **Lord Dunmore**, moved vigorously to assert its title to the colony's rapidly developing backcountry. Tensions mounted as Virginians surveyed land on the south side of the Ohio River—territory claimed by the Shawnees. In April, armed settlers attacked a Shawnee canoe carrying women and children as well as one man, murdering and scalping all nine. John Logan, a Mingo leader whose kin died in the attack, gathered warriors to retaliate against frontier settlements. When the governor dispatched some two thousand troops to move against Native villages along the Ohio, these skirmishes escalated into a conflict known as **Lord Dunmore's War**. Delawares, Miamis, Chippewas, and Wyandots allied with the Shawnee, and fighting continued throughout the summer. When the peace was settled in October, the Shawnee leader Cornstalk ceded the enormous territory that became the state of Kentucky to Dunmore's forces. Thousands of settlers then flooded across the mountains.

5-8 Government by Congress and Committee

▶ What did it mean to be "American" on the eve of the First Continental Congress?

▶ What tasks did the First Continental Congress complete?

▶ How did the First Continental Congress encourage and facilitate shared resistance to parliamentary actions by many of the seaboard colonies?

In the summer of 1774, while the Virginia backcountry bled and Boston suffered, fifty-six delegates from twelve very different mainland colonies readied for a "Grand Continental Congress" in Philadelphia. Because colonial governors had forbidden regular assemblies to conduct formal elections, most of the delegates had been chosen

Lord Dunmore Royal governor of Virginia who promised freedom to the slaves of rebel owners who fought to restore royal authority.

Lord Dunmore's War Confrontation between Virginians and the Shawnee people in 1774. During the peace conference that followed, Virginia gained uncontested rights to lands south of the Ohio country in exchange for its claims on the northern side.

by extralegal conventions. Thus the very act of designating representatives to attend the Congress asserted colonial autonomy in defiance of British authority. The lawyer John Adams, one of four delegates from hard-hit Massachusetts, anticipated that the Congress would serve as "a School of Political Prophets I Suppose—a Nursery of American Statesmen."

But what were American statesmen and what, indeed, was America? New England merchants, many of whom were descendants of stringent Puritans, and southern planters, with their slaves and their horse races and their finery, shared little common culture. (One Rhode Islander complained that because "Southern Gentlemen have been used to do no Business in the afternoon," Congress had to adjourn by three o'clock.) So distinct were the interests of the British West Indies that those thirteen colonies sent no official delegates—nor did Georgia. British North America had no capital city but London; until Congress met, more of the delegates had probably visited the English metropolis than had journeyed to Philadelphia. On the road to Pennsylvania, John Adams paused to admire the statue of the king looming over Battery Park in New York City, a town he had never before visited. Even in the fall of 1774, as tavern talk throughout the colonies turned to the imminence of civil war, Great Britain remained the only nation the congressmen shared. They called themselves "the Inhabitants of the English colonies," descendants of "free and natural-born subjects, within the realm of England." They pledged their fealty to George III. They pressed their claims not for American freedom but for "English liberty"; an image of the Magna Carta adorned the journal of their proceedings. "We uphold this, we lean upon this," read the Latin motto around the seal.

5-8a First Continental Congress

The colonies' leading political figures—most of them lawyers, merchants, and planters—attended the Philadelphia Congress. In addition to John Adams, the Massachusetts delegation included his elder cousin Samuel Adams. Among others, New York sent John Jay, a talented young attorney. John Dickinson, author of the homespun *Letters from a Farmer in Pennsylvania*, arrived in Philadelphia in a resplendent coach with four horses. Virginia elected Richard Henry Lee and Patrick Henry, both noted for their patriotic zeal, as well as George Washington. Most of these men had never met, but in the weeks, months, and years that followed they became the chief architects of a new nation.

The congressmen faced three tasks when they convened at Carpenters' Hall. The first two were explicit: defining American grievances and developing a plan for resistance. The third—articulating their constitutional relationship with Great Britain—was less clear-cut and proved nettlesome. The most radical congressmen, like Lee of Virginia, argued that colonists owed allegiance only to George III; Parliament had no legitimate authority over them. The conservatives—Pennsylvania's Joseph

Galloway and his allies—proposed a plan of union that would require Parliament and a new American legislature jointly to consent to laws governing the colonies. After heated debate, delegates narrowly rejected Galloway's proposal, but they were not prepared to embrace the radicals' position either.

Finally, they accepted wording proposed by John Adams. The crucial clauses in the Congress's Declaration of Rights and Grievances asserted that Americans would obey Parliament, but only voluntarily, and that they would resist all measures that were taxes in disguise. Only a few years before, such a position would have seemed radical. By the fall of 1774, it represented a compromise. The Americans had come a long way since the failure of the Albany Plan of Union in 1754, and even since their protests against the Sugar Act ten years later.

5-8b Continental Association

With the constitutional issue resolved, the delegates readily agreed on the laws they wanted repealed (notably the Coercive Acts) and decided to implement an economic boycott while petitioning the king for relief. They adopted fourteen Articles of Association calling for nonimportation of British goods (effective December 1, 1774), nonconsumption of British products (effective March 1, 1775), and nonexportation of American goods to Britain and the British West Indies (effective September 10, 1775).

The Articles of Association (also known as the Continental Association) were designed to appeal to different groups and regions. The nonimportation agreement banned commerce in slaves as well as manufactures, which accorded with a long-standing desire of the Virginia gentry to halt, or at least to slow, the arrival of enslaved Africans on their shores. (Leading Virginians were not opposed to slavery, but rather worried that continuing slave importations discouraged skilled Europeans from immigrating to their colony. They also knew that their enslaved workforce would continue to grow by natural increase.) Delaying nonconsumption for three months after implementing nonimportation gave merchants time to sell off the inventory they had acquired legally. The novel tactic of nonexportation and its postponement for nearly a year served other interests. In 1773, many Virginians had vowed to stop exporting tobacco in order to decrease supply and thus raise prices in a then-glutted market. Now, two years later, they welcomed an association that declared but delayed the export ban, allowing them to profit from higher prices for their current crop. Postponing the nonexportation agreement also benefited northern exporters of wood and foodstuffs to the Caribbean, giving them a final season of sales before the embargo began.

For all these concessions, the Continental Association was far more comprehensive than any previous economic measure adopted by the colonies, and it asked a great deal of the public. "We must change our Habits, our Prejudices, our Palates, our Taste in Dress, Furniture, Equipage, Architecture etc.," John Adams wrote. "Will, Can the People bear a total Interruption of the [We]st India Trade?" fretted one New York delegate. "Can [they] live without Rum, Sugar, and [Mo]lasses?" West Indian grandees worried about more than impatience. Severing their supply lines from North America could mean famine, and famine could provoke widespread slave insurrection. The *Antigua Gazette* chided the mainland colonists for "their folly, madness, and ingratitude" in adopting the new resolutions. "I look at them as dogs that will bark but dare not stand when opposed," wrote one Jamaican sugar planter who hoped Congress would prove "loud in mouth but slow to action."

5-8c Committees of Observation

To enforce the Continental Association, Congress recommended that every mainland locale elect committees of

Library of Congress, Prints & Photographs Division, Reproduction number LC-US262-45386 (b&w film copy neg.)

A New Method of MACARONY MAKING, as practised at BOSTON.

▲ This British cartoon, entitled "A New Method of Macaroni-Making, as Practised at Boston," satirizes the violence of patriot resistance. The practice of tarring and feathering those seen as enemies of American liberty was first recorded in 1766. Incidents multiplied after the Boston Tea Party. By the summer of 1774, vigilante justice against loyalists included many terrifying rituals: horses were poisoned, wives and children harassed. "One person was put in a coffin, and was near buried alive," a Boston customs official wrote.

observation and inspection. By specifying that committee members be chosen by all men qualified to vote for members of the lower houses of assembly, Congress guaranteed the committees a broad popular base. The seven to eight thousand committeemen—some experienced officeholders, some new to politics—became the local leaders of American resistance.

Such committees were officially charged only with overseeing implementation of the boycott, but during the next six months they became de facto governments. They examined merchants' records, publicizing the names of those who continued to import British goods. They promoted home manufactures, encouraging Americans to adopt simple modes of dress and behavior to symbolize their commitment to liberty. Because expensive leisure-time activities were believed to reflect vice and corruption, Congress urged Americans to forgo dancing, gambling, horse racing, card playing, cockfighting, and other forms of "extravagance and dissipation." Some committees extracted apologies from people caught gambling, drinking to excess, or racing. Everywhere, private activities acquired public significance.

The committees gradually extended their authority over many aspects of colonial life. They attempted to root out and sometimes terrorize opponents of American resistance, developed elaborate spy networks, and investigated reports of questionable activities. Suspected dissenters were urged to support the colonial cause publicly; if they refused, the committees had them watched, restricted their movements, or even tried to force them into exile. People engaging in political banter with friends one day could find themselves charged with "treasonable conversation" the next. One Massachusetts man was called before his local committee for maligning the Congress as "a Pack or Parcell of Fools" that was "as tyrannical as Lord North." When he refused to recant, the committee put him under surveillance.

5-8d Provincial Conventions

While the committees of observation expanded their power, the regular colonial governments edged toward collapse. By late 1774, only a few legislatures continued to meet without encountering challenges to their authority. In most colonies, popularly elected provincial conventions took over the task of running the government. In late 1774 and early 1775, these conventions approved the Continental Association, elected delegates to a Second Continental Congress (scheduled for May), organized militia units, and gathered arms and ammunition. British-appointed governors and councils saw their authority crumble. Royal officials suffered repeated humiliation. Courts were prevented from meeting, taxes were paid to convention agents rather than to provincial tax collectors, and militiamen mustered only when committees ordered. During the six months preceding the battles at Lexington and Concord, ordinary Americans forged independence at the local level, without formal acknowledgment and for the most part without bloodshed.

Women's Political Activism

In the twenty-first century, female citizens of the United States participate at every level of American public life. In 1984, Geraldine Ferraro was the Democratic candidate for vice president, the first woman on a major party ticket. In 2007, Nancy Pelosi was elected Speaker of the House, and Senator Hillary Rodham Clinton (D-NY) began her first run for the presidency. A record number of women were elected to the 114th Congress, whose term began in 2015: twenty serve in the Senate, and eighty-four in the House, or nearly 20 percent of each branch of the legislature. Three women currently serve as Supreme Court justices. After her losing presidential bid in 2008, Hillary Clinton was appointed Secretary of State from 2009-2013, and in 2016 accepted the Democratic nomination for president, the first woman to head a major party ticket. Often, the opposition to Clinton's failed bid to "shatter the highest glass ceiling," as she often put it, defaulted gendered stereotypes that would have been familiar to the men assembled in Congress in 1776.

Though the existence of female politicians today would have shocked those "founding fathers," the entrance of American women onto the political stage in some ways links back to the changes of the revolutionary era. Before the 1760s, women were seen as having no legitimate public role. A male essayist expressed the consensus in the mid-1730s: "Governing Kingdoms and Ruling Provinces are Things too difficult and knotty for the fair Sex." But when colonists began to resist British taxes and laws in the 1760s, traditional forms of protest (for example, assemblies' petitions to Parliament) came to seem too limited. Because women made purchasing decisions for American households, and because their labor in spinning and textile manufacture could replace imported clothing, it was vital for them to participate in the cause. For the first time in American history, women began to take formal political stands. Women of all ranks had to decide whether they would join or oppose the movement to boycott British goods. The groups they established to promote home manufactures—dubbed "Daughters of Liberty"—constituted the first American women's political organizations.

By the mid-nineteenth century, women's political involvement would begin to coalesce into a national "woman movement." In 1848, the leaders of a woman's rights convention at Seneca Falls, New York, drafted a Declaration of Sentiments, closely modeled on the language of the Declaration of Independence. The radical Victoria Woodhull, the first woman to run for president, declared her candidacy in 1871.

The legacy of revolutionary-era women for the nation continues today in such diverse groups as Emily's List and Concerned Women for America. Indeed, contemporary Americans would undoubtedly find it impossible to imagine their country without female activists of all political and partisan affiliations.

CRITICAL THINKING

- Despite great progress in terms of women's involvement in American politics, do vestiges of that consensus of the mid-1730s—the sense that "Governing Kingdoms and Ruling Provinces are Things too difficult and knotty for the fair Sex"—still remain? If so, provide examples.

Living in the muddle of the everyday without the clarity of hindsight, few Americans realized the extent of this political evolution. The vast majority still proclaimed their loyalty to Great Britain, denying that they sought to leave the empire. "Some People must have Time to look around them, before, behind, on the right hand, and on the left, then to think, and after all this to resolve," wrote John Adams in June 1776. "Others see, at one intuitive Glance into the past and the future, and judge with Precision at once. But remember you cant make thirteen Clocks, Strike precisely alike, at the Same Second." Even on the eve of the Declaration of Independence, each of the thirteen rebel colonies moved in its own way and time.

Summary

In 1754, at the outbreak of the Seven Years' War in the Ohio Country, no one could have predicted that the next two decades would bring such dramatic change to Britain's mainland colonies. Yet that conflict simultaneously removed France from North America and created a huge debt that Britain had to find means to pay, developments with major implications for the imperial relationship.

After the war ended in 1763, colonists experienced momentous changes in the ways they imagined themselves and their allegiances. The number who considered themselves political actors increased substantially. Once linked unquestioningly to Great Britain, many mainland colonists began slowly to develop a sense of their shared identity as Americans. They started to realize that their concept of the political process differed from that of people in the mother country, and that they held a different definition of what constituted representation and appropriate consent to government actions. Many also came to understand their economic interests as distinct from those of Great Britain. Colonial political leaders reached such conclusions only after a long train of events, some of them violent.

While many colonists questioned the imperial relationship with Britain, violence in the backcountry revealed persistent divisions *within* American society. From New England to the Carolinas, small western farmers sporadically battled large eastern landowners. In the 1760s and early 1770s, Regulator movements in the Carolinas assumed the proportions of guerilla warfare, as did battles between frontier settlers and displaced Native peoples in Virginia in 1774.

In late 1774, many Americans were committed to resistance but almost none to independence. Even so, they had begun to sever the bonds of empire. Over the next decades, they would forge a new American nationality to replace frayed Anglo-American ties.

Suggestions for Further Reading

Fred Anderson, *The War That Made America: A Short History of the French and Indian War* (2005)

Richard Archer, *As If an Enemy's Country: The British Occupation of Boston and the Origins of Revolution* (2010)

Christopher Leslie Brown, *Moral Capital: Foundations of British Abolitionism* (2006)

Nick Bunker, *An Empire on the Edge: How Britain Came to Fight America* (2014)

Stephen Brumwell, *Redcoats: The British Soldier and War in the Americas, 1755-1763* (2002)

Vincent Caretta, *Phillis Wheatley: Biography of a Genius in Bondage* (2011)

Benjamin H. Irvin, *Clothed in Robes of Sovereignty: The Continental Congress and the People out of Doors* (2011)

Marjoleine Kars, *Breaking Loose Together: The Regulator Rebellion in Pre-Revolutionary North Carolina* (2002)

Andrew Jackson O'Shaughnessy, *An Empire Divided: The American Revolution and the British Caribbean* (2000)

Peter Silver, *Our Savage Neighbors: How Indian War Transformed Early America* (2008)

MINDTAP
From Cengage

American Revolutions, 1775–1783

The Mohawks knew her as Konwatsitsiaenni, a leader in the Turtle clan. To the British, she was Molly Brant, common-law wife of the continent's most powerful Native American agent, Sir William Johnson. Their union—never formalized by a preacher or a judge—was a diplomatic alliance from which he gained as much as she did. After the Seven Years' War, Molly Brant became the first lady of Mohawk country, one of the busiest trading regions in the Atlantic world. Her power and influence, wrote one British official, was "far superior to that of all their Chiefs put together."

In the 1760s, people of all nations journeyed to Johnson Hall, the English-style manor that Brant shared with Johnson and their growing biracial family. Perched high above the Mohawk River, the house was the nerve center of an estate that stretched for miles. Iroquois diplomats, British officials, Dutch traders, Anglo-American speculators and politicians: all flocked to a place where they might smoke the calumet and drink tea served by African slaves, bury the hatchet and play billiards, and view a collection including English silver and Algonquian wampum. Worlds met and mingled at Johnson Hall, and in Molly Brant. She wore Mohawk dress and refused to speak English; Johnson spoke Mohawk and sometimes painted his face in the manner of Native warriors. Yet Brant and Johnson named four of their eight mixed-race children after British monarchs: Mary, Elizabeth, Anne, and George.

William Johnson died in 1774, on the eve of a war that would destroy the world he and Molly Brant had built at the western edge of Britain's empire. As Brant returned to her home village of Canajoharie, Mohawk country was transformed from a meeting ground into a battleground. When American rebels took up arms against King George, Molly and her younger brother Joseph rallied the Mohawks behind the British, who were grateful for her support. A leading loyalist noted, "one word from her is more taken notice of by the Five Nations than a thousand from any white man." The Oneidas threw in with

◄ No likeness of Molly Brant survives, but her brother Joseph was depicted by several leading artists. The American-born Gilbert Stuart painted this portrait in London, where Brant journeyed twice to plead the cause of his people. Brant wears the costume of a high-ranking Mohawk, along with a gorget (throat armor) and locket bearing the profile of George III. Fine Art/Getty Images

Chronology

1775	■ Battles of Lexington and Concord; first shots of war fired
	■ Siege of Boston begins
	■ Second Continental Congress begins
	■ Washington named commander-in-chief of Continental army
	■ "Olive Branch" petition seeks reconciliation with Britain
	■ Dunmore's proclamation offers freedom to Virginia patriots' slaves who join British forces
1776	■ Thomas Paine advocates American independence in *Common Sense*
	■ British evacuate Boston
	■ Second Continental Congress directs states to draft constitutions
	■ Declaration of Independence adopted
	■ Great Jamaica slave revolt
	■ New York City falls to British
1777	■ Articles of Confederation sent to states for ratification
	■ Philadelphia falls to British
	■ Burgoyne surrenders at Saratoga
1778	■ French alliance brings vital assistance to America
	■ British evacuate Philadelphia
1779	■ Sullivan expedition destroys Iroquois villages
1780	■ Charleston falls to British
1781	■ Articles of Confederation ratified
	■ Americans take Yorktown; Cornwallis surrenders
1782	■ British victory over French at Battle of the Saintes secures Jamaica
	■ Peace negotiations begin
1783	■ Treaty of Paris grants independence to the United States

the patriots, who professed themselves "afraid" that Brant's "influence may give us some trouble."

Through the summer of 1777, Mohawk country burned and bled. Johnson Hall stood empty, abandoned. As the Continentals advanced through the valley, Molly Brant apprised the British of the rebels' movements. Tipped off by Brant, pro-British militia and Mohawk warriors ambushed American forces and their Oneida allies at the village of Oriskany (Oriske) that August. The daylong battle left two hundred patriots and fifty loyalists dead. Joseph Brant's Mohawks torched what remained of Oriskany; Oneida and American troops razed Canajoharie. Soldiers plundered Molly Brant's house and carried off wagonloads of her possessions. Her people became refugees, hounded and sometimes horsewhipped by patriot forces as they marched north to seek shelter at Fort Niagara.

After the war, Molly Brant settled in the town of Kingston, in the new British colony of Upper Canada. She later told Britain's Loyalist Claims Commission that she was "not at all reconciled to this place & Country," where she found herself "an entire stranger." But there was no going back. In compensation for all she had done and for all she had lost, the British government awarded her an annual pension of £100. Her daughters married Canadian officials. Only her surviving son chose to live among the Iroquois, in the new Six Nations reserve on Grand River, north of the new national border dividing what had once been his mother's homeland.

Experience an interactive version of this story in MindTap®.

The American Revolution created an enduring republic from thirteen separate colonies—the "thirteen clocks" John Adams described in June 1776. But as Molly Brant's experience shows, it was also a bloody civil war affecting much of North America, often in unpredictable ways. The fighting uprooted countless families and forced roughly sixty thousand loyalists—black, white, and Native— into exile. The rupture of trading relationships between colonies and empire wreaked havoc upon the American economy. Much more than a series of clashes between armies, the war for independence marks the beginning of the history of the United States and, indeed, a significant turning point in the shaping of the modern world.

The struggle for independence required revolutionary leaders to accomplish three closely related aims. The first was political and ideological: transforming a loyal resistance into a movement demanding separation from Britain. Pursuing a variety of measures ranging from persuasion to coercion, the colonies' elected officials worked to enlist all European Americans in the patriot cause, and to ensure the neutrality of Native peoples and slaves in the conflict.

To win independence, patriot leaders also needed to secure international recognition and aid, particularly from France. Thus they dispatched to Paris the most experienced American diplomat, Benjamin Franklin, who had served for years as a colonial agent in London. Franklin skillfully negotiated the Franco-American alliance of 1778, which proved crucial to the American war effort.

Only the third task directly involved the British. George Washington, named commander-in-chief of the American army in the summer of 1775, soon recognized that his primary goal should be not to win battles so much as to avoid losing them decisively. The outcome of any one battle was less important than preserving his army to fight another day. Consequently, the story of the Revolutionary War often unfolds in British action and American reaction, British attacks and American defenses and withdrawals.

The challenges the rebellion presented to the British army aided the American war effort. King George's fighting forces—at least 100,000 men over the course of the war—had to cross 3,000 miles of ocean. Over such vast distances, men, materiel, and vital news traveled achingly slowly. The theater of war was immense, stretching from the Caribbean to the North Atlantic, and from the seacoast to the Appalachians. And the colonial disunity John Adams noted created challenges of its own. The United Colonies had no single capital whose conquest would crush the rebellion; instead of fighting a dragon, the British army confronted a many-headed Hydra. Against an enemy so various and dispersed, priorities were difficult to assign, especially after the entry of the French on the American side. Was it more important to punish Massachusetts than to preserve Jamaica? Faced with such strategic complexities, British military planners made grave errors. In the end, the Americans' improbable triumph owed as much to their geography, their endurance, and their enemy's missteps as to their own military prowess.

American victories on the battlefield violently severed the political bonds tying thirteen of the former colonies to Great Britain. But military success does not alone make a nation. To make thirteen clocks strike as one, as John Adams and other patriot leaders knew, required profound changes in politics, culture, and society. Through the years of war and long after the signing of the peace, Americans experimented with everything from the structure of their governments to the appearance of their money. The new nation layered new rituals and new identities atop older bonds of kin, church, and community. The triumph of the Continental army only began the long work of creating the United States.

- *What choices of allegiance confronted residents of North America after 1774? Why did people make the choices they did?*

- *What strategies did the British and American military forces adopt, and why?*

- *How did the United States win independence and forge the outlines of a new national government?*

6-1 Toward War

▶ **How did the military conflict between the British and the American colonies unfold in 1775–1776?**

▶ **What beliefs guided the British in prosecuting the war, and what were the consequences of those?**

▶ **What issues did the Second Continental Congress need to address?**

On January 27, 1775, Lord Dartmouth, Britain's secretary of state for America, addressed a fateful letter to General Thomas Gage in Boston, urging him to act. Opposition could not be "very formidable," Dartmouth wrote. Even if it were, "better that the Conflict should be brought on, upon such ground, than in a riper state of Rebellion." Gage, in short, should take the offensive. Now.

6-1a Battles of Lexington and Concord

Gage, the commander-in-chief of Britain's forces in America and, since the departure of Thomas Hutchinson, also the governor of Massachusetts, received Dartmouth's letter on April 14. He quickly dispatched an expedition to confiscate the stockpile of colonial military supplies at Concord. Bostonians learned of the impending seizure and sent two messengers, William Dawes and Paul Revere (later joined by Dr. Samuel Prescott), to rouse the countryside. When the vanguard of several hundred British regulars (a commonly used term for soldiers in the British Army) approached Lexington at dawn on April 19, they found a ragtag group of seventy

Plate II. A View of the Town of Concord.

▲ In 1775, an unknown artist painted the redcoats entering Concord. The fighting at North Bridge, which occurred just a few hours after this triumphal entry, signaled the start of open warfare between Britain and the colonies.

militiamen—about half the town's adult men—mustered on the common. Realizing that their small force could not halt the redcoats' advance, the Americans' commander ordered his force to withdraw. But as they dispersed, a shot rang out. British soldiers then fired several volleys. When they stopped, eight Americans lay dead, and another ten had been wounded. The British marched on to Concord, five miles away.

There the contingents of colonial militia were larger, reinforced by men from nearby towns. An exchange of gunfire at the North Bridge spilled the first British blood of the Revolution: three regulars were killed and nine wounded. Then thousands of militiamen hidden in houses and behind trees fired at the British forces as they retreated toward Boston. By day's end, the redcoats had suffered 272 casualties, including 70 deaths. The Americans suffered just 93 casualties.

The outbreak of war, long anticipated, was nonetheless shocking to those who experienced it. Subtle and shifting allegiances resolved, sometimes suddenly, into sides. Patriot printers decried the "Bloody Butchery" perpetrated by the British troops and eulogized "the deceased worthies, who died gloriously fighting in the cause of liberty." Others lost sympathy for the insurgents. "My hand trembles while I inform you that the Sword of Civil War is now unsheathd," wrote the engraver Henry Pelham to his half-brother, the painter John Singleton Copley, then in Italy. Pelham thought the British regulars "the Bravest and best Disciplined troops

that ever Europe Bred," while the patriot militia were blood-thirsty "Rebels" who "skulk'd behind trees."

6-1b The Siege of Boston

By April 20, some twenty thousand American militiamen had gathered around Boston. Many soon went home for spring planting, but those who remained, along with newer recruits, were organized into formal units. Officers under the command of General Artemas Ward of the Massachusetts militia ordered that latrines be dug, foodstuffs purchased, military discipline enforced, and defensive fortifications constructed.

Boston, which the colonists and the British alike saw as the cradle of the rebellion, was thus besieged by patriot militia whose presence effectively confined Gage's forces within the beleaguered town. Within weeks, some ten thousand of the city's sixteen thousand inhabitants—most of them patriot sympathizers—had fled into the surrounding countryside. "You'll see parents that are lucky enough to procure papers, with bundles in one hand and a string of children in the other, wandering out of the town … not knowing whither they'll go," wrote one man who hoped he too might "escape with the skin of my teeth." As supporters of the rebellion streamed over the narrow neck separating Boston from the mainland, loyalist refugees—subject to vigilant assaults in the countryside—flowed in the opposite direction, straggling into town to seek the protection of British troops. By late May, fresh food was running low. In August, smallpox claimed dozens; dysentery ravaged hundreds more. As winter descended, Gage's troops tore down houses, bridges, boardwalks, even the Old North Church, burning the lumber for fuel.

For nearly a year, the two armies eyed each other across the battlements. The redcoats attacked their besiegers only once, on June 17, when they drove the Americans from trenches atop Breed's Hill in Charlestown. In that misnamed Battle of Bunker Hill, the British incurred their greatest casualties of the entire war: more than 800 wounded and 228 killed. Though forced to abandon their position, the Americans lost less than half that number.

6-1c First Year of War

During the same eleven-month period, patriots easily captured Fort Ticonderoga, a British outpost on Lake Champlain, acquiring much-needed cannon. Trying to bring Canada into the war on the American side, they also mounted a northern campaign that ended in disaster at Quebec in early 1776. But the chief significance of the war's first year lay in the long lull in fighting between the main armies at Boston. The delay gave both sides a chance to organize and plan their strategies.

Prime Minister Lord North and his new American secretary, Lord George Germain, made three central assumptions about the war they faced. First, they forecast that patriot forces could not long withstand the assaults of trained British regulars, and that the 1776 campaign would therefore prove decisive. Accordingly, they dispatched to America the largest fighting force Great Britain had ever assembled: 370 transport ships carrying 32,000 troops, accompanied by 73 naval vessels and 13,000 sailors. Among the troops were thousands of professional German soldiers (many from the state of Hesse); the rulers of their principalities had hired them out to Britain. Second, British officials and army officers believed that capturing major cities—a central aim in European warfare—would defeat the rebel army. Third, they assumed that a clear-cut military victory would regain the colonies' allegiance.

All three assumptions proved false. North and Germain vastly underestimated Americans' commitment to armed resistance. Battlefield defeats did not lead patriots to abandon their political aims and sue for peace. London officials also failed to recognize the significance of the American population's dispersal over an area 1,500 miles long and more than 100 miles wide. Although Britain would control each of the largest mainland ports at some time during the war, less than 5 percent of the American population lived in those cities. The coast offered so many excellent harbors that essential commerce was easily rerouted. Capturing cities consumed vital British resources, but did relatively little damage to the American cause.

Most of all, London officials did not initially understand that military triumph would not bring political victory. Securing the colonies would require hundreds of thousands of rebel Americans to resume their allegiance to the empire. After 1778, King George's ministry determined to achieve that goal by expanding the use of loyalist forces and restoring civilian authority in occupied areas. But the new policy came too late. Britain's leaders never fully realized they were fighting an entirely new kind of conflict: not a conventional European war, but the first modern war of national liberation.

6-1d Second Continental Congress

At least Britain had a bureaucracy ready to supervise the war effort. The Americans had only the Second Continental Congress, originally convened to consider the ministry's response to the Continental Association. But much had changed between the fall of 1774 and the spring of 1775. The delegates who gathered in Philadelphia on May 10, 1775, had to assume the mantle of intercolonial government. As spring gave way to summer, Congress organized the United Colonies to prosecute the war that had escalated since the skirmishes in Lexington and Concord. The delegates authorized the printing of money, established a committee to oversee relations with foreign countries, strengthened the militia, and ordered ships built for a new Continental navy. In July, Pennsylvania's John Dickinson, who drafted Congress's Declaration on Taking Arms, proclaimed, "We are reduced to the alternative of chusing an unconditional submission to the tyranny of irritated ministers, or resistance by force.—The latter is our choice."

Yet for many delegates, hesitation remained. That same month, Dickinson drafted a petition beseeching the king to halt the growing conflict. Approved by Congress on July 5, 1775, the address, now known as the Olive Branch petition, began with the assertion that its 48 signatories remained "your Majesty's faithful subjects in the colonies," and concluded with a "sincere and fervent prayer" that the king would "enjoy a long and prosperous reign, and that your descendants may govern your dominions with honor to themselves and happiness to their subjects."

Even while preparing the Olive Branch petition—which the king would ultimately reject—Congress pursued the urgent task of creating the Continental army and appointing its leadership. In the first weeks after Lexington and Concord, the Massachusetts provincial congress supervised General Ward and the troops encamped at Boston. But that army, composed of men from all over New England, constituted a heavy drain on limited local resources, and Massachusetts soon asked Congress to take over. This meant Congress had to choose a commander-in-chief, and many delegates recognized the importance of naming someone who was not a New Englander. In mid-June, John Adams proposed the appointment of a fellow delegate to Congress, a Virginian (Adams later recalled) "whose Skill and Experience as an Officer, whose independent fortune, great Talents and excellent universal Character, would command the Approbation of all America": George Washington. Congress unanimously concurred.

6-1e George Washington

Neither a radical nor a reflective political thinker, Washington had played a minor role in the pre-revolutionary agitation. Devoted to the American cause, he was dignified, conservative, and respectable—a man of unimpeachable integrity. The early death of his older brother and his marriage to the landed, slave-owning widow Martha Custis had made him one of the wealthiest planters in Virginia. Hundreds of enslaved men, women, and children worked his Mount Vernon estate. Though a slaveholding aristocrat, Washington was unswervingly committed to representative government. After his mistakes at the beginning of the Seven Years' War, he had repaired his reputation by maintaining a calm demeanor under fire.

Washington both looked and acted like a leader. Standing more than six feet tall in an era when most men were five inches shorter, he displayed a stately and commanding presence. Even a loyalist admitted that Washington could "atone for many demerits by the extraordinary coolness and caution which distinguish his character."

Washington took command of the army surrounding Boston in July 1775. The new general continued Ward's efforts to organize and sustain those troops. In March 1776, the arrival of the cannon captured at Ticonderoga finally enabled him to put direct pressure on the redcoats, yet an assault on Boston proved unnecessary. Sir William Howe, Britain's new commander, had been considering an evacuation of the city; he wanted to transfer his men to New York, where he expected a warmer welcome in a city said to be well supplied with "friends to government," as the British called **loyalists**. The patriots' cannon mounted on Dorchester Heights decided the matter. On March 17, the British and more than a thousand of their supporters abandoned Boston forever.

6-2 Forging an Independent Republic

▶ **What were the main features of republican thought in the late eighteenth century?**

▶ **What values and principles guided the formation of new state constitutions and the Articles of Confederation?**

▶ **What role did the publication of Thomas Paine's Common Sense play in the imperial dispute?**

Well before the British fleet (along with many loyalist exiles) sailed north to await reinforcements in Halifax, the colonies were moving inexorably toward independence. By the late summer of 1775, Congress had begun to mold republican ideals into the structures, rituals, and symbols of a nation.

loyalists Colonists who retained their allegiance to the British crown through the upheavals of the revolution.

6-2a Varieties of Republicanism

Since its first meeting, in the autumn of 1774, Congress's actions had been strongly influenced by republican thought. The strenuous discipline required by the Articles of Association, for example, depended on Real Whig conceptions of self-sacrificing virtue. As John Dickinson recalled many years later, "We knew that the people of this country must unite themselves under some form of Government and that this could be no other than the republican form."

But *which* "republican form"? Three different definitions of republicanism animated Congress's thinking and continued to jockey for preeminence in the new United States. Despite their differences, the three strands shared many assumptions. All three contrasted the industrious virtue of America with the decadence of Britain and Europe. Most agreed that a virtuous country would be composed of hardworking citizens who would dress simply, live plainly, and elect wise leaders to public office.

Ancient history and political theory informed the first concept, embraced chiefly by members of the educated elite (such as the Adamses of Massachusetts). The histories of Greece and Rome suggested that republics fared best when they were small and homogeneous. Unless a republic's citizens were willing to sacrifice their private interests for the public good, government would collapse. A truly virtuous man, classical republican theory insisted, had the temperament—and the resources—to forgo personal profit and work for the best interests of the nation. Society would be governed by members of a "natural aristocracy," men whose talent elevated them to positions of power. Rank would not be abolished, but would be founded on merit rather than birth.

A second definition, advanced by other members of the elite and also by some skilled craftsmen, drew more on contemporary economic theory. Instead of perceiving the nation as an organic whole composed of people nobly sacrificing for the common good, this version of republicanism followed the Scottish thinker Adam Smith, whose treatise entitled *An Inquiry into the Nature and Causes of the Wealth of Nations* was published just weeks before Congress declared America's independence. Smith saw the pursuit of rational self-interest as inevitable and even salutary. Republican virtue would be achieved through the pursuit of private interests, rather than through the subordination of personal profit to communal ideals.

The third notion of republicanism was more egalitarian. Men who advanced this version—including many with scant formal education—wanted government to respond directly to the needs of ordinary folk, and rejected the notion that the "lesser sort" should defer to their "betters." They were, indeed, democrats in more or less the modern sense, in an era when "democracy" was typically a term of insult, roughly equivalent to mob rule. For them, the untutored wisdom of the people embodied republican virtue. The most prominent advocate of this variety of republicanism was a radical English printer named Thomas Paine, who

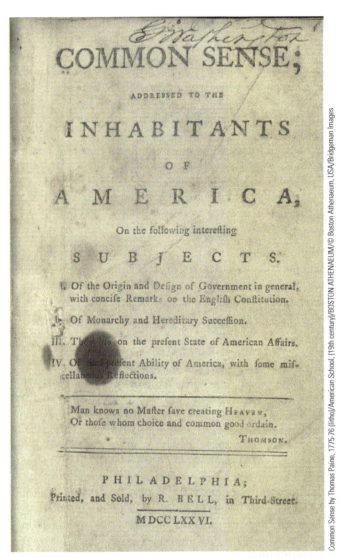

Common Sense by Thomas Paine, 1775-76 (litho)/American School, (19th century)/BOSTON ATHENAEUM/© Boston Athenaeum, USA/Bridgeman Images

▲ That America's patriot leaders read Thomas Paine's inflammatory *Common Sense* soon after it was published in early 1776 is indicated by this first edition, owned by George Washington himself.

sailed to Philadelphia in 1774 bearing letters of introduction from Benjamin Franklin. Throughout 1775, Paine scribbled in obscurity, publishing essays railing against the bloody excesses of English officials in India and attacking the "savage practice" of African slavery in America. In 1776, he would become one of the best-known writers in the world.

6-2b Common Sense

First printed in January 1776, Thomas Paine's **Common Sense** sold for as little as a shilling—about $7.50 in today's money. Perhaps 100,000 Americans bought copies or read sections of *Common Sense* reprinted in newspapers. Thousands more heard it read aloud in taverns, coffeehouses, and public squares. An estimated one in five American adults became familiar with Paine's arguments, far more than had read or

debated any previous patriot writings. Within months, copies surfaced not just in London and Edinburgh but also in Berlin and Warsaw.

Paine's best-seller did not create American independence, but it transformed the terms of debate. Even after they had been at war for months, many American leaders hesitated fully to break with Great Britain. "[D]o We aim at independency? or do We only ask for a Restoration of Rights putting of Us on Our old footing?" one South Carolina delegate asked Congress in May 1775. As late as March 1776, John Adams called independence "an Hobgoblin, of so frightful Mein, that it would throw a delicate Person into Fits to look it in the Face."

Thomas Paine was not a delicate person. He wrote with passion verging on rage, in straightforward prose that reflected the oral culture of ordinary folk. *Common Sense* took the Bible—the only book familiar to most Americans—as its primary source of authority. As its title suggested, *Common Sense* aimed to cut through a fog of received wisdom—to see clearly and speak plain.

Paine insisted that America's independence was inevitable. Just as all children one day grow up, the "authority of Great Britain over this continent, is a form of government, which sooner or later must have an end." Rejecting the widespread assumption that a balance among monarchy, aristocracy, and democracy preserved liberty, Paine said monarchs were "ridiculous," and aristocrats greedy and corrupt. No tender parent, Britain had exploited the colonies unmercifully, Paine argued. And for the frequently heard assertion that an independent America would be weak and divided, he substituted boundless confidence in its future. "The sun never shined on a cause of greater worth," he wrote. Independence was "not the affair of a City, a County, a province, or a kingdom; but of a continent—of at least one-eighth part of the habitable globe." America's struggle was "not the concern of a day, a year, or an age" but of "posterity . . . even to the end of time."

It is unclear how many were converted to the cause of independence by *Common Sense*. But by late spring, Adams's "hobgoblin" had become a given. Towns, grand juries, and provincial legislatures drafted at least ninety different statements demanding American independence. Then, on June 7, Congress confirmed the movement toward separation. Virginia's Richard Henry Lee introduced the crucial resolution: "that these United Colonies are, and of right ought to be, free and independent States, that they are absolved of all allegiance to the British Crown, and that all political connection between them and the State of Great Britain is, and ought to be, totally dissolved." Congress postponed a vote on Lee's resolution to allow time for consultation and public reaction. In the meantime, they directed a five-man committee—including Thomas Jefferson, John Adams, and Benjamin Franklin—to draft a declaration of American independence. The committee

Common Sense A pamphlet written by Thomas Paine that advocated freedom from British rule.

assigned primary responsibility for writing the document to Jefferson, a thirty-four-year-old Virginia lawyer known for his eloquence.

6-2c Jefferson and the Declaration of Independence

Thomas Jefferson had been educated at the College of William and Mary and trained in the law offices of a prominent attorney. A member of the House of Burgesses, he had read widely in history and political theory. That broad knowledge was evident not only in the Declaration of Independence but also in his draft of the Virginia state constitution, completed a few days before his appointment to the committee. An intensely private man, Jefferson loved his home and family deeply. This early stage of his political career was marked by his wife Martha's repeated difficulties in childbearing. Not until after her death in 1782, from complications following the birth of their third surviving child, did Jefferson fully commit himself to public service. He would not marry again. In the late 1780s, he began a long-lasting relationship with one of his slaves, Sally Hemings. Hemings was Martha Jefferson's half-sister, born of another relationship between a slave owner and enslaved woman. Between 1790 and 1808, Hemings bore seven children whose father was almost certainly Thomas Jefferson.

Jefferson's draft of the **Declaration of Independence** was laid before Congress on June 28, 1776. The delegates voted for independence four days later, on July 2, and then refined the wording of the Declaration for two more days, adopting it with some changes on July 4. Since Americans had long since ceased to see themselves as legitimate subjects of Parliament, the Declaration of Independence (see appendix) concentrated on the actions of George III. The document accused the king of attempting to destroy representative government in the colonies and of oppressing Americans through the use of excessive force.

The Declaration's chief long-term importance, however, did not lie in its lengthy catalogue of grievances against George III (including, in a section deleted by Congress, Jefferson's charge that the British monarchy had forced African slavery on America). It lay instead in the first lines of its second paragraph, ringing statements of principle that have served ever since as the ideal to which Americans aspire: "We hold these truths to be self-evident: That all men are created equal; that they are endowed by their Creator with certain unalienable rights; that among these are life, liberty and the pursuit of happiness; that, to secure these rights, governments are instituted among men, deriving their just powers from the consent of the governed; that whenever any form of government becomes destructive of these ends, it is the right of the people to alter or to abolish it, and to institute new government." These phrases have echoed down

Declaration of Independence Proposed by the Second Continental Congress, this document proclaimed independence of the Thirteen Colonies from British rule.

the centuries like no others: a clarion call taken up by many groups struggling for their rights within the United States, and well beyond it.

The congressmen who voted to accept the Declaration of Independence could not predict the consequences of their audacious act. By signing the Declaration, they committed treason, a capital offense. When they concluded with the assertion that they "mutually pledge[d] to each other our lives, our fortunes, and our sacred honor," they spoke no less than the truth. The real struggle lay before them, and few had Thomas Paine's confidence in their success.

6-2d Colonies to States

The Declaration dissolved an ancient set of political bonds with the stroke of a pen. Creating political entities to supplant the individual colonies, and to knit the newly united states together, would take much longer. Shortly before adopting the Declaration, Congress directed the individual provinces to replace their colonial charters with state constitutions, and to devise new republican bodies to supplant the conventions and committees that had governed since 1774.

The supporters of American independence wanted to create tangible documents specifying the fundamental structures of government, but at first legislators could not decide how to accomplish that goal. Political leaders eventually concluded that regular legislative bodies should not draft the constitutions that defined their powers. Following the models of Vermont in 1777 and Massachusetts in 1780, states began to elect conventions for the sole purpose of drafting constitutions. In this fashion, states sought authorization directly from the people—the theoretical sovereigns in a republic—to establish new governments. Delegates then submitted the constitutions they had drafted to voters for ratification.

Americans' experience with British rule permeated every provision of their new constitutions, which varied considerably in specifics while remaining broadly comparable in outline. Under their colonial charters, Americans had learned to fear the power of governors—usually the appointed agents of the king or proprietor—and to see their legislatures as defenders of the people. Accordingly, the first state constitutions typically provided for the governor to be elected annually (commonly by the legislature), limited the number of terms he could serve, and gave him little independent authority. The most radical of the state constitutions, adopted by Pennsylvania in late 1776, closely followed Paine's egalitarian thinking, and featured no executive or upper legislative house.

In every case, the state constitutions expanded the powers of the provincial legislatures. Each state except Pennsylvania and Vermont retained a two-house structure, with members of the upper house serving longer terms and required to own more property than their counterparts in the lower house. But they also redrew electoral districts to more accurately reflect population patterns and increased the number of members in both houses. Finally, most states lowered property qualifications for voting. As a result, state legislatures came to include members who earlier would not even have been eligible to cast a ballot. Thus, the revolutionary era witnessed the first deliberate attempt to broaden the base of American government, a process that continues in the present day.

6-2e Limiting State Governments

The authors of state constitutions knew that governments designed to be responsive to the people would not necessarily prevent tyrants from being elected to office. To protect what they regarded as the natural rights of citizens, they included explicit limitations on government authority in the documents they composed. Seven state constitutions contained formal bills of rights, and others had similar clauses. Most guaranteed freedom of the press, fair trials, the right to consent to taxation, and protection against general search warrants; an independent judiciary was charged with upholding such rights. Most states also safeguarded freedom of religion, but with restrictions. Seven states required that all officeholders be Christians, and some continued to support churches with tax revenues. (Not until 1833 did once-Puritan Massachusetts become the last state to remove all vestiges of a religious establishment.)

In general, state constitution makers put greater emphasis on preventing tyranny than on wielding political power effectively. Their approach was understandable, given the American experience with Great Britain. But establishing such weak political units, especially in wartime, all but ensured that the constitutions would require revision. Even before the war ended, some states began to rewrite the frameworks they had drafted in 1776 and 1777. Invariably, the revised versions increased the powers of the governor and reduced the legislature's authority.

American politicians initially concentrated on drafting state constitutions and devoted little attention to their national government. While officials were consumed with the military struggle against Britain, the powers and structure of the Continental Congress evolved by default. Not until late 1777 did Congress send the **Articles of Confederation**—the document outlining a national government—to the states for ratification, and those Articles simply wrote into law the unplanned arrangements of the Continental Congress.

6-2f Articles of Confederation

Under the Articles, the chief organ of national government was a unicameral (one-house) legislature in which each state had a single vote. Its powers included conducting foreign relations, mediating interstate disputes, controlling maritime affairs, regulating Native American trade, and setting the value of state and national money. Congress could request but not compel the payment of taxes. The United States of America was described as "a firm league of friendship" in which each state retained "its sovereignty, freedom and independence, and every Power, Jurisdiction and right, which is not by this confederation expressly delegated to the United States" (see the appendix for the text of the Articles of Confederation).

The Articles required the unanimous consent of state legislatures for ratification or amendment, and a clause concerning western lands quickly proved troublesome. The draft Congress accepted in 1777 allowed states to retain all land claims derived from their original charters. But states whose charters established definite western boundaries (such as Maryland and New Jersey) wanted the others to cede to the national government their landholdings west of the Appalachian Mountains, lest states with large claims grow to overpower their smaller neighbors. Maryland refused to accept the Articles until 1781, when Virginia finally surrendered its western holdings to national jurisdiction (see Map 7.1).

6-2g Funding a Revolution

In the 1770s as in the present day, fighting a war cost an enormous amount of money, of which the former colonies had precious little. To finance the American war, Britain possessed a well-developed fiscal-military state that could collect taxes effectively and issue sovereign debt in great quantity. It also had a stable national paper currency backed by substantial reserves of gold and silver coins, also known as hard money or specie. Because the newly created United States had none of these resources at its disposal, finance posed the most persistent problem faced by both state and national governments.

Congress borrowed what it could at home and abroad—from the American people, from Dutch investors, from Spain, and especially from France. But such mechanisms went only so far. The certificates purchased by domestic borrowers funded roughly 10 percent of the cost of the war, and the combined value of all foreign loans and gifts received between 1777 and 1783 totaled less than $10 million—about 7 percent of the Revolution's cost. With limited credit and even less power to tax, Congress turned to the only remaining alternative: printing money.

Through 1775 and the first half of 1776, these paper dollars—dubbed "Continentals"—passed at face value. But in late 1776, as the American army suffered reverses, prices rose, confidence in the nation's credit fell, and the Continental began to depreciate. State governments tried to prop up the ailing currency by controlling wages and prices and by requiring acceptance of paper money on an equal footing with specie. States borrowed funds, established lotteries, and levied taxes. But they also printed their own competing currencies, which further cluttered an already confusing monetary landscape. State currencies—issues totaling roughly $209 million—funded nearly 40 percent of the cost of the war. But as the conflict dragged on, they too plummeted in value.

Articles of Confederation The first document that framed the limited powers of an American national government. It reserved substantial powers for the states, granting to each state its "sovereignty, freedom and independence."

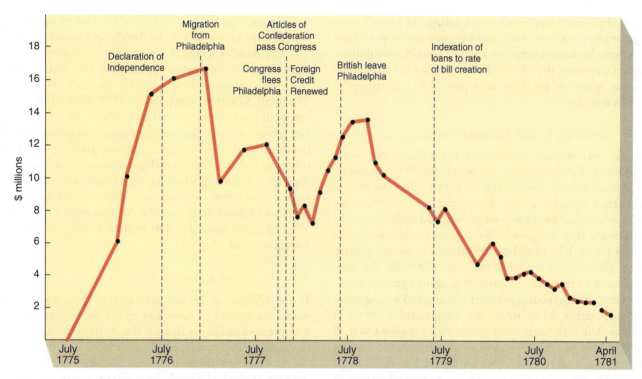

Figure 6.1 **The Changing Value of the Continental Dollar, 1777–1781**

This graph, illustrating the total value in silver coin of congressional bills of credit issued during the Revolution, shows that confidence in the new American currency was high at the beginning of the war. In 1777 and early 1778, the Continental's value sank with American defeats and rose with American victories. But after July 1778, the enormous number of bills in circulation caused their value to plummet. By the end of the war, they were virtually worthless. *Source: Adapted from Charles W. Calormis, "Institutional Failure, Monetary Scarcity, and the Depreciation of the Continental," Journal of Economic History, Vol. 48, No. 1 (Mar., 1988), p. 56.*

By the end of 1780, the value of the Continental had fallen so far that it took 100 paper dollars to purchase one Spanish silver dollar (see Figure 6.1). Congress responded by devaluating its notes, accepting Continental dollars in payment of taxes at one-fortieth of their face value. This scheme succeeded in retiring much of the "old tenor" paper, at an enormous cost to people who had taken the notes. All told, Congress issued more than $200 million worth of Continental dollars—funding about 40 percent of the cost of the war—before stopping the presses.

By the war's end, the phrase "not worth a Continental" had entered the American vernacular. Yet in many ways, the printing presses had offered the best possible answer to an impossible question: how could a new, underdeveloped nation finance a continental war with such limited powers of taxation? Benjamin Franklin—long a proponent of colonial paper money—called the Continental "a wonderful Machine": "it pays and clothes Troops, and provides Victuals and Ammunition; and when we are obliged to issue a Quantity excessive, it pays itself off by Deprecation," extracting a kind of tax on everyone who passes it. For better or worse, the new nation that created itself with a paper declaration also financed the great bulk of its war of independence with paper money.

6-2h Symbolizing a Nation

In addition to passing laws and mustering troops, Congress devised a wide array of symbols and ceremonies to embody the new nation in the daily lives of its citizens. The Continental dollar, for example, tried out a dizzying variety of images, including a harp with thirteen strings, a chain with thirteen links, and a beaver gnawing an enormous, unyielding oak. Some critics mocked the ever-changing face of American money as evidence of congressional fecklessness. But promoting a sense of "we" in the everyday interactions of ordinary citizens was one of Congress's most crucial tasks. The United States shared no common language or lineage. The Declaration of Independence called the new nation into being after a political crisis that had lasted barely a dozen years—an eye blink in historical time. When they printed money, coined medals, invented seals, designed uniforms, and proclaimed festivals, members of Congress worked to create unity from the astonishing diversity of former British subjects who must now become Americans. The crest for a proposed national coat of arms commissioned in September 1776 featured a scroll reading *E Pluribus Unum*: "out of many, one." Congress rejected the design, but the motto would reappear on the great seal of the United States in 1782.

Three-dollar bill, with the motto 'Exitus in Dubio Est' (The Outcome is in Doubt) c.1776 (colour litho)/American School, (18th century)/AMERICAN ANTIQUARIAN SOCIETY/American Antiquarian Society, Worcester, Massachusetts, USA/Bridgeman Images

◀ Among the first designs for Continental currency was this three-dollar bill, which featured the image of an eagle battling a crane. When it began circulating in 1776, people were unsure what the scene represented. Noted the *Pennsylvania Magazine*, "The eagle, I suppose, represents Great-Britain, the crane America." Benjamin Franklin, thought by some to have created the bill, later lamented that the eagle had come to symbolize the United States, calling it "a Bird of bad moral character." The turkey, he said, was "much more respectable." Not only was the national symbol up for grabs early in the war, so too was the result of the fighting. The motto on the bill, EXITUS IN DUBIO EST., translates to "*the outcome is in doubt.*"

6-3 Choosing Sides

▶ What motivated American colonists to remain loyal to Britain or remain neutral during the war?

▶ How did Native American and African American populations respond to the war?

▶ How did the United States and the British seek to engage Native American and African American populations in the war?

The endurance—and, indeed, the eventual global dominance—of the United States can obscure the chaos and tentativeness of its beginnings. American mythology sketches a conflict in which virtuous patriots, clearly in the right, squared off against villainous loyalists, clearly in the wrong, with the outcome preordained. In fact, the war of American independence was a long, bloody, and multisided conflict in which allegiance was often unstable and virtue often uncertain. Where patriots saw Sons of Liberty acting "with manly firmness" (as the Declaration put it) against British tyranny, those loyal to the Crown saw armed insurgents—"Sons of Anarchy," some called them—taking vigilante action against "Friends of Government" who defended the very notion of order. To Native Americans, land meant liberty, and the rise of the new nation threatened it. To African Americans—roughly a fifth of the mainland population—liberty meant freedom from slavery; their loyalty belonged to whoever would help them secure it. For Britain's ministers, the fate of twenty-six American colonies, not just the thirteen rebellious ones, hung in the balance.

And Spain and France knew that the balance of power in Europe as well as North America must change with the outcome of the rebels' fight for independence.

6-3a Patriots

Many though by no means most residents of the thirteen rebel colonies supported resistance and then backed independence. Active revolutionaries accounted for no more than two-fifths of the European American population. Among them were small and middling farmers, members of dominant Protestant sects (both Old and New Lights), Chesapeake gentry, merchants handling American commodities, urban artisans, elected officeholders, and people of English descent. Wives usually, but not always, fell in with their husbands about politics. Although such groups supported the Revolution, they pursued divergent goals within the broader coalition, much as they had in the 1760s. Some patriots sought more sweeping political reform than others; many fought for social and economic change instead or as well.

Some colonists, though, could not endorse independence. Like their patriot friends and neighbors, most had objected to parliamentary policies in the 1760s and 1770s, but they favored imperial reform rather than rupture. The events of the crucial year between the passage of the Coercive Acts in 1774 and the outbreak of fighting in 1775 crystallized their thinking. Their objections to violent protest, their desire to uphold legally constituted authority, and their fears of anarchy combined to make them sensitive to the dangers of independence.

6-3b Loyalists

Like patriots, loyalists comprised a diverse group of ordinary colonists, male and female, white, black, and Native. But loyalism, unlike patriotism, required no dramatic political conversion; those who supported the Crown merely sought to remain what they were born—subjects of the British sovereign and his empire—rather than to become something entirely new to modern history—citizens of an extensive republic.

Between one-fifth and one-third of the European American population rejected independence. Most who remained loyal to Great Britain had long opposed the men who became patriot leaders, for varying reasons. British-appointed government officials; Anglican clergy everywhere and lay Anglicans in the North; tenant farmers, particularly those whose landlords sided with the patriots; members of persecuted religious sects; backcountry southerners who had rebelled against eastern rule in the late 1760s and early 1770s; and non-English ethnic minorities, especially Scots: all these groups believed that the colonial assemblies had shown little concern for their welfare in the past. Joined by merchants whose trade depended on imperial connections, and by former officers and enlisted men from the British army who had settled in America after 1763, they formed a loyalist core who retained a political identity that revolutionaries proved willing to abandon.

Whole regions of British America, lying to the north and south of the familiar roster of thirteen colonies represented in Congress's many symbols (including the American flag), continued within the empire. Halifax, Quebec, and St. John (Prince Edward Island) in what became Canada; as well as East and West Florida, the Bahamas, Barbados, Dominica, Grenada, Jamaica, the Leeward Islands, and St. Vincent remained loyal to Britain, while Bermuda steered a precarious neutral course. The unfolding war cannot be understood without accounting for Britain's desire to protect its valuable Caribbean possessions, especially Jamaica.

Both Nova Scotians and West Indians had economic reasons for supporting the mother country. In the mid-1770s, the northerners had broken New England's domination of the northern coastal trade and entered the Caribbean market with their cargoes of dried, salted fish. Once the shooting started, they benefited greatly from Britain's retaliatory measures against rebel commerce. Sugar producers relied on Parliament's mercantilist trade laws for their profits, and counted on the British army's might for their security in a society where the enslaved, whom they brutalized, hugely outnumbered them. Neither Caribbean planters nor Nova Scotians had reason to believe they would be better off independent.

During the war, loyalists in the thirteen rebel colonies congregated in cities held by the British army. When those posts were evacuated, loyalists scattered to different parts of the empire—to Britain, the Bahamas, West Africa, and especially the Canadian provinces of Nova Scotia, New Brunswick, and Ontario. All told, roughly sixty thousand Americans

Courtesy of the Louisiana State Museum and the Louisiana Historical Society

▲ Bernardo de Gálvez, shown here in a twentieth-century copy of an earlier portrait, became governor of Spanish Louisiana in 1777, as the war between the United States and Britain moved south. Though Louisiana lay well to the west of the battle lines, its border with British West Florida made it strategically important to both the United States and the English crown. When representatives of the American Congress sought his assistance, Gálvez faced a delicate choice: to support the Americans—the enemy of his British enemies—might encourage colonial uprising in his own territories. He elected to throw in with the United States, recruiting Native allies to the cause, and attacking British ships in the Gulf to open supply lines to the fledgling American navy.

preferred exile to life in a republic independent of British rule. Their number included some eight to ten thousand escaped slaves who survived to the end of the war, a fraction of those who had trusted the British promise of freedom. In addition, slave-owning loyalists carried an estimated fifteen thousand enslaved African Americans along the varied paths of their exodus from the United States.

6-3c Neutrals

Between the patriots and the loyalists, there remained in the uneasy middle two-fifths to three-fifths of the European American population—a number equal to or greater than the patriots. Some who tried to avoid taking sides were committed pacifists, such as Quakers. Others shifted their allegiance to whichever side appeared to be winning, or cared little about politics and deferred to those in power. Their patriot neighbors

New Nations

The American Revolution that created the United States also led directly to the formation of three other nations: Canada, Sierra Leone, and Australia.

In modern Canada before the Revolution, only Nova Scotia had a sizable number of English-speaking settlers. Those people, largely New Englanders, had been recruited after 1758 to repopulate the region forcibly taken from the exiled Acadians. During and after the Revolution, many loyalist families, especially those from the northern and middle colonies, moved to the region that is now Canada, which remained under British rule. The provinces of New Brunswick and Upper Canada (later Ontario) were established to accommodate them, and some displaced loyalists settled in Quebec as well. In just a few years, the refugees transformed the sparsely populated former French colony, laying the foundation of the modern Canadian nation.

Sierra Leone, too, was founded by colonial exiles—African Americans who fled to the British army to seek their freedom during the war. Many of them ended up in London. Seeing the refugees' poverty, a group of charitable merchants—calling themselves the Committee for Relief of the Black Poor—developed a plan to resettle the African Americans elsewhere. After refusing to be sent to the Bahamas, where they might be re-enslaved, the refugees concurred in a scheme to return them to the continent of their ancestors. In early 1787, vessels carrying about four hundred settlers reached Sierra Leone in West Africa, where representatives of the Black Poor committee had acquired land from local rulers. The first years of the new colony were difficult, and many of the newcomers died of disease and deprivation. But in 1792, several thousand loyalist African Americans left Nova Scotia to join the struggling colony. The influx ensured Sierra Leone's survival; it remained a part of the British Empire until achieving independence in 1961.

▲ An early view of the settlement of black loyalists in West Africa, the foundation of the modern nation of Sierra Leone.

The New York Public Library/Art Resource, NY

While the Sierra Leone migrants were preparing to sail from London in late 1786, British prison ships were being readied for Australia. At the Paris peace negotiations in 1782, American diplomats refused to allow the United States to continue to serve as a dumping ground for British convicts. Needing another destination for the felons its courts sentenced to transportation, Britain decided to send them halfway around the world, to the continent Captain James Cook had explored and claimed in 1770. Britain continued to dispatch convicts to some parts of Australia until 1868, but long before then voluntary migrants also began to arrive. The modern nation was created from a federation of separate colonial governments on January 1, 1901.

Thus, the founding of the United States links the nation to the formation of its northern neighbor and to new nations in West Africa and the Pacific.

CRITICAL THINKING

■ The nations of Canada, Sierra Leone, and Australia were, in different ways, outgrowths of the American Revolution. How have the ideological underpinnings of the American Revolution affected other nations in the centuries since it occurred?

▲ Thomas Rowlandson, an English artist, sketched the boatloads of male and female convicts as they were being ferried to the ships that would take them to their new lives in the prison colony of Australia. Note the gibbet on the shore with two hanging bodies—symbolizing the fate these people were escaping.

National Library of Australia

sometimes derided them as "flexibles." On the whole, neutrals believed what the Boston-born painter John Singleton Copley wrote to his family from Europe in 1775: whether the new country would be "free or Dispotick is beyond the reach of human wisdom to decide." In such fluid circumstances, not taking sides might prove the best form of self-preservation. Thus Copley urged his kin to resist entreaties to take up arms and "be neuter at all events." Neutral colonists resisted British and Americans alike when the demands on them seemed too heavy—when taxes became too high or when calls for militia service came too often or lasted too long.

Found in every colony, neutrals made up an especially large proportion of the population in the backcountry, where Scots-Irish settlers had little love for either the patriot gentry or the British authorities. Understanding that backcountry settlers were likely to follow whichever side would better serve their interests, the Continental Congress moved to reoccupy the site of Fort Pitt and to establish other garrisons in the Ohio Country. Relying on such protection, as many as twenty thousand settlers poured into Kentucky and western Pennsylvania by 1780. Yet frontier affiliations were not clear: the growing town of Pittsburgh, for example, harbored many active loyalists.

To patriots, apathy or neutrality was as heinous as loyalism: those who were not with them were surely against them. In the winter of 1775–1776, the Second Continental Congress recommended that all "disaffected" persons be disarmed and arrested. State legislatures began to require voters (or, in some cases, all free adult men) to take oaths of allegiance; the penalty for refusal was usually banishment to England or extra taxes. After 1777, many states confiscated the property of banished persons, using the proceeds to fund the war effort. Enmities remained long after the fighting stopped. Some loyalists returning to the United States in the early 1780s were welcomed with tar and feathers, whippings, or even the noose.

The patriots' policies helped to prevent their opponents from banding together to threaten the revolutionary cause. But loyalists and neutrals were not the patriots' only worry, for revolutionaries could not assume that their longtime indigenous allies, or their enslaved laborers, would support their cause.

6-3d Native Americans

Their grievances against the tide of European American newcomers flooding the backcountry predisposed many Native Americans toward an alliance with Great Britain. Yet some chiefs urged caution: after all, Britain's earlier abandonment of Fort Pitt (and them) suggested that the Crown lacked the will—and perhaps the ability—to protect them. Moreover, Britain hesitated to make full, immediate use of its potential Native allies. Officials on the scene understood that neither the Native Americans' style of fighting nor their war aims necessarily coincided with British goals and methods. Accordingly, they at first sought from Native peoples only a promise of neutrality.

Patriots also sought to keep Native warriors out of the conflict. In 1775, the Second Continental Congress sent a general message to Native communities, describing the war as "a family quarrel between us and Old England" and requesting that Native warriors "not join on either side" because "you Indians are not concerned in it." The Iroquois Confederacy responded with a pledge of neutrality that proved short-lived. But a group of Cherokees led by Chief Dragging Canoe took advantage of the "family quarrel" to regain some land. In summer 1776, they attacked settlements in western Virginia and the Carolinas. After a militia campaign destroyed many Cherokee towns, along with crops and supplies, Dragging Canoe and his followers fled west, establishing new villages. Other Cherokees agreed to a treaty that ceded still more of their land to the United States. Bands of Shawnees and Cherokees continued to attack settlements in the backcountry throughout the war, but dissent within their ranks crippled their efforts.

The British victory over France in 1763 had restricted many Native American nations' most effective means of maintaining their independence: playing European powers against one another. Successful strategies were difficult to envision under these new circumstances, and Native leaders no longer concurred on a unified course of action. Communities split as older and younger men, or civilian and war leaders, disagreed over what policy to adopt. Only a few communities (among them the Stockbridge of New England and the Oneidas in New York) unwaveringly supported the American revolt; most Native villages either remained neutral or sporadically aligned with the British.

Warfare between settlers and Native peoples persisted in the backcountry long after fighting between patriot and redcoat armies had ceased. Indeed, the Revolutionary War constituted a brief chapter in the ongoing struggle for control of the region west of the Appalachians, which continued through the next century.

6-3e African Americans

So, too, the African Americans' Revolution formed but one battle in an epic freedom struggle that began with the first stirrings of race-based slavery and continues in the twenty-first century. Revolutionary ideology exposed one of the primary contradictions in colonial society. Both European Americans and African Americans saw the irony in slaveholders' claims that they sought to prevent Britain from "enslaving" them. Some patriot leaders, including Boston's James Otis and Philadelphia's Dr. Benjamin Rush, voiced the theme in their published writings. Common folk also pointed out the contradiction. When Josiah Atkins, a Connecticut soldier, saw George Washington's plantation, he observed in his journal: "Alas! That persons who pretend to stand for the rights of mankind for the liberties of society, can delight in oppression, & that even of the worst kind!"

African Americans did not need revolutionary ideology to tell them that slavery was wrong. But the pervasive talk of liberty added fuel to their struggle. Above all, the goal of bondspeople was *personal* independence—liberation from slavery. But could they best escape bondage by fighting with or against their masters? African Americans in different regions made different decisions. In New England, where blacks comprised the smallest share of the population, many joined the patriot ranks. Although they made up only 2 percent of the inhabitants of Massachusetts, African Americans comprised more than 12 percent of the militiamen who battled the British at Breed's Hill. During the crushing winter of 1777–1778, Washington, bogged down at Valley Forge, approved Rhode Island's plan to raise an enslaved regiment to reinforce his beleaguered troops. That state's legislature declared, "History affords us frequent precedents of the wisest, the freest, and bravest nations having liberated their slaves and enlisted them as soldiers to fight in defense of their country."

Most slaves in most colonies thought they stood a better chance by considering Britain to be "their country." As talk of war increased, groups of enslaved men from Massachusetts to South Carolina offered to assist the British army in exchange for freedom. Slave owners' worst fears were realized in Virginia, the mainland colony with the largest enslaved population. In late 1774, some Virginia slaves began meeting to discuss their response to the British troops who were soon expected to arrive. The following April, several Williamsburg slaves sent word to the royal governor, Lord Dunmore, that they were prepared to "take up arms" on his behalf. Dunmore quickly began to formulate the policy he announced in November 1775, with a proclamation offering to free any Virginia slaves and indentured servants who abandoned their patriot masters to join the British. In the months that followed, an estimated 2,500 enslaved Virginians—among them numerous women and children—rallied to the British standard. The surviving men (many perished in a smallpox epidemic) were organized into the British Ethiopian Regiment. White sashes across their uniforms bore the inscription, "Liberty to Slaves."

As other commanders renewed Dunmore's proclamation, and as the war and its attendant disruptions moved southward, thousands of escaped slaves—including people owned by George Washington and Thomas Jefferson—eventually joined the British. The best recent estimates suggest that some thirty to forty thousand people, more than two-thirds of whom were women and children, escaped their bondage during the conflict. Many died of battle wounds, starvation, and disease; those who survived till the war's end left with the redcoats, joining the global loyalist diaspora.

While the British sought to capitalize on the military potential of African Americans' freedom struggle, patriots turned rumors of slave uprisings to their own advantage. In South Carolina, resistance leaders argued that unity under the Continental Association would protect masters from their slaves at a time when royal government was unable to muster adequate defense forces. Georgia sent no delegates to the First Continental Congress and reminded its representatives at the second to remember the colony's circumstances, "with our blacks and tories [loyalists] within us," when voting on the question of independence.

In the Caribbean, the very real fear of slave uprising was a major determinant of the region's loyalism. In the summer of 1776, as news of American independence spread through the Atlantic world, more than one hundred Jamaican slaves—among them skilled artisans and house servants—led a carefully coordinated revolt that spread across much of the island. Sugar planters suspected that some of the rebels had overheard talk of revolution among their masters. "Can you be surprised that the Negroes in Jamaica should endeavour to Recover their Freedom," wrote one Kingston merchant, "when they dayly hear at the Tables of their Masters, how much the Americans are applauded for the stand they are making for theirs?" The conspirators, some of whom were burned alive for their crimes, demonstrated that there was ample reason for masters to fear the impact of the language of liberty upon their slaves.

◄ This watercolor appears in a diary kept by Jean Baptiste Antoine de Verger, a French officer serving in Rochambeau's army during the American campaigns of 1780 and 1781. The sketch depicts soldiers in varying uniforms, including a black infantryman and a scout in fringed buckskins with a tomahawk tucked in his belt.

Patriots could never completely ignore the threats posed by loyalists and neutrals, or the particular aims of Native peoples and African Americans. But only rarely did fear of these groups directly hamper the revolutionary movement. Occasionally, backcountry militiamen refused to turn out for duty on the seacoast because they worried that Native peoples would attack at home in their absence. Sometimes southern troops refused to serve in the North because they (and their political leaders) were unwilling to leave their regions unprotected against a slave insurrection. But the difficulties of a large-scale slave revolt on the mainland, coupled with dissension in Native communities and the patriots' successful campaign to disarm and neutralize loyalists, generally allowed the revolutionaries to remain in control of the countryside as they fought for independence.

6-4 The Struggle in the North

▶ **How did the British implement their military strategy in the North in 1776–1777?**

▶ **What were the consequences of the Battle of Saratoga?**

▶ **What were the outcomes of the French and American alliance?**

In June 1776, three months after they evacuated Boston, the first ships carrying Sir William Howe's troops from Halifax appeared off the coast of New York City (see Map 6.1).

Map 6.1 The War in the North, 1775–1778

The early phase of the Revolutionary War was dominated by British troop movements in the Boston area, the redcoats' evacuation to Nova Scotia in the spring of 1776, and the subsequent British invasion of New York and New Jersey.

Howe staked a great deal on "getting Possession of the Town of New York," his "principal Object" of the British campaign that year. Taking New York, home to numerous loyalists, would allow the British to consolidate their colonial allies and isolate New England, which they saw—not without reason—as the flinty soil from which the rebellion had sprung. The British also hoped that victory there would ensure their triumph in the psychological war—the struggle, as Howe's successor put it, to "gain the hearts & subdue the minds of America." On July 2, the day Congress voted for independence, redcoats landed on Staten Island, but Howe waited until more troops arrived from England before attacking. The delay gave Washington time to march his army of seventeen thousand south from Boston to defend Manhattan. "We expect a very bloody summer," he told his brother.

6-4a New York and New Jersey

Bloody it was. By August, when British forces reached full strength, they comprised some twenty-four thousand men at arms, including at least eight hundred fugitive slaves from as far south as Virginia. Washington and his men, still inexperienced in fighting and maneuvering, made major mistakes, losing battles at Brooklyn Heights—the war's largest, measured by number of participants—and on Manhattan. In September, New York City fell to the British, who captured nearly three thousand American soldiers. (Those men spent most of the rest of the war on British prison ships anchored in New York harbor, where many died of smallpox and other diseases.) As the British army remade New York into its military nerve center, the patriot population fled into the countryside, much as Boston's had done the previous year. The long occupation fostered intense, small-scale violence in and around the city. Vigilante loyalists lynched suspected rebel spies, and British and Hessian soldiers systematically raped female civilians in Westchester, Staten Island, and New Jersey.

As Washington and his men slowly retreated into Pennsylvania, British forces took control of most of New Jersey. Occupying troops met little opposition; the revolutionary cause appeared to be in disarray. "These are the times that try men's souls," read the opening line of Thomas Paine's periodical *The Crisis*, whose first issue was published on December 23, 1776.

Washington determined to strike back. Moving quickly, he crossed the Delaware River at night to attack a Hessian encampment at **Trenton** early on the morning of December 26, while the Germans were sleeping off their Christmas celebrations. The patriots captured more than nine hundred Hessians and killed another thirty; only three Americans were wounded. Several days later, Washington attacked again at Princeton, defeating a British fighting force of nearly 10,000 men. Having gained command of the field and buoyed American spirits with the two swift victories, Washington set up winter quarters at Morristown, New Jersey.

6-4b The Campaign of 1777

British strategy for 1777, sketched in London over the winter, still aimed to cut off New England from the other colonies. General John Burgoyne, a subordinate of Howe, would lead an invading force of redcoats and Native warriors down the Hudson River from Canada to rendezvous near Albany with a similar force moving east along the Mohawk River valley, through Molly Brant's homeland. The combined forces would then presumably link up with Howe's troops in New York City. Meanwhile, Howe simultaneously prepared his own plan to capture Philadelphia—the seat of Congress and functionally the patriot capital—and then pursue General Washington into Pennsylvania. Thus in 1777 the British armies in America would operate independently; the result would be disaster for the empire.

Howe delayed beginning the Philadelphia campaign for months, and then took precious weeks to transport his troops by sea. By the time British forces advanced, Washington had had time to prepare his defenses. The two armies clashed twice on the outskirts of the city, first at Brandywine Creek in September, and then at Germantown a month later. Although the British won both engagements, the Americans acquitted themselves well. The redcoats captured Philadelphia in late September, forcing Congress to move inland. But the campaign season was nearly over, and the Continental army had gained skill and confidence.

Far to the north, Burgoyne was headed toward defeat. He and his men had set out from Montreal in mid-June, sailing down Lake Champlain, then marching overland toward the Hudson. Giant trees felled by patriot militiamen slowed their progress to a crawl. An easy British triumph at Fort Ticonderoga in July was followed by two setbacks in August—the redcoats and Mohawks halted their march east after the bloody Battle at Oriskany, New York; and in a clash near Bennington, Vermont, American militiamen killed or captured over nine hundred of Burgoyne's troops, including a large number of German mercenaries.

6-4c Iroquois Confederacy Splinters

The August 1777 Battle at Oriskany revealed painful new divisions within the Six Nations of the Iroquois Confederacy, formally pledged to neutrality. The loyalist Mohawk bands led by **Molly and Joseph Brant** won over the Senecas and the Cayugas, all of whom contributed warriors to the British expedition. The Oneidas—committed to the American side—brought in the Tuscaroras before fragmenting into pro-British, pro-patriot, and neutral factions. At Oriskany, some Oneidas and Tuscaroras fought with patriot militiamen against their Mohawk brethren, shattering a three-hundred-year-old league of friendship.

Trenton New Jersey site of a battle where Continental forces took almost a thousand Hessian prisoners on December 26. The battle significantly boosted the flagging morale of Washington's troops, encouraging them to fight on.

Molly and Joseph Brant Mohawk leaders who supported the British.

A British View of the Continental Army

This cartoon, by the British satirist Matthew Darly, appeared in London print shops in August 1778. Six months earlier, France had entered the war on the American side, giving the rebels renewed hope of victory. Darly's image, entitled "A View in America, in 1778," mocks the state of the Continental Army. An officer, warmly dressed in a greatcoat and fitted with a ceremonial sash and sword of the sort that Congress used to establish the authority of the new fighting force, talks to a congressman robed in furs. The politician's eye wanders, seemingly blind to the suffering taking place on the other side of the scene: One soldier wearing a smart uniform mocks others who shiver in rags, without coats, while African American laborers huddle on the ground under blankets. A boy soldier holds a sign reading "Death or Liberty"; for him, death may loom closer than freedom.

Darly's view of the suffering of common soldiers in the American fighting forces was based in fact: Congress lacked sufficient funds to pay, clothe, and feed the Continental Army during the early stages of the war.

A View in America, 1778, by Matthew Darly

Library of Congress, Prints & Photographs Division, Reproduction number LC-US262-46659 [b&w film copy neg.]

CRITICAL THINKING

- How might such satires have served the British war effort?
- What details in the picture help the artist make his political point?

The collapse of Iroquois unity and the confederacy's abandonment of neutrality had devastating consequences. In 1778, British-allied warriors raided villages in western Pennsylvania and New York. To retaliate, Washington dispatched an expedition under General John Sullivan to burn Iroquois crops, orchards, and settlements the following summer. The advancing Americans torched dozens of towns and an estimated 160,000 bushels of corn. Some soldiers committed atrocities against the civilian population, mutilating bodies, desecrating graves, and raping Native women. An Onondaga chief later reported that Sullivan's troops had "put to death all the Women and Children, excepting some of the Young Women, whom they carried away for the use of their Soldiers & were afterwards put to death in a more shamefull manner." Sullivan's scorched-earth campaign forced many bands to seek food and shelter north of the Great Lakes. A large number of Iroquois followed Molly Brant's path into exile, leaving New York to settle permanently in Canada.

6-4d Burgoyne's Surrender

Burgoyne's sluggish progress from Montreal had given American troops time to prepare for his arrival. After several skirmishes with American soldiers commanded by General Horatio Gates, Burgoyne was surrounded near **Saratoga**, New York. On October 17, 1777, he surrendered his entire force, more than six thousand men.

Burgoyne's defeat buoyed patriots and disheartened Britons. When the news reached London, Thomas Hutchinson wrote of "universal dejection" among loyalist exiles there. "Everybody in a gloom," he commented, "most of us expect to lay our bones here." The disaster prompted Lord North to authorize a peace commission to offer the Americans what they had requested in 1774—in effect, a return to the imperial system as it stood in 1763. But the proposal came too late: the patriots rejected the overture, and the peace commission sailed back to England empty-handed in mid-1778.

Most important, the American victory at Saratoga drew France formally into the conflict. Since 1763, the French had sought to avenge their defeat in the Seven Years' War. The American War gave them the opportunity. Even before Benjamin Franklin arrived in Paris in late 1776, France covertly supplied the revolutionaries with military necessities. Indeed, 90 percent of the gunpowder used by the Americans during the war's first two years came from France, transported via its Caribbean colony in Martinique.

Saratoga Site of battles in September and October 1777 that marked a turning point in the American Revolution. The American victory at Saratoga convinced France that Americans could win the war, leading France to ally with the colonists.

6-4e Franco-American Alliance of 1778

Franklin worked tirelessly to strengthen ties between the two nations. He adopted a plain style of dress that played on the French image of Americans as virtuous farmers and made him conspicuous amid the luxury of the court of Louis XVI. His efforts culminated in February 1778, when the countries signed two treaties. In the Treaty of Amity and Commerce, France recognized American independence and established trading relations with the new nation. In the Treaty of Alliance, France and the United States pledged that neither would negotiate peace with the British without first consulting the other. France also abandoned any future claim to Canada and to North American territory east of the Mississippi River. In the years that followed, the most visible symbol of Franco-American cooperation was the Marquis de Lafayette, a young nobleman who volunteered for service with George Washington in 1777 and fought alongside American officers until the conflict ended.

The French alliance had two major benefits for the patriot cause. First, France began to aid the Americans openly, sending troops and warships in addition to arms, ammunition, clothing, and blankets. Second, the massing of French naval power on the patriots' behalf meant that Britain could no longer focus solely on the rebellious mainland colonies, for it had to fight France in the Caribbean and elsewhere. Spain's entry into the war as an ally of France (but not of the United States) in 1779, followed by Holland's in 1780, turned what had been a colonial rebellion into a global war. French, Spanish, Dutch, British, and American ships clashed in the West Indies, along the Atlantic coasts of North America and Africa, in India, the Mediterranean, and even in Britain's home waters. The French aided the Americans throughout the conflict, but in its latter half that assistance proved vital.

6-5 Battlefield and Home Front

▶ What kinds of Americans served as militiamen, common soldiers, and Continental Army officers?

▶ Why was life in the army difficult and hard for enlisted men and officers?

▶ How did the war reshape the lives of men and women on the home front?

As a series of military engagements, the American Revolution followed distinct regional and seasonal patterns. Beginning with Britain's early attempts to cut off the American insurgency at its New England roots, the shooting war remained in the northern and mid-Atlantic colonies through 1778. After France entered the conflict, Britain's attention shifted southward, and the colonies north of Pennsylvania saw little fighting. Yet the war also extended far beyond the battlefield; its insatiable demands for men and provisions, and the economic disruptions it caused, affected colonists across North America for eight long years. Roughly two hundred thousand men—nearly 40 percent of the free male population over the age of sixteen—served either in state militia units or in the Continental army over the course of the conflict. Their sacrifice and suffering changed their lives, and the lives of everyone in their households.

6-5a Militia Units

Only in the first months of the war was the revolutionaries' army manned primarily by the semi-mythical "citizen-soldier," the militiaman who swapped his plow for a musket. After a few months or at most a year, the early arrivals went home to their farms. They reenlisted briefly and only if the contending armies neared their farms and towns. In such militia units, elected officers and the soldiers who chose them reflected local status hierarchies, yet also retained a freedom and flexibility absent from the Continental army, composed of men in formally organized statewide units led by appointed officers.

6-5b Continental Army

The motley collection of former colonies that comprised the new United States could count only three entities of a national scope: the Congress, the navy, and the Continental army. Congress was able to mobilize a national fighting force so quickly in large part because its members drew on European—especially British—models for its structure, training, and tactics. As in Britain's military, the Continental army's officer corps was composed of gentlemen—men of property—who exercised strict control over the soldiers in their command. As in Britain, ordinary soldiers surrendered many of their liberties, including the right to trial by jury, when they joined the fight for American independence.

Continental soldiers were primarily young, single, or propertyless men. They enlisted for long periods or for the war's duration, and later expressed a variety of motivations for their choices. Some were ardent patriots. Pennsylvania's William Hutchinson, who signed up twice, recalled "being young and in love with the cause." But another soldier believed his prospects as an apprentice shoemaker were grim, and decided "to try my fortune by a Roving life" in the army. Some of these lower-status men saw the army as a chance to earn monetary bonuses or allotments of land after the war. As the fighting dragged on, such bounties grew. To meet their quotas, towns and states eagerly recruited everyone they could. Regiments from the middle states contained an especially large proportion of recent immigrants; nearly half of Pennsylvania soldiers were of Irish origin, and about 13 percent were German, some serving in German-speaking regiments.

Dunmore's proclamation led Congress in January 1776 to modify an earlier policy that had prohibited the enlistment of African Americans in the regular American army. Recruiters in northern states turned increasingly to enslaved men, often promising them freedom after the war. Southern states initially resisted the trend, but all except Georgia and South Carolina eventually enlisted black soldiers. Approximately five thousand African Americans served in the Continental army, commonly in racially integrated units.

▲ This receipt, dated April 21, 1778, documents the value of the blankets given to two black patriot soldiers from Glastonbury. One bears the name Prince Sambo, almost certainly a slave's name. The other, Sampson Freeman, may have claimed freedom and renamed himself by fighting in the American ranks. Collection of the Smithsonian National Museum of African American History and Culture

They were assigned tasks that others shunned, such as burying the dead, foraging for food, and driving wagons. At any given time they comprised about 10 percent of the regular army, but they seldom served in militia units.

Also attached to the American forces were a number of women, the wives and widows of poor soldiers, who came to the army with their menfolk because they were too impoverished to survive alone. Such camp followers—estimated to be about 3 percent of the total number of troops—worked as cooks, nurses, and laundresses in return for rations and low wages.

6-5c Officer Corps

Drawn from different ranks of American society, officers in the Continental army lived according to different rules of conduct and compensation than did enlisted men. A colonel earned seven times as much as a common soldier, and a junior officer was paid one and one-half times as much. Officers were discouraged from fraternizing with enlisted men, and sometimes punished for doing so.

In their tight-knit ranks, Continental officers developed an intense sense of pride and commitment to the revolutionary cause. The hardships they endured and the difficulties they overcame fostered an esprit de corps that outlasted the war. The realities of warfare were often dirty, messy, and corrupt, but the officers drew strength from a developing image of themselves as professionals who sacrificed personal gain for the good of the nation. Officers' wives, too, prided themselves on their and their husbands' service. Unlike poor women, they did not travel with the army but instead came for extended visits while the troops were in camp (usually during the winters). Martha Washington and other officers' wives, for example, lived at Valley Forge in the winter of 1777–1778. They brought with them food, clothing, and household furnishings to make their stay more comfortable, and they entertained each other and their menfolk at teas, dinners, and dances. In camp they created friendships later renewed in civilian life, when some of their husbands became the new nation's leaders.

6-5d Hardship and Disease

Ordinary soldiers endured more hardships than their officers, but life in the American army was difficult for everyone. Wages were low, and often the army could not meet the payroll. While in camp, soldiers occasionally hired themselves out as laborers to nearby farmers to augment their meager rations or earnings. Rations (a daily allotment of bread, meat, vegetables, milk, and beer) did not always appear, leaving men to forage for their own food. When conditions deteriorated, troops threatened mutiny (though only a few carried out that threat) or simply deserted. Punishments for desertion, theft, and assault were harsh; convicted soldiers were sentenced to hundreds of lashes, whereas officers were publicly humiliated, deprived of their commissions, and discharged in disgrace.

Disease—especially dysentery and, early in the war, smallpox—was a constant feature of camp life. Most native-born colonists had neither been exposed to smallpox nor inoculated against the disease, so soldiers and civilians were vulnerable when smallpox spread through the northern countryside beginning in early 1774. The disease ravaged residents of Boston during the British occupation, the troops attacking Quebec in 1775–1776, and the African Americans who fled to join Lord Dunmore (1775) and Lord Cornwallis (1781). Because most British soldiers had already survived smallpox (which was endemic in Europe), it did not pose as significant a threat to redcoat troops. In early 1777, Washington ordered that the entire regular army and all new recruits be inoculated. Some would die from the risky procedure, and survivors would be incapacitated for weeks. But those dramatic measures, coupled with the increasing numbers of foreign-born (and mostly immune) men who enlisted, helped to protect Continental soldiers later in the war, contributing significantly to the eventual American victory.

American soldiers and sailors unfortunate enough to be captured by the British endured great suffering, especially those held in makeshift prisons or on prison ships (known as hulks) in or near Manhattan. Because Britain refused to recognize the legitimacy of the American government,

◀ The horrors of the *Jersey* prison hulk survived in American memory for many years after the Revolution ended. This image of the interior of the ship, which depicts suffering American soldiers chained in filthy rags while a well-fed British regular stands guard with bayonet, was engraved in 1855, nearly eighty years after the war, as part of a book called *Life and Death on the Ocean: A Collection of Extraordinary Adventures.*

Library of Congress Prints and Photographs Division Washington, D.C., 20540 USA [LC-US262-5852]

redcoat officers regarded the patriots as rebellious traitors rather than as prisoners of war. Fed meager rations and kept in crowded, unsanitary conditions, over half of these prisoners eventually died of disease. Particularly notorious was the hulk *Jersey;* survivors reported fighting over scraps of disgusting food, and each day having to remove the bodies of their dead comrades.

6-5e Home Front

Wartime disruptions affected the lives of all Americans. Both American and British soldiers plundered farms and houses, looking for food or salable items; they burned fence rails in their fires and took horses and oxen to transport their wagons. A farmer from Tiverton, Rhode Island, later recalled that most of the town's "beasts of the plow had been carried off by the enemy from the shores, or were removed back into the country out of their reach, or had been converted for food for the use of our own army." Moreover, troops carried disease wherever they went, including when they returned home.

Those living far from the lines of march also suffered from shortages of salt, soap, flour, and other necessities. New clothing was essentially unavailable—nor could people afford it. Severe inflation eroded the worth of every penny (see Figure 6.1). With export markets drastically curtailed, income fell dramatically. While revenues plummeted, the cost of free labor increased as farmers and artisans competed with the army for available hands. That the military campaign season overlapped with the labor-intensive growing season compounded these challenges.

Even such basic social patterns as gender roles were profoundly altered by the scale and duration of the war. More men were absent from their homes for more time than ever before in the colonies. Wives who previously had handled only the "indoor affairs" of their households found themselves responsible for "outdoor affairs" as well. As the wife of a Connecticut soldier later recalled, her husband "was out more or less" from 1777 to the end of the war, "so much so as to be unable to do anything on our farm. What was done, was done by myself." Most white women did not work in the fields themselves, but they supervised field hands and managed their families' finances. These new responsibilities added to the burdens of wives and mothers, but also gave some of them a sense of independence that increased their sense of connection to the public life of the new nation.

6-6 The War Moves South

▶ Why did the British revise their military strategy?

▶ How was the British campaign in the South influenced by African American slaves and European powers?

▶ How did the island colonies of the West Indies affect the British campaign in the South?

Shortly after shots rang out at Lexington, the royal governor of Georgia had warned Lord Dartmouth that the concentration of British troops around Boston weakened the other provinces. If legal governments were to recover their powers, he argued, a sizeable redcoat presence was "absolutely necessary in every Province." Such warnings went unheeded through the siege of Boston and the long campaigns in New York, New Jersey, and Pennsylvania. By the end of 1777, the British had won New York City and Philadelphia. But they had lost Burgoyne's army in the process. The Americans, meanwhile, had gained an ally with a navy nearly as powerful as Britain's own.

In the wake of the Saratoga disaster, British military leaders reassessed their strategy. With France (and soon Spain) fighting on the rebel side, the North American theater shrank in importance; defending the West Indies, and even the home islands, became priorities. Britain's attention shifted toward the southern colonies in large part to create a base of operations from which to sustain and protect its Caribbean dominions. After 1778, Britain continued the American war chiefly to serve the ends of empire in the West Indies and in Europe. Sir Henry Clinton, who replaced Howe as Britain's commander, later recalled that the ministry had then "relinquished all thoughts of reducing the rebellious colonies by force of arms" so that "the collected strength of the realm might be more at liberty to act against this new enemy," France.

6-6a South Carolina and the Caribbean

In June 1778, Clinton ordered the evacuation of Philadelphia in order to redeploy some five thousand troops to capture St. Lucia from the French. Britain took St. Lucia in December of that year, and the island became the key to the empire's operations in the Caribbean. Clinton also dispatched a small expedition to Georgia. Savannah and then Augusta fell easily into British hands, convincing Clinton that a southern strategy could succeed, and might even provide a base from which to attack the northern rebel colonies. In late 1779, Clinton sailed a large force down the coast from New York to besiege Charleston (see Map 6.2). The Americans trapped in the seaport held out for months, but on May 12, 1780, General Benjamin Lincoln was forced to surrender the patriots' entire southern army—5,500 men.

The redcoats quickly spread through South Carolina, establishing garrisons at key points in the interior. Hundreds of South Carolinians renounced their allegiance to the United States, proclaiming renewed loyalty to the Crown. Thousands of escaped slaves streamed into Charleston, ready to assist the British in exchange for the freedom Clinton promised them. Fleeing from their patriot masters individually and as families, they seriously disrupted planting and harvesting in the Carolinas and Georgia in 1780 and 1781.

As smallpox ravaged besieged Charleston, Clinton organized both black and white loyalist regiments, and the process of pacifying the south began. Because there were three sides in this phase of the conflict—the British army seeking to subdue the rebels, the Continental army seeking to win American independence, and over twenty thousand African Americans seeking freedom from bondage—the southern campaign evolved into what one scholar calls a "triagonal war." Throughout 1780–1781, the specter of slave rebellion, and the certainty of massive property loss from the escape of so many enslaved people, heightened tensions between loyalists and patriots, making the war in the South especially brutal.

To a greater degree than the northern phase of the Revolution, the entry of France, Spain, and Holland made the southern campaign a naval as well as a land war. American privateers had long infested Caribbean waters, seizing valuable cargoes bound to and from British islands. Now France's powerful navy picked off those islands one by one, including Grenada—second only to Jamaica in sugar production—and, in 1781, St. Christopher. The British captured the Dutch island of St. Eustatius in early 1781, but the victory did them little good. Indeed, it cost them dearly, for Admiral Sir George Rodney, determined to secure (and to plunder) the island, remained in St. Eustatius and neglected to pursue the French fleet to Virginia, where it would play a major role in the **Battle of Yorktown**.

On land, the British army established only partial control of the areas it seized in South Carolina and Georgia. The fall of Charleston only spurred the patriots to greater exertions in the region. Patriot women in four states formed the Ladies Association, which collected money to purchase shirts for needy soldiers. Recruiting efforts were revitalized. Patriot bands operated freely, and loyalists could not be adequately protected. Nevertheless, the war in South Carolina went badly for the patriots throughout most of 1780. At Camden in August, forces under **Lord Cornwallis**, the new British commander in the South, crushingly defeated a reorganized southern army led by Horatio Gates.

6-6b Greene and the Southern Campaign

After Gates's defeat at Camden, George Washington (who remained in the North to contain the British garrison at New York) appointed General Nathanael Greene to command the southern campaign. Greene was appalled by the conditions he found in South Carolina. His troops lacked clothing, blankets, and food. He told a friend that "a great part of this country is already laid waste and in the utmost danger of becoming a desert." He lamented that incessant guerrilla warfare had "so corrupted the principles of the people that they think of nothing but plundering one another."

In such dire circumstances, Greene moved cautiously, adopting a conciliatory policy toward the many Americans who had switched sides. He ordered his troops to treat captives fairly and not to loot loyalist property. To convince a war-weary populace that the patriots could bring stability to the region, he helped the shattered provincial

Battle of Yorktown The Battle at Yorktown, Virginia, (September 28–October 19, 1781) which resulted in the defeat of British military leader Lord Cornwallis and his surrender to George Washington.

Lord Cornwallis British general whose surrender at Yorktown in 1781 marked the last major engagement between the British and Continental armies.

Map 6.2 The War in the South

The southern war—after the British invasion of Georgia in late 1778—was characterized by a series of British thrusts into the interior, leading to battles with American defenders in both North and South Carolina. Finally, after promising beginnings, Cornwallis's foray into Virginia ended with disaster at Yorktown in October 1781.

congresses of Georgia and South Carolina to reestablish civilian authority in the interior—a goal the British had failed to accomplish. Because he had so few regulars (only sixteen hundred when he took command), Greene had to rely on western volunteers. Because he could not afford to have frontier militia companies pinned down defending their homes from Native attack, he pursued diplomacy aimed at keeping the Cherokee and the Catawba out of the war. Although the British army initially won some Native allies, Greene's careful maneuvers eventually proved successful. By war's end, only the Creeks remained allied with Great Britain.

▲ British forces early recognized the strategic importance of Charleston, South Carolina. This battle plan dates from the first attack on the southern port city, which took place in the summer of 1776. Continental troops successfully repulsed the British assault, and Charleston remained under rebel control until 1779, when the city fell to General Henry Clinton's besieging forces. During its long occupation thereafter, Charleston became a loyalist stronghold, filled with black as well as white refugees from the bloody fighting in the South.

Even before Greene took command in December 1780, the tide had begun to turn. At King's Mountain, in western North Carolina, a force from the backcountry defeated a large party of redcoats and loyalists that October. Then in January 1781, Greene's trusted aide Daniel Morgan brilliantly routed the British regiment Tarleton's Legion at nearby Cowpens. Greene himself confronted the main body of British troops under Lord Cornwallis at Guilford Court House, North Carolina, in March. Although Cornwallis controlled the field at the end of the day, much of his army had been destroyed. He had to retreat to Wilmington, on the coast, to await supplies and fresh troops dispatched from New York by sea. Meanwhile, Greene returned to South Carolina, where, in a series of swift strikes, he forced the redcoats to abandon their interior posts and retire to Charleston.

6-6c Surrender at Yorktown

Cornwallis headed north into Virginia, where he joined forces with a detachment of redcoats commanded by Benedict Arnold, a one-time patriot who had returned to the British fold. But instead of acting decisively with his new army of 7,200 men, Cornwallis withdrew to the peninsula between the York and James rivers. He fortified Yorktown and awaited supplies and reinforcements from New York. The British commander Henry Clinton had dispatched 7,000 men and 25 battleships to relieve Cornwallis, explaining, "'Tis not a move of choice but of necessity. If Lord Cornwallis's army fails, I should have little hope of seeing British Dominion re-established in America" (Mackesy, p. 427). Events proved Clinton correct. Seizing the opportunity, Washington shipped more than seven thousand French and American troops south from New York. But it was French naval power that proved decisive. Admiral de Grasse's fleet arrived from the Caribbean just in time to defeat the Royal Navy vessels en route to relieve Cornwallis, and the British general found himself trapped. On October 19, 1781, Cornwallis surrendered. When news of the defeat reached London, Lord North's ministry fell, and negotiations for peace progressed rapidly.

Some thirty-five thousand British troops remained in America, and the king's forces continued to hold Halifax, New York City, Charleston, Savannah, and St. Augustine. But the catastrophe at Yorktown, coupled with losses in West Florida, Minorca, and India, and compounded by Spanish and French ships then besieging Gibraltar and menacing the English Channel, forced Britain to give up its thirteen rebel colonies for lost. In January 1782, Parliament voted to cease offensive operations in America and begin peace negotiations.

6-7 Uncertain Victories

▶ **Why did the British attach so much importance to retaining Jamaica and other Caribbean colonies?**

▶ **What challenges did the United States face in negotiating a peace treaty?**

The Battle of Yorktown marked the last engagement between the British and Continental armies, not the end of the Revolutionary War. Not until a year after news of Cornwallis's surrender reached Whitehall were preliminary peace terms settled; ratifying the **Treaty of Paris** took another nine months. In the long interim, sporadic guerilla warfare continued between loyalists and patriots from New York to Florida. In British-occupied New York, Charleston, and Savannah, some sixty thousand white and black loyalists awaited salvation. Meanwhile, the armies began the hard, slow work of withdrawing tens of thousands of British and Hessian troops and demobilizing tens of thousands of Continental soldiers and state militiamen, many of them wounded.

6-7a Saving Jamaica

Even after Yorktown, Britain remained reluctant to accept an independent United States. Indeed, George III threatened to relinquish the throne rather than recognize the new nation. "A separation from America would annihilate the rank in which the British empire stands among the European States," he wrote in January 1782. But that empire did not consist of thirteen rebel colonies alone. With the United States lost, British officials turned their full attention to the most valuable of all its American possessions: Jamaica. Jamaica produced two-fifths of Britain's sugar and nine-tenths of its rum. Its human capital—over 200,000 slaves—likewise added an enormous asset to the balance sheet of empire. Securing that prize had been a central British war aim since France entered the conflict. Through the autumn of 1781, while Cornwallis bumbled into Virginia, British strategists were consumed with the fate of Jamaica. From the perspective of the British Caribbean command, Yorktown was a disastrous distraction, allowing the French once again to mass their forces in the West Indies.

Treaty of Paris A treaty signed in 1783 when the British recognized the independence of the United States, established borders for the new nation, and agreed to withdraw all royal troops from the colonies.

▲ Admiral Sir George Rodney's triumph over the French navy at the Battle of the Saintes in April 1782 preserved Britain's control of Jamaica, a cornerstone of the empire. The victory—a crucial success that stood out amidst the broader pattern of British losses in the American War—was celebrated with heroic sculptures and maritime paintings like this one, part of a series of images of the battle that Nicholas Pocock began in 1782.

Revolutionary Rhetoric

The United States was created in an event termed the American Revolution as early as 1776. Yet many historians today contend that it was not truly "revolutionary," if *revolution* means overturning an existing power structure. The nation won its independence and established a republic, radical events in the context of the eighteenth century. But with the exception of British officials, the same men who had led the colonies also led the new country. In sharp contrast, the nearly contemporary French Revolution witnessed the execution of the monarch and many aristocrats, and a significant redistribution of authority. So the legacy of the American Revolution appears ambiguous, at once radical and conservative.

Throughout the more than two hundred years since the "Revolution," groups holding widely varying political views have claimed to represent its true meaning. From far left to far right, Americans frequently declare that they are acting in the spirit of 1776. People protesting discriminatory policies against women and minorities invoke the "created equal" language of the Declaration of Independence. Left-wing organizations rail against concentrations of wealth and power in the hands of a few, again citing the Revolution's egalitarian thrust. Those protesting higher taxes often adopt the symbolism of the Boston Tea Party, as in the "tea party" movement that arose in the spring of 2009 to oppose Obama administration policies. "Party Like It's 1773," read a sign popular at their rallies. Right-wing militias arm themselves, preparing to defend their homes and families against a malevolent government, as they believe the minutemen did in 1775. Indeed, vigilante groups styling themselves "minutemen" patrol the United States–Mexico border to defend it against illegal aliens. The message of the Revolution can be invoked to support extralegal demonstrations of any description, from invasions of military bases by antiwar protesters to demonstrations outside abortion clinics by prolife advocates.

Just as Americans in the eighteenth century disagreed over the meaning of their struggle against the mother country, so the legacy of revolution remains contested in the twenty-first century, both for the nation thus created and for today's American people.

CRITICAL THINKING

- Which American revolutionary ideas have been most inspiring to contemporary liberals, and which to conservatives?

If the patriots' revolution ended in British defeat in Virginia in October 1781, Britain's American war ended in victory over the French at the Battle of the Saintes in April 1782. Admiral Sir George Rodney, whose decision to linger in St. Eustatius had contributed to the defeat in Yorktown, redeemed himself by capturing the French admiral and his Jamaica-bound convoy in the narrow passage between Dominica and Guadeloupe. The victory made Rodney an English national hero, and it helped Britain obtain favorable peace terms from France in the negotiations under way in Paris.

6-7b Treaty of Paris

Americans rejoiced when they learned of the signing of the preliminary peace treaty in November 1782. The American diplomats—Benjamin Franklin, John Jay, and John Adams—ignored Congress's instructions to let France take the lead and instead negotiated directly with Great Britain. Their instincts were sound: the French government was at least as much an enemy to Britain as a friend to the United States. French ministers worked behind the scenes to try to prevent the establishment of a strong, unified government in America. Spain's desire to claim the region between the Appalachian Mountains and the Mississippi River further complicated the negotiations. But though new to the world stage, the American delegates proved adept at power politics, achieving their main goal: independence as a united nation. Weary of war, the new British government under Lord Shelburne made numerous concessions—so many, in fact, that Parliament forced Shelburne to resign shortly after peace terms were approved.

Signed on September 3, 1783, the Treaty of Paris granted unconditional independence to the United States of America. Generous boundaries delineated the new nation: to the north, approximately the present-day boundary with Canada; to the south, the 31st parallel (about the northern border of modern Florida); to the west, the Mississippi River. Florida, acquired by Britain in 1763, reverted to Spain (see Map 7.1). In ceding so much land to the United States, Britain ignored its Native American allies, sacrificing their territorial rights to the demands of European politics. British diplomats also poorly served loyalists and British merchants, who were disappointed in the peace terms.

Some provisions of the treaty rankled in the United States as well. Article Four, which allowed British merchants to recover prewar debts, and Article Five, which recommended that loyalists be allowed to recover their confiscated property, aroused considerable opposition in America. Sales of loyalists' confiscated land, houses, and possessions had helped to finance the war. Many of the purchasers were prominent patriots, and state officials hesitated to question the legitimacy of their property titles. State governments quickly passed laws denying British subjects the right to sue for recovery of debts or property in American courts, and town meetings decried the loyalists' homecoming. As residents of Norwalk, Connecticut, put it, few Americans wanted to permit the "Tory Villains" to return "while filial Tears are fresh upon our Cheeks and our Murdered Brethren scarcely cold in their Graves."

Tears were indeed plentiful. The war had been won at terrible cost. Over twenty-five thousand American soldiers had died of wounds and disease over the course of long conflict, the per capita equivalent of some 2.4 million deaths in today's United States. At least sixty thousand loyalists—the equivalent of more than 6 million people today—had fled. Years of guerrilla warfare and the escape of thousands of slaves shattered the southern economy. Everywhere, indebtedness soared, and few could afford to pay their taxes; local governments were crippled by lack of funds. It had taken thirteen rebel colonies eight years to complete the hard and violent work of demolishing a crucial part of Britain's empire. The work of building the new nation that would contain them was to last far longer.

Summary

The long war finally over, victorious Americans could contemplate their achievement with satisfaction and even awe. Having forged a working coalition among the disparate mainland colonies, they declared their membership in the family of nations and entered a successful alliance with France. An inexperienced army composed of militia and newly enlisted regulars had defeated the professional soldiers of the greatest military power in the world. They had won only a few battles—most notably, at Trenton, Saratoga, and Yorktown—but their army always survived to fight again, even after major losses at Manhattan and Charleston. Ultimately, the Americans wore down an enemy that had other parts of its empire to shore up.

In winning the war, the Americans reshaped the physical and mental landscapes in which they lived. They excluded from their new nation their loyalist neighbors who were unwilling to make a break with the mother country. They established republican governments at state and national levels. In the families of Continental army

soldiers in particular they began the process of creating new national loyalties. They laid claim to most of the territory east of the Mississippi River and south of the Great Lakes, thereby greatly expanding the land potentially open to their settlements and threatening Native dominance of the continent's interior. They had also begun, sometimes without recognizing it, the long national reckoning with slavery that would last nearly another century.

In achieving independence, Americans surmounted formidable challenges. But in the future they faced perhaps an even greater one: defining their nation and ensuring its survival in a world dominated by the bitter rivalries among Britain, France, and Spain, and threatened by divisions within the American people as well.

Suggestions for Further Reading

Emma Christopher, *A Merciless Place: The Fate of Britain's Convicts after the American Revolution* (2011)

Stephen Conway, *The British Isles and the War of American Independence* (2000)

Caroline Cox, *A Proper Sense of Honor: Service and Sacrifice in George Washington's Army* (2004)

Kathleen DuVal, *Independence Lost: Lives on the Edge of the American Revolution* (2015)

Edward G. Gray and Jane Kamensky, eds., *The Oxford Handbook of the American Revolution* (2012)

Maya Jasanoff, *Liberty's Exiles: American Loyalists in the Revolutionary World* (2011)

Jill Lepore, *The Whites of Their Eyes: The Tea Party's Revolution and the Battle over American History* (2010)

Piers Mackesy, *The War for America, 1775–1783* (1964)

Pauline Maier, *American Scripture: Making the Declaration of Independence* (1997)

Mary Beth Norton, *Liberty's Daughters: The Revolutionary Experience of American Women, 1750–1800* (2nd ed., 1996)

Andrew Jackson O'Shaughnessy, *The Men Who Lost America: British Leadership, the American Revolution, and the Fate of the Empire* (2013)

Robert G. Parkinson, *The Common Cause: Creating Race and Nation in the American Revolution* (2016).

Sophia Rosenfeld, *Common Sense: A Political History* (2011)

Alan Taylor, *American Revolutions: A Continental History, 1750-1804* (2016)

7

Forging a Nation, 1783–1800

The pullout began in March 1783, when news reached New York City that America and Britain had agreed upon preliminary terms of peace. Demilitarizing the occupied port posed a formidable challenge. Twenty thousand British troops had to be shipped to other corners of the empire, along with their cannons and mortars and guns. His Majesty's army sold its surplus, including 63,596 pairs of soldiers' boots. Every Wednesday and Sunday, the Wagon Office auctioned off the horses whose feed and transport the king's defeated cavalry could not afford.

Thirty-five thousand loyalist civilians also needed to find homes in a new world they had neither imagined nor embraced. As displaced patriots streamed back into the city, tensions flared. "Almost all those who have attempted to return to their homes have been exceedingly ill treated, many beaten, robbed of their money and clothing," lamented the British official in charge of the transfer. Ill treated or not, the patriots were home to stay. And so, like their counterparts in Savannah and Charleston, most of New York's loyalists would have to rebuild their shattered lives in exile. The fate of thousands of African American loyalists was especially insecure. A British commission met weekly in a tavern on Pearl Street to arbitrate the claims of people who had escaped slavery. Had they served the British cause and spent at least a year behind British lines, thus earning freedom by the terms of the treaty? Or would they be re-enslaved, recovered as lost property by their aggrieved owners?

Each Wednesday, the commissioners granted passage to the lucky ones whose names they recorded in a ledger called the "Book of Negroes." One of the first transport ships out, called *L'Abondance*, carried 132 free blacks to new lives in Nova Scotia. Among them was a man whom Lord Dunmore had

◄ This engraving of General George Washington's triumphant arrival in New York City was published in 1860. One of many popular versions of the scene, it offered an idealized image of American unity on the eve of the Civil War, when annual celebrations of New York's "Evacuation Day" would be absorbed by the new Union holiday of Thanksgiving. Library of Congress Prints and Photographs Division [LC-USZC4-524]

Chronology

1777	■ Vermont becomes first jurisdiction to abolish slavery
1783	■ British expelled from New York City
1784	■ United States signs treaty with Iroquois at Fort Stanwix; Iroquois repudiate it two years later
1785	■ Land Ordinance of 1785 provides for surveying and sale of national lands in Northwest Territory
1785–86	■ United States negotiates treaties with Choctaws, Chickasaws, and Cherokees
1786	■ Annapolis Convention discusses reforming government
1786–87	■ Shays's Rebellion in western Massachusetts raises questions about future of the republic
1787	■ Constitutional Convention drafts new form of government
1788	■ Hamilton, Jay, and Madison urge ratification of the Constitution in *The Federalist* ■ Constitution ratified
1789	■ Washington inaugurated as first president ■ Fall of the Bastille: French Revolution begins
1790	■ Hamilton's *Report on the Public Credit* proposes national assumption of state debts
1791	■ First ten amendments (Bill of Rights) ratified ■ First national bank chartered ■ Haitian Revolution begins
1793	■ France declares war on Britain, Spain, and the Netherlands ■ Washington proclaims American neutrality in Europe's war ■ Democratic societies founded, the first grassroots political organizations
1794	■ Whiskey Rebellion in western Pennsylvania protests taxation
1795	■ Jay Treaty with Britain resolves issues remaining from the Revolution ■ Pinckney's Treaty with Spain establishes southern boundary of the United States ■ Treaty of Greenville with Miami Confederacy opens Ohio to settlement
1796	■ First contested presidential election: Adams elected president, Jefferson vice president
1798	■ XYZ Affair arouses American opinion against France ■ Sedition Act penalizes dissent
1798–99	■ Quasi-War with France ■ Fries's Rebellion in Pennsylvania protests taxation
1800	■ Gabriel's Rebellion threatens Virginia slave owners
1800–01	■ Jefferson elected president by the House of Representatives after stalemate in electoral college

recruited from the workforce of a Virginia patriot when the war began. Harry Washington escaped Mount Vernon and never looked back, not even when his former owner assumed command of the Continental army. His exodus would take him from the Chesapeake to New York to a small settlement south of Halifax and eventually to the African American colony in Sierra Leone, whose capital the former slaves and their patrons named Freetown.

On November 25, 1783, months after *L'Abondance* spirited Harry Washington to lasting freedom, his onetime master—the commander-in-chief of the victorious American forces—rode into New York City in triumph. Sitting tall astride a tall gray charger, flanked by his officers and civilian leaders, General George Washington processed to the fort at the southern tip of Manhattan. At one o'clock, a cannon fired as the last British troops in the new United States climbed into longboats and rowed out to ships facing east, toward home.

Experience an interactive version of this story in MindTap®.

The evacuation of New York City marked one ending of the American Revolution. As the last British soldiers sailed out of New York harbor, Americans were left alone with the country whose independence they had won through eight years of bold and violent struggle against their erstwhile colonial parent. In the end, the transfer of power had been remarkably peaceful, noted one British officer who witnessed the evacuation. "These Americans are a curious original people," he quipped, "*they know how to govern themselves, but nobody else can govern them.*"

But *did* they know how to govern themselves? This "curious original people"—who were sovereign in the new American republic—now confronted urgent questions about their future: questions about liberty and property, about self-sacrifice and self-interest, about new allies and old enemies, about the states and the nation. How could Americans create and sustain that most fragile form of government, a virtuous republic? How would that republic take its place "among the powers of the earth," as the Declaration of Independence had put it? And how could the country's leaders foster consensus among a people so various in a nation so vast?

Fighting the British dissolved at least some of the boundaries that had long divided American colonists. But throughout the long civil war, Americans had remained stunningly diverse, even among the minority actively working for the patriot cause. Eastern planters held different priorities from western farmers. Native peoples battled backcountry settlers. Slaveholders found themselves at war with their bondspeople, and merchants contended with demands of poor laborers. Northern and southern interests, too, were increasingly distinct. *E Pluribus Unum*, the nation's new Great Seal proclaimed: "from many, one." Making one nation of many peoples—settling the Revolution—was the enormous task of the 1780s and 1790s. It remains unfinished still.

Nation-making involved formal politics and diplomacy, as the leading men of the United States set out to fashion a government from diverse polities and divergent republican ideals. The country's first such government, under the Articles of Confederation, proved too weak and decentralized. Political leaders tried another approach when they drafted the Constitution in 1787. Some historians have argued that the Articles of Confederation and the Constitution reflected opposing political philosophies, the Constitution representing an "aristocratic" counterrevolution against the more "democratic" Articles. The two documents are more accurately viewed as successive attempts to solve the same philosophical and practical problems. Neither succeeded in resolving those difficulties entirely.

Ratifying the Constitution provoked heated and sometimes violent contests in 1787 and 1788. Those battles between Federalists (supporters of the Constitution) and **Antifederalists** (its opponents) foreshadowed still deeper divisions over major questions confronting the republic: the relationship between national power and states' rights, the formulation of foreign policy, the future of Native territories encompassed within the borders of the United States, and the limits of dissent. Americans had not anticipated the acrimonious disagreements that roiled the 1790s, and could not fully accept the division of the nation's citizens into competing factions known as Federalists and Republicans (or Democratic–Republicans). In republics, they believed, consensus should prevail; the rise of factions signified corruption. Yet political leaders worked actively to galvanize supporters, thereby remaking the nation's political practice if not its theory. When the decade closed, Americans still had not come to terms with the implications of partisanship, as the election of 1800 vividly illustrated.

The hard work of settling the Revolution took place not only in the sphere of electoral politics and statecraft, but also in the realms of culture and ideas. In the early United States, novelists and playwrights, painters and architects, and educators at every level pursued explicitly moral goals. Women's education became newly important, for the mothers of the republic's "rising generation" were seen as responsible for ensuring the nation's future.

And then there were Thomas Jefferson's soaring words in the Declaration of Independence: "all men are created equal." Given that bold statement of principle, how could white republicans justify holding African Americans in perpetual bondage? During the war, thousands of enslaved men and women had answered that question by freeing themselves by any means necessary. Some white Americans, too, signed manumission papers, which freed particular slaves, or voted for state laws that abolished the institution of slavery. Others redoubled their defense of slavery, denying that blacks were "men" in the same sense as whites.

"We the People of the United States": in their name, and by their power, was the federal Constitution ratified. But who, precisely, were "the People," and how did various groups among them encounter the new nation? Some of the answers were clearer in 1800 than they had been in 1776. But as

Antifederalists So labeled by the Federalists, the Antifederalists were opposed to the Constitution because they feared it gave too much power to the central government and it did not contain a bill of rights.

Thomas Jefferson assumed the presidency, the long work of settling the Revolution had barely begun.

■ *What challenges confronted the new nation's leaders at home and abroad during the 1780s and 1790s?*

■ *What were the elements of the new national identity? How did poor farmers, women, Native peoples, and African Americans fit into that identity?*

■ *What disputes divided the nation's citizens, and how did Americans react to those disputes?*

7-1 Trials of the Confederation

▶ **What domestic and international issues exposed the weaknesses of the Articles of Confederation?**

▶ **How did state governments relate to the national government under the Articles of Confederation?**

▶ **How did relations between Native American peoples and the United States evolve under the Articles of Confederation?**

In late 1777, the Second Continental Congress sent to the states the first blueprint of the national government, the Articles of Confederation. But not until 1781, when Maryland finally accepted the Articles, had the document finally been ratified. The delay signaled the fate of the national government in the ensuing years. The unicameral legislature, called the Second Continental Congress until 1781 and the Confederation Congress thereafter, proved unwieldy. Under the Articles, Congress was simultaneously a legislative body and a collective executive; there was no judiciary. It had no independent income and no authority to compel the states to accept its rulings. In the 1780s, the limitations of the Articles would become obvious—indeed, glaring.

7-1a Foreign Affairs

Because the Articles denied Congress the power to establish a national commercial policy, the realm of foreign trade exposed the new government's weaknesses. Immediately after the war, Britain, France, and Spain restricted America's trade with their colonies. Members of Congress watched helplessly as British manufactured goods flooded the United States while American produce could no longer be sold in the British West Indies. Although the United States reopened commerce with other European countries and started a

profitable trade with China in 1784, neither substituted for access to closer and larger markets.

The Spanish presence on the nation's southern and western borders caused other difficulties. Determined to check the republic's expansion, Spain in 1784 closed the Mississippi River to American navigation, thereby depriving the growing settlements west of the Appalachians of access to the Gulf of Mexico. The United States began negotiations with Spain in 1785, but the talks collapsed when Congress divided. Southerners and westerners insisted on navigation rights on the Mississippi, whereas northerners focused on winning commercial concessions in the West Indies. The impasse made some congressmen question the possibility of a national consensus on foreign affairs.

The refusal of state and local governments to comply with provisions of the Treaty of Paris relating to the payment of prewar debts and the confiscated property of loyalists gave Britain an excuse to maintain military posts on the Great Lakes. Furthermore, Congress's inability to convince states to implement the treaty disclosed its lack of power, even in an area—foreign affairs—in which the Articles gave it clear authority. "Will foreign nations be willing to undertake anything with us or for us," asked New York's Alexander Hamilton, "when they find that the nature of our governments will allow no dependence to be placed on our engagements?"

7-1b Order and Disorder in the West

Congressmen confronted other knotty problems beyond the Appalachians, where individual states continued to jockey over the vague western boundaries indicated by their colonial charters (see Map 7.1). Native American nations advanced their territorial rights as well. The United States assumed the Treaty of Paris had cleared its title to all land east of the Mississippi except the area still held by Spain. Still, recognizing that land cessions should be obtained from powerful tribes, Congress initiated negotiations with northern and southern Native peoples (see Map 7.2).

At Fort Stanwix, New York, in 1784, American diplomats negotiated a treaty with chiefs who claimed to represent the Iroquois; at Hopewell, South Carolina, in late 1785 and early 1786, they did the same with emissaries from the Choctaw, Chickasaw, and Cherokee nations. In 1786, the Iroquois repudiated the Fort Stanwix treaty, denying that the men who negotiated the pact had been authorized to speak for the Six Nations. The confederacy threatened new attacks on frontier settlements, but everyone knew the threat was empty; the flawed treaty stood by default. At intervals until the end of the decade, New York purchased large tracts of land from individual Iroquois nations. By 1790, the once-dominant confederacy was confined to a few scattered reservations.

In the South, too, the United States took the treaties as confirmation of its sovereignty. European Americans poured over the southern Appalachians, provoking the Creeks—who had not agreed to the Hopewell treaties—to defend their territory by declaring war. Only in 1790 did they come to terms with the United States.

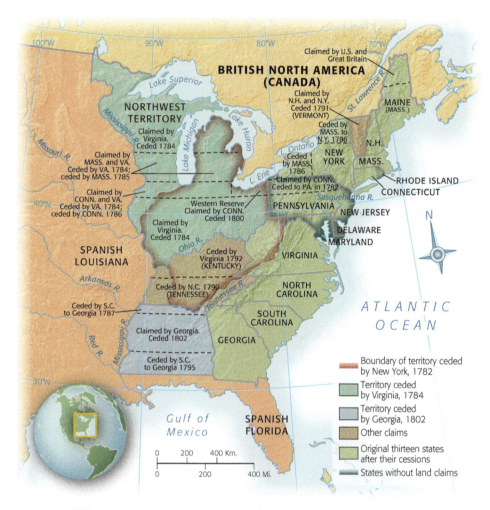

Map 7.1 Western Land Claims and Cessions, 1782–1802

After the United States achieved independence, states competed with one another for control of valuable lands to which their original charters granted them sometimes overlapping claims, largely ignoring the prior claims of Native American nations. That competition led to a series of compromises among the states or between individual states and the new nation, indicated on this map.

7-1c Ordinance of 1785

Western nations, such as the Shawnees, Chippewas, Ottawas, and Potawatomis, had begun to challenge Iroquois hegemony as early as the 1750s. After the collapse of Iroquois power in the late 1780s, they formed their own confederacy and demanded direct negotiations with the United States. At first, the American government ignored the western confederacy. Shortly after state land cessions were completed, Congress began to organize the Northwest Territory, bounded by the Mississippi River, the Great Lakes, and the Ohio River (see Map 7.1). Ordinances passed in 1784, 1785, and 1787 outlined the process through which the land would be governed and sold to settlers. The first of these laws, approved by Congress in April 1784, created procedures for settlers in the Northwest Territory to form governments and eventually organize new states that would join the federal union. To ensure orderly development, Congress in 1785 directed that

land in the Northwest Territory be surveyed into townships 6 miles square, each divided into thirty-six sections of 640 acres (one square mile). One dollar was the minimum price per acre; the minimum sale was one section. The resulting minimum outlay, $640, lay beyond the reach of small farmers, except for those veterans who received part of their army pay in land warrants. Proceeds from western land sales constituted the first independent revenues available to the national government.

7-1d Northwest Ordinance

The Northwest Ordinance of 1787 contained a bill of rights that guaranteed settlers in the territory freedom of religion and the right to jury trial, forbade cruel and unusual punishment, and prohibited slavery. Eventually, that prohibition became an important symbol for antislavery northerners, but at the time it had little effect. Some residents of the territory already held slaves,

Map 7.2 Cession of Tribal Lands to the United States, 1775–1790

The land claims of the United States meant little as long as Native American nations still controlled vast territories within the new country's formal boundaries. A series of treaties in the 1780s and 1790s spelled the end of Native territorial sovereignty over some lands, which were opened to white settlement.

U.S. population density per square mile, 1800

90 or more	6–18
45–90	2–6
18–45	Under 2

Indian land cessions, to 1799

1784 Date of cession

- Land ceded prior to 1768
- Land ceded 1768–1783
- Land ceded 1783–1799
- Unceded lands
- British territory
- Spanish territory

and Congress did not intend to seize their property. Moreover, the ordinance also contained a provision allowing slave owners to "lawfully reclaim" escaped slaves who took refuge in the territory—the first national fugitive slave law. Not until 1848 was enslavement abolished throughout the region, by then known as the Old Northwest. And by omission, Congress implied that slavery was legal in the territories south of the Ohio River.

The ordinance of 1787 also specified the process by which territorial residents could organize state governments and seek admission to the Union "on an equal footing with the original States," with the same rights held by citizens of the existing thirteen states. Having suffered under the rule of a colonial power, congressmen understood the importance of preparing the new nation's first "colony" for self-government.

Although the Northwest Ordinance is often viewed as one of the few lasting accomplishments of the Confederation Congress, its impact remained largely theoretical in 1787. Miamis, Shawnees, and Delawares in the region refused to acknowledge American sovereignty. They opposed the encroachment of the United States violently, attacking pioneers who ventured too far north of the Ohio River. Not until after the Articles of Confederation were replaced with a new constitution could the United States muster sufficient force to implement the ordinance.

7-1e The First American Depression

The Revolution wrought sudden and permanent change in the American economy, and the Articles—with their severe limitations around matters of taxation and finance—were ill equipped to confront the transformation. During the war, trade between Europe (especially Britain) and North America all but ceased. Between 1777 and 1782, the United States imported and exported about one-tenth what it had before the outbreak of fighting. New England fishermen, merchants in the British-held port cities, farm wives in the backcountry, tobacco growers in the Chesapeake, rice and indigo planters in the Lower South: everyone felt the disruption. As vital sources of income and goods dried up, the plummeting value of the Continental dollar sharply diminished purchasing

▲ A British cartoon ironically reflected Americans' hopes for postwar trade, hopes that were dashed after 1783. The Native woman symbolizing America sits on a pile of tobacco bales, near rice and indigo casks bound for Europe. The artist was satirizing the failed 1778 British peace commission and Britons' willingness to make concessions to the rebellious colonies, but his image captured Americans' belief in the importance of their produce.

power. After the peace, exporters of staple crops and importers of manufactured goods continued to suffer from restrictions that European powers imposed on American commerce.

Although recovery began by 1786, the war's effects proved hard to erase. Before the war broke out, per capita income in the rebel colonies had averaged roughly $2,130 (in today's dollars). In 1790, years after the war ended, per capita income averaged only $1,220. This drop of more than 40 percent nearly equaled the Americans' losses in the early years of the Great Depression. By 1805, average per capita income had rebounded to $1,830, but the recovery bypassed much of the countryside, especially in the Lower South.

The near-total cessation of foreign commerce during the war stimulated domestic manufacturing, and the postwar period witnessed the stirrings of American industrial development. The first American textile mill began production in Pawtucket, Rhode Island, in 1793. The country's export trade shifted from Europe and toward the West Indies, continuing a trend that began before the war. Foodstuffs shipped to the French and Dutch Caribbean colonies became America's largest single export, replacing tobacco (and thus accelerating the Chesapeake's conversion to grain production). South Carolina resumed importing slaves on a large scale, as planters sought to replace workers who fled during the war. Yet without British subsidies, American indigo could not compete with that produced in the Caribbean, and even rice planters struggled to find new markets.

7-2 From Crisis to the Constitution

▶ **How did Shays's Rebellion alter opinion about the Articles of Confederation?**

▶ **What issues divided the delegates at the Constitutional Convention?**

▶ **What were the respective positions of the Federalists and Antifederalists in the debates over the Constitution?**

Congress could not establish a uniform commercial policy or ensure compliance with the treaties it signed. Lacking the power to levy or collect taxes, it could not raise revenues needed to run the government. By the mid-1780s, Americans involved in overseas trade, western land speculation, foreign affairs, and finance had become acutely aware of the inadequacies of the Articles of Confederation.

7-2a Annapolis Convention

Recognizing the Confederation Congress's inability to deal with commercial matters, representatives of Virginia and Maryland met at George Washington's Mount Vernon plantation in March 1785 to negotiate an agreement about trade on the Potomac River. The meeting prompted an invitation to other states to discuss trade policy more broadly at a convention in Annapolis, Maryland. Although nine states named representatives to the gathering in September 1786, only five delegations attended—too few to have any significant impact. Those present issued a call for another convention, to be held in Philadelphia nine months later, "to devise such further provisions as shall . . . appear necessary to render the constitution of the federal government adequate to the exigencies of the Union."

At first, few other states responded. But the nation's economic problems also caused taxation woes. The states had run up huge debts to finance the war, issuing securities to pay soldiers, purchase supplies, and underwrite loans. During the hard times of the early 1780s, many veterans and other creditors sold those securities to speculators for pennies on the dollar. In 1785, Congress requisitioned still more taxes from the states to pay off foreign and domestic holders of national war bonds. When states tried to comply, they succeeded primarily in arousing popular protests. The most dramatic response came in Massachusetts, which levied heavy taxes to pay the securities (plus interest) at full price in specie before the end of the decade. Farmers faced with selling their land to pay the new taxes responded furiously. The actions of men from the state's western counties, many of them veterans from leading families, convinced doubters that reform was needed.

7-2b Shays's Rebellion

Daniel Shays, a former officer in the Continental army, assumed nominal leadership of the disgruntled westerners. On January 25, 1787, he led about fifteen hundred troops in an assault on the federal armory at Springfield. The militiamen mustered to defend the armory fired on their former comrades in arms, who suffered twenty-four casualties. Some (including Shays) fled the state; two were hanged; most paid fines and took oaths of allegiance to Massachusetts. The state legislature soon reduced the burden on landowners, easing tax collections and enacting new import duties instead.

Reprinted in newspapers throughout the United States, the words of the Shaysites reverberated around the new nation. Calling Massachusetts "tyrannical" and styling themselves "Regulators" (like backcountry Carolinians in the 1760s), they had linked their rebellion with the struggle for American independence, as political insurgents in the United States would do for decades to come.

7-2c Constitutional Convention

The words and actions of the Shaysites convinced many political leaders that only a much stronger federal government could solve the nation's problems. After most of the states had already appointed delegates, the Confederation Congress belatedly endorsed the proposed Philadelphia convention, "for the sole and express purpose of revising the Articles of Confederation." In mid-May 1787,

James Madison The Virginia congressman known as the "Father of the Constitution" and fourth president of the United States (1809–1817).

fifty-five men, representing all the states but Rhode Island, began to assemble in the Pennsylvania State House.

The vast majority of delegates to the Constitutional Convention were men of substantial property. Their ranks included merchants, planters, physicians, generals, governors, and especially lawyers—twenty-three had studied law. In an era when only a tiny handful of men had advanced education, more than half of them had attended college. The youngest delegate was twenty-six, the oldest—Benjamin Franklin—eighty-one. Like George Washington, whom they elected their presiding officer, most were in their vigorous middle years. All favored reform. Most wanted to give the national government new authority over taxation and foreign commerce. Yet they also sought to advance their states' divergent interests.

A dozen men did the bulk of the convention's work. Of those, **James Madison** of Virginia most fully deserves the title "Father of the Constitution." A Princeton graduate from western Virginia, he had served on the local Committee of Safety and was elected successively to the provincial convention, the state's lower and upper houses, and the Continental Congress (1780–1783). A promoter of the Annapolis Convention, he strongly supported further reform.

▲ James Madison (1751–1836), the youthful scholar and skilled politician who shaped the Constitution. The American artist Charles Willson Peale painted this miniature portrait of Madison. Madison presented it to Kitty Floyd, a young woman to whom he proposed marriage in the spring of 1783. She would have worn it as a pin until she broke off the engagement several months later. Library of Congress Prints and Photographs Division [LC-USZC4-4097]

Madison carefully prepared for the Philadelphia meeting. Through his close friend Thomas Jefferson, he ordered more than two hundred books on history and government from Paris, analyzing their accounts of past republics. A month before the convention began, Madison summed up his research in a paper entitled "Vices of the Political System of the United States." What the government most needed, he argued, was "such a modification of the sovereignty as will render it sufficiently neutral between the different interests and factions." Rejecting the common assertion that republics had to be small to survive, Madison asserted that a large, diverse republic was less likely to succumb to the influence of a particular faction. No one set of interests would be able to control it, and political stability would result from compromises among contending parties.

7-2d Virginia and New Jersey Plans

The so-called **Virginia Plan**, introduced on May 29 by that state's governor, Edmund Randolph, embodied Madison's conception of national government. The plan provided for a two-house legislature with the lower house elected directly by the people and the upper house selected by the lower; representation in both houses proportional to property or population; an executive elected by Congress; a national judiciary; and congressional veto over state laws. The Virginia Plan gave Congress broad power to legislate "in all cases to which the separate states are incompetent."

Many delegates believed the Virginia Plan went too far in the direction of national consolidation. After two weeks of debate on Randolph's proposal, disaffected delegates—particularly those from small states—united under the leadership of William Paterson of New Jersey. On June 15, Paterson presented an alternative scheme, the **New Jersey Plan**. He proposed retaining a unicameral Congress in which each state had an equal vote, while giving Congress new powers of taxation and regulation. Although the convention initially rejected Paterson's position, he and his allies won a number of victories in the months that followed.

The delegates began their work by discussing the structure and functions of Congress. They readily agreed that the new government should have a two-house (bicameral) legislature. Further, in accordance with Americans' long-standing opposition to virtual representation, they concurred that "the people," however defined, should directly choose the members of at least one house. But they differed widely in their answers to three key questions: Should representation in both houses of Congress be proportional to population? How was representation in either house to be apportioned among the states? And, finally, how would the members of the two houses be elected?

The last issue proved easiest to resolve. To quote Pennsylvania's John Dickinson, the delegates deemed it "essential" that members of the lower branch of Congress be elected directly by the people and "expedient" that members of the upper house be chosen by state legislatures. This strategy had the virtue of placing the election of one house of Congress a step removed from the "lesser sort," whose judgment the wealthy convention delegates did not wholly trust.

The possibility of proportional representation in the Senate caused greater disagreement. Small states, through their spokesman Luther Martin of Maryland, argued for equal representation in the Senate. Such a scheme, they rightly supposed, would give them relatively more power at the national level. Large states, on the other hand, supported a proportional plan, which would allot them more votes in the upper house. For weeks, the convention deadlocked. A committee appointed to work out a compromise recommended equal representation in the Senate, coupled with a proviso that all appropriation bills originate in the lower house. Only the absence of several opponents of the compromise at the time of the vote averted a breakdown.

7-2e Slavery and the Constitution

The remaining critical question divided the nation along sectional lines rather than by size of state: how was representation in the lower house to be apportioned? Delegates concurred that a census should be conducted every ten years to determine the nation's population, and they agreed that Native peoples, who paid no taxes, should be excluded for purposes of representation. Delegates from states like Virginia and South Carolina, with large numbers of slaves, wanted to count inhabitants of African descent and those of European descent equally for the purposes of representation, though not for taxation and certainly not for the rights of citizenship. Delegates from states with few slaves wanted to count only free people. Slavery thus became inextricably linked to the foundation of the new government.

The convention resolved the dispute by using a formula developed by the Confederation Congress in 1783 to allocate financial assessments among states: three-fifths of slaves would be included in population totals. (The formula reflected delegates' judgment that slaves were less efficient producers of wealth than free people, not that they were three-fifths human and two-fifths property.) What came to be known as the "three-fifths compromise" on representation won unanimous approval. Only two delegates, Gouverneur Morris of New York and George Mason of Virginia, later spoke out against the institution of slavery.

The **three-fifths clause** not only assured southern voters congressional representation out of proportion

Virginia Plan A proposal calling for the establishment of a strong central government. It gave Congress virtually unrestricted rights of legislation and taxation, power to veto any state law, and authority to use military force against the states.

New Jersey Plan A proposal calling for a single-chamber congress in which each state had an equal vote, just as in the Articles, and strengthening the taxing and commercial powers of Congress.

three-fifths clause Allowed states to count three-fifths of their enslaved population for the purposes of congressional representation, giving large slaveholding states disproportionate power in congress and in the electoral college.

to the free populations of their states, but also granted them disproportionate influence on the selection of the president. In return for southerners' agreement that Congress could pass commercial regulations by a simple majority vote, New Englanders agreed that Congress could not end the importation of slaves for at least twenty years. Further, the fugitive slave clause (Article IV, Section 2) required all states to return runaways to their masters. By guaranteeing that the national government would aid any states threatened with "domestic violence," the Constitution promised aid in putting down future slave revolts, as well as incidents like Shays's Rebellion. Although the words *slave* and *slavery* never appear in the Constitution (the framers used such euphemisms as "other persons"), eleven of its eighty-four clauses concerned slavery in some fashion. All but one of those eleven protected slaveholders and the institution on which their wealth and power rested.

7-2f Congressional and Presidential Powers

Having compromised on the knotty, conjoined problems of slavery and representation, the delegates readily achieved consensus on other issues. All concurred that the national government needed the authority to tax and to regulate foreign and interstate commerce, but the delegates stopped short of giving Congress the nearly unlimited scope Randolph had proposed. Discarding the congressional veto contained in the Virginia Plan, the convention implied but did not explicitly authorize a national judicial veto of state laws. Delegates also drafted a long list of actions forbidden to states, including impairing contractual obligations—in other words, preventing the relief of debtors. Contrary to many state constitutions, they stipulated that religious tests could never be required of U.S. officeholders.

The convention placed primary responsibility for the conduct of foreign affairs in the hands of a new official, the president, who was also designated commander-in-chief of the armed forces. With the Senate's consent, the president could appoint judges and other federal officers. To select the president, delegates established the electoral college, whose members would be chosen in each state by legislatures or qualified voters. If a majority of electors failed to unite behind one candidate, the House of Representatives (voting as states, not as individuals) would choose the president, who was to serve for four years and be eligible for reelection.

The Constitution created a national government less powerful than Madison and Randolph's Virginia Plan had envisioned. It distributed political authority among executive, legislative, and judicial branches of the national government, and divided power between states and nation (a system known as *federalism*). The president could veto congressional legislation, but that veto could be overridden by two-thirds majorities in both houses. Treaties and major appointments required the Senate's consent. Congress could impeach the president and federal judges, but courts appeared to have the final say on interpreting the Constitution. Two-thirds of Congress and three-fourths of the states had to concur on amendments. These checks and balances would prevent the

government from becoming tyrannical, yet the elaborate system would sometimes prevent the government from acting decisively. And the line between state and national powers remained so blurry that the United States fought a civil war in the next century over that very issue.

The convention held its last session on September 17, 1787. Benjamin Franklin had written a speech calling for unity; because his voice had grown weak, another delegate read it for him. "I confess that there are several parts of this constitution which I do not at present approve," Franklin admitted. Yet he urged its acceptance "because I expect no better, and because I am not sure, that it is not the best." All but three of the 42 delegates still present then signed the Constitution. Only then was the document made public. The convention's proceedings had been entirely secret—and remained so until the delegates' private notes were published in the nineteenth century (see the appendix for the text of the Constitution).

Congress submitted the Constitution to the states in late September. The ratification clause provided for the new system to take effect once it was approved by special conventions in at least nine states, with delegates elected by qualified voters. Thus, the national Constitution, unlike the Articles of Confederation, would rest directly on popular authority.

7-2g Federalists and Antifederalists

As states began to elect delegates to their special conventions, newspapers and pamphlets vigorously defended or attacked the Philadelphia convention's decisions. Every newspaper in the country printed the full text of the Constitution, and most supported its adoption. It quickly became apparent, though, that the disputes in Philadelphia had been mild compared to divisions of opinion within the populace as a whole. Although most citizens concurred that the national government needed more power over taxation and commerce, some believed the proposed government held the potential for tyranny. The vigorous debate between the two sides was unprecedented, and frequently spilled into the streets.

Those supporting the proposed Constitution called themselves Federalists. They drew upon the tenets of classical republicanism, promoting a virtuous, self-sacrificing republic led by a manly aristocracy of talent. They argued that the separation of powers among legislative, executive, and judicial branches, and the division of powers between states and nation, would preclude tyranny. The liberties of the people would be guarded by men of the "better sort" whose only goal (said George Washington) was "to merit the approbation of good and virtuous men."

The Federalists termed those who opposed the Constitution Antifederalists, thus casting them in a negative light. Antifederalists recognized the need for a national source of revenue but feared a powerful central government. They saw the states as the chief protectors of individual rights against the rise of arbitrary power. Heirs of the Real Whig ideology of the late 1760s and early 1770s, Antifederalists stressed the need for constant popular vigilance to avert oppression. Indeed, some of those who had originally pro-mulgated such ideas—Samuel Adams of Massachusetts, and Patrick Henry and Richard Henry Lee of Virginia—led the opposition to the Constitution. Older Americans, whose political opinions had been shaped prior to the Revolution, peopled the Antifederalist ranks. Joining them were small farmers determined to safeguard their property from excessive taxation, backcountry Baptists and Presbyterians, and ambi-tious, upwardly mobile men who would benefit from an eco-nomic and political system less tightly controlled than that the Constitution envisioned. Federalists denigrated such men as disorderly, licentious, and even "unmanly" because they would not follow the elites' lead in supporting the Constitution.

7-2h Bill of Rights

The Constitution's lack of specific guarantees to protect the rights of the people against the tyranny of a powerful cen-tral government troubled Antifederalists, who wanted the national governing document to incorporate a bill of rights, as did Britain's governing documents since the Glorious Rev-olution. Following the British model, most state constitutions had done so as well. *Letters of a Federal Farmer*, perhaps the most widely read Antifederalist pamphlet, listed the rights that should be enshrined: freedom of the press and religion, trial by jury, and protection from unreasonable searches. From Paris, Thomas Jefferson added his voice to the chorus. Reply-ing to Madison's letter conveying a copy of the Constitution, Jefferson declared, "I like much the general idea" but not "the omission of a bill of rights. . . . A bill of rights is what the people are entitled to against every government on earth."

7-2i Ratification

As state conventions debated ratification, the lack of a bill of rights loomed ever larger as a flaw in the proposed govern-ment. Four of the first five states to ratify did so unanimously, but then Massachusetts, where Antifederalist forces benefited from the backlash against the state's treatment of the Shays rebels, ratified by only a slender majority (see Table 7.1). In June 1788, when New Hampshire ratified, the Constitution's requirement of nine states was satisfied. But New York and Virginia had not yet voted, and everyone realized the new framework could not succeed unless those powerful states accepted it.

Despite a valiant effort by Antifederalist Patrick Henry, pro-Constitution forces won by ten votes in the Virginia con-vention, which, like Massachusetts, recommended that a list of specific rights be added. In New York, James Madison, John Jay, and Alexander Hamilton, writing under the pseudonym "Publius," published *The Federalist*, a series of eighty-five essays explaining the theory behind the Constitution and masterfully answering its critics. Their reasoned arguments, coupled with Federalists' promise to add a bill of rights to the Constitution, helped win the battle there. On July 26, 1788, New York rati-fied the Constitution by just three votes. Although the last states—North Carolina and Rhode Island—did not join the Union for over a year, the new government was a reality.

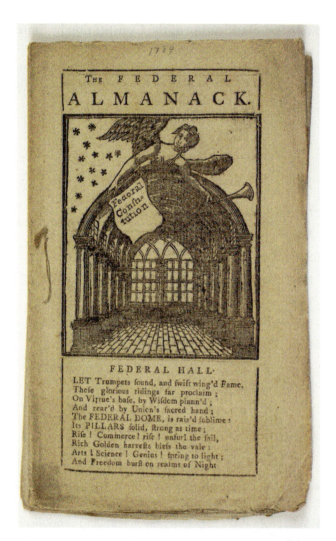

▲ *The Federal Almanack* for 1789 trumpeted the virtues of the new Constitution. Not all Americans were so certain that the national government, here symbolized as an edifice supported by thirteen pillars, was as "solid, strong as time" as the printer proclaimed. Federal Almanac Weatherwise Boston (litho)/American School, (18th century)/AMERICAN ANTIQUARIAN SOCIETY/American Antiquarian Society, Worcester, Massachusetts, USA/Bridgeman Images

In many towns and cities, Americans celebrated rati-fication (somewhat prematurely) with parades on July 4, 1788, thus linking the Constitution to the Declaration of Independence. In carefully choreographed parades, march-ers touted the unity of the new nation, seeking to drown out the dissent that had surfaced in recent years. Symbols expressing leaders' hopes for the industry and frugality of a virtuous public filled the Philadelphia celebration, planned by artist Charles Willson Peale. About five thousand people participated in the procession, which stretched for over a mile. Veterans trooped alongside farmers. Dozens of groups of tradesmen, including barbers, hatters, printers, cloth manufacturers, and clockmakers, sponsored elaborate floats. Lawyers, doctors, ministers, and congressmen followed the artisans. A final group of marchers symbolized the nation's future: students from the University of Pennsylvania and other schools carried a flag labeled "The Rising Generation."

Table 7.1 Ratification of the Constitution by State Conventions

State	Date	Vote
Delaware	December 7, 1787	30–0
Pennsylvania	December 12, 1787	46–23
New Jersey	December 18, 1787	38–0
Georgia	January 2, 1788	26–0
Connecticut	January 9, 1788	128–40
Massachusetts	February 6, 1788	187–168
Maryland	April 28, 1788	63–11
South Carolina	May 23, 1788	149–73
New Hampshire	June 21, 1788	57–47
Virginia	June 25, 1788	89–79
New York	July 26, 1788	30–27
North Carolina	November 21, 1789	194–77
Rhode Island	May 29, 1790	34–32

7-3 Promoting a Virtuous Citizenry

▶ How did Americans seek to infuse republican values in their society and culture?

▶ What role did education play in instilling republican values?

Citizens of the early United States believed they were embarking on an enterprise unprecedented in modern history, one that placed great moral burdens on the people. With pride in their new nation, they must replace the vices of monarchical Europe—luxury, decadence, and selfishness—with the sober virtues of republican America. They sought to embody republican principles not only in their governments but also in their society and culture, expecting painting, literature, drama, and architecture to promote national identity and virtue.

7-3a Virtue and the Arts

When the Revolution began, patriots toppled the gilded statue of George III that loomed over New York City's Bowling Green, melting the brass to make musket balls. Royalist icons had no place in the new republic. But what would American writers and artists erect in their places? Everywhere in the eighteenth-century world, artists struggled to find audiences and patronage for their work. Their task in the early United States was particularly fraught, for some republicans thought the fine arts signaled luxury and corruption, and questioned the very legitimacy of the enterprise.

Republican letters strove to edify. William Hill Brown's *The Power of Sympathy* (1789), the first novel published in the United States, unfolded a story of seduction as a warning to "the Young Ladies of United Columbia," and promised to "Inspire the Female Mind with a Principle of Self Complacency." Mason Locke Weems intended his *Life of Washington* to "hold up his great Virtues . . . to the imitation of Our Youth." Published in 1800, shortly after George Washington's death, Weems's moralizing biography—with its invented tale of the boy who chopped down the cherry tree and could not tell a lie—soon became the era's most popular secular work.

Painters and architects, too, used their works to elevate republican taste. Two of the most prominent artists of the period, Gilbert Stuart and Charles Willson Peale, painted innumerable portraits of upstanding republican citizens. Stuart's portraits of George Washington—three painted from life, from which the artist made scores of copies, which in turn spawned countless engravings—came to represent the face of the young republic around the world. Stuart's own motives were commercial as well as patriotic. When he sailed to the United States in 1793 after nearly two decades in Britain,

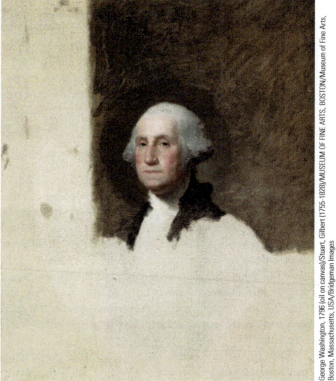

George Washington, 1796 (oil on canvas)/Stuart, Gilbert (1755-1828)/MUSEUM OF FINE ARTS, BOSTON/Museum of Fine Arts, Boston, Massachusetts, USA/Bridgeman Images

▲ During his second term as president, George Washington sat to the Rhode Island–born painter Gilbert Stuart three times in 1795 and 1796. The three sittings produced markedly different portraits, ranging from the formal full-length state portrait commissioned by the Marquis of Landsdowne to this ethereal unfinished bust, now known as the Athenaeum Washington, which became one of the most famous likenesses in the world even before it appeared on American currency. Copies of Stuart's portraits—painted as well as engraved—decorated homes throughout the early United States and surfaced as far away as Canton, China.

he told a friend, "I expect to make a fortune by Washington alone." Connecticut-born, London-trained painter John Trumbull's canvases depicted American milestones including Battle of Bunker Hill and the signing of the Declaration of Independence. Such portraits and historical scenes were intended to instill patriotic sentiments in their viewers, yet the artists rarely attracted public funding for their work, and struggled to make a living.

Architects likewise hoped to convey in their buildings a sense of the young republic's ideals. When the Virginia government asked Thomas Jefferson, then minister to France, for advice on the design of the state capitol in Richmond, Jefferson unhesitatingly recommended copying a Roman building, the Maison Carrée at Nîmes, an emblem of ancient republican simplicity. In Boston, Charles Bulfinch likewise designed his domed Massachusetts State House along classical lines.

Despite artists' efforts (or, some said, because of them), Americans began to detect signs of luxury and corruption by the mid-1780s. The resumption of European trade brought a return to imported fashions for both men and women. Elite families again attended balls and plays, threw parties, and played cards. Social clubs for young people multiplied. Especially alarming to fervent republicans like Samuel Adams was the establishment in 1783 of the Society of the Cincinnati, a hereditary association for Continental army officers and their firstborn male descendants. Although the organizers hoped to advance the notion of the citizen-soldier, opponents feared the group would become the nucleus of a native-born aristocracy.

7-3b Educational Reform

Americans' deep-seated concern for the future of the infant republic focused their attention on children, the "rising generation." Education had previously been seen as a private means to personal advancement, the concern of families. But if young people were to become useful citizens prepared for self-government, they would need a good education. In fact, the very survival of the nation depended on it. Inspired by such principles, some northern states began using tax money to support public elementary schools. In 1789, Massachusetts became one of the first states to require towns to offer their citizens free public elementary education.

To instruct their children adequately, mothers would have to be properly educated. Massachusetts insisted that town elementary schools teach girls as well as boys. Throughout the United States, private academies were founded to give teenage girls from well-to-do families an opportunity for advanced schooling. No one yet proposed opening colleges to women, but a few fortunate girls could study history, geography, rhetoric, and mathematics along with fancy needlework—the only artistic endeavor considered appropriate for ladies.

7-3c Judith Sargent Murray

Judith Sargent Murray of Gloucester, Massachusetts, became a leading theorist of women's education in the early republic.

Tierra Foundation for American Art, Chicago/Art Resource, NY

▲ Judith Sargent Stevens (later Murray), by John Singleton Copley, ca. 1769. The eventual author of essays advocating improvements in women's education sat for this portrait on the eve of her first marriage, some two decades before she began to publish her work. Her direct gaze and high forehead suggest both her intelligence and her seriousness of purpose.

In powerful essays published in the 1780s and 1790s, Murray argued that women and men had equal intellects but unequal schooling. If "an opportunity of acquiring knowledge hath been denied us," she declared, "the inferiority of our sex cannot fairly be deduced from thence." Boys and girls should be educated alike, Murray insisted, and girls should be taught to support themselves by their own labors: "Independence should be placed within their grasp." Murray's writings on female "independence" were part of a general rethinking of women's position that occurred in a climate of political upheaval. In 1798, Murray looked back on what she called "the happy revolution which the few past years have made" in women's "favour."

7-4 Building a Workable Government

▶ What challenges did Congress face in establishing a working government?

▶ How did Alexander Hamilton shape the United States' financial system?

▶ Why did Alexander Hamilton's financial plan cause division in Congress?

▶ What was the significance of the Whiskey Rebellion?

The first decade of government under the Constitution witnessed hesitant steps toward the creation of a United States that was more singular than plural. At first, consensus appeared possible. Only a few Antifederalists ran for office in the congressional elections held late in 1788; even fewer were elected. Thus, most members of the First U.S. Congress supported a strong national government. The drafters of the Constitution had deliberately left many key issues undecided, so the nationalists' domination of Congress meant that their views quickly prevailed.

7-4a First Congress

Congress faced four immediate tasks when it convened in April 1789: raising revenue, responding to calls for a bill of rights, setting up executive departments, and organizing the federal judiciary. The last duty was especially important. The Constitution established a Supreme Court but left it to Congress to decide whether to have other federal courts.

James Madison, representing Virginia in the House of Representatives, soon became as influential in Congress as he had been at the Constitutional Convention. During its first session, he persuaded Congress to adopt the Revenue Act of 1789, imposing a 5 percent tariff on certain imports. The First Congress thus quickly achieved what the Confederation Congress never had: an effective national tax law.

Madison also took the lead with respect to constitutional amendments. When introducing nineteen proposed amendments in June, he told his fellow representatives they needed to respond to the people's will as expressed in the state conventions, noting that North Carolina had vowed not to ratify the Constitution without a **Bill of Rights**. After lengthy, heated debates, Congress approved twelve amendments. The states ratified ten, which became part of the Constitution on December 15, 1791.

The First Amendment prohibited Congress from restricting freedom of religion, speech, the press, peaceable assembly, or petition. The next two amendments arose directly from the former colonists' fear of standing armies. Because a "well regulated Militia" was "necessary to the security of a free State," the Second Amendment guaranteed the right "to keep and bear arms." The Third Amendment limited the quartering of troops in private homes. The next five pertained to judicial procedures. The Fourth Amendment prohibited "unreasonable searches and seizures," the Fifth and Sixth established the rights of accused persons, the Seventh specified the conditions for jury trials in civil cases, and the Eighth forbade "cruel and unusual punishments." The Ninth and Tenth Amendments reserved to the people and the states other unspecified rights and powers. In short, the amendments' authors made clear that, in listing some rights, they had not precluded the exercise of others.

7-4b Executive and Judiciary

Congress also considered the organization of the executive branch, preserving the three administrative departments established under the Articles of Confederation: War, Foreign Affairs (renamed State), and Treasury. Congress also instituted two lesser posts: the attorney general—the nation's official lawyer—and the postmaster general. Controversy arose over whether the president alone could dismiss officials whom he had appointed with the Senate's advice and consent. The House and Senate eventually agreed that he had such authority, making the heads of executive departments accountable solely to the president.

The First Congress's most far-reaching law, the **Judiciary Act of 1789**, defined the jurisdiction of the federal judiciary and established a six-member Supreme Court, thirteen district courts, and three appellate courts. Its most important provision, Section 25, allowed appeals from state to federal courts when cases raised certain constitutional questions. In the nineteenth century, judges and legislators committed to states' rights would challenge the constitutionality of Section 25.

During its first decade, the Supreme Court handled few cases of any importance, and several members resigned. (John Jay, the first chief justice, served only six years.) But in a significant 1796 decision, *Ware v. Hylton*, the Court for the first time declared a state law unconstitutional. The most important case of the decade, *Chisholm v. Georgia* (1793), established that states could be sued in federal courts by citizens of other states. Five years later, the Eleventh Amendment to the Constitution overturned that decision, which was unpopular with state governments.

7-4c Washington's First Steps

George Washington did not seek the presidency. In 1783, he resigned his army commission and retired to Mount Vernon, a soldier trading his sword for his plough, as the Roman statesman Cinncinatus had done. (Of course, Washington's hundreds of bondspeople actually wielded the ploughs at Mount Vernon.) Even after he retired from command, Americans never regarded Washington as just another private citizen. After the adoption of the new government, only George Washington was thought to have sufficient stature to serve as the republic's first president, an office largely designed with him in mind. The unanimous vote of the electoral college merely formalized that consensus. Symbolically, Washington donned a suit of homespun for the inaugural ceremony in April 1789.

Washington acted cautiously during his first months in office, knowing that whatever he did would set precedents for the future. His first major task was to choose the heads of the executive departments. For the War Department, he selected an old comrade in arms, Henry Knox of Massachusetts. His choice for the State Department was fellow Virginian

Bill of Rights The first ten amendments of the Constitution, which guaranteed individual liberties.

Judiciary Act of 1789 Outlined the federal judiciary's jurisdiction and established the Supreme Court, as well as district and appellate courts.

▲ Alexander Hamilton, by James Sharpless, about 1796. This profile of Hamilton, painted near the end of Washington's presidency, shows the secretary of the treasury as he looked during the years of his first heated partisan battles with Thomas Jefferson and James Madison.

Thomas Jefferson, who had just returned to the United States from his post as minister to France. And for the crucial position of secretary of the treasury, the president chose the brilliant, intensely ambitious **Alexander Hamilton**.

7-4d Alexander Hamilton

The illegitimate son of a Scottish aristocrat, Hamilton—no relation to Dr. Alexander Hamilton, who toured the colonies in 1744 (see Chapter 4)—was born in the British West Indies in 1757. He spent his early years in poverty, but in 1773, financial support from friends allowed him to enroll at King's College (later Columbia University) in New York. Devoted to the patriot cause, Hamilton volunteered for service in the American army, where he came to Washington's attention. After the war, Hamilton practiced law in New York City and served as a delegate to the Annapolis Convention and later the Constitutional Convention. Although he exerted little influence at either gathering, his contributions to *The Federalist* in 1788 revealed him as one of the chief political thinkers in the republic.

Born in the Caribbean, Hamilton had no natal ties to any state; he neither sympathized with nor fully understood demands for local autonomy. In his dual role as treasury secretary and presidential adviser under Washington, Hamilton's primary loyalty lay with the nation. He never feared the exercise of centralized executive authority, and he favored close political and economic ties with Britain. Believing people to be motivated primarily by economic self-interest, his notion of republicanism placed little weight on self-sacrifice for the common good. Those beliefs significantly influenced the way he tackled the monumental task before him: straightening out the new nation's tangled finances.

7-4e National and State Debts

Congress ordered the new secretary of the treasury to assess the public debt and submit recommendations for supporting the government's credit. Hamilton found that the country's remaining war debts fell into three categories: those owed to foreign governments and investors, mostly to France (about $11 million); those owed to merchants, former soldiers, holders of revolutionary bonds, and the like (about $27 million); and those owed by state governments (roughly $25 million).

Americans agreed that their new government could establish its credit only by repaying at full face value the obligations the nation had incurred while winning independence. But the state debts were another matter. Some states—notably, Virginia, Maryland, North Carolina, and Georgia—had largely paid off their war debts. They would oppose the national government's assumption of responsibility for other states' debts because their citizens would be taxed to pay such obligations. Massachusetts, Connecticut, and South Carolina, by contrast, still had sizable unpaid debts and would welcome a system of national assumption. The possible assumption of state debts also had political implications. Consolidating state debt in the hands of the national government would concentrate economic and political power at the national level, thus raising the specter of tyranny.

7-4f Hamilton's Financial Plan

Hamilton's first **Report on the Public Credit**, sent to Congress in January 1790, proposed that Congress assume outstanding state debts, combine them with national obligations, and issue securities covering both principal and accumulated unpaid interest. Hamilton thereby hoped to ensure that holders of the public debt—many of them wealthy merchants and speculators—had a significant financial stake in the new government's survival. The opposition coalesced around James Madison, who opposed the assumption of state debts for two reasons. First, his state of Virginia had already paid off most of its obligations, and second, he wanted to avoid rewarding wealthy speculators who had purchased state and national debt certificates at deep discounts from needy veterans and farmers.

Prompted in part by Madison, the House initially rejected the assumption of state debts. But the Senate adopted Hamilton's plan largely intact. A series of compromises followed, in which the assumption bill became linked to the other major controversial issue of that congressional session: the location of the permanent national capital. A southern site on the Potomac River (favored by Washington and close to Mount Vernon) was selected, and the first part of Hamilton's financial program became law in August 1790.

Alexander Hamilton First U.S. secretary of the treasury, under President George Washington.

Report on the Public Credit Hamilton's plan to ensure the creditworthiness of the United States by having Congress assume state debts.

7-4g First Bank of the United States

Four months later, Hamilton submitted to Congress a second report on public credit, recommending the creation of a national bank modeled on the Bank of England. The Bank of the United States was to be chartered for twenty years with $10 million of paid-in capital—$2 million from public funds, and the balance from private investors. The bank would collect and disburse moneys for the treasury, and its notes would circulate as the nation's currency. Most political leaders recognized that such an institution would remedy America's perpetual shortage of an acceptable medium of exchange. But another issue loomed large: did the Constitution give Congress the power to establish such a bank?

Madison answered that question with a resounding no; the Constitutional Convention had specifically rejected a clause authorizing Congress to issue corporate charters. Madison's contention disturbed President Washington, who decided to request other opinions before signing the bill into law. Edmund Randolph, the attorney general, and Thomas Jefferson, the secretary of state, agreed with Madison that the bank was unconstitutional. Washington asked Hamilton to reply to their verdict. In his *Defense of the Constitutionality of the Bank*, Hamilton argued forcefully that Congress could choose any means not specifically prohibited by the Constitution to achieve a constitutional end. Washington concurred, and the bill became law.

The Bank of the United States initially aroused heated opposition. But it proved successful, as did Hamilton's scheme for funding the national debt and assuming the states' debts. The new nation's securities became desirable investments at home and abroad. The resulting influx of capital, coupled with the high prices that American grain now commanded in European markets, eased farmers' debt burdens and contributed to a new prosperity in the 1790s.

Hamilton's *Report on Manufactures* (1791) outlined an ambitious plan to nurture the United States' infant industries, such as shoemaking and textile manufacturing. Hamilton argued that the nation could never be truly independent as long as it relied so heavily on Europe for manufactured goods, and he urged Congress to promote industrial development through limited use of protective tariffs. Many of Hamilton's ideas were implemented in later decades, but few congressmen in 1791 saw much merit in his proposals. Convinced that America's future lay in agriculture and the carrying (shipping) trade and that the mainstay of the republic was the yeoman farmer, Congress rejected the report.

The Granger Collection

▲ The First Bank of the United States, constructed in the mid-1790s, as the building looked in Philadelphia in 1800. Its classical simplicity, meant to inspire confidence, concealed its contentious political origins.

Also controversial was another feature of Hamilton's financial program enacted in 1791: an excise tax on whiskey designed to provide additional income to the national government. The tax affected a relatively small number of westerners—the farmers who grew corn and the distillers who turned that corn into whiskey—and might also reduce the consumption of whiskey. (Eighteenth-century Americans consumed about twice as much alcohol per capita as Americans do today.) Moreover, Hamilton knew that western farmers and distillers tended to support Jefferson, and he saw the benefits of taxing them rather than the merchants who favored his own nationalist policies.

7-4h Whiskey Rebellion

News of the tax set off protests in the West, where residents were dissatisfied with the army's defense of their region from Native attack. To their minds, the same government that protected them inadequately was now proposing to tax them disproportionately. For two years, unrest continued on the frontiers of Pennsylvania, Maryland, and Virginia. Large groups of men drafted petitions protesting the tax, imitated crowd actions of the 1760s, and occasionally harassed tax collectors.

President Washington responded with restraint until July 1794, when western Pennsylvania farmers resisted two excisemen trying to collect the tax. On August 1, about seven thousand rebels convened to plot the destruction of Pittsburgh but decided not to face the heavy guns of the fort guarding the town. Washington then took decisive action to prevent a crisis reminiscent of Shays's Rebellion. On August 7, he called on the insurgents to disperse and summoned nearly thirteen thousand militiamen. Federal forces marched westward in October and November, led at times by Washington himself. The troops met no resistance and arrested only twenty suspects. Two men were convicted of treason; Washington pardoned both. The rebellion ended with little bloodshed.

The importance of the **Whiskey Rebellion** lay in the forceful message its suppression conveyed to the American people. The national government would not allow violent resistance to its laws. People dissatisfied with a given law should try to amend or repeal it, not take extralegal action as they had during the colonial era.

7-5 Building a Nation Among Nations

▶ What domestic and international events contributed to rivalry between the Federalists and Republicans?

▶ How did George Washington respond to international developments during his terms as president?

▶ How did political culture operate in the 1790s?

▶ What were the domestic and international ramifications of the XYZ Affair?

By 1794, some Americans were already beginning to seek change through electoral politics, even though traditional political theory regarded organized opposition—especially in a republic—as illegitimate. In a monarchy, formal opposition groups, commonly called factions, were expected. In a government of the people, by contrast, sustained factional disagreement was taken as a sign of corruption. Though widely held, such negative judgments did little to check partisan sentiment.

7-5a Republicans and Federalists

As early as 1792, Jefferson and Madison became convinced that Hamilton's policies, which favored wealthy commercial interests at the expense of agriculture, threatened the United States. Characterizing themselves as the true heirs of the Revolution, they charged Hamilton with plotting to subvert republican principles. To dramatize their point, Jefferson, Madison, and their followers in Congress began calling themselves Republicans. Hamilton accused Jefferson and Madison of the same offense: attempting to destroy the republic. To legitimize their claims and link themselves with the Constitution, Hamilton and his supporters called themselves Federalists. Newspapers aligned with each side fanned the flames of partisanship. Indeed, before parties fully coalesced, such newspapers served as the very foundation of political identity.

At first, President Washington tried to remain aloof from the dispute that divided his advisers. The growing controversy did help persuade him to promote unity by seeking office again in 1792. But after 1793, developments in Europe magnified the disagreements, as France (America's wartime ally) and Great Britain (America's essential trading partner) resumed the periodic hostilities that had originated centuries earlier.

7-5b French Revolution

In 1789, many American men and women welcomed the news of revolution in France. The French people's success in overthrowing an oppressive monarchy seemed to vindicate the United States' own revolution. Americans saw themselves as France's sister republic, the vanguard of a trend that would reshape the world. Dinners, public ceremonies, and balls celebrated the French revolutionaries; some began terming themselves "citizen" or, for women, "citesse," in the French manner.

But by 1793, the reports from France had grown alarming. Political leaders succeeded each other with bewildering rapidity. Executions mounted; the king himself was beheaded that January. Although many Americans, including Jefferson and Madison, retained sympathy for the revolution, others—Hamilton among them—began to cite France as a prime example of the perversion of republicanism into mob rule.

Whiskey Rebellion Tax protest by western farmers that turned violent. Washington's willingness to send troops in response demonstrated the increased power of the national government.

Newspapers of the Early Republic

In the 1790s newspapers did not attempt to present news objectively, and indeed, none of their readers expected them to do so. Instead, newspapers were linked to the rapidly expanding political factions of the new nation—the partisan groupings (not yet political parties in the modern sense) terming themselves *Federalists* and *Republicans*. The "official" paper of the Federalists was *The Gazette of*

the United States. (Colonial papers supported by individual governments too had been called *gazettes*—just as the *London Gazette* was tied to the English government.) Among the Republicans' many allied newspapers was *The New-York Journal, and Patriotic Register*. A reader comparing the front pages of any two issues could see at a glance the differences between them. *The Gazette of the United States* filled

its first page with sober news articles, whereas the face *The New-York Journal* presented to the world was consumed entirely with advertisements, some headed by intriguing design elements.

CRITICAL THINKING

- Which would appeal more directly to America's artisans and forward-thinking yeomen, and why?

Front Page of the New York Journal & Patriotic Register, August 21, 1793 (litho)/American School, (18th century)/CHICAGO HISTORY MUSEUM/© Chicago History Museum, USA/Bridgeman Images

Front Page of the Gazette of the United States, April 15, 1789 (litho)/American School, (18th century)/AMERICAN ANTIQUARIAN SOCIETY/American Antiquarian Society, Worcester, Massachusetts, USA/Bridgeman Images

Debates within the United States intensified when republican France declared war on Austria in 1792, and then on Britain, Spain, and Holland the following year. That confronted the Americans with a dilemma. The 1778 Treaty of Alliance with France bound them to that nation "forever," and a mutual commitment to republicanism created ideological bonds as well. Yet the United States remained connected to Great Britain through their shared history and language, and through commerce. By the 1790s, Americans again purchased most of their manufactured goods from Great Britain. Indeed, because the revenues of the United States depended heavily on import tariffs, vigorous trade with the former mother country became vital to the nation's economic health.

The political and diplomatic climate grew even more complicated in April 1793, when Edmond Charles Genêt, the French government's minister to the United States, landed in Charleston, South Carolina, carrying instructions to renegotiate the alliance of 1778 for the new French government. Genêt found himself thronged by well-wishers when he disembarked at the Charleston docks. Some weeks later, Secretary of State Thomas Jefferson welcomed Genêt warmly in Philadelphia. But President Washington was cooler to the French diplomat. He and other Federalists questioned the continuing obligations of the United States to the ever more radical French revolutionary regime. Before receiving Genêt, Washington issued a proclamation stating that the United States would adopt "conduct friendly and impartial toward the belligerent powers" in the European war.

Federalist newspapers vociferously defended the neutrality proclamation, and partisan leaders organized rallies to praise the president's action. Republicans who favored assisting France reluctantly accepted the policy of neutrality, which had overwhelming popular support. But by July, Genêt's support for French privateers in the Caribbean had cost him the support even of Jefferson's allies, and Washington requested his recall to France.

7-5c Democratic Societies

Genêt's faction fell from power in Paris, and he subsequently sought political asylum in the United States. But his disappearance from the diplomatic scene did not diminish the impact of the French Revolution in America. Clubs called Democratic societies, formed by Americans sympathetic to the French Revolution, perpetuated the domestic divisions Genêt had helped to widen. More than forty such societies organized between 1793 and 1800. Their members cast themselves in the mold of the 1760s resistance movement, as defenders of fragile liberty from corrupt and self-serving Federalist rulers.

The rapid spread of citizens' groups outspokenly critical of the administration disturbed Hamilton and Washington. Federalist writers charged that the societies' true intention was "to involve the country in war, to assume the reins of government and tyrannize over the people." The counterattack climaxed in the fall of 1794 when Washington accused the clubs of fomenting the Whiskey Rebellion. In retrospect, the administration's reaction seems disproportionately hostile. But as the first organized political dissenters in the United States, the Democratic societies alarmed officials who had not yet accepted the idea that one component of a free government was an organized loyal opposition.

7-5d Jay Treaty Debate

In 1794, George Washington dispatched Chief Justice John Jay to London to negotiate several unresolved questions in Anglo-American relations. The British had recently seized some American merchant ships trading in the French West Indies. The United States wanted to establish the principle of freedom of the seas and to assert its right, as a neutral nation, to unfettered trade with both combatants. Further, Great Britain still held posts in the American Northwest, thus violating the 1783 peace treaty. Settlers there believed the British responsible for renewed warfare with neighboring Native peoples, and they wanted that threat removed. Southern planters also wanted compensation for the slaves who left with the British army after the war.

Jay had little to offer the British in exchange for the concessions he sought. Britain agreed to evacuate the western forts and reduce restrictions on American trade to England and the Caribbean. The treaty established two arbitration commissions—one to deal with prewar debts Americans owed to British creditors and the other to hear claims for captured American merchant ships—but Britain adamantly refused to compensate slave owners for their lost human property. Under the circumstances, Jay had probably done the best he could. Nevertheless, most Americans, including the president, at first expressed dissatisfaction with the treaty.

The Senate debated the Jay Treaty in secret. Not until after its narrow ratification in June 1795 did the public learn its provisions in the pages of the leading Republican newspaper, Benjamin Franklin Bache's *Aurora*. Bache organized the protests that followed: publications and popular gatherings urging Washington to reject the treaty. Federalists countered with rallies and essays of their own, contending that Jay's treaty was preferable to no treaty at all. Displeased by the Republicans' organized opposition and convinced by pro-treaty arguments, Washington signed the pact in mid-August. Just one opportunity remained to prevent it from taking effect: Congress had to appropriate funds to carry out the treaty, and appropriation bills had to originate in the House of Representatives.

Hoping the opposition would dissipate, Washington delayed submitting the treaty to the House until March 1796. The treaty's congressional opponents initially commanded a majority, but pressure for appropriating the necessary funds built quickly. Federalists successfully linked the Jay Treaty with another, more popular pact that Thomas Pinckney of South Carolina had negotiated with Spain the previous year. Pinckney's Treaty gave the United States valuable navigation privileges on the Mississippi River and the right to land

and store goods at New Orleans tax-free. The Senate ratified it unanimously, and the overwhelming support it received helped to overcome opposition to the Jay Treaty. In late April, a divided House appropriated the money by a three-vote margin. All but two southerners opposed the treaty; all but three Federalists supported it.

Ironically, the Federalists' campaign to sway public opinion violated their fundamental philosophy of government. They believed ordinary people should defer to the judgment of elected leaders, yet in order to persuade the House to follow the president's lead, they actively engaged in grassroots politicking. Even Federalist women became involved by presenting patriotic banners to militia companies or by taking formal roles in July fourth celebrations. The Federalists won the battle, but in the long run they would lose the war, for Republicans ultimately proved far more effective in appealing to the citizenry at large.

To describe the growing partisanship in Congress and the nation is easier than to explain such fractures in the electorate. The terms used by Jefferson and Madison ("the people" versus "aristocrats") or by Hamilton and Washington ("true patriots" versus "subversive rabble") do not adequately describe the growing divisions. Simple economic differences between farmers and city folk do not provide the answer either, as more than 90 percent of Americans still lived in rural areas. Moreover, Jefferson's vision of a prosperous agrarian America rested on commercial farming, not rural self-sufficiency. Nor did the divisions in the 1790s simply repeat the ratification debates of 1787–1788. Even though most Antifederalists became Republicans, the party's leaders, Madison and Jefferson, had supported the Constitution.

Yet certain distinctions can be made. Republicans, especially strong in the southern and middle states, tended to be self-assured, confident, and optimistic. Southern planters, in control of their region and their bound labor force, foresaw a prosperous future fueled by continued westward expansion. Republicans employed democratic rhetoric to win the allegiance of small farmers in southern and mid-Atlantic states. Members of non-English ethnic groups found Republicans' message attractive. Artisans—like small farmers, fierce believers in household autonomy—joined the coalition. Republicans of all descriptions prized America's internal resources, remaining sympathetic to France but worrying less about the nation's place in the world than Federalists did.

By contrast, Federalists concentrated among the commercial interests of New England. They stressed the need for order, hierarchy, and obedience to political authority. Federalists, like their Republican opponents, realized that southern and middle-state interests would dominate western lands, so they had little incentive to focus on that potentially rich territory. Where Republicans faced West, Federalists faced East, toward London. In their eyes, the nation's internal and external enemies made alliance with Great Britain essential. Given the dangers posed to the nation by European warfare, Federalists' vision of international affairs may have been accurate, but it was also unappealing. Federalists offered voters little hope of a better future, and the Republicans prevailed in the end.

7-5e Washington's Farewell Address

After the treaty debate, wearied by the criticism to which he had been subjected, George Washington decided not to seek reelection. (Presidents had not yet been limited to two terms.) In September, Washington published his Farewell Address, most of which Hamilton wrote. The address outlined two principles that guided American foreign policy at least until the late 1940s: to maintain commercial but not political ties to other nations, and to reject permanent alliances. Washington also drew sharp distinctions between the United States and Europe, stressing America's uniqueness—its exceptionalism—and the need for independent action in foreign affairs, today called *unilateralism*.

Some interpret Washington's plea for an end to partisan strife as a call for politicians to consider the good of the whole nation. But in the context of the impending presidential election, the Farewell Address appears rather as an attack on the Republican opposition. Washington advocated unity behind the Federalist banner, which he viewed as the only proper stance. The Federalists (like the Republicans) continued to see themselves as the rightful heirs of the Revolution. Both sides perceived their opponents as illegitimate, unpatriotic troublemakers who sought to undermine revolutionary ideals. The Republican *Aurora* derided the address as empty words. Washington's administration had excelled at "the profession of republicanism, but the practice of monarchy and aristocracy," editor Bache wrote. Surely "the men of the revolution, who still feel its principles and its sympathies," would now follow a different and better course than the one the Federalists had charted.

7-5f Election of 1796

The two organized groups actively contending for office made the presidential **election of 1796** the first serious contest for the position. To succeed Washington, the Federalists in Congress put forward Vice President John Adams, with the diplomat Thomas Pinckney as his running mate. Congressional Republicans chose Thomas Jefferson as their presidential candidate; the lawyer, Revolutionary War veteran, and Republican politician Aaron Burr of New York agreed to stand for vice president. But the method of voting in the electoral college did not take into account the possibility of party slates. The Constitution's drafters had not foreseen the emergence of competing political organizations, so the document provided no way to express support for a ticket that included one candidate for president and another for vice president. The electors simply voted for two people. The man with the highest total became president; the second highest, vice president.

Election of 1796 Federalist John Adams won by three votes and, as the second-highest vote-getter in the electoral college, Thomas Jefferson became vice president.

Library of Congress Prints and Photographs Division [LC-USZC4-2711]

▲ This cartoon drawn during the XYZ Affair depicts the United States as a maiden being victimized by the five leaders of the French government's directorate. In the background, John Bull (England) watches from on high, while other European nations discuss the situation.

That procedure proved to be the Federalists' undoing. Adams won the presidency with 71 votes, but a number of Federalist electors failed to cast ballots for Pinckney. With 68 votes, the next highest total, Jefferson would become vice president. During the next four years, the new president and vice president, once allies and close friends, became bitter enemies.

7-5g XYZ Affair

As president, John Adams clung to an outdated notion discarded by George Washington as early as 1794: that the president should remain above politics. Thus, Adams kept Washington's cabinet intact, despite its key members' allegiance to his chief Federalist rival, Alexander Hamilton. Adams often adopted a passive posture, letting others (usually Hamilton) take the lead when the president should have acted decisively. But Adams's detachment from Hamilton's maneuverings did enable him to weather the greatest international crisis the republic had yet faced.

The Jay Treaty had improved America's relationship with Great Britain, but it provoked France to retaliate by seizing American vessels carrying British goods. In response, Congress authorized the building of ships and the stockpiling of weapons and ammunition. President Adams also sent three commissioners to Paris to negotiate a settlement. For months, the American commissioners sought talks with Talleyrand, the French foreign minister, but Talleyrand's agents demanded a bribe of $250,000

before negotiations could begin. The Americans retorted, "No, no; not a sixpence," and reported the incident in dispatches the president received in March 1798. Adams informed Congress and recommended further increases in military spending.

Convinced that Adams had deliberately sabotaged the negotiations, Republicans insisted that the dispatches be turned over to Congress. Adams complied, withholding only the names of the French agents, whom he labeled X, Y, and Z. The revelation that the Americans had been treated with contempt stimulated a wave of anti-French sentiment in the United States and became known as the **XYZ Affair**. One journalist's version of the commissioners' reply, "Millions for defense, but not a cent for tribute," became a national slogan. Congress formally abrogated the Treaty of Alliance and authorized American ships to commandeer French vessels.

7-5h Quasi-War with France

Thus began an undeclared war with France fought in Caribbean waters between warships of the U.S. Navy and French privateers. Although Americans initially suffered heavy losses, by early 1799 the U.S. Navy had established its superiority, easing the threat to America's vital Caribbean trade.

XYZ Affair French demand for bribes from American negotiators that triggered widespread anger in the United States and led to the ending of the American alliance with France.

The Republicans, who opposed war and continued to sympathize with France, could do little to stem the tide of anti-French feelings. Because Agent Y had boasted of the existence of a "French party in America," Federalists flatly accused Republicans of traitorous designs. John Adams wavered between denouncing the Republicans and acknowledging their right to oppose administration measures. His wife was less tolerant. "Those whom the French boast of as their Partizans," Abigail Adams declared, should be "adjudged traitors to their country."

7-5i Alien and Sedition Acts

Federalists saw an opportunity to deal a deathblow to their Republican opponents. Now that the country seemed to see the truth of what they had been saying ever since the Whiskey Rebellion in 1794—that Republicans were subversive foreign agents—Federalists would codify that belief. In 1798, the Federalist-controlled Congress adopted a set of four laws known as the **Alien and Sedition Acts**, intended to weaken the Republican faction.

Three of the acts targeted recently arrived immigrants, whom Federalists accurately suspected of sympathizing with Republicans. The Naturalization Act lengthened the residency period required for citizenship and ordered all resident aliens to register with the federal government. The two Alien Acts, though not immediately implemented, provided for the detention of enemy aliens during wartime and gave the president authority to deport any alien he deemed dangerous to the nation's security.

The fourth statute, the Sedition Act, sought to control both citizens and aliens. It outlawed conspiracies to prevent the enforcement of federal laws, setting the maximum punishment for such offenses at five years in prison and a $5,000 fine. The act also made writing, printing, or uttering "false, scandalous and malicious" statements "with intent to defame" the government or the president a crime punishable by as much as two years' imprisonment and a fine of $2,000. Today, a law punishing political speech would be unconstitutional. But in the eighteenth century, when organized opposition was suspect, many Americans supported such restrictions on free speech.

The Sedition Act led to fifteen indictments and ten guilty verdicts. Among those convicted were a congressman and former newspaper editor, Matthew Lyon of Vermont; and James Callender, a Scots immigrant and scandalmonger whose exposés forced Alexander Hamilton to acknowledge an extramarital affair. After turning his attention to President Adams, Callender was convicted, fined, and jailed for nine months. Energized rather than silenced by the persecution, growing numbers of Republican newspaper editors stepped up their relentless criticisms. One of the most outspoken, William Duane—successor to Bache as the *Aurora*'s editor—ignored a Sedition Act indictment, prosecutions in state and federal courts for other purported offenses, and even a vicious beating by Federalist thugs, to persist in partisan attacks. He and other Republicans created an informal network of newspapers that spread opposition ideas throughout the country.

Jefferson and Madison combated the acts in another way. Petitioning the Federalist-controlled Congress to repeal the laws would clearly fail, and Federalist judges refused to allow accused individuals to question the Sedition Act's constitutionality. Accordingly, Republican leaders turned to the only other forum available for formal protest: state legislatures. Carefully concealing their own roles, Jefferson and Madison drafted the **Virginia and Kentucky Resolutions**, which were introduced into those states' legislatures, respectively, in the fall of 1798. Because a compact among the states had created the Constitution, the resolutions contended, people speaking through their states had a legitimate right to judge the constitutionality of actions taken by the federal government. Both legislatures pronounced the Alien and Sedition Acts unconstitutional, thus advancing the doctrine later known as nullification.

Although no other state endorsed them, the Virginia and Kentucky Resolutions placed the opposition party squarely in the revolutionary tradition of resistance to tyrannical authority. Their theory of union inspired the Hartford Convention of 1814 and southern states' rights advocates in the 1830s and thereafter. Jefferson and Madison had identified a key constitutional issue: How far could states go in opposing the national government? How could conflicts between the two be resolved? These questions would not be definitively answered until the Civil War.

7-5j The Convention of 1800

Just as northern legislatures were rejecting the Virginia and Kentucky Resolutions, Federalists split over the course of action the United States should take toward France. Hamilton and his supporters called for a declaration legitimizing the undeclared naval war. Adams, though, received a number of private signals that the French government regretted its treatment of the American commissioners. In response, he dispatched William Vans Murray to Paris to negotiate with Napoleon Bonaparte, France's new leader. The United States wanted to receive compensation for ships the French had seized since 1793 and to abrogate the treaty of 1778. The Convention of 1800, which ended the Quasi-War, conceded only the latter point. Still, it freed the United States from its only permanent alliance, thus allowing the nation to follow the independent course George Washington had urged in his Farewell Address.

Alien and Sedition Acts
A series of laws passed in 1798 that were intended to suppress dissent and block the rise of the Republican faction.

Virginia and Kentucky Resolutions A republican response to the Alien and Sedition Acts, the resolutions asserted the right of state legislatures to judge the constitutionality of federal laws.

7-6 The West in the New Nation

▶ **How did the United States acquire additional lands in the 1790s?**

▶ **What was the national government's position toward Native peoples?**

By 1800, the nation had added three states (Vermont, Kentucky, and Tennessee) to the original thirteen and more than 1 million people to the nearly 4 million counted by the 1790 census. The United States claimed sovereignty east of the Mississippi River and north of Spanish Florida. But the nation controlled the Northwest Territory only after considerable bloodshed, as American troops battled a powerful confederacy of eight Native American nations led by the Miamis.

7-6a War in the Northwest Territory

In 1789, General Arthur St. Clair, first governor of the Northwest Territory, failed to open more land to settlement through treaty negotiations with the western confederacy. Subsequently, Little Turtle, the confederacy's able war chief, defeated forces led by General Josiah Harmar (1790) and by St. Clair himself (1791) in battles near the border between modern Indiana and Ohio. In the United States' worst defeat in the entire history of the American frontier, more than six hundred of St. Clair's men died, and scores more were wounded.

The Miami Confederacy declared that peace could be achieved only if the United States recognized the Ohio River as its northwestern boundary. But the national government refused to relinquish its claims in the region. In August 1794, a newly invigorated army under the command of General Anthony Wayne, a Revolutionary War hero, attacked and defeated the confederacy at the Battle of Fallen Timbers, near present-day Toledo, Ohio (see Map 7.2). Eager to avoid a costly and prolonged frontier conflict between settlers whom the government regarded as "white savages" and Native leaders whom Wayne called "red gentlemen," the general reached agreement with the confederacy in August 1795.

The resulting Treaty of Greenville gave each side a portion of what it wanted. The United States gained the right to settle much of what was to become Ohio. In exchange, the indigenous peoples won an acknowledgment they had long sought: the United States formally accepted the principle of Native sovereignty, by virtue of residence, over all lands the Native peoples had not ceded. Never again would

Little Turtle (colour litho)/American School, (19th century)/CHICAGO HISTORY MUSEUM,/© Chicago History Museum, USA/ Bridgeman Images

General Anthony Wayne (1745-96) [oil on linen]/Savage, Edward (1761-1817)/NEW YORK HISTORICAL SOCIETY/© Collection of the New-York Historical Society, USA/Bridgeman Images

▲ The two chief antagonists at the Battle of Fallen Timbers and negotiators of the Treaty of Greenville (1795). On the left, Little Turtle, the leader of the Miami Confederacy; on the right, General Anthony Wayne. Little Turtle, in a copy of a portrait painted two years after the battle, appears to be wearing a miniature of Wayne on a bear-claw necklace.

▲ In 1805, an unidentified artist painted Benjamin Hawkins, a trader and U.S. agent to the Creeks, near Macon, Georgia. Hawkins introduced European-style agriculture to the Creeks, who are shown here with vegetables from their fields. Throughout the eastern United States, Native peoples had to make similar adaptations of their traditional lifestyles in order to maintain their group identity.

the United States government claim that it had acquired Native American territory solely through negotiation with a European or North American country.

That same year, Pinckney's treaty with Spain established the 31st parallel as the boundary between the United States and Florida. Nevertheless, Spanish influence in the Old Southwest—where the Creeks, Cherokees, and other Native American nations continued to occupy much unceded territory—continued to raise questions about the loyalty of American settlers in the region. A Southwest Ordinance (1790) attempted to organize the territory; by permitting slavery, it made the region attractive to slaveholders.

7-6b "Civilizing" Native Peoples

Increasingly, even Native peoples who lived independent of federal authority came within the orbit of American influence. The nation's stated goal was to "civilize" them. "Instead of exterminating a part of the human race," Henry Knox contended in 1789, the government should "impart our knowledge of cultivation and the arts to the aboriginals of the country." To promote "a love for exclusive property"

among Native peoples, Knox proposed that the government give livestock and training in agriculture to people in native communities. Four years later, the Indian Trade and Intercourse Act of 1793 codified the secretary of war's proposals.

Knox's plan reflected federal officials' blindness to the realities of Native people's lives. Not only did it incorrectly posit that traditional commitment to communal notions of landowning could easily be overcome, it also ignored the centuries-old agricultural practices of eastern Native peoples. The policymakers focused only on Native American men: because they hunted, Native men were "savages" who had to be "civilized" by being taught to farm. That in these societies women traditionally raised the crops was irrelevant because, in the eyes of the officials, Native American women—like those of European descent—should properly confine themselves to child rearing, household chores, and home manufacturing.

Many indigenous nations responded cautiously to the "civilizing" plan. The Iroquois Confederacy had been devastated by the war; its people in the 1790s lived in what one historian has called "slums in the wilderness." Restricted to small reservations increasingly surrounded by Anglo-American farmlands, men could no longer hunt and often spent their days idle. Quaker missionaries started a demonstration farm among the Senecas, intending to teach men to plow, but they quickly learned that women showed greater interest in their message.

Iroquois men became more receptive to the reformers after the spring of 1799, when a Seneca named Handsome Lake experienced a remarkable series of visions. Like other Native prophets stretching back to Neolin in the 1760s, Handsome Lake preached that Native peoples should renounce alcohol, gambling, and other destructive European customs. Although he directed his followers to reorient men's and women's work assignments as the Quakers advocated, Handsome Lake aimed above all to preserve Iroquois culture. He recognized that, because men could no longer obtain meat through hunting, only by adopting the European sexual division of labor could the Iroquois retain their autonomy.

7-7 Created Equal?

▶ What contradictions lay at the heart of the Declaration's assertion that "all men are created equal"?

▶ How did the battle of women's rights develop in the new nation?

▶ What divisions emerged over the question of slavery and the slave trade?

The Constitution distinguished between "persons" and "citizens." All persons inhabiting the United States comprised, in some vague sense, *the people* who were sovereign in a republic. But only *citizens* voted; only citizens fully possessed the rights enumerated in the Constitution's first ten amendments. Slaves typically could not bear arms, for example. Women, like men, were entitled to "a speedy and public trial, by an impartial jury," but they could not themselves serve as jurors, let alone judges. The language of Jefferson's Declaration of Independence was far more sweeping: "all men are created equal." In eighteenth-century parlance, *all men* meant *all persons*; all *persons* had natural, "unalienable rights" including "life, liberty, and the pursuit of happiness." After independence, women, the enslaved, free people of color, and radical thinkers wrestled anew with the contradictions between such capacious notions of liberty and the laws and customs of the young United States.

7-7a Women and the Republic

"I long to hear that you have declared an independancy," wrote **Abigail Adams** to her husband John in March 1776, shortly after reading Paine's *Common Sense*. And "by the way," she continued, "in the new Code of Laws which I suppose it will be necessary for you to make I desire you would Remember the Ladies, and be more generous and favourable to them than your ancestors." She hoped that Congress would "not put such unlimited power into the Hands of the Husbands," who traditionally held near-absolute authority over their wives' property and persons. "Remember all Men would be tyrants if they could," Adams noted. "If perticuliar care and attention is not paid to the Laidies [*sic*] we are determined to foment a Rebellion, and will not hold ourselves bound by any Laws in which we have no voice, or Representation."

Two weeks later, John Adams responded: "As to your extraordinary Code of Laws, I cannot but laugh." But the widening circle of rights talk was not so easily dismissed. Like many other disfranchised Americans in the age of revolution, Abigail Adams adapted the ideology patriots had developed to combat Parliament to serve purposes revolutionary leaders had never intended.

Abigail Adams did not ask for woman suffrage, but others did, and some male and female authors began to discuss and define the "rights of women" in general terms. Judith Sargent Murray, Thomas Paine, and James Otis all published essays on the topic, as did many transatlantic radicals. The Philadelphia physician Benjamin Rush, a wide-ranging reformer who argued against capital punishment and slavery, began agitating for women's access to education in 1787. Five years later, Britain's Mary Wollstonecraft inflamed readers throughout the English-speaking world with her tract entitled *A Vindication of the Rights of Woman*.

Nor was the battle for women's rights confined to the page. The drafters of the New Jersey state constitution in 1776 defined voters as "all free inhabitants"; subsequent state laws explicitly enfranchised female voters. For several decades, women who met the state's property qualifications—as well as free black landowners—regularly voted in New Jersey's elections. The anomaly was noted elsewhere; in 1800, one Boston newspaper reported, "Single Females in the State of New Jersey, possessed of a certain property, and having paid taxes, are entitled to vote at elections," and "many exercised this privilege." Had Massachusetts been "equally liberal," Abigail Adams quipped, she too would have cast her ballot. That women who could vote chose to do so was evidence of their altered perception of their place in the political life of the country.

Like their brothers, sons, and husbands, many elite and middling women engaged in nascent partisanship in the 1790s. A 1798 play entitled *Politicians; or, A State of Things*, satirized female characters named Mrs. Violent and Mrs. Turbulent. As political contests grew more openly combative, women's role in the public sphere came to seem more threatening—both to the republic and to womanhood itself. Increasingly, thinkers emphasized the differences between men and women rather than their shared humanity. After an election marred

Abigail Adams Wife of Revolutionary figure (and second U.S. President) John Adams. Influenced by the ideology of the Revolution, her letter to her husband is considered an early effort for greater rights for women.

▲ Mary Wollstonecraft (1759–1797) was one of the most famous thinkers of her day. Her 1792 treatise, *A Vindication of the Rights of Woman*, argued that the radical equality envisioned by the revolutionaries in France should be extended to relations between the sexes. *Vindication* became an international bestseller, with French, German, and American editions printed within the year. Engravings based on this portrait of Wollstonecraft by John Opie served as the frontispiece to later editions of her works, and circulated widely in the United States.

by drunken violence, New Jersey's state legislature concluded that the polls were no place for ladies and abolished female voting in 1807. Throughout the nation, as property qualifications for white male voters shrank, the presumed distinction between white men and everyone else grew. "We hear no longer of the *alarming*, and perhaps justly obnoxious din, of the 'rights of women,'" wrote one conservative female historian in 1832.

7-7b Emancipation and Manumission

On the eve of independence, people of African descent comprised nearly 20 percent of the American population (see Map 7.3). How did approximately seven hundred thousand enslaved and free blacks—persons but not necessarily citizens—fit into the developing nation? Well before the Constitution was ratified, the question engaged white and black activists. In the late 1770s and early 1780s, enslaved men and women in New Hampshire, Connecticut, and Massachusetts petitioned their courts and legislatures for what some of them called "the sweets of freedom." "That liberty is a great thing we may know from our own feelings, and we may likewise judge so from the conduct of the white-people, in the late war," argued Jupiter Hammon, an enslaved New York writer. "I have hoped that God would open their eyes, when they were so much engaged for liberty, to think of the state of the poor blacks."

Such agitation catalyzed the gradual abolition of slavery in the North, a process now known as "the first emancipation." Vermont banned slavery in its 1777 constitution. Responding to lawsuits filed by enslaved men and women, Massachusetts courts ruled in 1783 that the state constitution prohibited slavery. Other states adopted gradual emancipation laws between 1780 (Pennsylvania) and 1804 (New Jersey). No southern state passed a general emancipation law, but the legislatures of Virginia (1782), Delaware (1787), and Maryland (1790 and 1796) altered statutes that restricted slave owners' ability to free their bondspeople.

7-7c Congress Debates Slavery

At the national level, too, the ideology and experience of Revolution transformed slavery from an unspoken assumption to an open question. In early 1790, three groups of Quakers submitted petitions to Congress calling for the abolition of slavery and the international slave trade. In the ensuing debates, the nation's political leaders directly addressed questions the Constitution had cloaked in euphemism. Southerners vigorously asserted that Congress should not even consider the petitions; had they imagined the federal government would interfere with slavery, they would never have ratified the Constitution. Insisting that slavery was integral to the Union and that abolition would cause more problems than it solved, such legislators developed a defense of slavery that forecast most of the arguments offered on the subject during the next seven decades. Congress accepted a committee report denying it the power to halt slave importations before 1808 or to emancipate slaves at any time, that authority "remaining with the several States alone." The precedent that Congress could not abolish slavery endured until the Civil War.

Revolutionary ideology thus had limited impact on the well-entrenched interests of large slaveholders. Only in the northern states—societies with slaves, not slave societies—did legislatures vote to abolish slavery. Even there, lawmakers' concern for the *property* rights of owners of human chattel—the Revolution, after all, was fought for property as well as for liberty—led them to favor gradual emancipation over immediate abolition. New York's law freed children born into slavery after July 4, 1799, but only after they reached their mid-twenties. And not until the

DEA PICTURE LIBRARY/Getty Images

late 1840s did Rhode Island and Connecticut abolish all vestiges of slavery. For decades, many African Americans in the North lived in an intermediate stage between slavery and freedom.

7-7d Growth of Free Black Population

Despite the slow progress of abolition, the number of free people of African descent grew dramatically after the Revolution. Wartime escapees from plantations, bondsmen who had served in the Continental army, and still others emancipated by their owners or by new state laws were now free. By 1790, nearly 60,000 free people of color lived in the United States; ten years later, they numbered more than 108,000, more than 10 percent of the African American population.

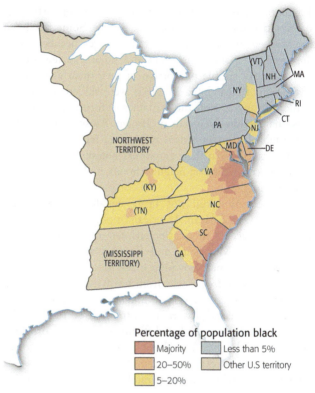

Percentage of population black

Majority	Less than 5%
20–50%	Other U.S territory
5–20%	

Map 7.3 African American Population, 1790: Proportion of Total Population

The first national census clearly indicated that the African American population was heavily concentrated in the coastal South. Although there were growing numbers of blacks in the backcountry—presumably taken there by migrating slave owners—most parts of the North and East had few African American residents. But slavery shaped the entire American economy in the early republic, and even in the mid-Atlantic and the North, its abolition took place gradually, sometimes over decades.

Heritage Images/Hulton Fine Art Collection/Getty Images

▲ A sailor of African descent posed proudly for this portrait around 1800. The name of the artist remains unknown, but the sitter has been tentatively identified as Paul Slocum, the Massachusetts-born son of a West African freedman and a Wampanoag woman. Slocum later changed his name to Cuffee, after his father's Akan day name. As a boat builder and maritime trader, he amassed a fortune, becoming perhaps the wealthiest African American of the early nineteenth century. Subject to racial violence and discrimination, he founded a school, Cuffee's School, to educate black children, and became involved with the free black colony of Sierra Leone, in Africa.

In the Chesapeake, manumissions were speeded by declining soil fertility and the shift from tobacco to grain production, as well as by the rising influence of Baptists and Methodists. Because grain cultivation was less labor intensive than tobacco growing, planters began to complain about "excess" slaves, and occasionally freed some of their less productive or more favored laborers. The enslaved also seized the opportunity to negotiate agreements allowing them to live and work independently until they could save enough to purchase themselves. The free black population of Virginia more than doubled in the two decades after 1790. By 1810, nearly one-quarter of Maryland's African American population lived outside of legal bondage.

7-7e Freedpeople's Lives

Freedpeople from rural areas often made their way to the port cities, especially Boston, Philadelphia, and the new boomtown of Baltimore. Women outnumbered men among the migrants, for they had better employment opportunities in the cities, especially in domestic service. Some freedmen also worked in domestic service, but larger numbers were employed as unskilled laborers and sailors. A few of the women and a sizable proportion of men (nearly one-third of those in Philadelphia in 1795) were skilled workers or retailers. Many cast off the surnames of former masters and chose names like Newman or Brown. As soon as possible they established independent two-parent families instead of continuing to live in their employers' households. They also began to occupy distinct neighborhoods, probably as a result of discrimination.

Emancipation did not bring equality. Even whites who recognized African Americans' right to freedom were unwilling to accept them as equals. Several states—including Delaware, Maryland, and South Carolina—adopted laws denying property-owning black men the vote. South Carolina forbade free blacks from testifying against whites in court. New Englanders used indenture contracts to control freed youths, who were also often barred from public schools. Freedmen found it difficult to purchase property and find good jobs. And though in many areas African Americans were accepted as members—even ministers—of evangelical churches, they were rarely allowed an equal voice in church affairs.

To survive and prosper, freedpeople came to rely on collective effort. In Charleston, mixed-race people formed the Brown Fellowship Society, which provided them insurance, financed a school, and helped to support orphans. In 1794, former slaves in Philadelphia and Baltimore, led by the African American clergyman Richard Allen, founded societies that eventually became the **African Methodist Episcopal (AME) Church**. AME congregations—along with African Baptist, African Episcopal, and African Presbyterian churches—became cultural centers of free black communities.

7-7f Development of Racist Theory

Their endeavors were all the more important because the post-revolutionary years witnessed the development of racist theory in the United States. European Americans had long regarded their slaves as inferior, but the most influential thinkers reasoned that bondspeople's seemingly debased character derived from their enslavement, rather than enslavement's being the consequence of inherited inferiority. In the Revolution's aftermath, though, slave owners became ever more defensive. To skirt the contradiction between slaveholding practice and the egalitarian implications of revolutionary theory, they redefined the theory, arguing that people of African descent were less than fully human and thus the principles of republican equality applied only to European Americans.

African Methodist Episcopal (AME) Church The first African American–led Protestant denomination.

A Philosophic Cock, 1804 (colour litho)/American School, (19th century)/AMERICAN ANTIQUARIAN SOCIETY/American Antiquarian Society, Worcester, Massachusetts, USA/Bridgeman Images

▲ A Federalist political cartoon from the election 1804 satirizes Jefferson's pretensions as a *philosophe* in the French mode, and lampoons his relationship with the enslaved Sally Hemings. The engraving, entitled (in a deliberately dirty pun) "A Philosophic Cock," depicts the president as a brightly-plumed rooster, with a turbaned Hemings cowering beside him as a little brown hen.

Simultaneously, the concept of "race" began to be applied to groups defined by skin color. The rise of egalitarian thinking among European Americans at once downplayed status distinctions within their own group, and distinguished all "whites" from all others. (That distinction soon manifested itself in new state laws forbidding whites from marrying blacks or Native peoples.) Notions of "whiteness," "redness," and "blackness" developed alongside beliefs in European Americans' superiority.

The new racial thought had several intertwined elements. First came the assertion that, as Thomas Jefferson insisted in 1781, blacks were "inferior to the whites in the endowments both of body and mind." (He was less certain about Native people.) There followed the belief that those with black skin were inherently lazy and disorderly. Owners had often argued, conversely, that slaves made "natural" workers, but no one seemed to notice the contradiction. Third was the notion that blacks were sexually promiscuous, and that African American men lusted after European American women. The specter of sexual intercourse between black men

Haitian Refugees

Although many European Americans welcomed the news of the French Revolution in 1789, few expressed similar sentiments about the slave rebellion that broke out two years later in the French colony of St. Domingue (later Haiti). A large number of refugees soon flowed into the new United States from that nearby revolt, bringing with them consequences deemed undesirable by most political leaders. Less than a decade after winning independence, the new nation confronted its first immigration crisis.

Among the approximately 600,000 residents of St. Domingue in the early 1790s were about 100,000 free people, almost all of them slave owners; half were whites, the rest of mixed race. In the wake of the French Revolution, those free mixed-race people split the slaveholding population by seeking greater social and political equality. Slaves then seized the opportunity to revolt. By 1793, they had triumphed under the leadership of a former bondsman, Toussaint L'Ouverture. In 1804 they finally ousted the French, establishing the republic of Haiti. Thousands of whites and free mixed-race people, accompanied by as many slaves as they could readily transport, sought asylum in the United States during those turbulent years.

Although willing to offer shelter to refugees, American political leaders nonetheless feared the consequences of their arrival. Southern plantation owners shuddered to think that slaves so familiar with ideas of freedom and equality would mingle with their own bondspeople. Many were uncomfortable with the arrival of numerous free people of color, even though the immigrants were part of the slaveholding class. Most southern states adopted laws forbidding the entry of Haitian slaves and free people of African descent, but the laws were difficult if not impossible to enforce, as was a later congressional act to the same effect. More than fifteen thousand refugees—white, black, and of mixed-race origins—flooded into the United States and Spanish Louisiana. Many ended up in Virginia (which did not pass an exclusion law) or in the cities of Charleston, Savannah, and New Orleans.

In both New Orleans and Charleston, the influx of Haitians of mixed race gave rise to a heightened color consciousness that placed light-skinned people atop a hierarchy of people of color. After the United States purchased Louisiana in 1803, the number of free people of color in the territory almost doubled in three years, largely because of a final surge of immigration from the new Haitian republic. And, in Virginia, stories of the successful revolt helped to inspire local slaves in 1800 when they planned the action that has become known as Gabriel's Rebellion.

The Haitian refugees thus linked European Americans and African Americans to current events in the West Indies, indelibly affecting both groups of people.

CRITICAL THINKING

- What threat did the free immigrant Haitian population present to American slavery defined by race?

Courtesy of the Collections of the Louisiana State Museum

◄ A free woman of color in Louisiana early in the nineteenth century, possibly one of the refugees from Haiti. Esteban Rodriguez Mir, named governor of Spanish Louisiana in 1782, ordered all slave and free black women to wear head wraps rather than hats—which were reserved for whites—but this woman and many others subverted his order by nominally complying, but nevertheless creating elaborate headdresses.

and white women haunted early American thought. The more common reverse circumstance—the sexual exploitation of enslaved women by their masters—generally aroused little concern, though Federalist newspaper editors did not hesitate to use Thomas Jefferson's long-standing relationship with Sally Hemings to inflame public opinion against him. "It is well known that the man, whom it delighteth the people to honor, keeps, and for many years has kept, as his concubine, one of his slaves. Her name is Sally," trumpeted the *Richmond Recorder* in September 1802.

African Americans did not allow developing racist notions to go unchallenged. Benjamin Banneker, a free black mathematical genius, disputed Thomas Jefferson's belief in Africans' intellectual inferiority. In 1791, Banneker sent Jefferson a copy of his latest almanac (which included his astronomical calculations) as an example of blacks' mental powers. Jefferson admitted Banneker's intelligence but regarded him as exceptional, and said he would need more evidence to change his mind about people of African descent.

7-7g A White Man's Republic

Though many men of African descent had served with honor in the Continental army, laws from the 1770s on linked male citizenship rights to "whiteness." Indeed, some historians argue that the subjugation of blacks, Native peoples, and women was a necessary precondition for theoretical equality among white men. Just as excluding women from the political realm reserved all power for men, so identifying common racial antagonists helped to foster white solidarity across class lines. After the Revolution, the division of American society between slave and free was transformed into a division between blacks—some of whom were free—and whites.

7-8 "Revolutions" at the End of the Century

▶ What did the "revolutions" at the end of the eighteenth century reveal about the government established in the United States?

▶ How did Fries's and Gabriel's Rebellion appropriate the language and experience of the Revolutionary Era?

Three events in the last two years of the eighteenth century can be deemed real or potential revolutions: Fries's Rebellion, Gabriel's Rebellion, and the election of Thomas Jefferson. Although they differed significantly, these events mirrored the tensions and uncertainties of the young republic. The Fries rebels resisted national authority to tax. Gabriel and his followers directly challenged the slave system so crucial to the Chesapeake economy. And the venomous, hard-fought

presidential election of 1800 exposed a flaw in the Constitution that would have to be corrected by amendment.

7-8a Fries's Rebellion

The tax resistance movement known by the name of one of its prominent leaders—Revolutionary War veteran John Fries—arose among German American farmers in Pennsylvania's Lehigh Valley in 1798–1799. To finance the Quasi-War against France, Congress taxed land, houses, and legal documents. German Americans, imbued with revolutionary ideals (nearly half were veterans), saw in the taxes a threat to

TOUSSAINT L'OUVERTURE
Chef des Noirs Insurgés de Saint Domingue

▲ This c. 1800 engraving depicts Toussaint L'Ouverture, leader of the movement for independence on the valuable sugar island of Saint Domingue, where slaves challenged French colonial rule in 1791. A decorated general on the Caribbean front of the French Revolution, L'Ouverture is shown as a hero in full military regalia. Newspapers in the United States followed his exploits closely; nearly 200 articles were printed about him during the year of Gabriel's rebellion. The uprising of the slaves of Saint Domingue—which became in 1804 the independent nation of Haiti—fascinated antislavery forces and terrified planters throughout the young United States.

Dissent During Wartime

The nation's first overseas conflict, the Quasi-War with France in 1798–1799, spawned its first attempt to suppress dissent. By criminalizing dissenting speech, the Sedition Act of 1798 tried to mute criticism of the war and President John Adams. Fifteen men were indicted and ten fined and jailed after being convicted under the statute's provisions.

Although Americans might assume that their right to free speech under the First Amendment, now more fully accepted than it was two centuries ago, protects dissenters during wartime, history suggests otherwise. Every conflict has stimulated efforts to suppress dissenters. During the Civil War, the Union jailed civilian Confederate sympathizers for long periods. During the First World War, a Sedition Act allowed the government to deport immigrant aliens who criticized the war effort, among them several outspoken Socialists and anarchists.

Moreover, angry neighbors subjected citizens who objected to government policies to a variety of formal and informal sanctions. World War II brought the silencing of those who had opposed American entry into the war. The consequences of antiwar protests in the Vietnam era still affect the nation today, for the American people remain divided over whether the proper course of action in the 1960s and 1970s was dissent from, or acquiescence to, government policy.

The USA PATRIOT Act, adopted after the terrorist attacks of September 11, 2001, removed long-standing restrictions on government surveillance of citizens, controversially granting access to library records. Criticism of the wars in Iraq and Afghanistan raised questions that arouse heated debate: Do newspapers that publish classified information or pictures of abused prisoners overstep the First Amendment? Can political figures censure the conduct

of the wars without being labeled unpatriotic?

Freedom of speech is never easy to maintain, and wartime conditions make it much more difficult. When the nation comes under attack, many argue that the time for dissent has ceased and that citizens should support the government. Others contend that, if American freedom is to mean anything, people must have the right to speak their mind at all times. Events in the United States since the 9/11 attacks suggest that this legacy remains contentious for the American people.

CRITICAL THINKING

- Over more than two centuries, the U.S. government has often passed laws to limit freedom of speech during times of national duress. What limitations on freedom of expression do Americans accept in the twenty-first century?
- How, besides enacting legislation, do we in the contemporary United States define the boundaries of acceptable political speech?

---

their liberties and livelihoods, as well as an echo of the hated Stamp Act of 1765. Asserting their right to resist unconstitutional laws, they raised liberty poles, petitioned Congress, and barred assessors from their homes.

When a federal judge ordered the arrest of twenty resisters, Fries led a troop of 120 militiamen to Bethlehem, where they surrounded a tavern temporarily housing the prisoners. President Adams described the militiamen's actions as acts of war. Fries and many of his neighbors were arrested and tried; he and two others were convicted of treason; thirty-two more of violating the Sedition Act. Although Fries and the other "traitors" were sentenced to hang, Adams pardoned them just two days before their scheduled execution. Despite clemency from a Federalist president, the region's residents became, and remained, Republican partisans.

7-8b Gabriel's Rebellion

Like their white compatriots in the Lehigh Valley and elsewhere, African Americans had witnessed the benefits of fighting collectively for freedom, a message reinforced by stunning news of the successful slave revolt in St. Domingue.

Gabriel, an enslaved Virginia blacksmith who planned the second end-of-the-century revolution, drew on both Haitian and American revolutionary experiences.

Gabriel first recruited to his cause other skilled African American artisans who lived, as he did, under minimal supervision. Next, he enlisted rural slaves. The rebels planned to attack Richmond on the night of August 30, 1800. They would set fire to the city, seize the capitol building, and capture the governor, James Monroe. At that point, Gabriel believed, other slaves and perhaps poor whites would join the movement.

The plan showed considerable political sophistication, but heavy rain forced a postponement. Several planters then learned of the plot and spread the alarm. Gabriel avoided arrest for weeks, but militia troops quickly apprehended and interrogated most of the rebellion's other leaders. Twenty-six rebels, including Gabriel himself, were hanged.

At his trial, one of Gabriel's followers made explicit the links that so frightened Chesapeake slaveholders. He told his judges that he, like George Washington, had "adventured my life in endeavouring to obtain the liberty of my country-men, and am a willing sacrifice in their cause." Southern state legislatures responded to such claims by passing increasingly severe laws regulating slavery, which soon became even more firmly entrenched as an economic institution and way of life in the region.

7-8c Election of 1800

The third end-of-the-century revolution was the election of Thomas Jefferson as president and a Congress dominated by Republicans after a decade of growing partisanship. Leading up to November 1800, Federalists and Republicans openly campaigned for congressional seats and maneuvered to control the outcome in the electoral college. Republicans again nominated Jefferson and Burr; Federalists named John Adams, with Charles Cotesworth Pinckney of South Carolina as vice president. The network of Republican newspapers forged in the fires of Sedition Act prosecutions vigorously promoted the Jeffersonian cause. When the votes were counted, Jefferson and Burr had tied with 73. Adams garnered 64 and Pinckney 63. Under the Constitution, the existing House of Representatives would decide the election; the newly elected Jeffersonians would not take office until the president did.

Voting in the House continued for six days. Through thirty-five ballots, Federalists supported Burr while Republicans held fast for Jefferson. Finally, James Bayard, a Federalist and Delaware's sole congressman, brokered a deal that gave the Virginian the presidency. The bitterly fought election prompted the adoption of the Twelfth Amendment, which provided that electors would thenceforth cast separate ballots for president and vice president.

Decades later, in a letter to then-president James Monroe, Jefferson looked back on his election as an accomplishment nearly as momentous as American independence. In an 1820 letter to then-president James Monroe, he linked "the revolution of 1776" to "that of 1800." Historians debate whether the so-called Revolution of 1800 deserves the name Jefferson later gave it. Many of the Republicans' promised reforms failed to materialize. The defeated Federalists retained and indeed strengthened their hold on the federal judiciary. But at the very least, Jefferson's inauguration—which marked the first peaceful transfer of power from one faction to another in a modern republic—ushered in a new era in American political culture, one in which republican theory and partisan practice could coexist. "We are all Republicans, we are all Federalists," the new president proclaimed in his first inaugural address.

Summary

During the 1780s, the republic's upheavals convinced many leaders that the United States needed a more powerful central government. Drafted in 1787, the Constitution created that stronger national framework. During heated debates over its ratification, the document's supporters—called Federalists—contended that their design was just as "republican" as the flawed Articles of Confederation had been. Those labeled Antifederalists argued otherwise, but ultimately lost the fight.

Inhabitants of the early United States faced changed lives as well as changed politics. Native peoples east of the Mississippi River found aspects of their cultures under assault. Enslaved African Americans faced increasingly restrictive laws in the southern colonies. In the North, freedom suits, manumissions, and gradual emancipation laws fostered a growing free black community. At the same time, a newly systematic and defensive pro-slavery argument emphasized race (rather than slave or free status) as the determinant of African Americans' standing in the nation. Imagined chiefly as mothers of the next generation and selfless contributors to the nation's welfare, white women played a limited role in the public life of the United States. Writers, artists, playwrights, and architects promoted feminine self-sacrifice and other such republican virtues.

The years between 1788 and 1800 established enduring precedents for Congress, the presidency, and the federal judiciary. Building on successful negotiations with Spain (Pinckney's Treaty), Britain (the Jay Treaty), and France (the Convention of 1800), the United States forged diplomatic independence. The French Revolution prompted vigorous debates over American foreign and domestic policy. In the 1790s, the United States saw the emergence of organized factionalism and grassroots politicking involving both men and women. In 1801, after more than a decade of struggle, the Jeffersonian view of an agrarian, decentralized republic prevailed over Alexander Hamilton's vision of a centralized economy and a strong national government.

Suggestions for Further Reading

Annette Gordon-Reed, *The Hemingses of Monticello: An American Family* (2008)

François Furstenberg, *When the United States Spoke French: Five Refugees Who Shaped a Nation* (2014)

Eliga Gould, *Among the Powers of the Earth: The American Revolution and the Making of a New World Empire* (2012)

Catherine O'Donnell Kaplan, *Men of Letters in the Early Republic: Cultivating Forums of Citizenship* (2008)

Pauline Maier, *Ratification: The People Debate the Constitution, 1787–1788* (2010)

Jeffrey L. Pasley, *"The Tyranny of Printers": Newspaper Politics in the Early American Republic* (2001)

Claudio Saunt, *West of the Revolution: An Uncommon History of 1776* (2014)

David Waldstreicher, *Slavery's Constitution: From Revolution to Ratification* (2009)

Caroline Winterer, *American Enlightenments: Pursuing Happiness in an Age of Reason* (2016)

Rosemarie Zagarri, *Revolutionary Backlash: Women and Politics in the Early American Republic* (2007)

MindTap®is a fully online personalized learning experience built upon Cengage Learning content. MindTap® combines student learning tools—readings, multimedia, activities, and assessments—into a singular Learning Path that guides students through the course and helps students develop the critical thinking, analysis, and communication skills that are essential to academic and professional success.

8

Defining the Nation, 1801–1823

E ager to set himself apart from the allegedly aristocratic ways of his Federalist predecessors, President Thomas Jefferson displayed impatience, even disdain, for ceremony. But on his first New Year's Day in office, the third president eagerly awaited the ceremonial presentation of a much-heralded tribute to his commitment, in the words of one of the gift's bearers, to "defend Republicanism and baffle all the arts of Aristocracy." Crafted in Massachusetts, the belated inaugural gift had been nearly a month en route, traveling amid much fanfare for more than 400 miles by sleigh, boat, and wagon. Weighing more than twelve hundred pounds and measuring four feet in diameter, it bore the inscription "THE GREATEST CHEESE IN AMERICA—FOR THE GREATEST MAN IN AMERICA."

The idea for the "mammoth cheese," as it became known, had been born the previous July in a small farming community in western Massachusetts. The "Ladies" of Cheshire—a town as resolutely Jeffersonian-Republican as it was Baptist—had made the cheese from the milk of nine hundred cows as "a mark of the exalted esteem" in which the town's residents held the Republican president. As members of a religious minority in New England, where Congregationalists still dominated the pulpits and statehouses, the Cheshire Baptists had much to celebrate in the election of a president whose vision for the nation featured not just agrarianism but also separation of church and state. Their fiery pastor, John Leland, presented the cheese to the president and, two days later, preached the Sunday sermon in the House of Representatives, where at least one genteel listener dismissed his brand of evangelicalism as "horrid."

Federalist editors delighted in poking fun at the mammoth cheese—especially at those who had made it. Its semirotten, maggot-infested condition upon delivery symbolized, they said, the

◀ Federalists derided the Cheshire cheese as the "mammoth" cheese, after the mastodon (similar to the "woolly mammoth") unearthed by naturalist Charles Willson Peale in 1801. Here, workers search for fossils while a specially designed machine pumps water from an excavation pit. Partially funded by the Jefferson administration, Peale's expedition was considered a boondoggle by Federalists. New York Public Library/Science Source

Chronology

1801	■ Marshall becomes chief justice
	■ Jefferson inaugurated as president
1801–05	■ United States defeats Barbary pirates
1803	■ *Marbury v. Madison*
	■ Louisiana Purchase
1804	■ Jefferson reelected president, Clinton vice president
1804–06	■ Lewis and Clark expedition
1805	■ Tenskwatawa emerges as Shawnee leader
1807	■ *Chesapeake* affair
	■ Embargo Act
1808	■ Congress bans slave importation
	■ Madison elected president
1808–13	■ Tenskwatawa and Tecumseh organize Native American resistance
1811	■ National Road begun
1812	■ Madison reelected president
1812–15	■ War of 1812
1813	■ Tecumseh's death
	■ Boston Manufacturing Company starts textile mill in Waltham, Massachusetts
1814	■ "The Star-Spangled Banner" is written
	■ Treaty of Ghent
1814–15	■ Hartford Convention
1815	■ Battle of New Orleans
1817	■ Regular steamboat travel begins on Mississippi
1817–25	■ Erie Canal constructed
1819	■ *McCulloch v. Maryland*
	■ Adams-Onís Treaty
1819–early 1820s	■ First major depression
1820–21	■ Missouri Compromise
1822	■ Colonization of Liberia begins (formally established in 1824)
1823	■ Monroe Doctrine

nation under Republican rule. Its very existence, to say nothing of its size, resulted from the excesses of democracy, in which even women and backwoods preachers could play leading roles. The cheese, they scoffed, had been made of "*asses'* milk."

Yet the Federalists' derision of the mammoth cheese won them few new supporters and instead inspired additional showy expressions of democratic pride. In the following months, a Philadelphia baker sold "Mammoth Bread," while two butchers sent the president a "Mammoth veal." In Washington, a "Mammoth Eater" consumed forty-two eggs in ten minutes. Nor did the "mammoth" craze prove ephemeral: two years later, in 1804, a "mammoth loaf" was served—along with whiskey, hard cider, and wine—in the Capitol to a raucous crowd of Federalist-disparaging Republicans, including President Jefferson himself.

Experience an interactive version of this story in MindTap®.

Seemingly frivolous in retrospect, political symbolism and rivalries were deadly serious in the early republic, as attested to by those (most famously, Alexander Hamilton) who died in duels. People excluded from formal political participation often joined voting citizens in expressing ideal visions for the nation's future when they petitioned legislatures, marched in parades, engaged in heated tavern debates—and sent the president a mammoth cheese. Behind such symbolism lay serious political ideologies. Jeffersonians believed virtue derived from agricultural endeavors, and they thus celebrated the acquisition of the Louisiana Territory. Their efforts to expand their agriculturally based "empire of liberty" westward were resisted, however, by Native Americans and their European allies, and sometimes by Federalists, too. Not until the War of 1812 largely removed such resistance would the United States begin its nearly unbridled expansion across the continent. Although it resolved few of the issues that caused it, that war held profound consequences for American development. It secured the United States' sovereignty, opened much of the West to European Americans and their African American slaves, and helped spur revolutions in transportation and industry.

Although contemporary observers noted that the postwar nationalism heralded an "Era of Good Feelings," it soon became apparent that good feelings had limits. When economic boom turned to bust, the postwar bubble of nationalistic optimism and ostensible unity may not have popped, but it never again proved quite so buoyant. No issue proved more divisive than slavery's future in the West, as Missouri's petition for statehood revealed. Even as President Monroe tried to bolster the nation's international standing, the nation's internal tensions festered not far beneath the surface.

- *What characterized the two main competing visions for national development?*

- *How did America's relationship with Europe influence political and economic developments?*

- *In what ways did nonvoting Americans—most African Americans, women, and Native Americans—take part in defining the new nation?*

8-1 Political Visions

▶ How did Democratic-Republicans seek to implement their political vision of the country after the election of Thomas Jefferson in 1800?

▶ How did the American political culture develop to encourage political activism and engagement?

▶ How did the Supreme Court develop as a branch of the federal government under Chief Justice John Marshall?

In his inaugural address, Jefferson appealed to his opponents. Standing in the Senate chamber, the Capitol's only completed part, he addressed the electorate not as party members but as citizens with common beliefs: "We are all republicans, we are all federalists." Nearly a thousand people strained to hear his vision of a restored republicanism: "A wise and frugal government, which shall restrain men from injuring one another, which shall leave them free to regulate their pursuits of industry and improvement, and shall not take from the mouth of labor the bread it had earned. This is the sum of good government."

But outgoing president John Adams did not hear Jefferson's call for unity, having left Washington before dawn. He and Jefferson, once close friends, now disliked each other intensely. Despite the spirit of Jefferson's inaugural address, the Democratic-Republicans—as the Republicans of the 1790s now called themselves, after the Democratic societies of the 1790s—and the Federalists remained bitter opponents. These parties held different visions of how society and government should be organized. The Federalists advocated a strong national government with centralized authority to promote economic development. The Democratic-Republicans sought to restrain the national government, believing that

limited government would foster republican virtue, which derived from agricultural endeavors. Nearly two decades later, Jefferson would call his election "the revolution of 1800," which was "as real a revolution in the principles of our government as that of 1776 was in its form."

8-1a Separation of Church and State

When the Cheshire farmers sent Jefferson a mammoth cheese, they did so largely to express gratitude for his commitment to the separation of church and state. On the very day he received the overripe cheese, Jefferson reciprocated by penning a letter to the Baptist association in Danbury, Connecticut, proclaiming that the Constitution's First Amendment supported a "wall of separation between church and state." Jefferson's letter articulated a core component of his vision of limited government. The president declared that "religion is a matter which lies solely between Man & his God." It lay beyond the government's purview. New England Baptists hailed Jefferson as a hero, but New England Federalists believed their worst fears were confirmed. During the election of 1800, Federalists had waged a venomous campaign against Jefferson, incorrectly labeling him an atheist. Their rhetoric proved so effective that, after Jefferson's election, some New England women hid their Bibles in their gardens and wells to foil Democratic-Republicans allegedly bent on confiscating them. Jefferson's letter to the Danbury Baptists seemingly vindicated such hysteria.

8-1b Religious Revivals

Jefferson became president during a period of religious revivalism, particularly among Methodists and Baptists, whose democratic preaching—all humans, they said, were equal in God's eyes—encouraged a growing democratic political culture. The most famous revival was at Cane Ridge, Kentucky, in August 1801. One report estimated 25,000 people attended, including men and women, free and enslaved, at a time when Kentucky's largest city, Lexington, had fewer than two thousand inhabitants. The call to personal repentance and conversion invigorated southern Protestantism, giving churches an evangelical base. All revivalists, both in the South and the North, shared a belief in individual self-improvement, but northern revivalists also emphasized communal improvement, becoming missionaries for both individual salvation and social reform (see "Revivals and Reform," Section 10-7).

Emboldened by secular and religious ideologies about human equality, society's nonelites articulated their own political visions. Rather than simply taking stands in debates defined by social and political betters, they worked to reshape the debates. When the Cheshire Baptists sent their cheese to President Jefferson, for example, they pointedly informed the Virginia planter that it had been made "without a single slave to assist."

8-1c Political Mobilization

The revolution of 1800, which gave the Democratic-Republicans majorities in both houses of Congress in addition to the presidency, did not reflect a revolution in the electorate, which remained limited largely, but not exclusively, to property-holding men. The Constitution left the regulation of voting to the individual states. In no state but New Jersey could women vote even when meeting property qualifications, and in New Jersey that right was granted inadvertently and was revoked in 1807. In 1800, free black men meeting property qualifications could vote in all states but Delaware, Georgia, South Carolina, and Virginia, but local custom often kept them from exercising that right. Nonetheless, partisan politics captured nearly all Americans' imaginations, and politicians actively courted nonvoters along with voters. Most political mobilization took place locally, where partisans rallied popular support for candidates and their ideologies on militia training grounds, in taverns and churches, at court gatherings, and during holiday celebrations. Voters and nonvoters alike expressed their views by marching in parades, signing petitions, singing songs, and debating politically charged sermons. Perhaps most important, they devoured a growing print culture of pamphlets, broadsides (posters), almanacs, and—especially—newspapers.

8-1d The Partisan Press

Newspapers provided a forum for sustained political conversation. Read aloud in taverns, artisans' workshops, and homes, newspapers gave national importance to local events. Without newspaper publicity, Cheshire's mammoth cheese would have

been little more than a massive hunk of curdled milk. With it, a cheese became worthy of presidential response. In 1800, the nation had 260 newspapers; by 1810, it had 396—virtually all of them unabashedly partisan.

The parties adopted official organs. Shortly after his election, Jefferson persuaded the *National Intelligencer* to move from Philadelphia to the new capital of Washington, where it became the Democratic-Republicans' voice. In 1801, Alexander Hamilton launched the *New York Evening Post* as the Federalist vehicle. It boosted Federalists while frequently calling Jefferson a liar and depicting him as the head of a slave harem. The party organs—published six or seven times a week, year in and year out—ensured that the growing American obsession with partisan politics extended beyond electoral campaigns.

8-1e Limited Government

Jefferson needed public servants as well as supporters. To bring into his administration men sharing his vision of individual liberty, an agrarian republic, and limited government, Jefferson refused to recognize appointments made by Adams in his presidency's last days and dismissed Federalist customs collectors. He awarded vacant treasury and judicial offices to Republicans. Federalists accused Jefferson of "hunting the Federalists like wild beasts" and abandoning the peaceful

Art Collection 3/Alamy

▲ Although most places limited the vote to property-owning white men, elections, such as this one in Philadelphia, drew multiracial crowds of men, women, and children.

overtures of his inaugural address. Jeffersonians worked to make the government leaner. If Alexander Hamilton had viewed the national debt as the engine of economic growth, Jefferson deemed it the source of government corruption. Secretary of the Treasury Albert Gallatin cut the army budget in half and reduced the 1802 navy budget by two-thirds. He moved to reduce the national debt from $83 million to $57 million, hoping to retire it altogether by 1817. Austerity motivated Jefferson to close two of the nation's five diplomatic missions abroad, at The Hague and in Berlin. Jeffersonians attacked taxes as well as spending: the Democratic-Republican–controlled Congress oversaw the repeal of all internal taxes, including the despised whiskey tax of 1791.

The Democratic-Republicans also struck down Federalists' efforts to stiffen citizenship requirements and to restrict speech critical of the government. Jefferson declined to use the Alien and Sedition Acts of 1798 against his opponents, instead pardoning those already convicted of violating them. Congress let the Sedition Act expire in 1801 and the Alien Act in 1802, and repealed the Naturalization Act of 1798, which had required fourteen years of residency for citizenship. The 1802 act that replaced it, while stipulating the registration of aliens, required of would-be citizens only five years of residency, loyalty to the Constitution, and the forsaking of foreign allegiances and titles. The new act remained the basis of naturalized American citizenship into the twentieth century.

8-1f Judicial Politics

To many Democratic-Republicans, the judiciary represented a centralizing and undemocratic force, especially because judges were appointed, not elected, and served for life. Partisan Democratic-Republicans thus targeted opposition judges. At Jefferson's prompting, the House impeached (indicted) and the Senate convicted Federal District Judge John Pickering of New Hampshire. Allegedly deranged and alcoholic, Pickering made an easy mark. On the same day in 1803 that Pickering was ousted from office, the House impeached Supreme Court Justice Samuel Chase for judicial misconduct. A staunch Federalist, Chase had pushed for prosecutions under the Sedition Act, had actively campaigned for Adams in 1800, and had repeatedly denounced Jefferson's administration from the bench. But in the Senate, the Democratic-Republicans failed to muster the two-thirds majority necessary for conviction. The failure to remove Chase preserved the Court's independence and established the precedent that criminal actions, not political disagreements, justified removal from office.

8-1g The Marshall Court

Although Jefferson appointed three new Supreme Court justices during his two administrations, the Court remained a Federalist stronghold under the leadership of his distant cousin John Marshall. Marshall adopted some outward trappings of Republicanism—opting for a plain black gown over the more colorful academic robes of his fellow justices—but

adhered steadfastly to Federalist ideology. Even after the Democratic-Republicans achieved a majority of Court seats in 1811, Marshall remained extremely influential as chief justice. Under the Marshall Court (1801–1835), the Supreme Court consistently upheld federal supremacy over the states while protecting the interests of commerce and capital.

Marshall made the Court an equal branch of the government in practice as well as theory. Previously regarded lightly, judicial service became a coveted honor for ambitious and talented men. Marshall, moreover, strengthened the Court by having it speak with a more unified voice; rather than issuing a host of individual concurring judgments, the justices now issued joint majority opinions. Marshall became the voice of the majority: from 1801 through 1805, he wrote twenty-four of the Court's twenty-six decisions; through 1810, he wrote 85 percent of the opinions, including every important one.

8-1h Judicial Review

One of the most important involved Adams's midnight appointments. In his last hours in office, Adams had named Federalist William Marbury a justice of the peace in the District of Columbia. But Jefferson's secretary of state, James Madison, declined to certify the appointment, allowing the new president to appoint a Democratic-Republican instead. Marbury sued, requesting a writ of mandamus (a court order forcing the president to appoint him). *Marbury v. Madison* presented a political dilemma. If the Supreme Court ruled in Marbury's favor, the president probably would not comply with the writ, and the Court could not force him to do so. Yet by refusing to issue the writ, the Federalist-dominated bench would hand the Democratic-Republicans a victory.

To avoid both pitfalls, Marshall brilliantly recast the issue. Writing for the Court, he ruled that Marbury had a right to his appointment but that the Supreme Court could not compel Madison to honor the appointment because the Constitution did not grant the Court power to issue a writ of mandamus. In the absence of any specific mention in the Constitution, Marshall wrote, the section of the Judiciary Act of 1789 authorizing the Court to issue writs was unconstitutional. Thus, the Supreme Court denied itself the power to issue writs of mandamus but established its far greater power to judge the constitutionality of laws passed by Congress. In doing so, Marshall fashioned the theory of judicial review. Because the Constitution was "the supreme law of the land," Marshall wrote, any federal or state act contrary to the Constitution must be null and void. The Supreme Court, whose duty it was to uphold the law, would decide whether a legislative act contradicted the Constitution. "It is emphatically the province and duty of the judicial department," Marshall ruled, "to say what the law is." This power of the Supreme Court to determine the constitutionality of legislation and presidential acts permanently enhanced the independence of the judiciary and breathed life into the Constitution. "Marshall

Marbury v. Madison Case that established the Supreme Court's power to determine the constitutionality of laws.

found the Constitution paper and made it power," President James A. Garfield later observed.

8-1i Election of 1804 and Burr-Hamilton Animosity

In the first election after the Twelfth Amendment's ratification, Jefferson took no chances: he dropped Burr as his running mate and, in keeping with the already established convention of having a North-South balance on the ticket, chose George Clinton of New York. They swamped their opponents—South Carolinian Charles Cotesworth Pinckney and New Yorker Rufus King—in the electoral college by 162 votes to 14, carrying fifteen of the seventeen states. That 1804 election escalated the long-standing animosity between Burr and Hamilton, who supported Burr's rival in the New York gubernatorial election. When Hamilton called Burr a liar, Burr challenged Hamilton to a duel. Believing his honor was at stake, Hamilton accepted the challenge even though his son Philip had died in 1801 from dueling wounds. Because New York had outlawed dueling, the encounter took place across the Hudson River in New Jersey. Details of the duel itself remain hazy—did Hamilton withhold his fire, as he claimed he would?—but the outcome was clear: Hamilton died the following day, after being shot by Burr. In New York and New Jersey, prosecutors indicted Burr for murder.

Facing arrest if he returned to either state, and with his political career in ruins, Burr fled to the West. While historians disagree about his motives, the "Burr Conspiracy" was understood at the time to involve a scheme with Brigadier General James Wilkinson to create a new empire by using military force to acquire what is now Texas and by persuading already existing western territories to leave the United States and join the new empire. Brought to trial in the U.S. Circuit Court in Richmond for treason in 1807, Burr faced a prosecution aided by President Jefferson but presided over by Jefferson's political rival Chief Justice Marshall. (At the time, Supreme Court justices presided over circuit courts.) Prompted by Marshall to interpret treason narrowly, the jury acquitted Burr, who fled to Europe.

8-1j Nationalism and Culture

As statesmen bickered over how to realize the nation's potential, other Americans touted their own nationalist visions with paintbrushes and pens. Nearly three decades after the Constitution's ratification, painters continued to memorialize great birth scenes of American nationhood, such as the Declaration of Independence's signing, Revolutionary War battle scenes, and the Constitutional Convention. Four of John Trumbull's revolutionary scenes, commissioned in 1817, still hang in the rotunda of the Capitol building in Washington.

With architecture, Americans self-consciously constructed a new, independent nation. Designed by Major Pierre Charles

Eli Whitney Inventor of the cotton gin, which made cleaning of southern cotton faster and cheaper.

L'Enfant, a French-born engineer who served under George Washington during the Revolution, the city of Washington was meant to embody a "reciprocity of sight": Each of the government's three branches—the legislative, judicial, and executive—should keep an eye on one another at all times. But nationalism could be easier to envision than to construct. Beset by pragmatic difficulties, L'Enfant's plan took nearly a century to implement. A French visitor in 1851 noted that Washington had "streets without houses," "houses without streets," and was "striking proof of this truth, that one cannot create a great city at will." In Washington and elsewhere, wealthier Americans commissioned homes in the "federal" style, which imitated classical architecture in its economy of decoration and which made use of indigenous, rather than imported, building materials.

The era's best-selling book was Noah Webster's spelling book, which proposed making English more "republican." By some estimates, the book sold nearly 100 million copies by the end of the nineteenth century. Webster believed Americans should speak and spell like one another—they should bind together by speaking a national language—but unlike "King's English," their language should not require elite training to master. Words should be spelled as they sound—for example, "honor" should replace "honour." A shared language would unite an increasingly far-flung population.

8-2 Continental Expansion and Native American Resistance

▶ Why was American access to New Orleans and the Mississippi Valley important in the early nineteenth century?

▶ What did the Lewis and Clark expedition through the Louisiana Territory achieve?

▶ How did Native American peoples respond to American encroachment on their lands?

Little excited Jeffersonians' nationalistic imaginations more than the West and its seeming abundance of unoccupied land ripe for agrarian expansion. Federalists, though, often urged caution, fearing uncontrolled expansion would impede commercial development and federal oversight.

By 1800, hundreds of thousands of white Americans had settled in the rich Ohio River and Mississippi River valleys, intruding on Native peoples' lands. In the Northwest they raised foodstuffs, primarily wheat, and in the Southwest they cultivated cotton. At the time of the American Revolution, cotton production was profitable only for the Sea Island planters in South Carolina and Georgia, who grew the long-staple variety. Short-staple cotton, which grew readily in the interior and in all kinds of soil, was unmarketable because its sticky seeds could be removed only by hand. After a young New England inventor named **Eli Whitney** designed a cotton

Huntington Library/SuperStock

▲ Because Washington, DC, was designed to maintain a symbolic "reciprocity of sight" between the federal government's branches, the White House and Capitol had little but a dirt road separating them in 1826, when a British diplomat painted the young nation's capital city.

gin (short for "engine") in 1793, allowing one person to remove the same number of seeds that previously required fifty people working by hand, the cultivation of short-staple cotton spread rapidly westward into the fertile lands of Louisiana, Mississippi, Alabama, Arkansas, and Tennessee. By exponentially increasing the efficiency with which cotton fiber could be extracted from raw cotton, the cotton gin greatly increased the demand for slaves who seeded, tended, and harvested cotton fields.

Whatever crops they marketed, American settlers depended on free access to the Mississippi River and its Gulf port, New Orleans. "The Mississippi," wrote Secretary of State James Madison, "is to them [western settlers] everything. It is the Hudson, the Delaware, the Potomac and all navigable rivers of the Atlantic States formed into one stream." Whoever controlled the port of New Orleans had a hand on the American economy's throat.

8-2a New Orleans

Spain, which had acquired France's territory west of the Mississippi in the settlement of the Seven Years' War (1763), secretly transferred it back to France in 1800 and 1801. American officials learned of the transfer only in 1802, when Napoleon seemed poised to rebuild a French

empire in the New World. "Every eye in the United States is now focused on the affairs of Louisiana," Jefferson wrote to Robert R. Livingston, the American minister in Paris. American concerns intensified when Spanish officials, on the eve of ceding control to the French, violated Pinckney's treaty by denying Americans the privilege of storing their products (or exercising their "right of deposit") at New Orleans prior to transshipment to foreign markets. Western farmers and eastern merchants, who traded through New Orleans, thought a devious Napoleon had closed the port; they talked war.

To relieve the pressure for war and win western farmers' support, Jefferson urged Congress to authorize the call-up of eighty thousand militiamen but at the same time sent Virginia's Governor James Monroe to join Robert Livingston in France with instructions to buy the port of New Orleans and as much of the Mississippi valley as possible. Arriving in Paris in April 1803, Monroe learned with astonishment that France had already offered to sell all 827,000 square miles of Louisiana to the United States for a mere $15 million. With St. Domingue torn from French control by revolution and slave revolt, Napoleon gave up dreams of a New World empire and no longer needed Louisiana as its breadbasket. His more urgent need was for money to wage war against

Map 8.1 Louisiana Purchase

The Louisiana Purchase (1803) doubled the area of the United States and opened the trans-Mississippi West for American settlement.

Britain. On April 30, Monroe and Livingston signed a treaty buying the vast territory, whose exact borders and land remained uncharted (see Map 8.1).

8-2b Louisiana Purchase

The **Louisiana Purchase** appealed to Americans with divergent ideas about how best to achieve national greatness and personal prosperity. The purchase ensured that the United States would control the Mississippi's mouth, giving peace of mind to western settlers who relied on the river to market their goods. It also inspired the commercial visions of those who imagined the United States as the nexus of international trade networks reaching between Europe and Asia. Louisiana promised to fulfill the dreams of easterners seeking cheap, fertile lands. Its vast expanse meant, too, that land could be set aside for Native peoples displaced by the incursion of white settlers and their black slaves, soothing the consciences of those white Americans who preferred to "civilize" rather than to exterminate the continent's first settlers. The purchase had its critics, though: some doubted its constitutionality (even Jefferson agonized over it); others worried that it belied the Democratic-Republicans' commitment to debt reduction; some New England Federalists complained that it undermined their commercial interests and threatened the sustainability of the republic by spreading the population beyond where it could be properly controlled.

Louisiana Purchase The U.S. purchase of the Louisiana Territory (the area from the Mississippi River to the Rocky Mountains) from France in 1803 for $15 million. The purchase virtually doubled the area of the United States.

Overall, though, the Louisiana Purchase was the most popular achievement of Jefferson's presidency.

Louisiana was not, however, the "vast wilderness" that some Federalists lamented and most Republicans coveted. When the United States acquired the territory, hundreds of thousands of people who had not been party to the agreement became American subjects. These included Native Americans from scores of nations who made their homes within the enormous territory, as well as people of European and African descent—or, often, a complex mixture of the two—who congregated primarily along the Gulf Coast. Around New Orleans, Louisiana's colonial heritage was reflected in its people: creoles of French and Spanish descent, slaves of African descent, free people of color, and Acadians, or Cajuns (descendants of French settlers in eastern Canada), as well as some Germans, Irish, and English. The 1810 census, the first taken after the purchase, reported that 97,000 non-Native Americans lived in the Louisiana Purchase area, of whom the great majority (77,000) lived in what is now the state of Louisiana. Not all these new Americans welcomed their new national identity. Although Jefferson imagined the West as an "empire of liberty," free people of color soon discovered their exclusion from the Louisiana Purchase treaty's provision that "the inhabitants of the ceded territory" would be accorded the rights of American citizenship. Denied the right to vote and serve on juries, New Orleans' people of color fought to retain their rights to form families and to bequeath as they pleased, and—with the help of sympathetic Anglos serving on juries, as justices, or as legislators—some of them succeeded.

▲ At the time of the Louisiana Purchase in 1803, New Orleans was already a bustling port, though boosters predicted an even brighter future under American "wings." View of New Orleans from the Plantation of Marigny, 1803 (oil on canvas), Woiseri, J. L. Bouquet de (fl.1797-1815) / © Chicago History Museum, USA / The Bridgeman Art Library

8-2c Lewis and Clark Expedition

Jefferson had a long-standing interest in the trans-Mississippi West, envisioning it as punctuated with volcanoes and mountains of pure salt, where llamas and mammoths roamed and Welshmen settled. He felt an urgent need to explore it, fearing that, if Americans did not claim it as their own, the British, who still claimed the northern reaches of the continent (in present-day Canada) and parts of the Pacific Northwest, surely would. He lost no time in launching a military-style mission that would chart the region's commercial possibilities—its water passages to the Pacific as well as its trading opportunities with Native peoples—while cataloging its geography, peoples, flora, and fauna.

The expedition, headed by Meriwether Lewis and William Clark, began in May 1804 and lasted for more than two years; it traveled up the Missouri River, across the Rockies, and then down the Columbia to the Pacific Ocean—and back. Along the way, the **Lewis and Clark expedition**'s members "discovered" (as they saw it) dozens of previously unknown Native peoples, many of whom had long before discovered Europeans. Lewis and Clark found the Mandans and Hidatsas already well supplied with European trade goods, such as knives, corduroy trousers, and rings. Although the Corps of Discovery, as the expedition came to be called, expected to find Native peoples and prepared for possible conflict, its goal was peaceable: to foster trade relations, win political allies, and take advantage of Native communities' knowledge of the landscape. Accordingly, Lewis and Clark brought with them twenty-one bags of gifts for Native American leaders, both to establish goodwill and to stimulate interest in trading for American manufactured goods. Most of the corps' interactions with Native peoples were cordial, but when the Native societies failed to be impressed by Lewis and Clark's gifts, tensions arose. After an encounter with the Lakota (or Sioux), Lewis denounced them as "the vilest miscreants of the savage race."

Although military in style, the Corps of Discovery proved unusually democratic in seating enlisted men on courts-martial and allowing Clark's black slave York as well as the expedition's female guide and translator **Sacagawea** to

Lewis and Clark expedition Expedition led by Meriwether Lewis and William Clark to explore the Louisiana Territory.

Sacagawea Female Native American guide who aided Lewis and Clark in exploring the Louisiana Territory.

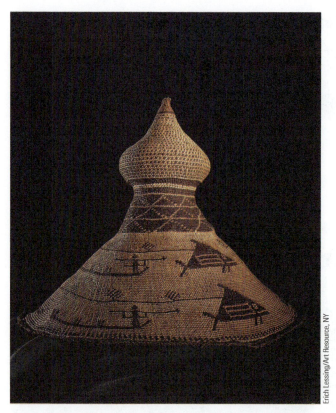

Made by the Nootka people, this wicker hat was collected—either as a trade item or a gift—by Lewis and Clark during their expedition to the Columbia River.

for a constitutional amendment that would transport them west of the Mississippi into the newly acquired Louisiana Territory. He became personally involved in efforts to pressure the Chickasaws to sell their land, and in the event that legal methods for removing Native peoples should fail, he advocated trickery. Traders, he suggested, might run the "good and influential individuals" into debt, which they would have to repay "by a cessation of lands."

8-2d Divisions Among Native Peoples

Some Native American nations decided to deal with white intruders by adopting white customs as a means of survival and often agreeing to sell their lands and move west. These "accommodationists" (or "progressives") were opposed by "traditionalists," who urged adherence to Native ways and refused to relinquish their lands. Distinctions between accommodationists and traditionalists were not always so clear-cut, however, as the Seneca Handsome Lake had demonstrated just a few years before. (see "'Civilizing' Native Peoples," Section 7-6b)

In the early 1800s, two Shawnee brothers, Tenskwatawa (1775–1837) and **Tecumseh** (1768–1813), led a traditionalist revolt against American encroachment by fostering a pan-Native American federation that centered in the Old Northwest and reached into parts of the South. During

vote on where to locate winter quarters in 1805. But unlike the expedition's other members, neither York nor Sacagawea drew wages, and when York later demanded his freedom for his services, Clark repaid him instead with—in Clark's own words—"a severe trouncing."

Lewis and Clark failed to discover a Northwest Passage to the Pacific, and the route they mapped across the Rockies proved more perilous than practical, but their explorations contributed to nationalist visions of American expansion. Fossils and Native American artifacts collected during the expedition were displayed in Charles Willson Peale's museum at Independence Hall in Philadelphia, an institution emphasizing the uniqueness of America's geography and, especially, its republican experiment; in addition to housing natural and human "curiosities," Peale's museum displayed his own renowned portraits of Revolutionary heroes. Nationalists generally overlooked Native peoples' claims to American lands. Although Jefferson had more sympathy for Native Americans than did many of his contemporaries—he took interest in their cultures and believed Native Americans to be intellectually equal to whites—he nonetheless lobbied, unsuccessfully,

Tecumseh The Shawnee leader who sought to unite several tribes from Canada to Georgia against encroachment on their lands by American settlers; allied with the British in the War of 1812.

At his museum in Philadelphia, Charles Willson Peale displays some of the "natural curiosities" that many Americans believed contributed to the nation's uniqueness.

the two brothers' lifetimes, the Shawnees had lost most of their Ohio land; by the 1800s, they occupied only scattered sites in Ohio and in the Michigan and Louisiana territories. Despondent, Lalawethika—as Tenskwatawa had been called as a youth—had turned to a combination of European remedies (particularly whiskey) and Native American ones, becoming a shaman in 1804. But when European diseases ravaged his village, he despaired.

8-2e Tenskwatawa and Tecumseh

Lalawethika emerged from his own battle with illness in 1805 as a new man, renamed Tenskwatawa ("the Open Door") or—by whites—"the Prophet." Claiming to have died and been resurrected, he traveled widely in the Ohio River valley as a religious leader, attacking the decline of moral values among Native Americans, warning against whiskey, condemning intertribal battles, and stressing harmony and respect for elders. He urged Native peoples to return to the old ways and to abandon white ways: to hunt with bows and arrows, not guns; to stop wearing hats; and to give up bread for corn and beans. Tenskwatawa was building a religious movement that offered hope to the Shawnees, Potawatomis, and other displaced western Native communities.

By 1808, Tenskwatawa and his older brother Tecumseh talked less about spiritual renewal and more about resisting American aggression. They invited Native peoples from all nations to settle in pan-Native American towns in Indiana, first at Greenville (1806–1808) and then at Prophetstown (1808–1812), near modern-day Lafayette. The new towns

challenged the treaty-making process by denying the claims of Native peoples who had been guaranteed the same land as part of the Treaty of Greenville of 1795 in exchange for enormous cessions. Younger Native Americans, in particular, flocked to Tecumseh, the more politically oriented of the two brothers.

Convinced that only a federation of Native peoples could stop the advance of white settlement, Tecumseh sought to unify northern and southern Native groups by preaching Native resistance across a wide swath of territory, ranging from Canada to Georgia. Among southern Native peoples, only one faction of the Creek nation welcomed him, but his efforts to spread his message southward nonetheless alarmed white settlers and government officials. In November 1811, while Tecumseh was in the South, Indiana governor William Henry Harrison moved against Tenskwatawa and his followers. During the Battle of Tippecanoe, the army burned their town; as they fled, the Native Americans exacted revenge on white settlers. "What other course is left for us to pursue," asked Harrison, "but to make a war of extirpation upon them?" With the stakes raised, Tecumseh entered a formal alliance with the British, who maintained forts in southern Ontario. This alliance in the West, combined with issues over American neutral rights on the high seas, were propelling the United States toward war with Britain.

8-3 The Nation in the Orbit of Europe

▶ How did "freedom of the seas" become a central international concern during Thomas Jefferson's presidency?

▶ How did the United States respond to threats to its sovereignty during Thomas Jefferson's presidency?

▶ What were the consequences of the end of the international slave trade?

▶ What political roles did women play in the early nineteenth century?

A decade earlier, in 1801, when Jefferson had sought to set a new course for the nation, he tried to put tensions with France to rest. "Peace, commerce, and honest friendship with all nations, entangling alliances with none," he had proclaimed in his first inaugural address. Yet, despite his wariness of foreign entanglements, the early republic's economy relied heavily on both fishing and the carrying trade, in which the American merchant marine transported commodities between nations. Merchants in Boston, Salem, and Philadelphia traded with China, sending cloth and metal to swap for furs with the Chinook people on the Oregon coast, and then sailing to China to trade for porcelain, tea, and silk. The slave trade lured American ships to Africa. America's commercial interests were clearly focused on the seas, and not long after Jefferson's first inaugural address, the United States was at war with Tripoli—a state

The Granger Collection

▲ Sacagawea, a bilingual Shoshone, guides Meriwether Lewis (center) and William Clark, along the Missouri River in 1805.

along the Barbary Coast of North Africa—over a principle that would long be a cornerstone of American foreign policy: freedom of the seas. In other words, outside national territorial waters, the high seas should be open for free transit of all vessels.

8-3a International Entanglements

In 1801, the *bashaw* (pasha) of Tripoli declared war on the United States for its refusal to pay tribute for safe passage of its ships, sailors, and passengers through the Mediterranean. Jefferson deployed a naval squadron to protect American ships. After two years of stalemate, Jefferson declared a blockade of Tripoli, but when the American frigate *Philadelphia* ran aground in the harbor, its three hundred officers and sailors were imprisoned. Jefferson refused to ransom them, and a small American force accompanied by Arab, Greek, and African mercenaries marched from Egypt to the "shores of Tripoli" (memorialized to this day in the Marine Corps anthem) to seize the port of Derne. A treaty ended the war in 1805, but the United States continued to pay tribute to the three other Barbary states—Algiers, Morocco, and Tunis—until 1815. In the intervening years, the United States became embroiled in European conflicts.

At first, Jefferson managed to distance the nation from the turmoil in Europe in the wake of the French Revolution. After the Senate ratified the Jay Treaty in 1795, the United States and Great Britain appeared to reconcile their differences. Britain withdrew from its western forts on American soil (while still retaining those in Canada) and interfered less in American trade with France. Then, in May 1803, two weeks after Napoleon sold Louisiana to the United States, France was at war against Britain and, later, Britain's continental allies, Prussia, Austria, and Russia. The Napoleonic wars again trapped the United States between belligerents on the high seas. But at first the United States—as the world's largest neutral shipping carrier—actually benefited from the conflict, and American merchants gained control of most of the West Indian trade. After 1805, however, when Britain defeated the French and Spanish fleets at Trafalgar, Britain's Royal Navy tightened its control of the oceans. Two months later, Napoleon crushed the Russian and Austrian armies at Austerlitz. Stalemated, France and Britain launched a commercial war, blockading each other's trade. As a trading partner of both countries, the United States paid a high price.

8-3b Threats to American Sovereignty

One British tactic in particular threatened American sovereignty. To replenish their supply of sailors, British vessels stopped American ships and impressed (forcibly recruited) British deserters, British-born naturalized American seamen, and other sailors suspected of being British. Perhaps six to eight thousand Americans were impressed between 1803 and 1812. Moreover, alleged deserters—many of them

Embargo Act of 1807 Act that forbade exports from the United States to any country.

American citizens—faced British courts-martial. Americans saw the principle of "once a British subject, always a British subject" as a mockery of U.S. citizenship and an assault on their national sovereignty. Americans also resented the British interfering with their West Indian trade as well as their searching and seizing American vessels within U.S. territorial waters.

In April 1806, Congress responded with the Non-Importation Act, barring British manufactured goods from entering American ports. Because the act exempted most cloth and metal articles, it had little impact on British trade; instead, it warned the British what to expect if they continued to violate American neutral rights. In November, Jefferson suspended the act temporarily while William Pinkney, a Baltimore lawyer, joined James Monroe in London to negotiate a settlement. But the treaty they carried home violated Jefferson's instructions—it did not so much as mention impressment—and the president never submitted it to the Senate for ratification.

Anglo-American relations steadily deteriorated, coming to a head in June 1807 when the USS *Chesapeake*, sailing out of Norfolk for the Mediterranean, was stopped by the British frigate *Leopard*, whose officers demanded to search the ship for British deserters. Refused, the *Leopard* opened fire, killing three Americans and wounding eighteen others, including the captain. The British then seized four deserters, three of whom were Americans; one of them was hanged. The *Chesapeake* affair outraged Americans while also exposing American military weakness.

8-3c The Embargo of 1807

Had the United States been better prepared militarily, public indignation might have resulted in a declaration of war. Instead, Jefferson opted for what he called "peaceable coercion." In July, the president closed American waters to British warships and soon thereafter increased military and naval expenditures. In December 1807, Jefferson again put economic pressure on Great Britain by invoking the Non-Importation Act, followed eight days later by a new restriction, the **Embargo Act of 1807**. Jefferson and his congressional supporters saw the embargo, which forbade all exports from the United States to any country, as a short-term measure to avoid war by pressuring Britain and France to respect American rights and by preventing confrontation between American merchant vessels and European warships.

The embargo's biggest economic impact, however, fell on the United States. Exports declined by 80 percent in 1808, squeezing New England shippers and their workers as economic depression set in. Manufacturers, by contrast, received a boost, as the domestic market became theirs exclusively, and merchants began to shift their capital from shipping to manufacturing. In 1807, there were twenty cotton and woolen mills in New England; by 1813, there were more than two hundred. Meanwhile, merchants who were willing to engage in smuggling profited enormously.

▲ *The Melee on Board the Chesapeake* (1813) portrays crew from the British frigate *Leopard* fighting to search the USS *Chesapeake* for British navy deserters. The sailors of the *Chesapeake* resisted, but the British overpowered them and seized four deserters, three of them American citizens. Americans were humiliated and angered by the British violation of American rights.

8-3d International Slave Trade

They had only to look at the vibrant slave trade to see how scarcity bred demand. With Jefferson's encouragement, Congress had voted in 1807 to abolish the international slave trade as of January 1, 1808—the earliest date permissible under the Constitution. South Carolina alone still allowed the legal importation of slaves, but most of the state's influential planters favored a ban on the trade, nervous (having seen what happened in St. Domingue) about adding to the black population of a state in which whites were already outnumbered. Congressional debate focused not on whether it was a good idea to abolish the trade, but on what should become of any Africans imported illegally after the ban took effect. The final bill provided that smuggled slaves would be sold in accordance with the laws of the state or territory in which they arrived. It underscored, in other words, that slaves (even illegal ones) were property. Had the bill not done so, threatened one Georgia congressman, the result might have

been "resistance to the authority of the Government," even civil war. Although the debate over the slave trade did not fall along strictly sectional (or regional) lines, sectional tensions never lay far beneath the surface in this era of heated partisan conflict.

In anticipation of the higher prices that their human property would fetch once the law took effect, traders temporarily withheld their slaves from the market in the months after the law's passage. During the last four months of 1807 alone, sixteen thousand African slaves arrived at Gadsden Wharf in Charleston, where they were detained by merchants eager to wait out the January 1 deadline. Although many of these slaves—hundreds, if not thousands—died in the cramped, disease-ridden holding "pens" before they could be sold, merchants calculated that the increased value of those who survived until the ban took effect would outweigh the losses. Not that January 1, 1808, brought an end to the international slave trade; a brisk—and profitable—illegal trade took over. As Justice Joseph Story noted in 1819, the slave trade "is still carried on with all the implacable ferocity and insatiable rapacity of former times. Avarice has grown more subtle in its evasions; and watches and seizes its prey with an appetite quickened rather than suppressed by its guilty vigils." In 1819, Congress passed a law authorizing the president to use force to intercept slave ships along the African coast, but even had the government been determined to enforce the law, the small American navy could not have halted the illicit trade in human beings.

8-3e Early Abolitionism and Colonization

The traffic in human beings helped galvanize early opposition to slavery, though African American abolitionists critiqued more than the slave trade itself; they also advocated slavery's immediate termination, assisted escaped slaves, and promoted legal equality for free blacks. From the

▲ In an effort to win support for measures to end the international slave trade and slavery itself, abolitionists published drawings of slaves being captured as well as images of the inhumanely cramped slave ships, where each person was allotted a space roughly the size of a coffin. Disease spread rapidly under such conditions, causing many slaves to die before reaching American shores.

nation's earliest days—in places like Philadelphia, New York, Albany, Boston, and Nantucket—free blacks formed societies to petition legislatures, seek judicial redress, stage public marches, and, especially, publish tracts chronicling slavery's horrors. By 1830, the nation had fifty African American abolitionist societies.

In the years after the Revolution, white abolitionists had also formed antislavery organizations in places like Boston and, especially, Philadelphia, with its large population of Quakers, whose religious beliefs emphasized human equality. These early antislavery advocates pressed for an end to the international slave trade and for slavery's gradual abolition. Although they aided African Americans seeking freedom through judicial decisions, their assumptions about blacks' racial inferiority kept them from advocating for equal rights. Early white abolitionists tended to be wealthy, socially prominent men whose societies excluded women, African Americans, and less elite white men.

More often, elites supported the colonization movement, which crystallized in 1816 with the organization of the American Colonization Society. Its members planned to purchase and relocate American slaves, as well as free blacks, to Africa or the Caribbean. Among its supporters were Thomas Jefferson, James Madison, James Monroe, and Henry Clay, as well as many lesser-known men and women from the North and, especially, the Upper South. In 1822, the society founded Liberia, on Africa's west coast, and began a settlement for African Americans who were willing to go. The society had resettled nearly twelve thousand people in Liberia by 1860. (More followed in upcoming decades.) Some colonizationists aimed to strengthen slavery by ridding the South of troublesome slaves or to purge the North of African Americans altogether. Others hoped colonization would improve African Americans' conditions. Although some African Americans supported the movement, black abolitionists generally denounced it.

8-3f Election of 1808

Once congressional discussion of the international slave trade subsided, however, politicians focused their attention not on slavery but rather on the embargo, especially with the approach of the 1808 presidential election. Democratic-Republicans suffered from factional dissent and dissatisfaction in seaboard states hobbled by the trade restrictions. Although nine state legislatures passed resolutions urging Jefferson to run again, the president followed George Washington's lead in declining a third term. He supported James Madison, his secretary of state, as the Democratic-Republican standard-bearer. For the first time, however, the Democratic-Republican nomination was contested. Madison won the endorsement of the party's congressional caucus, but Virginia Democratic-Republicans put forth James Monroe, who later withdrew, and some easterners supported Vice President George Clinton. Madison and Clinton headed the ticket. Charles Cotesworth Pinckney and Rufus King again ran on the Federalist ticket, but with new vigor.

Florilegius/SSPL/Getty Images

Emigration to Liberia

Even as European immigrants sought republican freedoms in the United States, Americans sought similar opportunities in Africa. For nearly thirteen thousand African Americans, the destination was Liberia—first a colony organized by the American Colonization Society (1822), then an independent nation (1847) along Africa's West Coast.

Excluded from the American Revolution's promises of equality, some African Americans advocated resettlement in the Caribbean, Canada, and, especially, Africa. In 1816, Paul Cuffee, an abolitionist and shipping merchant of African American and Native American descent, resettled nine African American families in Sierra Leone, a British colony established for freed slaves. After his death the following year, colonization efforts fell primarily to the newly organized American Colonization Society (ACS), whose membership included President James Monroe, Senator Henry Clay, and Supreme Court Justice Bushrod Washington (a nephew of George Washington). In 1824, the ACS formally established Liberia, to which it encouraged immigration of freeborn and recently freed African Americans.

The ACS's members held wide-ranging views; some saw slavery as a threat to American principles or prosperity, while others aimed primarily to deport free blacks, widely seen as a threat to slavery. Because ACS leaders called blacks "useless and pernicious" (Henry Clay) and reasoned that colonization would "secure the property of every master in the United States over his slaves" (John Randolph), many African Americans, including some who had endorsed Cuffee's efforts, denounced ACS-sponsored emigration.

But others seized what they saw as the best opportunity to secure their own freedom, one that might also allow them to help enlighten, as they saw it, native Africans. For many such emigrants, however, Liberia did not immediately prove a promised land. American transplants succumbed in large numbers to malaria, and when they attempted to wrestle land and power from indigenous populations, they met fierce resistance. Within a generation, though, the Americo-Liberians had established themselves as a social, economic, and political elite, subjecting the Native populations to the same sort of second-class citizenship that they had themselves experienced in the United States.

The Republic of Liberia declared its independence from the American Colonization Society in 1847, and today only about 5 percent of its population descends from original settlers. But the nation still bears many markers of its American heritage. Its constitution is modeled on the U.S. Constitution, its official language is English, its flag resembles the American stars-and-stripes design, its architecture has American vestiges, and the American dollar is accepted alongside the Liberian dollar. For the past three decades, the nation has suffered from violent political turmoil, at whose heart is the issue of who should rule: the descendants of the nineteenth-century Americo-Liberians or leaders of indigenous ethnic groups. Begun in the 1820s, African American emigration to Liberia forged a link with both immediate and enduring consequences.

CRITICAL THINKING

- How is the political turmoil that exists in modern Liberia a by-product of the legacies of both racism and freedom in the United States?

◀ Eager to persuade readers of Liberia's success as a colony for former American slaves, colonizationists published images such as this one of the president's house in Monrovia, in which sparsely clad African natives are juxtaposed with genteel American transplants. Even as the image lauds the supposed superiority of African Americans to Africans, it implies that African Americans will themselves fare much better in Africa than they could in the United States.

Library of Congress/Getty Images

The younger Federalists made the most of the widespread disaffection with Democratic-Republican policy, especially the embargo. Pinckney received only 47 electoral votes to Madison's 122, but he carried all of New England except Vermont, won Delaware, and carried some electoral votes in two other states. Federalists also gained seats in Congress and captured the New York State legislature. Although the Federalist future looked promising, the transition from one Democratic-Republican administration to the next went smoothly.

8-3g Women and Politics

This transition was eased, in part, by the wives of elected and appointed officials in the new capital, who encouraged political and diplomatic negotiation. Such negotiations often took place in social settings, even private homes, where people with divergent interests could bridge their ideological divides through personal relationships. Women played crucial roles, fostering conversation, providing an ear or a voice for unofficial messages, and—in the case of international affairs—standing as surrogates for their nation. Elite women hosted events that muted domestic partisan rivalries, events at which Federalists and Democratic-Republicans could find common ground in civility, if not always in politics. Political wives' interactions among themselves served political purposes, too: when First Lady Dolley Madison visited congressmen's wives, she cultivated goodwill for her husband while collecting recipes that allowed her to serve regionally diverse cuisine at White House functions. Mrs. Madison hoped her menus would help keep simmering sectional tensions from reaching a boiling point.

But it was women's buying power that may have proved most influential in the era of the embargo. Recalling women's support of revolutionary-era boycotts, Jeffersonians appealed directly for women's support of their embargo. Sympathetic women responded by spurning imported fabric and making (or directing their slaves to make) homespun clothing for themselves and their families. Federalists, however, encouraged women to "keep commerce alive," and sympathetic women bought smuggled goods.

8-3h Failed Policies

Under the pressure of domestic opposition, the embargo eventually collapsed. In its place, the Non-Intercourse Act of 1809 reopened trade with all nations except Britain and France, and authorized the president to resume trade with those two nations once they respected American neutral rights. In June 1809, President Madison reopened trade with Britain after its minister to the United States offered assurances that Britain would repeal restrictions on American trade. But His Majesty's government in London repudiated the minister's assurances, leading Madison to revert to nonintercourse.

War Hawks Militant Republicans of the early nineteenth century who demanded more aggressive policies and who wanted war with Britain.

When the Non-Intercourse Act expired in 1810, Congress substituted Macon's Bill Number 2, reopening trade with both Great Britain and France but providing that, when either nation stopped violating American commercial rights, the president would suspend American commerce with the other. When Napoleon accepted the offer, Madison declared nonintercourse on Great Britain in 1811. Although the French continued to seize American ships, Britain became the main focus of American hostility because its Royal Navy dominated the seas.

In spring 1812, the British admiralty ordered its ships not to stop, search, or seize American warships, and in June Britain reopened the seas to American shipping. But before word of the change in British policy reached American shores, Congress declared war.

8-3i Mr. Madison's War

The vote was sharply divided. The House voted 79 to 49 for war; the Senate, 19 to 13. Democratic-Republicans favored war by a vote of 98 to 23; Federalists opposed it 39 to 0. Those who favored war, including President Madison, pointed to assaults on American sovereignty and honor: impressment, violation of neutral trading rights, and British alliances with Native peoples in the West. Others saw an opportunity to conquer and annex British Canada. Most militant were land-hungry southerners and westerners—the "**War Hawks**"—led by John C. Calhoun of South Carolina and first-term congressman and House Speaker Henry Clay of Kentucky. John Randolph of Virginia, an opponent of war, charged angrily, "Agrarian cupidity, not maritime rights, urges war!" He heard "but one word" in Congress: "Canada! Canada! Canada!" Most representatives from the coastal states, and especially from the Northeast, feared disruption to commerce and opposed what they called "Mr. Madison's War."

Initially, the Federalists benefited from antiwar sentiment. They joined renegade Democratic-Republicans in supporting New York City mayor DeWitt Clinton for president in the election of 1812. Clinton lost to President Madison by 128 to 89 electoral votes—a respectable showing against a wartime president—and the Federalists gained some congressional seats and carried many local elections. But the South and the West—areas that favored the war—remained solidly Democratic-Republican.

8-4 The War of 1812

▶ **What challenges did the United States face in fighting the British during the War of 1812?**

▶ **How was the war in the South different from that in the North?**

▶ **What were the domestic and international consequences of the War of 1812?**

Lasting from 1812 to 1815, the war unfolded in a series of scuffles and skirmishes (see Map 8.2) for which the U.S. armed forces, kept lean by Jeffersonian fiscal policies,

Map 8.2 **Major Campaigns of the War of 1812**

The land war centered on the U.S.–Canadian border, the Chesapeake Bay, and the Louisiana and Mississippi Territories.

were ill prepared. With few experienced army officers—the U.S. Military Academy at West Point, founded in 1802, had produced only eighty-nine regular officers—campaigns were executed poorly. Although the U.S. Navy had a corps of experienced officers, it proved no match for the Royal Navy.

Nor did the United States succeed at enlisting sufficient forces. The government's efforts to lure recruits—with sign-up bonuses, and promises of three months' pay and rights to purchase 160 acres of western land upon discharge—met with mixed success. At first, recruitment went well among westerners, who were motivated by civic spirit, desire for land, strong anti-Native American sentiment, and fears of Tecumseh's pan-Native American organization. But after word spread of delays in pay, as well as inadequate supplies and rations, recruitment dwindled. In New England, raising an army was even more difficult. Federalists discouraged enlistments, and even some New England

Democratic-Republicans declined to raise volunteer companies. Others promised their men that they would serve only in defensive roles, as in Maine, where they would guard the coastline. Militias in New England and New York often refused to fight outside their own states. Desperate for soldiers, New York offered freedom to slaves who enlisted, and compensation to their owners, and the U.S. Army made the same offer to slaves in the Old Northwest and in Canada. In Philadelphia, black leaders formed a "Black Brigade" to defend the city. But in the Deep South, fear of arming slaves kept them out of the military except in New Orleans, where a free black militia dated back to Spanish control of Louisiana. The British, on the other hand, recruited slaves by promising freedom in exchange for service. In the end, British forces—made up of British regulars, their Native allies, fugitive slaves, and Canadians, many of whom were loyalists who had fled during the American Revolution—outnumbered the Americans overall.

8-4a Invasion of Canada

Despite their recruitment problems, Americans expected to take Canada easily. Canada's population was sparse, its army small, and the Great Lakes inaccessible to the Royal Navy in the Atlantic. Americans hoped, too, that French Canadians might welcome U.S. forces.

American strategy aimed to split Canadian forces and isolate pro-British Native peoples, especially Tecumseh, whom the British had promised a Native American nation in the Great Lakes region. In July 1812, U.S. general William Hull, territorial governor of Michigan, marched his troops, who outnumbered those of the British and their allies, into Upper Canada (modern Ontario), hoping to conquer Montreal. But by abandoning Mackinac Island and Fort Dearborn, and by surrendering Fort Detroit, he left the entire Midwest exposed to the enemy. Captain Zachary Taylor provided the only bright spot, giving the Americans a land victory with his September 1812 defense of Fort Harrison in Indiana Territory. But by the winter of 1812–1813, the British controlled about half of the Old Northwest. The United States had no greater success on the Niagara Front, where New York borders Canada, in large part because New York militiamen refused to leave their state to join the invasion of Canada.

8-4b Naval Battles

Despite victories on the Atlantic by the USS *Constitution* (nicknamed "Old Ironsides" after its rout of HMS *Guerrière*), the USS *Wasp*, and the USS *United States*, the American navy—which began the war with just seventeen ships—could not match the powerful Royal Navy. The Royal Navy blockaded the Chesapeake and Delaware bays in December 1812, and by 1814 the blockade covered nearly all American ports along the Atlantic and Gulf coasts. After 1811, American trade overseas declined by nearly 90 percent, and the decline in revenue from customs duties threatened to bankrupt the federal government and prostrate New England.

The contest for control of the Great Lakes, the key to the war in the Northwest, evolved as a shipbuilding race. Under Master Commandant Oliver Hazard Perry and shipbuilder Noah Brown, the United States outbuilt the British on Lake Erie and defeated them at the bloody Battle of Put-in-Bay on September 10, 1813, gaining control of Lake Erie.

8-4c Burning Capitals

General William Henry Harrison then began what would be among the United States' most successful land campaigns. A ragged group of Kentucky militia volunteers, armed only with swords and knives, marched 20 to 30 miles a day to join Harrison's forces in Ohio. Now 4,500 strong, Harrison's forces attacked and took Detroit before crossing into Canada, where they razed the capital of York (now Toronto), looting and burning the Parliament building in April of 1813. Six months later, at the Battle of the Thames, also in Canada, they defeated British, Shawnee, and Chippewa forces. Among the dead was Tecumseh. After defeating Napoleon in Europe in April 1814, the British launched a land counteroffensive against the United States, concentrating on the Chesapeake Bay region. In retaliation for the burning of York—and to divert American troops from Lake Champlain, where the British planned a new offensive—royal troops occupied Washington, D.C., in August and set it ablaze, leaving the presidential mansion and parts of the city burning all night. Chaos ruled. The president and cabinet fled. Dolley Madison stayed long enough to oversee the removal of cabinet documents and, famously, to save a Gilbert Stuart portrait of George Washington.

The British intended the attack on Washington only as a diversion. The major battle occurred in September 1814 at Baltimore, where the Americans held firm. Francis Scott Key, detained on a British ship, watched the bombardment of Fort McHenry from Baltimore harbor and the next morning wrote the verses of "The Star-Spangled Banner" (which became the national anthem in 1931). Although the British inflicted heavy damage, they achieved little militarily; their offensive on Lake Champlain proved equally unsuccessful. The war had reached a stalemate.

8-4d War in the South

To the south, two wars were happening simultaneously. In what one historian calls "the other War of 1812" (or the Patriot War), a private army of Americans, with secret support from the Madison administration, tried to seize East Florida from Spain's control. What started as a settlers' rebellion along the Georgia-Florida border—in an effort to grab more land, strike at the Spaniards' Native American allies, and later to protest the Spaniards' arming of black soldiers (increasing white settlers' fears of slave rebellion)—turned into a war, with the Patriots receiving support from U.S. regular forces (land and naval) and Georgia militia units. Federalists condemned the invasion of a neutral territory, and the Senate refused twice (in 1812 and 1813) to support a military seizure of Florida. Politically embarrassed, Madison withdrew his support, and the movement collapsed in May 1814. Historians disagree about whether the Patriot War ultimately helped or hindered American efforts to win Florida from the Spanish.

In the war with Britain, the southern theater proved much more successful. The war's final campaign began with an American attack on the Red Stick Creeks along the Gulf of Mexico and on the British around New Orleans, and it ended with Americans gaining new territory for white settlement. The Red Sticks had responded to Tecumseh's call (his mother was a Creek) to resist U.S. expansion. Some had died in Indiana Territory, when General Harrison's troops routed Shawnee forces at Tippecanoe in 1811. In 1813, the Red Sticks attacked Fort Mims, about forty miles from Mobile, killing hundreds of white men, women, and children seeking

Selling War

The War of 1812 was not always a popular war, but in its aftermath many Americans trumpeted the war's successes. To the left, we see a recruitment poster from 1812, in which General William Henry Harrison seeks additional cavalrymen. Hampered in part by transportation difficulties, Harrison is unable to offer much—soldiers are even requested to supply their own bacon as well as their own horses—but he does promise that the expedition will be short, undoubtedly a concern to men eager to return to the fall harvest. To the right, we see a handkerchief made in 1815, after the Treaty of Ghent and the Battle of New Orleans; it features the United States' victories against the world's greatest naval power, Great Britain. Made with a decorative border, the kerchief may have been for display.

CRITICAL THINKING

- What similar values do we see promoted in the two images, and what factors—such as their intended audiences, their purposes, and when they were created—might account for any differences between them?

▲ Made in 1815 from cotton textiles—whose domestic production soared during the War of 1812, with trade cut off from Britain—this handkerchief helps promote American "liberty and independence."

CIRCULAR.

ST. MARY's, September 20th, 1812.

SIR—As the force which I have collected at this place (of mounted men) is not sufficient to accomplish the object of the expedition, which it was proposed to set out from hence—You are hereby authorised to circulate through the country my wishes to be joined by any number of mounted men, (corps ready organ-ised would be preferred) under the authority hereto-fore given by Gov. Meigs. Companies which may join me to serve for the expedition and which will fur-nish their own horses will have credit for a tour of du-ty, and the expedition is not expected to continue more than thirty days, and will, at any rate, not ex-tend beyond forty.

> I am, respectfully,
> your humble servant,
> WM. H. HARRISON.

P. S. The men must bring on as much bacon as possible. Any one who will bring a spare horse, saddle and bridle, shall be allowed fifty cents per day for the use of them—The bearer is authorised to hire horses and give certificates which will be taken up and paid for by the Quarter Master.

WM. H. HARRISON.

▲ With a tiny regular army, the United States often had to rely on short-term recruits to wage war on the British.

protection there. Looking for revenge, General Andrew Jackson of Tennessee rallied his militiamen as well as Native American opponents of the Red Sticks (including other Creeks favoring accommodation with whites) and crushed the Red Sticks at Horseshoe Bend (in present-day Alabama) in March 1814, leading to the Treaty of Fort Jackson, in which the Creeks ceded 23 million acres of their land, or about half of their holdings, and withdrew to the southern and western part of Mississippi Territory.

Jackson became a major general in the regular army and continued south toward the Gulf of Mexico, with his eye on New Orleans. After seizing Pensacola (in Spanish Florida) and then securing Mobile, Jackson's forces marched to New Orleans, where for three weeks they played a game of cat and mouse with the British soldiers. Finally, on January 8, 1815, the two forces met head-on. In fortified positions, Jackson's poorly trained army held its ground against two British frontal assaults. At day's end, more than two thousand British soldiers lay dead or wounded (a casualty rate of nearly one-third), while the Americans suffered only twenty-one casualties.

The Battle of New Orleans took place two weeks after the war's official conclusion: word had not yet reached America that British and United States diplomats had signed the **Treaty of Ghent** on December 24,

Treaty of Ghent Treaty that ended the War of 1812, restoring the prewar status quo.

1814. Although militarily unnecessary, the Battle of New Orleans catapulted General Andrew Jackson to national political prominence, and the victory over a formidable foe inspired a sense of national pride.

8-4e Treaty of Ghent

The Treaty of Ghent, negotiated between the British and Americans with no Native Americans present, essentially restored the prewar status quo. It provided for an end to hostilities with the British and with Native Americans, release of prisoners, restoration of conquered territory, and arbitration of boundary disputes. But the United States received no satisfaction on impressment, blockades, or other maritime rights for neutrals, and the British demands for territorial cessions from Maine to Minnesota went unmet. The British dropped their promise to Tecumseh of an independent Native American nation.

Why did the negotiators settle for so little? Napoleon's defeat allowed the United States to discard its prewar demands because peace in Europe made impressment and interference with American commerce moot issues. Similarly, war-weary Britain—its treasury nearly depleted—stopped pressing for military victory.

8-4f American Sovereignty Reasserted

Yet the War of 1812 had significant consequences for America's status in the world. It affirmed the independence

▲ During the War of 1812, British forces and their Native American allies seized Fort Shelby in Wisconsin, renaming it Fort McKay. After the Treaty of Ghent (1814) restored the installation to American hands, British Captain W. Andrew Bulger bid farewell to his Native allies before withdrawing and burning the fort.

Rindisbacher, Peter/Wisconsin Historical Society, WHi-42292

of the American republic and ensured Canada's independence from the United States. Trade and territorial disputes with Great Britain continued, but they never again led to war. Americans strengthened their resolve to steer clear of European politics.

The return of peace allowed the United States to again focus on the Barbary Coast, where the *dey* (governor) of Algiers had taken advantage of the American preoccupation with British forces to declare his own war on the United States. In the Second Barbary War, U.S. forces captured and detained hundreds of Algerians while negotiating a treaty in the summer of 1815 that forever freed the United States from paying tributes for passage in the Mediterranean. The Second Barbary War reaffirmed America's sovereignty and its commitment to the principle of freedom of the seas.

8-4g Domestic Consequences

The War of 1812 had profound domestic consequences. The Federalists' hopes of returning to national prominence all but evaporated with the **Hartford Convention**, when delegates from New England—frustrated by the stalemated war and the shattered New England economy—met in Hartford, Connecticut, for three weeks in the winter of 1814–1815 to discuss revising the national compact or pulling out of the republic. Although moderates prevented a resolution of secession—a resolution to withdraw from the Union—the delegates condemned the war and the embargo while endorsing constitutional changes that would weaken the South's power vis-à-vis the North and make it harder to declare war. When news arrived in upcoming weeks of, first, Jackson's victory in New Orleans and, then, the Treaty of Ghent, the Hartford Convention made the Federalists look wrongheaded, even treasonous. Federalists survived in a handful of states until the 1820s, but the party faded from the national scene.

With Tecumseh's death, midwestern Native peoples lost their most powerful leader; with the withdrawal of the British, they lost their strongest ally. In the South, the Red Sticks had ceded vast tracts of fertile land. The war did not bring disaster to all Native Americans—some accommodationists, such as the Cherokees, temporarily flourished—but it effectively disarmed traditionalists bent on resisting American expansion. Although the Treaty of Ghent pledged the United States to end hostilities with Native peoples and to restore their prewar "possessions, rights, and privileges," Native groups could not make the United States adhere to the agreement.

For American farmers, the war opened vast tracts of formerly Native American land for cultivating cotton in the Old Southwest and wheat in the Old Northwest. For young industries, the war also ultimately proved a stimulant, as Americans could no longer rely on overseas imports of manufactured goods, particularly textiles. The War of 1812 thus fueled demand for raw cotton, and the newly acquired lands in the Southwest beckoned southerners, who migrated there with their slaves or with expectations of someday owning slaves. The war's conclusion accelerated three trends that would dominate U.S. history for upcoming decades: industrial takeoff, slavery's entrenchment, and westward expansion.

8-5 Early Industrialization

▶ **How was preindustrial labor organized?**

▶ **How did early industry begin to alter work routines and market relations?**

▶ **How was early industry in the North tied to slavery?**

As a result of the embargo and the War of 1812, the North underwent an accelerated industrial development even as the South became more dependent on cotton production (see Chapter 9). Although the two regions' economies followed different paths, however, they remained fundamentally interconnected.

8-5a Preindustrial Farms

Before the War of 1812, most American farmers practiced what is called mixed agriculture: they raised a variety of crops and livestock. Their goal was to procure what they called a "competence": everyday comforts and economic opportunities for their children. When they produced more than they needed, they traded the surplus with neighbors or sold it to local storekeepers. Such transactions often took place without money; farmers might trade eggs for shoes, or they might labor in their neighbor's fields in exchange for bales of hay.

Family members comprised the main source of farm labor, though some yeoman farmers, North and South, also relied on slaves or indentured servants. Work generally divided along gender lines. Men and boys worked in the fields, herded livestock, chopped firewood, fished, and hunted. Women and girls tended gardens, milked cows, spun and wove, processed and preserved food, prepared meals, washed clothes, and looked after infants and toddlers.

Farmers lent each other farm tools, harvested each other's fields, bartered goods, and raised their neighbors' barns and husked their corn. Little cash exchanged hands, in large part because money was in short supply. Still, farmers often kept elaborate accounts of their debts, whether in books (in New England) or in mental notes (in the South). Years might pass without debts repaid, and when they were, they were not always repaid directly. A farmer who owed a neighbor two days' labor might bring the local storekeeper his eggs, to be credited to the neighbor's account.

Many farmers engaged simultaneously in this local economy and in long-distance trade. In the local economy—where they exchanged goods with people

Hartford Convention Federalist meeting that was perceived as disloyalty during time of war and began the downfall of the party.

whom they knew—a system of "just price" prevailed, in which neighbors calculated value in terms of how much labor was involved in producing a good or providing a service. When the same farmers engaged in long-distance trade—when they sold their goods to merchants who resold them to other merchants before the goods eventually traveled as far away as coastal cities or even Europe—they set prices based on what the market would bear. In the long-distance market, credit and debt were reckoned in monetary value.

8-5b Preindustrial Artisans

Farmers who lived near towns or villages often purchased crafted goods from local cobblers, saddlers, blacksmiths, gunsmiths, silversmiths, and tailors. Most artisans, though, lived in the nation's seaports, where master craftsmen (independent businessmen who owned their own shops and tools) oversaw workshops employing apprentices and journeymen. Although the vast majority of craftsmen, North and South, were white, free blacks were well represented in some cities' urban trades, such as tailoring and carpentry in Charleston, South Carolina. Teenage apprentices lived with their masters, who taught them a craft, lodged and fed them, and offered parental oversight in exchange for labor. The master's wife, assisted by her daughters, cooked, cleaned, and sewed for her husband's

workers. The relationship between a master craftsmen and his workers was often familial in nature, if not always harmonious. When the term of their apprenticeship expired, apprentices became journeymen who earned wages, usually hoping to one day open their own shops. The workplace had little division of labor or specialization. A tailor measured, designed, and sewed an entire suit; a cobbler did the same with shoes.

Men, women, and children worked long days on farms and in workshops, but the pace of work was generally uneven and unregimented. During busy periods, they worked from dawn to dusk; the pace of work slowed after the harvest or after a large order had been completed. Market and court days were as much about exchanging gossip and offering toasts as exchanging goods and watching justice unfold. Husking bees and barn raisings brought people together not only to shuck corn and raise buildings, but also to eat, drink, dance, and flirt. Busy periods did not stop artisans from punctuating the day with grog breaks or from reading the newspaper aloud; they might even close their shops to attend a political meeting. Nor did each workday adhere to a rigid schedule; journeymen often staggered in late on Monday mornings, if they showed up at all, after a long night of carousing on their day off. Although the master craftsman was the boss, his workers exerted a good deal of influence over the workplace.

▲ Although separating flax fibers from their woody base could be arduous work, flax-scutching bees—much like corn-husking bees—brought together neighbors for frivolity as well as work.

National Gallery of Art, Washington, D.C. Gift of Edgar William and Bernice Chrysler Garbisch

8-5c Putting-Out and Early Factories

By the War of 1812, preindustrial habits were already changing, most noticeably in the Northeast, where early industry reorganized daily work routines and market relationships. Women and children had long made their family's clothing, hats, soap, and candles. In the late eighteenth and early nineteenth centuries, though, a "putting-out" system—similar to one existing in parts of western Europe—developed, particularly in Massachusetts, New Jersey, and Pennsylvania. Women and children continued to produce goods as they always had, but now did so in much greater quantities and for broader consumption. A merchant supplied them with raw materials, paid them a wage (usually a price for each piece they produced), and sold their wares in distant markets, pocketing the profit for himself. "Outwork," as it is sometimes called, appealed to women eager to earn cash, whether to secure some economic independence or to save money for land on which their children might establish their own farms. Particularly in New England—where population density, small farms, and tired soil constricted farming opportunities and thus created a surplus labor pool—the putting-out system provided cash with which to buy cheaper, more fertile western lands without requiring that family members seek employment away from home.

The earliest factories grew up in tandem with the putting-out system. When Samuel Slater helped set up the first American water-powered spinning mill in Rhode Island in 1790—using children to card and spin raw cotton into thread—he sent the spun thread to nearby farm families who wove it into cloth before sending it back to Slater, from whom they received a wage. Early shoe factories relied on a similar system: factory workers cut cowhide into uppers and bottoms that were sent to rural homes. There, women sewed the uppers while men lasted (or shaped) and pegged the bottoms, a process that also sometimes took place in small workshops. The change was subtle but significant: although the work remained familiar, women now operated their looms for wages and produced cloth for the market, not primarily for their families, while male cobblers made shoes for feet that would never walk into their shops or homes.

Despite their efforts to define themselves as a separate nation, Americans relied on British technology to bring together the many steps of textile manufacturing—carding (or disentangling) fibers, spinning yarn, and weaving cloth—under one factory roof. Slater, a British immigrant, had reconstructed from memory the complex machines he had used while working in a British cotton-spinning factory. But Slater's mill only carded and spun yarn; the yarn still needed

▲ This contemporary painting shows the Boston Manufacturing Company's 1814 textile factory at Waltham, Massachusetts. All manufacturing processes were brought together under one roof, and the company built its first factories in rural New England to tap roaring rivers as a power source.

to be hand-woven into cloth, work often done by farm women seeking to earn cash. In 1810, Bostonian Francis Cabot Lowell, determined to introduce water-powered mechanical weaving in the United States, visited the British textile center of Manchester, where he toured factories, later sketching from memory what he had seen. In 1813, he and his business associates, calling themselves the Boston Manufacturing Company, brought together all phases of textile manufacturing under one roof in Waltham, Massachusetts. A decade later, the Boston Manufacturing Company established what it saw as a model industrial village—named for its now-deceased founder—along the banks of the Merrimack River. At Lowell, Massachusetts, there would be boardinghouses for workers, a healthy alternative to the tenements and slums of Manchester. American industrialists envisioned America industrializing without the poverty and degradation associated with European industrialization.

Early industrialization, primarily in the northern states, was inextricably linked to slavery. Much of the capital came from merchants who made their fortunes at least in part through the trade in African slaves, and two of the most prominent industries—textiles and shoes—expanded alongside a growing southern cotton economy. Southern cotton fed northern textile mills, and northern shoe factories sold their "Negro brogans" (work shoes) to southern planters. Even in the putting-out system, the connections to the slave South were strong: New England farm girls wove palm-leaf hats for merchants who sold them to southern planters for their slaves. Yet despite these connections, northerners and southerners often saw their economies as developing in fundamentally distinct ways.

8-6 Sectionalism and Nationalism

▶ How did the federal government pursue a nationalist agenda to encourage domestic growth after the War of 1812?

▶ How did the North and South become more regionally distinct after the War of 1812?

▶ How did the United States seek to assert its position on the global stage after the War of 1812?

Following the War of 1812, Madison and the Democratic-Republicans embraced a nationalist agenda, absorbing the Federalist idea that the federal government should encourage growth. In his December 1815 message to Congress, Madison recommended economic development and military expansion. His agenda, which Henry Clay later called the American System, included a national bank, improved transportation, and a protective tariff—a tax on imported goods that was designed to protect American manufacturers from foreign competition. Yet Madison did not stray entirely from his Jeffersonian roots; only a constitutional

amendment, he argued, could authorize the federal government to build local roads and canals. Instead, the bulk of internal improvements would fall to the states, which would, in turn, exacerbate regional patterns of economic development.

8-6a American System

Clay and other congressional leaders, such as Calhoun of South Carolina, believed the American System would ease sectional divides. The tariff would stimulate New England industry, whose manufactured goods would find markets in the South and West. At the same time, the South's and West's agricultural products—cotton and foodstuffs—would feed New England mills and their workers. Manufactured goods and agricultural products would move in all directions along roads and canals—what contemporaries called "internal improvements"—which tariff revenues would fund. A national bank would handle the transactions.

In the Madison administration's last year, the Democratic-Republican Congress enacted much of the nationalist program. In 1816, it chartered the Second Bank of the United States (the charter on the first bank had expired in 1811) to serve as a depository for federal funds and to issue currency, collect taxes, and pay the government's debts. The Second Bank of the United States would also oversee state and local banks, ensuring that their paper money had backing in specie (precious metals). Like its predecessor, the bank mixed public and private ownership; the government provided one-fifth of the bank's capital and appointed one-fifth of its directors.

Congress also passed a protective tariff to aid industries that flourished during the War of 1812 but that now were threatened by the resumption of overseas trade. The Tariff of 1816 levied taxes on imported woolens and cottons as well as on iron, leather, hats, paper, and sugar. Foreshadowing a growing trend, though, the tariff did more to divide than to unify the nation. New England as well as the western and Middle Atlantic states stood to benefit from it and thus applauded it, whereas many southerners objected that it raised the price of consumer goods while opening the possibility that Britain would retaliate with a tariff on cotton.

Some southerners did promote roads and canals to "bind the republic together," as Calhoun put it. However, on March 3, 1817, the day before leaving office, President Madison, citing constitutional scruples, stunned Congress by vetoing Calhoun's "Bonus Bill," which would have authorized federal funding for such public works.

8-6b Early Internal Improvements

Constitutional scruples aside, Federalists and Democratic-Republicans agreed that the nation's prosperity depended on improved transportation. For Federalists, roads and canals were necessary for commercial development; for Jeffersonians, they would spur western expansion and

The Metropolitan Museum of Art / Art Resource, NY

▲ The young nation's dirt roads meant bumpy and dusty travel for goods as well as passengers, prompting calls for transportation innovations, such as canals and, later, railroads, to spur economic growth.

agrarian growth. In 1806, Congress had passed (and Jefferson had signed) a bill authorizing funding for the Cumberland Road (later, the National Road), running 130 miles between Cumberland, Maryland, and Wheeling, Virginia (now West Virginia). Construction began in 1811 and was completed in 1818. Two years later, Congress authorized a survey of the National Road to Columbus, Ohio, a project funded in 1825 and completed in 1833; the road would ultimately extend into Indiana.

After President Madison's veto of the Bonus Bill, though, most transportation initiatives received funding from states, private investors, or a combination of the two. Between 1817 and 1825, the State of New York constructed the **Erie Canal**, linking the Great Lakes to the Atlantic seaboard. Although southern states constructed modest canals, the South's trade depended on river-going steamboats after 1817, when steamboats began traveling regularly upriver on the Mississippi. With canals and steamboats, western agricultural products traveled to market much more quickly and inexpensively, fueling the nation's westward expansion. Unlike steamboats, though, canals expanded commercial networks into regions without natural waterways. Although the Mississippi provided the great commercial highway of the early Republic, canals began to reorient midwestern commerce through the North.

8-6c Panic of 1819

Immediately following the War of 1812, the American economy had boomed. The international demand for (and price of) American commodities reached new heights. Poor weather in Europe led to crop failures, increasing demand for northern foodstuffs and southern cotton, which, in turn, touched off western land speculation. Speculators raced to buy large tracts of land at modest, government-established prices and then to resell it at a hefty profit to would-be settlers. Easy credit made this expansion possible. With loans and paper money, farmers and speculators bought land, while manufacturers established or enlarged enterprises.

Prosperity proved short-lived. Now recovered from war as well as weather, by the late 1810s Europeans could grow their own food, and Britain's new Corn Laws established a high tariff on imported foodstuffs, further lessening demand for American agricultural

Erie Canal Major canal that linked the Great Lakes to the Atlantic seaboard, opening the upper Midwest to wider development.

exports. Cotton prices fell in England. Wars in Latin America interfered with mining and reduced the supply of precious metals, leading European nations to hoard specie; in response, American banks furiously printed paper money and expanded credit even further. Fearful of inflation, the Second Bank of the United States, which had itself issued more loans than it could back in hard currency, demanded in 1819 that state banks repay loans in specie. State banks in turn called in the loans and mortgages they had made to individuals and companies. The falling prices of commodities meant that farmers could not pay their mortgages, and the decline of land values—from 50 to 75 percent in portions of the West—meant they could not meet their debts even by selling their farms. The nation's banking system collapsed. The 1819 financial panic reminded Americans all too starkly that they still lived within the economic orbit of Europe.

Hard times came to countryside and city alike. Foreclosures soared. Unemployment skyrocketed, even in older manufacturing areas that had focused on industries like iron making and tobacco processing. In Philadelphia, unemployment reached 75 percent. The contraction devastated workers and their families. As a Baltimore physician noted in 1819, working people felt hard times "a thousand fold more than the merchants." They could not build up savings during boom times to get them through the hard times; often, they could not make it through the winter without drawing on charity for food, clothing, and firewood.

The depression sent tremors throughout American society. Americans from all regions contemplated the virtues and hazards of rapid market expansion, disagreeing most intensely on where to place the blame for its shortcomings. Westerners blamed easterners; farmers and workers blamed bankers. Even as the nation's economy began to rebound in the early 1820s amid a flurry of internal improvement projects, no one could predict with confidence where—in what region, in what sector—the nation's economic and political fortunes would lie.

8-6d Missouri Compromise

Just as financial panic struck the nation in 1819, so, too, did political crisis. The issue was slavery's westward expansion. Although economic connections abounded between North and South, slavery had long been politically explosive. Since the drafting of the Constitution, Congress had tried to avoid the issue; the one exception had been debates over the international slave trade. In 1819, however, slavery once again burst onto the national political agenda when residents of the Missouri Territory—carved out of the Louisiana Territory—petitioned Congress for admission to the Union

Missouri Compromise
Attempt to end the debate over the number of slave and free states admitted to the Union by admitting Missouri as a slave state and Maine as a free state and banning slavery in the Louisiana Territory north of the 36°30′ latitude line.

with a constitution permitting slavery. At stake was more than the future of slavery in an individual state. Missouri's admission to the Union would give the slaveholding states a two-vote majority in the Senate, and what happened in Missouri would set a precedent for all the new western states created from the vast Louisiana Purchase. "This momentous question," wrote former president Thomas Jefferson, fearful for the life of the Union, "like a fire bell in the night, awakened and filled me with terror."

Following the Louisiana Purchase and especially after the end of the War of 1812, the American population had surged westward, leading five new states to join the Union: Louisiana (1812), Indiana (1816), Mississippi (1817), Illinois (1818), and Alabama (1819). Of these, Louisiana, Mississippi, and Alabama permitted slavery. Because Missouri was on the same latitude as free Illinois, Indiana, and Ohio (a state since 1803), its admission as a slave state would thrust slavery not just westward but also northward, as well as tilt the uneasy balance in the Senate.

For two and a half years the issue dominated Congress, with the fiery debate transcending the immediate issue of slavery in Missouri. When Representative James Tallmadge Jr. of New York proposed gradual emancipation in Missouri, some southerners accused the North of threatening to destroy the Union. "If you persist, the Union will be dissolved," Thomas W. Cobb of Georgia shouted at Tallmadge. Only "seas of blood" could extinguish the fire Tallmadge had ignited, warned Cobb. "Let it come," retorted Tallmadge. The House, which had a northern majority, passed the Tallmadge Amendment, but the Senate rejected it.

House Speaker Henry Clay—himself a western slaveholder—put forward a compromise in 1820. Maine, carved out of Massachusetts, would enter as a free state, followed by Missouri as a slave state, maintaining the balance between slave and free states, at twelve to twelve. In the rest of the Louisiana Territory north of Missouri's southern border of 36°30′, slavery would be prohibited forever (see Map 8.3).

The compromise carried but almost unraveled when Missouri submitted a constitution barring free blacks from entering the state, a provision that opponents contended would violate the federal constitutional provision that citizens of each state were "entitled to all privileges and immunities of citizens in the several States." Proponents countered that many states, North and South, already barred free blacks from entering. In 1821, Clay proposed a second compromise: Missouri would guarantee that none of its laws would discriminate against citizens of other states. (The compromise carried, but once admitted to the Union, Missouri twice adopted laws barring free blacks.) For more than three decades, the **Missouri Compromise** would govern congressional policy toward admitting new slave states. But the compromise masked rather than suppressed the simmering political conflict over slavery's westward expansion.

Map 8.3 Missouri Compromise and the State of the Union, 1820

The compromise worked out by House Speaker Henry Clay established a formula that avoided debate over whether new states would allow or prohibit slavery. In the process, it divided the United States into northern and southern regions.

Map legend:
- Closed to slavery by Missouri Compromise
- Open to slavery by Missouri Compromise
- Free states and territories
- Slave states and territories

8-6e The Era of Good Feelings

So, too, did the so-called "**Era of Good Feelings**," as a Boston newspaper dubbed the presidency of James Monroe, Madison's successor, which was marked by a lack of partisan political discord. Monroe was the last president to have attended the Constitutional Convention and the third Virginian elected president since 1801. A former senator and twice governor of Virginia, he had served under Madison as secretary of state and of war and had used his close association with Jefferson and Madison to attain the presidency. In 1816, he and his running mate, Daniel Tompkins, trounced the last Federalist presidential nominee, Rufus King, garnering all the electoral votes except those of the Federalist strongholds of Massachusetts, Connecticut, and Delaware. In office, Monroe continued Madison's domestic program, supporting tariffs and vetoing the Cumberland Road Bill (for repairs) in 1822.

Led by Federalist chief justice John Marshall, the Supreme Court became the bulwark of the nationalist agenda. In **McCulloch v. Maryland** (1819), the Court struck down a Maryland law taxing banks within the state that were not chartered by its legislature—a law aimed at hindering the Baltimore branch of the federally chartered Second Bank of the United States. The bank refused to pay the tax and sued. At issue was state versus federal jurisdiction. Writing for a unanimous Court, Marshall asserted the supremacy of the federal government over the states. "The Constitution and the laws thereof are supreme," he declared. "They control the constitution and laws of the respective states and cannot be controlled by them." The Court ruled, too, that Congress had the power to charter banks under the Constitution's clause endowing it with the authority to pass "all laws which shall be necessary and proper for carrying into execution" the enumerated powers of government. The Marshall Court thus supported the Federalist view that the federal government could promote interstate commerce.

8-6f Government Promotion of Market Expansion

Later Supreme Court cases validated government promotion of economic development and encouraged business enterprise and risk taking. In *Gibbons v. Ogden* (1824), the Supreme Court overturned the New York law that had given Robert Fulton and Robert Livingston (and their successor, Aaron Ogden) a monopoly on the New York–New Jersey steamboat trade. Chief Justice Marshall ruled that the federal power to license new enterprises took precedence over New York's grant of monopoly rights and declared that Congress's power under the commerce clause of the Constitution extended to "every species of commercial intercourse," including transportation. The *Gibbons v. Ogden* ruling built on earlier Marshall Court decisions, such as those in *Dartmouth College v. Woodward* (1819), which

Era of Good Feelings Period of one-party politics during administration of James Monroe.

McCulloch v. Maryland Supreme Court decision that restated national supremacy over the states.

protected the sanctity of contracts against state interference, and *Fletcher v. Peck* (1810), which voided a Georgia law that violated individuals' rights to make contracts. Within two years of *Gibbons v. Ogden*, the number of steamboats operating in New York increased from six to forty-three. A later ruling under Chief Justice Roger Taney, *Charles River Bridge v. Warren Bridge* (1837), encouraged new enterprises and technologies by favoring competition over monopoly, and the public interest over implied privileges in old contracts.

Federal and state courts, in conjunction with state legislatures, encouraged the proliferation of corporations—organizations entitled to hold property and transact business as if they were individuals. Corporation owners, called shareholders, were granted limited liability, or freedom from personal responsibility for the company's debts beyond their original investment. Limited liability encouraged investors to back new business ventures.

The federal government assisted the development of a commercial economy in other ways. The U.S. Post Office fostered the circulation of information, a critical element of the market economy. The number of post offices grew from three thousand in 1815 to fourteen thousand in 1845. To promote individual creativity and economic growth, the government protected inventions through patent laws and domestic industries through tariffs on foreign imports.

8-6g Boundary Settlements

Monroe's secretary of state, John Quincy Adams, matched the Marshall Court in assertiveness and nationalism. Adams, the son of John and Abigail Adams, managed the nation's foreign policy from 1817 to 1825, pushing for expansion (through negotiations, not war), fishing rights for Americans in Atlantic waters, political distance from Europe, and peace. Under Adams's leadership, the United States settled points of conflict with both Britain and Spain. In 1817, the United States and Great Britain signed the Rush-Bagot Treaty limiting their naval forces to one ship each on Lake Champlain and Lake Ontario and to two ships each on Lakes Erie, Huron, and Superior. This first disarmament treaty of modern times demilitarized the border between the United States and Canada. Adams then pushed for the Convention of 1818, which fixed the U.S.–Canadian border from Lake of the Woods in Minnesota westward to the Rockies along the 49th parallel. When they could not agree on the boundary west of the Rockies, Britain and the United States settled on joint occupation of Oregon for ten years (renewed indefinitely in 1827).

Adams's negotiations resulted in the Adams-Onís Treaty, in which the United States gained Florida, already occupied by General Andrew Jackson under pretext of suppressing Seminole raids against American settlements across the border during the First Seminole War of 1817–1818. Although the Louisiana Purchase had omitted reference to Spanish-ruled West Florida, the United States claimed the territory as far east as the Perdido River (the present-day Florida-Alabama border). During the War of 1812, the United States had seized Mobile and the remainder of West Florida, and after the war—with Spain preoccupied with its own domestic and colonial troubles—Adams had laid claim to East Florida. In 1819, Don Luís de Onís, the Spanish minister to the United States, agreed to cede Florida to the United States without payment if the United States renounced its dubious claims to northern Mexico (Texas) and assumed $5 million of claims by American citizens against Spain. The Adams-Onís (or Transcontinental) Treaty also defined the southwestern boundary of the Louisiana Purchase and set the line between Spanish Mexico and Oregon Country at the 42nd parallel.

8-6h Monroe Doctrine

John Quincy Adams's desire to insulate the United States and the Western Hemisphere from European conflict brought about his greatest achievement: the **Monroe Doctrine**. The immediate issue was recognition of new governments in Latin America. Between 1808 and 1822, the United Provinces of Río de la Plata (present-day northern Argentina, Paraguay, and Uruguay), Chile, Peru, Colombia, and Mexico all broke free from Spain (see Map 8.4). In 1822, shortly after the ratification of the Adams-Onís Treaty, the United States became the first nation outside Latin America to recognize the new states, including Mexico. But in Europe, reactionary regimes were ascending, and with France now occupying Spain to suppress a liberal rebellion, the United States feared that continental powers would attempt to return the new Latin American states to colonial rule. Having withdrawn from an alliance with continental nations, Britain proposed a joint declaration with the United States against European intervention in the Western Hemisphere. Adams rejected Britain's offer as just the kind of entanglement he sought to avoid, despite clear advantages to allying with the British and their powerful navy.

Monroe presented to Congress in December 1823 what became known as the Monroe Doctrine. His message announced that the American continents "are henceforth not to be considered subjects for future colonization by any European power." This principle addressed American anxiety not only about Latin America but also about Russian expansion beyond Alaska and its settlements in California. Monroe demanded nonintervention by Europe in the affairs of independent New World nations, and he pledged noninterference by the United States in European affairs, including those of Europe's existing New World colonies. Although Monroe's words carried no force—European nations stayed out of New World affairs because they feared the Royal Navy, not the United States' proclamations—they proved popular at home, tapping American nationalism as well as anti-British and anti-European feelings.

Monroe Doctrine Foreign policy statement that proclaimed that the American continents were not to be subjected to European colonization and demanded nonintervention by Europe in New World nations.

OREGON
COUNTRY
(Joint U.S.-British
occupation)

BRITISH NORTH AMERICA
(CANADA)
(Gr. Br.)

Mississippi R.

New York

Colorado R.

UNITED STATES

Philadelphia
Washington, D.C.

40°N

40°W

MEXICO
1821

Rio Grande

San
Antonio

New Orleans

Charleston

N

ATLANTIC
OCEAN

Gulf of Mexico

BAHAMA IS.
(Gr. Br.)

Mexico City

Veracruz

Havana

CUBA
(Spain)

HAITI 1804

20°N

BRITISH
HONDURAS (Gr. Br.)

JAMAICA
(Gr. Br.)

PUERTO RICO (Spain)

GUATEMALA
Guatemala City

Caribbean Sea

UNITED PROVINCES OF
CENTRAL AMERICA
1823–1839

Panama

Caracas

TRINIDAD (Gr. Br.)

BR. GUIANA (Gr. Br.)

Magdalena R.

VENEZUELA

Orinoco R.

DUTCH GUIANA (Neth.)

Socorro

FRENCH GUIANA (France)

Bogotá

GRAN COLOMBIA
1819–1830

*Galápagos
Islands*

Quito

ECUADOR

Equator   0°

Amazon R.

EMPIRE OF BRAZIL
1822

PACIFIC
OCEAN

PERU
1824

Lima

BOLIVIA
1825

La Paz

Salvador

Sucre

20°S

PARAGUAY
1811

Paraná R.

Rio de Janeiro

São Paulo

CHILE
1817

UNITED
PROVINCES
OF THE RIO DE
LA PLATA
1816

URUGUAY
1828

Valparaíso

Montevideo

Santiago

ARGENTINA

Buenos Aires

Bahía
Blanca

0   500   1000 Km.

0   500   1000 Mi.

PATAGONIA
(Disputed between
Argentina and Chile)

Islas Malvinas
(Falkland Islands)

1811 Year independence gained

Colony

80°W

60°W

Map 8.4 Latin American Independence, 1840

With Central and South American colonies triumphing in their wars of independence against European colonial powers, President
Monroe sought to enhance the United States' security by warning European nations against meddling in the region.

The Star-Spangled Banner

Like many contemporaries, Francis Scott Key—a Maryland lawyer, slaveowner, and amateur poet—opposed America's second war with Britain, denouncing it as a "lump of wickedness." But in September 1814, after American forces withstood the British navy's bombardment of Fort McHenry, in Baltimore Harbor, Key experienced a renewed sense of national pride, which he captured in four verses that spread quickly throughout the states. Cadenced to match a British tavern song, the patriotic slaveowner's poem famously hailed the United States as the "land of the free."

As "The Star-Spangled Banner"'s popularity grew in ensuing decades, politicians and activists, of various leanings, substituted their own lyrics. Pennsylvania temperance reformers sang, "Oh! Who has not seen, by the dawn's early light/Some poor bloated drunkard to his home weakly reeling/With blear eyes and red nose most revolting to sight." An anti-immigrant group called itself The Order of the Star-Spangled Banner, and a German translation of the song—"Das Star-Spangled Banner"—circulated. During the Civil War, the song rallied Unionists, while Confederates parodied it: "Oh! say has the star-spangled banner become/The flag of the Tory and Vile Northern

scum?" Meanwhile, Confederate sympathizers in Maryland safeguarded the original star-spangled banner, the one spotted by Francis Scott Key atop Fort McHenry—the great symbol of the nation from which they hoped to separate but whose original values they cherished.

Union victory deepened northerners' attachment to Key's song, which became quasi-official when the Navy adopted it in 1889. Lobbyists, including many southerners, urged Congress to designate it the national anthem, but detractors voiced a variety of reservations: pragmatic (its difficult tune), emotional (its origins as a drinking song), and ideological (its militaristic tone and anti-British sentiments, problematic now that Britain was an ally). Finally, in 1931 Congress designated it the national anthem, and today it is routinely performed at sporting events, a practice that started during World War I and that became widespread by World War II.

During wartime, in particular, flags and anthems galvanize national pride and determination, but flags and anthems can also symbolize a nation's unfulfilled promises. At the 1968 Olympics in Mexico City, coinciding with the Black Power Movement, American medalists Tommie Smith and John Carlos raised their black-gloved fists

and bowed their heads in protest when the anthem played. The U.S. Olympic Committee suspended them, but nearly fifty years later, President Obama welcomed Smith and Carlos at the White House, amid renewed protests from athletes at all levels—from professional to children's leagues—in response to fatal police shootings of unarmed African Americans. As "taking a knee" during the anthem spread, so did the practice's critics.

Over two centuries, "The Star-Spangled Banner" has fueled passionate patriotism even as it has been mired in irony and controversy. Yet by providing a touchstone for discussions of what it means to be an American, and what it should mean to be an American, "The Star-Spangled Banner" has proved an enduring and evolving legacy for a people and a nation.

CRITICAL THINKING

■ As early as the 1960s but more frequently now, in the wake of what has been deemed an epidemic of police shootings of unarmed African American men, Americans have used the singing of "The Star-Spangled Banner" as an opportunity to protest what they see as the unfulfilled promise of freedom and equality in the United States Critics suggest that such protests are unpatriotic. Are such protests patriotic or unpatriotic, or can they be both?

Yet even as the nation pursued a nationalist economic agenda and defined its position on the world stage, sectional tensions remained a persistent threat to the nation's proclaimed unity.

Summary

The partisanship of the 1790s, though alarming to the nation's political leaders, captured Americans' imaginations, making the early republic a period of pervasive and vigorous political engagement. Troubled by vicious partisanship, President Jefferson sought both to unify the nation and to solidify Democratic-Republican control of the government. With a vision of an agrarian nation that protected individual liberty, Jeffersonians promoted a limited national government—one that stayed out of religious affairs and spent little on military forces, diplomatic missions, and economic initiatives. The rival Federalists, who exerted most of their influence through the judiciary, declared federal supremacy over the states even as the judiciary affirmed its own supremacy over other branches of the government. Federalists hoped a strengthened federal government would promote commerce and industry.

Despite his belief in limited government, Jefferson considered the acquisition of the Louisiana Territory and the commissioning of the Corps of Discovery among his most significant presidential accomplishments. The enormous expanse of fertile lands fueled the Jeffersonian dream of an agrarian republic: Americans soon streamed into the Louisiana Territory. Even more would have done so had it not been for the Native peoples (and their British allies) who stood in their way and for poorly developed transportation routes.

Jefferson's vision rested, too, on American disentanglement from foreign affairs. But with its economy so focused on international shipping, the United States soon faced its greatest threats from abroad, not from partisan or sectional divisions. In its wars with the Barbary states, the United States sought to guard its commerce and ships on the high seas. The second war with Britain—the War of 1812—was fought for similar reasons but against a much more formidable power. Although a military stalemate, the war inspired a new sense of nationalism and launched a new era of American development.

The Treaty of Ghent reaffirmed American independence; thereafter, the nation was able to settle disputes with Great Britain at the bargaining table. The war also dealt a serious blow to Native peoples' resistance in the Midwest and Southwest. At the same time, embargoes and war accelerated the pace of American industrial growth. Because the Federalists' opposition to the war undermined their political credibility, their party all but disappeared from the national political scene by 1820. The absence of well-organized partisan conflict created what contemporaries called an "Era of Good Feelings."

Although overt tension was muted in the heady postwar years, competing visions of America's route to prosperity and greatness endured. Under Chief Justice John Marshall, the Supreme Court supported the Federalist agenda, issuing rulings that stimulated commerce and industry through economic nationalism. The Democratic-Republicans looked instead toward the South and West, the vast and fertile Louisiana Territory. Whether they supported agrarian or industrial development, almost all Americans could agree on the need for improved transportation, though most internal improvements took place in the North.

Internal improvements could not guarantee national prosperity or unity, and in 1819 the postwar economic boom came to a grinding halt even as congressmen predicted that dire consequences could result from the dispute over whether to admit Missouri as a slave state. Henry Clay's compromise removed the issue of slavery's expansion from political center stage, but—by addressing only those territories already owned by the United States—it did not permanently settle the issue.

During the first quarter of the nineteenth century, the United States vastly expanded its territorial reach, not just through the Louisiana Purchase but also with the acquisition of Florida. Fearful of European intentions to reassert influence in the Americas and emboldened by the nation's expanding boundaries, President Monroe proclaimed that the United States would not tolerate European intervention in American affairs. But even as its expanding boundaries strengthened the United States' international presence, that same territorial expansion would, in decades to come, threaten the nation's newfound political unity at home.

Suggestions for Further Reading

Stephen Aron, *American Confluence: The Missouri Frontier from Borderland to Border State* (2006)

Claude A. Clegg III, *The Price of Liberty: African Americans and the Making of Liberia* (2004)

David Edmunds, *Tecumseh and the Quest for Indian Leadership* (2006)

Richard S. Newman, *The Transformation of American Abolitionism: Fighting Slavery in the Early Republic* (2002)

Kent Newmyer, *John Marshall and the Heroic Age of the Supreme Court* (2001)

Jeffrey Ostler, *The Plains Sioux and U.S. Colonialism from Lewis and Clark to Wounded Knee* (2004)

Jeffrey Pasley, Andrew Robertson, and David Waldstreicher, eds., *Beyond the Founders: New Approaches to the Political History of the Early American Republic* (2004)

Alan Taylor, *The Civil War of 1812: American Citizens, British Subjects, Irish Rebels, and Indian Allies* (2010)

Gordon S. Wood, *Empire of Liberty: A History of the Early Republic, 1789–1815* (2009)

The Rise of the South, 1815–1860

Thomas Jefferson died, as he had lived, in debt. Many Americans saw a providential hand at work when, on July 4, 1826, Jefferson and John Adams, rivals and founders of the American republic, died on the same day. But at Jefferson's home, Monticello, in Virginia, worldly anxiety abounded among the founder's white and black "families."

On January 15, 1827, a five-day estate sale took place at Monticello. Everything went up at auction, including paintings, furniture, and mementoes. Most expensive of all were "130 valuable negroes," described by Jefferson's grandson and executor, Thomas Jefferson Randolph, as "the most valuable for their number ever offered at one time in the state of Virginia." Large crowds gathered in frigid weather. Monticello's blacksmith, Joseph Fossett, watched his wife Edith and eight children sold at the auction to four different bidders.

Jefferson generally avoided separation of families and whipping except in rare cases. But he was intensely involved in the domestic lives and labor efficiency of his slaves, keeping production statistics on the young teenagers who worked in his nailery. After his wife, Martha (with whom he had two daughters), died in 1782, Jefferson also had at least six children, four of whom lived beyond infancy, with an enslaved woman whom he owned, Sally Hemings. Sally was the half-sister of Jefferson's wife, and part of a complex extended family of light-skinned Hemingses of Monticello.

Whole families of Jefferson's slaves were sold at the 1827 auction. Joseph Fossett, as promised by Jefferson, became free exactly one year after his master's death. Jefferson had already

◀ Peter Farley Fossett (1815–1901), born the son of Joseph and Edith Fossett, slaves owned by Thomas Jefferson. Joseph was head blacksmith and Edith head cook at Monticello. Peter had a stable family life in childhood until at age 10 when he was among Jefferson's 130 slaves sold at auction in 1827, including his mother and seven siblings. Peter lived 23 more years as a slave, obtaining his freedom and moving to Cincinnati to be near his parents in 1850. He became a successful caterer and an ordained Baptist minister, and in 1900 he returned to Monticello, was driven up the mountain by the son of the man who had taught him to read, and walked in the front door of the mansion. Thomas Jefferson Foundation at Monticello

Thomas Jefferson, President of the United States, author of the Declaration of Independence, slaveowner, three-quarter length portrait, seated at table. Library of Congress Prints and Photographs Division Washington, D.C.[LC-USZ62-8195]

Chronology

1810–20	■ An estimated 137,000 slaves are forced to move from the Upper South to Alabama, Mississippi, and other western regions
1822	■ Vesey's insurrection plot is discovered in South Carolina
1830s	■ Vast majority of African American slaves in America are native born
1830s–40s	■ Cotton trade grows into largest source of commercial wealth and America's leading export
1831	■ Turner leads a violent slave rebellion in Virginia
1832	■ Virginia holds the last debate in the South about the future of slavery; gradual abolition is voted down
	■ Publication of Dew's proslavery tract *Abolition of Negro Slavery*
1836	■ Arkansas gains admission to the Union as a slave state
1839	■ Mississippi's Married Women's Property Act gives married women some property rights
1845	■ Florida and Texas gain admission to the Union as slave states
	■ Publication of Douglass's *Narrative of the Life of Frederick Douglass, an American Slave, Written by Himself*
1850	■ Planters' share of agricultural wealth in the South is 90 to 95 percent
1850–60	■ Of some 300,000 slaves who migrate from the Upper to the Lower South, 60 to 70 percent go by outright sale
1857	■ Publication of Hinton R. Helper's *The Impending Crisis*, denouncing the slave system
	■ Publication of George Fitzhugh's *Southern Thought*, an aggressive defense of slavery
1860	■ There are 405,751 "mulattos" (biracial people) in the United States, accounting for 12.5 percent of the African American population
	■ Three-quarters of all southern white families own no slaves
	■ South produces largest cotton crop ever

earlier freed the four children he fathered with Sally Hemings: William Beverly Hemings, Harriet Hemings II, James Madison Hemings, and Thomas Eston Hemings. In 1822, Beverly and Harriet had left Monticello to pass as white people. Jefferson never freed Sally; Virginia law would have required him to attain, publicly, a dispensation from the state legislature in order to free her without removing her from the state. The Sage of Monticello wanted no more salacious publicity about his longtime house servant and mistress than had already occurred for many years. Sally died a slave, living in Charlottesville, Virginia, in 1835 at the age of sixty-two; she left numerous heirlooms for her children from her life with Jefferson: a pair of his eyeglasses, a shoe buckle, and an inkwell.

"Thank heaven the whole of this dreadful business is over," wrote Jefferson's granddaughter, Mary, when the auction had ended. She consoled herself that the vast majority of slaves had been sold within the state. She likened the "sad scene," though, to a "captured village in ancient times when all were sold as slaves." Monticello itself was sold in 1831. But across the South in the 1820s the "business" of slavery expansion and cotton production was hardly over at all.

Experience an interactive version of this story in MindTap®.

In 1815, the southern tier of states and territories, with fertile soil and a growing labor force of enslaved people to cultivate it, was poised for growth, prosperity, and power. New lands were settled, new states were peopled, and steadily the South emerged as the world's most extensive and vigorous commercial agricultural economy. The Old South's wealth came from export crops, land, and slaves, and its population was almost wholly rural. In the land where cotton became king, racial slavery affected not only economics but also values, customs, laws, class structure, and the region's relationship to the nation and the world. As slaves' bodies, labor, and lives came to be defined more and more as chattel, they struggled increasingly not only to survive but also to resist, sometimes overtly, but more often in daily life and cultural expression. By 1860, white southerners not only asserted the moral and economic benefits of slavery with a vigorous defense of the system, but also sought to sustain and advance their political power over the national government.

- *How and why was the Old South a "slave society," with slavery permeating every class and group within it, free or unfree?*

- *How and why did white southerners come to see cotton as "king" of a global economy, and how did the cotton trade's international reach shape southern society from 1815 to 1860?*

- *How did African American slaves build and sustain a meaningful life and a sense of community amid the potential chaos and destruction of their circumstances?*

- *How would you weigh the comparative significance of the following central themes in the history of the Old South: class, race, migration, power, liberty, wealth?*

9-1 The "Distinctive" South

▶ **What did the North and South share in common in the early nineteenth century?**

▶ **How did the South's social development and structure differ from that of the North because of the institution of slavery?**

▶ **How did the southern proslavery argument evolve over the first half of the nineteenth century?**

Not until the first half of the 1800s did the region of slave-holding states from the Chesapeake and Virginia to Missouri, and from Florida across to Texas, come to be designated as the South. Today, many still consider it America's most distinctive region. Historians have long examined how the Old South was like and unlike the rest of the nation. Because of its unique history, has the South, in the words of poet Allen Tate, always been "Uncle Sam's other province"? Or as southern writer W. J. Cash said in 1940, is the South "a tree with many age rings, with its limbs and trunk bent and twisted by all the winds of the years, but with its tap root in the Old South?" Analyzing just why the South seems more religious, more conservative, or more tragic than other regions of America has been an enduring practice in American culture and politics.

Certain American values, such as materialism, individualism, and faith in progress, have been associated with the North and values such as tradition, honor, and family loyalty,

with the South. The South, so the stereotype has it, was static, even "backward," and the North was dynamic in the decades leading up to the Civil War. There are many measures of just how different South was from North in the antebellum era. At the same time, there were many Souths: low-country rice and cotton regions with dense slave populations; mountainous regions of small farmers and subsistence agriculture; semitropical wetlands in the Southeast; **plantation** culture in the Cotton Belt and especially the Mississippi Valley; Texas grasslands; tobacco- and wheat-growing regions in Virginia and North Carolina; cities with bustling ports; and wilderness areas with only the rare homesteads of hillfolk.

9-1a South-North Similarity

The South was distinctive because of its commitment to slavery, but it also shared much in common with the rest of the nation. The geographic sizes of the South and the North were roughly the same. In 1815, white southerners shared with their fellow free citizens in the North a heritage of heroes and ideology from the era of the American Revolution and the War of 1812. With varying accents, southerners spoke the same language and worshiped the same Protestant God as northerners. Southerners lived under the same Constitution as northerners, and they shared a common mixture of nationalism and localism in their attitudes toward government. Down to the 1840s, northerners and southerners invoked with nearly equal frequency the doctrine of states' rights against federal authority. A sense of American mission inspired by the westward movement was as much a part of southern as of northern experience.

Indeed, some of the most eloquent visions of America as a land of yeomen—independent, self-sufficient farmers—expanding westward had come from a southerner, Thomas Jefferson. Jefferson believed that "virtue" rested in those who tilled the soil, that farmers made the best citizens. In 1804, Jefferson declared his "moral and physical preference of the agricultural over the manufacturing man." But as slavery and the plantation economy expanded (see Map 9.1), the South did not become a land of individual opportunity in the same manner as the North.

During the forty-five years before the Civil War, the South shared in the nation's economic booms and busts. Research has shown that, despite its enormous cruelties, slavery was a profitable labor system for planters. Southerners and northerners shared an expanding capitalist economy. As it grew, the slave-based economy reflected the rational choices of planters. More land and more slaves generally converted into more wealth. Slaveholders were good capitalists.

By the eve of the Civil War in 1860, the distribution of wealth and property in the two sections was almost identical: 50 percent of free adult males owned only 1 percent of real and personal property, and the richest 1 percent owned 27 percent of the wealth. One study comparing Texas and Wisconsin in 1850 shows that the richest 2 percent of families in

plantation Large landholding devoted to a cash crop such as cotton or tobacco.

Map 9.1 **Cotton Production in the South**

These two maps reveal the rapid westward expansion of cotton production and its importance to the antebellum South.

each state owned 31 to 32 percent of the wealth. So both North and South had ruling classes, even if their wealth was invested in different kinds of property. Entrepreneurs in both sections, whether forging plantations out of Mississippi Delta land or shoe factories and textile mills in New England river towns, sought their fortunes in an expanding market economy.

9-1b South-North Dissimilarity

There were important differences between the North and the South. The South's climate and longer growing season

gave it an unmistakably rural and agricultural destiny. Many great rivers provided rich soil and transportation routes to market. The South's people, white and black, developed an intense attachment to place, to the ways people were related to the land and to one another. The South developed as a biracial society of brutal inequality, where the liberty of one race depended directly on the enslavement of another. White wealth was built on highly valued black labor.

Cotton growers spread out over as large an area as possible to maximize production and income. As a result, population density in the South was low; by 1860, there were only 2.3 people per square mile in vast and largely unsettled Texas, 15.6 in Louisiana, and 18.0 in Georgia. By contrast, population density in the nonslaveholding states east of the Mississippi River was almost three times higher. The Northeast had an average of 65.4 people per square mile. Massachusetts had 153.1 people per square mile, and New York City compressed 86,400 people into each square mile. When, in the 1850s, young Frederick Law Olmsted of Connecticut, later renowned as a landscape architect, toured the South as a journalist, he traveled mostly on horseback along primitive trails. Between Columbus, Georgia, and Montgomery, Alabama, Olmsted found "a hilly wilderness, with a few dreary villages, and many isolated cotton farms." For one who would design Central Park in New York City, this was just too much ruralness.

Where people were scarce, it was difficult to finance and operate schools, churches, libraries, and even inns and restaurants. Similarly, the rural character of the South and the significance of the plantation as a self-sufficient social unit meant that the section put few resources into improving disease control and public health. Southerners were strongly committed to their churches, and some believed in the importance of universities, but all such institutions were far less developed than those in the North. Factories were rare because planters invested most of their capital in slaves. A few southerners did invest in iron or textiles on a small scale. But the largest southern "industry" was lumbering, and the largest factories used slave labor to make cigars. More decisively, the South was slower to develop a regional transportation network. Despite concerted efforts, the South had only 35 percent of the nation's railroad mileage in 1860.

The Old South never created its own banking and shipping capacity to any degree. If it had, its effort to be an international cartel might have succeeded longer. Most southern bank deposits were in the North, and southern cotton planters became ever more dependent on New York for shipping. As early as 1822, one-sixth of all southern cotton cleared for Liverpool or Le Havre from the port of New York and constituted two-fifths of all that city's exports. Many New York merchants and bankers developed deep interests in the fate of slavery and cotton prices. In a series of economic conventions held from 1837 to 1839, southern delegates debated the nature of foreign trade, dependence on northern importers and financiers, and other alleged threats to their commercial independence and security. But nothing, save rhetoric, came of these conventions; it was the last time southern planters would organize to break from their Yankee middlemen and shippers.

The South lagged far behind the North in nearly any measure of industrial growth. Its urban centers were mostly ports like New Orleans and Charleston, and to some extent Baltimore, which became crossroads of commerce and small-scale manufacturing. In the interior were small market towns dependent on agricultural trade—"urbanization without cities," as one historian has said. Slavery slowed urban growth. Likewise, because of a lack of manufacturing jobs, the South did not attract immigrants as readily as did the North. By 1860, only 13 percent of the nation's foreign-born population lived in the slave states.

Like most northerners, antebellum southerners were adherents to evangelical Christianity. Americans from all regions held in common a faith in a personal God and in conversion and piety as the means to salvation. But southern evangelicalism was distinct from its northern practice. In the South, Baptists and Methodists concentrated on personal rather than social improvement. By the 1830s in the North, evangelicalism was a major wellspring of reform movements (see "Revivals and Reform," Section 10-7); but in states where blacks were so numerous and unfree, and where the very social structure received increasingly aggressive attacks from abolitionists, religion, as one scholar has written, preached "a hands-off policy concerning slavery." Although slaves began to convert to Christianity in the early-nineteenth-century South, many southern whites feared a reform impulse that would foster what one historian has called an "interracial communion" in their churches. Moreover, those women who may have been reform minded were prevented from developing frequent associations with other reformers because of distance and sparse population.

The slave system made it inevitable that the interests and social structures of the North and the South would diverge after 1815. Because of its inherently conservative social structure, antebellum southern law restricted the authority of the courts, reinforcing a tradition of planter control. Penitentiaries tended to house only whites, as most blacks were under the authority of personal masters. Lawbreaking in the South tended to involve crimes of violence rather than crimes against property.

9-1c A Southern Worldview and the Proslavery Argument

Perhaps in no way was the South more distinctive than in its embrace of a particular worldview, a system of thought and meaning held especially by the planter class, but also influencing the entire society. Southerners' justifications for slavery were not so different from those of any other civilization trying to defend the institutions it inherits. But at the heart of the proslavery argument was a deep and abiding racism. The persistence of modern racism in all sections of the United States is all the more reason to comprehend antebellum southerners' rationalizations for human slavery.

In the wake of the American Revolution, the Enlightenment ideas of natural rights and equality did stimulate antislavery sentiment in the Upper South, produced a brief flurry of manumissions (the willful freeing of a slave by the owner), and led to considerable hope for gradual emancipation. In 1796, Virginian St. George Tucker argued that "slavery not only violates the laws of nature and of civil society, it also wounds the best forms of government." But confidence that the exercise of reason among gentlemen might end such a profitable system as slavery waned in the new nation. As slavery spread, southerners soon vigorously defended it. In 1816, George Bourne, a Presbyterian minister exiled from Virginia for his antislavery sermons and for expulsion of slaveholders

▲ *America, 1841*, lithograph and watercolor by Edward Williams Clay. An idealized portrayal of loyal and contented slaves, likely distributed by northern apologists for slavery. All is well on the plantation as well-dressed slaves dance and express their gratitude to their master and his perfect family. The text includes the old slave saying: "God bless you master! You feed and clothe us. When we are sick you nurse us, and when too old to work, you provide for us!" The master replies piously: "These poor creatures are a sacred legacy from my ancestors and while a dollar is left me, nothing shall be spared to increase their comfort and happiness."

Library of Congress Prints and Photographs Division[LC-US7C4-5950]

from his church, charged that, whenever southerners were challenged on slavery, "they were fast choked, for they had a Negro stuck fast in their throats." After walking home with South Carolina statesman and proslavery advocate John C. Calhoun from an 1820 cabinet meeting, John Quincy Adams confided to his diary that too many southerners "writhe in agonies of fear at the very mention of human rights as applicable to men of color."

By the 1820s, white southerners went on the offensive, actively justifying slavery as a "**positive good**" and not merely a "necessary evil." They used the antiquity of slavery, as well as the Bible's many references to slaveholding, to foster a historical argument for bondage. Slavery, they deemed, was the natural status of blacks. Whites were the more intellectual race, and blacks the race more inherently physical and therefore destined for labor. Whites were the creators of civilizations, blacks the appointed hewers of wood and drawers of water. Proslavery writers did not mince words. In a

positive good Southern justification for slavery as beneficial to the larger society, both to white owners and their black slaves.

proslavery tract written in 1851, John Campbell confidently declared that "there is as much difference between the lowest tribe of negroes and the white Frenchman, Englishman, or American, as there is between the monkey and the negro."

Some southerners defended slavery in practical terms; they simply saw their slaves as economic necessities and symbols of their quest for prosperity. In 1845, James Henry Hammond of South Carolina argued that slaveholding was essentially a matter of property rights. Unwilling to "deal in abstractions" about the "right and wrong" of slavery, Hammond considered property sacred and protected by the Constitution, because slaves were legal property—end of argument. The deepest root of the proslavery argument was a hierarchical view of the social order as slavery's defenders believed God or nature had prescribed it. Southerners cherished tradition, duty, and honor, believing social change should come only in slow increments, if at all. As the Virginia legislature debated the gradual abolition of slavery in 1831–1832, in the wake of Nat Turner's rebellion, Thomas R. Dew, a slaveholder and professor of law and history at the College of William and Mary, contended that "that which is the growth of *ages* may require ages to remove." Dew's widely read work *Abolition of Negro Slavery* (1832) ushered in an outpouring of proslavery writing that would intensify over the next thirty years. Until Turner's bloody rebellion, Dew admitted, emancipation in the South had "never been seriously discussed." But as slavery expanded westward and fueled national prosperity, Dew cautioned southerners that any degree of gradual abolition threatened the whole region's "irremediable ruin." Dew declared black slavery part of the "order of nature," an indispensable part of the "deep and solid foundations of society" and the basis of the "well-ordered, well-established liberty" of white Americans. Dew's well-ordered society also included his conception of the proper division of men and women into separate spheres and functions.

Proslavery advocates held views very different from those of northern reformers on the concepts of freedom, progress, and equality. They turned natural-law doctrine to their favor, arguing that the natural state of humankind was inequality of ability and condition, not equality. A former U.S. senator in South Carolina, William Harper, charged in 1837 that Jefferson's famous dictum about equality in the Declaration of Independence was no more than a "sentimental phrase." "Is it not palpably nearer the truth to say that no man was ever born free," Harper argued, "and that no two men were ever born equal?" Proslavery writers believed that people were born to certain stations in life; they stressed dependence over autonomy and duty over rights as the human condition. As Virginia writer George Fitzhugh put it in 1854, "Men are not born entitled to equal rights. It would be far nearer the truth to say, that some were born with saddles on their backs, and others booted and spurred to ride them."

Many slaveholders believed their ownership of people bound them to a set of paternal obligations as guardians of a familial relationship between masters and slaves. Although contradicted by countless examples of slave resistance and escape, as well as by slave sales, planters needed to believe in the idea of the contented slave. The slaveholders who promoted their own freedom and pursued personal profits through the bondage of blacks had to justify themselves endlessly.

9-1d A Slave Society

Slavery and race affected everything in the Old South. Whites and blacks alike grew up, were socialized, married, reared children, worked, conceived of property, and honed their most basic habits of behavior under the influence of slavery. This was true of slaveholding and nonslaveholding whites as well as of blacks who were enslaved and free. Slavery shaped the social structure of the South, fueled almost anything meaningful in its economy, and came to dominate its politics. Rudolphe Lucien Desdunes, a Louisiana sugar planter, remembered growing up in a society where "slavery was the pivot around which everything revolved."

The South was interdependent with the North, the West, and even with Europe in a growing capitalist market system. To keep the cotton trade flowing, southerners relied on northern banks, on northern steamship companies working the great western rivers, and on northern merchants. But there were elements of this system that southerners increasingly rejected during the antebellum era, especially urbanism, the wage labor system, a broadening right to vote, and any threat to their racial and class order.

In the antebellum era, as later, there were many Souths, but Americans have always been determined to define what one historian called the "Dixie difference." "The South is both American and something different," writes another historian, "at times a mirror or magnifier of national traits and at other times a counterculture." This was most acutely true in the decades before the Civil War.

Culturally, the South developed a proclivity to tell its own story. Its ruralness and its sense of tradition may have given southerners a special habit of telling tales. "Southerners . . . love a good tale," said Mississippi writer Eudora Welty. "They are born reciters, great memory retainers, diary keepers, letter exchangers, and letter savers, history tracers, and debaters, and—outstaying all the rest—great talkers." The South's story is both distinctive and national, and it begins in what we have come to call the Old South, a term only conceivable after the eviction of Native peoples from the region.

Taylor plantation, 1850 (b/w photo), American Photographer, (19th century)/Private Collection/Peter Newark American Pictures/Bridgeman Images

▲ Delia, an enslaved woman on the Edgehill plantation near Columbia, South Carolina, photographed in 1850 by daguerreotypist Joseph Zealy for natural scientist Louis Agassiz. Delia was among seven people Agassiz had photographed nude in an effort to investigate the alleged inferior physiognomy of Africans and African Americans. Delia's tearful gaze haunts the tragic process by which the "racial sciences" tried to categorize and rank human beings in the service of proslavery arguments.

9-2 Southern Expansion, Native American Resistance and Removal

▶ How did Native peoples respond to encroachments on their lands and southern expansion?

▶ How did state governments and the federal government treat Native peoples amid southern westward movement?

Americans were a restless, moving people when the trans-Appalachian frontier opened in the wake of the War of 1812. Some 5 to 10 percent of the booming population moved each year, usually westward. In the first two decades of the century, they poured into the Ohio Valley; by the 1820s, after the death of the Shawnee chief Tecumseh and the collapse of the pan-Indian federation, they were migrating into the Mississippi River Valley and beyond. By 1850, two-thirds of Americans lived west of the Appalachians.

9-2a A Southern Westward Movement

As much as in any other region, this surging westward movement was a southern phenomenon. After 1820, the heart of cotton cultivation and the slave-based plantation system shifted from the coastal states to Alabama and the newly settled Mississippi Valley—Tennessee, Louisiana, Arkansas, and Mississippi. Southern slaveholders forced slaves to move with them to the newer areas of the South, and **yeoman** farmers followed, also hoping for new wealth through cheap land and the ownership of other people.

A wave of migration was evident everywhere in the Southeast. As early

yeoman Independent small farmer, usually nonslaveholding.

as 1817, Georgian Samuel McDonald observed a "disease prevalent" in his region. "The patient," he said, first exhibited a "great love" of talking about "the new country" to the west. Then he tried to "make sale of his stock" and "lastly . . . to sell his plantation." Once attacked by this "Alabama fever," most never recovered and were carried "off to the westward." That same year, a Charleston, South Carolina, newspaper reported with alarm that migration out of that state had already reached "unprecedented proportions." Indeed, almost half of the white people born in South Carolina after 1800 left the state, most for the Southwest. And by 1833, Tyrone Power, an Irish actor riding a stagecoach from Georgia into Alabama, encountered many "camps of immigrants" and found the roads "covered" by such pilgrims.

The way to wealth for seaboard planters in the South was to go west to grow cotton for the booming world markets, by purchasing ever more land and slaves. The population of Mississippi soared from 73,000 in 1820 to 607,000 in 1850, with African American slaves in the majority. Across the Mississippi River, the population of Arkansas went from 14,000 in 1820 to 210,000 in 1850. By 1835, the American immigrant population in Texas reached 35,000, including 3,000 slaves, outnumbering Mexicans two to one. Aggressive American settlers declared Texas's independence from Mexico in 1836, spurring further American immigration into the region. By 1845, "Texas fever" had boosted the Anglo population to 125,000. Statehood that year opened the floodgates to more immigrants from the east and to a confrontation with Mexico that would lead to war.

As the **cotton kingdom** grew to what southern political leaders dreamed would be national and world dominion, this westward migration, fueled at first by an optimistic nationalism, ultimately made migrant planters more sectional and more southern. In 1817, Congressman John C. Calhoun embraced national expansion as the means to "bind the Republic together," as he provided the process its unquestioned assumption: "Let us conquer space." In time, political dominance in the South migrated westward into the Cotton Belt as well. By the 1840s and 1850s, these energetic capitalist planters, ever mindful of world markets and fearful that their slave-based economy was under attack, sought to protect and expand their system. Increasingly, they saw themselves, as one historian has written, less as "landowners who happened to own slaves" than as "slaveholders who happened to own land."

cotton kingdom A broad swath of territory where cotton was a mainstay that stretched from South Carolina, Georgia, and northern Florida in the east through Alabama, Mississippi, central and western Tennessee, and Louisiana, and from there on to Arkansas and Texas.

Long in advance of all this expansion, however, other, older groups of Americans already occupied much of this land. Before 1830, large swaths of upper Georgia belonged to the Cherokee, and huge regions of Alabama and Mississippi were either Creek, Choctaw, or Chickasaw land. Native peoples were also on the move, but in forced migrations. The indigenous cultures of the eastern and southern woodlands had to be uprooted to make way for white expansion. For the vast majority of white Americans, Native Americans were in the way of their growing empire. Taking Native peoples' land, so the reasoning went, merely reflected the natural course of history: the "civilizers" had to displace the "children of the forest" in the name of progress. National leaders provided all the rhetoric and justification needed. "Nothing," said General Andrew Jackson as early as 1816, "can promote the welfare of the United States, and particularly the southwestern frontier so much as bringing into market . . . the whole of this fertile country." As president in 1830, Jackson spoke with certainty about why Native peoples must go. "What good man would prefer a country," he asked, "covered with forests and ranged by a few thousand savages to our extensive Republic, studded with cities, towns, and prosperous farms?"

9-2b American Indian Treaty Making

In theory, under the U.S. Constitution, the federal government recognized Native peoples' sovereignty and treated these groups as foreign nations. Indeed, the United States received Native American delegations with pomp and ceremony, exchanging gifts as tokens of friendship. Agreements between American Indian nations and the United States were signed, sealed, and ratified like other international treaties. In practice, however, swindle and fraud dominated the government's approach to treaty making and Native peoples' sovereignty. As the country expanded, new treaties replaced old ones, shrinking Native peoples' landholdings.

Although Native American resistance persisted against such pressure after the War of 1812, it only slowed the process. In the 1820s, Native peoples in the middle West, Ohio Valley, Mississippi Valley, and other parts of the cotton South ceded lands totaling 200 million acres for a pittance.

9-2c American Indian Accommodation

Increasingly, American Indian nations east of the Mississippi sought to survive through accommodation. In the first three decades of the century, the Choctaw, Creek, and Chickasaw peoples in the lower Mississippi became suppliers and traders in the nation's expanding market economy. Under treaty provisions, Native American commerce took place through trading posts and stores that provided Native peoples with supplies, and purchased or bartered Native-produced goods. The trading posts extended credit to chiefs, who increasingly fell into debt that they could pay off to the federal government only by selling their land.

By 1822, the Choctaw nation had sold 13 million acres but still carried a debt of $13,000. The Choctaw people struggled to adjust, increasing agricultural production and hunting, working as farmhands and craftsmen, and selling produce at market stalls in Natchez and New Orleans. As

The Amistad Case

In April 1839, a Spanish slave ship, *Tecora*, sailed from Lomboko, the region of West Africa that became Sierra Leone. On board were Mende people, captured and sold by their African enemies. In June, they arrived in Havana, Cuba, a Spanish colony. Two Spaniards purchased fifty-three of the Mende and set sail aboard *La Amistad* for their plantations elsewhere in Cuba. After three days at sea, the Africans revolted. Led by a man the Spaniards called Joseph Cinque, they killed the captain and seized control of the vessel. They ordered the two Spanish owners to take them back to Africa, but the slaveholders sailed east by day and north by night, trying to reach the shores of the American South. Far off course, *La Amistad* was seized by the USS *Washington* in Long Island Sound and brought ashore in Connecticut.

The "Amistad Africans" were soon a celebrated moral and legal cause for abolitionists and slaveholders, as well as in U.S.–Spanish relations. The Africans were imprisoned in New Haven, and a prolonged dispute ensued around many questions: Were they slaves and murderers, and the property of their Cuban owners, or were they free people exercising their natural rights? Were they Spanish property, seized on the high seas in violation of a 1795 treaty? If a northern state could "free" captive Africans, what did it mean for enslaved African Americans in the South? Connecticut abolitionists immediately went to court, where a U.S. circuit court judge dismissed the charges of mutiny and murder but refused to release the Africans because their Spanish owners claimed them as property.

Meanwhile, the Mende were desperate to tell their own story. A Yale professor of ancient languages, Josiah Gibbs, visited the captives and learned their words for numbers. In New York, he walked up and down the docks repeating the Mende words until an African seaman, James Covey, responded. Covey journeyed to New Haven, conversed with the jubilant Africans, and soon their harrowing tale garnered sympathy all over Yankee New England.

In a new trial, the judge ruled that the Africans were illegally enslaved and ordered them returned to their homeland. Although slavery might be legal in Cuba, the slave trade between Africa and the Americas had been outlawed in a treaty between Spain and Great Britain. Spain's lawyers demanded the return of their "merchandise." In need of southern votes to win reelection, President Martin Van Buren supported the Spanish claims and advocated the Africans' return to a likely death in Cuba.

The administration appealed the case to the Supreme Court in February 1841. Arguing the abolitionists' case, former president John Quincy Adams famously pointed to a copy of the Declaration of Independence on the wall of the court chambers, invoked the natural rights to life and liberty, and chastised the Van Buren administration for its "immense array of power . . . on the side of injustice." In a 7-to-1 decision, the Court ruled that the Africans were "free-born" with the right of self-defense, while remaining silent on slavery's legality in the United States.

Fund-raising and speaking tours featuring Cinque made the return voyage possible. On November 27, 1841, thirty-five survivors and five American missionaries embarked for Africa. They arrived in Sierra Leone on January 15, 1842, whereupon Cinque wrote a letter to the Amistad Committee. "I thank all 'merican people," he said. "I shall never forget 'merican people." But the international meanings of the Amistad case would endure. Sarah Magru, one of the child captives on *La Amistad*, stayed in America to attend Oberlin College and later returned to work at the Mende mission in Sierra Leone.

The Amistad case showed how intertwined slavery was with freedom, and the United States with the world. It poisoned diplomatic relations between America and Spain for a generation, and stimulated Christian mission work in Africa.

CRITICAL THINKING

■ The *Amistad* case impacted Spanish-American diplomacy for a generation and led to wide-ranging change in Africa brought on by American missionary efforts. Why did the Supreme Court ruling declaring the *Amistad* captives free not impact the institution of slavery in the United States?

North Wind Picture Archives/Alamy

◄ Joseph Cinque, by Nathaniel Jocelyn, 1840. Cinque led the rebellion aboard *La Amistad*, a Spanish ship carrying captive Africans along the coast of Cuba in 1839. They commandeered the ship and sailed it north toward New England, where they were rescued off the coast of Connecticut. Cinque, celebrated as a great leader, sat for the painting while he and his people awaited trial. They were freed by a decision of the U.S. Supreme Court in 1841 and returned to their homeland in Sierra Leone in West Africa.

the United States expanded westward, white Americans promoted their assimilation, through education and conversion to Christianity, with renewed urgency. "Put into the hand of [Indian] children the primer and the hoe," the House Committee on Indian Affairs recommended in 1818, "and they will naturally, in time, take hold of the plough; and, as their minds become enlightened and expand, the Bible will be their book, and they will grow up in habits of morality and industry." In 1819, in response to missionary lobbying, Congress appropriated $10,000 annually for "civilization of the tribes adjoining the frontier settlements."

Within five years, thirty-two boarding schools enrolled Native American students. They substituted English for American Indian languages and taught agriculture alongside the Christian gospel. But this emphasis on agriculture and the value of private property did not deter settlers eyeing Native peoples' land. Wherever Native Americans lived, illegal settlers disrupted their lives. The federal government only halfheartedly enforced the integrity of treaties, as legitimate Native land rights gave way to the advance of white civilization.

Over time, however, Native Americans could not prevent the spread of the cotton economy that arose all around them. With loss of land came dependency. The Choctaw came to rely on white Americans not only for manufactured goods but even for food. Dependency, coupled with disease, facilitated removal of American Indian peoples to western lands. While the population of other groups increased rapidly, Native peoples' populations fell, some nations declining by 50 percent in only three decades. The French traveler and author Alexis de Tocqueville noticed the contrast. "Not only have these wild tribes receded, but they are destroyed," Tocqueville concluded, after personally observing the tragedy of forced removal in 1831, "and as they give way or perish, an immense and increasing people fill their place. There is no instance upon record of so prodigious a growth or so rapid a destruction." As many as 100,000 eastern and southern Native peoples were removed between 1820 and 1850; about 30,000 died in the process.

The wanderings of the Shawnee, the people of the Prophet and Tecumseh, illustrate the uprooting of Native peoples (see "Divisions Among American Indian Peoples," Section 8-2d and "Tenskwatawa and Tecumseh," Section 8-2e). After giving up 17 million acres in Ohio in a 1795 treaty, the Shawnee scattered to Indiana and eastern Missouri. After the War of 1812, some Shawnee sought protection from either the British in Canada or from Mexico. Yet another group moved to the Kansas territory in 1825. By 1854, Kansas was open to white settlement, and the Shawnee had to cede seven-eighths of their land, or 1.4 million acres.

Indian Removal Act Legislation authorizing Andrew Jackson to exchange public lands in the West for Native American territories in the East and appropriated federal funds to cover the expenses of removal.

Removal had a profound impact on all Shawnee. The men lost their traditional role as providers; their skills hunting woodland animals were useless on the prairies of Kansas. As grain became the tribe's dietary staple, Shawnee women played a greater role as providers, supplemented by government aid under treaty provisions. Remarkably, the Shawnee preserved their language and culture in the face of these devastating dislocations.

9-2d Indian Removal as Federal Policy

Much of the land of the southeastern tribes—Cherokee, Creek, Choctaw, Chickasaw, and Seminole—had remained intact after the War of 1812, and they had aggressively resisted white encroachment. In his last annual message to Congress in late 1824, President James Monroe proposed that all Native peoples be moved beyond the Mississippi River. Monroe described his proposal as an "honorable" one that would protect Native Americans' land from invasion and provide them with independence for "improvement and civilization." He believed force would be unnecessary.

But all four tribes unanimously rejected Monroe's proposition. Between 1789 and 1825, the four nations had negotiated thirty treaties with the United States, and they had reached their limit. Most wished to remain on what little was left of their ancestral land.

Pressure from Georgia had prompted Monroe's policy. In the 1820s, the state had accused the federal government of not fulfilling its 1802 promise to remove the Cherokee and Creek from northwestern Georgia in return for the state's renunciation of its claim to western lands. In 1826, under federal pressure, the Creek nation ceded all but a small strip of its Georgia acreage, but Georgians remained unmoved. Only the complete removal of the Georgia Creeks to the West could resolve the conflict between the state and the federal government. For the Creek, the outcome was devastating. In an ultimately unsuccessful attempt to hold fast to the remainder of their traditional lands, which were in Alabama, they radically altered their political structure. In 1829, at the expense of traditional village autonomy, they centralized tribal authority and forbade any chief from ceding land.

In 1830, after extensive debate and a narrow vote in both houses, Congress passed the **Indian Removal Act**, authorizing the president to negotiate treaties of removal with all tribes living east of the Mississippi. The bill, which provided federal funds for such relocations, would likely not have passed the House without the additional representation afforded slave states due to the three-fifths clause in the Constitution. Increasingly, slavery's expansion equated with political power and Native peoples' displacement in the South.

9-2e Cherokee

Adapting to American ways seemed no more successful than resistance in forestalling removal. No people met the challenge of assimilating to American standards more thoroughly than the Cherokee, whose traditional home centered on eastern Tennessee and northern Alabama and Georgia. Between 1819 and 1829, the tribe became economically self-sufficient and politically self-governing; during this Cherokee renaissance, the nearly fifteen thousand adult Cherokees came to think of themselves as a nation, not a collection of villages. In 1821 and 1822, Sequoyah, a self-educated Cherokee, devised an eighty-six-character phonetic alphabet that made possible a Cherokee-language Bible and a bilingual tribal newspaper, *Cherokee Phoenix* (1828). Between 1820 and 1823, the Cherokee created a formal government with a bicameral legislature, a court system, and a salaried bureaucracy. In 1827, they adopted a written constitution modeled after that of the United States. They transformed their economy from hunting, gathering, and subsistence agriculture to commodity trade based on barter, cash, and credit.

Cherokee land laws, however, differed from U.S. law. The nation collectively owned all Cherokee land and forbade land sales to outsiders. Nonetheless, economic change paralleled political adaptation. Many became individual farmers and slaveholders; by 1833, they held fifteen hundred black slaves, and over time Cherokee racial identity became very complex. Both before and after removal to the West, the designations of "mixed bloods" and "full bloods" were woven into the fabric of tribal society, and conflicts over membership as well as the legacy of Cherokee slaveholding still permeate the group today. But these Cherokee transformations failed to win respect or acceptance from white southerners. In the 1820s, Georgia pressed them to sell the 7,200 square miles of land they held in the state. Congress appropriated $30,000 in 1822 to buy the Cherokee land in Georgia, but the Cherokees resisted. Impatient with their refusals to negotiate cession, Georgia annulled the Cherokees' constitution, extended the state's sovereignty over them, prohibited the Cherokee National Council from meeting except to cede land, and ordered their lands seized. Then, the discovery of gold on Cherokee land in 1829 further whetted Georgia's appetite for Cherokee territory.

9-2f *Cherokee Nation v. Georgia*

Backed by sympathetic whites but not by President Andrew Jackson, the Cherokees under Chief John Ross turned to the federal courts to defend their treaty with the United States. Their legal strategy reflected their growing political sophistication. In *Cherokee Nation v. Georgia* (1831), Chief Justice John Marshall ruled that under the federal Constitution an American Indian tribe was neither a foreign nation nor a state and therefore had no standing in federal courts. American Indians' relationship with the United States was "marked," said Marshall, "by cardinal and peculiar distinctions which exist nowhere else." They were deemed "domestic, dependent nations." Legally, they were in but not of the United States.

Smithsonian American Art Museum/Art Resource, NY

▲ *Kutteeotubbee*, a prominent southeastern Native American warrior, 1834.

Nonetheless, said Marshall, the American Indians had an unquestionable right to their lands; they could lose title only by voluntarily giving it up.

A year later, in *Worcester v. Georgia*, Marshall defined the Cherokee position more clearly. The Cherokee nation was, he declared, a distinct political community in which "the laws of Georgia can have no force" and into which Georgians could not enter without permission or treaty privilege. The Cherokee celebrated. *Phoenix* editor Elias Boudinot called the decision "glorious news." Jackson, however, whose reputation had been built as an Indian fighter, did his best to usurp the Court's action. Newspapers widely reported that Jackson had said, "John Marshall has made his decision: now let him enforce it." Keen to open up new lands for settlement, Jackson favored expelling the Cherokees.

Georgians, too, refused to comply; they would not tolerate a sovereign Cherokee nation within their borders, and they refused to hear the pleas of Native peoples to share their American dream. A Cherokee census indicated that they owned thirty-three grist mills, thirteen sawmills, one powder mill, sixty-nine blacksmith shops, two tanneries, 762 looms, 2,486 spinning wheels, 172 wagons, 2,923 plows, 7,683 horses, 22,531 cattle, 46,732 pigs, and 2,566 sheep. "You asked us to throw off the hunter and warrior state," declared the Cherokee leader, John Ridge, in 1832. "We did so—you asked us to form a republican government: We did so—adopting your own as a model. You asked us to cultivate the earth, and learn the mechanic arts: We did so. You asked us to learn to read: We did so. You asked us to cast away our idols, and worship your God: We did so." But neither the plow nor the Bible earned the Cherokees respect in the face of the economic, imperial, and racial quests of their fellow southerners (see Map 9.2).

9-2g Trail of Tears

The Choctaw went first; they made the forced journey from Mississippi and Alabama to the West in the winter of 1831 and 1832. Alexis de Tocqueville was visiting Memphis when they passed through: "The wounded, the sick, newborn babies, and the old men on the point of death . . . . I saw them embark to cross the great river," he wrote, "and the sight will never fade from my memory. Neither sob nor complaint rose from

Trail of Tears Forced migration in 1838 of the Cherokee people from their homelands in the southeast to what is now Oklahoma.

that silent assembly. Their afflictions were of long standing, and they felt them to be irremediable." Other tribes soon joined the forced march. The Creeks in Alabama resisted removal until 1836, when the army pushed them westward. A year later, the Chickasaw followed.

Having fought removal in the courts, the Cherokee were divided. Some believed that further resistance was hopeless and accepted removal as the only chance to preserve their civilization. The leaders of this minority agreed in 1835 to exchange their southern home for western land, in the Treaty of New Echota. Most, though, wanted to stand firm. John Ross, with petitions signed by fifteen thousand Cherokee, lobbied the Senate against ratification of the treaty. He lost. But when the time for evacuation came in 1838, most Cherokee refused to move. President Martin Van Buren sent federal troops to round them up. About twenty thousand Cherokee were evicted, held in detention camps, and marched under military escort to Indian Territory in present-day Oklahoma. Nearly one-quarter of them died of disease and exhaustion on what came to be known as the **Trail of Tears**.

Map 9.2 Removal of Native Americans from the South, 1820–1840

Over a twenty-year period, the federal government and southern states forced Native Americans to exchange their traditional homes for western land. Some tribal groups remained in the South, but most settled in the alien western environment.

▲ *The Trail of Tears, 1838.* The epic and tragic drama of Cherokee removal is here depicted in *The Trail of Tears, 1838.* Oil on canvas, 1942, by Robert Lindneux. Courtesy Granger, NYC. All rights reserved.

When the forced march to the West ended, Native peoples had traded about 100 million acres east of the Mississippi for 32 million acres west of the river plus $68 million. Only a few scattered remnants, among them the Seminoles in Florida and the Cherokees in the southern Appalachian Mountains, remained east of the Mississippi River.

Forced removal had a disastrous impact on the Cherokee and other displaced American Indian nations. In the West, they encountered an alien environment. Unable to live off the land, many became dependent on government payments for survival. Removal also brought new internal conflicts. The Cherokees in particular struggled over their tribal government. In 1839, followers of John Ross assassinated the leaders of the protreaty faction. Violence continued sporadically until a new treaty in 1846 imposed a temporary truce. In time, the Cherokee managed to reestablish their political institutions and a governing body in Tahlequah, in northeastern Oklahoma.

9-2h Seminole Wars

In Florida, a small band of Seminoles continued to resist. Some Seminole leaders agreed in the 1832 Treaty of Payne's Landing to relocate to the West within three years, but others opposed the treaty, and some probably did not know it existed. A minority under Osceola, a charismatic leader, refused to vacate their homes and fought the pro-treaty group. When federal troops were sent to impose removal in 1835, Osceola waged a fierce guerrilla war against them.

The Florida Native peoples were a varied group that included many Creeks and people of mixed Native American and African American descent (mainly children of ex-slaves or descendants of fugitive slaves). The U.S. Army, however, considered them all Seminole, subject to removal. General Thomas Jesup believed that the fugitive slave population was the key to the war. "This, you may be assured, is a Negro, not an Indian war," he wrote a friend in 1836, "and if it be not speedily put down, the South will feel the effects of it on their slave population before the end of the next season."

Osceola was captured under a white flag of truce and died in an army prison in 1838, but the Seminole fought on under Chief Coacoochee (Wild Cat) and other leaders. In 1842, the United States abandoned the removal effort. Most of Osceola's followers agreed to move west to Indian Territory after another war in 1858, but some Seminoles remained in the Florida Everglades.

9-3 Social Pyramid in the Old South

▶ What were the socio-economic experiences of the groups that comprised the "social pyramid" of the Old South?

▶ What were the cultural experiences of the groups that comprised the "social pyramid" of the Old South?

▶ What tensions emerged among slaveholders and nonslaveholders in the Old South?

Native American lands were now open to restless and mobile white settlers. A large majority of white southern families (three-quarters in 1860) were yeoman farmers who owned their own land but did not own slaves. The social distance between poorer whites and the planter class could be great, although the line between slaveholder and nonslaveholder was fluid. Still greater was the distance between whites and blacks with free status. White yeomen, landless whites, and free blacks occupied the broad base of the social pyramid in the Old South.

9-3a Yeoman Farmers

Many of the white farmers pioneered the southern wilderness, moving into undeveloped regions or Native American land after removal. After the War of 1812, they moved in successive waves down the southern Appalachians into the Gulf lands or through the Cumberland Gap into Kentucky and Tennessee. In large sections of the South, especially inland from the coast and away from large rivers, small, self-sufficient farms were the norm. Lured by stories of good land, many men repeatedly uprooted their wives and children. So many shared the excitement over new lands that one North Carolinian wrote in alarm, "The Alabama Fever rages here with great violence . . . . I am apprehensive if it continues to spread as it has done, it will almost depopulate the country."

These farmers were individualistic and hardworking. Unlike their northern counterparts, their lives were not transformed by improvements in transportation. They could be independent thinkers as well, but their status as a numerical majority did not mean they set the political or economic direction of the larger society. Self-reliant and often isolated, absorbed in the work of their farms, they operated both apart from and within the slave-based staple-crop economy.

On the southern frontier, men cleared fields, built log cabins, and established farms while their wives labored in the household economy and patiently re-created the social ties—to relatives, neighbors, fellow churchgoers—that enriched everyone's experience. Women seldom shared the men's excitement about moving. They dreaded the isolation and loneliness of the frontier. "We have been [moving] all our lives," lamented one woman. "As soon as ever we get comfortably settled, it is time to be off to something new."

Some yeomen acquired large tracts of level land, purchased slaves, and became planters. They forged part of the new wealth of the cotton-boom states of Mississippi and Louisiana, where mobility into the slave-owning class was possible. Others clung to familiar mountainous areas or sought self-sufficiency because, as one frontiersman put it, they disliked "seeing the nose of my neighbor sticking out between the trees." As one historian has written, though they owned no slaves, yeomen were jealous of their independence, and "the household grounded their own claims to masterhood." Whatever the size of their property, they wanted control over their economic and domestic lives.

9-3b Yeoman Folk Culture

The yeomen enjoyed a folk culture based on family, church, and local region. Their speech patterns and inflections recalled their Scots-Irish and Irish backgrounds. They flocked to religious revivals called camp meetings, and in between they got together for house-raisings, logrolling, quilting bees, corn-shuckings, and hunting for both food and sport. Such occasions combined work with fun and fellowship, offering food and liquor in abundance.

A demanding round of work and family responsibilities shaped women's lives in the home. They worked in the fields to an extent that astonished travelers like Frederick Law Olmsted and British writer Frances Trollope, who believed yeomen had rendered their wives "slaves of the soil." Throughout the year, the care and preparation of food consumed much of women's time. Household tasks continued during frequent pregnancies and child care. Primary nursing and medical care also fell to mothers, who often relied on folk wisdom. Women, too, wanted to be masters of their household, the only space and power over which they could claim domain, although it came at the price of their health.

9-3c Yeomen's Livelihoods

Among the men, many aspired to wealth, eager to join the scramble for slaves and cotton profits. North Carolinian John F. Flintoff kept a diary of his struggle for success. At age eighteen in 1841, Flintoff went to Mississippi to seek his fortune. Like other aspiring yeomen, he worked as an overseer of slaves but often found it impossible to please his employers. At one point, he gave up and returned to North Carolina, where he married and lived for a while in his parents' house. But Flintoff was "impatient to get along in the world," so he tried Louisiana next and then Mississippi again.

Flintoff's health suffered in the Gulf region and, routinely, "first rate employment" alternated with "very low wages." Moreover, as a young man working on isolated plantations, Flintoff often felt lonely. Even at a revival meeting in 1844 he felt "little warm feeling." His employers found fault with his work, and in 1846 Flintoff concluded in despair that "managing negroes and large farms is soul destroying."

But a desire to succeed kept him going. At twenty-six, even before he owned any land, Flintoff bought his first slave, "a negro

▲ *Old Kentucky Home Life in the South*, by Eastman Johnson, 1859, oil on canvas. Collection of the New-York Historical Society/ the Bridgeman Art Gallery.

boy 7 years old." Soon he had purchased two more children, the cheapest slaves available. Conscious of his status as a slave owner, Flintoff resented the low wages he was paid. In 1853, with nine young slaves and a growing family, Flintoff faced "the most unhappy time of my life." Fired by his uncle, he returned to North Carolina, sold some of his slaves, and purchased 124 acres with help from his in-laws. As he began to pay off his debts, he looked forward to freeing his wife from labor and possibly sending his sons to college. Although Flintoff demonstrated that a farmer could move in and out of the slaveholding class, he never achieved the cotton planter status that he desired.

Probably more typical of the southern yeoman was Ferdinand L. Steel, who as a young man moved from North Carolina to Tennessee to work as a river boatman but eventually took up farming in Mississippi. Steel and his family raised corn and wheat, though cotton was their cash product: they sold five or six bales a year to obtain money for sugar, coffee, salt, calico, gunpowder, and a few other store-bought goods.

Thus, Steel entered the market economy as a small farmer, but with mixed results. He picked his own cotton and complained that it was brutal work and not profitable. He felt like a serf in cotton's kingdom. When cotton prices fell, a small grower like Steel could be driven into debt and lose his farm.

Steel's life in Mississippi in the 1840s retained much of the flavor of the frontier, and he survived on a household economy. He made all the family's shoes; his wife and sister sewed dresses, shirts, and "pantaloons." The Steel women also rendered their own soap and spun and wove cotton into cloth; the men hunted game. Steel doctored his illnesses with boneset tea and other herbs. As the nation fell deeper into crisis over the future of free or slave labor, and as the planter class strove ever more aggressively to preserve its slave society, this independent farmer never came close to owning a slave.

The focus of Steel's life was family and religion. Family members prayed together daily, and he studied Scripture for

North Carolina Emigrants: Poor White Folks, James Henry (1812-93)/CINCINNATI ART MUSEUM/Cincinnati Art Museum, Ohio, USA/Bridgeman Images

▲ *North Carolina Emigrants: Poor White Folks*, oil on canvas, 1845, by James Henry Beard. This depicts a yeoman family, their belongings all on one hungry horse, as they migrate westward in search of new land and livelihood.

an hour after lunch. "My Faith increases, & I enjoy much of that peace which the world cannot give," he wrote in 1841. Seeking to prepare himself for Judgment Day, Steel borrowed histories, Latin and Greek grammars, and religious books from his church. Eventually, he became a traveling Methodist minister. "My life is one of toil," he reflected, "but blessed be God that it is as well with me as it is."

9-3d Landless Whites

Toil with even less security was the lot of two other groups of free southerners: landless whites and free blacks. A sizable minority of white southern workers—from 25 to 40 percent, depending on the state—were hired hands who owned no land and worked for others in the countryside and towns. Their property consisted of a few household items and some animals—usually pigs—that could feed themselves on the open range. The landless included some immigrants, especially Irish, who did heavy and dangerous work, such as building railroads and digging ditches.

In the countryside, white farm laborers struggled to purchase land in the face of low wages or, if they rented, unpredictable market prices for their crops. By scrimping

and finding odd jobs, some managed to climb into the ranks of yeomen. When James and Nancy Bennitt of North Carolina succeeded in their ten-year struggle to buy land, they decided to avoid the unstable market in cotton; thereafter they raised extra corn and wheat as sources of cash. People like the Bennitts were both participants in and victims of an economy dominated by cotton producers who relied on slave labor.

Herdsmen with pigs and other livestock had a desperate struggle to succeed. By 1860, as the South anticipated war to preserve its society, between 300,000 and 400,000 white people in the four states of Virginia, North and South Carolina, and Georgia—approximately one-fifth of the total white population—lived in genuine poverty. Their lives were harsh. An early antebellum traveler in central South Carolina described the white folk he encountered in the countryside: they "looked yellow, poor, and sickly. Some of them lived the most miserably I ever saw any poor people live."

9-3e Yeomen's Demands and White Class Relations

Class tensions emerged in the western, nonslaveholding parts of the seaboard states by the 1830s. There, yeoman farmers resented their underrepresentation in state legislatures and the corruption in local government. After vigorous debate, the reformers won many battles. Voters in the more recently settled states of the Old Southwest adopted white manhood suffrage and other electoral reforms, including popular election of governors, legislative apportionment based on white population only, and locally chosen county government. Slave owners with new wealth, however, were determined to hold the ultimate reins of power.

Given such tensions, it was perhaps remarkable that slaveholders and nonslaveholders did not experience more overt conflict. Historians have offered several explanations. One of the most important factors was race. The South's racial ideology stressed the superiority of all whites to blacks. Thus, slavery became the basis of equality among whites, and white privilege inflated the status of poor whites and gave them a common interest with the rich. At the same time, the dream of upward mobility blunted some class conflict.

Most important, before the Civil War many yeomen were able to pursue their independent lifestyle largely unhindered by slaveholding planters. They worked their farms, avoided debt, and marked progress for their families in rural habitats of their own making. Likewise, slaveholders pursued their goals quite independently of yeomen. Planters farmed for the market but also for themselves. Suppression of dissent also played an increasing role. After 1830, white southerners who criticized the slave system out of moral conviction or class resentment were intimidated, attacked, or rendered politically powerless in a society held together in part by white racial solidarity.

Still, there were signs of class conflict in the late antebellum period. As cotton lands filled up, nonslaveholders faced narrower economic prospects; meanwhile, wealthy planters enjoyed expanding profits. The risks of entering cotton production were becoming too great and the cost of slaves too high for many yeomen to rise in society. From 1830 to 1860, the percentage of white southern families holding slaves declined steadily, from 36 to 25 percent. Although slave owners were a distinct minority in the white population, planters' share of the South's agricultural wealth remained between 90 and 95 percent. This long-standing American dilemma of severe inequality of wealth, combined with white racial solidarity, finds one of its deepest roots in the Old South.

Anticipating possible secession, slave owners stood secure. In the 1850s, they occupied from 50 to 85 percent of the seats in state legislatures and a similarly high percentage of the South's congressional seats. And planters' interests controlled all the other major social institutions, such as churches and colleges.

9-3f Free Blacks

The nearly quarter-million free blacks in the South in 1860 also yearned for mobility. But their condition was generally worse than the yeoman's and often little better than the slave's. The free blacks of the Upper South were usually descendants of men and women manumitted by their owners in the 1780s and 1790s. A remarkable number of slaveholders in Virginia and the Chesapeake region had freed their slaves because of religious principles and revolutionary ideals in the wake of American independence. Many free blacks also became free as fugitive slaves, especially by the 1830s, disappearing into the southern population; a few made their way northward. A small number of free blacks had purchased their own freedom.

White southerners were increasingly desperate to restrict this growing free black presence in their midst. "It seems the number of free Negroes," complained a Virginia slaveholder, "always exceeds the number of Negroes freed." Some free blacks worked in towns or cities, but most lived in rural areas and struggled to survive. They usually did not own land and had to labor in someone else's fields, often beside slaves. By law, free blacks could not own a gun, buy liquor, violate curfew, assemble except in church, testify in court, or (throughout the South after 1835) vote. Despite these obstacles, a minority bought land, and others found jobs as skilled craftsmen, especially in cities.

A few free blacks prospered and bought slaves. In 1830, there were 3,775 free black slaveholders in the South; 80 percent lived in the four states of Louisiana, South Carolina, Virginia, and Maryland, and approximately half of the total lived in the two cities of New Orleans and Charleston. Most of them purchased their own wives and children, whom they nevertheless could not free because laws required newly emancipated blacks to leave their state. In order to free family members whom they had purchased, hundreds of black slaveholders petitioned for exemption from the antimanumission laws passed in most southern states. At the same time, a few multiracial people in New Orleans were active slave traders in its booming market. The complex world of southern free blacks received new attention through Edward P. Jones's *The Known World*, a hugely successful novel published in 2003 about a Virginia family that rises from slavery to slave ownership. Although rare in the United States, the greed and the tragic quest for power that lay at the root of slavery could cross any racial or ethnic barrier.

9-3g Free Black Communities

In the Cotton Belt and Gulf regions, a large proportion of free blacks were of mixed race, the privileged offspring of wealthy white planters. Not all planters freed their mixed-race offspring, but those who did often recognized the moral obligation of giving their children a good education and financial backing. In a few cities like New Orleans, Charleston, and Mobile, extensive interracial sex, as well as migrations from the Caribbean, had produced a multiracial population that was recognized as a distinct class. Most multiracial people, however, experienced hardship. In the United States, "one drop" of black "blood" (any observable racial mixture to white people's eyes) made them black, and potentially enslaveable.

In many southern cities by the 1840s, free black communities formed, especially around an expanding number of churches. By the late 1850s, Baltimore had fifteen churches,

Louisville nine, and Nashville and St. Louis four each—most of them African Methodist Episcopal. Baltimore, from which **Frederick Douglass**, the slave, escaped in 1838 with his free-born fiancée, Anna Murray, developed an especially active free black society. In 1840, the city contained 17,967 free blacks and 3,199 slaves out of a total population of 102,313. Such a large assemblage of free people of color worked as all manner of menial laborer, from domestic servants to dockworkers and draymen, but they also suffered under a strict Black Code, denying any civil or political rights and restricting their movements.

9-4 The Planters' World

▶ **What were the social values of the planter class in the South?**

▶ **What was the relationship between slavery and global and domestic economy?**

▶ **What role did paternalism play in the relationships within the planter class?**

At the top of the southern social pyramid were slaveholding planters. Most lived in comfortable farmhouses, not on the opulent scale that legend suggests. The grand plantation mansions, with fabulous gardens and long rows of outlying slave quarters, are an enduring symbol of the Old South. But in 1850, 50 percent of southern slaveholders had fewer than five slaves; 72 percent had fewer than ten; 88 percent had fewer than twenty. Thus, the average slaveholder was not a wealthy aristocrat but an aspiring farmer.

9-4a The Newly Rich

Louisiana cotton planter Bennet Barrow, a newly rich planter of the 1840s, was preoccupied with moneymaking. He worried constantly over his cotton crop, filling his diary with weather reports and gloomy predictions of his yields. Yet Barrow also strove to appear above such worries. He hunted frequently and had a passion for racing horses and raising hounds. He could report the loss of a slave without feeling, but emotion broke through his laconic manner when illness afflicted his sporting animals. "Never was a person more unlucky than I am," he mourned. "My favorite pup never lives." His strongest feelings surfaced when his horse Jos Bell—equal to "the best Horse in the South"—"broke down running a mile . . . ruined for Ever." The same day, the distraught Barrow gave his human property a "general Whipping." In 1841 diary entries, he worried about a rumored slave insurrection. He gave a "severe whipping" to several of his slaves when they disobediently killed a hog. And when a slave named Ginney Jerry "sherked" his cotton-picking duties and was rumored "about to run off," Barrow whipped him one day and the next, which he recorded matter-of-factly: "took my gun found him in the Bayou

Frederick Douglass A former slave who was the leading black abolitionist during the antebellum period.

behind the Quarter, shot him in his thigh—etc. raining all around."

The richest planters used their wealth to model genteel sophistication. Extended visits, parties, and balls to which women wore the latest fashions provided opportunities for friendship, courtship, and display. Such parties were held during the Christmas holidays, but also on such occasions as molasses stewing, a bachelors' ball, a horse race, or the crowning of the May queen. These entertainments were especially important as diversions for plantation women, and at the same time they sustained a rigidly gendered society. Young women relished social events to break the monotony of their domestic lives. In 1826, a Virginia girl was ecstatic about the "week . . . I was in Town. . . . There were five beaux and as many belles in the house constantly," she declared, and all she and her companions did was "eat, visit, romp, and sleep."

Most of the planters in the cotton-boom states of Alabama and Mississippi were newly rich by the 1840s. As one historian put it, "a number of men mounted from log cabin to plantation mansion on a stairway of cotton bales, accumulating slaves as they climbed." They put their new wealth into cotton acreage and slaves even as they sought refinement and high social status.

William Faulkner immortalized the new wealthy planter in a fictional character, Thomas Sutpen, in his novel *Absalom, Absalom!* (1936). After a huge win at riverboat gambling, Sutpen arrives in a Mississippi county in the 1830s, buys a huge plantation he calls Sutpen's Hundred, and with his troop of slaves converts it into a wealthy enterprise. Sutpen marries a local woman, and although he is always viewed as a mysterious outsider by earlier residents of the county, he becomes a pillar of the slaveholding class, eventually an officer in the Confederate army. But Sutpen is a self-made man of indomitable will and slave-based wealth. Although his ambition is ultimately his undoing, one of the earliest lessons he learns about success in the South is that "you got to have land and niggers and a fine house."

The cotton boom in the Mississippi Valley created one-generation aristocrats. A nonfictional case in point is Greenwood Leflore, a Choctaw chieftain who owned a plantation in Mississippi with four hundred slaves. After selling his cotton on the world market, he spent $10,000 in France to furnish a single room of his mansion with handwoven carpets, furniture upholstered with gold leaf, tables and cabinets ornamented with tortoiseshell inlay, a variety of mirrors and paintings, and a clock and candelabra of brass and ebony.

9-4b Social Status and Planters' Values

Slave ownership was the main determinant of wealth in the South. Slaves were a commodity and an investment, much like gold; people bought them on speculation, hoping for a steady rise in their market value. Many slaveholders took out mortgages on their slaves and used them as collateral. Especially in the growing states, people who could not pay cash for slaves would ask the sellers to purchase the mortgage, just as banks give mortgages on houses today. The slaveholder would pay back the loan in installments with interest. Slaveholders and the people who lent them money put their faith in this "human collateral," believing it would increase in value. This was slaveholding capitalism as a growth industry. Hundreds of thousands of slaves were thus mortgaged, many several times and with full awareness of their masters' financial methods. In St. Landry's Parish, Louisiana, between 1833 and 1837, an eight-year-old slave boy named Jacques was mortgaged three times, sold twice, and converted into what one historian has called a "human cash machine and an investment vehicle" before the age of twelve.

Slavery's influence spread throughout the social system. The availability of slave labor tended to devalue free labor: where strenuous work under supervision was reserved for an enslaved race, few free people relished it. When Alexis de Tocqueville crossed from Ohio into Kentucky in his travels of 1831, he observed "the effect that slavery produces on society. On the right bank of the Ohio [River] everything is activity, industry; labor is honoured; there are no slaves. Pass to the left bank and the scene changes so suddenly that you think yourself on the other side of the world; the enterprising spirit is gone. There, work is not only painful; it is shameful." Tocqueville's own class impulses found a home in the South, however. There he found a "veritable aristocracy which . . . combines many prejudices with high sentiments and instincts."

The values of the aristocrat—lineage, privilege, pride, honor, and refinement of person and manner—commanded respect throughout the South. Many of those qualities were in short supply, however, in the recently settled portions of the cotton kingdom, where frontier values of courage and self-reliance ruled during the 1820s and 1830s. By the 1850s, a settled aristocratic group of planters did rule, however, in much of the Mississippi Valley. Indeed, by 1860 two-thirds of the millionaires in the United States were southern planters.

In this geographically mobile society, independence and codes of honor motivated both planter and frontier farmer alike. Instead of gradually disappearing, as it did in the North, the Code Duello, which required men to defend their honor through violence, lasted much longer in the South. In North Carolina in 1851, wealthy planter Samuel Fleming sought to settle disputes with lawyer William Waightstill Avery by "cowhiding" him on a public street. According to the code, Avery had two choices: to redeem his honor violently or to brand himself a coward through inaction. Three weeks later, he shot Fleming dead at point-blank range during a session of the Burke County Superior Court. A jury took only ten minutes to find Avery not guilty, and the spectators gave him a standing ovation.

In their pride, aristocratic planters expected not only to wield power but also to receive deference from poorer whites. But the sternly independent yeoman class resented infringements of their rights, and many belonged to evangelical faiths that exalted values of simplicity and condemned the planters' love of wealth.

9-4c King Cotton in a Global Economy

Planters always had their eyes on the international growth of the cotton markets. Cash crops such as cotton were for export; the planters' fate depended on world trade, especially with Europe. The American South so dominated the world's supply of cotton by the 1840s and 1850s that southern planters gained enormous confidence that the cotton boom was permanent and that the industrializing nations of England and France in particular would always bow to **King Cotton**.

American planters began producing cotton in the 1780s. Made possible in part by Eli Whitney's invention in 1793 of the cotton gin, a device for cleaning the short-staple variety of the crop that the British textile industry craved, American cotton production doubled in yield each decade after 1800 and provided three-fourths of the world's supply by the 1840s. Gins, which took on the scale of whole buildings with time, revolutionized cotton production and the investment of southern wealth in land and slaves. In the first decade of the nineteenth century in South Carolina alone, wrote one planter, cotton "trebled the price of land suitable to its growth" and "doubled" the annual income of growers. Southern staple crops were fully three-fifths of all American exports by 1850, and one of every seven workers in England depended on American cotton for his or her job. Indeed, cotton production made slaves the single most valuable financial asset in the United States—greater in dollar value than all of America's banks, railroads, and manufacturing combined. In 1860 dollars, the slaves' total value as property came to an estimated $3.5 billion. In early-twenty-first-century dollars, that would be approximately $75 billion.

"Cotton is King," the *Southern Cultivator* declared in 1859, "and wields an astonishing influence over the world's commerce." Until 1840, the cotton trade furnished much of the export capital to finance northern economic growth. After that date, however, the northern economy expanded without dependence on cotton profits. Free labor was in the long run more the engine of American capitalist growth than slave labor. Nevertheless, southern planters and politicians continued to boast of King Cotton's supremacy. "Our cotton is the most wonderful talisman in the world," announced a planter in 1853. "By its power we are transmuting whatever we choose into whatever we want." "No power on earth dares . . . to make war on cotton," James Hammond lectured the U.S. Senate in 1858; "Cotton is king."

9-4d Slavery and Capitalism

Historians have vigorously debated the relationship between slavery and capitalism in the Atlantic world. Slavery may not have caused the Industrial Revolution in the eighteenth and nineteenth centuries, one historian has written, but it "played an active role in its pattern and timing." Some historians once contended that American slavery was

King Cotton Term expressing the southern belief that the U.S. and British economies depended on cotton, making it "king."

pre-modern and pre-capitalist, but no longer. Although the debate can be ferocious over the extent and character of slavery's roots in capitalism, we no longer doubt that southern slaveholders were as intertwined in markets, investments, and the uses of credit and speculation as their northern industrializing counterparts. Especially with the westward movement of the domestic slave trade, slaveholders rationally organized the exploitation and sale of their human property on a huge scale for the production of commodities for a growing global market. Slaves were not only property, but moveable property in a system based on credit, debt, supply chains, and the reputations of both slave owners and slave traders. Slaves were virtually currency itself.

Cotton production, and therefore the productivity of slaves and the system they made possible, increased manifold in the forty years leading up to the Civil War. One historian has argued that such productivity was due to widespread "speed-ups" forced upon the enslaved and especially to increasing uses of "torture" to compel work. Other historians, however, have attributed the growth in cotton production over time to the use of hybrid seeds and other agricultural innovations that made the crop far more fruitful. Fewer than half of all slaves lived on cotton plantations by the late antebellum period; we must therefore be careful to paint pictures of slave experience and the capitalist system of American bondage with a broad brush. We must also be careful not to understand slavery and the southern or northern economies as products of impersonal economic forces alone. Systems do not commodify and sell people, people do. Slavery fueled capitalism and capitalism forged slavery. But ultimately the nation faced these issues as a deadly conflict in the only place it could—in political events and institutions, and at the ballot box.

9-4e Paternalism

Beyond cold economics, slaveholding men often embraced a paternalistic ideology that justified their dominance over both black slaves and white women. Instead of stressing the profitable aspects of commercial agriculture, they sometimes stressed their obligations, viewing themselves as custodians of the welfare of society in general, and of the black families they owned in particular. The paternalistic planter saw himself not as an oppressor but as the benevolent guardian of an inferior race.

Paul Carrington Cameron, North Carolina's largest slaveholder, exemplifies this mentality. After a period of sickness among his one thousand North Carolina slaves (he had hundreds more in Alabama and Mississippi), Cameron wrote, "I fear the Negroes have suffered much from the want of proper attention and kindness under this late distemper no love of lucre shall ever induce me to be cruel." On another occasion, he described to his sister the sense of responsibility he felt: "Do you remember a cold & frosty morning, during [our mother's] illness, when she said to me Paul my son the people ought to be shod' this is ever in my ears, whenever I see any ones shoes in bad order; and in my ears it will be, so long as I am master."

It was comforting to rich planters to see themselves in this way, and slaves—accommodating to the realities of power—encouraged their masters to think that their benevolence was appreciated. Paternalism also served as a defense against abolitionist criticism. Still, paternalism was often a matter of self-delusion, a means of avoiding some harsh dimensions of slave treatment. In reality, paternalism grew as a give-and-take relationship between masters and slaves, each extracting from the other what they desired—owners took labor from the bondsmen, while slaves, as best they could, obligated masters to provide them a measure of autonomy.

Charles Colcock Jones and his wife, Mary, were large slave owners on three Liberty County plantations south of Savannah, Georgia. A prominent Presbyterian minister and intellectual, trained in northeastern universities, Jones inherited and married into slaveholding. In the 1820s he and Mary thought slavery "one of the greatest curses," a terrible "wrong . . . unjust, contrary to nature and religion." Unable to imagine "total abolition" in the rice land of the low country, Jones sought a "middle way," believing slavery could be "reformed," that slaves, like whites, should be converted to evangelical Christianity.

In 1834 Jones published *Catechism for Colored Persons*, a manual for whites instructing slaves in Christian doctrine and obedience. But over time, his and Mary's theories about Christian reform of slavery fell to pieces. In 1857, desperately in debt and frustrated by sullen and runaway slaves, the Joneses resorted to what they claimed they would never do. They sold their longtime personal servants, Phoebe and Cassius, and their four children in the "least public" way possible at a Savannah slave market for $4,500. In long, wrenching letters the Joneses struggled with the morality of their decision, but congratulated themselves on selling Phoebe's family intact. They did not believe they had gotten the "best bargain," but Charles concluded: "Conscience is better than money."

Even Paul Cameron's benevolence vanished with changed circumstances. After the Civil War, he bristled at African Americans' efforts to be free and made sweeping economic decisions without regard for their welfare. Writing on Christmas Day 1865, Cameron showed little Christian charity (but a healthy profit motive) when he declared, "I am convinced that the people who gets rid of the free negro first will be the first to advance in improved agriculture. Have made no effort to retain any of mine." With that, he turned off his land nearly a thousand black people, rented his fields to several white farmers, and invested in industry.

Relations between men and women in the planter class were similarly defined by paternalism. The upper-class southern woman was raised and educated to be a wife, mother, and subordinate companion to men. South Carolina's Mary Boykin Chesnut wrote of her husband, "He is master of the house. To hear is to obey . . . . All the comfort of my life depends upon his being in a good humor." In a social system based on the coercion of an entire race, women found it very difficult to challenge society's rules on sexual or racial relations.

Planters' daughters usually attended one of the South's rapidly multiplying boarding schools. There, they formed friendships with other girls and received an education. Typically, the young woman had to choose a husband and commit herself for life to a man whom she generally had known for only a brief time. Young women were often alienated and emotionally unfulfilled. They had to follow the wishes of their family, especially their father. "It was for me best that I yielded to the wishes of papa," wrote a young North Carolinian in 1823. "I wonder when my best will cease to be painful and when I shall begin to enjoy life instead of enduring it."

Upon marriage, a planter-class woman ceded to her husband most of her legal rights, becoming part of his family. Most of the year she was isolated on a large plantation, where she had to oversee the cooking and preserving of food, manage the house, supervise care of the children, and attend sick slaves. All these realities were more rigid and confining on the frontier, where isolation was even greater. Women sought refuge in their extended family and associations with other women. Men on plantations could occasionally escape into the public realm—to town, business, or politics. Women could retreat from rural plantation culture only into kinship.

9-4f Marriage and Family Among Planters

It is not surprising that a perceptive young white woman sometimes approached marriage with anxiety. Women could hardly help viewing their wedding day, as one put it in 1832, as "the day to fix my fate." Lucy Breckinridge, a wealthy Virginia girl of twenty, lamented the autonomy she surrendered at the altar. In her diary, she recorded this unvarnished observation on marriage: "A woman's life after she is married, unless there is an immense amount of love, is nothing but suffering and hard work."

▲ *Virginian Luxuries*, folk painting, artist unknown. Abby Aldrich Rockefeller Folk Art Museum, the Colonial Williamsburg Foundation.

Lucy loved young children but knew that childbearing often involved grief, poor health, and death. In 1840, the birth rate for white southern women in their childbearing years was almost 30 percent higher than the national average. The average southern white woman could expect to bear eight children in 1800; by 1860, the figure had decreased to only six, with one or more miscarriages likely. Complications of childbirth were a major cause of death, occurring twice as often in the hot, humid South as in the cooler and drier Northeast.

Sexual relations between planters and slaves were another source of problems that white women had to endure but were not supposed to notice. "Violations of the moral law . . . made mulattos as common as blackberries," protested a woman in Georgia, but wives had to play "the ostrich game." "A magnate who runs a hideous black harem," wrote Mrs. Chesnut, ". . . poses as the model of all human virtues to these poor women whom God and the laws have given him." Such habits and dalliances, whatever the motives, such as at Jefferson's Monticello, produced a very large mixed-race population by the 1850s and a strained use of the term "family" across the South.

Southern men tolerated little discussion by women of the slavery issue. In the 1840s and 1850s, as abolitionist attacks on slavery increased, southern men published a barrage of articles stressing that women should restrict their concerns to the home. The *Southern Quarterly Review* declared, "The proper place for a woman is at home. One of her highest privileges, to be politically merged in the existence of her husband."

But some southern women were beginning to seek a larger role. A study of women in Petersburg, Virginia, a large tobacco-manufacturing town, revealed behavior that valued financial autonomy. Over several decades before 1860, the proportion of women who never married, or did not remarry after the death of a spouse, grew to exceed 33 percent. Likewise, the number of women who worked for wages, controlled their own property, and ran dressmaking businesses increased markedly.

9-5 Slave Life and Labor

▶ **What were the daily living conditions and work routines of slaves?**

▶ **How were slaves made to feel a sense of powerlessness in their lives?**

For African Americans, slavery was a burden that destroyed some people and forced others to develop modes of survival. Slaves knew a life of poverty, coercion, toil, and resentment. They provided the physical strength, and much of the know-how, to build an agricultural empire. But their daily lives embodied the nation's most basic contradiction: in the world's model republic, they were on the wrong side of a brutally unequal power relationship.

9-5a Slaves' Everyday Conditions

Although they generally had enough to eat, slaves' diet was monotonous and non-nutritious. Clothing, too, was plain, coarse, and inexpensive. Few slaves received more than one or two changes of clothing for hot and cold seasons, and one blanket each winter. Children of both sexes ran naked in hot weather and wore long cotton shirts in winter. Many slaves had to go without shoes until December, even as far north as Virginia. The bare feet of slaves were often symbolic of their status and one reason why, after freedom, many black parents were so concerned with providing their children with shoes. These conditions were generally better in cities, where slaves frequently lived in the same dwelling as their owners and were hired out to employers on a regular basis, enabling them to accumulate their own money.

Some of the richer plantations provided substantial houses, but the average slave lived in a crude, one-room cabin. The gravest drawback of slave cabins was not lack of comfort but an unhealthy environment. Each dwelling housed one or two entire families. Crowding and lack of sanitation fostered the spread of infection and such contagious diseases as typhoid fever, malaria, and dysentery. White plantation doctors were hired to care for sick slaves on a regular basis, but some "slave doctors" attained a degree of power in the quarters and with masters by practicing healing through herbalism and spiritualism.

9-5b Slave Work Routines

Hard work was the central fact of slaves' existence. The long hours and large work gangs that characterized Gulf Coast cotton districts operated almost like factories in the field. Overseers rang the morning bell before dawn, and black people of varying ages, tools in hand, walked toward the fields. Slaves who cultivated tobacco in the Upper South worked long hours picking the sticky, sometimes noxious, leaves under harsh discipline. And as one woman recalled when interviewed in the 1930s, "it was way after sundown 'fore they could stop that field work. Then they had to hustle to finish their night work [such as watering livestock or cleaning cotton] in time for supper, or go to bed without it."

Working "from sun to sun" became a norm in much of the South. As one planter put it, slaves were the best labor because "you could command them and make them do what was right." Profit took precedence over paternalism. Slave women did heavy fieldwork, even during pregnancy. Old people were kept busy caring for young children, doing light chores, or carding, ginning, and spinning cotton. The black abolitionist orator Frances Ellen Watkins captured the grinding economic reality of slavery in an 1857 speech, charging that slaveholders had "found out a fearful alchemy by which . . . blood can be transformed into gold. Instead of listening to the cry of agony, they listen to the ring of dollars and stoop down to pick up the coin."

task system Labor system in which each slave had a daily or weekly quota of tasks to complete.

By the 1830s, slave owners found that labor could be similarly motivated by the clock. Incentives had to be part of the labor regime. Planters like Charles Colcock Jones in the South Carolina and Georgia low country used a **task system** whereby slaves were assigned measured amounts of work to be performed in a given amount of time. So much cotton on a daily basis was to be picked from a designated field, so many rows hoed or plowed in a particular slave's specified section. When their tasks were finished, slaves' time was their own for working garden plots, tending hogs, even hiring out their own extra labor. From this experience and personal space, many slaves developed their own sense of property ownership. When the task system worked best, slaves and masters alike embraced it, fostering a degree of reciprocal trust.

Enslaved children were the future of the system and widely valued as potential labor. Of the 1860 population of 4 million slaves, fully half were under the age of sixteen. "A child raised every two years," wrote Thomas Jefferson, "is of more profit than the crop of the best laboring man." And in 1858, a slave owner writing in an agricultural magazine calculated that a slave girl he purchased in 1827 for $400 had borne three sons now worth $3,000 as his working field hands. Enslaved children gathered kindling, carried water to the fields, swept the yard, lifted cut sugar-cane stalks into carts, stacked wheat, chased birds away from sprouting rice plants, and labored at many levels of cotton and tobacco production. "Work," wrote one historian, "can be rightly called the thief who stole the childhood of youthful bond servants."

As enslaved children matured, they faced many psychological traumas. They faced a feeling of powerlessness as they became aware that their parents ultimately could not protect them. They had to muster strategies to fight internalizing what whites assumed was their inferiority. Thomas Jones, who grew up in North Carolina, remembered that his greatest struggle was with the sense of "suffering and shame" as he "was made to feel . . . degraded." Many former slaves resented foremost their denial of education. "There is one sin that slavery committed against me which I will never forgive," recollected the minister James Pennington. "It robbed me of my education." And for girls reaching maturity, the potential trauma of sexual abuse loomed over their lives.

9-5c Violence and Intimidation Against Slaves

Slaves could not demand much autonomy, of course, because the owner enjoyed a monopoly on force and violence. Whites throughout the South believed that slaves "can't be governed except with the whip." One South Carolinian frankly explained to a northern journalist that he whipped his slaves regularly, "say once a fortnight; . . . the fear of the lash kept them in good order." Evidence suggests that whippings were less frequent on small farms than on large plantations. But beatings symbolized authority to the master and tyranny to the slaves, who made them a benchmark for evaluating a master. In the words of former slaves, a good owner was one who did not "whip too much," whereas a bad owner "whipped till he's bloodied you and blistered you."

As these reports suggest, terrible abuses could and did occur. The master wielded virtually absolute authority on his plantation, and courts did not recognize the word of chattel slaves. Slaveholders rarely had to answer to the law or to the state. Yet physical cruelty may have been even more prevalent in other slaveholding parts of the New World than it was in the United States. In some of the sugar islands of the Caribbean in particular, treatment was so poor and death rates so high that the heavily male slave population shrank in size. In the United States, by contrast, the slave population experienced a steady natural increase, as births exceeded deaths and each generation grew larger.

The worst evil of American slavery was not its physical cruelty but the nature of slavery itself: coercion, belonging to another person, virtually no hope for mobility or change. Recalling their time in bondage, some former slaves emphasized the physical abuse, or the "bullwhip days," as one woman described her past. But memories of physical punishment focused on the tyranny of whipping as much as the pain. Delia Garlic made the essential point: "It's bad to belong to folks that own you soul an' body. I could tell you 'bout it all day, but even then you couldn't guess the awfulness of it." Thomas Lewis put it this way: "There was no such thing as being good to slaves. Many people were better than others, but a slave belonged to his master and there was no way to get out of it." To be a slave was to be the object of another person's will and material gain, to be owned, as the saying went, "from the cradle to the grave."

Most American slaves retained their mental independence and self-respect despite their bondage. Contrary to popular belief at the time, they were not loyal partners in their own oppression. They had to be subservient and speak honeyed words to their masters, but they talked and behaved quite differently among themselves. In *Narrative of the Life of Frederick Douglass, an American Slave, Written by Himself* (1845), Frederick Douglass wrote that most slaves, when asked about "their condition and the character of their masters, almost universally say they are contented, and that their masters are kind." Slaves did this, said Douglass, because they were governed by the maxim that "a still tongue makes a wise head," especially in the presence of unfamiliar people. Because they were "part of the human family," slaves often quarreled over who had the best master. But at the end of the day, Douglass remarked, when one had a bad master, he sought a better master; and when he had a better one, he wanted to "be his own master."

9-5d Slave-Master Relationships

Some former slaves remembered warm feelings between masters and slaves (they were sometimes related by blood), and some "special" bondsmen, such as highly skilled jockeys for planters who were great horsemen, enjoyed autonomy, privilege, and even fame. But the prevailing attitudes were distrust and antagonism. Slaves saw through acts of kindness. One woman said her mistress was "a mighty good somebody to belong to" but

only "'cause she was raisin' us to work for her." A man recalled that his owners took good care of their slaves, "and Grandma Maria say, 'Why shouldn't they—it was their money.'"

Slaves were alert to the thousand daily signs of their degraded status. One man recalled the general rule that slaves ate cornbread and owners ate biscuits. If blacks did get biscuits, "the flour that we made the biscuits out of was the third-grade sorts." A former slave recalled, "Us catch lots of 'possums," but "the white folks at [ate] 'em." If the owner took his slaves' garden produce to town and sold it for them, the slaves often suspected him of pocketing part of the profits.

Suspicion often grew into hatred. When a yellow fever epidemic struck in 1852, many slaves saw it as God's retribution. An elderly ex-slave named Minnie Fulkes cherished the conviction that God was going to punish white people for their cruelty to blacks. She described the whippings that her mother had to endure, and then she exclaimed, "Lord, Lord, I hate white people and the flood waters goin' to drown some more." On the plantation, of course, slaves had to keep such thoughts to themselves. Often they expressed one feeling to whites, another within their own household. In their daily lives, slaves created many ways to survive and to sustain their humanity in this world of repression.

9-6 Slave Culture and Resistance

▸ **What culture did slaves create amid the oppression of slavery?**

▸ **What role did religion play in the lives of slaves?**

▸ **What was the impact of slave resistance in the first half of the nineteenth century?**

A people is always "more than the sum of its brutalization," wrote African American novelist Ralph Ellison in 1967. What people create in the face of hard luck and oppression is what provides hope. The resource that enabled slaves to maintain such defiance was their culture: a body of beliefs, values, and practices born of their past and maintained in the present. As best they could, they built a community knitted together by stories, music, a religious worldview, leadership, the smells of their cooking, the sounds of their own voices, and the tapping of their feet. "The values expressed in folklore," wrote African American poet Sterling Brown, provided a "wellspring to which slaves . . . could return in times of doubt to be refreshed."

9-6a African Cultural Survival

Slave culture changed significantly after 1808, when Congress banned further importation of slaves and the generations born in Africa died out. For a few years, South Carolina illegally reopened the international slave trade, but by the 1830s, the vast majority of slaves in the South were native-born Americans. Many African Americans, in fact, can trace their American ancestry back further than most white Americans.

Yet African influences remained strong, despite lack of firsthand memory, especially in appearance and forms of expression. Some enslaved men plaited their hair into rows and fancy designs; enslaved women often wore their hair "in string"—tied in small bunches secured by a string or piece of cloth. A few men and many women wrapped their heads in kerchiefs of the styles and colors of West Africa. In burial practices, slaves used jars and other glass objects to decorate graves, following similar African traditions.

Music, religion, and folktales were parts of daily life for most slaves. Borrowing partly from their African background, as well as forging new American folkways, they developed what scholars have called a sacred worldview, which affected all aspects of work, leisure, and self-understanding. Slaves made musical instruments with carved motifs that resembled African stringed instruments. Their drumming and dancing followed African patterns that made whites marvel. One visitor to Georgia in the 1860s described a ritual dance of African origin: "A ring of singers is formed . . . . They then utter a kind of melodious chant, which gradually increases in strength, and in noise, until it fairly shakes the house, and it can be heard for a long distance." This observer of the "ring shout" also noted the agility of the dancers and the African call-and-response pattern in their chanting.

Many slaves continued to believe in spirit possession. Their belief resembled the African concept of the living dead—the idea that deceased relatives visit the earth for many years until the process of dying is complete. Slaves also practiced conjuration and quasi-magical root medicine. By the 1850s, the most notable conjurers and root doctors were reputed to live in South Carolina, Georgia, Louisiana, and other isolated coastal areas with high slave populations.

These cultural survivals provided slaves with a sense of a past. Such practices and beliefs were not static "Africanisms" or mere "retentions." They were cultural adaptations, living traditions re-formed in the Americas in response to new experience. African American slaves in the Old South were a people forged by two centuries of cultural mixture in the Atlantic world, and the South itself was a melding of many African and European cultural forces.

As they became African Americans, slaves also developed a sense of racial identity. In the colonial period, Africans had arrived in America from many different states and kingdoms, represented in distinctive languages, body markings, and traditions. Planters had used ethnic differences to create occupational hierarchies. By the early antebellum period, however, old ethnic identities gave way as American slaves increasingly saw themselves as a single group unified by race. Africans had arrived in the New World with virtually no concept of "race"; by the antebellum era, however, their descendants had learned through bitter experience that race was now the defining feature of their lives. They were a transplanted and transformed people.

9-6b Slaves' Religion and Music

As African culture gave way to a maturing African American culture, more and more slaves adopted Christianity. But they fashioned Christianity into an instrument of support and resistance. Theirs was a religion of justice and deliverance, quite unlike their masters' religious messages directed at them as a means of control. "You ought to have heard that preachin,'" said one man. "'Obey your master and mistress, don't steal chickens and eggs and meat,' but nary a word about havin' a soul to save." Slaves believed that Jesus cared about their souls and their plight. In their interpretations of biblical stories, as one historian has said, they were "literally willing themselves reborn." Just like their white owners or poorer whites in their region, blacks were drawn to revivalism, often attending the same Methodist camp meetings as their masters.

For slaves, Christianity was a religion of personal and group salvation. Devout men and women worshiped every day, "in the field or by the side of the road" or in special "prayer grounds" that afforded privacy. Some slaves held fervent secret prayer meetings that lasted far into the night. Many slaves nurtured an unshakable belief that God would enter history and end their bondage. They appropriated many of the Old Testament figures, such as Moses, and its greatest narratives, such as the Exodus story, to their own ends.

Slaves also adapted Christianity to African practices. In West African belief, devotees are possessed by a god so thoroughly that the god's own personality replaces the human personality. In the late antebellum era, Christian slaves experienced possession by the Protestant "Holy Spirit." The combination of shouting, singing, and dancing that seemed to overtake black worshipers formed the heart of their religious faith. "The old meeting house caught fire," recalled an ex-slave preacher. "The spirit was there . . . . God saw our need and came to us. I used to wonder what made people shout but now I don't. There is a joy on the inside and it wells up so strong that we can't keep still. It is fire in the bones. Any time that fire touches a man, he will jump." Out in brush arbors or in meetinghouses, slaves took in the presence of God, thrust their arms to heaven, made music with their feet, and sang away their woes. Many post-slavery black choirs could not perform properly without a good wooden floor to use as their "drum."

Rhythm and physical movement were crucial to slaves' religious experience. In black preachers' chanted sermons, which reached out to gather the sinner into a narrative of meanings and cadences along the way to conversion, an American tradition was born. The chanted sermon was both a message from Scripture and a patterned form that required audience response punctuated by "yes sirs!" and "amens!" But it was in song that the slaves left their most sublime gift to American culture.

Through the spirituals, slaves tried to impose order on the chaos of their lives. Many themes run through the lyrics of slave songs. Often referred to later as the "sorrow songs," they also anticipate imminent rebirth. Sadness could immediately give way to joy: "Did you ever stan' on a mountain, wash yo' hands in a cloud?" Rebirth was at the heart as well of the famous hymn "Oh, Freedom": "Oh, Oh,

Abby Aldrich Rockefeller Folk Art Museum, The Colonial Williamsburg Foundation. Gift of Dr. and Mrs. Richard M. Kain in memory of George Hay Kain.

▲ Drawing by Lewis Miller of a *Lynchburg Negro Dance*, Lynchburg, Virginia, August 18, 1853. This work of art shows the slaves' use of elaborate costumes, string instruments, and "the bones"—folk percussion instruments of African origin, held between the fingers and used as clappers.

Freedom / Oh, Oh, Freedom over me— / But before I'll be a slave, / I'll be buried in my grave, / And go home to my Lord, / And Be Free!"

This tension and sudden change between sorrow and joy animates many songs: "Sometimes I feel like a motherless chile … / Sometimes I feel like an eagle in the air, / … Spread my wings and fly, fly, fly!" Many songs also express a sense of intimacy and closeness with God. Some songs display an unmistakable rebelliousness, such as the enduring "He said, and if I had my way / If I had my way, if I had my way, / I'd tear this building down!" And some spirituals reached for a collective sense of hope in the black community as a whole.

> O, gracious Lord! When shall it be,
> That we poor souls shall all be free;
> Lord, break them slavery powers—
> Will you go along with me?
> Lord break them slavery powers,
> Go sound the jubilee!

In many ways, African American slaves converted the Christian God to themselves. They sought an alternative world to live in—a home other than the one fate had given

them on earth. In a thousand variations of songs, they fashioned survival out of their own cultural imagination.

9-6c The Black Family in Slavery

African American slaves clung tenaciously to the personal relationships that gave meaning to life. Although American law did not recognize slave families, masters permitted them; in fact, slave owners *expected* slaves to form families and have children. As a result, even along the rapidly expanding edge of the cotton kingdom, there was a normal ratio of men to women, young to old. On some of the largest cotton plantations of South Carolina, when masters allowed their slaves increased autonomy through work on the task system, the property accumulation in livestock, tools, and garden produce thus fostered led to more stable and healthier families.

Following African kinship traditions, African Americans avoided marriage between cousins (commonplace among aristocratic slave owners). By naming their children after relatives of past generations, African Americans emphasized their family histories. Kinship networks and broadly extended families are what held life together in many slave communities.

For enslaved women, sexual abuse and rape by white masters were ever-present threats to themselves and their family life. By 1860, there were 405,751 biracial people in the United States, comprising 12.5 percent of the African American population. White planters were sometimes open with their sexual abuse of slave women, but not in the way they talked about it. As Mary Chesnut remarked, sex between slaveholding men and their slave women was "the thing we can't name." Buying slaves for sex was all too common at the New Orleans slave market. In what was called the "fancy trade" (a "fancy" was a young, attractive slave girl or woman), females were often sold for prices as much as 300 percent higher than the average.

Enslaved women had to negotiate this confused world of desire, threat, and shame. Harriet Jacobs, who spent much of her youth and early adult years dodging her owner's relentless sexual pursuit, described this circumstance as "the war of my life." In recollecting her desperate effort to protect her children and help them find a way north to freedom, Jacobs asked a haunting question that many enslaved women carried with them to their graves: "Why does the slave ever love? Why allow the tendrils of the heart to twine around objects which may at any moment be wrenched away by the hand of violence?"

9-6d The Domestic Slave Trade

Separation by violence from those they loved, sexual appropriation, and sale were what enslaved families most feared and hated. Many struggled for years to keep their children together and, after emancipation, to reestablish contact with loved ones lost by forced migration and sale. Between 1820 and 1860, an estimated 1 million slaves were moved into the region extending from western Georgia to eastern Texas. When the Union army registered thousands of black marriages in Mississippi and Louisiana in 1864 and 1865, fully 25 percent of the men over the age of forty reported that they had been forcibly separated from a previous wife. Thousands of black families were disrupted every year to serve the needs of the expanding cotton economy.

▲ This photograph of five generations of an enslaved family, taken in Beaufort, South Carolina, in 1862, is silent but powerful testimony to the importance that enslaved African Americans placed on their ever-threatened family ties.

Library of Congress

Many antebellum white southerners made their living from the slave trade. A large slave trading firm such as Franklin & Armfield established its own credit system and a far-flung buying and distribution network from Richmond and Norfolk in Virginia, across Tennessee, and to the New Orleans market. They also owned their own ships for maritime transport of slaves, as well as jails for housing captives before their departures. The average time spent in a Norfolk jail for a slave awaiting transport in the Franklin & Armfield system was 117 days. Such firms ran businesses with full control over financing and supply chains of their objects of sale, all firmly within the law.

In South Carolina alone by the 1850s, there were more than one hundred slave-trading firms selling an annual average of approximately 6,500 slaves to southwestern states. Although southerners often denied it, vast numbers of slaves moved west by outright sale and not by migrating with their owners. A typical trader's advertisement read, "NEGROES WANTED. I am paying the highest cash prices for young and likely NEGROES, those having good front teeth and being otherwise sound." One estimate from 1858 indicated that slave sales in Richmond, Virginia, netted $4 million that year alone. A market guide to slave sales that same year in Richmond listed average prices for "likely ploughboys," ages twelve to fourteen, at $850 to $1,050; "extra number 1 fieldgirls" at $1,300 to $1,350; and "extra number 1 men" at $1,500.

Slave traders were practical, roving businessmen. They were sometimes considered degraded by white planters, but many slave owners did business with them. Market forces drove this commerce in humanity. At slave "pens" in cities like New Orleans, traders promoted "a large and commodious showroom … prepared to accommodate over 200 Negroes for sale." Traders did their utmost to make their slaves appear young, healthy, and happy, cutting gray whiskers off men, using paddles as discipline so as not to scar their merchandise, and forcing people to dance and sing as buyers arrived for an auction. When transported to the southwestern markets, slaves were often chained together in "coffles," which made journeys of 500 miles or more on foot.

The complacent mixture of racism and business among traders is evident in their own language. "I refused a girl 20 year[s] old at 700 yesterday," one trader wrote to another in 1853. "If you think best to take her at 700 I can still get her. She is very badly whipped but good teeth." Some sales were transacted at owners' requests, often for tragically inhumane reasons. "Bought a cook yesterday that was to go out of state," wrote a trader; "she just made the people mad that was all." Some traders demonstrated how deeply slavery and racism were intertwined. "I have bought the boy Isaac for 1100," wrote a trader in 1854 to his partner. "I think him very prime . . . . He is a . . . house servant . . . first rate cook . . . and splendid carriage driver. He is also a fine painter and varnisher and . . . says he can make a fine panel door . . . . Also he performs well on the violin . . . . He is a genius and its strange to say I think he is smarter than I am."

Missouri Historical Museum

▲ A bill of sale documents that this enslaved woman, Louisa, was owned by the young child whom she holds on her lap. In the future, Louisa's life would be subject to the child's wishes and decisions.

9-6e Strategies of Resistance

Slaves brought to their efforts at resistance the same common sense and determination that characterized their struggle to secure their family lives. The scales weighed heavily against overt revolution, and they knew it. But they seized opportunities to alter their work conditions. They sometimes slacked off when they were not being watched. Thus, owners complained that slaves "never would lay out their strength freely."

Daily discontent and desperation were also manifest in sabotage of equipment; in wanton carelessness about work; in theft of food, livestock, or crops; or in getting drunk on stolen liquor. Some slaves might just fall into recalcitrance. "I have a boy in my employ called Jim Archer," complained a Vicksburg, Mississippi, slaveholder in 1843. "Jim does not want to be under anyones control and says . . . he wants to go home this summer." A woman named Ellen, hired as a cook in Tennessee in 1856, quietly put mercury poison into a roasted apple for her unsuspecting mistress. And some enslaved women resisted as best they could by trying to control their

A slave coffle marching across the USA, before the Civil War (coloured engraving)/American School, (19th century)/PETER NEWARK'S PICTURES/Private Collection/Bridgeman Images

▲ A slave coffle on the march toward newly settled states of the Southwest.

own pregnancy, either by avoiding it or by seeking it as a way to improve their physical conditions.

Many individual slaves attempted to escape to the North, and some received assistance from the loose network known as the Underground Railroad (see "The Underground Railroad," Section 12-7d). But it was more common for slaves to escape temporarily to hide in the woods. Approximately 80 percent of fugitive slaves were male; women simply could not flee as readily because of their responsibility for children. Fear, disgruntlement over treatment, or family separation might motivate slaves to risk all in flight. Only a minority of those who tried such escapes ever made it to freedom in the North or Canada, but these fugitives made slavery a very insecure institution by the 1850s.

American slavery also produced some fearless revolutionaries. Gabriel's Rebellion involved as many as a thousand slaves when it was discovered in 1800, just before it would have exploded in Richmond, Virginia (see "Gabriel's Rebellion," Section 7-8b). According to controversial court testimony, a similar conspiracy existed in Charleston in 1822, led by a free black named Denmark Vesey. Born a slave in the Caribbean, Vesey won a lottery of $1,500 in 1799, bought his own freedom, and became a religious leader in the black community. According to one long-argued interpretation, Vesey was a heroic revolutionary

Nat Turner A slave who led a bloody rebellion in Southampton County, Virginia, in 1831.

determined to free his people or die trying. But in a recent challenge, historian Michael Johnson points out that the court testimony is the only reliable source on the alleged insurrection. Might the testimony reveal less of reality than of white South Carolina's fears of slave rebellion? The court, says Johnson, built its case on rumors and intimidated witnesses, and "conjured into being" an insurrection that was not about to occur in reality. Whatever the facts, when the arrests and trials were over, thirty-seven "conspirators" were executed, and more than three dozen others were banished from the state.

9-6f Nat Turner's Insurrection

The most famous rebel of all, **Nat Turner**, struck for freedom in Southampton County, Virginia, in 1831. The son of an African woman who passionately hated her enslavement, Nat Turner was a precocious child who learned to read when he was very young. Encouraged by his first owner to study the Bible, he enjoyed certain privileges but also endured hard work and changes of masters. His father successfully escaped to freedom.

Young Nat eventually became a preacher with a reputation for eloquence and mysticism. After nurturing his plan for several years, Turner led a band of rebels from farm to farm in the predawn darkness of August 22, 1831. The group severed limbs and crushed skulls with axes or killed their victims with guns. Before alarmed planters stopped them, Nat Turner and his followers had in forty-eight hours slaughtered sixty whites of both sexes and all ages. The rebellion was soon put down, and in retaliation whites killed slaves at random all over the region, including in adjoining states. Turner was eventually caught and then hanged. As many as two hundred African Americans, including innocent victims of marauding whites, lost their lives as a result of the rebellion.

Nat Turner remains one of the most haunting symbols in America's unresolved history with racial slavery and discrimination. While in jail awaiting execution, Turner was interviewed by a Virginia lawyer and slaveholder, Thomas R. Gray. Their intriguing creation, *The Confessions of Nat Turner*, became a best seller within a month of Turner's hanging. Turner told of his early childhood, his religious visions, his zeal to be free; Gray called the rebel a "gloomy fanatic," but in a manner that made him fascinating and produced one of the most remarkable documents in the annals of American slavery. In the wake of Turner's insurrection, many states passed stiffened legal codes against black education and religious practice.

Most important, in 1832 the state of Virginia, shocked to its core, held a full-scale legislative and public debate over gradual emancipation as a means of ridding itself of slavery and of blacks. The plan debated would not have freed any slaves until 1858, and it provided that eventually all blacks would be colonized outside Virginia. But when the House of Delegates voted, gradual abolition lost, 73 to 58. In the end, Virginia opted to do nothing except reinforce its own moral and economic defenses of slavery. It was the last time white southerners would debate any kind of emancipation until war forced their hand. And the United States itself, in its laws and institutions, fueled by the seemingly permanent, prosperous cotton South, remained a proslavery nation.

Imagining Nat Turner's Rebellion

Below is the title page from *The Confessions of Nat Turner*, by Thomas R. Gray, 1831. This document of nearly twenty pages was published by the lawyer, Gray, who recorded and likely refashioned Turner's lengthy statement during an interview in his jail cell before his execution. *The Confessions* became a widely sold and sensational documentation of Turner's identity and especially his motivations and methods during the rebellion. It portrayed Turner as a religious mystic and fanatic and allowed the broad public to imagine the mind of a religiously motivated slave rebel. Below and to the right is "Horrid Massacre in Virginia," 1831, woodcut. This composite of scenes depicts the slaughter of innocent women and children, as well as white men as both victims and resistants. The fear, confusion, and fierce retribution that dominated the aftermath of the Turner rebellion are on display here.

CRITICAL THINKING

■ Why was Nat Turner's insurrection such a shock to the nation as well as to the South?

■ What kind of impact did Nat Turner's rebellion have on the South's evolving defense of slavery in the coming decades?

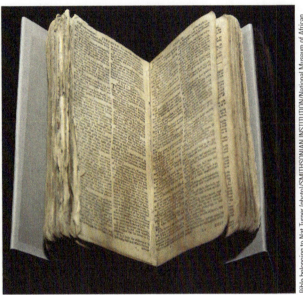

Bible belonging to Nat Turner (photo)/SMITHSONIAN INSTITUTION/National Museum of African American History & Culture, Smithsonian Institution, USA/Bridgeman Images

THE CONFESSIONS OF NAT TURNER, THE LEADER OF THE LATE INSURRECTION IN SOUTHAMPTON, VA.

AS FULLY AND VOLUNTARILY MADE TO THOMAS R. GRAY,

In the prison where he was confined, and acknowledged by him to be such when read before the Court of Southampton; with the certificate, under seal of the Court convened at Jerusalem, Nov. 5, 1831, for his trial.

ALSO, AN AUTHENTIC ACCOUNT OF THE WHOLE INSURRECTION, WITH Lists of the Whites who were Murdered, AND OF THE Negroes brought before the Court of Southampton, and there sentenced, &c.

RICHMOND:
PUBLISHED BY THOMAS R. GRAY.
T. W. WHITE, PRINTER.
1832.

Everett Collection

The Library of Congress

Reparations for Slavery

How should the United States come to terms with 250 years of racial slavery? Is this period best forgotten as a terrible passage that African Americans as well as the country transcended over time? Or does the nation owe a long-overdue debt to black people for their oppression? In the wake of emancipation in 1865, and rooted in vague federal promises, many former slaves believed they were entitled to "forty acres and a mule," but for most these never materialized.

In 1897, Callie House, a poor mother of four who had been born in 1865 in a contraband camp for ex-slaves, organized the National Ex-Slave Pension and Bounty Association, modeled after the pension system established for soldiers. House traveled all over the South, recruiting 250,000 members at 10-cent dues. Her lobbying of the federal government for slave pensions failed; she was accused of mail fraud and imprisoned for one year in 1916.

More recently, a widespread debate over "reparations" for slavery has emerged. In the rewriting of slavery's history since the 1960s, Americans have learned a great deal about how slave labor created American wealth: how insurance companies insured slaves, how complicit the U.S. government was in slavery's defense and expansion, and how slaves built the U.S. Capitol while their owners received $5 a month for their labor.

The debate is fueled by a wealth of analogies: the reparations paid to Japanese Americans interned during World War II; the reparations paid to many Native American tribes for their stolen land; the reparations paid to thousands of Holocaust survivors and victims of forced labor; and a suit settled in 1999 that will pay an estimated $2 billion to some twenty thousand black farmers for discrimination practiced by the Agriculture Department in the early twentieth century.

On the other side, some argue that, because there are no living former slaves or slaveholders, reparations for slavery can never take the form of money. But in 2002, a lawsuit was filed against three major corporations that allegedly profited from slavery. Some city councils have passed resolutions forcing companies that do business in their jurisdictions to investigate their possible past complicity with slave trading or ownership, which has prompted some banks and other firms to establish scholarship programs for African Americans.

Critics argue that resources would be better spent "making sure black kids have a credible education" and rebuilding inner cities. And some now say that the new Smithsonian Museum of African American History and Culture on the Mall in Washington, DC is, as a living memorial, a kind of reparations. Yet advocates contend that, when "government participates in a crime against humanity," it is "obliged to make the victims whole." The movement for reparations has strong support in grassroots black communities, and the issue has become the subject of broad public debate. The legacy of slavery for a people and a nation is America's most traumatic test of how to reconcile its history with justice.

CRITICAL THINKING

- What are the arguments for and against reparations for slavery?
- If the United States did implement some form of "reparations," would it lead to improved or worsened race relations in the nation?

Summary

During the four decades before the Civil War, the South grew in land, wealth, and power along with the rest of the country. Although the southern states were deeply enmeshed in the nation's heritage and political economy, they also developed as a distinctive region, ideologically and economically, because of slavery. Far more than the North, the antebellum South was a biracial society; whites grew up directly influenced by black folkways and culture; and blacks, the vast majority of whom were slaves, became predominantly native-born Americans and the cobuilders with whites of a rural, agricultural society. From the Old South until modern times, white and black southerners have always shared a tragic mutual history, and many are blood relatives.

With the cotton boom, as well as state and federal policies of Indian Removal, the South grew into a huge slave society. The coercive influence of slavery affected virtually every element of southern life and politics, and increasingly produced a leadership determined to preserve a conservative, hierarchical social and racial order. Despite the white supremacy that united them, the democratic values of yeomen often clashed with the profit motives of aristocratic planters. The benevolent self-image and paternalistic ideology of slaveholders ultimately had to stand the test of the slaves' own judgments. African American slaves responded by fashioning over time a rich, expressive folk culture and a religion of personal and group deliverance. Their experiences could be profoundly different from one region and kind of labor to another. Some blacks were crushed by bondage; many others transcended it in an epic of survival and resistance.

By 1850, through their own wits and on the backs of African labor, white southerners had aggressively built one of the last profitable, expanding slave societies on earth. North of them and deeply intertwined with them in the same nation, economy, constitutional system, and history, a different kind of society had grown even faster—driven by industrialism and free labor. The clash of these two deeply connected—yet mutually fearful and divided—societies would soon explode in political storms over the nation's future.

Suggestions for Further Reading

Ira Berlin, *Generations of Captivity: A History of African American Slaves* (2003)

David Brion Davis, *Inhuman Bondage: The Rise and Fall of Slavery in the New World* (2006)

Erskine Clarke, *Dwelling Place: A Plantation Epic* (2005)

Steven Deyle, *Carry Me Back: The Domestic Slave Trade in American Life* (2005)

Annette Gordon-Reed, *The Hemingses of Monticello: An American Family* (2008)

Charles Joyner, *Down by the Riverside: A South Carolina Slave Community* (1984)

James D. Miller, *South by Southwest: Planter Emigration and Identity in the Slave South* (2002)

James Oakes, *Slavery and Freedom: An Interpretation of the Old South* (1991)

Michael O'Brien, *Conjectures of Order: Intellectual Life and the American South, 1810–1860*, 2 vols. (2004)

Seth Rockman, *Scraping By: Wage Labor, Slavery, and Survival in Early Baltimore* (2009)

Calvin Schermerhorn, *The Business of Slavery and the Rise of American Capitalism, 1815-1860* (2015)

Daniel H. Usner Jr., *American Indians in the Lower Mississippi Valley* (1998)

MINDTAP
From Cengage

MindTap® is a fully online personalized learning experience built upon Cengage Learning content. MindTap® combines student learning tools—readings, multimedia, activities, and assessments—into a singular Learning Path that guides students through the course and helps students develop the critical thinking, analysis, and communication skills that are essential to academic and professional success.

10

The Restless North, 1815–1860

The four children, all under the age of ten, struggled to find their land legs. It was April 17, 1807, and they had spent the last twenty-five days on a stormy voyage from Scotland to New York. Their parents, Mary Ann and James Archbald, had left their ancestral homeland reluctantly, but envisioned a future in which their children would be beholden to no one—neither landlord nor employer. They had set sail in search of the Jeffersonian dream of republican independence.

The Archbalds bought a farm in central New York, along a tributary of the Hudson River, where they raised a large flock of sheep, grew hay and vegetables, skinned rabbits for their meat and fur—and then sold whatever food or fur the family did not need to feed or clothe itself. From the wool shorn by her husband and sons, Mary Ann and her daughters spun thread and wove cloth for their own use and for sale. They used the cash to pay their mortgage. Twenty-one years after leaving Scotland, Mary Ann, in anticipation of making their last payment, declared herself wealthy: "being out of debt is, in my estimation, being rich." By then, though, her sons were young adults and had their own visions of wealth. Theirs centered on water, not land.

Ten years earlier, on April 17, 1817—a decade to the day after the Archbalds had stepped onto American shores—the New York State legislature authorized construction of a canal that would connect Lake Erie to the Hudson River, and surveyors mapped a route that ran through the Archbalds' farm. The sons (one in his early twenties, the other a teenager) helped dig the canal, while Mary Ann and her daughters cooked and cleaned for the twenty Irish laborers whom the sons hired. Bitten by canal fever, the Archbald sons soon tried their hands at commercial speculation, borrowing

◀ Farm families transported their surplus produce and handicrafts to local marketplaces, where merchants purchased them for resale. American Scenes: Preparing for Market, published by N. Currier, 1856 (colour litho), Maurer, Louis (1832–1932) (after)/Private Collection/Peter Newark American Pictures/The Bridgeman Art Library

Chronology

1790s–1840s	■ Second Great Awakening
1820s	■ Model penitentiaries established
1820s–1840s	■ Utopian communities founded
1824	■ *Gibbons v. Ogden* prohibits steamboat monopolies
1825	■ Erie Canal completed
1826	■ American Society for Promotion of Temperance founded
1827	■ Construction begins on Baltimore and Ohio (B&O) Railroad
1830	■ First locomotive runs on B&O Railroad
	■ Joseph Smith organizes Mormon Church
1830s	■ Penny press emerges
1830s–1850s	■ Urban riots commonplace
1833	■ American Antislavery Society founded
1834	■ Women workers strike at Lowell
1837–42	■ Croton Aqueduct constructed
1839–43	■ Hard times spread unemployment and deflation
1840	■ Split in abolitionist movement; Liberty Party founded
1840s	■ Female mill workers' publications appear
1844	■ Federal government sponsors first telegraph line
	■ Lowell Female Reform Association formed
1845	■ Massive Irish immigration begins
1846	■ Smithsonian Institute founded
1848	■ American Association for the Advancement of Science established
1850s	■ Free-labor ideology spreads

money to buy wheat and lumber in western New York with the idea of reselling it at substantial profits to merchants in Albany and New York City. This was not the future Mary Ann had envisioned for her sons, and their ventures distressed, but did not surprise, her. As early as 1808, she had reached an unpleasant conclusion about her new home: "We are a nation of traders in spite of all Mr. Jefferson can say or do."

The United States may have already been a "nation of traders" as early as 1808, but in the years after the War of 1812, the market economy took off in ways few could have anticipated when the Archbald family decided to seek its independence in America. In the North, steamboats, canals, and then railroads remapped the young republic's geography and economy, setting off booms in westward migration, industry, commerce, and urban growth, and fueling optimism among commercially minded Americans.

Experience an interactive version of this story in MindTap®.

Although the transportation revolution would foster commercial exchange, technology alone could not make it happen. Even after the War of 1812, the United States' financial connections to Europe, particularly Britain, remained profound. When Europeans suffered hard times, so, too, did American merchants, manufacturers, farmers, workers—and their families. Particularly for those Americans who relied on wages for their livelihood, economic downturns often meant unemployment and destitution.

Economic downswings could shake even the most commercially committed northerners, as could other consequences of the economy's rapid expansion in the years after the War of 1812. Market expansion, some worried, threatened the nation's moral fiber if not properly controlled. It upset traditional patterns of family organization, and it relied heavily on unskilled workers—many of whom were immigrants and free African Americans—who at best seemed unfit for republican citizenship and at worst seemed threatening. The burgeoning cities spawned by market expansion seemed to bear out Thomas Jefferson's opinion that they were "pestilential to the morals, the health and the liberties of man." Like Jefferson, who also acknowledged that cities nourished the arts, commercially minded Americans could see cities as both exemplars of civilization and breeding grounds of depravity and conflict.

Anxious about the era's rapid changes, many Americans turned to evangelical religion, which in turn launched many of the era's myriad reform movements. Believing in the notion of human perfectibility, reformers worked to free individuals and society from sin. In the Northeast and Midwest, in particular, women and men organized to end the abuses of prostitution and alcohol, to improve conditions in prisons and asylums, and to establish public schools. Some embraced science as fervently as religion. Other reformers, instead of trying to fix society, established separate experimental communities that might model a new form of social relations. Opponents of slavery, meanwhile, worked within the existing system but sought to radically alter Americans' premises about the practical implications of the revolutionary declaration that "all men are created equal."

Only by maintaining a strong faith in improvement, progress, and upward mobility could these Americans remain hopeful that the nation's greatness lay with commercial expansion. They did so in part by articulating a free-labor ideology that at once rationalized the negative aspects of market expansion while promoting the northern labor system as superior to the South's.

- *What factors contributed to the commercialization of northern society, and why did they have less of an influence on the South?*

- *How did the daily lives—work, family, leisure—of northerners (rural and urban) change between 1815 and 1860?*

- *In what ways did reformers try to preserve existing American ideals, and in what ways did they try to change them?*

10-1 Or Was the North Distinctive?

▶ **What developments contributed to the divergence between the North and the South after the War of 1812?**

Historian James McPherson has proposed a new twist to the old question of southern distinctiveness: perhaps it was the *North*—New England, the Middle Atlantic, and the Old Northwest—that diverged from the norm. At the republic's birth, the North and South had much in common, with some similarities persisting for decades: slavery, religious heritage, an overwhelming proportion of the population engaged in agricultural pursuits, a small urban population. As late as the War of 1812, the regions were more similar than dissimilar. But all that started to change

with postwar economic development. Although often couched in nationalist terms, such development was undertaken mostly by state and local governments as well as private entrepreneurs, and it took place much more extensively and rapidly in the North. As the North embraced economic progress, it—rather than the South—diverged from the international norm. The North, writes McPherson, "hurtled forward eagerly toward a future that many Southerners found distasteful if not frightening." With its continual quest for improvement, the North—much more so than the South—embodied what Frenchman Alexis de Tocqueville, who toured the United States in 1831–1832, called the nation's "restless spirit."

While the South expanded as a slave society, the North changed rapidly and profoundly. It transformed, as one historian has put it, from a society with markets to a market society. In the colonial era, settlers lived in a society with markets, one in which they engaged in long-distance trade—selling their surpluses to merchants, who in turn sent raw materials to Europe, using the proceeds to purchase finished goods for resale—but in which most settlers remained self-sufficient. During and after the War of 1812, the North became more solidly a market society, one in which participation in long-distance commerce fundamentally altered individuals' aspirations and activities. With European trade largely halted during the war, entrepreneurs invested in domestic factories, setting off a series of changes in the organization of daily life. More men, women, and children began working for others in exchange for wages—rather than for themselves on a family farm—making the domestic demand for foodstuffs soar. The result was a transformation of agriculture itself. Farming became commercialized, with individual farmers abandoning self-sufficiency and specializing instead in crops that would yield cash on the market. With the cash that farmers earned when things went well, they now bought goods they had once made for themselves, such as cloth, candles, and soap as well as some luxuries. Unlike the typical southern yeoman, they were not self-reliant, and isolation was rare. In the North, market expansion altered, sometimes dramatically, virtually every aspect of life. Some historians see these rapid and pervasive changes as a market revolution.

10-2 The Transportation Revolution

▶ **What were the limitations of transportation methods prior to the War of 1812?**
▶ **How did transportation innovations developed after the War of 1812 shape American society?**
▶ **What regional connections were created because of transportation developments?**

To market goods at substantial distances from where they were produced, Americans needed internal improvements. Before the War of 1812, natural waterways provided the most readily available and cheapest transportation routes for people and goods, but with many limitations. Boatmen poled bateaux (cargo boats) down shallow rivers or floated flatboats down deep ones. Cargo generally moved downstream only, and most boats were broken up for lumber once they reached their destination. On portions of a few rivers, including the Mississippi and the Hudson, sailing ships could tack upstream under certain wind conditions, but upstream commerce was very limited.

10-2a Roads

Overland transport was limited, too. Roads, constructed during the colonial and revolutionary eras, often became obstructed by fallen trees, soaked by mud, or clouded in dust. To reduce mud and dust, turnpike companies built "corduroy" roads, whose tightly lined-up logs resembled ribbed cotton fabric. But the continual jolts caused nausea among passengers and discouraged merchants from shipping fragile wares. Land transportation was slow and expensive, demanding a good deal of human and animal power. In 1800, according to a report commissioned by the federal government, it cost as much to ship a ton of goods thirty miles into the country's interior as to ship the same goods from New York to England. The lack of cheap, quick transportation impeded westward expansion as well as industrial growth. When the Archbald family decided against moving to Ohio in 1810, Mary Ann Archbald explained, "It is at a great distance from markets."

After the American Revolution, some northern states chartered private stock companies to build turnpikes. These toll roads expanded commercial possibilities in southern New England and the Middle Atlantic, but during the War of 1812 the nation's paucity of roads in its more northerly and southerly reaches impeded the movement of troops and supplies, prompting renewed interest—in the name of defense—in building roads. Aside from the National Road (see "Early Internal Improvements," Section 8-6b), the financing fell on states and private investors, and generally the enthusiasm for building turnpikes greatly outpaced the money and manpower expended. Turnpike companies sometimes adopted improvements, such as laying hard surfaces made of crushed stone and gravel, but many of the newly built roads suffered from old problems. An urgent need arose not just for more, but also for better transportation.

10-2b Steamboats

The first major innovation was the steamboat. In 1807, Robert Fulton's *Clermont* traveled between New York and Albany on the Hudson River in thirty-two hours, demonstrating the feasibility of using steam engines to power boats. After the Supreme Court's ruling against steamboat monopolies in *Gibbons v. Ogden* (1824), steamboat companies flourished on eastern rivers and, to a lesser extent, on the Great Lakes. These boats carried more passengers than freight, transporting settlers to the Midwest, where they would grow grain and raise pigs that fed northeastern factory workers. Along western rivers like the Mississippi and the Ohio, steamboats played a more direct commercial role, carrying midwestern timber and grain and southern cotton to New Orleans,

Erie Canal Major canal that linked the Great Lakes to New York City, opening the upper Midwest to wider development.

where they were transferred to oceangoing vessels destined for northern and international ports. In the 1850s, steamboats began plying rivers as far west as California and Washington Territory. Privately owned and operated, steamboats became subject to federal regulations after frequent and deadly accidents in which boilers exploded, fires ignited, and boats collided.

To travel between Ohio and New Orleans by flatboat in 1815 took several months; in 1840, the same trip by steamboat took just ten days. But the steamboat did not supplant the flatboat. Rather, the number of flatboats traveling downstream to New Orleans more than doubled between 1816 and 1846. Now that flatboat crews could return upstream by steamboat rather than by foot, the greatest investment in flatboat travel—time—had been greatly reduced.

10-2c Canals

In the late eighteenth and early nineteenth centuries, private companies (sometimes with state subsidies) built small canals to transport goods and produce to and from interior locations previously accessible only by difficult-to-navigate rivers or by poorly maintained roads. These projects rarely reaped substantial profits, discouraging investment in other projects. In 1815, only three canals in the United States measured more than 2 miles long; the longest was 27 miles. After Madison's veto of the Bonus Bill (see "Sectionalism and Nationalism," Section 8-6) dashed commercially minded New Yorkers' hopes for a canal connecting Lake Erie to the port of New York, Governor DeWitt Clinton pushed for a state-sponsored initiative. What later became known as the **Erie Canal** was to run 363 miles between Buffalo and Albany, and was to be four feet deep. Skeptics derided it as "Clinton's Big Ditch."

But the optimists prevailed. Construction began—amid much symbolism and fanfare—on July 4, 1817. The canal, its promoters emphasized, would help fulfill the nation's revolutionary promise by demonstrating how American ingenuity and hard work could overcome any obstacle, including imposing natural ones, such as the combined ascent and descent of 680 feet between Buffalo and Albany. By so doing, it would help unify the nation and secure its commercial independence from Europe.

Over the next eight years, nearly nine thousand laborers felled forests, shoveled and piled dirt, picked at tree roots, blasted rock, heaved and hauled boulders, rechanneled streams, and molded the canal bed. Stonemasons and carpenters built aqueducts and locks. The work was dangerous, sometimes fatal, with workers succumbing to malaria, rattlesnake bites, gunpowder explosions, falls, and asphyxiation from collapsed canal beds.

The canal's promoters celebrated the waterway as the work of "republican free men," but few canal workers would have perceived their construction work as fulfilling Jefferson's notion of republican freedom. Unskilled laborers—including many immigrants and some convicts—greatly outnumbered artisans. Once completed, the Erie Canal relied on child labor: Boys led the horses who pulled the canal boats between the canal's eighty-three locks, while girls cooked and cleaned on the boats. When the canal froze shut in winter, many canal workers found themselves destitute, with neither employment nor shelter.

Once completed in 1825, the Erie Canal proved immediately successful. Horse-drawn boats, stacked with bushels of wheat, barrels of oats, and piles of logs, streamed eastward from Lake Erie and western New York. Tens of thousands of passengers—forty thousand in 1825 alone—traveled the waterway each year. The canal shortened the journey between Buffalo and New York City from twenty days to six and reduced freight charges by nearly 95 percent—thus securing New York City's position as the nation's preeminent port. Other states rushed to construct canals, and by 1840 canals crisscrossed the Northeast and Midwest, with mileage totaling 3,300. Southern states, with many easily navigable rivers, dug fewer canals. None of the new canals, North or South, enjoyed the Erie's financial success. As the high cost of construction combined with an economic contraction, investment slumped in the 1830s. Several midwestern states could not repay their canal loans, leading them to bankruptcy or near-bankruptcy. By midcentury, more miles were abandoned than built. The canal era had ended, though the Erie Canal (by then twice enlarged and rerouted) continued to prosper, remaining in commercial operation until the late twentieth century and even undergoing a minor resurgence today.

10-2d Railroads

The future belonged to railroads. Trains moved faster than canal boats and operated year-round. Railroads did not need to be built near natural sources of water, allowing them to connect remote locations to national and international markets. By 1860, the United States had 60,000 miles of track, most of it in the North. Railroads dramatically reduced the cost and the time involved in shipping goods, and excited the popular imagination.

The railroad era in the United States began in 1830 when Peter Cooper's locomotive, Tom Thumb, first steamed along 13 miles of Baltimore and Ohio Railroad track. In 1833, the nation's second railroad ran 136 miles from Charleston to Hamburg in South Carolina. Not until the 1850s, though, did railroads offer long-distance service at reasonable rates. Even then, the lack of a common standard for the width of track thwarted development of a national system. Pennsylvania and Ohio railroads, for example, had no fewer than seven different track widths. A journey from Philadelphia to Charleston involved eight different gauges, requiring passengers and freight to change trains seven times. Only at Bowling Green, Kentucky, did northern and southern railroads connect to one another. Although northerners and southerners alike raced to construct internal improvements, the nation's canals and railroads did little to unite the regions and promote nationalism, as the earliest proponents of government-sponsored internal improvements had hoped.

Northern governments and investors spent substantially more on internal improvements than did southerners.

▲ Railroads, introduced in the 1830s, soon surpassed canals. Easier, quicker, and cheaper to build than canals, they moved goods and people faster. The Mohawk & Hudson, pictured here, offered competition to the slower Erie Canal boats, yet its passenger cars (on the left) were styled after an even older technology: the stagecoach.

Map 10.1 Major Roads, Canals, and Railroads, 1850

A transportation network linked the seaboard to the interior. Settlers followed those routes westward, and they sent back grain, grain products, and cotton to the port cities.

Pennsylvania and New York together accounted for half of all state monies invested. Southern states did invest in railroads, but—with smaller free populations—they collected fewer taxes, leaving them with less to spend.

The North and South laid roughly the same amount of railroad track per person before the Civil War, but when measured in terms of overall mileage, the more populous North had a web of tracks that stretched considerably farther, forming an integrated system of local lines branching off major trunk lines. In the South, railroads remained local in nature, leaving southern travelers to patch together trips on railroads, stagecoaches, and boats. Neither people nor goods moved easily across the South, unless they traveled via steamboat or flatboat along the Mississippi River system—and even then, flooded banks disrupted passage for weeks at a time.

10-2e Regional Connections

Unlike southern investments in river improvements and steamboats, which disproportionately benefited planters whose lands bordered the region's riverbanks, the North's frenzy of canal and railroad building expanded transportation networks far into the hinterlands, proving not only more democratic but also more unifying. In 1815, nearly all the produce from the Old Northwest floated down the Mississippi to New Orleans, tying that region's fortunes to the South. By the 1850s, though, canals and railroads had strengthened the economic, cultural, and political links between the Old Northwest—particularly the more densely populated northern regions—and the Northeast (see Map 10.1).

Internal improvements hastened the population's westward migration. They eased the journey itself while also making western settlement more appealing by providing easy access to eastern markets and familiar comforts. News, visitors, and luxuries now traveled regularly to previously remote areas of the Northeast and Midwest. Delighted that the Erie Canal brought fresh seafood to central New York, hundreds of miles from the sea, Mary Archbald explained that "distance … is reduced to nothing here."

Samuel F. B. Morse's invention of the telegraph in 1844 made the compression of distance and time even starker. News traveled almost instantaneously along telegraph wires. By 1852, the nation had more than 23,000 miles of telegraph lines, which enabled the birth of modern business practices involving the coordination of market conditions, production, and supply across great distances. Together, internal improvements and the telegraph allowed people in previously isolated areas to proclaim themselves—as did one western New Yorker—a "citizen of the world."

10-2f Ambivalence Toward Progress

Many northerners hailed internal improvements as symbols of progress. Northerners proclaimed that, by building canals and railroads, they had completed God's design for the North American continent. On a more practical level, canals and railroads allowed them to seek opportunities in the West.

But people who welcomed such opportunities could find much to lament. Mary Ann Archbald savored her fresh seafood dinners but regretted that her sons turned to speculation. Others decried the enormous numbers of Irish canal diggers and railroad track layers, whom they deemed depraved and inherently inferior. Still others worried that, by promoting urban growth, transportation innovations fostered social ills.

The degradation of the natural world proved worrisome, too. When streams were rerouted, swamps drained, and forests felled, natural habitats were disturbed, even ruined. Humans soon felt the consequences. Deprived of waterpower, mills no longer ran. Without forests to sustain them, wild animals—on which many rural people (Native American and European American) had relied for protein—sought homes elsewhere. Fishermen, too, found their sources of protein (and cash) dried up when natural waterways were dammed or rerouted to feed canals. If many northerners embraced progress, they also regretted its costs.

10-3 Factories and Industrialization

▶ **How did the experience of work change with industrialization?**

▶ **What patterns of work and living were established in textile mills?**

▶ **How did factory workers seek to improve their workplace conditions and wages?**

By dramatically lowering transportation costs, internal improvements made possible the Northeast's rapid manufacturing and commercial expansion. After canals and railroads opened the trans-Appalachian West for wide-scale settlement, western farmers supplied raw materials and foodstuffs for northeastern factories and their workers. They also created a larger domestic market for goods manufactured in the Northeast. With most of their time devoted to cultivating their land, western settlers preferred to buy rather than make cloth, shoes, and other goods.

10-3a Factory Work

In many industries, daily life changed dramatically. Much early industrialization involved processing raw materials—milling flour, turning hogs into packaged meat, sawing lumber—

and the pork-packing industry illustrates strikingly how specialization turned skilled craftsmen into laborers. Traditionally, each butcher carved an entire pig. Under the new industrial organization, each worker performed a particular task—such as cutting off the right front leg or scooping out the entrails—as the pig traveled down a "disassembly line."

Factory work, with its impersonal and regimented nature, contrasted sharply with the informal atmosphere of artisan shops and farm households. The bell, the steam whistle, or the clock governed work. In large factories, laborers never saw owners, working instead under paid supervisors, nor did they see the final product of their labor. Factory workers lost their sense of autonomy in the face of impersonal market forces. Competition from cheaper, less-skilled workers—particularly after European immigration soared in the 1840s—created job insecurity and few opportunities for advancement.

Machinery made mass production possible. Although initially Americans imported or copied British machines, they soon built their own. The **American System of Manufacturing**, as the British called it, produced interchangeable parts that did not require individual adjustment to fit. Eli Whitney, the cotton gin's inventor, promoted the idea of interchangeable parts in 1798, when he contracted with the federal government to make ten thousand rifles in twenty-eight months. In the 1820s, the United States Ordnance Department contracted with private firms to introduce machine-made interchangeable parts for firearms. The American System quickly produced the machine-tool industry—the manufacture of machines for the purpose of mass production. The new system permitted large-scale production at low costs, with items such as Waltham watches becoming inexpensive but high-quality household items.

10-3b Textile Mills

Mechanization was most dramatic in textiles, with production centered in New England, near water sources to power spinning machines and looms. After 1815, New England's rudimentary cotton mills developed into modern factories with mass-produced goods. Cotton cloth production rose from 4 million yards in 1817 to 323 million in 1840. Mechanization did not make workers obsolete; rather, it demanded more workers to monitor the machines. In the mid-1840s, the cotton mills employed approximately eighty thousand "operatives," more than half of them women. Mill owners employed a resident manager, thus separating ownership from management.

With labor scarce near the mills, managers recruited New England farm daughters, whom they paid wages and housed in dormitories and boardinghouses in what became known as the **Waltham** or **Lowell** plan of industrialization. People

American System of Manufacturing System of manufacturing that used interchangeable parts.

Waltham, Lowell Sites of early textile mills in New England, which were precursors to modern factories. Nearly 80 percent of the workers in Waltham, Lowell, and similar mills were young, unmarried women who sought economic opportunities and social independence in the mill towns.

Internal Improvements

On July 4, 1827, ninety-one-year-old Charles Carroll, the only surviving signer of the Declaration of Independence, shoveled the first spadeful of earth on the Baltimore and Ohio Railroad, the nation's first westward railroad. "I consider this moment the most important act of my life," he declared, "second only to my signing the Declaration of Independence, if even it be second to that." Internal improvements, he and many others believed, would cement the United States' economic independence by supplying the nation's growing industrial centers with food and raw materials, while transporting manufactured goods back to its far-flung rural population.

Although boosters championed the era's canals and railroads as the triumph of American republicanism, such transportation projects often depended on technology, funding, and labor from abroad. American engineers scrutinized canals and, later, railroads in France, the Low Countries, and particularly England; one Erie Canal engineer spent nearly two years walking 2,000 miles alongside British canals. Railroad companies purchased locomotives from English manufacturers. Foreign investors, meanwhile, financed significant portions of projects heralded as symbols of American independence. In addition to borrowing know-how and money from abroad, Americans looked overseas for people to build their canals and railroads. Thousands of immigrants, mostly from Ireland, worked sunup to sundown blasting boulders, draining malaria-filled swamps, picking at roots and rocks, and heaving dirt. After the Civil War, Chinese immigrants performed similarly arduous and dangerous tasks on the transcontinental railroad.

When completed, internal improvements allowed people, raw materials, and goods to move inexpensively and quickly across the continent, spurring the young nation's growth—but also strengthening its ties to Europe. Eastward from the American heartland came cotton and grain, much of which was transferred to oceangoing vessels. The cotton fed European textile mills; the grain fed their workers. Thus, whenever economic conditions constricted in Europe, slowing textile production and leaving workers with smaller incomes with which to purchase food, reverberations could be felt on cotton and wheat farms across America.

Canals and railroads, hailed as great symbols of American independence, linked American farmers to an increasingly complex and volatile international economy.

CRITICAL THINKING

■ At mid-century, the United States, particularly the northern part, was undergoing tremendous change in terms of transportation and industrialization. What domestic and international forces drove these changes?

Erie Canal, NY, 1831 (graphite, w/c and gouache on paper), Hill, John William (1812-79) / © Collection of the New York Historical Society, USA / The Bridgeman Art Library

▲ Workers repair a section of the Erie Canal, near Little Falls, in 1831. While hailed as a great achievement of human progress, the canal required frequent repairs, frustrating travelers, merchants, boat workers, and people living along its banks.

who made their living from farming often harbored suspicions of those who did not—particularly in the young United States, where an agrarian lifestyle was often associated with virtue itself—so some rural parents resisted sending their daughters to textile mills. To ease such concerns, mill managers offered paternalistic oversight; they enforced curfews, prohibited alcohol, and required church attendance.

Despite its restrictions, the Waltham system offered farm girls opportunities to socialize and to earn wages, which they used to help their families buy land or send a brother to college, to save for their own dowries or education, or to spend on personal items, such as fashionable clothing. Workers wrote literary pieces for the owner-subsidized *Lowell Offering* and attended educational lectures in the evenings. Still, most women imagined factory work as temporary, and factory conditions—the power looms' deafening roar, the long hours, the regimentation—made few change their minds. The average girl arrived at sixteen and stayed five years, usually leaving to get married, often to men they met in town rather than to farm boys at home.

Although the Waltham plan drew international attention for its novelty, more common was the Rhode Island (or Fall River) plan employed by Samuel Slater, among others. Mills hired entire families, lodging them in boardinghouses. Men often worked farm plots near the factories while their wives and children worked in the mills, though as the system developed, men increasingly worked in the factories full time, directly supervising the labor of their wives and children in small, family-based work units.

10-3c Labor Protests

Mill life grew more difficult, especially during the depression of 1837 to 1843, when demand for cloth declined, causing most mills to run part time. To increase productivity, managers sped up machines and required each worker to operate more machines. In the race for profits, owners lengthened hours, cut wages, tightened discipline, and packed the boardinghouses.

Workers organized, accusing their bosses of treating them like wage slaves. In 1834, in reaction to a 25 percent wage cut, they unsuccessfully "turned out" (struck) against the Lowell mills. Two years later, when boardinghouse fees increased, they again turned out, unsuccessfully. With conditions worsening and strikes failing, workers resisted in new ways. In 1844, Massachusetts mill women formed the Lowell Female Reform Association and joined other workers in pressing, unsuccessfully, for state legislation mandating a ten-hour day—as opposed to the fourteen-hour days that some workers endured.

Women aired their complaints in worker-run newspapers: in 1842, the *Factory Girl* appeared in New Hampshire, the *Wampanoag, and Operatives' Journal* in Massachusetts. Two years later, mill workers founded the *Factory Girl's Garland* and the *Voice of Industry*, nicknamed "the factory girl's voice." Even the *Lowell Offering*, the owner-sponsored paper that was the pride of mill workers and managers alike, became embroiled in controversy when workers charged its editors with suppressing articles criticizing working conditions.

Worker turnover weakened organizational efforts. Few militant native-born mill workers stayed to fight the managers and owners, and gradually, fewer New England daughters entered the mills. In the 1850s, Irish immigrant women replaced them. Technological improvements made the work less skilled, enabling mills to hire inexperienced, lower-paid laborers. Male workers, too, protested changes wrought by the **market economy** and factories. But, unlike women, they could vote. Labor political parties first formed in Pennsylvania, New York, and Massachusetts in the 1820s, and then spread elsewhere; they advocated free public education and an end to imprisonment for debt, and opposed banks and monopolies. Some advocated free homesteads, a reminder that most early industrial workers still aspired to land ownership.

10-3d Labor Unions

The courts provided organized labor's greatest victory: protection from conspiracy laws. When journeyman shoemakers organized during the century's first decade, their employers accused them of criminal conspiracy. The cordwainers' (shoemakers') cases between 1806 and 1815 left labor organizations in an

> **market economy** Newly developing commercial economy that depended on the long-distance exchange of goods and crops produced for sale rather than for personal consumption.

▲ Published between 1840 and 1845, the *Lowell Offering* showcased women mill workers' essays, stories, and letters.

uncertain position. Although the courts acknowledged the journeymen's right to organize, judges viewed strikes as illegal until a Massachusetts case, **Commonwealth v. Hunt** (1842), ruled that Boston journeyman bootmakers could strike "in such manner as best to subserve their own interests," in the words of the state's chief justice Lemuel Shaw. Although the ruling applied to Massachusetts only, Shaw's national eminence extended the ruling's influence beyond the state's boundaries.

The first unions represented journeymen in printing, woodworking, shoemaking, and tailoring. Locally organized, they resembled medieval guilds, with members seeking protection against competition from inferior workmen by regulating apprenticeships and establishing minimum wages. Umbrella organizations composed of individual craft unions, like the National Trades' Union (1834), arose in several cities in the 1820s and 1830s. But the movement disintegrated amid wage reductions and unemployment in the hard times of 1839–1843.

Permanent labor organizations were difficult to sustain. Skilled craftsmen disdained less-skilled workers. Moreover, workers divided along ethnic, religious, racial, and gender lines.

10-4 Consumption and Commercialization

▶ What factors contributed to the emergence and development of the ready-made clothing industry in the first half of the nineteenth century?

▶ How did agricultural production and work change in the first half of the nineteenth century?

▶ What were the social and economic consequences of the emergence of commercial production?

By producing inexpensive cloth, New England mills spawned the ready-made clothing industry. Before the 1820s, women sewed most clothing at home, and some people purchased used clothing. Tailors and seamstresses made wealthy men's and women's clothing to order. By the 1820s and 1830s, much clothing was mass-produced for sale in retail clothing stores. The process often involved little more than the reorganization of work; tailors no longer performed every task involved in making an article of clothing, from measuring to finishing work. Standard sizes replaced measuring, and a division of labor took hold: one worker cut patterns all day, another sewed hems, another affixed buttons, still another attached collars. The sewing machine, invented in 1846 and widely available in the 1850s, accelerated the process. Although many farm families still made their own clothing, they bought clothes when they could afford to do so, freeing time for raising both crops and children.

Commonwealth v. Hunt An 1842 court case in which the Massachusetts Supreme Judicial Court ruled that labor unions were not illegal monopolies that restrained trade.

10-4a The Garment Industry

Market expansion created a demand for mass-produced clothing. Girls who left farms for factories no longer had time to sew clothes. Young immigrant men—often separated by thousands of miles from mothers and sisters—bought the crudely made, loose-fitting clothing. But the biggest market for ready-made clothes, at least initially, was in the cotton South. With the textile industry's success driving up the demand and price for raw cotton, planters bought ready-made shoes and clothes for slaves, in whose hands they would rather place a hoe than a needle and thread. Doing so made good economic sense.

Retailers often bought goods wholesale, though many manufactured shirts and trousers in their own factories. Lewis and Hanford of New York City boasted of cutting more than 100,000 garments in the winter of 1848–1849. The New York firm did business mostly in the South and owned a retail outlet in New Orleans. Paul Tulane, a New Orleans competitor, owned a New York factory that made goods for his Louisiana store. In the Midwest, Cincinnati became the center of the men's clothing industry. Nationally, though, New York remained the garment industry's capital.

The garment industry often took the form of what some historians call metropolitan industrialization, a form relying not on mechanization but on reorganization of labor, similar to the earlier putting-out system. Much production of ready-made clothing, for example, took place in tenements throughout New York City, where women spent hour after hour sewing on buttons for a piece of ready-made clothing, while others sewed hem after hem. In 1860, more than 16,000 women worked in New York's garment industry.

10-4b Specialization of Commerce

Commerce expanded with manufacturing. Commercial specialization transformed some traders in big cities, especially New York, into virtual merchant princes. After the Erie Canal opened, New York City became a stop on every major trade route from Europe, southern ports, and the West. New York traders were the intermediaries for southern cotton and western grain. Merchants in other cities played a similar role. Traders in turn sometimes invested their profits in factories, further stimulating urban manufacturing. Some cities specialized: Rochester became a milling center ("The Flour City"), and Cincinnati ("Porkopolis") became the first meatpacking center.

Merchants who engaged in complex commercial transactions required large office staffs, mostly all male. At the bottom of the hierarchy were messenger boys, often preteens, who delivered documents. Above them were copyists, who hand-copied documents. Clerks processed documents and shipping papers and did translations. Above them were the bookkeeper and the confidential chief clerk. Those seeking employment in such an office, called a countinghouse, often studied under a writing master to acquire a "good hand." Most hoped to become partners, but their chances of success grew increasingly slim.

Commerce specialized more quickly in cities than in small towns, where merchants continued to exchange goods with local farm women—trading flour or pots and pans for eggs and other produce. Local craftsmen continued to sell their own finished goods, such as shoes and clothing. In some

Everett Collection Historical/Alamy

▲ Although many women in New York's garment industry worked in their tenements, others labored in factories, where regimentation and close supervision characterized the work day.

rural areas, particularly newly settled ones, peddlers acted as general merchants. But as transportation improved and towns grew, small-town merchants increasingly specialized.

10-4c Commercial Farming

Even amid the manufacturing and commercial booms, agriculture remained the northern economy's backbone. But the **transportation revolution** and market expansion transformed formerly semisubsistence farms into commercial enterprises, with families abandoning mixed agriculture for specialization in cash crops. By the 1820s, eastern farmers had cultivated nearly all the available land, and their small farms, often with uneven terrains, were ill suited for the labor-saving farm implements introduced in the 1830s, such as mechanical sowers, reapers, and threshers. Many northern farmers thus either moved west or quit farming for jobs in merchants' houses and factories.

Those farmers who remained, however, proved as adaptable on the farm as were their children working at water-powered looms or in countinghouses. In 1820, about one-third of all northern produce was intended for the market, but by 1850 the amount surpassed 50 percent. As farmers shifted toward specialization and market-oriented production, they often invested in additional land (buying the farms of neighbors who moved west), new farming equipment (such as improved

iron and steel plows), and new sources of labor (hired hands). Many New England and Middle Atlantic farm families faced steep competition from midwestern farmers after the opening of the Erie Canal, and began abandoning wheat and corn production. Instead, they raised livestock, especially cattle, and specialized in vegetable and fruit production. Much of what they produced ended up in the stomachs of the North's rapidly growing urban and manufacturing populations.

Farmers financed innovations through land sales and debts. Indeed, increasing land values, not the sale of agricultural products, promised the greatest profit. Farm families who owned their own land flourished, but it became harder to take up farming in the first place. The number of tenant farmers and hired hands increased, providing labor to drive commercial expansion. Farmers who had previously employed unpaid family members and enslaved workers now leased portions of their farms or hired paid labor to raise their livestock and crops.

10-4d Farm Women's Changing Labor

As the commercial economy expanded, rural women assumed additional responsibilities, increasing

transportation revolution
Innovations in the movement of people and goods—via canals, steamships, and railroads—that greatly increased the speed of travel even as they greatly decreased its cost.

their already substantial farm and domestic work. Some did outwork (see "Putting-Out and Early Factories," Section 8-5c). Many increased their production of eggs, dairy products, and garden produce for sale; others raised bees or silkworms.

With the New England textile mills producing more and more finished cloth, farm women and children often abandoned time-consuming spinning and weaving, bought factory-produced cloth, and dedicated the saved time to producing larger quantities of marketable products, such as butter and cheese. Some mixed-agriculture farms converted entirely to dairy production, with men taking over formerly female tasks. Canals and railroads carried cheese to eastern ports, where wholesalers sold it around the world, shipping it to California, England, and China. In 1844, Britain imported more than 5 million pounds of cheese from the United States.

10-4e Rural Communities

Although agricultural journals and societies exhorted farmers to manage their farms like time-efficient businesses, not all farmers abandoned the old practices of gathering at market, general stores, taverns, and church. They did not forgo barn raisings and husking bees, but by the 1830s there were fewer young people at such events to dance and flirt. Many young women had left for textile mills, and young men often worked as clerks or factory hands. Those who stayed behind were more likely to come dressed in store-bought clothing and to consume pies made with store-bought flour.

Even as they continued to swap labor and socialize with neighbors, farmers became more likely to reckon debts in dollars. They kept tighter accounts and watched national and international markets more closely. When financial panics hit, cash shortages almost halted business activity, casting many farmers further into debt, sometimes to the point of bankruptcy. Faced with the possibility of losing their land, farmers did what many would have considered unthinkable before: they called in debts with their neighbors, sometimes causing fissures in long-established relationships.

10-4f Cycles of Boom and Bust

The market economy's expansion led to cycles of boom and bust. Prosperity stimulated demand for finished goods, such as clothing and furniture. Increased demand in turn led not only to higher prices and still higher production, but also, because of business optimism and expectations of higher prices, to land speculation. Investment money was plentiful as Americans saved and foreign, mostly British, investors bought U.S. bonds and securities. Then production surpassed demand, causing prices and wages to fall; in response, land and stock values collapsed, and investment money flowed out of the United States. This boom-and-bust cycle influenced the entire country, but particularly the Northeast, where even the smallest localities became enmeshed in regional and national markets.

Panic of 1837 Financial crisis of international origins that led to bankruptcies, bank failures, and unemployment

Although the 1820s and 1830s were boom times, financial panic triggered a bust cycle in 1837, the year after the Second Bank of the United States closed. Economic contraction remained severe through 1843. Internal savings and foreign investments declined sharply. Many banks could not repay their depositors, and states, facing deficits because of the economy's decline, defaulted on their bonds. Because of the **Panic of 1837**, European, especially British, investors became suspicious of all U.S. loans and withdrew money from the United States.

Hard times had come. Philadelphia took on an eerie aura. "The streets seemed deserted," Sidney George Fisher observed in 1842. "The largest [merchant] houses are shut up and to rent, there is no business . . . no money, no confidence." New York countinghouses closed their doors. Former New York mayor Philip Hone later observed, "A deadly calm pervades this lately flourishing city. No goods are selling, no businesses stirring." The hungry formed lines in front of soup societies, and beggars crowded the sidewalks. Some workers looted. Crowds of laborers demanding their deposits gathered at closed banks. Sheriffs sold seized property at one-quarter of its former value. In smaller cities like Lynn, Massachusetts, shoemakers weathered hard times by fishing and tending gardens, while laborers became scavengers, digging for clams and harvesting dandelions. Once-prosperous businessmen—some victims of the market, others of their own recklessness—lost nearly everything, prompting Congress to pass the Federal Bankruptcy Law of 1841; by the time the law was repealed two years later, 41,000 bankrupts had sought protection under its provisions.

10-5 Families in Flux

▶ How did the emergence of the market economy contribute to changes in families and familial organization?

▶ What role did women play in the management of the home and in the family economy?

▶ How did the role of children in the family change in the first half of the nineteenth century?

Anxieties about economic fluctuations reverberated beyond factories and countinghouses into northern homes. Sweeping changes in the household economy, rural as well as urban, led to new family ideals. In the preindustrial era, the family had been primarily an economic unit; now it became a moral and cultural institution, though in reality few families could live up to the new ideal.

10-5a The "Ideal" Family

In the North, the market economy increasingly separated the home from the workplace, leading to a new middle-class ideal in which men functioned in the public sphere while women oversaw the private or domestic sphere. The home became, in theory, an emotional retreat from the competitive, selfish world of business, where men increasingly focused on their work, eager to prosper yet fearful of failure in the unpredictable market economy. At the home's center was a couple that married for love rather than for economic considerations. Men provided and protected,

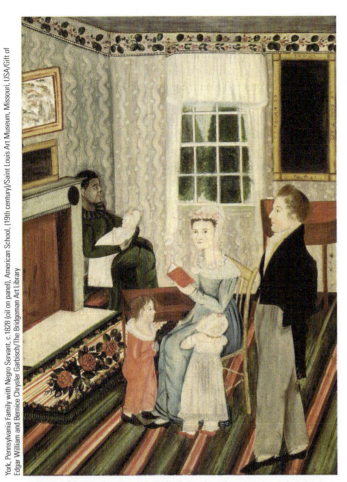

York, Pennsylvania Family with Negro Servant, c.1828 (oil on panel), American School, (19th century)/Saint Louis Art Museum, Missouri, USA/Gift of Edgar William and Bernice Chrysler Garbisch/The Bridgeman Art Library

▲ As they strove to live according to new domestic ideals, middle-class families often relied on African American or immigrant servants, who sacrificed time with their own children in order to care for their employers' children.

while women nurtured and guarded the family's morality, making sure that capitalism's excesses did not invade the private sphere. Childhood focused more on education than on work, and the definition of childhood itself expanded: children were to remain at home until their late teens or early twenties. This ideal became known as separate-sphere ideology, or sometimes the cult of domesticity or the cult of true womanhood. Although it rigidly separated the male and female spheres, this ideology gave new standing to domestic responsibilities. In her widely read *Treatise on Domestic Economy* (1841), Catharine Beecher approached housekeeping as a science even as she trumpeted mothers' role as their family's moral guardian. Although Beecher advocated the employment of young, single women as teachers, she believed that, once married, women belonged at home. She maintained that women's natural superiority as moral, nurturing caregivers made them especially suited for teaching (when single) and parenting (once married). Although Beecher saw the public sphere as a male domain, she insisted that the private sphere be elevated to the same status as the public.

10-5b Shrinking Families

These new domestic ideals depended on smaller families in which parents, particularly mothers, could offer children

greater attention, education, and financial help. With the market economy, parents could afford to have fewer children because children no longer played a vital economic role. Urban families produced fewer household goods, and commercial farmers, unlike self-sufficient ones, did not need large numbers of workers year-round, turning instead to hired laborers during peak work periods. Although smaller families resulted in part from first marriages' taking place at a later age—shortening the period of potential childbearing—they also resulted from planning, made easier when cheap rubber condoms became available in the 1850s. Some women chose, too, to end accidental pregnancies with abortion.

In 1800, American women bore seven or eight children; by 1860, five or six. This decline occurred even though many immigrants with large-family traditions were settling in the United States; thus, the birth rate among native-born women declined even more sharply. Although rural families remained larger than urban ones, birth rates among both groups declined comparably.

Yet even as birth rates fell, few northern women could fulfill the middle-class ideal of **separate spheres**. Most wage-earning women provided essential income for their families and could not stay home. They often saw domestic ideals as oppressive, as middle-class reformers mistook poverty for immorality, condemning working mothers for letting their children work or scavenge rather than attend school. Although most middle-class women stayed home, new standards of cleanliness and comfort proved time-consuming. These women's contributions to their families were generally assessed in moral terms, even though their economic contributions were significant. When they worked inside their homes, they provided, without remuneration, the labor for which wealthier women paid when they hired domestic servants to perform daily chores. Without servants, moreover, women could not devote themselves primarily to their children's upbringing, placing the ideals of the cult of domesticity beyond the reach of many middle-class families.

10-5c Women's Paid Labor

In working-class families, girls left home as early as age twelve to begin a lifetime of wage earning, with only short respites for bearing and rearing children. Unmarried girls and women worked primarily as domestic servants or in factories; married and widowed women worked as laundresses, seamstresses, and cooks. Some hawked food and wares on city streets; others did piecework at home, earning wages in the putting-out system; and some became prostitutes. Few such occupations enabled women to support themselves or a family comfortably.

separate spheres Middle-class ideology that emerged with the market revolution and divided men's and women's roles into distinct and separate categories based on their perceived gender differences, abilities, and social functions. Men were assigned the public realm of business and politics, while women were assigned to the private world of home and family. In practice, however, few families adhered strictly, if at all, to this ideology.

Middle-class Americans sought to keep daughters closer to home, except for brief stints as mill girls or, especially, as teachers. In the 1830s, Catharine Beecher successfully campaigned for teacher-training schools for women. She argued in part for women's moral superiority and in part for their economic value; because these women would be single, she contended, they need not earn as much as their male counterparts, whom she presumed to be married, though not all were. Unmarried women earned about half the salary of male teachers. By 1850, school-teaching had become a woman's profession. Many women worked as teachers, usually for two to five years.

The proportion of single women in the population increased significantly in the nineteenth century. In the East, some single women would have preferred to marry but market and geographic expansion worked against them: more and more young men headed west in search of opportunity, leaving some eastern communities disproportionately female in makeup. Other women chose to remain independent, seeking opportunities opened by the market economy and urban expansion. Because women's work generally paid poorly, those who forswore marriage faced serious challenges, leaving many single women dependent on charitable or family assistance.

10-6   The Growth of Cities

▶ How did urban environments emerge and expand in the first half of the nineteenth century?

▶ What strains did urban development place on the city and its residents?

▶ How did ethnic and racial tensions manifest themselves in urban environments?

▶ What forms of culture emerged in urban environments?

To many contemporary observers, cities symbolized what market expansion had wrought—for better or for worse—on northern society. No period in American history saw more rapid urbanization than the years between 1820 and 1860. The percentage of people living in urban areas (defined as a place with a population of 2,500 or more) grew from just over 7 percent in 1820 to nearly 20 percent in 1860. Most of this growth took place in the Northeast and the Midwest. Although most northerners continued to live on farms or in small villages, the population of individual cities boomed. Many of those residents were temporary—soon moving on to another city or the countryside—and many came from foreign shores.

10-6a   Urban Boom

Even as new cities sprang up, existing cities grew tremendously (see Map 10.2). In 1820, the United States had thirteen places with a population of ten thousand or more; in 1860, it had ninety-three. New York City, already the nation's largest city in 1820, saw its population grow from 123,706 people in that year to 813,669 in 1860—a growth factor of six and a half times. Philadelphia, the nation's second-largest city in both 1820 and 1860, saw the size of its population multiply ninefold during that same forty-year period. In 1815, Rochester, New York, had a population of just 300 persons. By 1830, the Erie Canal had turned the sleepy agricultural town into a bustling manufacturing center; now the nation's twenty-fifth-largest city, its population was just over 9,000 and continued to multiply at fantastic rates. By 1860, it had more than 48,000 residents.

Cities expanded geographically as well. In 1825, Fourteenth Street was New York City's northern boundary. By 1860, 400,000 people lived above that divide, and Forty-second Street was the city's northern limit. Gone were the cow pastures, kitchen gardens, and orchards. Public transit made city expansion possible. Horse-drawn omnibuses appeared in New York in 1827, and the Harlem Railroad, completed in 1832, ran the length of Manhattan. By the 1850s, all big cities had horse-drawn streetcars, allowing wealthier residents who could afford the fare to settle on larger plots of land on the cities' outskirts.

10-6b   Market-Related Development

The North urbanized more quickly than the South, but what was most striking about northern urbanization was where it took place. With only a few exceptions, southern cities were seaports, whereas the period between 1820 and 1860 saw the creation of many inland cities in the North—usually places that sprang to life with the creation of transportation lines or manufacturing establishments. The Boston Manufacturing Company, for example, selected the site for Lowell, Massachusetts, because of its proximity to the Merrimack River, whose rapidly flowing waters could power its textile mill. Incorporated in 1826, by the 1850s Lowell was the second-largest city in New England.

Northern cities developed elaborate systems of municipal services but lacked adequate taxing power to provide services for all. At best, they could tax property adjoining new sewers, paved streets, and water mains. New services and basic sanitation depended on residents' ability to pay. Another solution was to charter private companies to sell basic services, such as providing gas for lights. Baltimore first chartered a private gas company in 1816. By midcentury, every major city had done so. Private firms lacked the capital to build adequate water systems, though, and they laid pipe only in commercial and well-to-do residential areas, bypassing the poor. The task of supplying water ultimately fell on city governments.

10-6c   Extremes of Wealth

Throughout the United States, wealth was concentrating with a relatively small number of people. By 1860, the top 5 percent of American families owned more than half of the nation's wealth, and the top 10 percent owned nearly three-quarters. In the South, the extremes of wealth were most apparent on rural plantations, but in the North, cities provided the starkest evidence of economic inequities.

Despite the optimistic forecasts of early textile manufacturers that American industrialization need not engender the poverty and degradation associated with European industrialization, America's industrial cities soon resembled European ones. A number of factors contributed to widespread poverty: poor wages, the inability of many workers to secure full-time

Map 10.2 Major American Cities in 1820 and 1860

The number of Americans who lived in cities increased rapidly between 1820 and 1860, and the number of large cities grew as well. In 1820, only New York City had a population exceeding 100,000; forty years later, eight more cities had surpassed that level.

Female Guardian Society, Home for the Friendless, 29th Street, New York, July 4, 1864 (b/w photo)/American Photographer, (19th century)/NEW YORK HISTORICAL SOCIETY,/© Collection of the New-York Historical Society, USA/Bridgeman Images

▲ Visible signs of urban poverty in the 1850s were the homeless and orphaned children, most of them immigrants, who wandered the streets of New York City. The Home for the Friendless Orphanage, at Twenty-ninth Street and Madison Avenue, provided shelter for some of the orphan girls.

employment, and the increasingly widespread employment of women and children, which drove down wages for everyone. Women and children, employers rationalized, did not need a living wage because they were—in the employers' way of thinking—dependent by nature and did not require a wage that allowed self-sufficiency. In reality, though, not all women or children had men to support them, nor were men's wages always adequate to support a family comfortably.

New York provides a striking example of the extremes of wealth accompanying industrialization. Where workers lived, conditions were crowded, unhealthy, and dangerous. Houses built for two families often held four; tenements built for six families held twelve. Some of those families took in lodgers

to pay the rent, adding to the unbearably crowded conditions that encouraged poorer New Yorkers to spend as much time as possible outdoors. But streets in poor neighborhoods were filthy. Excess sewage from outhouses drained into ditches, carrying urine and fecal matter into the streets. People piled garbage into gutters or dumped it in backyards or alleys. Pigs, geese, dogs, and vultures scavenged the streets, while enormous rats roamed under wooden sidewalks and through large buildings. Typhoid, dysentery, malaria, and tuberculosis thrived in such conditions, and epidemics of cholera struck in 1832, 1849, and again in 1866, claiming thousands of victims.

But within walking distance of poverty-stricken neighborhoods were lavish mansions, whose residents could escape

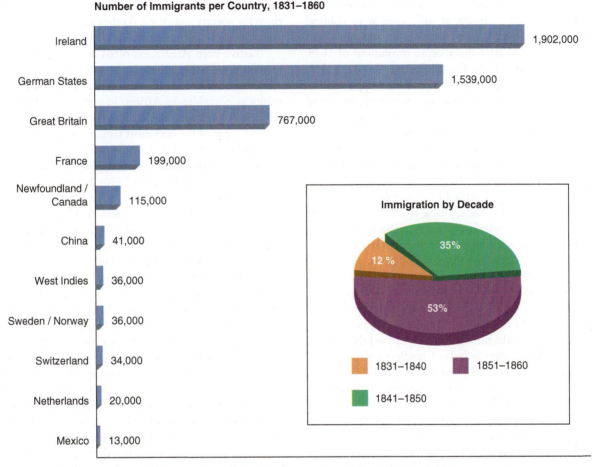

Number of Immigrants per Country, 1831–1860

Ireland	1,902,000
German States	1,539,000
Great Britain	767,000
France	199,000
Newfoundland / Canada	115,000
China	41,000
West Indies	36,000
Sweden / Norway	36,000
Switzerland	34,000
Netherlands	20,000
Mexico	13,000

Immigration by Decade

- 1831–1840: 12%
- 1841–1850: 35%
- 1851–1860: 53%

Figure 10.1 **Major Sources of Immigration to the United States, 1831–1860**

Most immigrants came from two areas: Great Britain, of which Ireland was a part, and the German states. These two areas sent more immigrants between 1830 and 1860 than the inhabitants of the United States enumerated at the first census in 1790. By 1860, 15 percent of the white population was of foreign birth. *Data from Stephan Thernstrom, ed., Harvard Encyclopedia of American Ethnic Groups [Cambridge, Mass., and London: Harvard University Press, 1980], 1047.*

to country estates during the summer's brutal heat or during epidemics. Much of this wealth was inherited. For every John Jacob Astor, who became a millionaire in the western fur trade after beginning life in humble circumstances, ten others had inherited or married money. These rich New Yorkers were not idle, though; they worked at increasing their fortunes and power by investing in commerce and manufacturing.

Between the two extremes of wealth sat a distinct middle class, larger than the wealthy elite but substantially smaller than the working classes. They were businessmen, traders, and professionals, and the rapid turn toward industrialization and commercial specialization made them a much larger presence in northern cities than in southern ones. Middle-class families enjoyed new consumer items: wool carpeting, fine wallpaper, and rooms full of furniture replaced the bare floors, whitewashed walls, and relative sparseness of eighteenth-century homes. Houses were large, from four to six rooms. Middle-class children slept one to a bed, and by the 1840s and 1850s, middle-class families used indoor toilets that were mechanical, though not yet flushing. Middle-class families formed the backbone of urban clubs and societies,

filled the family pews in church, and sent their sons to college. They were as distinct from the world of John Jacob Astor as they were from the milieu of the working class and the poor.

10-6d Immigration

Many of the urban poor were immigrants. The 5 million immigrants who came to the United States between 1830 and 1860 outnumbered the country's entire population in 1790. The vast majority came from Europe, primarily Ireland and the German states (see Figure 10.1). During the peak period of pre–Civil War immigration (1847–1857), 3.3 million immigrants entered the United States, including 1.3 million Irish and 1.1 million Germans. By 1860, 15 percent of the white population was foreign born, with 90 percent of immigrants living in northern states. Not all planned to stay permanently, and many, like the Irish, saw themselves as exiles.

A combination of factors "pushed" Europeans from their homes and "pulled" them to the northern United States. In Ireland, the potato famine (1845–1850)—a period of widespread starvation caused by a diseased potato crop—drove millions from their homeland. Although economic conditions pushed most Germans as well, some were political refugees—liberals, freethinkers, socialists, communists, and anarchists—who fled after the abortive revolutions of 1848. Europeans' awareness of the United States grew as employers, states, and shipping companies promoted opportunities across the Atlantic. Often the message was stark: work and prosper in America, where everyone could aspire to be an independent farmer, or starve in Europe. Although boosters promised immigrants a land of milk and honey, many soon became disillusioned; hundreds of thousands returned home.

Many early immigrants lived or worked in rural areas. Like the Archbalds, a few settled immediately on farms and eventually bought land. Others, unable to afford even a modest down payment, worked as hired farmhands, canal diggers, or railroad track layers—often hoping to buy land later. Pádraig Cúndún was among the lucky. The Irishman used his earnings as a canal laborer to buy land in western New York, proclaiming proudly in 1834 that "I have a fine farm of land now, which I own outright. No one can demand rent from me. My family and I can eat our fill of bread and meat, butter and milk any day we like throughout the year, so I think being here is better than staying in Ireland, landless and powerless, without food or clothing." By the 1840s and 1850s—when the steady stream of immigration turned into a flood—the prospects of buying land became more remote.

By 1860, most immigrants settled in cities, often the port at which they arrived. The most destitute could not afford the fare to places farther inland. Others arrived with resources but fell victim to swindlers who preyed on newly arrived immigrants. Some liked the cities' ethnic flair. In 1855, 52 percent of New York's 623,000 inhabitants were immigrants, with 28 percent of the city's population from Ireland and 16 percent from the German states. Boston, another major entry port, took on a European tone; throughout the 1850s, the city was about 35 percent foreign born, of whom more than two-thirds were Irish.

Most of the new immigrants from Ireland were young, poor, rural, and Roman Catholic. Women worked as domestic servants or mill hands, while men labored in construction or transportation. Very few Germans settled in New England; most came with enough resources to head to the upper Mississippi and Ohio valleys, to states such as Ohio, Illinois, Wisconsin, and Missouri. Although some southern cities like Charleston and Savannah had significant numbers of Irish immigrants, the vast majority of European immigrants, many of whom arrived with aversions to slavery and to semitropical heat, settled in the Northeast or Midwest.

10-6e Ethnic Tensions

Tension—often resulting from anxieties over the era's economic changes—characterized the relationship between native-born Americans and immigrants, particularly Irish Catholics. Native-born workers blamed immigrants for scarce job opportunities and low wages. Middle-class whites blamed them for poverty and crime. As they saw it, immigrants' moral depravity—not poor wages—led to poverty.

Native-born Americans often associated the Irish with another group whom they deemed morally inferior: African Americans. White northerners often portrayed Irish immigrants as nonwhite, as African in appearance. But Irish and African Americans did not develop a sense of solidarity. Instead, some of the era's most virulent riots erupted between Irish immigrants and African Americans.

Closely related to racial stereotyping was anti-Catholicism, which became strident in the 1830s. In Boston, anti-Catholic riots occurred frequently. Nearby Charlestown, Massachusetts, saw a mob burn a convent in 1834. In Philadelphia, a crowd attacked priests and nuns and vandalized churches in 1844, and in Lawrence, Massachusetts, a mob leveled the Irish neighborhood in 1854. Anti-Catholic violence spread beyond urban areas—riots between native-born and Irish workers erupted along the nation's canals and railroads—but urban riots usually attracted more newspaper attention, fueling fears that cities were violent, depraved places.

German immigrants, at least the majority who were Protestants, mostly fared better. In part because Germans generally arrived with some resources and skills, Americans stereotyped them as hardworking, self-reliant, and intelligent. But non-Protestant Germans—Catholics and Jews (whom white Americans considered a separate race) frequently encountered hostility fed by racial and religious prejudice.

Immigrants often lived in ethnic enclaves. Intolerance between Protestants and Catholics ran both ways, and Irish Catholics tended to live in their own neighborhoods, where they established Catholic churches and schools. In larger cities, immigrants from the same German states clustered together. Immigrants set up social clubs and mutual-aid societies, such as the Hibernian Society and Sons of Erin (Irish), and B'nai B'rith (Jewish).

10-6f People of Color

African Americans also forged their own communities and culture. As late as the 1830s, significant numbers of them remained enslaved in New York and New Jersey, but the numbers of free African Americans grew steadily, and by 1860 nearly 250,000 (many of them refugees from southern slavery) lived in the urban North. Despite differences in status, occupation, wealth, education, and religion, African Americans often felt a sense of racial solidarity. **African Methodist Episcopal Churches** and preachers helped forge communities. Chapels and social halls functioned as town halls and school buildings. Ministers were political leaders, and their halls housed political forums, conventions, and protest meetings.

But white racism impinged on every aspect of northern African Americans' lives. Streetcars, hotels, restaurants, and theaters could turn away African Americans with no legal penalty. City laws barred African Americans from entering public buildings. Even where more liberal laws existed, popular attitudes often constrained African Americans' opportunities.

African Methodist Episcopal Churches First American denomination established by and for African Americans.

▲ Domestic servants await their fate at a hiring office. Because servants resided with their employers, concerns about honesty often topped an employer's list of priorities for a suitable servant.

In Massachusetts, for example, African Americans enjoyed more legal rights than anywhere else, yet laws protecting civil and political rights could not make whites shop at black businesses. "Colored men in business in Massachusetts receive more respect, and less patronage than in any place I know of," proclaimed a prominent African American lawyer.

African Americans were excluded from factory and clerical jobs. Women worked as house servants, cooks, washerwomen, and child nurses. Most African American men worked as construction workers, porters, longshoremen, or day laborers—all jobs subject to frequent periods of unemployment. Others found employment in the lower-paying but more stable service industry, working as servants, waiters, cooks, barbers, and janitors. Many African American men became sailors and merchant seamen, as commercial sailing offered regular employment and opportunities for advancement, though not protection from racial taunts.

In the growing cities, African Americans turned service occupations into businesses, opening their own restaurants, taverns, hotels, barbershops, and employment agencies for domestic servants. Some became caterers. Others sold used clothing or were junk dealers or small-job contractors. A few became wealthy, invested in real estate, and loaned money. With professionals—ministers, teachers, physicians, dentists, lawyers, and newspaper editors—they formed a small but growing African American middle class.

In cities large and small, African Americans became targets of urban violence. White rioters clubbed and stoned African Americans, destroying their houses, churches, and businesses. Philadelphia experienced the most violence, with five major riots in the 1830s and 1840s, and major riots occurred in Providence and New York, where in July of 1834 many buildings were vandalized or destroyed during a three-day riot.

▲ Born in Saint-Domingue and brought to New York as a slave in the early 1790s, Pierre Toussaint became a very successful hairdresser catering to the city's fashion-conscious, wealthy white women. After being freed, Toussaint bought his wife (Juliette, pictured on the right) and other relatives, established orphanages, and supported the city's Catholic church. (left) The New York Historical Society /Archive Photos/Getty Images (right) The New York Historical Society/Getty Images

10-6g Urban Culture

Living in cramped, squalid conditions, working-class families—white and black, immigrant and native-born—spent little time indoors. In the 1840s, a working-class youth culture developed on the Bowery, one of New York's entertainment strips. The lamp-lit promenade, lined with theaters, dance halls, and cafés, became an urban midway for the "Bowery boys and gals." The Bowery boys' greased hair, distinctive clothing, and swaggering gait frightened many middle-class New Yorkers, as did the Bowery girls' colorful costumes and ornate hats, which contrasted with genteel ladies' own modest veils and bonnets. Equally scandalous to an older generation were the middle-class clerks who succumbed to the city's temptations, most notably prostitution.

Gangs of garishly dressed young men and women—flaunting their sexuality, using foul language, sometimes speaking in foreign tongues, and drinking to excess—drove self-styled respectable citizenry to establish private clubs and associations. Some joined the Masonic order, which offered everything the bustling, chaotic city did not: an elaborate hierarchy, an older code of deference between ranks, harmony, and shared values. Although the Masons admitted men only, women organized their own associations, including literary clubs and benevolent societies.

Increasingly, urban recreation and sports became formal commodities. One had to buy a ticket to go to the theater, the circus, P. T. Barnum's American Museum in New York City, the racetrack, or the ballpark. Horse racing, walking races, and, in the 1850s, baseball attracted large urban male crowds.

Starting in 1831, enthusiasts could read the all-sports newspaper, *Spirit of the Times.* A group of Wall Street office workers formed the Knickerbocker Club in 1842 and in 1845 drew up rules for the game of baseball. By 1849, news of boxing was so much in demand that a round-by-round account of a Maryland boxing match was telegraphed throughout the East.

A theater was often the second public building constructed in a town, after a church. Large cities boasted two or more theaters catering to different classes. Some plays cut across class lines—Shakespeare was performed so often and appreciated so widely that even illiterate theatergoers knew his plays well—yet the same taste in plays did not soothe class tensions. In 1849, a dispute between an American and a British actor about how to properly stage Shakespeare's *Macbeth* escalated into a working-class riot at New York City's elitist Astor Place Opera House, which hosted the British actor. It was, as one observer explained, "the rich against the poor—the aristocracy against the people." As the disorder escalated, bringing thousands into the streets, militia fired into the working-class crowd, killing at least twenty-seven and injuring about 150.

In the 1840s, singing groups, theater troupes, and circuses traveled from city to city. Minstrel shows were particularly popular, featuring white men (often Irish) in burnt-cork makeup imitating African Americans in song, dance, and patter. In the early 1830s, Thomas D. Rice of New York became famous for his role as Jim Crow, an old southern slave. In ill-fitting patched clothing and torn shoes, the blackface Rice shuffled, danced, and sang. Minstrel performers told jokes mocking economic

▲ On May 10, 1849, a working-class protest at the elitist Astor Place Theater in New York City led to a clash with state militia, resulting in at least 22 deaths and over 150 injuries.

and political elites, and evoked nostalgia for preindustrial work habits and morality, as supposedly embodied by carefree black men. At the same time, the antics of blackface actors encouraged a racist stereotyping of African Americans as sensual and lazy.

10-6h The Penny Press

Accounts of urban culture peppered the penny press, a new journalistic form that emerged in the 1830s, soon sweeping northern cities, particularly the ports of New York, Boston, Philadelphia, and Baltimore. Made possible by technological advances—the advent of the steam-powered press, improved methods for producing paper, and transportation innovations—the penny press (each newspaper cost one cent) contrasted fundamentally to the established six-cent newspapers. The older papers covered mostly commercial news and identified strongly with a political party; politicians themselves supplied much of the content, often reprinting their speeches. The penny press, by contrast, proclaimed political independence and dispersed paid reporters to cover local, national, and even international stories. Unlike six-cent newspapers, which relied primarily on mail subscriptions and contributions from political parties for their revenue, penny newspapers were sold by newsboys on the street, earned money by selling advertising, and circulated to a much larger and economically diverse readership. For the first time, working-class people could regularly buy newspapers.

Penny newspapers focused on daily life, what today would be called "human interest stories," giving individuals of one social class the opportunity to peer into the lives of different classes, ethnicities, and races. Working- and middle-class readers, for example, could read about high society—its balls, its horse racing, its excesses of various sorts. Wealthy and middle-class readers encountered stories about poorer neighborhoods—their crime, poverty, and insalubrious conditions. The penny press often sensationalized or slanted the news, and, in the process, influenced urban dwellers' views of one another, and of cities themselves.

10-6i Cities as Symbols of Progress

Many northerners saw cities—with their mixtures of people, rapid growth, municipal improvements, and violence—as symbolizing at once progress and decay. On the one hand, cities represented economic advancement; new ones grew at the crossroads of transportation and commerce. Cities nurtured churches, schools, civil governments, and museums—all signs of civilization and culture. As canals and railroads opened the West for mass settlement, many white northerners applauded the appearance of what they called "civilization"—church steeples, public buildings—in areas that had recently been what they called "savage wilderness," or territory controlled by Native Americans. One Methodist newspaper remarked in 1846 that the nation's rapid expansion westward would outpace "our means of moral and intellectual improvement." But the remedies, the editor noted, were evident: bring churches, schools, and moral reform societies to the West. "Cities, civilization, religion, mark our progress," he declared. To many nineteenth-century white Americans, cities represented the moral triumph of civilization over savagery and heathenism.

Yet some of the same Americans deplored the everyday character of the nation's largest cities, which they saw as havens of disease, poverty, crime, and vice. To many middle-class observers, disease and crime represented moral decline. They considered epidemics to be divine scourges, striking primarily those who were filthy, intemperate, and immoral. Theft and prostitution provided evidence of moral vice, and wealthy observers perceived these crimes not as by-products of poverty but as signs of individual failing. They pressed for laws against vagrancy and disturbing the peace, and pushed city officials to establish the nation's first police forces. Boston hired daytime policemen in 1838 to supplement its part-time night watchmen and constables, and New York formed its own police force, modeled on London's, in 1845.

How did northerners reconcile urban vice and depravity with their view of cities as symbols of progress? Middle-class reformers focused on purifying cities of disease and vice. If disease was a divine punishment, then Americans would have to become more godly. Middle-class reformers took to the streets and back alleys, trying to convince the urban working classes that life would improve if they gave up alcohol, worked even harder, and prayed frequently. This belief in hard work and virtuous habits became central to many northerners' ideas about progress.

10-7 Revivals and Reform

▶ How did religion influence the emergence of reform efforts in the first half of the nineteenth century?

▶ What role did women play in the reform movements?

▶ How were individual reform efforts in American society similar to one another?

Second Great Awakening Period of the religious revivals that swept the nation from the 1790s into the 1830s; these helped inspire northern reform movements.

Charles G. Finney A lawyer-turned-Presbyterian minister who conducted revivals in towns like Rochester along the Erie Canal, and who stressed individual responsibility for making moral decisions.

For many, those ideas were grounded in evangelical religion. During the late eighteenth and early nineteenth centuries, a series of religious revivals throughout the nation raised people's hopes for the Second Coming of the Christian messiah and the establishment of the Kingdom of God on earth. Sometimes called the **Second Great Awakening** for their resemblance to revivals of the Great Awakening of the eighteenth century, these revivals created communities of believers who resolved to combat sin in an effort to speed the millennium, or the thousand years of peace on earth that would accompany Christ's Second Coming. Some believed the United States had a special mission in God's design and a special role in eliminating evil. If sin and evil could be eliminated, individuals and society could be perfected, readying the earth for Christ's return.

Because it was not enough for an individual to embrace God and godliness, revivalists strove for large-scale conversions. Rural women, men, and children traveled long distances to camp meetings, where they listened to fiery sermons preached day and night from hastily constructed platforms and tents in forests or open fields. In cities, women in particular attended daily church services and prayer meetings, sometimes for months on end. Converts renounced personal sin, vowed to live sanctified lives, and committed themselves to helping others see the light.

10-7a Revivals

Northern revivalists emphasized social reform in a way that their southern counterparts did not. The most prominent northern preachers were Lyman Beecher, who made his base in New England before moving to Cincinnati, and **Charles G. Finney**, who traveled the canals and roads linking the Northeast to the Midwest. They, like many lesser-known preachers, argued that evil was avoidable, that Christians were not doomed by original sin, and that anyone could achieve salvation. In everyday language, Finney—a former lawyer who became a Presbyterian minister—preached that "God has made man a moral free agent." Finney's brand of revivalism transcended sects, class, and race. Revivalism thrived among Methodists and Baptists, whose denominational structures maximized democratic participation and drew ministers from ordinary folk.

Finney achieved his greatest successes in the area of western New York that had experienced rapid changes in transportation and industrialization—in what he called the "Burned-Over District" because of the region's intense evangelical fires. Rapid change raised fears of social disorder—family dissolution, drinking, swearing, and prostitution. Many individuals worried, too, whether their status would improve or decline in an economy cycling through booms and busts.

When northern revivalist preachers emphasized the importance of good works—good deeds and piety—they helped ignite many of the era's social reform movements, which began in the Burned-Over District and spread eastward to New England and the Middle Atlantic and westward to the upper Midwest. Evangelically inspired reform associations together constituted what historians call the "benevolent empire." While advocating for distinct causes, these associations shared a commitment to human perfectibility, and they often turned to the same wealthy men for financial resources and advice.

Camp Meeting of the Methodists in N. America

▲ Often attracting worshippers in the thousands, revivalist meetings became known as "camp meetings" because the faithful camped out for days at a time to hear charismatic preachers, who offered sermons day and night.

10-7b Moral Reform

Those resources enabled them to make good use of the era's new technologies—steam presses and railroads—to spread the evangelical word. By mass-producing pamphlets and newspapers for distribution far into the country's interior, reformers spread their message throughout the Northeast and Midwest, strengthening cultural connections between regions increasingly tied together economically. With canals and railroads making travel easier, reformers could attend annual conventions and contact like-minded people personally, and local reform societies could host speakers from distant places. Most reform organizations, like political parties, sponsored weekly newspapers, creating a virtual community of reformers.

While industrialists and merchants provided financial resources for evangelical reform, their wives and daughters solicited new members and circulated petitions. Reforms sought to expand the cult of domesticity, which assigned women the role of moral guardianship of their families, into the public realm. Rather than simply providing moral guidance to their own children, women would establish reformatories for wayward youth or asylums for orphans. Participation in reform movements allowed women to exercise moral authority outside the household, giving them a new sense of influence. They might both improve people's lives and hasten the millennium. Women also enjoyed the friendships and intellectual camaraderie with other women that participation in benevolent societies fostered.

Many female reformers had attended a female academy or seminary, where the curriculum included arts of "refinement"—music, dance, penmanship—but focused on science and literature. Based on the notion that women were men's intellectual equals, the curriculum was modeled on that of men's colleges, and by 1820, approximately the same number of men and women attended institutions of higher education. At the female academies and seminaries, and at the hundreds of reading circles and literary societies in which their alumnae participated, women honed their intellectual and persuasive skills, preparing themselves to influence public opinion even as many of them maintained substantial domestic responsibilities. A few of these women became prominent editors and writers, but most influenced society as educators and, especially, reformers.

The aftermath of an 1831 exposé of prostitution in New York City illustrates reformers' public influence. Even as female reformers organized a shelter for the city's prostitutes and tried to secure respectable employment for them, they publicized the names of brothel clients to shame the men contributing to the women's waywardness. The New York women organized themselves into the Female Moral Reform

Society, expanding their geographic scope and activities. By 1840, the society had 555 affiliated chapters across the nation. In the next few years, it entered the political sphere by lobbying successfully for criminal sanctions in New York State against men who seduced women into prostitution. If only prostitutes could be freed from the corrupting reach of the men who preyed on them, reformers believed, so-called "fallen women" might be morally uplifted.

10-7c Penitentiaries and Asylums

A similar belief in perfectibility led reformers to establish penitentiaries for criminals and delinquents that aimed not simply to punish, as jails did, but to transform criminals into productive members of society through disciplined regimens. Under the "Auburn system," prisoners worked together in the daytime but were isolated at night, while under the "Philadelphia system," utter silence and isolation prevailed day and night. Isolation and silence were meant to enable reflection and redemption—to provide opportunities for penitence—within individual prisoners. When Frenchman Alexis de Tocqueville came to America in 1831 to study its prisons, he noted that the Philadelphia system made him feel as if he "had traversed catacombs; there were a thousand living beings, and yet it was desert solitude."

Other reformers sought to improve treatment of the mentally ill, who were frequently imprisoned, often alongside criminals, and put in cages or dark dungeons, chained to walls, brutalized, or held in solitary confinement. **Dorothea Dix**, the movement's leader, exemplifies the early-nineteenth-century reformer who started with a religious belief in individual self-improvement and human perfectibility, and moved into social action by advocating collective responsibility. Investigating asylums, petitioning the Massachusetts legislature, and lobbying other states and Congress, Dix helped create a new public role for women. In response to Dix's efforts, twenty-eight of thirty-three states built public institutions for the mentally ill by 1860.

10-7d Temperance

Temperance reformers, who pushed for either partial or full abstinence from alcoholic beverages, likewise crossed into the political sphere. Drinking was widespread in the early nineteenth century, when men gathered in public houses and rural inns to drink whiskey, rum, and hard cider while they gossiped, talked politics, and played cards. Contracts were sealed, celebrations commemorated, and harvests toasted with liquor. "Respectable" women did not drink in public, but many tippled alcohol-based patent medicines promoted as cure-alls.

Evangelicals considered drinking sinful, and in many denominations, forsaking alcohol was part of conversion. Preachers condemned alcohol for violating the Sabbath—the only day workers had off, which some spent at the public house. Factory owners condemned alcohol for making workers unreliable. Civic leaders connected alcohol with crime. Middle-class reformers, often women, condemned it for squandering wages, diverting men from their family responsibilities, and fostering abusive behavior at home. In the early 1840s, thousands of ordinary women formed Martha Washington societies to protect families by reforming alcoholics, raising children as teetotalers, and spreading the temperance message. Abstinence from alcohol, reformers believed, would foster both religious perfectibility and secular progress.

As the temperance movement gained momentum, its goal shifted from moderation to voluntary abstinence and finally to prohibition. By the mid-1830s, five thousand state and local temperance societies touted teetotalism, and more than a million people had taken the pledge of abstinence, including several hundred thousand children who enlisted in the Cold Water Army. Per capita consumption of alcohol fell from five gallons per year in 1800 to below two gallons in the 1840s. The American Society for the Promotion of Temperance, organized in 1826 to promote pledges of abstinence, became a pressure group for legislation to end alcohol manufacture and sale. In 1851, Maine became the first state to ban alcohol except for medicinal purposes; by 1855, similar laws had been enacted throughout New England and in New York, Pennsylvania, and the Midwest.

The temperance campaign had a nativist—or anti-immigrant and anti-Catholic—strain to it. The Irish and Germans, complained the *American Protestant Magazine* in 1849, "bring the grog shops like the frogs of Egypt upon us." Along the nation's canals, reformers lamented the hundreds of taverns catering to the largely Irish workforce, and in the cities, they expressed outrage at the Sunday tradition of urban German families' gathering at beer gardens to eat and drink, to dance and sing, and sometimes to play cards. Some Catholics heeded the message, pledging abstinence and forming their own organizations, such as the St. Mary's Mutual Benevolent Total Abstinence Society in Boston.

But temperance spawned strong opposition, too. Many workers—Protestants as well as Catholics—rejected what they saw as reformers' efforts to impose middle-class values on people whose lives they did not understand, and they steadfastly defended their right to drink whatever they pleased. Workers agreed that poverty and crime were problems but believed that poor wages, not drinking habits, were responsible. Even some who abstained from alcohol opposed prohibition, believing that drinking should be a matter of self-control, not state coercion.

10-7e Public Schools

Protestants and Catholics often quarreled over education as well. Public education usually included religious education, but when teachers taught Protestant beliefs and used the King James version of the Bible, Catholics established their own schools, which taught Catholic doctrines. Some Protestants began

Dorothea Dix Leader of movement to improve conditions for the mentally ill.

temperance Abstinence from alcohol; the temperance movement advocated against using alcohol for nonmedicinal reasons.

Engaging Children

Hundreds of thousands of children joined the temperance movement, often by enlisting in the so-called Cold Water Army. Like adult temperance societies, the Cold Water Army advocated for complete abstinence from alcoholic beverages. On holidays such as George Washington's birthday and the Fourth of July, they marched at public gatherings, singing temperance songs and carrying banners and fans such as the one pictured at the right. Reverend Thomas P. Hunt, a Presbyterian minister, founded the Cold Water Army because he believed that by recruiting children, he stood a much greater chance of eradicating alcohol consumption than if he aimed his temperance efforts directly at adults.

CRITICAL THINKING

- What might have been Hunt's logic? Why might children have wanted to join a Cold Water Army?

- Do the images on the certificate and fan offer any clues? What were the benefits of participating in the movement?

- What were the implied consequences of failing to do so? Why might Hunt have chosen the term *army*, and what about that choice might have proved appealing to his young recruits?

▲ Children who participated in a Cold Water Army often received a certificate that acknowledged their commitment to the cause while reiterating the pledge they had taken. Cold Water Army Pledge (litho)/American School, (19th century)/NEW YORK HISTORICAL SOCIETY/© Collection of the New-York Historical Society, USA/Bridgeman Images

▲ Children in Cold Water Army parades sometimes carried decorative fans, which they may have displayed in their homes as well, as reminders to themselves and their parents of temperance's virtues. Museum of American Political Life, University of Hartford

to fear that Catholics would never assimilate into American culture, and some charged Catholics with being exclusionists, plotting to undermine the republic and impose papal control. Yet even as these conflicts brewed, public education touched the lives of more Americans than did any other reform movement.

The movement's leader was **Horace Mann**, a Massachusetts lawyer and reformer from humble beginnings. Mann advocated free, tax-supported education to replace church schools and the private schools set up by untrained, itinerant young men. Universal education, Mann proposed, would end misery and crime, and would help Americanize immigrants. "If we do not prepare children to become good citizens," he argued, "if we do not develop their capacities, imbue their hearts with the love of truth and duty, and a reverence for all things sacred and holy, then our republic must go down to destruction."

During Mann's tenure as secretary of the Massachusetts Board of Education from 1837 to 1848, Massachusetts led the "common school" movement, establishing schools for training teachers (the "normal school," modeled on the French *école normale*, and the forerunner of teacher-training colleges); lengthening the school year; and raising teachers' salaries to make the profession more attractive. In keeping with the era's notions that women had special claims to morality and that they could be paid less because they were by nature dependents, Mann envisioned a system in which women would prepare future clerks, farmers, and workers with a practical curriculum that deemphasized classics in favor of geography, arithmetic, and science. Like other reform movements, educational reform rested on the notions of progress and perfectibility; given the proper guidance, individuals could educate themselves out of their material and moral circumstances.

Thanks in part to expanding public education in the North, by 1850 the vast majority of native-born white Americans were literate. Newspapers and magazines proliferated, and bookstores spread. Power printing presses and better transportation made possible wide distribution of books and periodicals. The religious press—of both traditional sects and revivalists—produced pamphlets, hymnals, Bibles, and religious newspapers. Secular newspapers and magazines—political organs, the penny press, and literary journals—also abounded from the 1830s on.

Horace Mann First secretary of the newly created Massachusetts Board of Education who presided over sweeping reforms to transform schools into institutions that occupied most of a child's time and energy.

Mormons Members of the Church of Jesus Christ of Latter-day Saints, the first major religion founded in the United States; members were persecuted for many years.

Joseph Smith Founder of the Mormon Church.

10-7f Engineering and Science

Public education's emphasis on science reflected a broader tendency to look not just to moral reform but also to engineering and science to remedy the nation's problems. Not everyone blamed epidemics on immorality, for example; scientists and doctors saw unclean, stagnant water as the culprit. With its

Fairmount Water Works, constructed between 1812 and 1815, Philadelphia took the lead in building municipal waterworks. After the devastating cholera epidemic of 1832, New York City planned its own massive waterworks: between 1837 and 1842, it built the 41-mile Croton Aqueduct, an elaborate system of iron pipes encased in brick masonry that brought water from upstate New York to Manhattan.

Science became increasingly important nationally, too, with the founding of institutions that still exist today. After James Smithson, a wealthy British scientist, left his estate to the United States government, Congress established the Smithsonian Institution (1846), which acquired and disseminated scientific knowledge. The Smithsonian's director was Joseph Henry, one of the nation's most talented scientists; his experiments in electromagnetism helped make possible both the telegraph and, later in the century, the telephone. In 1848, Henry helped found the American Association for the Advancement of Science to promote scientific collaboration and, thus, advancement. That Henry was a devoutly religious man did not deter him from seeking scientific knowledge. For many nineteenth-century Americans, particularly those in non-revivalist sects, religious devotion and scientific inquiry were compatible. They saw scientific discoveries as signs of progress, reassuring them that the millennium was approaching. God had created the natural world, they believed, and it was their Christian duty to perfect it in preparation for God's return.

10-8 Utopian Experiments

▶ **What did utopian communities seek to achieve in the first half of the nineteenth century?**

▶ **What were the features of the American Renaissance?**

Some idealists dreamed of an entirely new social order. They established dozens of utopian communities—ideal communities designed as models for broader society—based on either religious principles, a desire to resist what they deemed the market economy's excessive individualism, or both. Some groups, like the **Mormons**, arose during the Second Great Awakening, while others, like the Shakers, had originated in eighteenth-century Europe. Utopian communities attempted to recapture what they perceived as the past's more communal nature, even as they offered sometimes-radical departures from established practices of marriage and child rearing.

10-8a Mormons

No utopian experiment had a more lasting influence than the Church of Jesus Christ of Latter-day Saints, whose members were known as the Mormons. During the religious ferment of the 1820s in western New York, **Joseph Smith**, a young farmer, reported that an angel called Moroni had given him divinely engraved gold plates. Smith published his revelations as the *Book of Mormon* and organized a church in 1830. The next year, the community moved west to Ohio to build a "New Jerusalem" and await the Second Coming of Jesus.

▲ The Croton Aqueduct, shown here near Harlem, New York, was an engineering marvel of its time. It brought fresh water to New York City.

After angry mobs drove the Mormons from Ohio, they settled in Missouri. Anti-Mormons charged that Mormonism was a scam by Joseph Smith, and feared Mormon economic and political power. In 1838, Missouri's governor charged Smith with fomenting insurrection and worked to indict him and other leaders for treason.

Smith and his followers left for Nauvoo, Illinois. The state legislature gave them a city charter making them self-governing and authorized a local militia. But again the Mormons met antagonism, especially after Smith introduced the practice of polygamy in 1841, allowing men to have several wives at once. The next year, Smith became mayor, and this consolidation of religious and political power, as well as Nauvoo's petition to the federal government to be a self-governing territory, further antagonized opponents, now including some former Mormons. In 1844, after Smith and his brother were charged with treason and jailed, and then murdered, the Mormons left Illinois to seek security in the western wilderness. Under the leadership of Brigham Young, they established a cooperative community in the Great Salt Lake Valley.

10-8b Shakers

The **Shakers**, the largest communal utopian experiment, reached their peak between 1820 and 1860, with six thousand members in twenty settlements in eight states. Shaker communities emphasized agriculture and handcrafts, selling their products beyond their own community; most became self-sufficient and profitable enterprises. The community's craft tradition contrasted with the new factory regime. But the Shakers were essentially a spiritual community. Founded in England in the early 1770s by Ann Lee, their name derived from their worship service, which included shaking their entire bodies, singing, dancing, and shouting. Ann Lee's children had died in infancy, and she saw their deaths as retribution for her sin of intercourse; thus, she advocated celibacy. After imprisonment in England in 1773–1774, she settled in America.

In religious practice and social relations, Shakers offered an alternative to the era's rapid changes. Shakers lived communally, with men and women in separate quarters; individual families were abolished. Men and women shared leadership equally. Many Shaker settlements became temporary refuges for orphans, widows, runaways, abused wives, and laid-off workers. Their settlements depended on new recruits,

Shakers Utopian sect that stressed celibacy and emphasized agriculture and handcrafts; became known for furniture designs long after the community itself ceased to exist.

not only because the practice of celibacy meant no reproduction, but also because some members left, unsuited to either communal living or the Shakers' spiritual message.

10-8c Oneidans, Owenites, and Fourierists

Other utopian communities joined in resisting the social changes accompanying industrialism. John Humphrey Noyes, a lawyer converted by Finney's revivals, established two perfectionist communities: first in Putney, Vermont, in 1840, and then—after being indicted for adultery—in Oneida, New York, in 1848. Noyes decried individualism, advocating instead communal property ownership, communal child rearing, and "complex marriage," in which all the community's men were married to all its women, but in which a woman could accept or reject a sexual proposition. The Oneida Colony forbade exclusive sexual relationships and required men to practice "male continence," or intercourse without ejaculation, in order to promote relationships built on more than sexual fulfillment. Pregnancies were to be planned; couples applied to Noyes for permission to have a child, or Noyes assigned two people to reproduce with each other. Robert Dale Owen's community in **New Harmony**, Indiana (1825–1828), also abolished private property and advocated communal child rearing. The Fourierists, named after French philosopher Charles Fourier, established more than two dozen communities in the Northeast and Midwest; these communities, too, resisted individualism and promoted equality between the sexes.

The most famous Fourier community was Brook Farm, in West Roxbury, Massachusetts, near Boston. Inspired by **transcendentalism**—the belief that the physical world is secondary to the spiritual realm, which human beings can reach not by custom and experience but only by intuition—Brook Farm's members rejected materialism. Their rural communalism combined spirituality, manual labor, intellectual life, and play. Originally founded in 1841 by the Unitarian minister George Ripley, Brook Farm attracted farmers, craftsmen, and writers, among them the novelist Nathaniel Hawthorne. Brook Farm residents contributed regularly to the *Dial*, the leading transcendentalist journal. Although Unitarians were not evangelicals, their largely middle- and upper-class followers had a long-standing "devotion to progress," as one of their most influential ministers put it. In 1845, Brook Farm's one hundred members organized themselves into phalanxes (working-living units), following a model suggested by Fourier. As rigid regimentation replaced individualism, membership dropped. A year after a disastrous fire in 1846, the experiment collapsed.

New Harmony A utopian community founded in Indiana by Robert Owen; it advocated communal property and child-rearing.

transcendentalism The belief that the physical world is secondary to the spiritual realm, which humans can reach only by intuition.

After visiting Brook Farm in 1843, transcendentalist Henry David Thoreau decided that organized utopian communities did not suit him: "As for these communities, I think I had rather keep bachelor's hall in hell than go to board in heaven." Two years later, Thoreau constructed his own one-man utopia in a small cabin along the shores of Walden Pond, in Massachusetts, where he meditated and wrote about nature, morality, spirituality, progress, society, and government.

10-8d American Renaissance

Thoreau joined a literary outpouring known today as the American Renaissance. Ralph Waldo Emerson, a pillar of the transcendental movement, was its prime inspiration. After quitting his Boston Unitarian ministry in 1832, followed by a two-year sojourn in Europe, Emerson returned to lecture and write, preaching individualism and self-reliance. Widely admired, he influenced Hawthorne, *Dial* editor Margaret Fuller, Herman Melville, and Thoreau, among many others. In philosophical intensity and moral idealism, the American Renaissance was both distinctively American and an outgrowth of the European romantic movement. It addressed universal themes using American settings and characters. Hawthorne, for instance, used Puritan New England as a backdrop, and Melville wrote of great spiritual quests as seafaring adventures.

Perhaps more than any other American Renaissance author, Thoreau emphasized individualism and its practical applications. In his 1849 essay on "Resistance to Civil Government" (known after his death as "Civil Disobedience"), Thoreau advocated individual resistance to a government engaged in immoral acts. Thoreau had already put into practice what he preached: In the midst of the War with Mexico (see Chapter 12, "Politics and the Fate of the Union, 1824–1859"), Thoreau refused to pay his taxes, believing they would aid an immoral war to expand slavery, and was briefly jailed. "I cannot for an instant recognize that political organization as my government which is the *slave's* government also," Thoreau wrote. Later, in defiance of federal law, Thoreau aided escaped slaves on their way to freedom.

10-9 Abolitionism

▶ How did evangelical abolitionism differ from its antislavery predecessors?

▶ What role did women and African Americans play in the abolitionist movement?

▶ What internal and external challenges did the abolitionist movement face?

Thoreau joined evangelical abolitionists in trying to eradicate slavery, which they deemed both an individual and a communal sin suffusing American society. Their efforts built on an earlier generation of antislavery activism among blacks and whites.

10-9a   Evangelical Abolitionism

In the early 1830s, a new group of radical white abolitionists—most prominently, **William Lloyd Garrison**—rejected the gradual approaches of an earlier generation of white legal reformers and colonizationists (see "Early Abolitionism and Colonization," Section 8-3e). Instead, these overwhelmingly northern reformers demanded immediate, complete, and uncompensated emancipation. In the first issue of the abolitionist newspaper *The Liberator*, which he began publishing in 1831, Garrison declared, "I am in earnest—I will not equivocate—I will not excuse—I will not retreat a single inch—and *I will be heard.*" Two years later, he founded the American Antislavery Society, which became the era's largest abolitionist organization.

Immediatists, as they came to be called, believed slavery was an absolute sin needing urgent eradication. They were influenced by African American abolitionist societies and by evangelicals' notion that humans, not God, determined their own spiritual fate by deciding whether to choose good or evil. In that sense, all were equal before God's eyes. When all humans had chosen good over evil, the millennium would come. Slavery, however, denied enslaved men and women the ability to make such choices, the ability to act as what Finney called "moral free agents." For every day that slavery continued, the millennium was postponed.

Because the millennium depended on *all* hearts being won over to Christ, because it depended on the perfectibility of everyone, including slave owners, Garrison advocated "moral suasion." He and his followers hoped to bring about emancipation not through coercion, but by winning the hearts of slave owners as well as others who supported or tolerated slavery. Evangelical abolitionism depended, then, on large numbers of ministers and laypeople spreading the evangelical message all across the nation. Many of them joined local organizations affiliated with the American Antislavery Society.

10-9b   The American Antislavery Society

By 1838, at its peak, the society reported 1,300 local affiliates and a membership of 250,000. Unlike earlier white abolitionist societies, the immediatist organizations welcomed men and women of all racial and class backgrounds. Lydia Maria Child, Maria Chapman, and Lucretia Mott served on its executive committee; Child edited its official paper, the *National Anti-Slavery Standard*, from 1841 to 1843, and Chapman coedited it from 1844 until 1848. The society sponsored black and female speakers, and women undertook most of the day-to-day conversion efforts. In rural and small-town northern and midwestern communities, women addressed mail, collected signatures, raised money, organized boycotts of textiles made from slave-grown cotton, and increased public awareness. With the "great postal campaign," launched in 1835, the society's membership flooded the mails with antislavery tracts. Women went door to door collecting signatures on antislavery petitions; by 1838, more than 130,000 petitions, each with numerous signatures, had been sent to Congress. Abolitionist-minded women met in "sewing circles," making clothes for escaped slaves while organizing future activities, such as antislavery fairs at which they sold goods—often items they had made themselves—whose proceeds they donated to antislavery causes. These fairs increased their cause's visibility and drew more Americans into direct contact with abolitionists and their ideas.

10-9c   African American Abolitionists

Even as white abolitionist societies opened membership to African Americans and sponsored speaking tours by former slaves, African Americans continued their independent efforts to end slavery and to improve the status of free African Americans. Former slaves—most famously, Frederick Douglass, Henry Bibb, Harriet Tubman, and Sojourner Truth—dedicated their lives to ending slavery through their speeches, publications, and participation in a secret network known as the Underground Railroad, which spirited enslaved men, women, and children to freedom. By the thousands, less famous African Americans continued the work of the post-revolutionary generation and established their churches, founded moral reform societies, published newspapers, created schools and orphanages for African American children, and held conventions to consider tactics for improving African Americans' status within the free states.

Although genuine friendships emerged among white and black abolitionists, many white abolitionists treated blacks as inferiors, driving some African Americans to reject white antislavery organizations and to form their own. Others lacked the patience for the supposed immediatism of

▲ Women played an activist role in reform, especially in abolitionism. A rare daguerreotype from August 1850 shows women and men, including Frederick Douglass, on the podium at an abolitionist rally in Cazenovia, New York.

The Art Archive /Art Resource, NY

William Lloyd Garrison
Founder of *The Liberator* and a controversial white advocate of abolition, he demanded an immediate end to slavery and embraced civil rights for blacks on par with those of whites.

William Lloyd Garrison; they did not object to moral suasion, but they sought even more immediate solutions, such as legislation, to African Americans' problems in both the South and the North. African American abolitionists nonetheless took heart in the immediatists' success at winning converts.

10-9d Opposition to Abolitionism

But that very success gave rise to a virulent, even violent, opposition, not only among southerners but also among northerners who recognized cotton's vital economic role, and who feared emancipation would prompt an enormous influx of freed slaves into their own region. Like many southerners, they questioned the institution's morality but not its practicality: they believed blacks to be inherently inferior and incapable of acquiring the attributes—virtue and diligence—required of freedom and citizenship. Some northerners, too, objected to white women's involvement in abolitionism, believing that women's proper role lay within the home.

Opposition to abolitionism could become violent. In Boston, David Walker, a southern-born free black, died under mysterious circumstances in 1830, one year after advocating the violent overthrow of slavery in his *Appeal . . . to the Colored Citizens*. Among those northerners who most despised abolitionists were "gentlemen of property and standing"—a nineteenth-century term for commercial and political elites—who often had strong economic connections to the southern cotton economy and political connections to leading southerners. Northern gentlemen incited anti-abolitionist riots. In Utica, New York, in 1835 merchants and professionals broke up the state Anti-Slavery Convention, which had welcomed blacks and women. Mob violence peaked that year, with more than fifty riots aimed at

Destruction by Fire of Pennsylvania Hall,

On the night of the 17th May, 1838

▲ Three days after its dedication in 1838, Pennsylvania Hall—an abolitionist center in Philadelphia—was burned to the ground by anti-abolitionist rioters.

P. T. Barnum's Publicity Stunts

Usually remembered for the Ringling Brothers and Barnum & Bailey Circus, P. T. Barnum (1810–1891) left another legacy: the publicity stunt. Using hoaxes and spectacles, Barnum's American Museum in New York City drew tens of millions of visitors between 1841 and 1868, making Barnum the era's second wealthiest American.

"I am indebted to the press . . . for almost every dollar that I possess," Barnum declared. Barnum first gained widespread publicity in 1835 with his traveling exhibition of Joice Heth, whom he claimed was the 161-year-old former slave of George Washington. When interest petered out, Barnum planted a rumor that she was a fake, a machine made of leather and bones. The penny press reveled in the ensuing controversy, swelling admissions and earning Barnum enough to purchase the American Museum, whose "500,000 natural and artificial curiosities" he promoted through similar stunts. The "Feejee [Fiji] Mermaid," for example, caused a national stir, as scientists debated its authenticity. (It was a monkey's head sewn to a fish's body.) Barnum hosted promotional events, too, including the nation's first beauty pageant in 1854. Offensive to middle-class sensibilities, it flopped, but Barnum persevered with pageants featuring dogs, babies, and chickens. The baby show alone attracted 61,000 visitors. As Barnum wrote, "Without promotion, something terrible happens . . . Nothing!" Selling more than a million copies, Barnum's autobiography inspired generations of entrepreneurs.

Many of today's cultural icons began as promotional gimmicks, including the Miss America Pageant (1921), the Macy's Thanksgiving Day parade (1924), and the Goodyear blimp (1925). Since 1916, Nathan's has hosted an annual Fourth of July hot dog–eating contest, now attracting forty thousand live spectators and a national television audience; until recently, the event also included acts from the circus that bore Barnum's name until its closing in 2017. Nathan's rival, Oscar Mayer, launched its Wienermobile in 1936; seven hot dog–shaped cars now tour the country, with drivers selected from a nationally publicized competition. The *Guinness Book of World Records*, begun as an Irish beer company's promotional brochure, inspires pizza makers to attempt to make the world's largest pizza; ice-cream makers, to create the largest sundae; and billionaires to cross oceans in hot-air balloons sporting their conglomerate's logos. Even failed attempts generate publicity.

By staging stunts designed to garner free media exposure, today's entrepreneurs reveal the enduring legacy of P. T. Barnum, the self-proclaimed greatest showman on earth.

CRITICAL THINKING

- While the use of publicity stunts has become the norm in the entertainment industry and is used widely in the promotion of various products, it also has a legacy of use in American politics for good or ill. How has the advent of instant communication and (especially) social media altered the nature and influence of publicity stunts in our own era, compared to those of the 1840s–1860s?

Paul Fearn/Alamy

◀ In the 1840s, P.T. Barnum stirred controversy by exhibiting one of his most famous hoaxes, the "Feejee Mermaid," which he fabricated by sewing a monkey's head to a fish's body.

abolitionists or African Americans. In 1837, in Alton, Illinois, a mob murdered white abolitionist editor Elijah P. Lovejoy, and rioters sacked his printing office. The following year, rioters in Philadelphia hurled stones and insults at three thousand black and white women attending the Anti-Slavery Convention of American Women in the brand-new Pennsylvania Hall, a building constructed to house abolitionist meetings and an abolitionist bookstore. The following day, a mob burned the building to the ground, three days after its dedication.

10-9e Moral Suasion Versus Political Action

Such violence made some immediatists question whether moral suasion was a realistic tactic. Men like James G. Birney, the son of a Kentucky slave owner, embraced immediatism but believed abolition could be effected only in the male sphere of politics. Involving women violated the natural order of things and detracted from the ultimate goal: freedom for slaves. Thus, when William Lloyd Garrison, an ardent supporter of women's rights, endorsed Abby Kelly's appointment to the American Antislavery Society's business committee in 1840, he provoked an irreparable split in the abolitionist movement. Arthur Tappan and Theodore Weld led a dissident group that established the American and Foreign Anti-Slavery Society. That society in turn formed a new political party: the Liberty Party, which nominated Birney for president in 1840 and 1844.

Although committed to immediate abolitionism, the Liberty Party doubted the federal government's authority to abolish slavery where it already existed. States, not the federal government, had the jurisdiction to determine slavery's legality within their bounds. Where the federal government could act was in the western territories, and the party demanded that all new territories prohibit slavery. Some prominent black abolitionists, including Frederick Douglass, endorsed the party, whose leaders emphasized, too, the need to combat northern prejudice as a crucial step in allowing African Americans to achieve their full potential.

10-9f Free-Labor Ideology

Secular and religious beliefs in progress—and upward mobility—coalesced into the notion of free labor, the concept that, in a competitive marketplace, those who worked hard and lived virtuous lives could improve their status. Free-labor ideology appealed especially to manufacturers and merchants eager to believe that their own success emerged from hard work and moral virtue—and eager as well to encourage their factory hands and clerks to work hard and live virtuously, to remain optimistic despite current hardships. Many laborers initially rejected free-labor ideology, seeing it as a veiled attempt to tout industrial work habits, to rationalize poor wages, to denigrate Catholicism, and to quell worker protest. But by the 1850s, when the issue of slavery's expansion into the West returned to the political foreground, more and more northerners would embrace free-labor ideology and come to see slavery as antithetical to it. It was this way of thinking, perhaps more than anything else, that made the North distinctive.

Summary

During the first half of the nineteenth century, the North became rapidly enmeshed in a commercial culture. Northern states and capitalists invested heavily in internal improvements, which lay the groundwork for market expansion. Most northerners now turned either toward commercial farming or, in smaller numbers, toward industrial wage labor. Farmers gave up mixed agriculture and specialized in cash crops, while their children often went to work in factories or countinghouses.

To many northerners, the market economy symbolized progress, in which they found much to celebrate: easier access to cheap western lands, employment for surplus farm laborers, and the ready commercial availability of goods that had once been time-consuming to produce. At the same time, though, the market economy led to increased specialization, a less personal workplace, complex market relationships, more regimentation, a sharper divide between work and leisure, and a degradation of natural resources. Northerners' involvement in the market economy also tied them more directly to fluctuating national and international markets, and during economic downturns, many northern families experienced destitution.

With parents relying less directly on children's labor, northerners began producing smaller families. Even as working-class children continued to work as canal drivers and factory hands (or to scavenge urban streets), middle-class families created a sheltered model of childhood in which they tried to shield children from the perceived dangers of the world outside the family. Their mothers, in theory, became moral guardians of the household, keeping the home safe from the encroachment of the new economy's competitiveness and selfishness. Few women, though, had the luxury to devote themselves entirely to nurturing their children and husbands.

Immigrants and free African Americans performed much of the lowest-paying work in the expanding economy, and many native-born whites blamed them for the problems that accompanied the era's rapid economic changes. Anti-immigrant (especially anti-Catholic) and antiblack riots became commonplace. At the same time, immigrants and African Americans worked to form their own communities.

Cities came to symbolize for many Americans both the possibilities and the limits of market expansion. Urban areas were marked by extremes of wealth, and they fostered vibrant working-class cultures even as they encouraged poverty, crime, and mob violence. Driven by a belief in human perfectibility, many evangelicals, especially women, worked tirelessly to right the wrongs of American society. They hoped to trigger the millennium, the thousand years of earthly peace accompanying Christ's return. Reformers battled the evils of prostitution and alcohol, and they sought to reform criminals and delinquents, improve insane asylums, and establish public schools. Some rejected the possibility of reforming American society from within and instead joined experimental communities that modeled radical alternatives to the social and economic order. Abolitionists combined the reformers' and utopians' approaches; they worked to perfect American society from within but through radical means—the eradication of slavery. Drawing on both secular and religious ideals, middle-class northerners increasingly articulated an ideology of free labor, touting the possibility for upward mobility in a competitive marketplace. This ideology would become increasingly central to northern regional identity.

Suggestions for Further Reading

Jeanne Boydston, *Home and Work: Housework, Wages, and the Ideology of Labor in the Early Republic* (1990)

Nancy Cott, *The Bonds of Womanhood: "Women's Sphere" in New England, 1780–1835* (1977)

Daniel Walker Howe, *What Hath God Wrought: The Transformation of America, 1815–1848* (2007)

Mary Kelley, *Learning to Stand and Speak: Women, Education, and Public Life in America's Republic* (2006)

Bruce Laurie, *Artisans into Workers: Labor in Nineteenth-Century America* (1989)

Steven Mintz, *Moralists and Modernizers: America's Pre–Civil War Reformers* (1995)

Carol Sheriff, *The Artificial River: The Erie Canal and the Paradox of Progress, 1817–1862* (1996)

Christine Stansell, *City of Women: Sex and Class in New York, 1789–1860* (1986)

Melvyn Stokes and Stephen Conway, eds., *The Market Revolution in America: Social, Political, and Religious Expressions, 1800–1880* (1996)

George Rogers Taylor, *The Transportation Revolution, 1815–1860* (1951)

The Contested West, 1815–1860

To eight-year-old Henry Clay Bruce, moving west was an adventure. In April 1844, the Virginia boy began a 1,500-mile, two-month trip to his new home in Missouri. Henry marveled at the newness of it all—beautiful natural terrain, impressive towns, different styles of dress. Nothing awed him more than the steamboat ride from Louisville to St. Louis; it felt like "a house floating on the water." Upon his arrival in Missouri, Henry was struck by how much the West differed from the East. The farms lay at much greater distances apart, and the countryside abounded with berries, wild fruits, game, and fish. But it was not paradise. Rattlesnakes, wolves, and vicious hogs roamed the countryside, keeping Henry and his playmates close to home.

Only one thing matched the wildlife's ferocity: Jack Perkinson, the owner of the plantation on which Henry now lived. For Henry was a slave boy who had been relocated, along with his mother and siblings, because his master decided to seek a new beginning in the West. Pettis Perkinson (Jack's brother and Henry's owner) and three other white Virginians had crammed their families, their slaves, and whatever belongings they could fit into three wagons—two for slaves, one for whites. Once in Missouri, Pettis resided with Jack Perkinson, who—according to Henry—readily yelled at and whipped his own slaves. Henry's first year in Missouri was as carefree as a slave child's life could be. The boy fished, hunted (with dogs, not guns), and gathered prairie chickens' eggs. But as his ninth birthday approached, Henry was hired out, first to a brickmaker, then to a tobacco factory. He worked sunup to sundown, and when he failed to satisfy his bosses, he was whipped.

Meanwhile, Pettis Perkinson, unenamored with Missouri, returned home to Virginia, only later summoning some of his slaves, including Henry, who returned "contrary to our will." A less

◀ Like Henry Clay Bruce, many emigrants in the 1840s traveled west by steamboat for part of their journey, making the rest of the trip on foot, horseback, wagon, canal boat, or—often—by some combination of means.
Joslyn Art Museum, Omaha, Nebraska

Chronology

1812	▪ General Land Office established
1820	▪ Price lowered on public lands
1821	▪ Santa Fe Trail charted
	▪ Mexico's independence
1823	▪ Mexico allows Stephen Austin to settle U.S. citizens in Tejas
1824	▪ Congressional General Survey Act
	▪ Jedediah Smith's South Pass publicized
	▪ Indian Office established
1825–32	▪ *Empresario* contracts signed
1826	▪ Fredonia rebellion fails
1830	▪ Indian Removal Act (see Chapter 9)
1830–46	▪ Comanche, Navajo, and Apache raiders devastate northern Mexican states
1832	▪ Black Hawk War
1834	▪ McCormick reaper patented
1836	▪ Lone Star Republic founded
	▪ U.S. Army Corps of Topographical Engineers established
1840–60	▪ 250,000 to 500,000 migrants travel overland
1841	▪ Log Cabin Bill
	▪ Texas annexed (see Chapter 12)
1846–48	▪ War with Mexico (see Chapter 12)
1847	▪ Mormons settle Great Salt Lake valley
1848	▪ California gold discovered
1849–50s	▪ Migrants stream into Great Plains and Far West
1849–1855	▪ Border between United States and Mexico demarcated
1855	▪ Ash Hollow Massacre
1857–58	▪ Mormons and U.S. Army in armed conflict
1862	▪ Homestead Act passed

rigorous work routine awaited the Perkinson slaves in Virginia, but that did not compensate for leaving loved ones behind in Missouri.

Soon Pettis Perkinson again grew weary of the tired, rocky soil on his Virginia farm, and with renewed determination to seek opportunity in the West, he moved to Mississippi, where his sister lived. But life on a cotton plantation suited neither Henry nor his master, who now decided—to his slaves' joy—to give Missouri a second chance.

Henry's master remained restless: two years after returning to Missouri, he decided to head for Texas. Henry, now in his late teens, and his brothers refused to go. Although livid, Pettis Perkinson abandoned his plans, apparently not wishing to contend with recalcitrant slaves. After being hired out several more times, Henry became the foreman on Perkinson's Missouri farm, where he remained until escaping during the Civil War to the free state of Kansas. Finally, Henry Clay Bruce found the opportunity and freedom that so many sought when they first headed westward.

Experience an interactive version of this story in MindTap®.

In 1820, about 20 percent of the nation's population lived west of the Appalachian Mountains. By 1860, nearly 50 percent did. Most white people and free blacks moved west because they—or their heads of household—believed better opportunities awaited them there. When easterners envisioned the West, they generally saw enormous tracts of fertile, uncultivated land. Or, beginning in the late 1840s, they imagined getting rich quick in the West's gold or silver mines. Some saw opportunities for lumbering or ranching or for selling goods or services to farmers, miners, lumbermen, and cattlemen.

For some white Americans, mostly from the South, the ability to own slaves in the West signaled the epitome of their own freedom. For others, from both the North and the South, slavery's westward expansion frustrated dreams for a new beginning in a region free from what they saw as slavery's degrading influence on white labor. Northerners, in particular, often set their sights on the Oregon Territory.

They believed the sacrifices brought about by an arduous transcontinental journey would be outweighed by the rewards: agricultural prosperity in a land free from blacks, enslaved and free.

Many of those heading west had no say in the matter. Men often made the decision without consulting their wives and children, and slaves' wishes received even less consideration. Nor did western settlers give much, if any, thought to how their migration would influence the Native peoples already living in the West—on lands they had occupied in some cases for generations and, in other cases, since being relocated by the U.S. government.

The federal government's involvement in westward expansion extended far beyond removing Native peoples. The government sponsored exploration, made laws regulating settlement and the establishment of territorial governments, surveyed and fixed prices on public lands, sold those lands, invested in transportation routes, and established a military presence (see Map. 11.1).

The Mexican government, too, played a role in Anglo-American settlement in the West—one it would later regret—by encouraging immigration to its northern borderlands in the 1820s. From the United States came settlers who vied with the region's other inhabitants—Native Americans, Hispanics, and people of mixed heritage—for land and other natural resources. A decade later, Texas, one of Mexico's northern provinces, declared its independence and sought annexation by the United States. Thus began an era of heightened tensions—not only between the United States and Mexico, but also within the United States as Texas's future became entangled with the thorny issue of slavery.

Human interactions in the West involved both cooperation and conflict. But with each passing decade, conflict—between expectations and reality, between people with different aspirations and worldviews—would increasingly define daily life.

- *How did conditions and tensions in the East influence western migration and settlement?*

- *How did public, private, and individual initiatives converge to shape the West's development?*

- *What motivated cooperation in the West, and what spurred conflict?*

11-1 The West in the American Imagination

▶ **What was the "West" to early-nineteenth-century Americans and emigrants?**

▶ **How did literature and art shape Americans' and Europeans' imaginations of the West?**

▶ **How did Euro-American artists portray Native peoples and their cultures?**

For historian Frederick Jackson Turner, writing in the late nineteenth century, it was the West, not the South or the North, that was distinctive. With its abundance of free land, the western frontier—what he saw as the "meeting point between savagery and civilization"—bred American democracy, shaped the American character, and made the United States exceptional among nations. Modern historians generally eschew the notion of American exceptionalism, stressing instead the deep and complex connections between the United States and the rest of the world. Although today's scholars also reject the racialist assumptions of Turner's definition of *frontier*, some see continued value in using the term to signify a meeting place of different cultures. Others see the West as fundamentally a place, not a process, though they disagree over what delineates it.

11-1a Defining the West

For early-nineteenth-century Americans of European descent, the West included anything west of the Appalachian Mountains. But it was, first and foremost, a place representing the future—a place offering economic and social betterment for themselves and their children. For many, betterment entailed landownership; the West's seeming abundance of land meant that anyone could hope to own a farm and achieve economic and political independence. Men who already owned land, like Pettis Perkinson, looked westward for cheaper, bigger, and more fertile landholdings. With the discovery of gold in California in 1848, the West became a place to strike it rich before returning home to live in increased comfort or even opulence.

Many people arrived in the West under the threat of force. These included enslaved men, women, and children whose owners moved them, often against their will, as well as Native peoples removed from their eastern homelands by the U.S. military under provisions of the Indian Removal Act of 1830.

To others, the very notion of the West would have been baffling. Emigrants from Mexico and Central or South America traveled north to get to what European Americans called the West. Chinese nationals traveled eastward to California. Many Native Americans simply considered the West home. Other Native peoples and French Canadians journeyed southward to the West. All these people, much like European Americans, arrived in the western portion of the North American continent because of a combination of factors pushing and pulling them.

11-1b Frontier Literature

For European Americans, Daniel Boone became the archetypal frontiersman, a man whose daring individualism opened the Eden-like West for virtuous and hard-working freedom lovers. Through biographies published by John Filson (1784) and by Timothy Flint (1833), Boone became a familiar figure in American and European households. The mythical Boone lived in the wilderness, became "natural" himself, and shrank from society, feeling compelled to relocate upon seeing smoke billowing from a neighboring cabin. He single-handedly overpowered bears and Indians. Even as he adopted wilderness ways, according to legend, Boone became the pathfinder for civilization. As a friend wrote, Boone "has been the instrument of opening the road to millions of the human family from the pressure of sterility and want, to a Land flowing with milk and honey." By borrowing biblical language—the land of milk and honey denoting the Promised Land, the idyllic place that God promised to the beleaguered Israelites—Boone's friend

suggested that Boone was Moses-like, leading his people to a land of abundance.

Such stories mythologized not only Boone, but the West itself. The Indian-fighting Boone, according to Flint's best-selling biography, had wrested for civilized society "the great west—the garden of the earth." Little matter that the real Boone regretted having killed Native peoples and often struggled to support his family. When Boone became the heroic model for James Fenimore Cooper's *Leatherstocking Tales* (1823–1841)—set on the frontier of western New York—he came to symbolize not only American adventure but also individualism and freedom.

With the invention of the steam press in the early 1830s, western adventure stories became cheap and widely read. Davy Crockett, another real-life figure turned into mythical hero, was featured in many of them. In real life, Crockett had first fought the Creeks under Andrew Jackson but later championed Native peoples' rights, rebuking the removal bill. After losing his life defending the Alamo mission during Texas's fight for

Map 11.1 Westward Expansion, 1800–1860

Through exploration, purchase, war, and treaty, the United States became a continental nation, stretching from the Atlantic to the Pacific.

independence (1836), though, Crockett often appeared in stories portraying the West as violent, a place where one escaped civilized society and fought Indians and Mexicans. But even in this version of the western myth, the American West symbolized what white Americans saw as their nation's core value: freedom.

11-1c Western Art

Inspired partly by such literature, many easterners yearned to see the West and its Native peoples, and artists hastened to accommodate them. Yet the images they produced often revealed more about white Americans' ideals than about the West itself. In these portrayals, the West was sometimes an untamed wilderness inhabited by savages (noble or otherwise), and sometimes a cultivated garden, a land of milk and honey where the Jeffersonian agrarian dream was realized.

The first Anglo-American artists to travel west were Samuel Seymour and Titian Ramsay Peale, whom the federal government hired to accompany explorer Stephen H. Long on his 1820 expedition to the Rocky Mountains. They pioneered an influential art genre: facsimiles in government reports. Between 1840 and 1860, Congress published nearly sixty works on western exploration, featuring hundreds of lithographs and engravings of plants, animals, and people. Some reports became best sellers. The most popular was the twelve-volume Pacific Railway Survey (1855–1860), chronicling expeditions to explore four possible railroad routes. The government distributed more than 53,000 copies, helping easterners visualize for themselves the continent's western reaches.

Although government reports often faithfully reproduced original paintings, they sometimes made telling alterations. When Richard Kern accompanied explorer James H. Simpson in 1849 to the Southwest, for example, he painted a Navajo man in a submissive pose. The painting's reproduction for general distribution transformed the man's pose into a rebellious one. In other cases, the government reports transformed artists' depictions of Native American-occupied landscapes into empty terrain seemingly free for the taking.

Yet the original artwork did not necessarily offer an accurate view of the West either. Artists' own cultural assumptions colored their portrayals, and commercial artists produced what they thought the public craved. When **George Catlin** traveled west in the early 1830s, he may have genuinely hoped to paint what he saw as Native peoples' vanishing way of life. But he also aimed to attract a paying public of easterners to his exhibitions. Traveling and painting immediately following the Indian Removal Act of 1830, Catlin painted the West with a moral in mind: Native peoples came in two varieties—those who preserved their original, almost noble qualities, characterized by freedom and moderation, and those who, after coming in contact with whites, had become "dissolute." Native peoples, he implied, benefited from removal from white Americans' corrupting influence.

Western artwork became widely viewed as facsimiles appeared in magazines and books and even on banknotes. Such images nurtured easterners' curiosities and fantasies— and sometimes their itch to move westward.

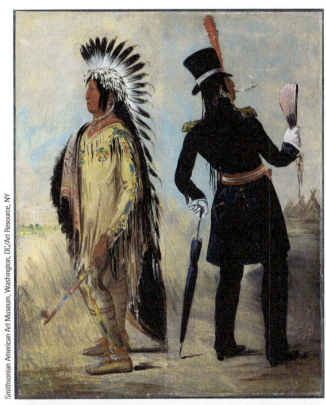

Smithsonian American Art Museum, Washington, DC/Art Resource, NY

▲ In one of his most famous portraits, George Catlin painted Wi-Jun-Jon, an Assiniboine man, both before and after he had mingled with white men. In the "before" stance, Wi-Jun-Jon is a dignified, peace-pipe-bearing warrior; in the "after" portrait, the "corrupted" Assiniboine has abandoned dignity for vanity and his peace pipe for a cigar.

11-1d Countering the Myths

But western realities often clashed with promoters' promises, and disappointed settlers sometimes tried to clarify matters for future migrants. From Philadelphia in the 1850s came a song parodying the familiar call of "to the West":

> At the west they told me there was wealth to be won,
> The forest to clear, was the work to be done;
> I tried it—couldn't do it—guv it up in despair,
> And just see if you'll ever again catch me there.
> The little snug farm I expected to buy,
> I quickly discovered was just all in my eye,
> I came back like a streak—you may go—but I'm bless'd
> If you'll ever again, sirs, catch me at the west.

Rebecca Burlend, an English immigrant in Illinois, encountered hardships aplenty—intemperate weather, difficult working conditions, swindlers—and with her son wrote an autobiographical account, *A True Picture of Emigration* (1848), alerting her countrymen to what awaited them in the American West. The Burlends had been lured to

George Catlin American painter who traveled throughout the West and produced numerous portraits of Native Americans that reflected his fascination with and beliefs about them.

Illinois by an Englishman's letters extolling "a land flowing with milk and honey." Burlend reckoned that he must have "gathered his honey rather from thorns than flowers." Her account sought not to discourage emigration but to substitute a realistic for a rosy description.

11-2 Expansion and Resistance in the Trans-Appalachian West

▶ How did individuals decide to move west?

▶ How did Native Americans respond to white settlement in the West?

▶ What were the realities of work in the West?

▶ How was the economy of the West linked to the East?

Americans had always been highly mobile, but never to the extent following the War of 1812, which weakened Native peoples' resistance and set off a flurry of transportation projects. In the 1820s and 1830s, settlers streamed west of the Appalachian Mountains into the Old Northwest and the Old Southwest. They traveled by foot, horseback, wagon, canal boat, steamboat, or—often—by some combination of means. Many people, like Pettis Perkinson and his slaves, moved several times, looking for better opportunities, and when opportunities failed to materialize, some returned home.

Both the Old Northwest and the Old Southwest saw population explosions during the early nineteenth century (see Map 11.2). But while the Old Southwest grew by an impressive 50 percent each decade, the Northwest's population grew exponentially. In 1790, the region's white population numbered just a few hundred people. By 1860, nearly 7 million people called the region home. Between 1810 and 1830, the population of Ohio more than quadrupled, while Indiana and Illinois grew fourteenfold and thirteenfold, respectively. Michigan's population multiplied by more than fifty times in the thirty years between 1820 and 1850. Migration rather than birth rates accounted for most of this growth, and once in the Old Northwest, people did not stay put. By the 1840s, more people left Ohio than moved into it. Geographic mobility, the search for more and better opportunities, and connections to the market economy defined the region that became known as the Midwest following the acquisition of U.S. territory farther west. This region came to symbolize, for many northerners, the heart of American values: freedom and upward mobility, both of which could be achieved (for white Americans and European immigrants) through hard work and virtuous behavior.

11-2a Deciding Where to Move

The decision to move west—and then to move again—could be difficult, even heartrending. Moving west meant leaving behind worn-out soil and settled areas with little land available for purchase, but it also meant leaving behind family, friends, and communities. One woman remembered how on the evening before her departure for the West, her entire family gathered together for the last time "looking as if we were all going to our graves the next morning." The journey promised to be arduous and expensive, as did the backbreaking labor of clearing new lands. The West was a land of opportunity but also of uncertainty. What if the soil proved less fertile than anticipated? What if neighbors—white as well as Native American—proved unfriendly, or worse? What if homesickness became unbearable?

Given all that western settlers risked, they tried to control as many variables as possible. Like Pettis Perkinson, people often relocated to communities where they had relatives or friends, and they often traveled with acquaintances from home. They moved to climates similar to those they left behind. Massachusetts farmers headed to western New York or Ohio, Virginians and North Carolinians went to Missouri, Georgians populated Mississippi and Texas, and Europeans—mostly Germans and Irish—headed to the Old Northwest in much larger numbers than to the Old Southwest. Migrants settled in ethnic communities or with people of similar religious values and affiliations. As a result, the Midwest was—in the words of two of its historians—"more like an ethnic and cultural checkerboard than the proverbial melting pot."

When westward-bound Americans fixed on particular destinations, their decisions often rested on slavery's status there. Some white southerners, tired of the planter elite's social and political power, sought homes in areas free from slavery—or at least where there were few plantations. Many others, though, went west to improve their chances of owning slaves, or of purchasing additional slaves. White northerners also resented elite slaveowners' economic and political power and hoped to distance themselves from slavery as well as from free blacks. One Bostonian captured the viewpoint of many white northerners who contemplated moving west: "As a great evil, I detest slavery, but what will you do with the blacks when it is abolished; they cant [sic] hold their own & if given a fair land would ruin it & relapse into African barbarism." Influenced by such sentiments, many midwestern states passed "black laws" in the 1850s prohibiting African Americans, free or enslaved, from living within their boundaries. (Oregon passed a similar law.) Ironically, many free blacks migrated west to free themselves from eastern prejudice. Enslaved men, women, and children moved west in enormous numbers in the years after 1815. Some traveled with their owners, either young couples whose parents had given them slaves as wedding gifts, or established planters who had headed west in search of more fertile soil. When white parents presented their westward-bound children with slaves, they often tore apart those slaves' own families, as spouses, children, parents, or siblings stayed behind. Many slaves moved west with slave traders, who manacled them to a chain connecting them to dozens of other slaves, "urged on by the whip," as one white observer described the slave coffle he encountered in a Mississippi swamp. Their first destination in

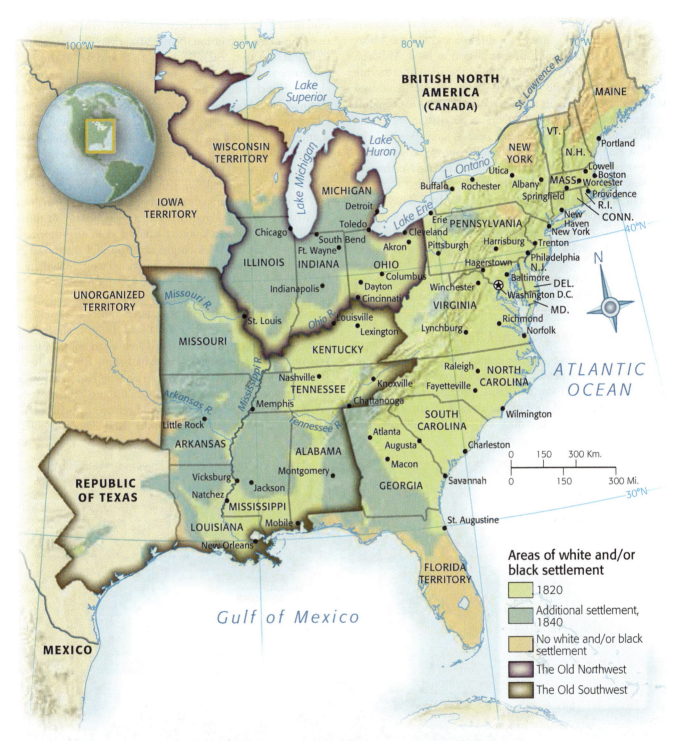

Map 11.2 Settlement in the Old Southwest and Old Northwest, 1820 and 1840

Removal of Native peoples and a growing transportation network opened up land to white and black settlers in the regions known as the Old Southwest and the Old Northwest, as the U.S. population grew from 9.6 million in 1820 to 17.1 million in 1840.

the West was the slave pen, often in New Orleans, where they were auctioned to the highest bidder, who became their new owner and took them farther west. Despite the hardships that slaves faced in the West, some took advantage of frontier conditions—tangled and vast forests, the comparative thinness of

law enforcement and slave patrol, and the proximity of Native American communities willing to harbor runaway slaves—to seize their freedom.

Between 1815 and 1860, few western migrants, white or black, settled on the Great Plains, a region reserved for

Native peoples until the 1850s, and relatively few easterners risked the overland journey to California and Oregon before the transcontinental railroad's completion in 1869. Although at first the Southwest seemed to hold the edge in attracting new white settlers, the Midwest—with its better-developed transportation routes, its more democratic access to economic markets, its smaller African American population, its smaller and cheaper average landholding, and its climatic similarity to New England and northern Europe—proved considerably more attractive in the decades after 1820. The Old Northwest's thriving transportation hubs also made good first stops for western migrants lacking cash to purchase land. They found work unloading canal boats, planting and harvesting wheat on nearby farms, grinding wheat into flour, or sawing trees into lumber—or, more often, cobbling together a combination of these seasonal jobs. The South offered fewer such opportunities. With the Old Northwest's population growing more quickly, white southerners worried increasingly about congressional representation and laws regarding slavery.

11-2b Indian Removal and Resistance

In both the Midwest and the Southwest, the expansion of white settlement depended on Native peoples' removal. Even as the U.S. Army escorted Native peoples from the Old Southwest, the federal government arranged treaties in which northeastern American Indian nations relinquished their land titles in exchange for lands west of the Mississippi River (see "Southern Expansion, Native American Resistance and Removal," Section 9-2). Between 1829 and 1851, the U.S. government and northern American Indian tribes signed eighty-six such treaties. Some northern Native peoples evaded removal, including the Miamis in Indiana, the Ottawas and Chippewas in the upper Midwest, and the Winnebagos in southern Wisconsin. In 1840, for example, Miami chiefs had acceded to pressure to exchange 500,000 acres in Indiana for equivalent acreage in Indian Country. Under the treaty's terms, their people had five years to move. When they did not, federal troops arrived to escort them. But about half of the Miami nation dodged the soldiers—and many of those who did trek to Indian Country later returned unauthorized. In Wisconsin, some Winnebagos similarly eluded removal or returned to Wisconsin after being escorted west by soldiers.

11-2c Black Hawk War

The Sauks (or "Sacs") and Fox fared much less well. In a series of treaties between 1804 and 1830, their leaders exchanged lands in northwestern Illinois and southwestern Wisconsin for lands across the Mississippi River in Iowa Territory. Black Hawk, a Sauk warrior who had sided with the British during the War of 1812, disputed the treaties' validity and vowed his people would return to their ancestral lands. "My reason teaches me that land cannot be sold,"

▲ In 1834, Karl Bodmer painted a farm on the Illinois prairie, depicting the more permanent, if still modest, structures that farmers built after the initial urgency to clear fields for cultivation had subsided.

Joslyn Art Museum, Omaha, Nebraska

Black Hawk later recalled. "The Great Spirit gave it to his children to live upon, and cultivate, as far as is necessary for their subsistence … Nothing can be sold but such things as can be carried away." In 1832, Black Hawk led a group of Sauk and Fox families to Illinois, causing panic among white settlers. The state's governor activated the militia, who were later joined by militia from surrounding states and territories as well as by U.S. Army regular soldiers. Over the next several months, hundreds of Sauk and Fox individuals and dozens of white settlers died under often gruesome circumstances in what is known as the Black Hawk War. As the Sauks and Fox tried to flee across the Mississippi River, American soldiers on a steamboat and on land fired indiscriminately. Those men, women, and children who survived the river crossing met gunfire on the western shore from Lakota (Sioux), their longtime enemies, now allied with the Americans.

Black Hawk survived to surrender, and U.S. officials undertook to impress on him and the uprising's other leaders the futility of resistance. After being imprisoned, then sent to Washington, D.C., along a route meant to underscore the United States' immense size and population, and then imprisoned again, the Sauk and Fox peoples were returned to their homes. The Black Hawk War marked the end of militant Native American uprisings in the Old Northwest, adding to the region's appeal to white settlers.

11-2d Selling the West

Land speculators, developers of "paper towns" (ones existing on paper only), steamboat companies, and manufacturers of farming implements all promoted the Midwest as a tranquil place of unbounded opportunity. Land proprietors emphasized the region's connections to eastern customs and markets. They knew that, when families uprooted themselves and headed west, they did not—the mythical Daniel Boone and Davy Crockett aside—seek to escape civilization. When Michael D. Row, the proprietor of Rowsburg in northern Ohio, sought to sell town lots in 1835, he emphasized that Rowsburg was in a "thickly settled" area, stood at the crossroads of public transportation leading in every direction, and had established mills and tanning yards.

Western settlement generally followed rather than preceded connections to national and international markets. Eastern farmers, looking to escape tired soil or tenancy, sought fertile lands for growing commercial crops. Labor-saving devices, such as Cyrus McCormick's reaper (1834) and John Deere's steel plow (1837), made the West more alluring. McCormick, a Virginia inventor, patented a horse-drawn reaper that allowed two men to harvest the same number of acres of wheat that previously required between four and sixteen men, depending on which handheld tool they wielded. Because the reaper's efficiency achieved its greatest payoffs on the prairies, where tracts of land were larger and flatter than in the Shenandoah Valley, McCormick relocated his factory to Chicago in 1847 and began a dogged campaign to sell his reaper—which at $100 was an expensive investment for the average farmer—and, along with it, the West itself.

Without John Deere's steel plow, which unlike wooden and iron plows could break through tough grass and roots and did not require constant cleaning, "breaking the plains" might not have been possible at all.

11-2e Clearing the Land

Most white migrants intended to farm. After locating a suitable land claim, they immediately constructed a rudimentary cabin if none already existed. Time did not permit more elaborate structures, for—contrary to McCormick reaper ads—few settlers found plowed fields awaiting them. First they had to clear the land.

For those settling in wooded areas, the quickest and easiest way to get crops in the ground was to girdle, or to cut deep notches with an ax around a tree's base, cutting off the flow of sap. A few weeks later, the trees would lose their leaves, which farmers burned for fertilizer. As soon as enough light came through, settlers planted corn—a durable and nutritious crop. Eventually the dead trees fell and were chopped for firewood and fences, leaving stumps whose removal was a backbreaking task. At the rate of five to ten acres a year, depending on a family's size, the average family needed ten years to fully clear a farm, assuming the family did not relocate sooner. Prairie land took less time. Throughout the 1850s, though, many farmers dismissed lands free of timber as equivalent to deserts, unfit for cultivation.

Whereas farming attracted families, lumbering and, later, mining appealed mostly to single young men. Lumbering involved long hours—sunup to sundown—and backbreaking labor; lumber workers not only felled trees, but hauled, hoisted, sawed, and stacked the wood. Although employers believed that married men constituted the most stable workforce, they did not want women encumbered by children in the camps. Instead, they looked for "good Families without children," whose wives would work as cooks or laundresses. As one Chicago mill owner informed his manager, "my Business will not warrant the payment of wages sufficient for any one to keep his wife as a Laidy [sic]." Few family men found lumbering to be attractive work.

By the 1840s, the nation's timber industry centered around the Great Lakes. As eastern forests became depleted, northeastern lumber companies and their laborers migrated to Wisconsin, Michigan, and Minnesota. Recently arrived Scandinavians and French Canadians also worked in the booming lumber industry, which provided construction materials for growing cities and wooden ties for expanding railroads. As the Great Lakes forests thinned, lumbermen moved again—some to the Gulf States' pine forests, some to Canada, and some to the Far West, where Mexicans in California and British in Canada had already established flourishing lumber industries. With the rapid growth of California's cities following the **Gold Rush of 1849**, timber's demand soared, drawing midwestern lumbermen farther west.

Gold Rush of 1849 After an American carpenter discovered gold in the foothills of California's Sierra Nevada range in 1848, Americans and people from around the world moved to California to look for gold.

▲ The horse-drawn McCormick reaper made the harvesting of wheat far more efficient, increasing the allure of western prairie lands. McCormick's Patent Virginia Reaper Advert, 1850 (litho), American School, (19th century) /Private Collection/ Peter Newark American Pictures/ Bridgeman Images.

The Midwest's own cities nurtured the surrounding countryside's settlement. Steamboats turned river settlements like Louisville and Cincinnati into vibrant commercial centers, while Chicago, Detroit, and Cleveland grew up on the Great Lakes' banks. By the mid-nineteenth century, Chicago, with its railroads, stockyards, and grain elevators, dominated the region's economy; western farmers transported livestock and grain by rail to that city, where pigs became packed meat and grain became flour before being shipped east. The promise of future flour and future pigs gave rise to commodities markets. Some of the world's most sophisticated and speculative economic practices took place in Chicago.

11-3　The Federal Government and Westward Expansion

▶ What was the significance of early explorations and encounters in the West?

▶ What role did the federal government play in the exploration of and expansion into the West?

▶ Why did tensions emerge between the federal government and white settlers over the distribution of land?

Few white Americans considered settling in the West before the region had been explored, surveyed, secured, and "civilized," by which they meant not only the removal of Native populations but also the establishment of churches, businesses, and American legal structures. Although some individuals headed west in advance of European civilization, wide-scale settlement depended on the federal government's sponsorship.

11-3a　The Fur Trade

No figure better represents the mythical westerner than the mountain man: the loner who wandered the mountains, trapping beaver, living off the land, casting off all semblance of civilization, and daring to go where no white person had ever trod. Fur trappers were, in fact, among the first white Americans in the trans-Appalachian West, but in reality, their lives bore faint resemblance to the myth. Although many had little contact with American society, they interacted regularly with the West's Native peoples. Fur trappers lived among Native peoples, became multilingual, and often married Native American women. Native women transformed animal carcasses into finished pelts, and they also smoothed trade relations between their husbands and their own Native communities. The offspring of such marriages—métis or mestizos (people of mixed Native American and European heritage)—often entered the fur trade and added to the West's cultural complexity.

The fur trade was an international business, with pelts from deep in the American interior finding their way to Europe and Asia. Until the 1820s, British companies dominated the trade, but American ventures prospered in the 1820s and 1830s. The American Fur Company made John Jacob Astor the nation's wealthiest man. While Astor lived lavishly in his New York City mansion, his business employed hundreds of trappers and traders who lived and worked among Native peoples in the Great Lakes and Pacific Northwest regions. From its base in Astoria on the Columbia River, just a few miles from the Pacific Ocean in present-day Oregon, the American Fur Company made millions by sending furs to China.

Even for the great majority of trappers who never made it to Astoria, the fur trade had an international dimension. Beginning in the 1820s, they came together annually for a "rendezvous"—a multiday gathering where they traded fur for guns, tobacco, and beads that they could later exchange with Native peoples. They also shared stories and alcohol, and gambled. Modeled on similar Native American gatherings that had occurred for generations, the rendezvous brought together Americans, Native peoples, Mexicans, and people of mixed heritage from all over the West—as far north as Canada and as far south as Mexico—in numbers that could reach up to one thousand. Rendezvous took place in remote mountain locations but were cosmopolitan affairs.

By 1840, when the final rendezvous took place, the American fur trade was fading. Beavers had been over-hunted and fashions had shifted, with silk supplanting

◀ In 1837, Alfred Jacob Miller, a noted painter of the American West, visited an annual rendezvous, where fur trappers and Native peoples exchanged goods and shared conviviality. Here, Miller portrays the fanfare with which he and his fellow travelers were greeted.

Gift of The Coe Foundation/Buffalo Bill Center of the West

beaver fur as the preferred material for hats. The traders' legacy includes setting a pattern of resource extraction and depletion (and boom and bust), introducing Native peoples to devastating diseases, and developing trails across the trans-Mississippi West.

11-3b Transcontinental Exploration

A desire for quicker and safer routes for transporting goods to trading posts drove much early exploration (see Map 11.3). William Becknell, an enterprising merchant, helped in 1821 to chart the **Santa Fe Trail** running between Missouri and Santa Fe, New Mexico, where it connected to the Chihuahua Trail running southward into Mexico, allowing American and Mexican merchants to develop a vibrant exchange of American manufactured goods for furs and other items. Fur trader Jedediah Smith rediscovered in 1824 the South Pass; this twenty-mile break in the Rocky Mountains in present-day Wyoming had previously been known only to Native Americans and a handful of fur trappers from the Pacific Fur Company who had passed through in 1812. The South Pass became the route followed by most overland travelers to California and Oregon. Less well-known traders, trappers, missionaries, and gold seekers, often assisted by Native American guides, also discovered traveling routes throughout the West, and some—most famously, mountain man Kit Carson—aided government expeditions.

Lewis and Clark's Corps of Discovery was only the first of many federally sponsored expeditions to chart the trans-Mississippi West. These expeditions often had diplomatic goals, aiming to establish cordial relations with Native groups with whom Americans might trade or enter military alliances. Some had scientific missions, charged with recording information about the region's Native inhabitants, flora, and fauna. But they were always also commercial in purpose. Just

as Lewis and Clark had hoped to find what proved to be an elusive Northwest Passage to the Pacific, so, too, did later explorers hope to locate land, water, and rail routes that would allow American businessmen and farmers to trade nationally and internationally.

In 1805, the U.S. Army dispatched Zebulon Pike to find the Mississippi River's source and a navigable route west. He was instructed to collect information on natural resources and Native peoples, and to foster diplomatic relationships with Native American leaders. Pike, like other explorers, was also instructed by government officials to identify and purchase Native peoples' lands suitable for military garrisons.

Although Pike failed to identify the Mississippi's source and had limited success in cultivating relationships and purchasing land, he nonetheless gathered important information. Shortly after returning from present-day Minnesota, he left for what are now Missouri, Nebraska, Kansas, and Colorado. After Pike and his men wandered into Spanish territory to the south, military officials held Pike captive for several months in Mexico, inadvertently giving him a tour of areas that he might not have otherwise explored. After his release, Pike wrote an account of his experiences describing a potential market in southwestern cities as well as bountiful furs and precious metals. The province of Tejas (Texas), with its fertile soil and rich grasslands, enchanted him. At the same time, Pike dismissed the other northern provinces of Mexico, whose boundaries stretched to the northern borders of present-day Nevada and Utah, as unsuitable for human habitation. Although nomadic Native peoples might sustain themselves there, he explained, the region was unfit for cultivation by civilized people.

Santa Fe Trail Trading route from St. Louis, Missouri, to Santa Fe, New Mexico, that enabled commerce to expand its reach farther west.

Map 11.3 Western Native Peoples and Routes of Exploration

Although western explorers believed they were discovering new routes and places, Native peoples had long lived in most of the areas through which explorers traveled.

Stephen Long, another army explorer, similarly declared in 1820 that the region comprising modern-day Oklahoma, Kansas, and Nebraska was "the Great American Desert," incapable of cultivation. Until the 1850s, when a transcontinental railroad was planned, this "desert" was reserved for Native peoples' settlement, and most army-sponsored exploration focused elsewhere. In 1838, Congress established the U.S. Army Corps of Topographical Engineers to systematically explore the West in advance of widespread settlement. As a second lieutenant in that corps, **John C. Frémont**

John C. Frémont Explorer who played a role in a California rebellion against Mexico; later a senator and presidential candidate and force in national politics.

undertook three expeditions to the region between the upper Mississippi and Missouri rivers, the Rockies, the Great Basin, Oregon, and California. He helped survey the Oregon Trail. With the assistance of his wife, Jessie Benton Frémont, Frémont published best-selling accounts of his explorations, earning him the nickname "The Pathfinder" and paving the way for a political career. The Corps of Topographical Engineers' most significant contributions came in the 1850s with its surveying of possible routes for a transcontinental railroad.

The federal government spent millions publicizing the results of its explorations, much more than it allotted for exploration itself. Westward migrants often carried two books with them: the Bible and Frémont's account of his army explorations.

11-3c A Military Presence

The army did more than explore. It also helped ready the West for settlement. With the General Survey Act of 1824, Congress empowered the military to chart transportation improvements deemed vital to the nation's military protection or commercial growth. In addition to working on federally funded projects, army engineers helped design state- and privately sponsored roads, canals, and railroads, and army soldiers cleared forests and lay roadbeds. A related bill, also in 1824, authorized the army to improve the Ohio and Mississippi rivers; a later amendment did the same for the Missouri.

By the 1850s, 90 percent of the U.S. military was stationed west of the Mississippi River. When Native peoples refused to relinquish their lands, the army escorted them westward; when they inflicted harm on whites or their property, the army waged war. The army sometimes destroyed the crops and buildings of white squatters refusing to vacate lands settled without legal title. But, primarily, the army assisted overland migration. Army forts on the periphery of Indian Country intimidated Native peoples, defended settlers and migrants from Native attacks, and supplied information and provisions. In theory, the army was also supposed to protect Native Americans by driving settlers off Native lands and enforcing laws prohibiting the sale of alcohol to Native peoples. Yet even when officers were disposed to enforce such policies, the army's small size relative to the territory it regulated made it virtually impossible to do so.

The Office of Indian Affairs handled the government's other interactions with Native peoples, including treaty negotiations, school management, and trade oversight. Created in 1824 as part of the War Department, the Indian Office cooperated with the military in removing Native peoples from lands that stood in the way of American expansion and in protecting those citizens who staked their future in the West. In 1849 the Indian Office became part of the newly established Department of the Interior and soon shifted its focus from removal to civilization, through a reservation system. Whereas some Native individuals accepted reservations as the best protection from white incursion, others rejected them, sometimes setting off deadly intratribal disagreements.

11-3d Public Lands

The federal government controlled vast tracts of land, procured either from the states' cessions of their western claims after the Revolution or through treaties with foreign powers, including American Indian nations. The General Land Office, established in 1812 as part of the Treasury Department, handled those lands' distribution. Its earliest policies, designed to raise revenue, divided western lands into 640-acre tracts to be sold at public auction at a minimum price of $2 an acre. These policies favored speculators over individual, cash-poor farmers. Speculators bought up millions of acres of land. Unable to afford federal lands, many settlers became squatters, prompting Congress

The Squatters, 1850 (oil on canvas)/Bingham, George Caleb (1811–79)/MUSEUM OF FINE ARTS, BOSTON/Museum of Fine Arts, Boston, Massachusetts, USA/Bridgeman Images

▲ In this 1850 painting, George Caleb Bingham portrays squatters, or settlers who improved public lands before they went on sale, often in the hope that the government would later allow them to purchase the lands at low prices.

in 1820 to lower the price of land to $1.25 per acre and to make available tracts as small as 80 acres. Twelve years later, it began selling 40-acre tracts. Yet it demanded that the land be bought outright, and in a cash-poor society (particularly in the aftermath of the Panic of 1819), few would-be western settlers had enough cash to purchase government land. Because speculators sold land on credit, many small-time farmers bought from them instead, but at inflated prices.

Farmers pressed for a federal policy of preemption—that is, the right to settle on land without obtaining title, to improve it, and to buy it later at the minimum price ($1.25 an acre) established by law. Without such a law, farmers who had "squatted" on land—settled and improved it without legal title—risked losing it to speculators who could outbid them once the land became officially open for sale. One congressman explained the squatter's plight: "he would see his little home, on which he had toiled for years, where he hoped to rear his children and find a peaceful grave, pass into the hands of a rich moneyed company."

Although some states offered lands through preemption, and although Congress authorized preemption of federal lands in particular instances in the 1820s and 1830s, the first general preemption law, the so-called Log Cabin Bill, came in 1841, and even then, it applied only to surveyed land. The right of preemption extended to unsurveyed lands with the **Homestead Act of 1862**, which provided that land would be provided free to any U.S. citizen (or foreigner who had declared the intention of becoming a citizen), provided he or she resided on it for five years and improved it. Alternatively, settlers could buy the land

Homestead Act of 1862
Passed in 1862, it embodied the Republican Party's ideal of "free soil, free labor, free men" by granting 160 acres of public land to settlers who resided on it for five years and improved it.

Gold in California

When James Marshall discovered gold in Sutter's Mill, California, in January 1848, word spread quickly—and quite literally around the world. Within a year, tens of thousands of adventurers from other countries rushed to California, making it the most cosmopolitan place in North America, and perhaps the entire world.

In an era before the telegraph crossed the oceans, the news traveled surprisingly fast. Mexicans heard first. Next, word spread to Chile, Peru, and throughout South America; then across the Pacific to Hawai'i, China, and Australia; and then to Europe— Ireland, France, and the German states. How did the news travel? Overland travelers brought the news south to Baja California and Sonora in Mexico. By spring 1849, some six thousand Mexicans were panning for gold around the newly established town of Sonora, California. Many of the Mexicans came north seasonally to seek gold, spreading news of California on every trip home.

Sailing ships brought news of California gold to Hawai'i. The newspaper *Honolulu Polynesian* announced it in the kingdom on June 24, 1848. "Honolulu has never before witnessed such an excitement as the gold fever has created," the *Polynesian* reported later that summer. Gold seekers and merchants sailed from Hawai'i to California, and their letters home recruited others. The constant traffic led to regular steamship service between Hawai'i and California as early as 1853.

A ship brought news of California gold discoveries to Valparaiso, Chile, in August 1848. More dramatically, a few weeks later, another sailing vessel landed with $2,500 in gold dust aboard. Although Chilean newspapers initially ignored the discovery, people in Chile's cities talked feverishly about gold. By November, newspapers reported rumors of California's overnight riches. Before year's end, two thousand Chileans had left for California, and many Chilean merchants opened branch stores in San Francisco.

Word of gold and California reached Australia in December 1848. Gold seekers quickly made travel arrangements, and by 1850 every ship in Sydney Harbour was destined for California. News had already reached China in mid-1848. A San Francisco merchant headed for the gold fields, Chum Ming, had written a cousin about his hopes for wealth. Four months later, the cousin arrived in San Francisco—with fellow villagers. Widespread poverty and gold's allure prompted many other Chinese to follow. By the mid-1850s, one in five gold miners was Chinese.

Californians, new and old, foreign and native-born, expressed amazement at the ethnic variety. One described it as "the most curious Babel of a place imaginable." In 1850, the new state of California had nearly 40 percent foreign-born inhabitants, the majority non-European. Through word of mouth, rumor, letters home, and newspaper reports, the discovery of gold in 1848 linked California to millions of ordinary people around the globe.

CRITICAL THINKING

- Reading this feature and section 11-2f on the Gold Rush, evaluate the extent to which the influx of immigrants from countries around the world as well as the arrival of Americans from the East unsettled patterns of migration that had existed up until this point. How did California's gold rush change life there for newcomers, existing residents, and Native peoples?

◀ This 1855 Frank Marryat drawing of a San Francisco saloon dramatizes the international nature of the California gold rush. Like theater performers, the patrons of the saloon dress their parts as Yankees, Mexicans, Asians, and South Americans.

The Art Archive at Art Resource, NY

outright at $1.25 an acre after six months of residency, an arrangement that allowed them to use the land as collateral for loans to purchase additional land, farming supplies, or machinery. By the time of the Homestead Act, though, much of the remaining federal land was arid, and 160 acres was not always enough for an independent farm. Most of the best land, moreover, ended up in speculators' hands.

11-4 The Southwestern Borderlands

▶ **What was life like for Hispanics and Native peoples prior to settlement by white Americans?**

▶ **How did white settlement and expansion in the Southwest and Texas influence Native peoples?**

▶ **How did the relationship between Mexico and Americans evolve amid efforts to obtain Texas independence?**

Along the Louisiana Territory's southwestern border lay vast provinces controlled mostly by the Comanches and other Native American groups but claimed first by Spain and then—after 1821—by the newly independent nation of Mexico (see Map 11.4). **New Mexico**, with its bustling commercial centers of Albuquerque and Santa Fe, remained under Mexican federal control until the United States conquered the territory during its War with Mexico. Texas, by contrast, had a much more attenuated relationship with the Mexican government; in 1824, it became an autonomous state (Coahuila y Tejas), giving it substantially more political independence from federal authorities than New Mexico enjoyed. This situation fostered Texas's struggle for national independence and then annexation to the United States, which in turn returned the divisive issue of slavery to the forefront of American political debate (see Chapter 12).

11-4a Southwestern Slavery

By the time Anglo-Americans became interested in Mexico's northern reaches, slavery in the Southwest was centuries old. Yet as practiced by indigenous peoples—Comanches, Apaches, Kiowas, Navajos, Utes, and Pueblos—and by Spaniards, slavery differed from the chattel slavery of Africans and African Americans in the American South. Southwestern slavery was no less violent, but it centered on capturing women and children, who were then assimilated into their captors' communities, where they provided labor and status while fostering economic and diplomatic exchanges with the communities from which they had been captured.

This system of "captives and cousins," as one scholar terms it, was built on racial mixing—a practice anathema to most white Americans. As white slaveholders from the Southeast pushed their way into Mexican territory during the 1820s and 1830s, they often justified their conquest in racial

terms. Even the region's Hispanic settlers, they reasoned, had been rendered lazy and barbarous by racial intermixing and were thus destined to be supplanted, whether peaceably or otherwise.

11-4b The New Mexican Frontier

When Mexico gained independence from Spain in 1821, the Hispanic population of New Mexico outnumbered the indigenous Pueblo peoples by three to one. There were 28,000 Hispanics, including people born in Spain and, especially, *criollos*, people born in New Spain to parents of Spanish descent. Whether Spanish, Native American, criollo, or mestizo, most New Mexicans engaged in irrigated agriculture. To the north of Santa Fe, they farmed small plots, but to the south, larger farms and ranches predominated. Rancheros' wealth came from selling their wool and corn in distant markets, and from relying on unpaid laborers: farmhands, often their own relatives, bound to the rancheros by debt. United by a threat from the province's raiding Native groups—Apaches, Utes, Navajos, and Comanches—Hispanics, Pueblos, and mestizos sometimes united in common defense. But relations among Hispanics and the sedentary Pueblos were not always peaceful. Their numerical superiority allowed Hispanics to seize many of the Pueblos' villages and lands in the rich northern river valleys of an otherwise arid region.

The Santa Fe Trail caused a commercial explosion in New Mexico, doubling the value of imports in just two years. Whereas the Spanish had tried to keep foreigners out, the Mexican government offered enormous land grants to Anglo-American and French entrepreneurs, sometimes in partnership with the region's Hispanic residents, hoping they would develop the region's industry and agriculture, and strengthen commercial ties with the United States.

Although commercial ties did strengthen, very few Americans settled permanently in New Mexico during the 1820s and 1830s. Most of the best lands had already been taken by Native peoples and Hispanics. And Americans in search of cheap, fertile land did not need to travel that far west; they could find what they were looking for in Texas.

11-4c The Texas Frontier

That they would do so, however, was not evident at the time of Mexican independence. Unlike in New Mexico, indigenous peoples remained the dominant group in Texas in 1821, though the population also included Hispanics, Anglos, mestizos, and immigrant Native Americans. Of the thirty thousand indigenous people, most were Comanches, but there were also Coahuiltecans, Tonkawas, Karankawas, Apaches, Caddos, and Wichitas. Texas was part of what one historian has called the Comanche Empire, an enormous territory spreading from northern Mexico to Louisiana that the Comanches dominated through a combination of kinship ties, trade, diplomacy, and violence. People of European heritage were a relatively

New Mexico Former Spanish colony in the upper Rio Grande Valley that became part of Mexico after 1821.

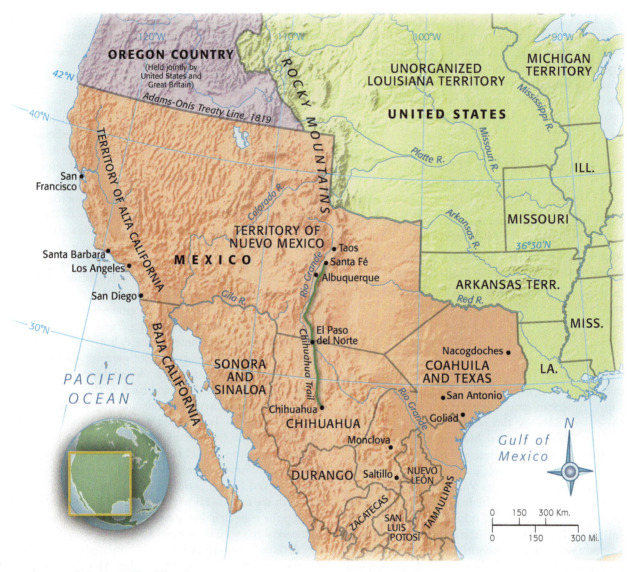

Map 11.4 Mexico's Far North

What is now considered the American Southwest was made up of the northern provinces of Mexico until the United States conquered the territory during the Mexican War (1846–1848).

small presence in Texas in 1821. Hispanic peoples had been there since the 1500s, establishing missions and presidios, but by 1820, they numbered only two thousand. Most raised livestock on ranches, while others made their living from trading with Native peoples. Living so distant from the Spanish colonial capital in Mexico City, they formed a distinctive identity, seeing themselves as **Tejanos** (or Texans) rather than as Spaniards. Many intermarried with Native peoples.

After the War of 1812, Anglo-Americans had begun entering Texas, where they sought furs, silver, or adventure. They traded manufactured goods—such as guns, ammunition, and kettles—for animal hides, horses, and mules; soon they largely supplanted the Tejanos as Native peoples' trading partners. Although

some Anglos settled in Texas, often living among Native peoples, most simply traveled the Santa Fe and Chihuahua trails without settling. They were deterred in part by the region's violence.

11-4d The Comanche Empire

As Native Americans competed with one another for resources, the southwestern borderlands experienced intermittent but often brutal violence. Mounted on horses, the Comanches hunted bison, took captives, and stole horses, livestock, and crops from their enemies, among whom were the Pawnees, Arapahos, Cheyennes, and Osage. Other, smaller Native groups, such as the Wichitas and Caddos, mostly farmed, growing enough corn, beans, squash, and

Tejanos Native Texans of Mexican descent.

Smithsonian American Art Museum, Washington, DC/Art Resource, NY

▲ The Comanche controlled a vast empire along the Louisiana Territory's southwestern with Mexico. Here, in a George Catlin painting from 1834, Comanche women dress robes and dry meat.

pumpkin to feed themselves and to trade with the more mobile Comanches. When crops failed, farmers often turned to bison hunting as well, sometimes causing conflict with the Comanches.

Tensions increased around the time of Mexican independence, when another ten thousand Native Americans began migrating into the region. From the Old Northwest came Shawnees and Kickapoos—former members of Tecumseh's confederacy—who after their defeat during the War of 1812 had headed north to Canada before heading back southward into Kansas, Indian Territory, and then Texas. From the Old Southwest came Cherokees, Creeks, Choctaws, Chickasaws, and Seminoles, some with African American slaves. Native newcomers often clashed with indigenous Native peoples, with whom they vied for land and animals. The conflict was cultural, too: some Native American immigrants, having adopted Anglo clothing and racial ideologies, dismissed as "savage" the indigenous Native peoples who hunted buffalo, wore skins, and did not value land as a commodity.

Because such violence threatened the viability of southeastern Native peoples' removal and disrupted trade, the U.S. government brokered a treaty in 1835: the Comanches agreed to allow immigrants onto their lands in exchange for trade opportunities. Before long, trade boomed. Native American immigrants swapped agricultural products and manufactured goods, such as rifles and ammunition, for the Comanches' meats, robes, and horses. The Comanches also traded human captives, seized in Texas or northern Mexico. That same year, the Comanches ended more than a century of war with the Osages. As peace returned, so too did American traders, who now built permanent trading posts. Meanwhile, the U.S. government's Indian removal continued apace, fueling Americans' commitment to cotton cultivation and expansionism. Mexican officials feared for the region's future.

11-4e American *Empresarios*

More than a decade earlier, before Mexican independence, the Spanish had worried about the security of Texas, which they saw as a buffer between hostile Native peoples, particularly Comanches, and the United States. Their solution was to populate the region. Thus when Moses Austin, a miner and

Paintings and Cultural Impressions

Although few people of Spanish descent settled in Texas, those who did developed a distinctive and proud cultural identity. Calling themselves Tejanos, they adapted their inherited culture—music, dances, and cuisine—to their new surroundings. In the painting below of an 1844 celebration in San Antonio, French-born painter Theodore Gentilz captures the mixture of cultural carryovers and frontier adaptations.

CRITICAL THINKING

■ Which elements of the scene seem reminiscent of life in Spain or in the colonial capital of Mexico City?

■ Which elements seem to be adaptations to life along a cultural frontier and political borderland?

■ Which elements of the painting seem to celebrate Tejano culture, and which, if any, seem critical of it?

■ If you were using this painting as a source of information about Tejano culture and its influence on contemporary music and dance, what else would you want to know about the artist and the scene he has captured?

bpk, Berlin/Art Resource, NY

◀ Although the musician in Gentilz's painting is playing the fiddle, other artistic depictions record the widespread use of the guitar, which helped give rise to the corrido, a folk ballad whose legacy is still apparent in today's country and western music.

Daughters of the Republic of Texas Library

▲ Theodore Gentilz arrived in Texas in the 1840s and soon began portraying the region's culture with his paintbrush. Here, Tejano settlers perform the fandango, a Spanish dance.

trader from Missouri, approached Spanish authorities in December 1820 about settling Americans in Texas, they were willing to make a deal, finalized the following month, as long as Austin brought with him Americans willing to assimilate into Texas society. In exchange for promising to bring three hundred Catholic families—and no slaves—Austin would receive an enormous land grant of approximately two hundred thousand acres along the Brazos River. Before Austin could act, though, he died, and Mexico won its independence from Spain in September 1821.

Austin's son, Stephen, pursued his father's scheme, pressing the new Mexican government to honor the grant, which it did in 1823, provided that the younger Austin renounce his American citizenship and become a Mexican national. Recruiting families proved challenging, however, because of fears of Native peoples' attacks. When Mexican officials expressed frustration at Austin's slow progress in settling the area, he complained, "the Situation I am placed in near the frontiers of two Nations, and surrounded on every side by hostile Indians and exposed to their attacks . . . vexatious pilfering and robbing . . . renders my task particularly laborious." But by 1825, Stephen Austin had settled three hundred families (1,357 white people) and, despite the promise of no slaves, 443 "contract laborers" of African descent. With contracts that ran for ninety-nine years, these African Americans were essentially slaves. Still, faced with the urgency of peopling the region, the Mexican government signed three more contracts granting Austin land in exchange for his bringing nine hundred additional families.

Generally satisfied with the Austin experiment, in 1824 Mexico passed a Colonization Law providing land and tax incentives to future foreign settlers and leaving the details of colonization to the individual Mexican states. Coahuila y Texas specified that the head of a family could have either 177 acres (if just farming), 4,251 acres (if just grazing), or 4,428 acres (if both farming and grazing). The land was cheap, and—unlike land in the United States—could be paid for in installments over six years, with no money due until the fourth year. To be eligible, foreigners had to be upstanding Christians with "good habits," and they had to establish permanent residency. As an incentive for these new settlers to assimilate into Mexican society, the Coahuila y Texas government provided additional land to those who married Mexican women.

Most U.S. citizens who settled in Mexico did so under the auspices of an *empresario*, or immigration agent, who took responsibility for selecting "moral" colonists, distributing lands, and enforcing regulations. In exchange, he received nearly 25,000 acres of grazing land and 1,000 acres of farming land for every hundred families that he settled. Between 1825 and 1832, approximately twenty-four empresario contracts (seventeen of which went to foreigners, mostly Anglo-Americans) had been signed, with the empresarios agreeing to bring eight thousand families total. The

land grants were so vast that together they covered almost all of present-day Texas.

During the 1820s, Anglo-Americans emigrated, with their slaves, to Texas, motivated by a combination of push and pull factors. Some felt pushed by the hard times following the Panic of 1819; at the same time, they were drawn by cheap land and, especially, generous credit terms. Despite Mexican efforts to encourage assimilation, these Americans tended to settle in separate communities and to interact little with the Tejanos. Even more troubling to the Mexican government, the Anglo-Americans outnumbered the Tejanos two to one. Authorities worried that the transplanted Americans would try to make Texas part of the United States.

11-4f Texas Politics

In 1826, their fears seemed to materialize when an empresario named Haden Edwards called for an independent Texas, the "Fredonia Republic." Other empresarios, reasoning that they had more to gain than to lose from peaceful relations with the Mexican government, resisted Edwards's secessionist movement. Austin even sent militia to help quash the rebellion. Although the Fredonia revolt failed, Mexican authorities dreaded what it might foreshadow.

The answer to the secessionist threat, Mexican authorities thought, was to weaken the American presence in Texas. In 1830, they terminated legal immigration from the United States while simultaneously encouraging immigration from Europe and other parts of Mexico in order to dilute the American influence. They prohibited American slaves from entering Texas, a provision that brought Texas in line with the rest of Mexico—where slavery had been outlawed the previous year—and that was meant to repel American slaveholders. Yet these laws did little to discourage Americans and their slaves from coming; soon they controlled most of the Texas coastline and its border with the United States. Mexican authorities repealed the anti-immigration law in 1833, reasoning that it discouraged upstanding settlers but did nothing to stem the influx of undesirable settlers. By 1835, the non-Native population of Texas was nearly thirty thousand, with Americans outnumbering Tejanos seven to one.

White Texans divided into two main factions. There were those, like Stephen Austin, who favored staying in Mexico but demanding more autonomy, the legalization of slavery, and free trade with the United States. Others pushed for secession from Mexico and asked to be annexed to the United States. In 1835, the secessionists overtook a Mexican military installation charged with collecting taxes at Galveston Bay. Austin advocated a peaceful resolution to the crisis, but Mexican authorities nonetheless considered him suspicious and jailed him for eighteen months, an act that helped convert him to the independence cause. But it would be Sam Houston and Davy Crockett—newly arrived Americans—who would lead the movement.

The Center for American History, The University of Texas at Austin

▲ Like George Allen, many Texas settlers relied on slave labor to work their fields and maintain their households.

11-4g The Lone Star Republic

With discontent increasing throughout Mexico, Mexican president **General Antonio Lopez de Santa Anna** declared himself dictator and marched his army toward Texas. Fearing Santa Anna would free their slaves, and citing similarities between their own cause and that of the American colonies in the 1770s, Texans staged an armed rebellion. After initial defeats at the Alamo mission in San Antonio and at Goliad in March 1836, the Texans easily triumphed by year's end. They declared themselves the Lone Star Republic and elected **Sam Houston** as president. Their constitution legalized slavery and banned free blacks from living within Texas.

Texas then faced the challenge of nation building, which to its leaders involved Indian removal. When Native peoples refused to leave, Mirabeau Lamar, the nation's second president, mobilized the Texas Rangers—mounted nonuniformed militia—to drive them out through terror. Sanctioned by the Texas government, but sometimes acting on their own, the Rangers raided Native peoples' villages, where they robbed, raped, and murdered. Although some Texas officials tried to negotiate with the Native peoples and Tejanos, it was what one historian has called "ethnic cleansing" that cleared the land of its Native settlers to make room for white Americans and their African American slaves. Before long, the surviving Comanches would face starvation and depopulation—weakened by European disease, drought, and overhunting. First, though, they would ravage the northern Mexico countryside and its inhabits, inadvertently paving the way for American conquest.

11-4h "War of a Thousand Deserts"

Since the early 1830s, Mexico's ten northern states had been wracked by raiding warfare perpetrated by Native peoples of the Plains—Comanches, Navajos, and Apaches. Even as the Comanches negotiated with Texans and agreed to peace with the Cheyenne and Arapaho to their north, they intensified their raids into Mexico, sending raiders on horseback to seize bounties of horses, goods, and human captives that they then traded throughout the Plains, bringing them and their families status and wealth. When Mexicans resisted their attacks by killing Comanches or their Kiowa allies, the Comanches escalated their violence, ravishing the countryside and its inhabitants in what one historian has deemed vengeance killings, those in which the victims often bore no individual responsibility for the Comanches' deaths. When additional Comanches fell in the course of avenging a killing, then another round of revenge killing ensued, in what became an ongoing, vicious cycle. The raiders devastated Mexican settlements, where once-thriving farms became man-made "deserts," as Mexico's minister of war called them. Passing through one abandoned village in 1846, a British traveler noted that "a dreary stillness reigned over the whole place, unbroken by any sound, save the croaking of a bullfrog in the spring."

General Antonio Lopez de Santa Anna Mexican president and dictator whose actions led Texans to revolt.

Sam Houston Military and political leader of Texas during and after the Texas Revolution.

▲ Native peoples of the Plains, including the Apaches portrayed here, frequently and brutally raided the northern provinces of Mexico beginning in the 1830s, leading to a cycle of vengeance killings that devastated the region and made it more vulnerable to invasion by the U.S. army during the War with Mexico in the mid-1840s.

With the Mexican government's concerns trained more directly on threats from the United States and France, individual Mexican states pursued their own responses to the raids, and in the process they often turned against one another, with Mexicans killing other Mexicans. The resulting carnage, with Mexicans falling at one another's hands and at the hands of Native peoples, gave fodder to proponents of **manifest destiny** in the United States—those who believed that racially superior (white) Americans were destined to spread their culture westward to regions inhabited by inferior races (Native Americans and Mexicans). Using the rationale of manifest destiny, the United States would justify its war with Mexico from 1846 to 1848 (see "The War with Mexico and Its Consequences," Section 12-6). When American soldiers marched to Mexico's capital with seeming ease, they did so because they traversed huge swaths of Mexican territory that had been devastated or deserted by fifteen years of Native American raiding.

11-4i Wartime Losses and Profits

After annexing Texas in 1845, the United States, seeking to further expand its territorial reach, waged war against Mexico. In the borderlands, as in Mexico itself, civilians—Native peoples, Tejanos, Californios, and Mexicans—got caught in the fray. Some lost their lives, and many more, precariously caught between the two sides, suffered wartime depredations. If they aided the Mexicans,

manifest destiny Coined by editor John L. O'Sullivan, it was the belief that the United States was endowed by God with a mission to spread its republican government and brand of freedom and Christianity to less fortunate and uncivilized peoples; it also justified U.S. territorial expansion.

the U.S. Army destroyed their homes; if they refused aid to the Mexicans, then the Mexicans destroyed their homes. A U.S. Army report in 1847 acknowledged that its "wild volunteers … committed … all sorts of atrocities on the persons and property of Mexicans." Many civilians fled. Even once the war ended in the borderlands, violence did not stop. From 1847 to 1848, Texas Rangers slaughtered Native peoples. "They think that the death of an Indian is a fair offsett [*sic*] to the loss of a horse," wrote one Anglo-American.

Yet some civilians profited from the war. Farmers sold provisions and mules to the armies, peddlers sold alcohol and food to soldiers, and others set up gambling and prostitution businesses near army camps. Still, tension generally characterized the relationship between civilians and soldiers, largely because of the American soldiers' attitude of racial superiority.

11-5 Cultural Frontiers in the Far West

▶ How did religion shape the culture of the Far West?

▶ What was the nature of emigrant interactions with Native peoples along the overland migration routes?

▶ What actions did the federal government take to ease westward migration and commerce?

▶ What impact did European American migration and settlement have on Native Americans in the Far West?

▶ How did the discovery of mineral wealth transform the society and economy of California?

Even before the United States seized tremendous amounts of new territory during the war with Mexico, some Americans took the gamble of a lifetime and moved to the Far West, often to places—such as California and Utah—that Mexico controlled. Some sought religious freedom or to convert others to Christianity, but most wanted fertile farmland. Whatever their reasons for moving west, they often encountered people from different cultures. Such encounters sometimes led to cooperation, but more often to tension or open conflict.

11-5a Western Missionaries

Catholic missionaries maintained a strong presence in the Far West. In the Spanish missions, priests treated Native peoples as "spiritual children," introducing them to Catholic sacraments; holding them to a rigid system of prayer, sexual conduct, and work; and treating them as legal minors. When they failed to live up to priests' or soldiers' expectations, they were subject to corporal punishment. When they ran away, they were forcibly returned. With no political voice and few other choices, Native peoples often responded to abusive practices with armed uprisings, in the process helping to weaken the mission system itself.

A Mexican law secularized the California missions in 1833, removing them from ecclesiastical control and using them primarily to organize Indian labor. Some Native peoples stayed at the missions, while others left to farm their own land or to find employment elsewhere, but for almost all, secularization brought enhanced personal freedom despite persistent limitations to their legal rights.

Even after the missions' secularization, Catholic missionaries—Americans, Europeans, and Native converts—continued ministering to immigrants, working to convert other Native peoples, and encouraging specifically Roman Catholic colonies. Missionaries founded schools and colleges, introduced medical services, and even aided in railroad explorations.

In the Pacific Northwest, Catholics vied directly with Protestants for Native peoples' souls. Although evangelicals focused on the Midwest, a few hoped to bring Christianity to the Native peoples of the Far West. Under the auspices of the American Board of Commissioners for Foreign Missions, two missionary couples—generally credited as being the first white migrants along the Oregon Trail—traveled to the Pacific Northwest in 1836. Narcissa and Marcus Whitman built a meetinghouse for the Cayuse in Waiilatpu, near present-day Walla Walla, Washington, while Eliza and Henry Spalding worked to convert the Nez Percé at Lapwai, in what is now Idaho. The Whitmans did little to endear themselves to the Cayuses, whom Narcissa deemed "insolent, proud domineering arrogant and ferocious"; their dark skin, she concluded, was fitting of their "heathenism." The Cayuse, in turn, saw the Whitmans as "very severe and hard," and none converted. The Whitmans redirected their efforts toward the ever-increasing stream of white migrants flowing into Oregon beginning in the 1840s.

These migrants' arrival escalated tensions with the Cayuses, and when a devastating measles epidemic struck in 1847, the Cayuses saw it as a calculated assault. They retaliated by murdering the Whitmans and at least ten other missionaries. After the Whitmans' violent deaths, the Spaldings abandoned their own, more successful mission; blamed Catholics for inciting the massacre; and became farmers in Oregon, not returning to Lapwai for another fifteen years.

11-5b Mormons

The Mormons, who had been persecuted in Missouri and Illinois, sought religious sanctuary in the West. In 1847, Brigham Young led them to their "Promised Land" in the Great Salt Lake valley, still under Mexican control but soon to become part of the unorganized U.S. territory of Utah. As non-Mormons began to settle in Utah, Brigham Young tried to dilute their influence by attracting new Mormon settlers to what he called the state of Deseret. In 1849, Young and his associates established the Perpetual Emigration Fund, which sponsored "handcart companies" of poor migrants, particularly from Europe, who pushed all their belongings to Utah in small handcarts.

The Mormons' arrival in the Great Basin complicated the region's already complex relations among Native peoples. The Utes, for example, had long traded in stolen goods and captured people, particularly Paiutes. After Mormons tried to curtail the slave trade, Ute slavers tortured their Paiute captives, particularly children, calculating that Mormons would buy them. The ploy

▲ This rare stereocard shows an emigrant train, including two women and possibly a child, dwarfed by the natural landscape in Strawberry Valley, California, in the 1860s.

often worked; when it did not, Ute slavers sometimes killed the children, in one case dangling them by their feet and thrashing them against stones. The purchased children often worked as servants in Mormon homes, which encouraged their distraught families, eager for proximity to their children, to settle near Mormon villages. Although the Mormons tried to bring the Paiutes into their religious fold, they—much like Catholic missionaries in California—treated adult Native Americans as children, causing friction, even violence, when the Paiutes sought to secure their autonomy. Sharing the Utes as a common enemy, the Mormons and Paiutes nonetheless formed an uneasy alliance in the early 1850s.

With their slave trade threatened and their economy in shambles, the Utes attacked Mormon and Paiute settlements to steal livestock and horses for resale, and then to vandalize their crops and property in an effort to drive away the Mormons. War erupted in 1853, and although an uneasy truce was reached in 1854, tensions continued between the Mormons and their Native neighbors.

And between Mormons and their white neighbors. Although Mormons prospered from providing services, such as ferries, and supplies to tens of thousands of California-bound settlers and miners passing by their settlements, Young discouraged "gentiles" (his term for non-Mormons) from settling in Deseret and advocated boycotts of gentile businesses. When in 1852 the Mormons openly sanctioned polygamy, which some followers had practiced for more than a decade, anti-Mormon sentiment increased throughout the nation. After some young Mormons vandalized federal offices in Utah, President James Buchanan—hoping to divert Americans' attention from the increasingly divisive slavery issue—dispatched 2,500 federal troops in June 1857 to suppress an alleged Mormon rebellion.

Anxious over their own safety, a group of Mormons joined some Paiutes in attacking a passing wagon train of non-Mormon migrants. Approximately 120 men, women, and children died in the so-called Mountain Meadows Massacre in September 1857. In the next two years, the U.S. Army and the Mormons engaged in armed conflict, resulting in much property destruction but no fatalities. As the Mormons' relationships with their neighbors and passersby indicate, western violence often emerged from complex interactions and alliances that did not simply pit Native communities against newcomers.

11-5c Oregon and California Trails

Nor were all encounters between natives and newcomers violent. From 1840 until 1860, between 250,000 and 500,000 people, including many children, walked across much of the continent, a trek that took seven months on average. Although they traveled armed for conflict, most of their encounters with Native peoples were peaceful, if tense.

The overland journeys began at one of the so-called jumping-off points—towns such as Independence, St. Joseph, and Westport Landing—along the Missouri River, where migrants bought supplies for the 2,000-mile trip still ahead of them. After cramming supplies into wagons already overflowing with household possessions, they set out either in organized wagon trains or on their own. While miners frequently traveled alone or in groups of fortune-seeking young men, farmers—including many women migrating only at their husbands' insistence—often traveled with relatives, neighbors, fellow church members, and other acquaintances.

They timed their departures to be late enough that they could find forage grass for their oxen and livestock, but not so late that they would encounter the treacherous snows that came early to the Rockies and the Sierra Nevada. Not all were successful. From 1846 to 1847, the Donner Party took a wrong turn, got caught in a blizzard, and resorted to cannibalism. More fortunate overland migrants trudged alongside their wagons, beginning their days well before dawn, pausing only for a short midday break, and walking until late afternoon. They covered on average fifteen miles a day, in weather ranging from freezing cold to blistering heat. In wagon trains composed of families, men generally tended livestock during the day, while women—after an energy-draining day on the trail—set up camp, prepared meals, and tended small children. Many women gave birth on the trail, where an always-difficult experience could become excruciating. "Her sufferings were so great," one woman wrote about her sister. "It all seems like a jumble of jolting wagon, crying baby, dust, sagebrush and the never ceasing pain." Even under normal circumstances, trail life was exhausting, both physically and emotionally. Overlanders worried about attack by Native peoples, getting lost, running out of provisions or water, and losing loved ones, who would have to be buried along the trail, in graves never again to be visited. But for most adults, trail life did not prove particularly dangerous, with Native attacks rare and death rates approximating those of society at large. Children, though, had a greater risk than adults of being crushed by wagon wheels or drowning during river crossings.

Native peoples were usually peaceful, if cautious. Particularly during the trails' early days, Native peoples provided food and information or ferried migrants across rivers; in exchange, migrants offered wool blankets, knives, metal pots, tobacco, ornamental beads, and other items in short supply in Native societies. When exchanges went wrong—when one of the parties misunderstood the other's cultural practices or tried to swindle the other—relationships grew tense, not just between the particular persons involved, but between Native peoples and migrants more generally. Native peoples grew suspicious of all white people, just as migrants failed to distinguish between different native bands or tribes.

A persistent aggravation among migrants was the theft of livestock, which they usually blamed on Native peoples even though white thieves stole livestock, too. Native peoples who took livestock often did so when whites failed to offer gifts in exchange for grazing rights. One such incident, the so-called Mormon Cow Incident (or the Grattan Massacre), resulted in human bloodshed, forever altering relationships along the Oregon Trail.

In August 1854, a Lakota in present-day Wyoming slaughtered a cow that had strayed from a nearby Mormon camp. When Lakota leaders offered compensation, U.S. Army Lieutenant John Grattan, intent on making a point, refused the offer. Tempers flared, Grattan ordered his men to shoot, and after a Lakota chief fell dead, the Lakotas returned the fire, killing Grattan, all twenty-nine of his men, and a French interpreter. In retaliation, the following year General William Harney led six hundred soldiers to a village near Ash Hollow, where migrants and Native peoples had traded peaceably for many years. When the Lakota leaders refused to surrender any of their people to Harney, the general ordered his men to fire. Thirty minutes later, eighty-five Lakotas lay dead, with more wounded, and seventy women and children had been taken prisoner. The event disrupted peaceful exchange along the trail and laid the groundwork for nearly two decades of warfare between the Lakotas and the U.S. Army.

11-5d Treaties with Native Peoples

Even as the U.S. Army became embroiled in armed conflict, the Indian Office worked to negotiate treaties to keep Native peoples—and their intertribal conflicts—from interfering with western migration and commerce. The **Fort Laramie Treaty of 1851** (or the Horse Creek Council Treaty) was signed by the United States and eight northern Plains tribes—the Lakotas, Cheyennes, Arapahos, Crows, Assiniboines, Gros-Ventres, Mandans, and Arikaras—who occupied the Platte River valley through which the three great overland routes westward—the Oregon, California, and Mormon Trails—all passed. Two years later, in 1853, the United States signed a treaty with three southwestern nations, the Comanches, Kiowas, and Apaches, who lived in the vicinity of the Sante Fe Trail. Under the terms of both treaties, these Native groups agreed to maintain peace among themselves, to recognize government-delineated tribal boundaries, to allow the United States to construct roads and forts within those boundaries, to refrain from depredations against western migrants, and to issue restitution for any depredations nonetheless committed. In return, they

Fort Laramie Treaty of 1851 Also known as the Horse Creek Council Treaty; a treaty between the United States and eight northern Plains tribes in which the Native Americans agreed to maintain intertribal peace, accepted the U.S.-defined territorial regions for each tribe, and allowed the United States to construct roads. In exchange, they received annual payouts of provisions and agricultural necessities.

Interior of Fort Laramie, 1858–60 (w/c on paper), Miller, Alfred Jacob (1810–74) / Walters Art Museum, Baltimore, USA / Bridgeman Images

▲ Established in 1834 in eastern Wyoming, Fort Laramie—pictured here three years later by Alfred Jacob Miller— served as a fur-trading site, where Native peoples and trappers of European or mixed heritage came together not only to exchange goods but also to socialize. In 1849, as interactions between Native peoples and overland migrants to Oregon grew increasingly tense, the U.S. Army took over the fort, now designed to protect overland emigrants.

would receive annual allotments from the U.S. government for ten years, to be paid with provisions, domestic animals, and agricultural implements. These allotments could be renewed for another five years at the discretion of the president of the United States.

But these treaties often meant different things to their American Indian signatories and to the U.S. officials who brokered them. Contrary to U.S. expectations, Native American chiefs did not see such treaties as perpetually binding. Government officials, meanwhile, promised allotments but did little to ensure their timely arrival, often leaving Native peoples starving and freezing. The treaties did not end intertribal warfare, nor did they fully secure the overlanders' safety. But they did represent the U.S. government's efforts to promote expansion and to protect those citizens who caught the western fever.

11-5e Ecological Consequences of Cultural Contact

Armed conflict took relatively few lives compared to cholera, smallpox, and other maladies. The trails' jumping-off points, where migrants camped in close quarters while preparing for their journeys, bred disease, which migrants inadvertently carried to the Native peoples with whom they traded. Fearful of infection, Native peoples and migrants increasingly shied away from trading.

The disappearance of the buffalo (American bison) from the trails' environs further inflamed tensions. The buffalo not only provided protein to Native peoples of the Plains; they also held great spiritual significance. Many Native Americans blamed the migrants for the buffalo's disappearance, even though most overlanders never laid eyes on a buffalo. By the

▲ The vibrant trade in buffalo hides prompted both Native Americans and whites to overhunt the American bison, leading to near extinction for the animal by the latter part of the nineteenth century.

time the overland migration reached its peak in the late 1840s and 1850s, the herds had already been overhunted, in part by Native Americans eager to trade their hides. As traffic increased along the trail, the surviving buffalo scattered to where the grass was safe from the voracious appetites, and trampling feet, of the overlanders' livestock. But on those rare occasions when wagon trains did stumble upon bison herds, men rushed to fulfill their frontier fantasies—nurtured by the literature they had read—and shot the animals; such buffalo chases provided diversions from the trail's drudgery. Overlanders hunted other animals for sport, too, leaving behind rotting carcasses of antelopes, wolves, bears, and birds—animals that held spiritual significance for many Native Americans.

Overland migrants also sparked prairie fires. Native peoples had long used fire to clear farmland, to stimulate the growth of grasslands, and to create barren zones that would discourage bison from roaming into a rival nation's territory. But now emigrants—accustomed to stoves, not open fires—accidentally started fires that raged across the prairies, killing animals and the vegetation on which they survived. On rarer occasions, Native peoples started fires in the hope of capturing the migrants' fleeing livestock. Stories about intentionally lit fires exaggerated their extent, but they, too, contributed to increasing hostility between the two groups.

11-5f Gold Rush

Nowhere did migrants intrude more deeply on Native American life than near the California gold strikes. In January 1848, James Wilson Marshall discovered gold on John Sutter's property along a shallow tributary to the American River near present-day Sacramento, California. During the next year, tens of thousands of "forty-niners" rushed to California, where they practiced what is called placer mining, panning and dredging for gold in the hope of instant riches.

Some did indeed make fortunes. Peter Brown, a black man from Ste. Genevieve, Missouri, wrote his wife in 1851 that "California is the best country in the world to make money. It is also the best place for black folks on the globe." But not

The Mexican-United States Border

Under the Treaty of Guadalupe Hidalgo (1848), ending the United States' war with Mexico, Mexico ceded modern-day California, Arizona, and New Mexico, and parts of Utah, Nevada, and Colorado. The task of delimiting the new border, including adjustments made in a subsequent treaty, fell to the Joint United States and Mexican Boundary Commission, whose crew of more than one hundred men labored through rugged terrain, climactic extremes, and Native American raids. Where the boundary strayed from natural features and human settlements, as it often did along its western end, the Commission demarcated it with scattered, often-improvised markers, in one instance erecting just seven markers along a 140-mile stretch. Completing its field work between 1849 and 1855, the Commission created the nearly 2,000-mile border that exists today.

The border's contested nature manifested itself immediately, as Native peoples recognized neither Mexico's nor the United States' sovereignty in the region. In 1882, Mexico and the United States agreed to reciprocal border crossings, allowing the U.S. Army to defeat the powerful Chiricahua Apaches four years later. Only then did the United States begin restricting border crossings, with efforts focused on Chinese, not Mexican, nationals. In 1897, President McKinley established a sixty-foot-wide clearance through Nogales, a

town on the Arizona-Mexico border; the government stripped the area of homes and businesses to improve surveillance of cattle rustlers and drug smugglers, and to ease tariff collection and immigration controls. Four years later, President Teddy Roosevelt extended McKinley's "reservation strip" into New Mexico, Arizona, and California, foreshadowing increasing division of binational communities. Yet in 1904, only eighteen U.S. immigration inspectors patrolled the 550-mile border dividing Mexico from Arizona and New Mexico, and fences built in the early twentieth century restricted cattle, not people.

With the Mexican Revolution (1910–1920), the two governments agreed to construct more substantial fences. Mexico aimed to block smuggled military supplies; the United States, to staunch the influx of refugees from wartime devastation. With the Great Depression, pressure to control immigration increased alongside U.S. workers' fear of job competition. When labor surpluses turned into shortages during World War II, the United States implemented its Bracero (guestworker) program, but many employers preferred undocumented workers, whose susceptibility to deportation led to lower wages and poorer working conditions. To protect the Bracero program, the United States deported undocumented Mexicans; in 1954 alone, the Border Patrol reported more than one million deportations. Later

initiatives focused more on erecting barriers and increasing patrols. In 2006, the Secure Fence Act mandated 700 miles of fencing, designed to "reform" immigration while enhancing national security post-9/11. The extremely expensive project remains unfinished, though during the 2016 election Donald J. Trump promised to "build a wall" to stop illegal Mexican immigration. If built, such a wall would entail formidable fiscal and logistical challenges. "Often," according to the U.S. Border Patrol's official website, "the border is a barely discernible line in uninhabited deserts, canyons, or mountains."

In the mid-nineteenth century, while trekking through those deserts, canyons, and mountains, the Boundary Commissioners never imagined that their scattered and makeshift markers would be replaced with fences and walls, reinforced with aerial surveillance and electronic sensors. Yet by demarcating a border governed by neither natural nor human geography, they created a legacy for a people and a nation.

CRITICAL THINKING

- Consider the legacy of "a border governed by neither natural nor human geography" from a scattering of random markers to the promise made in 2016 by then-candidate Donald Trump to "build a wall" along the border, a feat with both logistical and financial complexities. What other solutions might there be to the "problem" of the Mexican/U.S. border?

---

everyone reveled in the gold strikes. John Sutter complained that gold "destroyed" his milling and tanning businesses, as his Native American and Mormon workers left him for the mines and vandals stole his property. Most forty-niners never found enough gold to pay their expenses. "The stories you hear frequently in the States," one gold seeker wrote home, "are the most extravagant lies imaginable—the mines are a humbug." With their dreams dashed—and too poor or embarrassed to return home—many forty-niners took wage-paying jobs with

large mining companies that used dangerous machinery to cut deep into the earth's surface to reach mineral veins.

The discovery of gold changed the face of California (see Map 11.5). As a remote Mexican province, California had a chain of small settlements surrounded by military forts (presidios) and missions. It was inhabited mostly by Native peoples, along with a small number of Mexican rancheros, who raised cattle and sheep on enormous landholdings worked by coerced Native American laborers. As word spread of gold strikes, new

Map 11.5 The California Gold Rush

Gold was discovered at Sutter's Mill in 1848, sparking the California gold rush that took place mostly along the western foothills of the Sierra Nevada Mountains.

migrants—from South America, Asia, Australia, and Europe—rushed to California. Although a California Supreme Court ruling—*People v. Hall* (1854)—made it virtually impossible to prevent violence against Chinese immigrants, Chinese citizens continued to seek their fortunes in California; by 1859, approximately 35,000 of them worked in the goldfields.

With so many hungry gold miners to feed, California experienced an agricultural boom. Although the immediate vicinity of mines became barren, when hydraulic mining washed away surface soil to expose buried lodes, California agriculture thrived overall, with wheat becoming the preferred crop: it required minimal investment, was easily planted, and had a relatively short growing season. In contrast to the Midwest's and Oregon's family farms, though, California's large-scale wheat farming depended on bonded Native American laborers.

11-5g Mining Settlements

Mining brought a commercial and industrial boom, too, as enterprising merchants rushed to supply, feed, and clothe the new settlers. Among them was Levi Strauss, a German Jewish immigrant, whose tough mining pants found a ready market among the prospectors. Because men greatly outnumbered

women, women's skills (and company) were in great demand. Even as men set up all-male households and performed tasks that bent prevailing notions of gender propriety, women received high fees for cooking, laundering, and sewing. Women also ran boardinghouses, hotels, and brothels.

Cities sprang up. In 1848, San Francisco had been a small mission settlement of about 1,000 Mexicans, Anglos, soldiers, friars, and Native Americans. With the gold rush, it became an instant city, ballooning to 35,000 people in 1850. It was the West Coast gateway to the interior, and ships bringing people and supplies jammed the harbor. A French visitor in that year wrote, "At San Francisco, where fifteen months ago one found only a half-dozen large cabins, one finds today a stock exchange, a theater, churches of all Christian cults, and a large number of quite beautiful homes."

Yet as the Anglo-American, European, Hispanic, Asian, and African American populations swelled, the Native American population experienced devastation. Although California was admitted into the Union as a free state in 1850, its legislature soon passed "An Act for the Government and Protection of Indians" that essentially legalized Native peoples' enslavement. The practice of using enslaved Native Americans in the mines between 1849 and 1851 ended only when newly arrived miners brutally attacked the Native American workers, believing they degraded white labor and gave an unfair advantage to established miners. Those slaves who survived the violence were sent to work instead as field workers and house servants. Between 1821 and 1860, the Native American population of California fell from 200,000 to 30,000, as Native peoples died from disease, starvation, and violence. Because masters separated male and female workers, even Native Americans who survived failed to reproduce in large numbers.

Summary

Encouraged by literary and artistic images of the frontier, easterners often viewed the West as a place of natural abundance, where hardworking individuals could seek security, freedom, and perhaps even fortune. By the millions they poured into the Old Southwest and Old Northwest in the early decades of the nineteenth century. Although the federal government promoted westward expansion—in the form of support for transportation improvements, surveying, cheap land, and protection from Native peoples—western migrants did not make the decision to head west lightly. Nor did they always find what they were looking for. Some returned home, some moved to new locations, and some—too poor or too embarrassed—stayed in the West, where they reluctantly abandoned their dreams of economic independence. Others found what they were looking for in the West, though often the road to success proved much slower and more circuitous than they had anticipated.

Not everyone who went west did so voluntarily, nor did everyone in the West think of it as an expanding region. African American slaves were moved westward by their owners or slave traders in enormous numbers in the years between 1820 and 1860. Native Americans saw their lands and their livelihoods constrict, and their environments so altered that their economic and spiritual lives were threatened. Some Native peoples responded to the white incursion through accommodation and peaceful overtures; others resisted, sometimes forcefully. If their first strategy failed, then they tried another. But the sheer force of numbers favored whites. For Native Americans in Texas and California, white incursions brought devastation, yet not before the Comanches and their allies had ravaged farming settlements along the borderland between Mexico and the United States, paving the way for the U.S. Army to invade its southern neighbor with little resistance. That war, lasting from 1846 to 1848, would bring to the brink of collapse the system of political rivalries that had emerged during the 1829–1837 presidency of a frontier Indian fighter and slave owner: Andrew Jackson.

Suggestions for Further Reading

Gary Clayton Anderson, *The Conquest of Texas: Ethnic Cleansing in the Promised Land, 1820–1875* (2005)

Stuart Banner, *How the Indians Lost Their Land: Law and Power on the Frontier* (2005)

Ned Blackhawk, *Violence over the Land: Indians and Empires in the Early American West* (2006)

Andrew R. L. Cayton and Peter S. Onuf, *The Midwest and the Nation: Rethinking the History of an American Region* (1990)

William Cronon, *Nature's Metropolis: Chicago and the Great West* (1991)

Brian DeLay, *War of a Thousand Deserts: Indian Raids and the U.S.-Mexican War* (2008)

Pekka Hämäläinen, *The Comanche Empire* (2008)

Robert V. Hine and John Mack Faragher, *The American West: A New Interpretive History* (2000)

Albert L. Hurtado, *Indian Survival on the California Frontier* (1998)

Anne F. Hyde, *Empires, Nations & Families: A History of the North American West, 1800–1860* (2011)

Susan L. Johnson, *Roaring Camp: The Social World of the California Gold Rush* (2000)

Andrés Reséndez, *Changing National Identities at the Frontier: Texas and New Mexico, 1800–1850* (2005)

Rachel St. John, *Line in the Sand: A History of the Western U.S.-Mexico Border* (2011)

Michael L. Tate, *Indians and Emigrants: Encounters on the Overland Trails* (2006)

MINDTAP
From Cengage

MindTap® is a fully online personalized learning experience built upon Cengage Learning content. MindTap® combines student learning tools—readings, multimedia, activities, and assessments—into a singular Learning Path that guides students through the course and helps students develop the critical thinking, analysis, and communication skills that are essential to academic and professional success.

Politics and the Fate of the Union, 1824–1859

I n *Uncle Tom's Cabin* (1852), Harriet Beecher Stowe created countless scenes and characters remembered through the ages, but none more than this: "A thousand lives seemed to be concentrated in that one moment to Eliza. Her room opened by a side door to the river. She caught her child and sprang down the steps toward it. The trader caught a full glimpse of her just as she was disappearing down the bank." No scene in American literature has been more often depicted in the visual arts than the young slave Eliza, child in arms, escaping across the Ohio River, after her owner had just sold the infant to a slave trader. Never has a work of popular literature so caught the roiling tide of politics. "Nerved with strength such as God gives only to the desperate," continued Stowe, "with one wild cry and flying leap, she [Eliza] vaulted clear over the turbid current . . . on to the raft of ice beyond. . . . With wild cries and desperate energy she leaped to another. . . . Her shoes are gone—her stockings cut from her feet—while blood marked every step; but she . . . felt nothing, till dimly, as in a dream, she saw the Ohio side, and a man helping her up the bank."

As the United States slowly collapsed into disunion, millions of Americans either loved or hated *Uncle Tom's Cabin*; many of the book's characters and episodes entered household, as well as public, conversation. The daughter and sister of some of the nation's most prominent preachers and theologians, Harriet Stowe (she married a pious theology professor, Calvin Stowe) was

◄ *Eliza Crossing the Ice Flows of the Ohio River*, depicting one of the most famous scenes in American literature, illustration from *Uncle Tom's Cabin*, engraved by Charles Bour. Private collection, the John Bridgeman Library.

Eliza crossing the ice floes of the Ohio river to freedom, illustration from *Uncle Tom's Cabin* by Harriet Beecher Stowe, engraved by Charles Bour (1814–81) (litho) (see also 90903)/Bayot, Adolphe Jean-Baptiste (1810–66) (after)/Private Collection/Bridgeman Images

Chronology

1824	■ No electoral college majority in presidential election
1825	■ House of Representatives elects Adams president
1828	■ Tariff of Abominations
	■ Jackson elected president
1830s–40s	■ Democratic-Whig competition gels in second party system
1831	■ Antimasons hold first national political convention
1832	■ Jackson vetoes rechartering Second Bank of the United States
	■ Jackson reelected president
1832–33	■ Nullification Crisis
1836	■ Specie Circular
	■ Van Buren elected president
1837	■ Financial panic ends boom of the 1830s
1839–43	■ Hard times spread unemployment and deflation
1840	■ Whigs win presidency under Harrison
1841	■ Tyler assumes presidency after Harrison's death
1845	■ Texas annexed
	■ "Manifest destiny" term coined
1846	■ War with Mexico begins
	■ Oregon Treaty negotiated
	■ Wilmot Proviso inflames sectional divisions
1847	■ Cass proposes idea of popular sovereignty
1848	■ Treaty of Guadalupe Hidalgo gives United States new territory in the Southwest

	■ Free-Soil Party formed
	■ Taylor elected president
	■ Gold discovered in California, which later applies for admission to Union as free state
	■ Seneca Falls Woman's Rights Convention
1850	■ Compromise of 1850 passes, containing controversial Fugitive Slave Act
1852	■ Stowe publishes *Uncle Tom's Cabin*
	■ Pierce elected president
1854	■ "Appeal of the Independent Democrats" published
	■ Kansas-Nebraska Act approved, igniting controversy
	■ Republican Party formed
	■ Fugitive Burns returned to slavery in Virginia
1856	■ Bleeding Kansas troubles nation
	■ Brooks attacks Sumner in Senate chamber
	■ Buchanan elected president, but Republican Frémont wins most northern states
1857	■ *Dred Scott v. Sanford* endorses white southern views on black citizenship and slavery in territories
	■ Economic panic and widespread unemployment begin
1858	■ Kansas voters reject Lecompton Constitution
	■ Lincoln-Douglas debates
	■ Douglas contends popular sovereignty prevails over *Dred Scott* decision in territories
1859	■ Brown raids Harpers Ferry

a little-known writer and mother of seven children when she began to conceive her classic. Serialized in a Washington, D.C., newspaper, the *National Era*, in 1851, and published as a book in 1852, the sentimental but highly charged political novel captured the agonies of slave families broken apart and sold, and now ever more endangered by the Fugitive Slave Act of 1850. Stowe ingeniously indicted the institution of slavery more than any individuals, while spreading the blame widely. The most evil slaveholder (Simon Legree) is a transplanted New Englander, and in Miss Ophelia, a Vermont woman whose visit to a southern plantation reveals her squeamishness about blacks, we see northern racism fully exposed. The story's most humane slaveholder, St. Clair, is southern bred, but almost too good for this corrupt world, and dies before he can reform it. In Eliza, Little Eva, Topsy, and Uncle Tom himself, a Christ-like figure whom the story ultimately ushers toward unforgettable martyrdom, the nation and the world vicariously experienced not only slavery's inhumanity, but its destruction of the human soul itself, as it also threatened the life of the republic.

No book had ever exposed so effectively the nation's gravest problem—slavery and its hold on America's institutions and collective psyche. Although it can seem romantic and sugar-coated to modern readers, *Uncle Tom's Cabin* was the nineteenth century's best seller. By mid-1853, the book had sold over 1 million copies. A publishing sensation in England, too, the book was soon translated into numerous foreign languages, and recreated for the dramatic stage and performed nonstop well into the twentieth century.

The popularity of *Uncle Tom's Cabin* alarmed anxious white southerners, prompting a forceful defense of slavery's morality. Nearly twenty anti–Uncle Tom novels were published in the 1850s, providing a cultural counterpart to the heightened ideological defense of slavery in the realm of politics. Southern writers defended slavery as more humane than northern wage labor, blamed slave trading on the "outside interference" of Yankee speculators, and attacked Stowe for breaking gender conventions as a woman engaging in such a public critique of the South's integrity. In stories such as J. W. Page's *Uncle Robin in His Cabin and Tom Without One in Boston*, fiendish abolitionists induced slaves to run away, leaving them to all but starve in northern cities. In these novels, masters are benevolent and slaves loyal as they perform roles dictated by nature and God. One narrator made clear blacks' destiny: "Africans hate civilization, and are never happier . . . than when allowed to live in the abandonment, nakedness, and filth their instincts crave." Many of the novels let slaves philosophize on slavery's behalf. In *Aunt Phillis's Cabin*, Phillis accompanies her owners on a visit to the North, where wicked abolitionists encourage her to escape. "I want none of your help," she declares; she refuses to "steal" herself, longing instead for her southern "home." Yet another slave character speaks for all proslavery philosophers: "The Declaration of 'Dependence may do . . . for white folks . . . but isn't worth a chaw of backer to a nigger . . . . I don't b'leeve it was ever 'tended for them."

Experience an interactive version of this story in MindTap®.

n *Uncle Tom's Cabin,* Stowe had thrown down a feminist, abolitionist, Christian thunderbolt into the national debate over slavery's future. Although potentially explosive, that debate had been largely submerged in the political system dominated, beginning in the 1830s, by the Jacksonian Democrats and the Whigs.

Despite this, the Democrats and **Whigs** took distinct positions on many salient issues. With certain exceptions, such as removing Native peoples from ancestral lands, Democrats emphasized small government, whereas Whigs advocated an activist federal government to promote economic development and maintain social order. Democrats championed the nation's agricultural expansion into the West, while Whigs urged industrial and commercial growth in the East, fostered through their "American System" of high protective tariffs, centralized banking, and federally funded internal improvements. Together, Whigs and Democrats forged the second party system, characterized by strong organizations in both North and South, intense loyalty, and religious and ethnic voting patterns.

Sectional conflict resurfaced after the annexation of Texas in 1845. From 1846 to 1848, the United States went to war against Mexico, unleashing the problem of slavery's expansion as never before. As part of the Compromise of 1850, a new fugitive slave law sent thousands of free and fugitive blacks fleeing into Canada, and prompted Mrs. Stowe to

Uncle Tom's Cabin Harriet Beecher Stowe's best-selling 1852 novel that aroused widespread northern sympathy for slaves (especially fugitives) and widespread southern anger.

Whigs Formerly called the National Republicans; a major political party in the 1830s.

write her controversial novel. By 1855, open warfare exploded in Kansas Territory between proslavery and antislavery settlers. On the U.S. Senate floor, a southern representative beat a northern senator senseless in 1856. The following year, the Supreme Court issued a dramatic decision about slavery's constitutionality, as well as the status of African American citizenship—to the delight of most white southerners and the anger of many northerners. And by 1858, violence brewed under the surface of the country; abolitionist John Brown was planning a raid into Virginia to start a slave rebellion.

The political culture of the American republic was disintegrating. As the 1850s advanced, slavery pulled Americans, North and South, into a maelstrom of dispute that its best statesmen could not subdue. The old nationwide political parties fractured, and a realignment that reinforced a virulent sectionalism took their place.

A feeling grew in both North and South that America's future was at stake—the character of its economy, its definition of constitutional liberty, and its racial self-definition. In 1855, the famous black leader Frederick Douglass spoke for the enslaved when he wrote that "the thought of only being a creature of the *present* and the *past*, troubled me, and I longed to have a *future*—a future with hope in it." In those words, Douglass spoke as well to the entire nation's central dilemma.

■ *What were the main issues dividing Democrats and Whigs?*

■ *After 1845, how and why did westward expansion become so intertwined with the future of slavery and freedom?*

■ *During the 1850s, why did Americans (voters and nonvoters alike) care so deeply about electoral politics?*

12-1 Jacksonianism and Party Politics

▶ How did the American political culture become more democratic in the 1820s and 1830s?

▶ What impact did the elections of 1824 and 1828 have on the country's political parties?

▶ What were the defining characteristics of Jacksonian Democrats?

Throughout the 1820s and 1830s, politicians reframed their political visions to appeal to an increasingly broad-based electorate. Hotly contested elections helped make politics the great nineteenth-century American pastime, drawing the interest and participation of voters and nonvoters alike. Voter turnout skyrocketed, and elections really mattered in the expanding republic. But intense interest also fueled bitter, even deadly, rivalries.

12-1a Expanding Political Participation

Property restrictions for voters, which states began abandoning during the 1810s, remained in only seven of twenty-six states by 1840. Some states even allowed foreign nationals who had officially declared their intention of becoming American citizens to vote. The net effect was a sharply higher number of votes cast in presidential elections. Between 1824 and 1828, that number increased threefold, from 360,000 to over 1.1 million. In 1840, 2.4 million men cast votes. The proportion of eligible voters who cast ballots also grew, from about 27 percent in 1824 to more than 80 percent in 1840.

At the same time, the method of choosing presidential electors became more democratic. Previously, a caucus of party leaders had done so in most states, but by 1824 eighteen out of twenty-four states chose electors by popular vote, compared to just five of sixteen in 1800. Politicians thus appealed directly to voters, and the election of 1824 saw the end of the congressional caucus, when House and Senate members of the same political party came together to select their candidate.

12-1b Election of 1824

As a result, five candidates, all of whom identified as Democratic-Republicans, entered the presidential campaign of 1824. The poorly attended Republican caucus chose William H. Crawford of Georgia, secretary of the treasury, as its presidential candidate. But other Democratic-Republicans boycotted the caucus as undemocratic, ending Congress's role in nominating presidential candidates. Instead, state legislatures nominated candidates, offering the expanded electorate a slate of sectional candidates. John Quincy Adams drew support from New England, while westerners backed House Speaker Henry Clay of Kentucky. Some southerners at first supported Secretary of War John C. Calhoun, who later dropped his bid for the presidency and ran for the vice presidency instead. The Tennessee legislature nominated Andrew Jackson, a military hero with unknown political views.

Among the four candidates remaining in the race until the election, Jackson led in both electoral and popular votes, but no candidate received an electoral college majority. Adams finished second; Crawford and Clay trailed far behind. Under the Constitution, the House of Representatives, voting by state delegation, one vote to a state, would select the next president from among the three leaders in electoral votes. Clay, with the fewest votes, was dropped, and the three others courted his support, hoping he would influence his electors to vote for them. Crawford, disabled from a stroke suffered before the election, never received serious consideration. Clay dramatically backed Adams, who won with thirteen of the twenty-four state delegations and thus became president (see Map 12.1). Adams named Clay to the cabinet position of secretary of state, the traditional stepping-stone to the presidency.

Angry Jacksonians denounced the election's outcome as a "corrupt bargain," claiming Adams had stolen the election by offering Clay a cabinet position in exchange for his votes. Jackson's bitterness fueled his later emphasis on the people's will. The Republican Party split. The Adams wing emerged as the National Republicans, and the Jacksonians became the **Democrats**; as an insurgent political force, they immediately began planning for 1828.

As president, Adams proposed a strong nationalist policy incorporating Henry Clay's American System, a program of protective tariffs, a national bank, and internal improvements. Adams believed the federal government's active role should extend to education, science, and the arts, and he proposed a national university in Washington, D.C. Brilliant as

▲ Presidential candidate Andrew Jackson is portrayed on a trinket or sewing box in 1832. This is an example both of how campaigns entered popular culture and of the active role of women, excluded from voting, in politics.

a diplomat and secretary of state, Adams fared less well as chief executive. He underestimated the lingering effects of the Panic of 1819 and the resulting staunch opposition to national banks and tariffs.

12-1c Election of 1828

The 1828 election pitted Adams against Jackson in a rowdy campaign. Nicknamed "Old Hickory" after the toughest of American hardwood, Jackson was a rough-and-tumble, ambitious man. Born in South Carolina in 1767, he rose from humble beginnings to become a wealthy Tennessee planter and slaveholder. After leading the Tennessee militia campaign to remove Creeks from the Alabama and Georgia frontier, Jackson burst onto the national scene in 1815 as the hero of the Battle of New Orleans; in 1818, he enhanced his glory in an expedition against Seminoles in Spanish Florida. Jackson served as a congressman from Tennessee, then as the first territorial governor of Florida, and then returned to Washington as a senator from Tennessee, before running for president in 1824.

Both voters and non-voters displayed enthusiasm

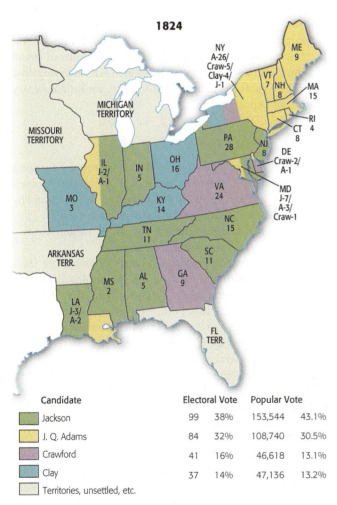

1824

Candidate		Electoral Vote		Popular Vote	
Jackson		99	38%	153,544	43.1%
J. Q. Adams		84	32%	108,740	30.5%
Crawford		41	16%	46,618	13.1%
Clay		37	14%	47,136	13.2%
Territories, unsettled, etc.					

Map 12.1 **Presidential Election, 1824**

Andrew Jackson led in both electoral and popular votes but failed to win a majority of electoral college votes. The House elected John Quincy Adams president.

Democrats Members of the party that emerged from Jefferson's Republican Party as one of the two dominant parties in the second party system.

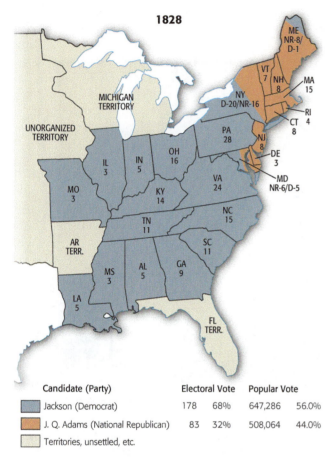

1828

Candidate (Party)		Electoral Vote		Popular Vote	
■ Jackson (Democrat)		178	68%	647,286	56.0%
■ J. Q. Adams (National Republican)		83	32%	508,064	44.0%
□ Territories, unsettled, etc.					

Map 12.2 Presidential Election, 1828

In 1828, Andrew Jackson swept the presidential election, avenging his defeat in 1824.

for Jackson with badges, medals, and other campaign paraphernalia, mass-produced for the first time. In an intensely personal contest, Jackson's supporters accused Adams of stealing the 1824 election and, when he was envoy to Russia, of having secured prostitutes for the czar. Adams supporters countered with reports that Jackson's wife, Rachel, had married Jackson before divorcing her first husband, making her an adulterer and a bigamist. In 1806 Jackson, attempting to defend Rachel's integrity, had killed a man during a duel, and the cry of "murderer!" was revived in the election. Such elements of this campaign were harbingers of many modern elections to come.

Although Adams kept all but one of the states (New York) he had won in 1824, his opposition now unified behind a single candidate, and Jackson swamped him, polling 56 percent of the popular vote and winning in the electoral college by 178 to 83 votes (see Map 12.2). Jacksonians believed the people's will had finally prevailed. Through a lavishly financed coalition of state parties, political leaders, and newspaper editors, a popular movement had elected the president. The Democrats became the nation's first well-organized national party.

spoils system Practice of rewarding political supporters with public office.

12-1d Democrats

The Democrats represented a wide range of views but shared a fundamental commitment to the Jeffersonian concept of an agrarian society. They viewed a strong central government as antithetical to individual liberty, and they condemned government intervention in the economy as favoring the rich at the expense of the artisan and the ordinary farmer. When it came to westward expansion, though, Jacksonians called for federal intervention, with Jackson initiating removal of Native peoples despite protests from northeastern reformers.

Like Jefferson, Jackson strengthened the government's executive branch even as he advocated limited government. In combining the roles of party leader and chief of state, he centralized power in the White House. He relied on political friends, his "Kitchen Cabinet," for advice, rarely consulting his official cabinet. Jackson commanded enormous loyalty and rewarded his followers handsomely. Rotating officeholders, Jackson claimed, made government more responsive to the public will, and he appointed loyal Democrats to office, a practice his critics called the **spoils system**, in which the victor gives power and place to his supporters, valuing loyalty above all else. Although not the first president to do so—Jefferson had replaced many of John Adams's appointees—Jackson's own outcry against corrupt bargains made him an easy target for inflammatory charges of hypocrisy.

12-1e King Andrew

Opponents mocked Jackson as "King Andrew I," charging him with abuse of power by ignoring the Supreme Court's ruling on Cherokee rights, by sidestepping his cabinet, and by replacing officeholders with his own political cronies. They rejected his claim of restoring republican virtue and accused him of recklessly destroying the economy.

Perhaps nothing rankled Jackson's critics more than his frequent use of the veto, which he employed to promote his vision of a limited government. In 1830, he vetoed the Maysville Road bill, which would have funded construction of a sixty-mile turnpike from Maysville to Lexington, Kentucky. Constitutionally, he insisted, states and not the federal government bore responsibility for funding internal improvements confined to a single state. The veto undermined Henry Clay's American System, personally embarrassed Clay because the project was in his home district, and drew lines of stark difference between the two parties.

From George Washington to John Quincy Adams, the first six presidents had vetoed nine bills; Jackson alone vetoed twelve. Previous presidents believed vetoes were justified only on constitutional grounds, but Jackson considered policy disagreements legitimate grounds as well. He made the veto an effective weapon for controlling Congress, which had to weigh the possibility of a presidential veto as it deliberated.

12-2 Federalism at Issue: The Nullification and Bank Controversies

▶ **What did the Nullification Crisis reveal about the relationship between state versus federal power?**

▶ **What role did violence play in American politics in the 1820s and 1830s?**

▶ **How did Andrew Jackson use presidential power in the dispute over the Second Bank of the United States?**

Soon after the Maysville Road veto, Jackson directly faced the question of state versus federal power. The slave South feared federal power, and no state more so than South Carolina, where the planter class was the strongest and slavery the most concentrated. Southerners also resented protectionist tariffs, one of the foundations of Clay's American System, which in 1824 and 1828 bolstered manufacturers by imposing import duties on foreign cloth and iron. In protecting northern factories, the tariff raised the costs of manufactured goods to southerners, who quickly labeled the high tariff of 1828 the **Tariff of Abominations**.

12-2a Nullification

South Carolina's political leaders rejected the 1828 tariff, invoking the doctrine of nullification, maintaining that a state had the right to overrule, or nullify, federal legislation. Nullification drew from the idea expressed in the Virginia and Kentucky Resolutions of 1798—that the states, representing the people, have a right to judge the constitutionality of federal actions. Jackson's vice president, John C. Calhoun of South Carolina, argued in his unsigned *Exposition and Protest* that, in any disagreement between the federal government and a state, a special state convention—like the conventions called to ratify the Constitution—should decide the conflict by either nullifying or affirming the federal law. Only the power of nullification, Calhoun asserted, could protect the minority against the majority's tyranny.

As Jackson's running mate in 1828, Calhoun had avoided endorsing nullification and thus embarrassing the Democratic ticket; he also hoped to win Jackson's support as the Democratic presidential heir apparent. Thus, in early 1830, Calhoun presided silently over the Senate and its packed galleries when Senator Daniel Webster of Massachusetts and Senator Robert Y. Hayne of South Carolina debated states' rights. The debate started over a resolution to restrict western land sales, soon turned to the tariff, and from there focused on the nature of the Union, with nullification a subtext. Hayne charged the North with threatening to bring disunity. For two days, Webster eloquently defended New England and the republic. Although debating Hayne, he aimed his remarks at Calhoun. At the debate's climax, Webster invoked two powerful images. One was the outcome of nullification: "states

dissevered, discordant, belligerent; on a land rent with civil feuds, or drenched . . . in fraternal blood!" The other was a patriotic vision of a great nation flourishing under the motto "Liberty and Union, now and forever, one and inseparable."

Though sympathetic to states' rights and distrustful of the federal government, Jackson rejected the idea of state sovereignty. He strongly believed sovereignty rested with the people. Believing deeply in the Union, he shared Webster's dread of nullification. Soon after the Webster-Hayne debate, the president made his position clear at a Jefferson Day dinner with the toast "Our Federal Union, it must be preserved." Vice President Calhoun, when his turn came, toasted "The Federal Union—next to our liberty the most dear," revealing his adherence to states' rights. Calhoun and Jackson grew apart, and Jackson looked to the secretary of state, Martin Van Buren, not Calhoun, as his successor.

Tension resumed in 1832 when Congress passed a new tariff, reducing some duties but retaining high taxes on imported iron, cottons, and woolens. Although a majority of southern representatives supported the new tariff, South Carolinians did not, insisting that the constitutional right to control their own destiny had been sacrificed to northern industrialists' demands. They feared the act could set a precedent for congressional legislation on slavery. In November 1832, a South Carolina state convention nullified both the 1828 and the 1832 tariffs, declaring it unlawful for federal officials to collect duties in the state. Differing visions of states' rights and the practice of federalism would remain an eternal conflict in American political life. Both Jackson and Calhoun were slaveholders with differing conceptions of how best to protect it within or outside the Union.

12-2b The Force Bill

Jackson soon issued a proclamation opposing nullification. He moved troops to federal forts in South Carolina and prepared U.S. marshals to collect the duties. At Jackson's request, Congress passed the Force Bill, authorizing the president to call up troops but also offering a way to avoid force by collecting duties before foreign ships reached Charleston's harbor. Jackson also extended an olive branch by recommending tariff reductions.

Calhoun resigned as vice president and soon won election to the U.S. Senate, where he worked with Henry Clay to draw up the compromise Tariff of 1833. Quickly passed by Congress and signed by the president, the new tariff lengthened the list of duty-free items and reduced duties over nine years. Satisfied, South Carolina's convention repealed its nullification law. In a final salvo, it also nullified Jackson's Force Bill. Jackson ignored the gesture.

Nullification offered a genuine debate on the nature and principles of the republic. Each side believed it was upholding the Constitution and opposing subversion of republican values. South Carolina's leaders opposed the tyranny of the federal government and manufacturing interests, while long term, they

Tariff of Abominations Protective tariff of 1828 that infuriated southerners and spawned the Nullification Crisis.

also sought to protect slavery. Jackson fought the tyranny of South Carolina, whose refusal to bow to federal authority threatened to split the republic. Neither side won a clear victory, though both claimed to have done so. It took another crisis, over a central bank, to define the powers of the federal government more clearly.

12-2c Second Bank of the United States

At stake was survival of the Second Bank of the United States, whose twenty-year charter would expire in 1836. The bank served as a depository for federal funds and provided credit for businesses. Its notes circulated as currency throughout the country; they could be readily exchanged for gold, and the federal government accepted them as payment in all transactions. Through its twenty-five branch offices, the Second Bank acted as a clearinghouse for state banks, refusing to accept bank notes of any local bank lacking sufficient gold reserves. Most state banks resented the central bank's police role. Moreover, state banks could not compete equally with the Second Bank, which had greater reserves.

Many state governments regarded the national bank as unresponsive to local needs, and many western settlers and urban workers remembered bitterly the bank's conservative credit policies during the Panic of 1819. As a private, profit-making institution, its policies reflected the interest of its owners, especially its powerful president, Nicholas Biddle. An eastern patrician, Biddle symbolized all that westerners feared about the bank, and all that eastern workers despised about the commercial elite.

12-2d Political Violence

Controversy over the Second Bank inflamed long-standing political animosities, igniting street violence. Elections often involved fraud, and with no secret ballot, political parties employed operatives to intimidate voters. New York City was home to the most powerful political machine, the Democrats' Tammany Hall, and in New York's mayoral election of 1834, the first in which the mayor was elected by popular vote, this combination of machine politics and the bank controversy's exacerbation of tensions nationwide led to mayhem.

Three days of rioting began when Democratic operatives attacked Whig headquarters in the sixth ward. After beating some Whigs unconscious, the Democrats turned their ire on the police, injuring eight of them severely; even the mayor suffered wounds. Vowing revenge, more than five hundred Whigs stole weapons from the armory, but before they could use them, the state militia restored order.

A few months later, an election-day riot in Philadelphia left two dead and five buildings burned to the ground. Although these two riots stood out for their proportions and intensity, voter intimidation and fraud—initiated by both Democrats and Whigs—characterized the second party system.

12-2e Antimasonry

Violence was a catalyst for the formation of the Antimason Party, which formed in upstate New York in the mid-1820s as a grassroots movement against Freemasonry, a secret male fraternity that attracted middle- and upper-class men prominent in commerce and civic affairs. Opponents of Masonry claimed the fraternity to be unrepublican; Masons colluded to bestow business and political favors on each other, and—in the incident that sparked the organized Antimasonry movement—Masons had obstructed justice in the investigation of the 1826 disappearance and presumed murder of a disgruntled former member who had written an exposé of the society. Evangelicals denounced Masonry, claiming its members neglected their families for alcohol and ribald entertainment.

Antimasonry, rooted in the deep American fear of concentrated power and conspiracy, soon developed into a vibrant political movement in the Northeast and parts of the Midwest. In the 1828 presidential election, the Antimasons opposed Jackson, himself a Mason. With their confidence bolstered by strong showings in gubernatorial elections in 1830, the Antimasons held the first national political convention in Baltimore in 1831, nominating William Wirt of Maryland for president and Amos Ellmaker of Pennsylvania for vice president.

12-2f Election of 1832

Following the Antimasons' lead, the Democrats and National Republicans held their own conventions. The Democrats reaffirmed the choice of Jackson, who had already been nominated by state legislatures, for president and nominated Martin Van Buren of New York for vice president. (In the election, however, South Carolina's electors would break from the rest of the party and support John Floyd and Henry Lee of Virginia; as Virginia's governor, Floyd had supported nullification, making him popular in the South Carolina legislature, which chose its state electors.) The National Republican convention selected Clay and John Sergeant of Pennsylvania. The Bank of the United States became the election's main issue. Jacksonians denounced it as a vehicle for special privilege and economic power, while the Republicans supported it as a pillar of their plan for economic nationalism. The bank's charter was valid until 1836, but as part of his campaign strategy, Clay persuaded Biddle to ask Congress to approve an early rechartering. If Jackson signed the rechartering bill, then Clay could attack the president's inconsistency on the issue. If he vetoed it, then—Clay reasoned—the voters would give Clay the nod. The plan backfired. The president vetoed the bill and issued a pointed veto message appealing to voters who feared that the era's rapid economic development spread its advantages undemocratically. Jackson acknowledged that prosperity could never be evenly dispersed, but he took a strong stand against special interests that tried to use the government to their own advantage. "It is to be regretted," he wrote, "that the rich and powerful too often bend the acts of government to their selfish purposes." The message proved powerful and successful. Jackson won 54 percent of the popular vote to Clay's 37 percent, and he captured 76 percent of the electoral college. Although the Antimasons won just one state, Vermont, they nonetheless helped galvanize the anti-Jackson opposition.

12-2g Jackson's Second Term

After a sweeping victory, Jackson began in 1833 to dismantle the Second Bank and to deposit federal funds in state-chartered banks (termed "pet banks" by critics). When its federal charter expired in 1836, it became just another Pennsylvania-chartered private bank, closing five years later. As Congress allowed the Second Bank to die, it passed the Deposit Act of 1836, authorizing the secretary of the treasury to designate one bank in each state and territory to provide services formerly performed by the Bank of the United States. The act also provided that the bulk of the federal surplus—income derived from the sale of public lands to speculators, who bought large quantities of land to resell at a profit—be distributed to the states as interest-free loans (or "deposits") beginning in 1837. (The loans were understood to be forgiven and, in fact, they were never repaid.) Eager to use the money for state-funded internal improvements, Democrats joined Whigs in supporting the measure overwhelmingly. Fearing that the act would fuel speculation, promote inflation, and thus undermine farmers' interests, Jackson opposed it. Because support was strong enough to override a veto, Jackson signed the bill but first insisted on a provision prohibiting state banks from issuing or accepting small-denomination paper money. Jackson hoped that by encouraging the use of coins, the provision would prevent unscrupulous businessmen from defrauding workers by paying them in devalued paper bills.

12-2h Specie Circular

The president then ordered treasury secretary Levi Woodbury to issue the Specie Circular, which provided that, after August 1836, only settlers could use paper money to buy land; speculators would have to use specie (gold or silver). The policy proved disastrous, significantly reducing public land sales, which in turn reduced the federal government's surplus and its loans to the states. Meanwhile, a banking crisis emerged. Fearful that bank notes would lose value, people sought to redeem them for specie, creating a shortage that forced the banks to suspend payment. Jackson's opponents were irate. Now "King Andrew" had used presidential powers to defy legislative will, and with disastrous consequences. In the waning days of Jackson's administration, Congress repealed the circular, but the president pocket-vetoed the bill by holding it unsigned until Congress adjourned. Finally, in May 1838, after Jackson had left office, a joint resolution of Congress overturned the circular.

Library of Congress Prints & Photographs Division, [LC-USZC4-12983]

▲ Whigs, who named themselves after the loyal opposition in Britain, delighted in portraying Andrew Jackson as a power-hungry leader eager to turn a republic into a monarchy.

12-3 The Second Party System

▶ **What were the main differences between the Democrats and Whigs?**

▶ **How did economic challenges influence electoral politics in the 1830s?**

▶ **What factors influenced Americans in choosing their political affiliation?**

In the 1830s, opponents of the Democrats, including remnants of the National Republican and Antimason parties, joined together to become the Whig Party. Resentful of Jackson's domination of Congress, the Whigs borrowed the name of the eighteenth-century British party that opposed the Hanoverian monarchs' tyranny. They, too, were the loyal opposition. From 1834 through the 1840s, the Whigs and the Democrats competed on nearly equal footing, and each drew supporters from all regions. The era's political competition—the second party system—thrived on intense ideological rivalry.

12-3a Democrats and Whigs

The two parties held very different visions of the route to national prosperity. For Democrats, the West's fertile and abundant lands were essential for creating a society in which white men could establish independent livelihoods and receive equal rights, freed from the undue influence of established slaveholders or urban elites. Whigs were more suspicious of rapid westward expansion, though they welcomed the commercial opportunities it might bring. Instead, they pushed for industrial and commercial development within the nation's current boundaries. Henry Clay, a leading Whig, explained that it "is much more important that we unite, harmonize, and improve what we have than attempt to acquire more."

The Whigs' vision of economic expansion demanded an activist government, while Democrats reaffirmed the Jeffersonian principle of limited government. Whigs supported corporate charters, a national bank, and paper currency; Democrats opposed all three. Whigs generally professed a strong belief in progress and perfectibility, and they favored social reforms, including public schools, prison and asylum reform, and temperance. Jacksonians criticized reform associations for undermining the people's will by giving undue influence to political minorities; Whigs countered they served the common good. Nor did Whigs object to helping special interests if doing so promoted the general welfare. The chartering of corporations, they argued, expanded economic opportunity for everyone, laborers and farmers alike. Democrats distrusted concentrated economic power as well as moral and economic coercion. Whigs stressed a "harmony of interests" among all classes and interests while Democrats saw society as divided into the "haves" and the "have nots." Whigs feared the "excesses of democracy" and preferred to see society ruled from the top down; they touted self-improvement and thought that society's wealthy and powerful had risen by their own merits. Democrats embraced a motto of "equal rights," alleging that the wealthy and powerful had often benefited from special favors.

12-3b Political Coalitions

But religion and ethnicity, as much as class, influenced party affiliation. The Whigs' support for energetic government and moral reform appealed to evangelical Protestants. In many locales, the membership rolls of reform societies overlapped those of the party. Indeed, Whigs practiced a kind of political revivalism. Their rallies resembled camp meetings; their speeches employed pulpit rhetoric; their programs embodied reformers' perfectionist beliefs.

By appealing to evangelicals, Whigs alienated members of other faiths. The evangelicals' ideal Christian state had no room for nonevangelical Protestants, Catholics, Mormons, or religious freethinkers. Those groups opposed Sabbath laws and temperance legislation in particular, and state interference in moral and religious questions in general. In fact, they preferred to keep religion and politics separate. As a result, more than 95 percent of Irish Catholics, 90 percent of Reformed Dutch, and 80 percent of German Catholics voted Democratic.

The parties' platforms thus attracted what might seem to be odd coalitions of voters. Democrats' promises to open additional lands for settlement—and to remove the Native peoples on those lands—attracted yeoman farmers, wage earners, frontier slave owners, and immigrants. The Whigs' preference for a slower, controlled settlement of western lands attracted groups as diverse as African American New Englanders and well-settled slave owners, especially in the Upper South; the former hoped Whig policies would undercut slavery itself, and the latter wanted to protect their investments in land and slaves from cheap western competition. With such broad coalitions of voters, room existed within each party for a wide spectrum of beliefs, particularly in relation to slavery.

Yet slavery also had a long history of being politically divisive, leading some politicians to take extreme measures to remove it from national political debate. In response to the American Antislavery Society's petitioning campaign, the House of Representatives in 1836 adopted what abolitionists labeled the "gag rule," which automatically tabled abolitionist petitions, effectively preventing debate on them. Former president John Quincy Adams, now a representative from Massachusetts, dramatically defended the right to petition and took to the floor many times to decry the gag rule, which was ultimately repealed in 1844.

12-3c Election of 1836

Vice President Martin Van Buren, handpicked by Jackson, headed the Democratic ticket in the 1836 presidential election. A career politician, Van Buren had built a political machine—the Albany Regency—in New York and joined Jackson's cabinet in 1829, first as secretary of state and then as American minister to Great Britain.

Because the Whigs in 1836 had not yet coalesced into a national party, they entered three sectional candidates: Daniel Webster (from New England), Hugh White (from the South), and William Henry Harrison (from the West). By splintering the vote, they hoped to throw the election into the House of Representatives. Van Buren, however, comfortably captured the electoral college even though he had only a 25,000-vote edge out of a total of 1.5 million votes cast. No vice presidential candidate received a majority of electoral votes, and for the only time in American history, the Senate decided a vice presidential race, selecting Democratic candidate Richard M. Johnson of Kentucky.

12-3d Van Buren and Hard Times

Just weeks after Van Buren took office, the American credit system collapsed. With banks refusing to redeem paper currency with gold in response to the Specie Circular, a downward economic spiral curtailed bank loans and strangled business confidence. After a brief recovery, hard times persisted from 1839 until 1843.

Van Buren followed Jackson's hard-money, antibank policies, proposing the Independent Treasury Bill, which became law in 1840 but which was repealed in 1841 when Whigs regained congressional control. The independent treasury—so named for its independence from both the Bank of the United States and British capital—created regional treasury branches that accepted and dispersed only gold and silver coin; they did not accept paper currency or checks drawn on state banks, and thus accelerated deflation.

The issue of the government's role in economic development sharply divided the parties. Whigs favored new banks, more paper currency, and readily available corporate and bank charters. Democrats favored eliminating paper currency altogether. Increasingly, the Democrats became distrustful even of state banks; by the mid-1840s, a majority favored eliminating all bank corporations.

12-3e William Henry Harrison and the Election of 1840

With the nation gripped by hard times, the Whigs confidently approached the election of 1840 with a simple strategy: maintain loyal supporters and court independents by blaming hard times on the Democrats. The Whigs rallied behind a military hero, General William Henry Harrison, conqueror of the Shawnees at Tippecanoe Creek in 1811. The Democrats renominated President Van Buren, and the newly formed Liberty Party ran James Birney on its antislavery, free-soil platform.

Harrison, or "Old Tippecanoe," and his running mate, John Tyler of Virginia, ran a "log cabin and hard cider" campaign—a people's crusade—against the aristocratic president in "the Palace." Although descended from a Virginia plantation family, Harrison presented himself as an ordinary farmer. While party hacks blamed Democrats for hard times, Harrison remained silent, earning the nickname "General Mum." Whigs wooed voters with huge rallies, parades, songs, posters, campaign mementos, and a party newspaper, *The Log Cabin*.

They appealed to voters as well as nonvoters, including women, who attended their rallies and speeches, and women actively promoted the Whig cause; one Virginia woman, for example, published two pamphlets backing Harrison's candidacy. In a huge turnout, 80 percent of eligible voters cast ballots. Narrowly winning the popular vote, Harrison swept the electoral college, 234 to 60. The Whigs had beaten the Jacksonians at their own game.

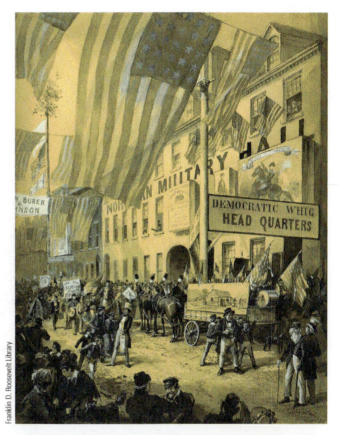

Franklin D. Roosevelt Library

▲ Even as the Whigs opposed the Democrats, they adopted many of the Democrats' campaign techniques, appealing to the common man with their "log cabin and cider" campaign of 1840. The band in this street scene is riding a wagon decorated with a log-cabin painting. The campaign's excitement appealed to nonvoters as well as voters, and 80 percent of eligible voters cast ballots.

12-4 Women's Rights

▶ What were the origins of the women's rights movement?

▶ How did women's legal status change in the first half of the nineteenth century?

▶ What were the connections between the women's rights movement and the abolitionist movement?

Although women participated in electoral campaigns, states denied them the right to vote, along with other rights afforded male citizens. Some radical reformers, such as Fanny Wright, had long decried such inequality, but the movement for women's rights did not pick up steam until the religious revivalism and reform movements of the 1830s (see "Revivals and Reform," Section 10-7). While revivals emphasized human equality, reform movements brought middle-class women into the public sphere.

By the 1840s, female abolitionists took the lead in demanding women's legal and political rights. Committed

Smithsonian American Art Museum, Washington, DC/Art Resource, NY

▲ This 1861 painting captures the notion of manifest destiny, in which European Americans displace Native Americans in a divinely ordained mission to spread "civilization" into the West.

to the general notion of human equality, they were especially frustrated by their subordinated status within the abolitionist movement itself. Dismayed that female abolitionists were denied seats in the main hall at the first World Anti-Slavery Convention in London in 1840, Lucretia Mott and Elizabeth Cady Stanton joined together eight years later to help organize the first American women's rights convention. Other early women's rights activists included **Angelina and Sarah Grimké**, sisters who were born into a South Carolina slaveholding family and who became abolitionists in the North, where critics attacked them for speaking to audiences that included men. Lesser-known women also developed their political consciousness from abolitionist activities. After Congress voted to automatically table antislavery petitions with the "gag rule" of 1836, women defended their right to petition, employed more demanding language, and began offering specific legislative advice. Some thought the next step was obvious: full citizenship rights for women.

absolute control over the family. Husbands owned their wives' personal property and whatever their wives or their children produced or earned. Fathers were their children's legal guardians and could deny their daughters' choice of husband, though by 1800 few did.

Married women made modest legal gains beginning in the 1830s. Arkansas in 1835 passed the first married women's property law, and by 1860 sixteen states allowed women—single, married, or divorced—to own and convey property. When a wife inherited property, it was hers, not her husband's, though money earned or acquired in other ways still belonged to her husband. Women could also write wills. Wealthy Americans, South and North, favored such laws, hoping to protect family fortunes during periods of economic boom and bust; a woman's property was safe from her husband's creditors. In the 1830s, states also liberalized divorce laws, adding cruelty and desertion as grounds for divorce, but divorce remained rare.

Angelina and Sarah Grimké
Southern-born sisters who were powerful antislavery speakers; later leaders of the women's rights movement.

12-4a Legal Rights

After independence, American states carried over traditional English marriage law, giving husbands

12-4b Political Rights

The organized movement to secure women's political rights was launched in July 1848, when abolitionists Elizabeth Cady Stanton, Lucretia Mott, Mary Ann McClintock, Martha Wright, and Jane Hunt organized the first Woman's Rights

Convention at **Seneca Falls**, New York. The three hundred women and men in attendance demanded women's social and economic equality, with some advocating political equality, too. They protested women's legal disabilities and social restrictions, such as exclusion from many occupations. Their Declaration of Sentiments, modeled on the Declaration of Independence, broadcast the injustices suffered by women: "All men and women are created equal," the declaration proclaimed. The similar premises of abolitionism and women's rights led many reformers, including former slaves like Sojourner Truth, to work simultaneously for both movements in the 1850s. Even among those supporting the movement's general aims, though, the question of female suffrage became divisive. Abolitionists William Lloyd Garrison and Frederick Douglass supported women's right to vote, but most men actively opposed it. At Seneca Falls, the resolution on woman suffrage passed only after Douglass, one of only a few men to take an active role at the convention, passionately endorsed it, but some participants still refused to sign. In 1851, **Elizabeth Cady Stanton** joined with **Susan B. Anthony**, a temperance advocate, to become the most vocal and persistent activists for woman suffrage. They won relatively few converts, but they continued to gather many critics even as other national issues eclipsed women's rights.

12-5 The Politics of Territorial Expansion

▶ **What developments fueled westward expansion?**

▶ **What role did the federal government play in territorial acquisition?**

▶ **How were westward expansion and territorial acquisition issues in party politics?**

Fiscal policy and westward expansion dominated national politics. Immediately after taking office in 1841, President Harrison convened Congress in special session to pass the Whig program: repeal of the independent treasury system and adoption of a new national bank and a higher protective tariff. But the sixty-eight-year-old Harrison caught pneumonia and died within a month of his inauguration. His vice president, John Tyler, who had left the Democratic Party to protest Jackson's nullification proclamation, now became the first vice president to succeed to the presidency. The Constitution did not stipulate what should happen, but Tyler quickly took full possession of executive powers, setting a crucial precedent that would not be codified in the Constitution until 1967 with the Twenty-fifth Amendment's ratification.

12-5a President Tyler

In office, Tyler became more a Democrat than a Whig. He repeatedly vetoed Clay's protective tariffs, internal improvements, and bills to revive the Bank of the United States. Two days after Tyler's second veto of a bank bill, the entire cabinet resigned, with the exception of Secretary of State Webster, who would soon step down, but not until completing treaty negotiations with Britain over the eastern end of the Canadian-U.S. boundary. Tyler became a president without a party, and the Whigs lost the presidency without losing an election. Disgusted Whigs referred to Tyler as "His Accidency."

Like Jackson, Tyler expanded presidential powers and emphasized westward expansion. His expansionist vision contained Whig elements, though: he eyed commercial markets in Hawai'i and China. During his presidency, the United States negotiated its first treaties with China, and Tyler expanded the Monroe Doctrine to include Hawai'i (or the Sandwich Islands, as they had been named by the English explorer James Cook). Tyler was a Virginia slaveholder; his vision for the nation's path to greatness fixed mostly on Texas and westward expansion.

12-5b Texas and "Manifest Destiny"

Soon after establishing the Lone Star Republic in 1836, Sam Houston approached American authorities to propose annexation as a state. But a new slave state would upset the balance of slave and free states in the Senate, a balance maintained since before the Missouri Compromise. Neither Whigs nor Democrats, wary of causing sectional divisions within their ranks, were inclined to confront the issue. In the 1830s, Democratic presidents Andrew Jackson and Martin Van Buren—one a strong proponent of slavery, the other a mild opponent—sidestepped the issue. But by the mid-1840s—with cotton cultivation expanding rapidly—some Democratic politicians equated the annexation of Texas with the nation's manifest destiny.

The belief that American expansion westward and southward was inevitable, just, and divinely ordained dated to the nation's founding but was first labeled "manifest destiny" in 1845, amid the debate over Texas annexation, by John L. O'Sullivan, editor of the *United States Magazine and Democratic Review*. O'Sullivan claimed that Texas annexation would be "the fulfillment of our manifest destiny to overspread the continent allotted by Providence for the free development of our yearly multiplying millions." The nation's destiny, he and others believed, was to encompass the continent. Manifest destiny implied that Americans had a God-given right, perhaps even an obligation, to expand their republican and Christian institutions to less fortunate and less civilized peoples. Manifest destiny provided a political and ideological rationale for territorial expansion.

Implicit in the idea of manifest destiny was the belief that Native Americans and Hispanics, much like people of African descent, were inferior peoples best controlled or conquered. White racial theorists believed that, unlike white people, Native peoples and blacks were not capable of self-improvement. Nor, according to these racial theorists, were Hispanics, because intermarriage with Native Americans had left

Seneca Falls Town in New York which hosted a women's rights convention in 1848.

Elizabeth Cady Stanton, Susan B. Anthony Vocal advocates of women's suffrage.

them incapable of improvement. Many white Americans believed that in their conquest of the West they were implementing God's will.

Not all white Americans subscribed to such views, however. During debates over Texas annexation, transcendentalist William Ellery Channing argued that the United States should expand its empire by example, not conquest: It should "assume the role of sublime moral empire, with a mission to diffuse freedom by manifesting its fruits, not to plunder, crush, and destroy."

In June 1846, impatient expansionists, including John C. Frémont, staged an armed rebellion against Mexican authorities and declared California an independent republic. Because the U.S. military soon conquered California in its War with Mexico, the "Bear Flag Rebellion"—so named for the symbol on the revolutionaries' flag—was short-lived but further inflamed racial tensions in California.

12-5c "Fifty-Four Forty or Fight"

To the north, Britain and the United States had jointly occupied the disputed Oregon Territory since 1818. Beginning with John Quincy Adams's administration, the United States had tried to fix the boundary at the forty-ninth parallel, but Britain was determined to maintain access to Puget Sound and the Columbia River. As migrants streamed into Oregon in the early 1840s, expansionists demanded the entire Oregon Country for the United States, up to its northernmost border at latitude 54° 40'. Soon "fifty-four forty or fight" became their rallying cry.

President Tyler wanted both Oregon and Texas, but was obsessed with Texas. He argued that there was little to fear from slavery's expansion, for it would spread the nation's black population more thinly, causing the institution's gradual demise. But when word leaked out that Secretary of State John Calhoun had written to the British minister in Washington to justify Texas annexation as a way of protecting slavery—"a political institution essential to the peace, safety, and prosperity of those States in which it exists"—the Senate rejected annexation in 1844 by a vote of 35 to 16.

12-5d Polk and the Election of 1844

Worried southern Democrats persuaded their party's 1844 convention to adopt a rule requiring that the presidential nominee receive two-thirds of the convention votes, effectively giving the southern states a veto and allowing them to block the nomination of Martin Van Buren, an opponent of annexation. Instead, the party ran "Young Hickory," House Speaker **James K. Polk,** an avid expansionist and slaveholding cotton planter from Tennessee. The Democratic platform

James K. Polk Eleventh president of the United States (1845–1849); supporter of immediate annexation of Texas who wanted to gain California and Oregon for the United States as well.

called for occupation of the entire Oregon Territory and annexation of Texas. The Whigs, who ran Henry Clay, argued that the Democrats' belligerent nationalism would trigger war with Great Britain or Mexico or both. Clay favored expansion through negotiation, whereas many northern Whigs opposed annexation altogether, fearful it would add slave states and strain relations with vital trading partners.

Polk won the election by 170 electoral votes to 105, though with a margin of just 38,000 out of 2.7 million votes cast. Polk won New York's 36 electoral votes by just 5,000 popular votes. Abolitionist James G. Birney, the Liberty Party candidate, had drawn almost 16,000 votes from Clay by running on a Free-Soil platform. Without Birney, Clay might have won New York, giving him an edge of 141 to 134 in the electoral college. Abolitionist forces thus unwittingly helped elect a slaveholder as president, and some antislavery Whigs, such as Abraham Lincoln, never forgave the abolitionists for helping defeat Clay.

12-5e Annexation of Texas

Interpreting Polk's victory as a mandate for annexation, President Tyler proposed that Texas be admitted by joint resolution of Congress. The usual method of annexation, by treaty negotiation, required a two-thirds majority in the Senate—which annexationists did not have because of opposition to slavery's expansion. Joint resolution required only a simple majority in each house. On March 1, 1845, the resolution passed the House by 120 to 98 and the Senate by 27 to 25. Three days before leaving office, Tyler signed the measure. Mexico, which had never recognized Texas independence, immediately broke relations with the United States. In October, the citizens of Texas ratified annexation, and Texas joined the Union, with a constitution permitting slavery. The nation was on the brink of war with Mexico. That conflict—like none other before it—would lay bare the inextricable relationships among westward expansion, slavery, and sectional discord.

12-6 The War with Mexico and Its Consequences

▶ What actions and decisions drew the United States into war with Mexico?

▶ How did Americans respond to the war with Mexico?

▶ How did the Wilmot Proviso and the election of 1848 change the debate on the issue of slavery?

The annexation of Texas did not necessarily make war with Mexico inevitable, but through a series of calculated decisions, President Polk triggered the conflict. During the annexation process, Polk urged Texans to seize all land to the Rio Grande and claim the river as their southern and western border. Mexico held that the Nueces River was the border; hence, the stage was set for conflict. Polk wanted Mexico's territory all the way to the Pacific, and all of Oregon Country as well. He and his expansionist cabinet achieved their goals, largely unaware of the price in domestic harmony that expansion would exact.

12-6a Oregon

During the 1844 campaign, Polk's supporters had threatened war with Great Britain to gain all of Oregon. As president, however, Polk turned first to diplomacy. Not wanting to fight Mexico and Great Britain simultaneously, he tried to avoid bloodshed in the Northwest, where America and Britain had since 1819 jointly occupied disputed territory. In 1846, the Oregon Treaty gave the United States all of present-day Oregon, Washington, and Idaho, and parts of Wyoming and Montana (see Map 12.3). Thus, a new era of land acquisition and conquest had begun under the eleventh president of the United States, the sixth to be a slaveholder and one who, through an agent, secretly bought and sold slaves from the White House.

12-6b "Mr. Polk's War"

Toward Mexico, Polk was particularly aggressive. In early 1846, he ordered American troops under "Old Rough and

Ready," General Zachary Taylor, to march south and defend the contested border of the Rio Grande across from the town of Matamoros, Mexico (see Map 12.4). Polk especially desired California as the prize in his expansionist strategy, and he attempted to buy from Mexico a huge tract of land extending to the Pacific. When that effort failed, Polk waited for war. Negotiations between troops on the Rio Grande were awkwardly conducted in French because no American officer spoke Spanish and no Mexican spoke English. After a three-week standoff, the tense situation came to a head. On April 24, 1846, Mexican troops ambushed a U.S. cavalry unit on the north side of the river; eleven Americans were killed, and sixty-three were taken captive. On April 26, Taylor sent a dispatch overland to Washington, D.C., which took two weeks to arrive, announcing, "Hostilities may now be considered as commenced."

Polk now drafted a message to Congress: Mexico "passed the boundary of the United States, has invaded our territory and shed American blood on American soil." In the bill accompanying the war message, Polk deceptively declared that "war exists by the act of Mexico itself" and summoned the nation to arms. On May 12, the Senate voted 40 to 2 (with numerous abstentions) for war, reaffirming the House's similarly lopsided vote of 174-14. Some antislavery Whigs in Congress had tried to oppose the war, but they were barely allowed to speak. Because Polk withheld key facts, the full reality of what had happened on the distant Rio Grande was not known. But the theory and practice of manifest destiny had launched the United States into its first major war on foreign territory.

12-6c Foreign War and the Popular Imagination

The idea of war unleashed great public celebrations. Huge crowds gathered in southern cities, such as Richmond and Louisville, to voice support for the war effort. Twenty thousand Philadelphians and even more New Yorkers rallied in the same spirit. After news came of General Taylor's first two battlefield victories at Palo Alto and Resaca de la Palma, volunteers swarmed recruiting stations. From his home in Lansingburgh, New York, writer Herman Melville remarked that "the people here are all in a state of delirium. . . . A military ardor pervades all ranks. . . . Nothing is talked of but the Halls of the Montezumas." Publishers rushed books about Mexican geography into print; "Palo Alto" hats and root beer went on sale. And new daily newspapers, now printed on rotary presses, boosted their sales by giving the war a romantic appeal.

Here was an adventurous war of conquest in a far-off, exotic land. Here was the fulfillment of an Anglo-Saxon–Christian destiny to expand and possess the North American continent and to take civilization to the "semi-Indian" Mexicans. For many, racism fueled the expansionist spirit. In 1846, an Illinois newspaper justified the war on the basis that Mexicans were "reptiles in the path of progressive democracy." For those who read newspapers, the War with Mexico became the first national

Map 12.3 **American Expansion in Oregon**

The slogan of Polk's supporters had been "fifty-four forty or fight," but negotiation of a boundary at the forty-ninth parallel avoided the danger of war with Great Britain.

Map 12.4 **The War with Mexico**

This map shows the territory disputed between the United States and Mexico. After U.S. gains in northeastern Mexico, in New Mexico, and in California, General Winfield Scott captured Mexico City in the decisive campaign of the war.

event experienced with immediacy. War correspondents reported the battles south of the border. From Veracruz on the Gulf Coast of Mexico, ships carried news dispatches to New Orleans, whose nine daily newspapers ran a faster steamer out to meet them. With stories set in type before they even reached shore, riders carried the news to the North. By war's end, news traveled by telegraph in only three days from New Orleans to Washington, D.C., as war fueled the communication revolution.

The war spawned an outpouring of poetry, song, drama, travel literature, and lithographs that captured the popular imagination and glorified the conflict. New lyrics to the tune of "Yankee Doodle" proclaimed: "They attacked our men upon our land / and crossed our river too sir / now show them all with sword in hand / what yankee boys can do sir." Most of the war-inspired flowering of the popular arts was patriotic. But not everyone cheered. Abolitionist James Russell Lowell considered the war a "national crime committed in behoof of slavery, our common sin." Ralph Waldo Emerson confided to his journals in 1847, "The United States will conquer Mexico, but it will be as the man swallows arsenic, which brings him down in turn. Mexico will poison us." Even proslavery spokesman John C. Calhoun saw the perils of expansionism. Mexico, he said, was "the forbidden fruit; the penalty of eating it would be to subject our institutions to political death."

12-6d Conquest

The U.S. troops proved unruly and undisciplined, and their politically ambitious commanders quarreled among themselves. Nevertheless, early in the war, U.S. forces made significant gains. In May 1846, Polk ordered Colonel Stephen Kearny and a small detachment to invade the remote and thinly populated provinces of New Mexico and California. General Zachary Taylor's forces attacked and occupied Monterrey, which surrendered in September, securing northeastern Mexico (see Map 12.4).

New Mexico proved more difficult to subdue, however. In January 1847, in Taos, northwest of Santa Fe, Hispanics and Native Americans led by Pablo Montoya and Tomas Romero rebelled against the Americans and killed numerous government officials. In what came to be known as the Taos Revolt, some 500 Mexican and Native American insurgents laid siege to a mill in Arroyo Hondo, outside Taos. The U.S. command acted swiftly to suppress the revolt with 300 heavily armed troops. The growing band of insurgents eventually retreated to Taos Pueblo and held out in a thick-walled church. With cannon, the U.S. Army succeeded in killing some 150 and capturing 400 of the rebels. Approximately 28 insurgent leaders were hanged in the Taos plaza, ending the bloody resistance to U.S. occupation of lands still claimed by Mexican and Native peoples.

Before the end of 1846, American forces had also established dominion over California. General Winfield Scott then carried the war to the enemy's heartland. Landing at Veracruz, he led fourteen thousand men toward Mexico City. This daring invasion proved the war's decisive campaign. Scott's men, outnumbered and threatened by yellow fever, encountered a series of formidable Mexican defenses, but engineers repeatedly discovered flanking routes around their foes. After a series of hard-fought battles, U.S. troops captured the Mexican capital.

12-6e Treaty of Guadalupe Hidalgo

Representatives of both countries signed the **Treaty of Guadalupe Hidalgo** in February 1848. The United States gained California and New Mexico (including present-day Nevada, Utah, and Arizona, and parts of Colorado and Wyoming), and recognition of the Rio Grande as the southern boundary of Texas. In return, the American government agreed to settle the $3.2 million in claims of its citizens (mostly Texans) against Mexico and to pay Mexico a mere $15 million.

The war's costs included the lives of thirteen thousand Americans (mostly from disease) and, according to some estimates, fifty thousand Mexicans. Moreover, enmity between Mexico and the United States endured into the twenty-first century. The domestic cost to the United States was even higher. Public opinion was sharply divided. Southwesterners were enthusiastic about the war, as were most southern planters; New Englanders strenuously opposed it. Whigs in Congress charged that Polk, a

Democrat, had "provoked" an unnecessary war and "usurped the power of Congress." The aged John Quincy Adams denounced the war, and an Illinois Whig named Abraham Lincoln called Polk's justifications the "half insane mumbling of a fever-dream." Abolitionists and a small minority of antislavery Whigs charged that the war was a plot to extend slavery.

12-6f "Slave Power Conspiracy"

These charges fed northern fear of the "Slave Power." Abolitionists had long warned of a slaveholding oligarchy that intended to dominate the nation through its hold on federal power. Slaveholders had gained control of the South by suppressing dissent. They had forced the gag rule on Congress in 1836 and threatened northern liberties. To many white northerners, even those who saw nothing wrong with slavery, it was the battle over free speech that first made the idea of a Slave Power credible. The War with Mexico deepened such fears.

Northern opinion on slavery's expansion began to shift, but the war's impact on southern opinion was even more dramatic. At first, some southern Whigs attacked the Democratic president for causing the war, and few southern congressmen saw slavery as the paramount issue. Many whites, North and South, feared that large land seizures would bring thousands of nonwhite Mexicans into the United States and upset the racial order. An Indiana politician did not want "any mixed races in our Union, nor men of any color except white, unless they be slaves." And the *Charleston* (South Carolina) *Mercury* asked if the nation expected "to melt into our population eight millions of men, at war with us by race, by language, by religion, manners and laws." Yet, despite their racism and such numerical exaggerations, many statesmen soon saw other prospects in the outcomes of a war of conquest in the Southwest.

12-6g Wilmot Proviso

In August 1846, David Wilmot, a Pennsylvania Democrat, proposed an amendment, or proviso, to a military appropriations bill: that "neither slavery nor involuntary servitude shall ever exist" in any territory gained from Mexico. Although the proviso never passed both houses of Congress, its repeated introduction by northerners transformed the debate over the expansion of slavery. Southerners suddenly circled their wagons to protect the future of a slave society. Alexander H. Stephens, until recently "no defender of slavery," now declared that slavery was based on the Bible and above moral criticism, and John C. Calhoun took an aggressive stand. The territories, Calhoun insisted, belonged to all the

Treaty of Guadalupe Hidalgo Agreement that ended the U.S. War with Mexico, in which Mexico ceded vast amounts of its territory and was forced to recognize the Rio Grande as Texas's southern boundary.

Table 12.1 New Political Parties

Party	Period of Influence	Area of Influence	Outcome
Liberty Party	1839–1848	North	Merged with other antislavery groups to form Free-Soil Party
Free-Soil Party	1848–1854	North	Merged with Republican Party
Know-Nothings (American Party)	1853–1856	Nationwide	Disappeared, freeing most to join Republican Party
Republican Party	1854–present	North (later nationwide)	Became rival of Democratic Party and won presidency in 1860

states, and the federal government could not limit the spread of slavery there. Southern slaveholders had a constitutional right rooted in the Fifth Amendment, Calhoun claimed, to take their slaves (as property) anywhere in the territories.

This position, often called "state sovereignty," which quickly became a test of orthodoxy among southern politicians, was a radical reversal of history. In 1787, the Confederation Congress had discouraged if not fully excluded slavery from the Northwest Territory; Article IV of the U.S. Constitution had authorized Congress to make "all needful rules and regulations" for the territories; and the Missouri Compromise had barred slavery from most of the Louisiana Purchase. Now, however, southern leaders demanded future guarantees for slavery.

In the North, the **Wilmot Proviso** became a rallying cry for abolitionists. Eventually the legislatures of fourteen northern states endorsed it—and not because all of its supporters were abolitionists. David Wilmot, significantly, was neither an abolitionist nor an antislavery Whig. He denied having any "squeamish sensitiveness upon the subject of slavery" or "morbid sympathy for the slave." Instead, he sought to defend "the rights of white freemen" and to obtain California "for free white labor."

As Wilmot demonstrated, it was possible to be both a racist and an opponent of slavery. The vast majority of white northerners were not active abolitionists, and their desire to keep the West free from slavery was often matched by their desire to keep blacks from settling there. Fear of the Slave Power was thus building a potent antislavery movement that united abolitionists and antiblack voters. At stake was an abiding version of the American Dream: the free individual's access to social mobility through acquisition of land in the West. This sacred ideal of free labor, and its dread of concentrated power, fueled a new political persuasion.

Wilmot Proviso A proposed amendment to an 1846 military appropriations bill that would have prohibited slavery in territories acquired from Mexico; though it never passed, it transformed the national debate over slavery.

Free-Soil Party A political party that sprang from and represented the movement to prevent slavery in the western territories.

Slave labor, thousands of northerners had come to believe, would degrade the honest toil of free men and render them unemployable.

12-6h The Election of 1848 and Popular Sovereignty

The divisive slavery question now infested national politics. After Polk renounced a second term as president, the Democrats nominated Senator Lewis Cass of Michigan for president and General William Butler of Kentucky for vice president. Cass, a party loyalist who had served in Jackson's cabinet, had devised in 1847 the idea of "popular sovereignty"—letting residents in the western territories decide the slavery question for themselves. His party's platform declared that Congress lacked the power to interfere with slavery's expansion. The Whigs nominated General Zachary Taylor, a southern slaveholder and war hero; Congressman Millard Fillmore of New York was his running mate. The Whig convention similarly refused to assert that Congress had power over slavery in the territories.

But the issue could not be avoided. Many southern Democrats distrusted Cass and eventually voted for Taylor because he was a slaveholder. Among northerners, concern over slavery led to the formation of a new party. New York Democrats committed to the Wilmot Proviso rebelled against Cass and nominated former president Martin Van Buren. Antislavery Whigs and former supporters of the Liberty Party then joined them to organize the **Free-Soil Party**, with Van Buren as its candidate (see Table 12.1). This party, which sought to restrict slavery expansion to any western territories and whose slogan was "Free Soil, Free Speech, Free Labor, and Free Men," won almost 300,000 northern votes. For a new third party to win 10 percent of the national vote was unprecedented. Taylor polled 1.4 million votes to Cass's 1.2 million and won the White House, but the results were more ominous than decisive.

American politics had split along sectional lines as never before. Religious denominations, too, severed into northern and southern wings. As the 1850s dawned, the legacies of the War with Mexico threatened the nature of the Union itself.

The Mexican War in Popular Imagination

The War with Mexico was the first American foreign conflict to be covered by the press with actual correspondents and the first to stimulate the creation of widespread promotional popular art and commemorative objects. General Zachary Taylor, the American commander in Mexico, became the hero of the war, and in its wake, was elected president in 1848 in a campaign that featured countless forms of this art.

CRITICAL THINKING

■ Why was the War with Mexico the first American foreign war to be covered by journalists and so widely depicted in political and military art?

■ Do you think the artistic depictions of the War with Mexico increased or decreased the popularity of the war?

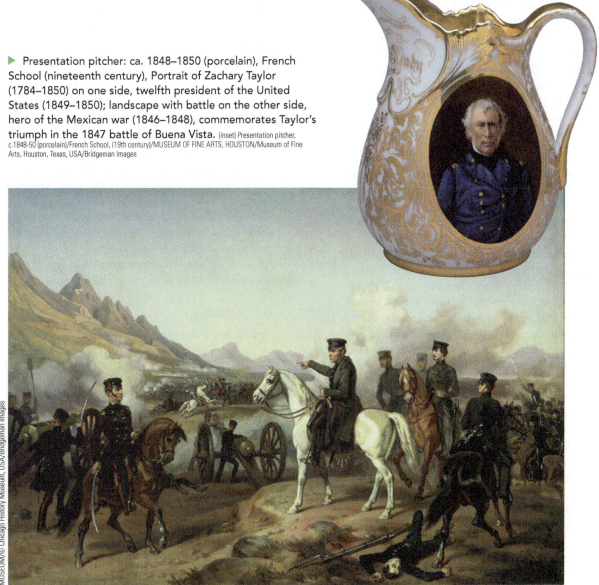

▶ Presentation pitcher: ca. 1848–1850 (porcelain), French School (nineteenth century), Portrait of Zachary Taylor (1784–1850) on one side, twelfth president of the United States (1849–1850); landscape with battle on the other side, hero of the Mexican war (1846–1848), commemorates Taylor's triumph in the 1847 battle of Buena Vista. (inset) Presentation pitcher, c.1848-50 (porcelain)/French School, (19th century)/MUSEUM OF FINE ARTS, HOUSTON/Museum of Fine Arts, Houston, Texas, USA/Bridgeman Images

General Zachary Taylor at the Battle of Buena Vista in 1847 (oil on canvas)/Powell, William Henry (1823-79)/CHICAGO HISTORY MUSEUM/© Chicago History Museum, USA/Bridgeman Images

▲ Painting, General Zachary Taylor in command at the Battle of Buena Vista, in Mexico, 1847, oil on canvas, by William Henry Powell (1823–1879).

12-7 1850: Compromise or Armistice?

▶ **Why was the debate over slavery in newly acquired territories so contentious?**

▶ **How did northerners respond to the Fugitive Slave Law?**

▶ **How did Franklin Pierce's election contribute to increased conflicts over slavery?**

The new decade's first sectional battle involved California. More than eighty thousand Americans flooded into California during the gold rush of 1849. With Congress unable to agree on a formula to govern the territories, President Taylor urged these settlers to apply directly for admission to the Union. They promptly did so, proposing a state constitution that did not permit slavery. Because California's admission as a free state would upset the Senate's sectional balance of power (the ratio of slave to free states was fifteen to fifteen), southern politicians wanted to postpone admission and make California a slave territory, or at least extend the Missouri Compromise line west to the Pacific.

12-7a Debate Over Slavery in the Territories

Henry Clay, the venerable Whig leader, sensed that the Union was in peril. Twice before—in 1820 and 1833—Clay, the "Great Pacificator," had taken the lead in shaping sectional compromise; now he struggled again to preserve the nation. To hushed Senate galleries, Clay presented a series of compromise measures in the winter of 1850. At one point, he held up what he claimed was a piece of George Washington's coffin as a means of inspiring unity. Over the weeks that followed, he and Senator Stephen A. Douglas of Illinois steered their compromise package through debate and amendment.

The problems to be solved were numerous and difficult. Would California, or part of it, become a free state? How should the territory acquired from Mexico be organized? Texas, which allowed slavery, claimed large portions of the new land as far west as Santa Fe. Southerners complained that fugitive slaves were not returned as the Constitution required, and northerners objected to slave auctions held in the nation's capital. Most troublesome of all, however, was the status of slavery in the territories.

Clay and Douglas hoped to avoid a specific formula, and in the idea of popular sovereignty they discovered what one historian called a "charm of ambiguity." Ultimately Congress would have to approve statehood for a territory, but "in the meantime," said Lewis Cass, it should allow the people living there "to regulate their own concerns in their own way."

Those simple words proved all but unenforceable. When could settlers prohibit slavery? To avoid dissension within their party, northern and southern Democrats explained Cass's statement to their constituents in two incompatible ways. Southerners claimed that neither Congress nor a territorial legislature could bar slavery. Only late in the territorial process, when settlers were ready to draft a state constitution, could they take that step, thus allowing time for slavery to take root. Northerners, however, insisted that Americans living in a territory were entitled to local self-government and thus could outlaw slavery at any time.

The cause of compromise gained a powerful supporter when Senator Daniel Webster committed his prestige and eloquence to Clay's bill. "I wish to speak today," Webster declaimed on March 7 in a scene of high drama, "not as a Massachusetts man, nor as a Northern man, but as an American. I speak today for the preservation of the Union." Abandoning his earlier support for the Wilmot Proviso, Webster urged northerners not to "taunt or reproach" the South with antislavery measures. To southern firebrands, he issued a warning that disunion inevitably would cause violence and destruction. For his efforts at compromise, Webster was condemned by many former abolitionist friends in New England who accused him of going over to the "devil."

Only three days earlier, with equal drama, Calhoun had been carried from his sickbed to deliver a speech opposing the compromise. As Calhoun was unable to stand and speak, Senator James Mason of Virginia read his address for him. Grizzled and dying, the South's intellectual defender warned that the "cords which bind these states" were "already greatly weakened." Calhoun did not address the specific measures in the bill; he predicted disunion if southern demands were not met, thereby frightening some into support of compromise.

With Clay sick and absent from Washington, Douglas reintroduced the compromise measures one at a time. Although there was no majority for compromise, Douglas shrewdly realized that different majorities might be created for the separate measures. Because southerners favored some bills and northerners the rest, a small majority for compromise could be achieved on each distinct issue, and for now, the strategy worked.

12-7b Compromise of 1850

The compromise had five essential measures:

1. California became a free state.
2. The Texas boundary was set at its present limits, and the United States paid Texas $10 million in compensation for the loss of New Mexico Territory (see Map 12.5).
3. The territories of New Mexico and Utah were organized on a basis of popular sovereignty.
4. The fugitive slave law was strengthened.
5. The slave trade was abolished in the District of Columbia.

Jubilation greeted passage of the compromise; crowds in Washington and other cities celebrated the happy news. "On one glorious night," records one modern historian, "the word went abroad that it was the duty of every patriot to get drunk. Before the next morning many a citizen had proved his patriotism."

In reality, there was less cause for celebration than people hoped. At best, the Compromise of 1850 was an artful evasion. As one historian has argued, the legislation was more an "armistice," delaying greater conflict, than a compromise. Douglas had found a way to pass the five proposals without convincing northerners and southerners to agree on fundamentals; narrow majorities emerged as

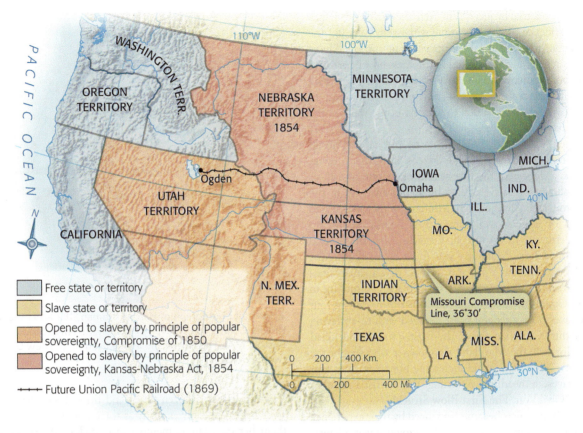

Map 12.5 The Kansas-Nebraska Act and Slavery Expansion, 1854

The vote on the Kansas-Nebraska Act in the House of Representatives (see also Table 12.2) demonstrates the sectionalization of American politics due to the slavery question.

Congressmen and Senators voted on the measures one by one. The compromise bought time for the nation, but it did not provide a real settlement of the territorial questions.

Furthermore, the compromise had two basic flaws. The first concerned the ambiguity of popular sovereignty. Southerners insisted there would be no prohibition of slavery during the territorial stage, and northerners declared that settlers could bar slavery whenever they wished. The compromise even allowed for the appeal of a territorial legislature's action to the Supreme Court. One

Table 12.2 The Vote on the Kansas-Nebraska Act

The vote was 113 to 100 in favor.

Party	Aye	Nay
Northern Democrats	44	42
Southern Democrats	57	2
Northern Whigs	0	45
Southern Whigs	12	7
Northern Free-Soilers	0	4

witty politician remarked that the legislators had enacted a lawsuit instead of a law.

12-7c Fugitive Slave Act

The second flaw lay in the **Fugitive Slave Act**, which gave new—and controversial—protection to slavery. The law empowered slave owners to make a legal claim in their own states that a person owing them "service" or "labor" had become a fugitive. That claim would then serve as legal proof of a person's slave status, even in free states and territories. Specially appointed federal commissioners adjudicated the identity of the alleged fugitives, and those commissioners were paid fees that favored slaveholders: $10 if they found the person to be a fugitive, and $5 if they judged that he or she was not. The law also made it a felony to harbor fugitives, and required that citizens, even in free states and territories, could be summoned to hunt fugitives.

Abolitionist newspapers quickly attacked the Fugitive Slave Act as a violation of fundamental American rights. Why were alleged

Fugitive Slave Act Part of the Compromise of 1850, this controversial measure gave additional powers to slave owners to recapture slaves and angered northerners by requiring their complicity in the return of fugitive slaves.

fugitives denied a trial by jury? Why were they given no chance to present evidence or cross-examine witnesses? Why did the law give authorities a financial incentive to send suspected fugitives into bondage, and why would northerners now be arrested if they harbored runaways? The "free" states, moreover, were no longer a safe haven for black folk, whatever their origins; an estimated twenty thousand fled to Canada in the wake of the Fugitive Slave Act.

Between 1850 and 1854, protests and violent resistance to slave catchers occurred in dozens of northern towns. Sometimes a captured fugitive was broken out of jail or from the clutches of slave agents by abolitionists, as in the 1851 Boston case of Shadrach Minkins, who was spirited by a series of wagons and trains across Massachusetts, up through Vermont, to Montreal, Canada. Also in 1851, a fugitive named Jerry McHenry was freed by an abolitionist mob in Syracuse, New York, and hurried to Canadian freedom. That same year as well, the small black community in Lancaster County, Pennsylvania, took up arms to defend four escaped slaves from a federal posse charged with re-enslaving them. At this "Christiana riot," the fugitives shot and killed Edward Gorsuch, the Maryland slave owner who sought the return of his "property." Amid increasing border warfare over fugitive slaves, a headline reporting the Christiana affair screamed, "Civil War, The First Blow Struck!"

Many abolitionists became convinced by their experience of resisting the Fugitive Slave Act that violence was a legitimate means of opposing slavery. In an 1854 column entitled "Is It Right and Wise to Kill a Kidnapper?," Frederick Douglass said that the only way to make the fugitive slave law "dead letter" was to make a "few dead slave catchers." Into this new and volatile mixture of violence, lawbreaking, and sectional as well as racial fear, Harriet Beecher Stowe's *Uncle Tom's Cabin* became a literary sensation.

12-7d The Underground Railroad

In reality, by the 1850s slaveholders were especially disturbed over what was widely called the **Underground Railroad**. This loose, illegal network of civil disobedience, spiriting runaways to freedom, had never been very organized, with the possible exception of routes from the eastern shore of Maryland through Delaware to New York City. Thousands of slaves did escape by these routes, but largely through their own wits and courage, and through the assistance of blacks in some northern cities. Lewis Hayden in Boston, David Ruggles in New York, William Still in Philadelphia, John Parker in Ripley, Ohio, and Jacob Gibbs in Washington, D.C., were some of the many black abolitionists who assisted fugitive slaves. Moreover, William Howard Gay, editor of a major antislavery newspaper, provided an effective sanctuary and escape means to many fugitives through New York.

Famously, Harriet Tubman, herself an escapee in 1848, returned to her native Maryland and to

Underground Railroad A loosely organized route by which fugitive slaves escaped to freedom in the northern United States and Canada.

▲ Portrait photograph of Harriet Tubman (1823–1913, Ohio History Connection, 1887, by H. G. Smith, Smith Studio, Boston, MA). This will be the image used on the new U.S. twenty dollar bill.

Ohio History Connection

Virginia at least a dozen times, and through clandestine measures helped possibly as many as three hundred slaves, some of them her own family members, to freedom. Maryland planters were so outraged that they offered a $40,000 reward (nearly $1,200,000 today) for her capture.

In Ohio, numerous white abolitionists, often Quakers, joined with blacks as agents of slave liberation at various points along the river border between slavery and freedom. The Underground Railroad also had numerous maritime routes, as coastal slaves escaped aboard ships out of Virginia or the Carolinas, or from New Orleans, and ended up in northern port cities, the Caribbean, or England. Many fugitive slaves from the Lower South and Texas escaped to Mexico, which had abolished slavery in 1829. Some slaves escaped by joining the Seminole communities in Florida, where they joined forces against the U.S. Army in the Seminole Wars of 1835–1842 and 1855–1858.

This constant, dangerous flow of humanity was a testament to human courage and the will for freedom. Although it never reached the scale believed by some angry slaveholders and claimed today by some northern towns that harbored runaways in safe houses and hideaways, the Underground Railroad applied pressure to the institution of slavery and provided slaves with a focus for hope.

12-7e Election of 1852 and the Collapse of Compromise

The 1852 election gave southern leaders hope that slavery would be secure under the new presidential administration. Franklin Pierce, a Democrat from New Hampshire, won an easy victory over the Whig nominee, General Winfield Scott. Because Scott's views on the compromise had been unknown and the Free-Soil candidate, John P. Hale of New Hampshire, had openly rejected it, Pierce's victory suggested widespread support for the compromise.

The Whig Party was weak, however, and by 1852 sectional discord had rendered it all but dead. President Pierce's embrace of the compromise appalled many northerners. His vigorous enforcement of the Fugitive Slave Act provoked outrage and fear of the Slave Power, especially in the case of the fugitive slave Anthony Burns, who had fled Virginia by stowing away on a ship in 1852. In Boston, thinking he was safe in a city known for abolitionism, Burns began a new life. But in 1854, federal marshals found and placed him under guard in Boston's courthouse. An interracial crowd of abolitionists attacked the courthouse, killing a jailer in an unsuccessful attempt to free Burns, whose case attracted nationwide attention.

Pierce moved decisively to enforce the Fugitive Slave Act. He telegraphed local officials to "incur any expense to insure the execution of the law" and sent marines, cavalry, and artillery to Boston. U.S. troops marched Burns to Boston harbor through streets that his supporters had draped in black and hung with American flags at half-mast. At a cost of $100,000, a single black man was returned to slavery through the power of federal law.

The national will to sustain slavery was now tested at every turn. This demonstration of federal support for slavery radicalized opinion, even among many conservatives. Textile manufacturer Amos A. Lawrence observed that "we went to bed one night old fashioned, conservative, Compromise Union Whigs & waked up stark mad Abolitionists." Juries refused to convict the abolitionists who had stormed the Boston courthouse, and New England states passed personal-liberty laws that absolved local judges from enforcing the Fugitive Slave Act, in effect nullifying federal authority. What northerners now saw as evidence of a dominating Slave Power, outraged slaveholders saw as the legal defense of their rights.

Pierce confronted sectional conflict at every turn. His proposal for a transcontinental railroad derailed when congressmen fought over its location, North or South. His attempts to acquire foreign territory stirred more trouble. An annexation treaty with Hawai'i failed because southern senators would not vote for another free state, and efforts to acquire slaveholding Cuba through the Ostend Manifesto angered northerners. Written after a meeting among the U.S. foreign ministers to Britain, France, and Spain, the document advocated conquest of Cuba if it could not be "purchased." The ministers predicted that Cuba "would be Africanized and become a second St. Domingo, with all its attendant horrors to the white race." Antislavery advocates once again saw schemes of the Slave Power as political division and social fear deepened.

12-8 Slavery Expansion and Collapse of the Party System

▸ **What were the consequences of the passage of the Kansas-Nebraska Act?**

▸ **What was the ideological foundation of the Republican Party?**

▸ **How did southern Democrats respond to the dissolution of the Whig Party?**

▸ **Why did violence erupt in Kansas and on the floor of the U.S. Senate?**

An even greater controversy over slavery expansion began in a surprising way. Stephen A. Douglas, one of the architects of the Compromise of 1850, introduced a bill to establish the Kansas and Nebraska Territories. Talented and ambitious for the presidency, Douglas was known for compromise, not sectional quarreling. But he did not view slavery as a fundamental problem, and he was willing to risk some controversy to win economic benefits for Illinois, his home state. A transcontinental railroad would encourage settlement of the Great Plains and stimulate the Illinois economy. Thus, with these goals in mind, Douglas inflamed sectional passions to new levels.

12-8a The Kansas-Nebraska Act

The **Kansas-Nebraska Act** exposed the conflicting interpretations of popular sovereignty. Douglas's bill left "all questions pertaining to slavery in the Territories . . . to the people residing therein." Northerners and southerners, however, still disagreed violently over what territorial settlers could constitutionally do. Moreover, the Kansas and Nebraska Territories lay within the Louisiana Purchase, and the Missouri Compromise of 1820 prohibited slavery in all that land from latitude 36° 30′ north to the Canadian border. If popular sovereignty were to mean anything in Kansas and Nebraska, it had to mean that the Missouri Compromise was no longer in effect and that settlers could establish slavery there.

Southern congressmen, anxious to establish slaveholders' right to take slaves into any territory, pressed Douglas to concede this point. They demanded an explicit repeal of the 36° 30′ limitation as the price of their support. During a carriage ride with Senator Archibald Dixon of Kentucky, Douglas debated the point at length. Finally, he made an impulsive decision: "By God, Sir, you are right. I will incorporate it in my bill, though I know it will raise a hell of a storm."

Perhaps Douglas underestimated the storm because he believed that conditions of climate and soil would keep slavery out of Kansas and Nebraska. Nevertheless, his bill threw open to slavery land from which it had been prohibited for thirty-four years. Opposition from Free-Soilers and antislavery forces was immediate and enduring; many considered this turn of events a betrayal of a sacred trust. The struggle in Congress lasted three and a half months. Douglas won the support of President Pierce and eventually prevailed: the bill became law in

Kansas-Nebraska Act
Repealed the Missouri Compromise and inflamed sectional disputes around the expansion of slavery in the territories. The act left the decision of whether to allow slavery in the new territories of Kansas and Nebraska up to the voters residing there (popular sovereignty).

May 1854 by a vote that demonstrated the dangerous sectionalization of American politics (see Map 12.5 and Table 12.2).

But the storm was just beginning. Northern fears of slavery's influence deepened. Opposition to the Fugitive Slave Act grew dramatically; between 1855 and 1859, Connecticut, Rhode Island, Massachusetts, Michigan, Maine, Ohio, and Wisconsin passed personal-liberty laws. These laws enraged southern leaders by providing counsel for alleged fugitives and requiring trial by jury. More important was the devastating impact of the Kansas-Nebraska Act on political parties. The weakened Whig Party broke apart into northern and southern wings that could no longer cooperate nationally. The Democrats survived, but their support in the North fell drastically in the 1854 elections. Northern Democrats lost sixty-six of their ninety-one congressional seats and lost control of all but two free-state legislatures.

12-8b Birth of the Republican Party

The beneficiary of northern voters' wrath was a new political party. During debate on the Kansas-Nebraska Act, six congressmen had published an "Appeal of the Independent Democrats." Joshua Giddings, Salmon Chase, and Charles Sumner—the principal authors of this protest—attacked Douglas's legislation as a "gross violation of a sacred pledge" (the Missouri Compromise) and a "criminal betrayal of precious rights" that would make free territory a "dreary region of despotism." Their appeal tapped a reservoir of deep concerns in the North, cogently expressed by Abraham Lincoln of Illinois.

Lincoln did not personally condemn southerners— "They are just what we would be in their situation"—but exposed the meaning of the Kansas-Nebraska Act. Lincoln argued that the founders, from love of liberty, had banned slavery from the Northwest Territory, kept the word *slavery* out of the Constitution, and treated it overall as a "cancer" on the republic. Rather than encouraging liberty, the Kansas-Nebraska Act put slavery "on the high road to extension and perpetuity," and that constituted a "moral wrong and injustice." America's future, Lincoln warned, was being mortgaged to slavery and all its influences.

Thousands of ordinary white northerners agreed. During the summer and fall of 1854, antislavery Whigs and Democrats, Free-Soilers, and other reformers throughout the Old Northwest met to form the new Republican Party, a coalition dedicated to keeping slavery out of the territories. The influence of the Republicans rapidly spread to the East, and they won a stunning victory in the 1854 elections. In their first appearance on the ballot, Republicans captured a majority of northern House seats. Antislavery sentiment had created a new party and caused roughly a quarter of northern Democrats to desert their party.

For the first time, too, a sectional party had gained significant power in the political system. Now the Whigs were gone, and only the Democrats struggled to maintain national membership. The Republicans absorbed the Free-Soil Party and grew rapidly in the North. Indeed, the emergence of the Republican coalition of antislavery interests is the most rapid transformation in party allegiance and voter behavior in American history.

12-8c Know-Nothings

Republicans also drew into their coalition a fast-growing nativist movement that called itself the American Party, or **Know-Nothings** (because its first members kept their purposes secret, answering, "I know nothing" to all questions). This group exploited fear of foreigners and Catholics. Between 1848 and 1860, nearly 3.5 million immigrants entered the United States—proportionally the heaviest inflow of foreigners ever in American history. Democrats courted the votes of these new citizens, but many native-born Anglo-Saxon Protestants believed that Irish and German Catholics would owe primary allegiance to the pope in Rome and not to the American nation.

In 1854, anti-immigrant fears gave the Know-Nothings spectacular success in some northern states. They triumphed

▲ Throughout the North, the Kansas-Nebraska Act kindled fires of alarm over the Slave Power's "determination to extend its dominion" and "control the government of the nation." Public meetings like the one announced here, held in West Chester, Pennsylvania, aided the new Republican Party.

Know-Nothings Anti-Catholic and anti-immigrant party whose influence peaked in the mid-1850s.

especially in Massachusetts, electing 11 congressmen, a governor, all state officers, all state senators, and all but 2 of 378 state representatives. The temperance movement also gained new strength early in the 1850s with its promises to stamp out the evils associated with liquor and immigrants (a particularly anti-Irish campaign). In this context, the Know-Nothings strove to reinforce Protestant morality and to restrict voting and office holding to the native born. As the Whig Party faded from the scene, the Know-Nothings temporarily filled the void, inaugurating a long tradition of cycles of nativism in party politics. But like the Whigs, the Know-Nothings could not keep their northern and southern wings together on the issue of slavery's expansion, and they dissolved after 1856. The growing Republican coalition wooed the nativists with temperance ordinances and laws postponing suffrage for naturalized citizens (see Table 12.1).

12-8d Party Realignment and the Republicans' Appeal

With nearly half of the old electorate up for grabs, the demise of the Whig Party ensured a major political realignment. The remaining parties appealed to various segments of the electorate on such issues as immigration, temperance, homestead bills, the tariff, and internal improvements. The Republicans appealed strongly to those interested in the economic development of the West. Commercial agriculture was booming in the Old Northwest, but residents of that region desired more canals, roads, and river and harbor improvements. Because credit was scarce, a homestead program—the idea that western land should be free to individuals who would farm it and make a home on it—attracted many voters. The Republicans seized on these political desires.

Partisan ideological appeals characterized the realigned political system. As Republicans preached, "Free Soil, Free Labor, Free Men," they captured a self-image of many northerners. These phrases resonated with traditional ideals of equality, liberty, and opportunity under self-government—the heritage of republicanism. Invoking that heritage also undercut charges that the Republican Party was radical and abolitionist.

The northern economy was booming, and thousands of migrants had moved west to establish productive farms and growing communities. Midwesterners multiplied their yields by using new machines, such as mechanical reapers. Railroads were carrying their crops to urban markets. And industry was beginning to perform wonders of production, making available goods that only recently had been beyond the reach of the average person.

12-8e Republican Ideology

The key to progress appeared, to many people, to be free labor—the dignity of work and the incentive of opportunity. Any hardworking and virtuous man, it was thought, could improve his condition and achieve economic independence. Republicans argued that the South, with little industry and slave labor, remained backward.

Traditional republicanism hailed the virtuous common man as the backbone of the country. In Abraham Lincoln, a man of humble origins who had become a successful lawyer and political leader, Republicans had a symbol of that tradition. They portrayed their party as the guardian of economic opportunity, giving individuals a chance to work, acquire land, and attain success. In the words of an Iowa Republican, the United States was thriving because its "door is thrown open to all, and even the poorest and humblest in the land, may, by industry and application, gain a position which will entitle him to the respect … of his fellow-men."

At stake in the crises of the 1850s were thus two competing definitions of "liberty": southern planters' claims to protection of their liberty in the possession and transport of their slaves anywhere in the land, and northern workers' and farmers' claims to protection of their liberty to seek a new start on free land, unimpeded by a system that defined labor as slave and black.

Opposition to slavery's extension had brought the Republicans into being, but they carefully broadened their appeal. Their coalition ideology consisted of many elements: resentment of southern political power, devotion to unionism, antislavery convictions based on free-labor arguments, moral revulsion to slavery, and racial prejudice. As *New York Tribune* editor Horace Greeley wrote in 1856, "It is beaten into my bones that the American people are not yet anti-slavery." Four years later, Greeley again observed that "an Anti-Slavery man *per se* cannot be elected." But, he added, "a Tariff, River-and-Harbor, Pacific Railroad, Free Homestead man, may succeed although he is Anti-Slavery."

12-8f Southern Democrats

In the South, the disintegration of the Whig Party had left many southerners at loose ends politically; they included a good number of wealthy planters, smaller slaveholders, and urban businessmen. In the increasingly tense atmosphere of sectional crisis, these people were highly susceptible to strong states' rights positions and the defense of slavery. The security of their own communities seemed at stake, and in the 1850s, most formerly Whig slaveholders converted to the Democratic Party.

Since Andrew Jackson's day, however, nonslaveholding yeomen had been the heart of the Democratic Party. Democratic politicians, though often slave owners themselves, lauded the common man and argued that their policies advanced his interests. According to the southern version of republicanism, white citizens in a slave society enjoyed liberty and social equality because black people were enslaved. As Jefferson Davis put it in 1851, in other societies distinctions were drawn "by property, between the rich and the poor." But in the South, slavery elevated every white person's status and allowed the nonslaveholder to "stand upon the broad level of equality with the rich man." To retain the support of ordinary whites, southern Democrats appealed to racism, warning starkly of the main issue: "shall negroes govern white men, or white men govern negroes?"

Southern leaders also portrayed sectional controversies as matters of injustice and insult to the South's honor and prestige. The rights of all southern whites were in jeopardy, they argued, because antislavery and Free-Soil forces threatened an institution protected in the Constitution. The stable, well-ordered South was the true defender of constitutional principles; the rapidly changing North, their destroyer.

Racial fears and traditional political loyalties helped keep the volatile political alliance between yeoman farmers and planters largely intact through the 1850s. Across class lines, white southerners joined together in the interest of community security against what they perceived as the Republican Party's capacity to cause slave unrest in their midst. In the South, no viable party emerged to replace the Whigs, and as in the North, political realignment sharpened sectional identities.

Political leaders of both sections used race in their arguments about opportunity, but northerners and southerners saw different futures. The *Montgomery* (Alabama) *Mail* warned southern whites in 1860 that the Republicans intended "to free the negroes and force amalgamation between them and the children of the poor men of the South. The rich will be able to keep out of the way of the contamination." Republicans warned northern workers that, if slavery entered the territories, the great reservoir of opportunity for ordinary citizens would be poisoned.

12-8g Bleeding Kansas

The Kansas-Nebraska Act spawned hatred and violence as land-hungry partisans in the sectional struggle clashed repeatedly in Kansas Territory. Abolitionists and religious groups sent in armed Free-Soil settlers; southerners sent in their reinforcements to establish slavery and prevent "northern hordes" from stealing Kansas. Conflicts led to vicious bloodshed, and soon the whole nation was talking about "Bleeding Kansas."

During elections for a territorial legislature in 1855, thousands of proslavery Missourians—known as Border Ruffians—invaded the polls and won a large but fraudulent majority for proslavery candidates. They murdered and intimidated free-state settlers. At one rally of such ruffians with other southerners, flags flapped in the breeze with the mottoes "Southern Rights," "Supremacy of the White Race," and "Alabama for Kansas." The resulting legislature legalized slavery, and in response Free-Soilers held an unauthorized convention at which they created their own government and constitution. Kansas was a tinderbox. By the spring of 1856, newspapers screamed for violence. "In a fight, let our motto be War to the knife, and knife to the hilt," demanded the proslavery *Squatter Sovereign*. Slavery's advocates taunted their adversaries as cowards and likened "abolitionists" to "infidels" worthy only of "total extermination."

In May, a proslavery posse sent to arrest the Free-Soil leaders sacked the Kansas town of Lawrence, killing several people and destroying a hotel with cannon shot. In revenge, John Brown, a radical abolitionist with a band of followers, murdered five proslavery settlers living along Pottawatomie Creek. The victims were taken in the dark of night from the clutches of their families, their heads and limbs hacked to pieces by heavy broadswords, their bodies heaved into dead brush. Brown himself did not wield the swords, but he did fire a single shot into the head of one senseless foe to ensure his death. Soon, armed bands of guerrillas roamed the territory, battling over land claims as well as slavery.

These passions brought violence to the U.S. Senate in May 1856, when Charles Sumner of Massachusetts denounced "the Crime against Kansas." Radical in his anti-slavery views, Sumner bitterly assailed the president, the South, and Senator Andrew P. Butler of South Carolina. Soon thereafter, Butler's cousin, Representative Preston Brooks, approached Sumner at the latter's Senate desk, raised his cane, announced the defense of his kin's honor, and mercilessly beat Sumner on the head. The senator collapsed, bleeding, on the floor while unsympathetic colleagues watched.

Shocked northerners recoiled from what they saw as another case of wanton southern violence and an assault on free speech. William Cullen Bryant, editor of the *New York Evening Post,* asked, "Has it come to this, that we must speak with bated breath in the presence of our southern masters?" As if in reply, the *Richmond Enquirer* denounced "vulgar Abolitionists in the Senate" who "have been suffered to run too long without collars. They must be lashed into submission." Popular opinion in Massachusetts strongly supported Sumner; South Carolina voters reelected Brooks and sent him dozens of commemorative canes.

12-8h Election of 1856

The election of 1856 showed how extreme such polarization had become. For Republicans, "Bleeding Sumner" and "Bleeding Kansas" had become rallying cries. When Democrats met to select a nominee, they shied away from prominent leaders whose views on the territorial question invited controversy. Instead, they chose James Buchanan of Pennsylvania, whose chief virtue was that for the past four years he had been ambassador to Britain, uninvolved in territorial controversies. Superior party organization helped Buchanan win 1.8 million votes and the election, but he owed his victory to southern support. Hence, he was tagged with the label "a northern man with southern principles."

Eleven of sixteen free states voted against Buchanan, and Democrats did not regain ascendancy in those states for decades. The Republican candidate, John C. Frémont, famous as a western explorer, won those eleven free states and 1.3 million votes; Republicans had become the dominant party in the North after only two years of existence. The Know-Nothing

William Walker and Filibustering

Between 1848 and 1861, the United States was officially at peace with foreign nations. But that did not stop private citizens, sometimes with the support of politicians and businessmen, from launching adventurous attempts to take over foreign lands, especially in Mexico, Central America, and the Caribbean. The 1850s was the heyday of "filibustering," defined in this era as private military expeditions designed to destabilize or conquer foreign lands in the name of manifest destiny, commerce, the spread of slavery and white supremacy, or masculine daring.

At least a dozen filibustering schemes emerged in this era of expansion and sectional crises, all of them illegal and often opposed by American presidents as blatant violations of the Neutrality Act of 1818 that outlawed the attempted overthrow of foreign "dominions." Such laws did not stop some senators, railroad and shipping entrepreneurs, and especially self-styled soldier of fortune William Walker from flaunting the law and seeking the "Southern dream" of a Latin American empire. The law also did not stop several American presidents from engaging in numerous more official attempts to annex Cuba in these years.

Born in Tennessee, Walker traveled and studied in Europe as the 1848 revolutions rocked that continent. After a short stint editing a newspaper in New Orleans, he moved to California, practiced law, and courted conflict by fighting at least three duels. After an ill-fated but determined attempt in 1853 to create by force an American "colony" in Sonora and the Baja peninsula in Mexico, Walker turned his sights to Nicaragua, already of great interest to thousands of Americans using its isthmus as the fastest route to the California gold fields.

With a small army of mercenaries, Walker invaded Nicaragua in 1856, exploited its ongoing civil war, seized its government, declared himself president, and reintroduced slavery into a society that had banned it. Defeated by a coalition of Nicaraguans and British in 1857, Walker returned to the United States and launched a fund-raising and speaking campaign on which he was often treated as a romantic hero. On his return to Nicaragua, he was arrested by a U.S. Navy squadron, brought once again to American soil, tried, and acquitted.

In 1860, Walker published an account of his exploits, *War in Nicaragua*. His wide fame was due in part to his swashbuckling character; some saw him as a pirate serving the "Slave Power Conspiracy," and others as the "grey-eyed man of destiny" advancing the causes of slavery and American hegemony. Walker became more aggressively proslavery in Nicaragua when he desperately needed southern political support to supply his plots. On Walker's third return to Central America in 1860 to pursue his insatiable dream of fame and power, he was arrested by a British captain who turned him over to Honduran authorities, who promptly executed him by firing squad. These filibustering adventures fired the imagination of manifest destiny and were merely small precursors of a larger Latin American exploitation and conquest by the United States in the century to follow. Walker's legend, both heroic and notorious, lives on today in Central America, as well as in two American movies, *Burn* (1969), starring Marlon Brando, and *Walker* (1987), starring Ed Harris. Filibusters were links to the world that gave the United States a difficult legacy to overcome with its neighbors from Cuba to Hawai'i.

CRITICAL THINKING

- Although Walker and others' attempts to overthrow foreign dominions in the first half of the nineteenth century were illegal, how are they reflective of larger ideas and beliefs about American exceptionalism?

Library of Congress Prints and Photographs Division[LC-USZC4-10802]

◀ Portrait of William Walker, Tennessee-born filibusterer, a self-styled soldier of fortune who attempted to create his own empire in Nicaragua, where he reinstituted slavery. To some, especially white southerners, he was a romantic hero, but to others, especially northerners and the U.S. government, he was a notorious villain and arch proponent of the worst aspects of manifest destiny.

candidate, Millard Fillmore, won almost 1 million votes, but this election was that party's last hurrah. The coming battle would pit a sectional Republican Party against an increasingly divided Democratic Party. With huge voter turnouts, as high as 75 to 80 percent in many states, Americans were about to learn that elections really matter.

12-9 Slavery and the Nation's Future

▶ How did abolitionists and the Republican Party respond to the Supreme Court's decision in *Dred Scott v. Sanford*?

▶ Why did the Democratic Party become fractured in the wake of *Dred Scott v. Sanford*?

▶ Why did John Brown's position on slavery and his actions anger white southerners?

For years, the issue of slavery in the territories had convulsed Congress, and Congress had tried to settle the issue with vague formulas. In 1857, the Supreme Court entered the fray, took up this emotionally charged subject, and attempted to silence controversy with a definitive verdict.

12-9a Dred Scott Case

A Missouri slave named Dred Scott and his wife, Harriet Robinson Scott, had sued for their freedom. Scott based his claim on the fact that his former owner, an army surgeon, had taken him for several years into Illinois, a free state, and to Fort Snelling in the Minnesota Territory, from which slavery had been barred by the Missouri Compromise. Scott first won and then lost his case as it moved on appeal through the state courts into the federal system and, finally, after eleven years, to the Supreme Court.

The impetus for the lawsuit likely came as much from Harriet as from Dred Scott. They were legally married at Fort Snelling (free territory) in 1836 when Dred was forty and Harriet seventeen. She had already lived as a slave on free soil for at least five years and had given birth to four children, also born on free soil: two sons who died in infancy and two daughters, Eliza and Lizzie, who lived. In all likelihood, the quest to achieve "freedom papers" through a lawsuit—begun in 1846 as two separate cases, one in his name and one in hers—came as much from Harriet's desire to sustain her family and protect her two teenage daughters from potential sale and sexual abuse as from the aging and sickly Dred. Indeed, her legal case for freedom may have been even stronger than Dred's, but their lawyers subsumed her case into his during the long appeal process.

Normally, Supreme Court justices were reluctant to inject themselves into major political issues. An 1851 decision had declared that state courts determined the status of blacks who lived within their jurisdictions. The Supreme Court had only

▲ Frank Leslie's *Illustrated Newspaper*, June 27, 1857. Dred Scott and his wife, Harriet, below, and their two children, Eliza and Lizzie, above. Such dignified pictures and informative articles provided Americans broadly with images of the otherwise mysterious Dred Scott and his family in the landmark Supreme Court case.

to follow this precedent to avoid ruling on substantive, and very controversial, issues: Was a black person like Dred Scott a citizen of the United States and thus eligible to sue in federal court? Had residence in a free state or territory made him free? Did Congress have the power to prohibit or promote slavery in a territory?

After hesitation, the Supreme Court agreed to hear *Dred Scott v. Sanford* and decided to rule on the Missouri Compromise after all. Two northern justices indicated they would dissent from the assigned opinion and argue for Scott's freedom and the constitutionality of the Missouri Compromise. Their decision emboldened southerners on the Court, who were growing eager to declare the 1820 geographical restriction on slavery unconstitutional. Southern sympathizers in Washington were pressing for a proslavery verdict, and several justices felt they should simply try to resolve sectional strife once and for all.

In March 1857, Chief Justice Roger B. Taney of Maryland delivered the majority opinion of a divided Court (the vote was 7 to 2). Taney declared that Scott was not a citizen of either the United States or Missouri, that residence in free territory did not make Scott free, and that Congress had no power to bar slavery from any territory. The decision not only overturned a sectional compromise that had been honored for thirty-seven years, it also invalidated the basic ideas of the Wilmot Proviso and popular sovereignty.

The Slave Power seemed to have won a major constitutional victory. African Americans were especially dismayed, for Taney's decision asserted that the founders had never intended for black people to be citizens. At the nation's founding, the chief justice wrote, blacks had been regarded "as beings of an inferior order" with "no rights which the white man was bound to respect." Taney was mistaken, however. African Americans had been citizens in several of the original states and had in fact voted.

Nevertheless, the ruling seemed to shut the door permanently on black hopes for justice. After 1857, African Americans lived in the land of the **Dred Scott decision**. In northern black communities, rage and despair prevailed. Many who were still fugitive slaves sought refuge in Canada; others considered emigration to the Caribbean or even to Africa. Mary Ann Shadd Cary, who was free and the leader of an emigration movement to Canada, advised her fellow blacks, "Your national ship is rotten and sinking, why not leave it?" Another black abolitionist said that the *Dred Scott* decision had made slavery "the supreme law of the land and all descendants of the African race denationalized." In this state of social dislocation and fear, blacks contemplated whether they had any future in the United States.

Northern whites who rejected the decision's content were suspicious of the circumstances that had produced it. Five of the nine justices were southerners; three of the northern justices actively dissented or refused to concur in parts of the decision. The only northerner who supported Taney's opinion, Justice Robert Grier of Pennsylvania, was known to be close to President Buchanan. A storm of angry reaction broke in the North. The decision seemed to confirm every charge against the aggressive Slave Power. "There is such a thing as the slave power," warned the *Cincinnati Daily Commercial*. "It has marched over and annihilated the boundaries of the states. We are now one great homogenous slaveholding community." The *Cincinnati Freeman* asked, "What security have the Germans and the Irish that their children will not, within a hundred years, be reduced to slavery in this land of their adoption?" Poet James Russell Lowell expressed the racial and economic anxieties of poor northern whites when he had his Yankee character Ezekiel Biglow say, in the language of the day,

> Wy, it's just ez clear ez figgers,
> Clear ez one an' one make two,
> Chaps thet make black slaves o' niggers,
> Want to make wite slaves o' you.

12-9b Abraham Lincoln and the Slave Power

Republican politicians used these fears to strengthen their antislavery coalition. Abraham Lincoln stressed that the territorial question affected every citizen. "The whole nation," he had declared as early as 1854, "is interested that the best use shall be made of these Territories. We want them for homes of free white people. This they cannot be, to any considerable extent, if slavery shall be planted within them." The territories must be reserved, he insisted, "as an outlet for free white people everywhere" so that immigrants could come to America and "find new homes and better their condition in life."

More important, Lincoln warned of slavery's increasing control over the nation. The founders had created a government dedicated to freedom, Lincoln insisted. Admittedly they had recognized slavery's existence, but the public mind, he argued in the "House Divided" speech of 1858, by which he launched his campaign against Stephen Douglas for the U.S. Senate from Illinois, had always rested in the belief that slavery would die either naturally or by legislation. The next step in the unfolding Slave Power conspiracy, Lincoln alleged, would be a Supreme Court decision "declaring that the Constitution does not permit a State to exclude slavery from its limits…. We shall lie down pleasantly, dreaming that the people of Missouri are on the verge of making their State free; and we shall awake to the reality instead, that the Supreme Court has made Illinois a slave State." This charge was not hyperbole, for lawsuits soon challenged state laws that freed slaves brought within their borders. Countless northerners heeded Lincoln's warnings, as events convinced them that slaveholders were intent on making slavery a national institution. Southerners, fatefully, never forgot Lincoln's use of the direct words "ultimate extinction."

They also never forgot the epic Lincoln-Douglas debates, staged before massive crowds in September-October, 1858. Both candidates crisscrossed Illinois, with Lincoln traveling 4,350 miles and delivering some 63 major speeches, and Douglas logging over 5,000 miles and speaking 130 times. These two talented candidates, one tall and lean, the other short and stocky, squared off over the great issues dividing the country: the westward expansion of slavery, the meaning of abolitionism, the character of federal power over property in slaves, whether the Declaration of Independence had signaled some kind of racial equality, and ultimately the future existence of the American republic. Tens of thousands of people attended these outdoor events, arriving by foot, by wagon, on trains, and accompanied by brass bands. Perhaps never before or since have Americans demonstrated such an appetite for democratic engagement. "The prairies

***Dred Scott* decision**
Controversial 1857 Supreme Court decision that stated that no black Americans, whether enslaved or free, were U.S. citizens. It also declared that the Missouri Compromise had been unconstitutional because Congress lacked the authority to ban slavery in the territories.

are on fire," wrote an eastern journalist. "It is astonishing how deep an interest in politics this people takes."

As Lincoln showed in these debates, politically, Republicans were now locked in conflict with the *Dred Scott* decision. By endorsing the South's doctrine of state sovereignty, the Court had in effect declared that the central position of the Republican Party—no extension of slavery—was unconstitutional. Republicans could only repudiate the decision, appealing to a "higher law," or hope to change the personnel of the Court.

12-9c The Lecompton Constitution and Disharmony Among Democrats

For northern Democrats like Stephen Douglas, the Court's decision posed an awful dilemma. Northern voters were alarmed by the prospect that the territories would be opened to slavery. To retain their support, Douglas had to find some way to reassure these voters. Yet given his presidential

ambitions, Douglas could not afford to alienate southern Democrats.

Douglas chose to stand by his principle of popular sovereignty, even if the result angered southerners. In December 1857, Kansans voted on a proslavery constitution that had been drafted at Lecompton. Believing the election to be rigged, most "free staters"—those who opposed legalizing slavery—boycotted the election, giving the proslavery constitution an overwhelming victory. The free staters, who controlled the territorial legislature, quickly called for a new referendum in January; this time, the proslavery forces boycotted, resulting in an overwhelming defeat of the constitution. Although evidence suggests that most Kansans opposed slavery, President Buchanan tried to force the Lecompton Constitution through Congress in an effort to hastily organize the territory.

Never had the Slave Power's influence over the government seemed more blatant; the Buchanan administration and southerners demanded a proslavery outcome, contrary to the majority will in Kansas. Breaking with the administration,

▲ Abraham Lincoln (right) and Stephen A. Douglas (left), 1860. The formal studio photographs depict each man in a stance he might have assumed in the famous debates of 1858 as they squared off for the U.S. Senate election in Illinois.

Douglas threw his weight against the Lecompton Constitution. But his action infuriated southern Democrats. After the *Dred Scott* decision, southerners like Senator Albert G. Brown of Mississippi believed slavery was protected in the territories: "The Constitution as expounded by the Supreme Court awards it. We demand it; we mean to have it." Increasingly, though, many southerners believed their sectional rights and slavery would be safe only in a separate nation. And northern Democrats, led by Douglas, found it harder to support the territorial protection for slavery that southern Democrats insisted was theirs as a constitutional right. Thus, in North and South, the issue of slavery in the territories continued to destroy moderation and promote militancy. (After numerous additional votes on its constitution, Kansas would ultimately enter the Union in 1861 as a free state.)

12-9d John Brown's Raid on Harpers Ferry

Soon after the Congressional showdown on the Lecompton Constitution, the entire nation's focus would be drawn to a new dimension of the slavery question—armed rebellion, led by the abolitionist who had killed proslavery settlers along Pottawatomie Creek in "Bleeding Kansas." Born in Connecticut in 1800, John Brown had been raised by staunchly religious antislavery parents. Between 1820 and 1855, he engaged in some twenty business ventures, including farming, nearly all of them failures. But Brown had a distinctive vision of abolitionism. He relied on an Old Testament conception of justice—"an eye for an eye"—and he had a puritanical obsession with the wickedness of others, especially southern slave owners. Brown believed that slavery was an "unjustifiable" state of war conducted by one group of people against another. He also believed violence in a righteous cause was a holy act, even a rite of purification for those who engaged in it. To Brown, the destruction of slavery in America required revolutionary ideology and revolutionary acts.

On October 16, 1859, Brown led a band of eighteen whites and blacks in an attack on the federal arsenal at Harpers Ferry, Virginia. Hoping to trigger a slave rebellion, Brown failed miserably and was quickly captured. In a celebrated trial in November and a widely publicized execution in December, in Charles Town, Virginia, Brown became one of the most enduring martyrs, as well as villains, of American history. His attempted insurrection struck fear into the South.

Then it became known that Brown had received financial backing from several prominent abolitionists. When such northern intellectuals as Ralph Waldo Emerson and Henry David Thoreau praised Brown as a holy warrior who "would make the gallows as glorious as the cross," white southerners' outrage intensified. The white South almost universally interpreted Brown's attack at Harpers Ferry as an act of midnight terrorism, as the fulfillment of their long-stated dread of "abolition emissaries" who would infiltrate the region to incite slave rebellion.

Perhaps most telling of all was the fact that the pivotal election of 1860 was less than a year away when Brown went so eagerly to the gallows, handing a note to his jailer with the

▲ *The Last Moments of John Brown*, depicting Brown's mythical kissing of the black child while leaving the jail for his journey to the gallows, by Thomas Hovenden, oil on canvas, 1882. Metropolitan Museum of Art, New York, Art Resource New York.

famous prediction "I John Brown am now quite certain that the crimes of this guilty land will never be purged away, but with blood." Most troubling to white southerners, perhaps, was their awareness that, though Republican politicians condemned Brown's crimes, they did so in a way that deflected attention onto the still-greater crime of slavery. After eighty-four years of growth from its birth in a revolution against monarchy and empire, the American republic now faced its most dire test of existence—whether the expansion of freedom or slavery would define its future. As both hero and villain on the two sides of the slavery question, John Brown had driven a stake into the American Union.

Summary

During the 1820s, politicians reshaped public discourse to broaden their appeal to an expanding electorate of white men, helping give birth to the second party system with its heated rivalry between the Democrats and Whigs. The two parties competed almost equally in the 1830s and 1840s for voter loyalty by building strong organizations that vied in national and local elections often characterized by fraud, and sometimes by violence. Both parties favored economic development but by different means: the Whigs advocated centralized government initiative to spur commercial growth, whereas

Coalition Politics

In a democracy, constituencies with diverse interests often form coalition parties in the hope of winning elections. Although the Jacksonian Democrats and Whigs in the 1830s and 1840s demonstrated their sharp differences over the nature of government, banking, reform, and expansion, each party's constituents held a wide range of beliefs, particularly regarding slavery. From the Mexican War into the 1850s, when significant third parties (the Free-Soilers and nativists) threatened the two-party system, and with the ultimate triumph of the Republicans in forging a new antislavery alliance that destroyed the second party system, the antebellum era provided a lasting model of coalition politics and realignment.

The most potent and rapidly successful third-party movement in American history was the Republican Party, founded in 1854 in the wake of the Kansas-Nebraska Act and its potential opening of the entire American West to slavery. Never before or since has a coalition of politicians and voters from previously long-standing parties and persuasions coalesced so successfully around a cluster of interests aimed at a single goal—in this case, stopping slavery's spread.

So many northern Democrats bolted to the Republicans that by the 1856 election, they formed perhaps 25 percent of the new party's vote. Northern Whigs, with their historic advocacy of activist government and social reform, also joined the Republicans. Radical abolitionists who had entered politics through the old Liberty or Free-Soil parties now found leadership positions among the exclusively northern Republicans.

This antislavery coalition forged numerous divergent outlooks into a new worldview: resentment of southern society and political power; an aggressive antislavery stance based on the free-labor argument and a celebration of the wage earner and small farmer; devotion to the Union against increasing southern threats of disunion; moral revulsion to slavery as inhumane and a threat to the country's future; a racist urge to keep the West open for white immigrant laborers and free of black competition; and finally, commitment to the northern social order as the model of progress, capitalist enterprise, and social mobility. Such a multipart ideology coalesced against the common foe of the "Slave Power Conspiracy,"

an alleged southern oligarchy of concentrated power determined to control the nation's future.

Whether in the diverse alliances of rural and urban reformers that formed the Populist and Progressive movements of the late nineteenth and early twentieth centuries; the mixture of urban working classes, labor unions, rural southern whites, African Americans, and artists and intellectuals that formed the New Deal coalition that reshaped America from the Great Depression to the 1970s; the Obama coalition of 2008–2016 that combined racial minorities, women, and young voters; or the modern conservative counterrevolution, with its antigovernment determination to dismantle the New Deal's social contract, all such coalitions have drawn upon this enduring legacy of pre–Civil War American politics. In the wake of the stunning election of Donald Trump in 2016, we may find new coalitions forming or dissolving.

CRITICAL THINKING

- Does the election of Donald Trump represent the rise of a new coalition?
- If so, what causes are driving this political realignment?

Democrats advocated limited government and sought agricultural expansion. Andrew Jackson did not hesitate, however, to use presidential authority, leading his opponents to dub him "King Andrew." The controversies over the Second Bank of the United States and nullification exposed different interpretations of the nation's founding principles and intensified political rivalries. Although women participated in political campaigns, activists for women's legal and political equality won few supporters. Instead, the nation focused its attention on economic development and westward expansion.

Long submerged, political debate over slavery was forced into the open after the annexation of Texas led to the War with Mexico, during which the United States acquired massive amounts of new land. The Compromise of 1850 attempted to settle the dispute but only added fuel to the fires of sectional contention, leading to the fateful Kansas-Nebraska Act of

1854, which tore asunder the political party system and gave birth to a genuine antislavery coalition. With Bleeding Kansas and the *Dred Scott* decision, by 1857 Americans North and South faced clear and dangerous choices about the future of labor and the meaning of liberty in an ambitious and expanding society. And finally, by 1859, when radical abolitionist John Brown attacked Harpers Ferry to foment a slave insurrection, southerners and northerners came to see each other in conspiratorial terms. Meanwhile, African Americans, slave and free, fled from slave catchers in unprecedented numbers and grew to expect violent if uncertain resolutions to their dreams of freedom in America. No one knew the future, but all knew the issues and conflicts were real.

Throughout the 1840s and 1850s, many able leaders had worked to avert the outcome of disunion. As late as 1858, even Jefferson Davis had declared, "This great country will continue united." But within two years he found himself in the midst of a movement for disunion in order to preserve his section's slave society and their definition of states' rights.

During the 1850s, every southern victory in territorial expansion increased fear of the Slave Power, and each new expression of Free-Soil sentiment prompted slaveholders to harden their demands. In the profoundest sense, slavery was the root of the conflict. As a people and a nation, Americans had reached the most fateful turning point in their history. Answers would now come from a completely polarized election, disunion, and the battlefield.

Suggestions for Further Reading

Edward L. Ayers and Carolyn R. Martin, eds., *America on the Eve of the Civil War* (2010)

Donald B. Cole, *Vindicating Andrew Jackson: The 1828 Election and the Rise of the Two-Party System* (2009)

Marc Egnal, *Clash of Extremes: The Economic Origins of the Civil War* (2009)

Nicole Etcheson, *Bleeding Kansas: Contested Liberty in the Civil War Era* (2004)

Don E. Fehrenbacher, *The Slaveholding Republic: An Account of the United States Government's Relations to Slavery* (2001)

Joan D. Hedrick, *Harriet Beecher Stowe: A Life* (1994)

Daniel Walker Howe, *What Hath God Wrought: The Transformation of America, 1815–1848* (2007)

Robert W. Johannsen, *To the Halls of the Montezumas: The Mexican War and the American Imagination* (1985)

Lynn Hudson Parsons, *The Birth of Modern Politics: Andrew Jackson, John Quincy Adams, and the Election of 1828* (2009)

Richard H. Sewell, *Ballots for Freedom: Antislavery Politics Before the Civil War* (1976)

Elizabeth R. Varon, *Disunion! The Coming of the American Civil War, 1789–1859* (2008)

Harry L. Watson, *Liberty and Power: The Politics of Jacksonian America* (2006)

Susan Zaeske, *Signatures of Citizenship: Petitioning, Antislavery, and Women's Political Identity* (2003)

Transforming Fire: The Civil War, 1860–1865

S lave prisons, known as slave pens, were the dark and ugly crossroads of American history. To see, hear, and smell one was to understand why the Civil War happened. Wallace Turnage, a seventeen-year-old slave from a cotton plantation in Pickens County, Alabama, entered wartime Mobile in December 1862 through the slave traders' yard; he would leave Mobile from that same yard a year and eight months later.

Turnage was born in 1846 on a remote tobacco farm near Snow Hill, North Carolina. In mid-1860, as the nation teetered on the brink of disunion, he was sold to a Richmond, Virginia, slave trader named Hector Davis. Turnage worked in Davis's three-story slave jail, organizing daily auctions until he was sold for $1,000 in early 1861 to a cotton planter from Pickens County, Alabama. Frequently whipped and longing for escape, the desperate teenager tried four times over the next two years to escape to Mississippi, seeking the lines of the Union armies. Although he remained at large for months, he was captured each time and returned to his owner in southeastern Alabama.

In frustration, his owner took Turnage to the Mobile slave traders' yard, where the youth was sold for $2,000 to a wealthy merchant in the port city. During 1864, as Union admiral David Farragut prepared his fleet for an assault on Mobile Bay and the city came under siege, its

◄ A fugitive slave chased by dogs and slave catchers, a 19th century illustration. The escaped slave, or "runaway," was one of the most oft-depicted visual images of American slavery. The Granger Collection, NYC — All rights reserved.

Chronology

slaves were enlisted to build elaborate trenchworks. Meanwhile, Turnage labored at all manner of urban tasks for his new owner's family, including driving their carriage on errands.

One day in early August, Turnage crashed the old carriage on a Mobile street. In anger, his owner took him to the slave pen and hired the jailer to administer thirty lashes in the special "whipping house." Stripped naked, his hands tied in ropes, Turnage was hoisted up on a hook on the wall. At the end of the gruesome ritual, his owner instructed Wallace to walk home. Instead, Turnage "took courage," as he wrote in his postwar narrative, "prayed faithfully," and walked steadfastly southwest, right through the Confederate encampment and trenchworks. The soldiers took the bloodied and tattered black teenager for simply one among the hundreds of slaves who did camp labor.

For the next three weeks, Turnage crawled and waded for twenty-five miles through the snake-infested swamps of the Foul River estuary, down the west edge of Mobile Bay. Nearly starved and narrowly escaping Confederate patrols, Turnage made it all the way to Cedar Point, where he could look out at the forbidding mouth of Mobile Bay to Dauphin Island, now occupied by Union forces. Alligators swam in their wallows nearby, delta grass swayed waist high in the hot breezes, and the laughing gulls squawked around him as Turnage hid from Confederate lookouts in a swampy den. He remembered his choices starkly: "It was death to go back and it was death to stay there and freedom was before me; it could only be death to go forward if I was caught and freedom if I escaped."

Turnage barely survived a desperate attempt to ride a log out into the ocean and narrowly made it back to shore. Then, one day at the water's edge, he noticed an old rowboat that had rolled in with the tide. The veteran fugitive now took a "piece of board" and began to row out into the bay. As a squall with "water like a hill coming" at him nearly swamped him, he suddenly "heard the crash of oars and behold there was eight Yankees in a boat." Following the rhythm of the oars, Turnage jumped into the Union gunboat. For a stunning few moments, he remembered, the oarsmen in blue "were struck with silence" as they contemplated the frail young black man crouched in front of them. Turnage turned

his head and looked back at Confederate soldiers on the shore and measured the distance of his bravery at sea. Then he took his first breaths of freedom.

Experience an interactive version of this story in MindTap®.

The Civil War brought astonishing changes to individuals everywhere in the North and South. It obliterated the normal patterns of life. Millions of men were swept away into training camps and regiments. Armies numbering in the hundreds of thousands marched over the South, devastating the countryside. Families struggled to survive without their men; businesses tried to cope with the loss of workers. Women on both sides took on extra responsibilities in the home and moved into new jobs in the workforce, including the ranks of nurses and hospital workers. No sphere of life went untouched.

But southern soldiers and their families also experienced what few other groups of Americans have—utter defeat. For most of them, wealth changed to poverty and hope to despair as countless southern farms were ruined. Late in the war, many southerners yearned only for an end to inflation, to shortages, to the escape of their slaves, and to the death that visited nearly every family. Even the South's slaves, who eventually placed great hope in the war, did not always encounter sympathetic liberators such as those who took Turnage from his drowning boat, fed and clothed him in a tent, and took him before a Union general, where the freedman was given two choices: join a black regiment or become a camp servant for a white officer. For the remainder of the war, Turnage cooked for a Maryland captain.

In the North, farm boys and mechanics from all regions would be asked for heretofore unimagined sacrifices. The conflict ensured vast government expenditures and lucrative federal contracts. *Harper's Monthly* reported that an eminent financier expected a long and prosperous war. "The battle of Bull Run," predicted the financier, "makes the fortune of every man in Wall Street who is not a natural idiot."

Change was most drastic in the South, where secessionists had launched a conservative revolution for their section's national independence. Born of states' rights doctrine, the Confederacy now had to be transformed into a centralized nation to fight a vast war. Southern whites had feared that a peacetime government of Republicans would interfere with slavery and ruin plantation life. Instead, their own actions led to a war that turned southern society upside down and imperiled the very existence of slavery.

The war created social strains in both North and South. Disaffection was strongest, though, in the Confederacy, where poverty and class resentment threatened the South from within as federal armies assailed it from without. In the North, dissent against the rising powers of the federal government also flourished, and antiwar sentiment occasionally erupted into violence.

Ultimately, the Civil War forced on the nation a social and political revolution regarding race. Its greatest effect was to compel leaders and citizens to finally face the great question of slavery. And blacks themselves embraced what was for them the most fundamental turning point in their experience as Americans.

- *How and why did the Civil War bring social transformations to both South and North?*

- *How did the war to preserve the Union or for southern independence become the war to free the slaves?*

- *By 1865, when Americans on all sides searched for the meaning of the war they had just fought, what might some of their answers have been?*

13-1 Election of 1860 and Secession Crisis

▶ **How did slavery affect the election of 1860 and the immediate aftermath of the election?**

▶ **What were the varying positions on secession in the South after the election of 1860?**

▶ **How did Abraham Lincoln address the dilemma regarding Fort Sumter?**

Many Americans believed the election of 1860 would decide the fate of the Union. The Democratic Party was the only party that was truly national in scope. "One after another," wrote a Mississippi editor, "the links which have bound the North and South together, have been severed . . . [but] the Democratic party looms gradually up . . . and waves the olive branch over the troubled waters of politics." But, fatefully, at its 1860 convention in Charleston, South Carolina, the Democratic Party split.

Stephen Douglas wanted his party's presidential nomination, but he could not afford to alienate northern voters by accepting the southern position on the territories. Southern Democrats, however, insisted on recognition of their rights—as the *Dred Scott* decision had defined them—and they moved to block Douglas's nomination. When Douglas obtained a majority for his version of the platform, delegates from the Deep South walked out of the convention. After efforts at compromise failed, the Democrats presented two nominees: Douglas for the northern wing, and Vice President John C. Breckinridge of Kentucky for the southern.

The Republicans nominated Abraham Lincoln at a rousing convention in Chicago. The choice of Lincoln reflected the growing power of the Midwest, and he was perceived as more moderate on slavery than the early front-runner, Senator William H. Seward of New York. A Constitutional Union Party, formed to preserve the nation but strong only in the Upper South, nominated John Bell of Tennessee.

Bell's only issue in the ensuing campaign was the urgency of preserving the Union; Constitutional Unionists hoped to appeal to history and sentiment to hold the country together. Douglas desperately sought to unite his northern and southern supporters, but the slavery question and the Breckinridge candidacy had permanently divided the party. Although Lincoln and the Republicans denied any intent to interfere with slavery in the states where it existed, they stood firm against the extension of slavery into the territories.

But the election of 1860 was sectional in character, and the only one in American history in which the losers refused to accept the result. Lincoln won, but Douglas, Breckinridge, and Bell together received a majority of the votes. Douglas had broad-based support but won few states. Breckinridge carried nine southern states, all in the Deep South. Bell won pluralities in Virginia, Kentucky, and Tennessee. Lincoln prevailed in the North, but in the four slave states that ultimately remained loyal to the Union (Missouri, Kentucky, Maryland, and Delaware—the border states) he gained only a plurality, not a majority (see Table 13.1). Lincoln's victory was won in the electoral college. He polled only 40 percent of the total vote and was not even on the ballot in ten slave states.

Opposition to slavery's extension was the core issue for Lincoln and the Republican Party. Meanwhile, in the South, proslavery advocates and secessionists whipped up public opinion and demanded that state conventions assemble to consider secession.

Lincoln made the crucial decision not to soften his party's position on the territories. He wrote of the necessity of maintaining the bond of faith between voter and candidate and of declining to set "the minority over the majority." Although many conservative Republicans—eastern businessmen and former Whigs who did not feel strongly about slavery— hoped for a compromise, the original and most committed Republicans—old

Jefferson Davis President of the Confederacy.

Free-Soilers and antislavery Whigs—held the line on slavery expansion.

In the winter of 1860–1861, numerous compromise proposals were floated in Washington, including resurrecting the Missouri Compromise line, 36°30', and even initiating a "plural presidency," with one president from each section. When Lincoln ruled out concessions on the territorial issue, these peacemaking efforts, based largely on old or discredited ideas, collapsed.

13-1a Secession and the Confederate States of America

Meanwhile, on December 20, 1860, South Carolina passed an ordinance of secession amid jubilation and cheering. By reclaiming its "independence," South Carolina raised the stakes in the sectional confrontation. No longer was secession an unthinkable step; the Union was broken. Secessionists now argued that other states should follow South Carolina and that those who favored compromise could make a better deal outside the Union than in it. Moderates from regions with fewer slaves and more diversified economies than the cotton belt (such as upstate Georgia, as opposed to the southern tier of the state), fearing economic chaos and arguing for "resistance short of secession," still felt deep affection for the Union and had family ties in the North; secession was by no means inevitable or widely popular in Upper South states like Virginia or Tennessee.

Southern extremists soon got their way in the Deep South. Overwhelming their opposition, they called separate state conventions and passed secession ordinances in Mississippi, Florida, Alabama, Georgia, Louisiana, and Texas. By February 1861, these states had joined South Carolina to form a new government in Montgomery, Alabama: a revolutionary movement now called the Confederate States of America. The delegates at Montgomery chose **Jefferson Davis** of Mississippi as their president.

This apparent unanimity of action was deceiving. Confused and dissatisfied with the alternatives, many

Table 13.1 **Presidential Vote in 1860**

Lincoln (Republican)*	Carried all northern states and all electoral votes except 3 in New Jersey
Breckinridge (Southern Democrat)	Carried all slave states except Virginia, Kentucky, Tennessee, Missouri
Bell (Constitutional Union)	Carried Virginia, Kentucky, Tennessee
Douglas (Northern Democrat)	Carried only Missouri

*Lincoln received only 26,000 votes in the entire South and was not even on the ballot in ten slave states. Breckinridge was not on the ballot in three northern states.

southerners—perhaps even 40 percent of those in the Deep South—opposed immediate secession. In some state conventions, the secession vote was close and decided by overrepresentation of plantation districts. In Georgia, where more than three in five voters were nonslaveholders, the secession convention voted 166–130 to secede after a bitterly divided debate. Four states in the Upper South where wheat production and commercial ties to the North had grown steadily in the 1850s—Virginia, North Carolina, Tennessee, and Arkansas—flatly rejected secession and did not join the Confederacy until after fighting had begun. In Augusta County, Virginia, in the Shenandoah Valley, where one-fifth of households held slaves, the majority steadfastly sought alternatives to secession until after Fort Sumter. In the border states, popular sentiment was deeply divided; minorities in Kentucky and Missouri tried to secede, but these slave states ultimately came under Union control, along with Maryland and Delaware (see Map 13.1).

Such misgivings were not surprising. Secession posed enormous challenges for southerners. Analysis of election returns from 1860 and 1861 indicates that slaveholders and nonslaveholders were beginning to part company politically. Heavily slaveholding counties strongly supported secession. But nonslaveholding areas that had favored Breckinridge in the presidential election proved far less willing to support secession: economic interests and fear of war on their own soil provided a potent, negative reaction to abstractions such as "state rights."

As for why the Deep South bolted, we need look no further than the speeches and writings of the secession commissioners sent out by the seven seceded states to try to convince the other slave states to join them. Repeatedly, they stressed independence as the only way to preserve white racial security and the slave system against the hostile Republicans. Upon "slavery," said the Alabama commissioner, Stephen Hale, to the Kentucky legislature, rested "not only the wealth and prosperity of the southern people, but their very existence as a political community." Only secession, Hale contended, could sustain the "heaven-ordained superiority of the white over the black race." This combination of economic interests and beliefs fueled the tragedy about to happen. Southern states seceded from the Union to preserve slavery and white supremacy.

13-1b Fort Sumter and Outbreak of War

President Lincoln's dilemma on Inauguration Day in March 1861 was unprecedented—how to maintain the authority of the federal government without provoking war. Proceeding

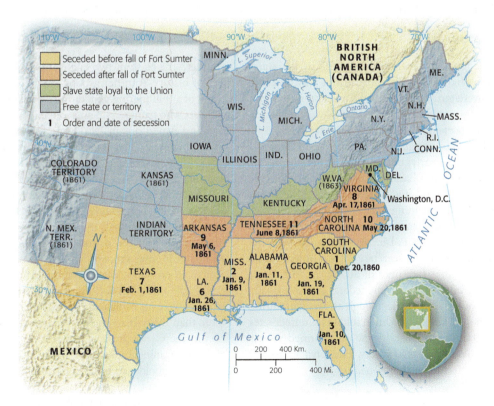

Map 13.1 The Divided Nation—Slave and Free Areas, 1861

After fighting began, the Upper South joined the Deep South in the Confederacy. The nation's pattern of division corresponded to the distribution of slavery and the percentage of black people in the population.

National Archives

▲ Photograph of interior of Fort Sumter, in Charleston Harbor, April 14, 1861, the day Major Robert Anderson and his troops surrendered and the Civil War began.

cautiously, he sought only to hold onto forts in the states that had left the Union, reasoning that in this way he could assert federal sovereignty while waiting for a restoration. But Jefferson Davis, who could not claim to lead a sovereign nation if the Confederate ports were under foreign (that is, U.S.) control, was unwilling to be so patient. A collision soon came.

It arrived in the early morning hours of April 12, 1861, at **Fort Sumter** in Charleston harbor. A federal garrison there ran low on food, and Lincoln notified the South Carolinians that he was sending a ship to resupply the fort. For the Montgomery government, the alternatives were to attack the fort or to acquiesce to Lincoln's authority. After the Confederate cabinet met, the secretary of war ordered local commanders to obtain a surrender or attack the fort. After two days of heavy bombardment, the federal garrison finally surrendered. No one died in battle, though an accident during postbattle ceremonies killed two Union soldiers. Confederates permitted the U.S. troops to sail away on unarmed vessels while Charlestonians celebrated wildly. The Civil War—the bloodiest war in America's history—had begun.

13-1c Causation

Historians have long debated the immediate and long-term roots of the Civil War. Some have interpreted it as an "irrepressible conflict," the clash of two civilizations on divergent trajectories of history. Another group saw the war as "needless," the result of a "blundering generation" of irrational politicians and activists who trumped up an avoidable conflict. But the issues dividing Americans in 1861 were fundamental to the future of the republic. The logic of Republican ideology tended in the direction of abolishing slavery. The logic of southern arguments led to establishing slavery potentially everywhere.

Republicans were devoted to promoting the North's free-labor economy, burgeoning in the Great Lakes region through homesteading, internal improvements, and protective tariffs. The lords of the cotton kingdom, owners of more than $3 billion in slave property and the largest single asset in the American economy, were determined to protect and expand their "way of life." Small investors in land and large investors in slaves were on a collision course. Both sides had watched for more than thirty years the consequences of British emancipation in the Caribbean and had reached different conclusions about its meaning. Indeed, the American antislavery movement had been emboldened by emancipation in the British empire.

Lincoln put these facts succinctly. In a postelection letter to his old congressional colleague, Alexander Stephens of Georgia, soon to be vice president of the Confederacy, Lincoln offered assurance that Republicans would not attack slavery in the states where it existed. But Lincoln continued, "You think slavery is right and ought to be expanded; while we think it is wrong and ought to be restricted. That I suppose is the rub."

Fort Sumter Federal fort in Charleston harbor, South Carolina where the first shots of the Civil War were fired when the Union attempted to resupply troops.

As a matter of *interests* and *morality*, disunion and war came because of the great political struggle over slavery. Without slavery, there would have been no war. Many Americans still hold to a belief that the war was about states' rights, the theory and practice of the proper relationship of state to federal authority. But the significance of states' rights, then as now, is always in the cause in which it is employed. Americans still debate this question because its implications never seem to subside in the present.

13-2 America Goes to War, 1861–1862

▶ What were the respective strategies of the Union and Confederacy in fighting the war?

▶ How did the war in the West differ from that in Virginia during the first year of the war?

▶ What were the Confederate objectives in bringing the war to Maryland and Kentucky?

Few Americans understood what they were getting into when the war began. The onset of hostilities sparked patriotic sentiments, optimistic speeches, and joyous ceremonies in both North and South. Northern communities raised companies of volunteers eager to save the Union and sent them off with fanfare. In the South, confident recruits boasted of whipping the Yankees and returning home before Christmas. Southern women sewed dashing uniforms for men who would soon be lucky to wear drab gray or butternut homespun. Americans went to war in 1861 with decidedly romantic notions of what they would experience.

13-2a First Battle of Bull Run

Through the spring of 1861, both sides scrambled to organize and train their undisciplined armies. On July 21, 1861, the first battle took place outside Manassas Junction, Virginia, near a stream called **Bull Run**. General Irvin McDowell and thirty thousand Union troops attacked General P. G. T. Beauregard's 22,000 southerners (see Map 13.3). As raw recruits struggled amid the confusion of their first battle, federal forces began to gain ground. Then they ran into a line of Virginia troops under General Thomas Jackson. "There is Jackson standing like a stone wall," shouted one Confederate. "Stonewall" Jackson's line held, and the arrival of nine thousand Confederate reinforcements by train won the day for the South. Union troops fled back to Washington, observed by shocked northern congressmen and spectators who had watched the battle; a few sightseers were actually captured for their folly.

The unexpected rout at Bull Run gave northerners their first hint of the nature of the war to come. Although the United States enjoyed an enormous advantage in resources, victory would not be easy. Pro-Union feeling was growing in western Virginia, and loyalties were divided in the four border slave states—Missouri, Kentucky, Maryland,

and Delaware. But the rest of the Upper South—the states of North Carolina, Virginia, Tennessee, and Arkansas—joined the Confederacy in the wake of the attack on Fort Sumter. Moved by an outpouring of regional loyalty, half a million southerners volunteered to fight—so many that the Confederate government could hardly arm them all. The United States therefore undertook a massive mobilization of troops around Washington, D.C.

Lincoln gave command of the army to General **George B. McClellan**, an officer who proved better at organization and training than at fighting. McClellan put his growing army into camp and devoted the fall and winter of 1861 to readying a formidable force of nearly two hundred thousand men whose mission would be to take Richmond, established as the Confederate capital by July 1861. "The vast preparation of the enemy," wrote one southern soldier, produced a "feeling of despondency" in the South for the first time. But southern morale remained high early in the war.

13-2b Grand Strategy

While McClellan prepared, the Union began to implement other parts of its overall strategy, which called for a blockade of southern ports and eventual capture of the Mississippi River. Like a constricting snake, this "**Anaconda plan**" would strangle the Confederacy (see Map 13.2). At first, the Union navy had too few ships to patrol 3,550 miles of coastline and block the Confederacy's avenues of supply. Gradually, however, the navy increased the blockade's effectiveness, though it never stopped southern commerce completely.

The Confederate strategy was essentially defensive. A defensive posture was not only consistent with the South's claim of independence, but also reasonable in light of the North's advantage in resources (see Figure 13.1). But Jefferson Davis called the southern strategy an "offensive defensive," taking advantage of opportunities to attack and using its interior lines of transportation to concentrate troops at crucial points. In its war aims, the Confederacy did not need to conquer the North; the Union effort, however, as time would tell, required conquest of the South.

Strategic thinking on both sides slighted the importance of the West, that vast expanse of territory between Virginia and the Mississippi River and beyond. Guerrilla warfare broke out in 1861 in the politically divided state of Missouri, and key locations along the Mississippi and other major western rivers would prove crucial prizes in the North's eventual victory. Beyond the Mississippi River, the Confederacy hoped to gain an advantage by negotiating treaties with the Creeks, Choctaws,

Bull Run The location of the first major land battle in the Civil War.

George B. McClellan Union general very popular with troops who proved better at organization and training than at fighting.

"Anaconda plan" Called for the Union to blockade southern ports, capture the Mississippi River, and, like a snake, strangle the Confederacy.

Map 13.2 The War in the West

An overview of the Union's successful campaigns in the West and its seizure of the key points on the Mississippi River, as well as along the Atlantic coast in 1862 and 1863. These actions were decisive in paving the way for ultimate northern victory.

Chickasaws, Cherokees, Seminoles, and smaller groups of Native peoples on the Plains. At the same time, the Republican U.S. Congress carved the West into territories in anticipation of state making. For most Native Americans west of the Mississippi, the Civil War marked the beginning of nearly three decades of offensive warfare against them, an enveloping strategy of conquest, relocation, and slaughter. Meanwhile, Native Americans would fight on both sides in the Civil War, and in some cases (especially the Cherokee) they would have their own deep struggles over emancipation of their own slaves.

13-2c Union Naval Campaign

The last half of 1861 brought no major land battles, but the North made gains by sea. Late in the summer, Union naval forces captured Cape Hatteras and then Hilton Head, one of the Sea Islands off Port Royal, South Carolina. A few months later, similar operations secured vital coastal points in North Carolina as well as Fort Pulaski, which defended Savannah. Federal naval operations established significant beachheads along the Confederate coastline (see Map 13.2).

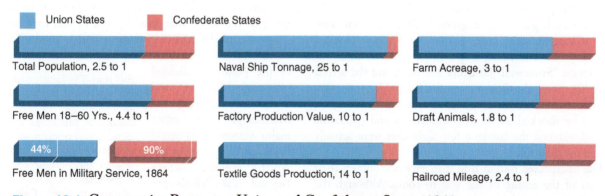

Figure 13.1 Comparative Resources, Union and Confederate States, 1861

The North had vastly superior resources. Although the North's advantages in manpower and industrial capacity proved very important, the South still had to be conquered, its society and its will crushed. Source: *The Times Atlas of World History*

The coastal victories off South Carolina foreshadowed a revolution in slave society. At the federal gunboats' approach, planters abandoned their land and fled. For a while, Confederate cavalry tried to round up slaves and move them to the interior as well. But thousands of slaves greeted what they hoped to be freedom with rejoicing and broke the hated cotton gins. Some entered their masters' homes and took clothing and furniture, which they conspicuously displayed. A growing stream of fugitive slaves poured into Union lines. Unwilling at first to wage a war against slavery, the federal government did not acknowledge the slaves' freedom—though it began to use their labor in the Union cause. This swelling tide of emancipated slaves, defined by many Union officers as "contraband" of war (confiscated enemy property), forced first a bitter debate within the Union army and government over how to treat the freedmen, and then a forthright attempt to harness their labor and military power.

The coastal incursions worried southerners, but the spring of 1862 brought even stronger evidence of the war's gravity. In March, two ironclad ships—the USS *Monitor* (a Union warship) and the CSS *Virginia* (a Confederate warship built on the hull of the Union steam frigate USS *Merrimack*, which had been burned and abandoned by Union forces when they evacuated Norfolk)—fought each other for the first time off the coast of Virginia. Their battle, though indecisive, ushered in a new era in naval design. In April, Union ships commanded by Admiral David Farragut smashed through log booms blocking the Mississippi River and fought their way upstream to capture New Orleans. The city at the mouth of the Mississippi, the South's greatest seaport and slave-trading center, was now in federal hands.

13-2d War in the Far West

Farther west, three full Confederate regiments were organized, mostly of Cherokees, from Indian Territory, but a Union victory at Elkhorn Tavern, Arkansas, shattered southern control of the region. Thereafter, Confederate operations in Indian Territory amounted to little more than guerrilla raids.

In the westernmost campaign of the war, from February to May 1862, some three thousand Confederate and four thousand Union forces fought for control of New Mexico Territory. The military significance of the New Mexico campaign was limited, but the Confederate invasion had grander aims: access to the trade riches of the Santa Fe Trail and possession of gold mines in Colorado and California. If the campaign had succeeded, the Confederacy would have been much stronger with a western empire. But Colorado and New Mexico Unionists fought for their region, and in a series of battles at Glorieta Pass, twenty miles east of Santa Fe, on March 26 through 28, they blocked the Confederate invasion. By May 1, Confederate forces straggled down the Rio Grande River back into Texas, ending their effort to take New Mexico.

▲ Monument to fallen soldiers, near Water Oaks Pond, Shiloh National Battlefield Park, near Pittsburg Landing, TN.

13-2e Grant's Tennessee Campaign and the Battle of Shiloh

Meanwhile, in February 1862, land and river forces in northern Tennessee won significant victories for the Union. A Union commander named **Ulysses S. Grant** saw the strategic importance of Fort Henry and Fort Donelson, the Confederate outposts guarding the Tennessee and Cumberland rivers. If federal troops could capture these forts, Grant realized, they would open two prime routes into the heartland of the Confederacy. In just ten days, he seized the forts—completely cutting off the Confederates and demanding "unconditional surrender" of Fort Donelson. A path into Tennessee, Alabama, and Mississippi now lay open before the Union army. Grant's achievement of such a surrender from his former West Point classmate, Confederate commander Simon Bolivar Buckner, inspired northern public opinion.

Grant moved on into southern Tennessee and the first of the war's shockingly bloody encounters, the **Battle of Shiloh** (see Map 13.2). On April 6, Confederate general Albert Sidney Johnston caught federal troops with their backs to the water awaiting reinforcements along the Tennessee River. The Confederates attacked early in the morning and inflicted heavy damage all day. Close to victory, General Johnston was shot from his horse and killed. Southern forces almost achieved a breakthrough, but Union reinforcements arrived that night. The next day, the tide of battle turned and, after ten hours of terrible combat, Grant's men forced the Confederates to withdraw.

Neither side won a decisive victory at Shiloh, yet the losses were staggering, and the Confederates were forced to retreat into northern Mississippi.

"Ulysses S. Grant Union general who, in 1864, became Commanding General of the United States Army.

Battle of Shiloh The bloodiest battle in American history to that date (April 6–7, 1862)

Northern troops lost thirteen thousand men (killed, wounded, or captured) out of sixty-three thousand; southerners sacrificed eleven thousand out of forty thousand. Total casualties in this single battle exceeded those in all three of America's previous wars combined. Now both sides were beginning to sense the true nature of the war. "I saw an open field," Grant recalled, "over which Confederates had made repeated charges . . . so covered with dead that it would have been possible to walk across the clearing, in any direction, stepping on dead bodies, without a foot touching the ground." Shiloh utterly changed Grant's thinking about the war. He had hoped that southerners would soon be "heartily tired" of the conflict. After Shiloh, "I gave up all idea of saving the Union except by complete conquest." Memories of the Shiloh battlefield, and many others to come, would haunt the soldiers who survived for the rest of their lives. Herman Melville's "Shiloh, A Requiem" captures the pathos of that spring day when armies learned the truth about war:

> Skimming lightly, wheeling still,
> The swallows fly low
> Over the field in clouded days,
> The forest-field of Shiloh—
> Over the field where April rain
> Solaced the parched ones stretched in pain
> Through the pause of night
> That followed the Sunday fight
> Around the church of Shiloh—
> The church so lone, the log-built one,
> That echoed to many a parting groan
> And natural prayer
> Of dying foemen mingled there—
> Foemen at morn, but friends at eve—
> Fame or country least their care:
> (What like a bullet can undeceive!)
> But now they lie low,
> While over them the swallows skim,
> And all is hushed at Shiloh.

13-2f McClellan and the Peninsula Campaign

On the Virginia front, President Lincoln had a different problem. General McClellan was slow to move. Only thirty-six, McClellan had already achieved notable success as an army officer and railroad president. Habitually overestimating the size of enemy forces, he called repeatedly for reinforcements and ignored Lincoln's directions to advance. McClellan advocated war of limited aims that would lead to a quick reunion. He intended neither disruption of slavery nor war on noncombatants. Finally, the cautious, even insubordinate, McClellan chose to move by a water route, sailing his troops down the Chesapeake, landing them on the peninsula between the York and James rivers, and advancing on Richmond from the east (see Map 13.3).

Robert E. Lee Confederate general who, in 1862, commanded the Army of Northern Virginia. In 1865 he became general-in-chief of the Confederate army.

Map 13.3 McClellan's Campaign

This map shows the water route chosen by McClellan to threaten Richmond during the Peninsula Campaign.

After a bloody but indecisive battle at Fair Oaks on May 31 through June 1, the federal armies moved to within seven miles of the Confederate capital. They could see the spires on Richmond churches. The Confederate commanding general, Joseph E. Johnston, was badly wounded at Fair Oaks, and President Jefferson Davis placed his chief military adviser, **Robert E. Lee**, in command. The fifty-five-year-old Lee was an aristocratic Virginian, a lifelong military officer, and a decorated veteran of the War with Mexico. Although he initially opposed secession, Lee loyally gave his allegiance to his state and became a staunch Confederate nationalist. He soon foiled McClellan's legions.

First, Lee sent Stonewall Jackson's corps of seventeen thousand northwest into the Shenandoah Valley behind Union forces, where they threatened Washington, D.C., and with rapid-strike mobility drew some federal troops away from Richmond to protect their own capital. Further, in mid-June, in an extraordinary four-day ride around the entire Union army, Confederate cavalry under J. E. B. Stuart, a self-styled Virginia cavalier with red cape and plumed hat, confirmed the exposed position of a major portion of McClellan's army north of the rain-swollen Chickahominy River. Then, in a series of engagements known as the Seven Days Battles, from June 26 through July 1, Lee struck at McClellan's army. Lee never managed to close his pincers around the retreating Union forces, but the daring move of taking the majority of his army northeast and attacking the Union right flank, while leaving only a small force to defend Richmond, forced McClellan (who always believed he was outnumbered) to retreat toward the James River.

During the sustained fighting of the Seven Days, the Union forces suffered 20,614 casualties and the Confederates, 15,849. After repeated rebel assaults against entrenched positions on high ground at Malvern Hill had been beaten back, an officer concluded, "It was not war, it was murder." By August 3, McClellan withdrew his army back to the Potomac and the environs of Washington. Richmond remained safe for almost two more years.

13-2g Confederate Offensive in Maryland and Kentucky

Buoyed by these results, Jefferson Davis conceived an ambitious plan to turn the tide of the war and gain recognition of the Confederacy by European nations. He ordered a general offensive, sending Lee north into Maryland and Generals Kirby Smith and Braxton Bragg into Kentucky. Calling on residents of Maryland and Kentucky, still slave states, to make a separate peace with his government, Davis also invited northwestern states like Indiana, which sent much of their trade down the Mississippi to New Orleans, to leave the Union. This was a coordinated effort to take the war to the North and to try to force both a military and a political turning point.

The plan was promising (it almost worked), but in the end the offensive failed. Lee's forces achieved a striking success at the Second battle of Bull Run, August 29 through 30, just southwest of Washington, D.C. On the same killing fields along Bull Run Creek where federal troops had been defeated the previous summer, an entire Union army was sent in retreat back into the federal capital. Thousands of wounded occupied schools and churches, and two thousand suffered on cots in the rotunda of the U.S. Capitol.

But in the bloodiest day of the entire war, September 17, 1862, McClellan turned Lee back from Sharpsburg, Maryland. In this **Battle of Antietam**, five thousand men died, and another eighteen thousand were wounded in the course of eight horrible hours. Lee was lucky to escape destruction, for McClellan had intercepted a lost battle order, wrapped around cigars for each Confederate corps commander and inadvertently dropped by a courier. But McClellan moved slowly, failed to use

Battle of Antietam First major battle on northern soil.

◄ Photograph of "Sunken Road," Antietam battlefield, taken shortly after the battle, September, 1862, often called "the Harvest of Battle."

Library of Congress Prints and Photographs Division Washington, D.C.[LC-DIG-ppmsca-07751]

his larger forces in simultaneous attacks, and allowed Lee's stricken army to retreat to safety across the Potomac. In the wake of Antietam, Lincoln, after long frustration, removed McClellan from command.

In Kentucky, Generals Smith and Bragg secured Lexington and Frankfort, but their effort to force the Yankees back to the Ohio River was stopped at the Battle of Perryville on October 8. Bragg's army retreated back into Tennessee, where—from December 31, 1862, to January 2, 1863—they fought an indecisive but much bloodier battle at Murfreesboro. Casualties exceeded even those of Shiloh, and many lives were sacrificed on a bitter winter landscape.

Confederate leaders marshaled all their strength for a breakthrough but failed. Outnumbered and disadvantaged in resources, the South could not continue the offensive. Profoundly disappointed, Davis admitted to a committee of Confederate representatives that southerners were entering "the darkest and most dangerous period we have yet had."

But 1862 also brought painful lessons to the North. Confederate general J. E. B. Stuart executed a daring cavalry raid into Pennsylvania in October. Then, on December 13, Union general Ambrose Burnside, now in command of the Army of the Potomac, unwisely ordered his soldiers to attack Lee's army, which held fortified positions on high ground at Fredericksburg, Virginia. Lee's men performed so efficiently in killing northerners that Lee was moved to say, "It is well that war is so terrible. We should grow too fond of it." Burnside's repeated assaults up Marye's Heights shocked even the opponents. "The Federals had fallen like the steady dripping of rain from the eaves of a house," remarked Confederate general James Longstreet. And a Union officer observed of the carnage of thirteen hundred dead and ninety-six hundred wounded Union soldiers, "The whole plain was covered with men, prostrate and dropping. . . . I had never before seen fighting like that . . . the next brigade coming up in succession would do its duty, and melt like snow coming down on warm ground." The scale of carnage now challenged people on both sides to search deeply for the meaning of such a war. At the front, some soldiers lost their sense of humanity in the face of the challenge. In the wake of Antietam's death toll, one Union burial crew, exhausted and perhaps inebriated, threw fifty-eight Confederate bodies down the well of a local farmer.

13-3 War Transforms the South

▶ How did the Confederacy manage to create a functioning federal government while fighting an all-out war?

▶ How did the war affect Southern civilian populations?

▶ How did wartime needs reveal inequities in the Confederacy?

The war caused tremendous disruptions in civilian life and altered southern society beyond all expectations. One of the first traditions to fall was the southern preference for local and limited government. States' rights had been a formative ideology for the Confederacy, but state governments were weak operations. To withstand the massive power of the North, the South needed to centralize; like the colonial revolutionaries, southerners faced a choice of joining together or dying separately.

13-3a The Confederacy and Centralization

Jefferson Davis moved promptly to bring all arms, supplies, and troops under centralized control. But by early 1862, the scope and duration of the conflict required something more. Tens of thousands of Confederate soldiers had volunteered for just one year's service, planning to return home in the spring to plant their crops. More recruits were needed constantly to keep southern armies in the field. However, as one official admitted, "the spirit of volunteering had died out." Finally, faced with a critical shortage of troops, in April 1862 the Confederate government enacted the first national conscription (draft) law in American history. Thus, the war forced unprecedented change on states that had seceded out of fear of change.

Davis adopted a firm leadership role toward the Confederate Congress, which raised taxes and later passed a tax-in-kind—paid in farm products. Nearly forty-five hundred agents dispersed to collect the tax. Where opposition arose, the government suspended the writ of habeas corpus (which prevented individuals from being held without trial) and imposed martial law. Despite Davis's unyielding stance, this tax system proved inadequate as well as unpopular for the South's war effort.

Davis further exhorted state governments to require farmers to switch from cash crops to food crops. But the army remained short of food and labor. The War Department resorted to impressing slaves to work on fortifications, and after 1861 the government relied heavily on confiscation of food to feed the troops. Officers swooped down on farms in the line of march and carted away grain, meat, wagons, and draft animals. Such raids caused increased hardship and resentment for women managing farms in the absence of husbands and sons.

Soon, the Confederate administration in Richmond gained virtually complete control over the southern economy. The Confederate Congress also gave the central government a great deal of control of the railroads. A large bureaucracy sprang up to administer these operations: over seventy thousand civilians staffed the Confederate administration. By war's end, the southern bureaucracy, a "big government" by any measure, was larger in proportion to population than its northern counterpart.

13-3b Confederate Nationalism

Historians have long argued over whether the Confederacy itself was a "rebellion," a "revolution," or the creation of a genuine "nation." Whatever label we apply, Confederates created a culture and an ideology of nationalism. Southerners immediately tried to forge their own national symbols and identity. In flags, songs, language, seals, school readers, and other national characteristics, Confederates created their own story.

In its conservative crusade to preserve states' rights, the social order, and racial slavery, southerners believed the Confederacy was the true legacy of the American Revolution—a bulwark against centralized power. In this view, southern "liberty" was no less a holy cause than that of the patriots of 1776. To southerners, theirs was a continuing revolution against the excesses of Yankee democracy, and George Washington (a Virginian) on horseback formed the center of the official seal of the Confederacy.

Also central to Confederate nationalism was a refurbished defense of slavery as a benign, protective institution. In wartime schoolbooks, children were instructed in the divinely inspired, paternalistic character of slavery. And the idea of the "faithful slave" was key to southerners' nationalist cause. A poem popular among whites captured an old slave's rejection of the Emancipation Proclamation:

Now, Massa, dis is berry fine, dese words
You've spoke to me,
No doubt you mean it kindly, but ole Dinah
Won't be free . . .
Ole Massa's berry good to me—and though I am
His slave,
He treats me like I'se kin to him—and I would
Rather have
A home in Massa's cabin, and eat his black
Bread too,
Dan leave ole Massa's children and go and
Lib wid you.

In the face of defeat and devastation, this and other forms of Confederate nationalism collapsed in the final year of the war. But much of the spirit and substance of Confederate nationalism would revive in the postwar period in a new racial ideology of the Lost Cause.

13-3c Southern Cities and Industry

Clerks and subordinate officials crowded the towns and cities where Confederate departments set up their offices. The sudden urban migration that resulted overwhelmed the housing supply and stimulated new construction. The pressure was especially great in Richmond, whose population increased 250 percent. Mobile's population jumped from 29,000 to 41,000; Atlanta, too, began to grow; and 10,000 people poured into war-related industries in little Selma, Alabama.

As the Union blockade disrupted imports of manufactured products, the traditionally agricultural South forged new industries. Many planters shared Davis's hope that industrialization would bring "deliverance, full and unrestricted, from all commercial dependence" on the North or the world. Indeed, beginning almost from scratch, the Confederacy achieved tremendous feats of industrial development. Chief of Ordnance Josiah Gorgas increased

the capacity of Richmond's Tredegar Iron Works and other factories to the point that by 1865, his Ordnance Bureau was supplying all Confederate small arms and ammunition. Meanwhile, the government constructed new railroad lines and ironworks, and much of the labor consisted of slaves relocated from farms and plantations.

13-3d Changing Roles of Women

White women, restricted to narrow roles in antebellum society, gained substantial new responsibilities in wartime. The wives and mothers of soldiers now headed households and performed men's work, including raising crops and tending animals. Women in nonslaveholding families cultivated fields themselves, while wealthier women suddenly had to perform as overseers and manage field work. In the cities, white women—who had been largely excluded from the labor force—found a limited number of respectable paying jobs, often in the Confederate bureaucracy, where some found clerks' jobs as "government girls." And female schoolteachers appeared in the South for the first time.

Women experienced both confidence and agony from their new responsibilities. Among them was Janie Smith, a young North Carolinian. Raised in a rural area by prosperous parents, she now faced grim realities as the war reached her farm and troops turned her home into a hospital. "It makes me shudder when I think of the awful sights I witnessed that morning," she wrote to a friend. "Ambulance after ambulance drove up with our wounded. . . . Under every shed and tree, the tables were carried for amputating the limbs. . . . The blood lay in puddles in the grove; the groans of the dying . . . were horrible." But Janie Smith learned to cope with crisis. She ended her account with the proud words, "I can dress amputated limbs now and do most anything in the way of nursing wounded soldiers."

Patriotic sacrifice appealed to some women, but others resented their new burdens. A Texas woman who had struggled to discipline slaves pronounced herself "sick of trying to do a man's business." Others grew angry over shortages, scornful of the war itself, and demanded that their men return to help provide for their families.

13-3e Human Suffering, Hoarding, and Inflation

For millions of ordinary southerners, the war brought privation and suffering. Mass poverty descended for the first time on a large minority of the white population. Many yeoman families had lost their breadwinners to the army. As a South Carolina newspaper put it, "The duties of war have called away from home the sole supports of many, many families. . . . Help must be given, or the poor will suffer." Women on their own sought help from relatives, neighbors, friends, anyone. Sometimes they pleaded their case to the Confederate government. "In the name of humanity," begged one woman, "discharge my husband he is not able to do your government much good and he might do his children some

▲ Five Texans in the Confederate cavalry sitting for a formal photograph. Four have the "lone star" on their hats. Like thousands of others, these men posed to send their image to the folks back home, but also perhaps as an act of comradeship at the war front.

good . . . my poor children have no home nor no Father." To the extent that the South eventually lost the will to fight in the face of defeat, women played a role in demanding an end to the war.

The South was in many places so sparsely populated that the conscription of one skilled craftsman could wreak hardship on the people of an entire county. Often, they begged in unison for the exemption or discharge of the local miller, or the neighborhood tanner or wheelwright. Physicians were also in short supply. Most serious, however, was the loss of a blacksmith. As a petition from Alabama explained, "Our Section of County [is] left entirely Destitute of any man that is able to keep in order any kind of Farming Tules."

The blockade of Confederate shipping created shortages of important supplies—salt, sugar, coffee, nails—and speculation and hoarding made the shortages worse. Greedy businessmen cornered the supply of some commodities; prosperous citizens stocked up on food. The *Richmond Enquirer* criticized a planter who purchased so many wagonloads of supplies that his "lawn and paths looked like a wharf covered with a ship's loads."

Inflation raged out of control, fueled by the Confederate government's heavy borrowing and inadequate taxes, until prices had increased almost 7,000 percent. Inflation particularly imperiled urban dwellers without their own sources of food. As early as 1862, newspapers reported that "want and starvation are staring thousands in the face," and troubled officials predicted that "women and children are bound to come to suffering if not starvation." A rudimentary relief program organized by the Confederacy failed to meet the need.

13-3f Inequities of the Confederate Draft

As their fortunes declined, people of once-modest means looked around and found abundant evidence that all classes were not sacrificing equally. The Confederate government enacted policies that decidedly favored the upper class. Until the last year of the war, for example, prosperous southerners could avoid military service by hiring substitutes. Prices for substitutes skyrocketed until it cost a man $5,000 or $6,000 to send someone to the front in his place. Well over fifty thousand upper-class southerners purchased such substitutes. Mary Boykin Chesnut knew of one young aristocrat who

Panhandle-Plains Historical Museum

"spent a fortune in substitutes. . . . He is at the end of his row now, for all able-bodied men are ordered to the front. I hear he is going as some general's courier."

Anger at such discrimination exploded in October 1862, when the Confederate Congress exempted from military duty anyone who was supervising at least twenty slaves. "Never did a law meet with more universal odium," observed one representative. "Its influence upon the poor is most calamitous." Protests poured in from every corner of the Confederacy, and North Carolina's legislators formally condemned the law. Its defenders argued, however, that the exemption preserved order and aided food production.

This "twenty Negro" law is indicative of the racial fears many Confederates felt as the war threatened to overturn southern society. But it also fueled desertion and stimulated new levels of overt Unionism in nonslaveholding regions of the South. In Jones County, Mississippi, an area of piney woods and few slaves or plantations, Newt Knight, a Confederate soldier, led a band of renegades who took over the county, declared their allegiance to the Union, and called their district the "Free State of Jones." They held out for the remainder of the war as an interracial enclave of independent Union sympathizers.

The bitterness of letters to Confederate officials suggests the depth of the dissension and class anger. "If I and my little children suffer [and] die while there Father is in service," threatened one woman, "I invoke God Almighty that our blood rest upon the South." War magnified existing social tensions in the Confederacy, and created a few new ones.

13-4 Wartime Northern Economy and Society

▶ What was the nature of the partnership between the Union government and businesses?

▶ How did the war affect labor relations and expectations?

▶ What role did women play in the Union war effort, on homefronts and warfronts?

With the onset of war, a tidal wave of change rolled over the North as well. Factories and citizens' associations geared up to support the war, and the federal government and its executive branch gained new powers. The energies of an industrializing society were harnessed to serve the cause of the Union. Idealism and greed flourished together, and the northern economy proved its awesome productivity.

13-4a Northern Business, Industry, and Agriculture

At first, the war was a shock to business. Northern firms lost their southern markets, and many companies had to change their products and find new customers. Southern debts became uncollectible, jeopardizing not only northern

merchants but also many western banks. Farm families struggled with a shortage of labor caused by army enlistments. A few enterprises never pulled out of the tailspin caused by the war. Cotton mills lacked cotton; construction declined; and shoe manufacturers sold few of the cheap shoes that planters had bought for their slaves. Those manufacturers that provided all manner of slave clothing and farm implements for the South had to diversify into other products.

Certain entrepreneurs, such as wool producers, benefited from shortages of competing products, and soaring demand for war-related goods swept some businesses to new success. To feed the hungry war machine, the federal government pumped unprecedented sums into the economy. The Treasury issued $3.2 billion in bonds and paper money called "greenbacks," and the War Department spent over $360 million in revenues from new taxes, including the nation's first income tax.

War-related spending revived business in many northern states. In 1863, a merchants' magazine examined the effects of the war in Massachusetts: "Seldom, if ever, has the business of Massachusetts been more active or profitable than during the past year. . . . In every department of labor the government has been, directly or indirectly, the chief employer and paymaster." Government contracts saved Massachusetts shoe manufacturers, as well as many firms in other states, from ruin.

The northern economy also grew because of a complementary relationship between agriculture and industry. Mechanization of agriculture had begun before the war. Wartime recruitment and conscription, however, gave western farmers an added incentive to purchase laborsaving machinery. The boom in the sale of agricultural tools was tremendous. Cyrus and William McCormick built an industrial empire in Chicago from the sale of their reapers. Between 1862 and 1864, the manufacture of mowers and reapers doubled to 70,000 yearly; by war's end, 375,000 reapers were in use, triple the number in 1861. Thus, northern farm families whose breadwinners went to war did not suffer as much as did their counterparts in the South. "We have seen," one magazine observed, "a stout matron whose sons are in the army, cutting hay with her team . . . and she cut seven acres with ease in a day, riding leisurely upon her cutter." Northern farms, generally not ravaged by foraging armies and devastation, thrived during wartime.

13-4b The Quartermaster and Military-Government Mobilization

This government-business marriage emerged from a greatly empowered Quartermaster Department, which as a bureaucracy grew to be the single largest employer in the United States, issuing thousands of manufacturing contracts to hundreds of firms. The 100,000 civilian employees of the Quartermaster Department labored throughout a network of procurement centers, especially in the cities of Washington, D.C., Philadelphia, New York, Cincinnati, and St. Louis.

A portion of Secretary of War Edwin M. Stanton's list of the weapons supplies alone needed by the Ordnance Department indicates the scope of the demand for government

▲ Despite initial problems, the task of supplying a vast war machine kept the northern economy humming. This photograph shows businesses on the west side of Hudson Street in New York City in 1865.

Lower Hudson Street, N.Y.C., 1865 (gelatin silver print)/American Photographer, (19th century)/NEW YORK HISTORICAL SOCIETY/© Collection of the New-York Historical Society, USA/Bridgeman Images

and business cooperation: "7,892 cannon, 11,787 artillery carriages, 4,022,130 small-arms, . . . 1,022,176,474 cartridges for small-arms, 1,220,555,435 percussion caps, . . . 26,440,054 pounds of gunpowder, . . . and 90,416,295 pounds of lead." In an unprecedented military mobilization, the government also purchased huge quantities of uniforms, boots, food, camp equipment, saddles, horses, ships, and other necessities. By 1865, the government had purchased some 640,000 horses and 300,000 mules at a cost well over $100 million.

Two-thirds of all U.S. war spending went to supply the forces in the field and, to command that process, President Lincoln appointed the talented West Point–trained engineer Montgomery Meigs. Meigs, whose experience included overseeing the building of the Capitol dome, insisted on issuing government contracts only with competitive bidding. He spent $1.8 billion of the public's money to wage the war, a figure larger than all previous U.S. government

expenditures since independence combined. His efforts, argued one historian, made the Union army "the best fed, most lavishly supplied army that had ever existed." Many historians consider Meigs the "unsung hero of Northern victory," a claim hard to deny, although he benefited from his corps of Quartermaster officers, who won the war one contract at a time. The success of such military mobilization left an indelible mark on American political-economic history and provided perhaps the oldest root of the modern American military-industrial state.

Nothing illustrated the wartime partnership between business and government better than the work of Jay Cooke, a wealthy New York financier. Cooke threw himself into the marketing of government bonds to finance the war effort. With imagination and energy, he convinced both large investors and ordinary citizens to invest enormous sums, in the process earning hefty commissions for himself. But the financier's profit served the Union cause, as the interests of capitalism and government successfully merged in American history's first era of "big government."

13-4c Northern Workers' Militancy

Northern industrial and urban workers did not fare as well as many of the companies for which they labored. After the initial slump, jobs became plentiful, but inflation ate up much of a worker's paycheck. The price of coffee had tripled; rice and sugar had doubled; and clothing, fuel, and rent had all climbed. Between 1860 and 1864, consumer prices rose at least 76 percent, while daily wages rose only 42 percent. Workers' families consequently suffered a substantial decline in their standard of living.

As their real wages shrank, industrial workers lost job security. To increase production, some employers replaced workers with laborsaving machines. Other employers urged the government to promote immigration to secure cheap labor. Workers responded by forming unions and sometimes by striking. Skilled craftsmen organized to combat the loss of their jobs and status to machines; women and unskilled workers, who were excluded by the craftsmen, formed their own unions. Indeed, thirteen occupational groups—including tailors, coal miners, and railway engineers—formed national unions during the Civil War, and the number of strikes climbed steadily.

Employers reacted with hostility to this new labor independence. Manufacturers viewed labor activism as a threat to their freedom of action and accordingly formed statewide or craft-based associations to cooperate and pool information. These employers shared blacklists of union members and required new workers to sign "yellow dog" contracts (promises not to join a union). To put down strikes, they hired strikebreakers, and sometimes used federal troops to break the unions' will.

Labor militancy, however, prevented employers neither from making profits nor from profiteering on government contracts. Unscrupulous businessmen took advantage of the suddenly immense demand for army supplies by selling clothing and blankets made of "shoddy"—wool fibers reclaimed from rags or worn cloth. Shoddy goods often came apart in the rain; most of the shoes purchased in the early months of the war were worthless. Contractors sold inferior guns for double the usual price and passed off tainted meat as good. Corruption was so widespread that it led to a yearlong investigation by the House of Representatives.

13-4d Economic Nationalism and Government-Business Partnership

Legitimate enterprises also made healthy profits. The output of woolen mills increased so dramatically that dividends in the industry nearly tripled. Some cotton mills made record profits on what they sold, even though they reduced their output. Brokerage houses worked until midnight and earned unheard-of commissions. Railroads carried immense quantities of freight and passengers, increasing their business to the point that railroad stocks skyrocketed in value.

Railroads were also a leading beneficiary of government largesse. With southern representatives absent from Congress, the northern route of the transcontinental railroad quickly prevailed. In 1862 and 1864, Congress chartered two corporations—the Union Pacific Railroad and the Central Pacific Railroad—and assisted them financially in connecting Omaha, Nebraska, with Sacramento, California. For each mile of track laid, the railroads received a loan of from $16,000 to $48,000 in government bonds plus 20 square miles of land along a free 400-foot-wide right of way. Overall, the two corporations gained approximately 20 million acres of land and nearly $60 million in loans. Railroad owners never decried government involvement in the economy.

Other businessmen benefited handsomely from the **Morrill Land Grant** Act (1862). To promote public education in agriculture, engineering, and military science, Congress granted each state thirty thousand acres of federal land for each of its congressional districts. The law eventually fostered sixty-nine colleges and universities as it also enriched a few prominent speculators. At the same time, the Homestead Act of 1862 offered cheap, and sometimes free, land to people who would settle the West and improve their property.

Before the war, adequate national banking, taxation, and currency did not exist. Banks operating under state charters issued no fewer than seven thousand different kinds of notes. During the war, Congress and the Treasury Department established a national banking system empowered to issue national bank notes and, by 1865, most state banks were forced by a prohibitive tax to join the national system. This process created sounder currency but also inflexibility in the money supply and an eastern-oriented financial structure that, later in the century, pushed farmers in need of credit and cash to revolt.

Republican economic policies expanded the scope of government and bonded people to the nation as never before. Yet ostentation coexisted with idealism. In the excitement of wartime moneymaking, an eagerness to display one's wealth flourished in the largest cities. *Harper's Monthly* reported that "the suddenly enriched contractors, speculators, and stock-jobbers ... are spending money with a profusion never before witnessed in our country.... The men button their waistcoats with diamonds ... and the women powder their hair with gold and silver dust." The *New York Herald* summarized that city's atmosphere: "This war has entirely changed the American character.... The individual who makes the most money—no matter how—and spends the most—no matter for what—is considered the greatest man."

13-4e The Union Cause

In thousands of self-governing towns and communities, northern citizens felt a personal connection to representative government. Secession threatened to destroy their system, and northerners rallied to its defense. In the first two years of the war, northern morale remained

Morrill Land Grant Act Law in which Congress granted land to states to establish colleges focusing on agriculture, engineering, and military science.

National Archives

▲ Union women's volunteer defense unit, ca. 1864. The soldiers' caps and muskets make this a rare image of women's lives on the home front during the Civil War.

remarkably high for a cause that today may seem abstract—the Union—but at the time meant the preservation of a social and political order that people cherished.

Secular and church leaders supported the cause, and even ministers who preferred to separate politics and pulpit denounced "the iniquity of causeless rebellion." Abolitionists campaigned to turn the war into a crusade against slavery. Free black communities and churches, both black and white, responded to the needs of slaves who flocked to the Union lines, sending clothing, ministers, and teachers to aid the freedpeople. Indeed, northern blacks gave wholehearted support to the war, volunteering by the thousands at first, despite the initial rejection they received from the Lincoln administration.

Thus, northern society embraced strangely contradictory tendencies. Materialism and greed flourished alongside idealism, religious conviction, and self-sacrifice. In decades to come, Americans would commemorate and build monuments to soldiers' sacrifice and idealism, not to opportunism and sometimes not even to the causes for which they fought, which provided a way of forgetting the deeper

U.S. Sanitary Commission Civilian organization in the North, staffed by large numbers of women, that was a major source of medical and nutritional aid for soldiers.

Clara Barton Nurse who worked for the Sanitary Commission and later founded the Red Cross.

nature of the conflict. But almost no one on the Northern side ever forgot the preservation of the Union, even as the larger society struggled mightily to face the legacies of emancipation and the beginnings of black equality.

13-4f Northern Women on Home Front and Battlefront

Northern women, like their southern counterparts, took on new roles. Those who stayed home organized over ten thousand soldiers' aid societies, rolled bandages, and raised $3 million to aid injured troops. Women were instrumental in pressing for the first trained ambulance corps in the Union army, and they formed the backbone of the **U.S. Sanitary Commission**, a civilian agency officially recognized by the War Department in 1861. The Sanitary Commission provided crucial nutritional and medical aid to soldiers. Although most of its officers were men, the bulk of the volunteers who ran its seven thousand auxiliaries were women. Women organized elaborate "Sanitary Fairs" to raise money and awareness for soldiers' health and hygiene.

Approximately thirty-two hundred women also served as nurses in frontline hospitals. Yet women had to fight for a chance to serve at all; the professionalization of medicine since the Revolution had created a medical system dominated by men, and many male physicians did not want women's aid. Even **Clara Barton**, famous for her persistence in working

Corbis Historical/Getty Images

▲ Nurse Anne Bell tending to wounded soldiers in a federal hospital, Nashville, Tennessee, ca. 1863. The distant gaze of the man on the left and the grateful gaze of the one on the right realistically represent the agonies of military hospitals.

in the worst hospitals at the front, was ousted from her post in 1863. But along with Barton, women such as the stern Dorothea Dix, well known for her efforts to reform asylums for the insane, and an Illinois widow, Mary Ann Bickerdyke, who served tirelessly in Sherman's army in the West, established a heroic tradition for Civil War nurses. They also advanced the professionalization of nursing, as several schools of nursing were established in northern cities during or after the war.

Women also wrote popular fiction about the war. In sentimental war poetry, short stories, and novels, and in printed war songs that reached thousands of readers, women produced a commercial literature in illustrated weeklies, monthly periodicals, and special "story papers." In many stories, female characters seek recognition for their loyalty and service to the Union, while others probe the suffering and death of loved ones at the front. One female writer, Louisa May Alcott, arrived at her job as a nurse in Washington, D.C., just after the horrific Union defeat at Fredericksburg, in December 1862. She later immortalized her experience in *Hospital Sketches* (1863), a popular book in which she described shattered men, "riddled with shot and shell," who had "borne suffering for which we have no name." Alcott provided northern readers a clear-eyed view of the hospitals in which so many of their loved ones agonized and perished.

At its heart, in what one historian has called a "feminized war literature," women writers explored the relationship between individual and national needs, between home and "the cause." And by 1863, many women found the liberation of slaves an inspiring subject, as did Julia Ward Howe in her immortal "Battle Hymn of the Republic":

> As He died to make men holy
> Let us die to make men free.

13-4g Walt Whitman's War

The poet **Walt Whitman** also left a record of his experiences as a volunteer nurse in Washington, D.C. As he dressed wounds and tried to comfort suffering and lonely men, Whitman found "the marrow of the tragedy concentrated in those Army Hospitals." But despite "indescribably horrid wounds," he also found inspiration in such suffering and a deepening faith in American democracy. Whitman celebrated the "incredible dauntlessness" and sacrifice of the common soldier who fought for the Union. As

Walt Whitman Well-known poet and author of *Leaves of Grass;* Whitman wrote about his experiences as a nurse and his renewed faith in democracy.

he had written in the preface to his great work *Leaves of Grass* (1855), "The genius of the United States is not best or most in its executives or legislatures, but always most in the common people." Whitman worked this idealization of the common man into his poetry, which also explored homoerotic themes and rejected the lofty meter and rhyme of European verse to strive for a "genuineness" that would appeal to the masses.

In "The Wound Dresser," Whitman meditated unforgettably on the deaths he had witnessed on both sides:

On, on I go, (open doors of time! open hospital doors!)
The crush'd head I dress, (poor crazed hand tear not the bandage away,)
The neck of the cavalry-man with the bullet through and through I examine,
Hard the breathing rattles, quite glazed already the eye, yet life struggles hard, (Come sweet death! be persuaded O beautiful death! In mercy come quickly.)

Whitman mused for millions in the war who suffered the death of a husband, brother, father, or friend. Indeed, the scale of death in this war shocked many Americans into believing that the conflict had to be for purposes larger than themselves.

13-5 The Advent of Emancipation

▶ **What was the relationship between Abraham Lincoln's personal views of, and official acts on, slavery?**

▶ **What competing views and policies emerged within the Union government on the issue of slavery?**

▶ **How was the Emancipation Proclamation both a legal and a moral document?**

▶ **How did African Americans seek to enact their own emancipation and advancement in society?**

Despite the sense of loyalty to cause that animated soldiers and civilians on both sides, the governments of the United States and the Confederacy lacked clarity about the purpose of the war. Throughout the first several months of the struggle, both Davis and Lincoln studiously avoided references to slavery. Davis realized that emphasis on the issue could increase class conflict in the South. To avoid identifying the Confederacy only with the interests of slaveholders, he articulated a broader, traditional ideology. Davis told southerners they were fighting for constitutional liberty: northerners had betrayed the founders' legacy, and southerners had seceded to preserve it. As long as Lincoln also avoided making slavery an issue, Davis's strategy seemed to work.

Lincoln had his own reasons for avoiding slavery. It was crucial at first not to antagonize the Union's border slave states, whose loyalty was tenuous. Also, for many months

Lincoln hoped that a pro-Union majority would assert itself in the South. It might be possible, he thought, to coax the South back into the Union and stop the fighting, short of what he later called "the result so fundamental and astounding"—emancipation. Raising the slavery issue would severely undermine both goals. Powerful political considerations also dictated Lincoln's reticence. The Republican Party was a young and unwieldy coalition. Some Republicans burned with moral outrage over slavery; others were frankly racist, dedicated to protecting free whites from the Slave Power and the competition of cheap slave labor. No Republican, or even northern, consensus on what to do about slavery existed early in the war.

13-5a Lincoln and Emancipation

The president's hesitancy ran counter to some of his personal feelings. Lincoln's compassion, humility, and moral anguish during the war were evident in his speeches and writings. But as a politician, Lincoln distinguished between his own moral convictions and his official acts. His political positions were studied and complex, calculated for maximum advantage.

Many black people attacked Lincoln furiously during the first year of the war for his refusal to convert the struggle into an "abolition war." When Lincoln countermanded General John C. Frémont's order of liberation for slaves owned by disloyal masters in Missouri in September 1861, the *Anglo-African* declared that the president, by his actions, "hurls back into the hell of slavery thousands . . . rightfully set free." As late as July 1862, Frederick Douglass condemned Lincoln as a "miserable tool of traitors and rebels," and characterized administration policy as reconstruction of "the old union on the old and corrupting basis of compromise, by which slavery shall retain all the power that it ever had." Douglass wanted the old Union destroyed and a new one created in the crucible of a war that would destroy slavery and rewrite the Constitution in the name of human equality. To the black leader's own amazement, within a year, just such a profound result began to take place.

Lincoln first broached the subject of slavery in a substantive way in March 1862, when he proposed that the states consider emancipation on their own. He asked Congress to promise aid to any state that decided to emancipate, appealing especially to border state representatives. What Lincoln proposed was gradual emancipation, with compensation for slaveholders and colonization of the freed slaves outside the United States. To a delegation of free blacks in August 1862, in perhaps his worst racial moment, he explained that "it is better for us both . . . to be separated."

Until well into 1864, Lincoln's administration promoted schemes to colonize black people in Central America or the Caribbean. Lincoln saw colonization as one option among others in dealing with the impending freedom of America's 4 million slaves. He was as yet unconvinced that America had any prospect as a biracial society, and he desperately feared that white northerners might not support a war for black freedom. Led by Frederick Douglass, black abolitionists vehemently opposed these machinations by the Lincoln administration.

▲ A group of "contrabands" (liberated slaves), photographed at Cumberland Landing, Virginia, May 14, 1862, at a sensitive point in the war when their legal status was still not fully determined. The faces and generations of the women, men, and children represent the human drama of emancipation.

Other politicians had much greater plans for a struggle against slavery. A group of Republicans in Congress, known as the **Radical Republicans** and led by men such as George Julian, Charles Sumner, and Thaddeus Stevens, dedicated themselves to a war for emancipation. They were instrumental in creating a special House–Senate committee on the conduct of the war, which investigated Union reverses, sought to make the war effort more efficient, and prodded the president to take stronger measures against slavery.

13-5b Confiscation Acts

In August 1861, at the Radicals' instigation, Congress passed its first confiscation act. Designed to punish the Confederates, the law confiscated all property used for "insurrectionary purposes." Thus, if the South used slaves in a hostile action, those slaves were seized and liberated as "contraband" of war. A second confiscation act (July 1862) went much further: it confiscated the property of anyone who supported the rebellion, even those who merely resided in the South and paid Confederate taxes. Their slaves were declared "forever free of their servitude." These acts stemmed from the logic that, in order to crush the southern rebellion, the government had to use extraordinary powers.

Although he signed the second confiscation act, Lincoln refused to adopt that view in the summer of 1862; he stood by his proposal of voluntary gradual emancipation by the states. His stance provoked a public protest from Horace Greeley, editor of the powerful *New York Tribune*. In an open letter to the president entitled "The Prayer of Twenty Millions,"

Greeley pleaded with Lincoln to "execute the laws" and declared, "On the face of this wide earth, Mr. President, there is not one . . . intelligent champion of the Union cause who does not feel that all attempts to put down the Rebellion and at the same time uphold its inciting cause are preposterous and futile." Lincoln's reply was an explicit statement of his calculated approach to the question. He disagreed, he said, with all those who would make slavery the paramount issue of the war. "I would save the Union," announced Lincoln. "If I could save the Union without freeing any slave I would do it, and if I could save it by freeing all the slaves I would do it; and if I could save it by freeing some and leaving others alone I would also do that. What I do about slavery, and the colored race, I do because I believe it helps to save the Union." Lincoln closed with a personal disclaimer: "I have here stated my purpose according to my view of official duty; and I intend no modification of my oft-expressed personal wish that all men everywhere could be free."

When he wrote those words, Lincoln had already decided to boldly issue a presidential **Emancipation Proclamation**. He was waiting, however, for a Union victory so that it would not appear to be an act of desperation. Yet the

Radical Republicans A group of Republicans who assailed President Lincoln early in the war for failing to make emancipation a war goal and, later, for making it too easy for defeated rebel states to return to the Union.

Emancipation Proclamation Lincoln's decree freeing all slaves in Confederate-held territories. It exempted border slave states that remained within the Union.

letter to Greeley represents Lincoln's concern with conditioning public opinion as best he could for the coming social revolution, and he needed to delicately consider international opinion as well.

13-5c Emancipation Proclamations

On September 22, 1862, shortly after Union success at the Battle of Antietam, Lincoln issued the first part of his two-part proclamation. Invoking his powers as commander-in-chief of the armed forces, he announced that on January 1, 1863, he would emancipate the slaves in the states "in rebellion." Lincoln made plain that he would judge a state to be in rebellion in January if it lacked legitimate representatives in the U.S. Congress. Thus, his September 1862 proclamation was less a declaration of the right of slaves to be free than a threat to southerners: unless they put down their arms and returned to Congress, they would lose their slaves. "Knowing the value that was set on the slaves by the rebels," said Garrison Frazier, a black Georgia minister, "the President thought that his proclamation would stimulate them to lay down their arms . . . and their not doing so has now made the freedom of the slaves a part of the war." Lincoln had little expectation that southerners would give up their effort, but he was determined to make them reply.

In the fateful January 1, 1863, proclamation, Lincoln declared that "all persons held as slaves" in areas in rebellion "shall be then, thenceforward, and forever free." But he excepted (as areas in rebellion) every Confederate county or city that had fallen under Union control. Those areas, he declared, "are, for the present, left precisely as if this proclamation were not issued." Nor did Lincoln liberate slaves in the border slave states that remained in the Union. "The President has purposely made the proclamation inoperative in all places where . . . the slaves [are] accessible," charged the anti-administration *New York World*. "He has proclaimed emancipation only where he has notoriously no power to execute it." Partisanship aside, even Secretary of State Seward said sarcastically, "We show our sympathy with slavery by emancipating slaves where we cannot reach them and holding them in bondage where we can set them free."

But Lincoln was worried about the constitutionality of his acts, and he anticipated that after the war southerners might sue in court for restoration of their "property." Making the liberation of the slaves "a fit and necessary war measure" raised a variety of legal questions: How long did a war measure remain in force? Did it expire with the suppression of a rebellion? The proclamation did little to clarify the status or citizenship of the freed slaves, although it did open the possibility of military service for blacks. How, indeed, would this change the character and purpose of the war? Just what kind of revolution would it launch?

Thus the Emancipation Proclamation was legally an ambiguous document. But as a moral and political document it had great meaning. Because the proclamation defined the war as a war against slavery, congressional Radicals could applaud it. Yet at the same time, it protected Lincoln's position with conservatives, leaving him room to retreat if he chose and forcing no immediate changes on the border slave states. It was a delicate balancing act, but one from which there was no turning back.

Most important, though, thousands of slaves had already reached Union lines in various sections of the South. They had "voted with their feet" for emancipation, as many said, well before the proclamation. And now, every advance of federal forces into slave society was a liberating step.

Across the North and in Union-occupied sections of the South, black people and their white allies celebrated the Emancipation Proclamation with unprecedented fervor. Full of praise songs, these celebrations demonstrated that, whatever the fine print of the proclamation, black folks knew they had lived to see a new day. At a large "contraband camp" in Washington, D.C., some six hundred black men, women, and children gathered at the superintendent's headquarters on New Year's Eve and sang through the night. In chorus after chorus of "Go Down, Moses" they announced the magnitude of their painful but beautiful exodus. One newly supplied verse concluded with "Go down, Abraham, away down in Dixie's land, tell Jeff Davis to let my people go!"

13-5d African American Recruits

The need for men soon convinced the administration to recruit northern and southern blacks for the Union army. By the spring of 1863, African American troops were answering the call of a dozen or more black recruiters barnstorming the cities and towns of the North. Lincoln came to see black soldiers as "the great available and yet unavailed of force for restoring the Union."

African American leaders hoped that military service would secure equal rights for their people. Once the black soldier had fought for the Union, wrote Frederick Douglass, "there is no power on earth which can deny that he has earned the right of citizenship in the United States." If black soldiers turned the tide, asked another man, "would the nation refuse us our rights?"

In June 1864, with thousands of black former slaves in blue uniforms, Lincoln gave his support to a constitutional ban on slavery. On the eve of the Republican national convention, Lincoln called on the party to "put into the platform as the keystone, the amendment of the Constitution abolishing and prohibiting slavery forever." The party promptly called for the **Thirteenth Amendment**. Republican delegates probably would have adopted such a plank without his urging, but Lincoln demonstrated his commitment by lobbying Congress for quick approval of the measure. The proposed amendment passed in early 1865 and was sent to the states for ratification. The war to save the Union had also become the war to free the slaves.

13-5e Who Freed the Slaves?

It has long been debated whether Abraham Lincoln deserved the label (one he never claimed for himself) of "Great Emancipator." Was Lincoln ultimately a reluctant emancipator,

Thirteenth Amendment
Ratified in December 1865, it permanently abolished slavery in all U.S. territories.

following rather than leading Congress and public opinion? Or did Lincoln give essential presidential leadership to the most transformative and sensitive aspect of the war by going slow on emancipation but, once moving, never backpedaling on black freedom? Once he had realized the total character of the war and decided to prosecute it to the unconditional surrender of the Confederates, Lincoln made the destruction of slavery central to the war's purpose.

Others have argued, however, that the slaves themselves are the central story in the achievement of their own freedom. When they were in proximity to the war zones or had opportunities as traveling laborers, slaves fled for their freedom by the thousands. Some worked as camp laborers for the Union armies, and eventually more than 180,000 black men served in the Union army and navy. Sometimes freedom came as a combination of confusion, fear, and joy in the rural hinterlands of the South. Some found freedom as individuals in 1861, and some not until 1865, as members of trains of refugees trekking great distances to reach contraband camps. And tragically, war always causes disease among large numbers of displaced people; thousands of freedmen died from exposure and illness in their quest for liberation.

However freedom came to individuals, emancipation was a historical confluence of two essential forces: one, a policy directed by and dependent on the military authority of the president in his effort to win the war; and the other, the will and courage necessary for acts of self-emancipation. Wallace Turnage's escape in Mobile Bay in 1864 demonstrates that emancipation could result from both a slave's own extraordinary heroism and the liberating actions of the Union forces. Most African Americans comprehended their freedom as both given and taken, but also as their human right. "I now dreaded the gun and handcuffs . . . no more," remembered Turnage of his liberation. "Nor the blowing of horns and running of hounds, nor the threats of death from rebels' authority." He was free in body and mind. "I could now speak my opinion," Turnage concluded, "to men of all grades and colors."

13-5f A Confederate Plan of Emancipation

Before the war was over, the Confederacy, too, addressed the issue of emancipation. Late in the war, Jefferson Davis himself was willing to sacrifice slavery to achieve independence. He proposed that the Confederate government purchase forty thousand slaves to work for the army as laborers, with a promise of freedom at the end of their service. Soon Davis upgraded the idea, calling for the recruitment and arming of slaves as soldiers, who likewise would gain their freedom at war's end. The wives and children of these soldiers, he made plain, must also receive freedom from the states. Davis and his advisers envisioned an "intermediate" status for ex-slaves of "serfage or peonage." Thus, at the bitter end, a few southerners were willing to sacrifice some of the racial, if not class, destiny for which they had launched their revolution.

Bitter debate over Davis's plan resounded through the Confederacy. When the Confederate Congress finally approved slave enlistments in March 1865, owners had to comply only on a "voluntary" basis. In sheer desperation for manpower, General Lee also supported the idea of slave soldiers. Against the reality all around them of slaves fleeing to Union lines, some southern leaders mistakenly hoped that they could still count on the "loyalty" of the South's bondsmen. Most Confederate slaveholders and editors vehemently opposed the enlistment plan; those who did support it acknowledged that the war had already freed some portion of the slave population. Their aim was to fight to a stalemate, achieve independence, and control the postwar racial order through their limited wartime emancipation schemes. It was too late. As a Mississippi planter wrote to his state's governor, the plan seemed "like a drowning man catching at straws."

By contrast, Lincoln's Emancipation Proclamation stimulated a vital infusion of forces into the Union armies. As both policy and process, emancipation had profound practical and moral implications for the new nation to be born out of the war.

13-6 The Soldiers' War

▶ **What motivated soldiers to fight in the Union army?**

▶ **What were the characteristics of camp life and combat for soldiers?**

▶ **How did the recruitment of African American soldiers change race relations in the Union army?**

The intricacies of policymaking and social revolutions were often far from the minds of most ordinary soldiers. Military service completely altered their lives. Enlistment took young men from their homes and submerged them in large organizations whose military discipline ignored their individuality. Army life meant tedium, physical hardship, and separation from loved ones. Yet the military experience had powerful attractions as well.

13-6a Ordinary Soldiers and Ideology

Most common soldiers, according to recent studies, were also committed to the ideological purposes of the war on both sides and not merely pawns caught up in a struggle they did not comprehend. The thousands of soldiers' letters, as well as regimental newspapers, indicate a deep awareness, if varying degrees of resolve, about slavery as the principal reason for the war.

The old idea that Civil War soldiers fought largely because of unit cohesion and the devotion of the men next to them is no longer an adequate explanation of why so many endured so much hardship for so long. Comradeship, duty, and honor were all powerful motivators for the men of the line. So were "union," "home," "the government," "freedom," "flag," "liberty," and "states' rights." But multitudes of literate soldiers left testimony of how much they saw slavery at the heart of the matter. In typical phrasing, members of the Thirteenth Wisconsin Infantry declared the conflict "a war of, by and for Slavery . . . as plain as the noon day sun." And their foes in Morgan's Confederate Brigade from Virginia agreed with different intentions: "any man who pretends to believe that this is not a war for the emancipation of the blacks . . . is either a fool or a liar."

13-6b Hospitals and Camp Life

The soldiers' lot was often misery. They benefited from certain new products, such as canned condensed milk, but blankets, clothing, and arms were often of poor quality. Hospitals were badly managed at first. Rules of hygiene in large camps were scarcely enforced; latrines were poorly made or carelessly used. One investigation turned up "an area of over three acres, encircling the camp as a broad belt, on which is deposited an almost perfect layer of human excrement." Water supplies were unsafe and typhoid epidemics common. About 57,000 men died from dysentery and diarrhea; in fact, 224,000 Union troops died from disease or accidents, far more than the 110,100 who died as a result of battle. Confederate troops were less well supplied, especially in the latter part of the war. Still, an extensive network of hospitals, aided by many white female volunteers and black female slaves, sprang up to aid the sick and wounded.

On both sides, troops quickly learned that soldiering was far from glorious. "The dirt of a camp life knocks all its poetry into a cocked hat," wrote a North Carolina volunteer in 1862. One year later, he marveled at his earlier innocence. Fighting had taught him "the realities of a soldier's life. We had no tents after the 6th of August, but slept on the ground, in the woods or open fields. . . . I learned to eat fat bacon raw, and to like it. . . . Without time to wash our clothes or our persons . . . the whole army became lousy more or less with body lice."

Few had seen violent death before, but war soon exposed them to the blasted bodies of their friends and comrades. "Any one who goes over a battlefield after a battle," wrote one Confederate, "never cares to go over another. . . . It is a sad sight to see the dead and if possible more sad to see the wounded—shot in every possible way you can imagine." Many men died gallantly; there were innumerable striking displays of courage. But often soldiers gave up their lives in mass sacrifice, in tactics that made little sense.

Still, Civil War soldiers developed deep commitments to each other and to their task. As campaigns dragged on, many soldiers grew determined to see the struggle through. "We now, like true Soldiers go determined not to yield one inch," wrote a New York corporal. When at last the war was over, "it seemed like breaking up a family to separate," one man observed. Another admitted, "We shook hands all around, and laughed and seemed to make merry, while our hearts were heavy and our eyes ready to shed tears."

13-6c The Rifled Musket

Advances in technology made the Civil War particularly deadly. By far the most important were the rifle and the "minie ball." Bullets fired from a smoothbore musket tumbled and wobbled as they flew through the air, and thus were not accurate at distances over eighty yards. Cutting spiraled grooves inside the barrel gave the projectile a spin and much greater accuracy, but rifles remained difficult to load and use until Frenchman Claude Minie and American James Burton developed a new kind of bullet. Civil War bullets were lead slugs with a cavity at the bottom that expanded on firing so that the bullet "took" the rifling and flew accurately. With these bullets, rifles were deadly at four hundred yards.

This meant, of course, that soldiers assaulting a position defended by riflemen were in greater peril than ever before; the defense thus gained a significant advantage. While artillery now fired from a safe distance, there was no substitute for the infantry assault or the popular turning movements aimed at an enemy's flank. Thus, advancing soldiers had to expose themselves repeatedly to accurate rifle fire. Because medical knowledge was rudimentary, even minor wounds often led to amputation and death through infection. Never before in Europe or America had such massive forces pummeled each other with weapons of such destructive power. As losses mounted, many citizens wondered at what Union soldier (and future Supreme Court justice) Oliver Wendell Holmes Jr. called "the butcher's bill."

13-6d The Black Soldier's Fight for Manhood

At the outset of the war, most white soldiers wanted nothing to do with black people and regarded them as inferior. "I never came out here for to free the black devils," wrote one soldier, and another objected to fighting beside African Americans because "[w]e are a too superior race for that." For many, acceptance of black troops grew only because they could do heavy labor and "stop Bullets as well as white people." A popular song celebrated "Sambo's Right to Be Kilt" as the only justification for black enlistments.

But among some, a change occurred. While recruiting black troops in Virginia in late 1864, Massachusetts soldier Charles Brewster sometimes denigrated the very men he sought to enlist. But he was delighted at the sight of a black cavalry unit because it made the local "secesh" furious, and he praised black soldiers who "fought nobly" and filled hospitals with "their wounded and mangled bodies." White officers who volunteered to lead segregated black units only to gain promotion found that experience altered their opinions. After just one month with black troops, a white captain informed his wife, "I have a more elevated opinion of their abilities than I ever had before. I know that many of them are vastly the superiors of those . . . who would condemn them all to a life of brutal degradation." One general reported that his "colored regiments" possessed "remarkable aptitude for military training."

Black troops created this change through their own dedication. They had a mission to destroy slavery and demonstrate their equality. "When Rebellion is crushed," wrote a black volunteer from Connecticut, "who will be more proud than I to say, I was one of the first of the despised race to leave the free North with a rifle on my shoulder, and give the lie to the old story that the black man will not fight." Corporal James Henry Gooding of Massachusetts's black Fifty-fourth Regiment explained that his unit intended "to live down all prejudice against its color, by a determination to do well in any position it is put." After an engagement, he was proud that "a regiment of white men gave us three cheers as we were passing them" because "it shows that we did our duty as men should."

Black Soldiers in the Civil War

The image below is of the storming of Fort Wagner in July 1863 by the Fifty-fourth Massachusetts regiment, in Charleston, South Carolina, by Chicago printmakers Kurtz and Allison. Kurtz and Allison issued vivid and colorful chromolithographs in the 1880s, celebrating the military valor of African Americans. This scene depicts the most famous combat action of black troops in the Civil War; the Fifty-fourth was the first northern-recruited black unit, and their bravery and sacrifice served as a measure of African American devotion to the Union cause. At left is the Robert Gould Shaw memorial commemorating the Fifty-fourth Massachusetts Regiment.

CRITICAL THINKING

- Why was this regiment such a symbolic test case for the military ability and political meaning of black soldiers in the Civil War?
- Why did black men have to die on battlefields for many Americans in the Civil War era to consider them fully men and citizens?

STORMING FORT WAGNER

Library of Congress Prints and Photographs Division[LC-DIG-pga-01949]

▲ The image is of the storming of Fort Wagner in July 1863 by the Fifty-fourth Massachusetts regiment, in Charleston, South Carolina, by Chicago printmakers Kurtz and Allison. Kurtz and Allison issued vivid and colorful chromolithographs in the 1880s, celebrating the military valor of African Americans. This scene depicts the most famous combat action of black troops in the Civil War; the Fifty-fourth was the first northern-recruited black unit, and their bravery and sacrifice served as a measure of African American devotion to the Union cause.

Jerry L. Thompson / Art Resource, NY

▲ Robert Gould Shaw Memorial, Boston Common, by Augustus Saint Gaudens, unveiled in 1897, and considered his Civil War masterpiece. Depicts the march of the Fifty-fourth Massachusetts black regiment when then departed for war in May, 1863.

Through such experience under fire, the blacks and whites of the Fifty-fourth Massachusetts forged deep bonds. Just before the regiment launched its costly assault on Fort Wagner in Charleston harbor, in July 1863, a black soldier called out to abolitionist Colonel Robert Gould Shaw, who would perish that day, "Colonel, I will stay by you till I die." "And he kept his word," noted a survivor of the attack. "He has never been seen since." Indeed, the heroic assault on Fort Wagner was celebrated for demonstrating the valor of black men. This bloody chapter in the history of American racism proved many things, not least of which was that black men had to die in battle to be acknowledged as men.

Such valor emerged despite persistent discrimination. The Union government paid white privates $13 per month plus a clothing allowance of $3.50, whereas black privates earned only $10 per month less $3 for clothing. Outraged by this injustice, several regiments refused to accept any pay whatsoever, and Congress eventually remedied the inequity. In this instance at least, the majority of legislators agreed with a white private that black troops had "proved their title to manhood on many a bloody field fighting freedom's battles."

13-7 1863: The Tide of Battle Turns

▶ Why were Vicksburg and Gettysburg significant defeats for the Confederacy, and therefore turning points in the war?

▶ Despite major Union victories during 1863, why or how could the Confederacy still have won the war in their terms during the following year?

The fighting in the spring and summer of 1863 did not settle the war, but it began to suggest the outcome as it provided bloody turning-points. The campaigns began in a deceptively positive way for Confederates, as Lee's army performed brilliantly in battles in central Virginia.

13-7a Battle of Chancellorsville

For once, a large Civil War army was not slow and cumbersome, but executed tactics with speed and precision. On May 2 and 3, west of Fredericksburg, Virginia, some 130,000 members of the Union Army of the Potomac bore down on fewer than 60,000 Confederates. Boldly, Lee and Stonewall Jackson divided their forces, ordering 30,000 men under Jackson on a daylong march westward to prepare a flank attack.

This classic turning movement was carried out in the face of great numerical disadvantage. Arriving at their position late in the afternoon, Jackson's seasoned "foot cavalry" found unprepared Union troops laughing, smoking, and playing cards. The Union soldiers had no idea they were under attack until frightened deer and rabbits bounded out of the forest, followed by gray-clad troops. The Confederate attack drove the entire right side of the Union army back in confusion. Eager to press his advantage, Jackson rode forward with a few officers to study the ground. As they returned at twilight, southern troops mistook them for federals and fired, fatally wounding their commander. The next day, Union forces left in defeat. Chancellorsville was a remarkable southern victory, but costly because of the loss of Stonewall Jackson, who would forever remain a legend in Confederate memory.

13-7b Siege of Vicksburg

July brought crushing defeats for the Confederacy in two critical battles that severely damaged Confederate hopes for independence. One of these battles occurred at **Vicksburg**, Mississippi. Vicksburg was a vital western citadel, the last major fortification on the Mississippi River in southern hands (see Map 13.2). After months of searching through swamps and bayous, General Ulysses S. Grant found an advantageous approach to the city. He laid siege to Vicksburg in May, bottling up the defending army of General John Pemberton. If Vicksburg fell, Union forces would control the river, cutting the Confederacy in two and gaining an open path into its interior. To stave off such a result, Jefferson Davis gave command of all other forces in the area to General Joseph E. Johnston and beseeched him to go to Pemberton's aid. Meanwhile, at a council of war in Richmond, General Robert E. Lee proposed a Confederate invasion of the North. Although such an offensive would not relieve Vicksburg directly, it could stun and dismay the North and, if successful, possibly even lead to peace. By invading the North a second time, Lee hoped to take the war out of war-weary Virginia, garner civilian support in Maryland, win a major victory on northern soil, threaten major cities, and thereby force a Union capitulation on his terms.

As Lee's emboldened army advanced through western Maryland and into Pennsylvania, Confederate prospects to the south along the Mississippi darkened. Davis repeatedly wired General Johnston, urging him to concentrate his forces and attack Grant's army. Johnston, however, did little, telegraphing back: "I consider saving Vicksburg hopeless." Grant's men, meanwhile, were supplying themselves from the abundant crops of the Mississippi River valley and could continue their siege indefinitely.

13-7c Battle of Gettysburg

In such circumstances, the fall of Vicksburg was inevitable, and on July 4, 1863, its commander surrendered. The same day, the other battle, which had been raging for three days, concluded at **Gettysburg**, Pennsylvania (see Map 13.4). On July 1, Confederate forces hunting for a supply of shoes had collided with part of the Union army. Heavy fighting on the second day over two steep hills left federal forces in possession

Vicksburg Union victory that gave the North complete control of the Mississippi River.

Gettysburg Union victory that halted the Confederate invasion of Pennsylvania; turning point in the war in the East.

Map 13.4 Battle of Gettysburg

In the war's greatest battle, fought around a small market town in southern Pennsylvania, Lee's invasion of the North was repulsed. Union forces had the advantage of the high ground, shorter lines, and superior numbers. The casualties for the two armies—dead, wounded, and missing—exceeded 50,000 men.

of high ground along Cemetery Ridge, running more than a mile south of the town. There, they enjoyed the protection of a stone wall and a clear view of their foe across almost a mile of open field.

Undaunted, Lee believed his reinforced troops could break the Union line and, on July 3, he ordered a direct assault. Full of foreboding, General James Longstreet warned Lee that "no 15,000 men ever arrayed for battle can take that position." But Lee stuck to his plan. Virginians under General George E. Pickett and North Carolinians under General James Pettigrew methodically marched up the slope in a doomed assault known as Pickett's Charge. For a moment, a few hundred Confederates breached the enemy's line, but most fell in heavy slaughter. On July 4, Lee had to withdraw, having suffered almost 4,000 dead and about 24,000 missing

and wounded. The Confederate general reported to President Davis that "I am alone to blame" and offered to resign. Davis replied that to find a more capable commander was "an impossibility." The Confederacy had reached what many consider its "high-water mark" on that ridge at Gettysburg.

Southern troops displayed unforgettable courage and dedication at Gettysburg, and under General George G. Meade, the Union army, which suffered 23,000 casualties (nearly one-quarter of the force), exhibited the same bravery in stopping the Confederate invasion. But the results there and at Vicksburg were disastrous for the South. The Confederacy was split in two; west of the Mississippi, General E. Kirby Smith had to operate on his own, virtually independent of Richmond. Moreover, the heartland of Louisiana, Tennessee, and Mississippi lay exposed to invasion. Far to the north, Lee's defeat spelled the end of major southern offensive actions. By refusing to give up, and by wearing down northern morale while fighting defensively, the South might yet win, but its prospects were darker than before.

13-8 Disunity: South, North, and West

▶ How did internal stresses and external pressures contribute to disaffection and defeat in the Confederacy?

▶ How did the Confederacy disintegrate internally over the course of the war?

▶ How did Northerners demonstrate their disaffection with the government and opposition to the war?

▶ What was the significance of the election of 1864?

Both northern and southern governments waged the final two years of the war in the face of increasing opposition at home. Dissatisfactions that had surfaced earlier grew more intense and sometimes violent. The gigantic costs of a civil war that neither side seemed able to win fed the unrest. But protest also arose from fundamental stresses in the social structures of North and South.

13-8a Union Occupation Zones

Wherever Union forces invaded, they imposed a military occupation consisting roughly of three zones: garrisoned towns, with large numbers of troops in control of civilian and economic life; the Confederate frontier, areas still under southern control but also with some federal military penetration; and "no man's land," the land between the two armies, beyond Confederate authority and under frequent Union patrols.

As many as one hundred southern towns were garrisoned during the war, causing severe disruption to the social landscape. Large regions of Tennessee, Virginia, Louisiana, Mississippi, and Georgia fell under this pattern of occupation and suffered food shortages, crop and property destruction, disease, roadway banditry, guerrilla warfare, summary executions, and the random flow of escaped slaves. After two years of occupation, a southern white woman wrote to a kinsman about their native Clarksville, Tennessee. "You would scarcely know the place," she lamented, "it is nothing but a dirty hole filled . . . with niggers and Yankees."

13-8b Disintegration of Confederate Unity

Vastly disadvantaged in industrial capacity, natural resources, and labor, southerners felt the cost of the war more directly and more painfully than northerners. But even more fundamental were the Confederacy's internal problems; the southern class system threatened the Confederate cause.

One ominous development was the planters' increasing opposition to their own government. Along with new taxation, Confederate military authorities also impressed slaves to build fortifications. And when Union forces advanced on plantation areas, Confederate commanders burned stores of cotton that lay in the enemy's path. Many planters bitterly complained about such interference with their interests.

The Confederate constitution had granted substantial powers to the central government, especially in time of war. But many planters took the position articulated by R. B. Rhett, editor of the *Charleston Mercury*, that the Confederate constitution "leaves the States untouched in their Sovereignty, and commits to the Confederate Government only a few simple objects, and a few simple powers to enforce them." Governor Joseph E. Brown of Georgia took a similar states' rights position, occasionally prohibiting supplies and that state's soldiers from leaving its borders.

Years of opposition to the federal government within the Union had frozen southerners in a defensive posture. Now they erected the barrier of states' rights as a defense against change, hiding behind it while their capacity for creative statesmanship atrophied. As secession revolutionized their world and hard war took so many lives, some could never fully commit to the cause.

Confused and embittered planters struck out at Jefferson Davis. Conscription, thundered Governor Brown, was "subversive of [Georgia's] sovereignty, and at war with all the principles for the support of which Georgia entered into this revolution." Searching for ways to frustrate the law, Brown ordered local enrollment officials not to cooperate with the Confederacy. The *Charleston Mercury* told readers that "conscription . . . is . . . the very embodiment of Lincolnism, which our gallant armies are today fighting." In a gesture of stubborn selfishness, Robert Toombs of Georgia, a former U.S. senator, refused to switch from cotton to food crops, defying the wishes of the government, the newspapers, and his neighbors' petitions.

13-8c Food Riots in Southern Cities

Meanwhile, for ordinary southerners, the dire predictions of hunger and suffering were becoming a reality. Food riots occurred in the spring of 1863 in Atlanta, Macon, Columbus, and Augusta, Georgia, and in Salisbury and High Point, North Carolina. On April 2, a crowd assembled in Richmond to demand relief. A passerby, noticing the excitement, asked a young girl, "Is there some celebration?" "We celebrate our right to live," replied the girl. "We are starving. As soon as enough of us get together we are going to the bakeries and each of us will take a loaf of bread." Soon they did just that, sparking a riot that Davis ordered quelled at gunpoint.

Throughout the rural South, ordinary people resisted more quietly—by refusing to cooperate with conscription, tax collection, and impressments of food. "In all the States impressments are evaded by every means which ingenuity can suggest, and in some openly resisted," wrote a commissary officer. Farmers who did provide food for the army refused to accept payment in certificates of credit or government bonds, as required by law. Conscription officers increasingly found no one to draft. "The disposition to avoid military service is general," observed one of Georgia's senators in 1864. In some areas, tax agents were killed in the line of duty.

Jefferson Davis was ill equipped to deal with such discontent. Austere and private by nature, he failed to communicate with the masses. His class perspective also distanced him from the sufferings of the common people. While his social circle in Richmond dined on duck and oysters, ordinary southerners recovered salt from the drippings on their smokehouse floors and went hungry.

13-8d Desertions from the Confederate Army

Such discontent was certain to affect the Confederate armies. "What man is there that would stay in the army and no that his family is sufring at home?" an angry citizen wrote anonymously to the secretary of war. Worried about their loved ones and resentful of what they saw as a rich man's war, large numbers of men did indeed leave the armies. Their friends and neighbors gave them support. Mary Chesnut observed a man being dragged back to the army as his wife looked on. "Desert agin, Jake!" she cried openly. "You desert agin, quick as you kin. Come back to your wife and children."

Desertion did not become a serious problem for the Confederacy until mid-1862, and stiffer policing solved the problem that year. But from 1863 on, the number of men on duty fell rapidly. By mid-1863, John A. Campbell, the South's assistant secretary of war, wondered whether "so general a habit" as desertion could be considered a crime. Campbell estimated that 40,000 to 50,000 troops were absent without leave and that 100,000 were evading duty in some way. Furloughs, amnesty proclamations, and appeals to return had little effect; by November 1863, Secretary of War James Seddon admitted that one-third of the army could not be accounted for.

The defeats at Gettysburg and Vicksburg dealt a heavy blow to Confederate morale. When the news reached Josiah Gorgas, the genius of Confederate ordnance operations, he confided to his diary, "Today absolute ruin seems our portion. The Confederacy totters to its destruction." In desperation, President Davis and several state governors resorted to threats and racial scare tactics to drive southern whites to further sacrifice. Defeat, Davis warned, would mean "extermination of yourselves, your wives, and children." Governor Charles Clark of Mississippi predicted "elevation of the black race to a position of equality—aye, of superiority, that will make them your masters and rulers." Confederate leaders knew they were facing an apocalyptic revolution in the world as they had known it.

From this point on, the internal disintegration of the Confederacy quickened. Confederate leaders began to realize they were losing the support of the common people. It is, indeed, remarkable how long and how effectively the Confederacy sustained a military effort in the face of such internal division.

13-8e Antiwar Sentiment, South and North

In North Carolina, a peace movement grew under the leadership of William W. Holden, a popular Democratic politician and editor. He and his followers convened over one hundred public meetings in support of peace negotiations, which took place during the summer of 1863. In Georgia early in 1864, Governor Brown and Alexander H. Stephens, vice president of the Confederacy, led a similar effort. Ultimately, however, these movements came to naught. The lack of a two-party system threw into question the legitimacy of any criticism of the government; even Holden and Brown could not entirely escape the taint of dishonor and disloyalty.

The results of the 1863 congressional elections strengthened dissent in the Confederacy. Everywhere, secessionists and supporters of the administration lost seats to men not identified with the government. In the last years of the war, Davis's support in the Confederate Congress dwindled. Some newspaper editors and a core of courageous, determined soldiers, especially in Lee's Army of Northern Virginia, kept the Confederacy alive in spite of disintegrating popular support.

By 1864, much of the opposition to the war had moved entirely outside the political sphere. Southerners were simply giving up the struggle. Deserters dominated some whole towns and counties. Active dissent was particularly common in upland and mountain regions, where support for the Union had always been genuine. "The condition of things in the mountain districts of North Carolina, South Carolina, Georgia, and Alabama," admitted Assistant Secretary of War Campbell, "menaces the existence of the Confederacy as fatally as either of the armies of the United States."

Opposition to the war, though less severe, existed in the North as well. Alarm intensified over the growing centralization of government and, by 1863, war weariness was widespread. Resentment of the draft sparked protest, especially among poor citizens, and the Union army, too, struggled with a troubling desertion rate. But the Union was so much richer than the South in human resources that none of these problems ever threatened the effectiveness of the government.

Moreover, Lincoln possessed a talent that Davis lacked: he knew how to stay in touch with the ordinary citizen. Through public letters to newspapers and private ones to soldiers' families, he reached the common people. The battlefield carnage, the tortuous political problems, and the ceaseless criticism weighed heavily on him, but his administration never lost control of the federal war effort.

13-8f Peace Democrats

Much of the wartime protest in the North was political in origin. The Democratic Party fought to regain power by blaming Lincoln for the war's death toll, the expansion of federal powers, inflation and the high tariff, and the emancipation of blacks. Appealing to tradition, its leaders called for an end to the war and reunion on the basis of "the Constitution as it is and the Union as it was." The Democrats denounced conscription and martial law and defended states' rights. They charged repeatedly that Republican policies were designed to flood the North with blacks, threatening white men's privileges. In the 1862 congressional elections, the Democrats made a strong comeback, with peace Democrats wielding influence in New York State and majorities in the legislatures of Illinois and Indiana.

Led by outspoken men like Representative Clement L. Vallandigham of Ohio, the peace Democrats became highly visible. Vallandigham criticized Lincoln as a "dictator" who had suspended the writ of habeas corpus without congressional authority, arrested thousands of innocent citizens, and shut down opposition newspapers (which was true). He condemned both conscription and emancipation, and urged voters to use their power at the polls to depose "King Abraham." Vallandigham stayed carefully within legal bounds, but his attacks seemed so damaging to the war effort that military authorities arrested him for treason. Lincoln wisely decided against punishment—and martyr's status—for the Ohioan and exiled him to the Confederacy. Vallandigham eventually returned to the North through Canada.

Some antiwar Democrats did encourage draft resistance, discourage enlistment, sabotage communications, and generally plot to aid the Confederacy. Likening such groups to a poisonous snake, Republicans sometimes branded them—and by extension the peace Democrats—as **"Copperheads"**. Although some Confederate agents were active in the North and Canada, they never genuinely threatened the Union war effort and their suppression remains a vexing legal legacy.

13-8g New York City Draft Riots

More violent opposition to the government arose from ordinary citizens facing the draft, which became law in 1863. Although many soldiers risked their lives willingly out of a desire to preserve the Union or extend freedom, others openly sought to avoid service.

The urban poor and immigrants in strongly Democratic areas were especially hostile to conscription. Federal enrolling officers made up the lists of eligibles, a procedure open to personal favoritism and

"Copperheads" Poisonous snakes; also the Republican nickname for antiwar northern Democrats. Some were pacifists, while others were activists who encouraged draft resistance, sabotage, and efforts to aid the Confederacy.

prejudice. The North's poor viewed the system as discriminatory, and many immigrants suspected (wrongly, on the whole) that they were called in disproportionate numbers. (Approximately 200,000 men born in Germany and 150,000 born in Ireland served in the Union army.)

As a result, there were scores of disturbances. Enrolling officers received rough treatment in many parts of the North, and riots occurred in New Jersey, Ohio, Indiana, Pennsylvania, Illinois, and Wisconsin. By far the most serious outbreak of violence occurred in New York City in July 1863. The war was unpopular in that Democratic stronghold, and racial, ethnic, and class tensions ran high. Shippers had recently broken a longshoremen's strike by hiring black strikebreakers to work under police protection. Working-class New Yorkers feared an inflow of black labor from the South and regarded blacks as the cause of the war. Poor Irish workers resented being forced to serve in the place of others who could afford to avoid the draft by paying a substitute.

Military police officers came under attack first, and then mobs crying, "Down with the rich" looted wealthy homes and stores. But blacks became the special target. The mob rampaged through African American neighborhoods, beating and murdering people in the streets, and burning an orphan asylum. At least seventy-four people died in the violence, which raged out of control for three days. Only the dispatch of army units directly from Gettysburg ended this tragic episode of racism and class resentment.

13-8h War Against Native Americans in the Far West

East and West, over race, land, and culture, America was a deeply divided country. A civil war of another kind raged on the Great Plains and in the Southwest. By 1864, U.S. troops under the command of Colonel John Chivington waged full-scale war against the Sioux, Arapaho, and Cheyenne in order to eradicate Native peoples' title to all of eastern Colorado. Native American chiefs sought peace, but American commanders had orders to "burn villages and kill Cheyennes whenever and wherever found." A Cheyenne chief, Lean Bear, was shot from his horse as he rode toward U.S. troops, holding in his hand papers given him by President Lincoln during a visit to Washington, D.C. Another chief, Black Kettle, was told by the U.S. command that, by moving his people to Sand Creek, Colorado, they would find a safe haven. But on

THE RIOTS IN NEW YORK : DESTRUCTION OF THE COLOURED ORPHAN ASYLUM.

▲ A contemporary wood engraving of the destruction of the Colored Orphan Asylum during the New York City draft riots, July 13–16, 1863.

The Granger Collection, NYC

November 29, 1864, 700 cavalrymen, many drunk, attacked the Cheyenne village. With most of the men absent hunting, the slaughter included 105 Cheyenne women and children and 28 men. American soldiers scalped and mutilated their victims, carrying women's body parts on their saddles or hats back to Denver. The Sand Creek Massacre, and the retaliation against white ranches and stagecoaches by Native peoples in 1865, would live in western historical memory forever.

In New Mexico and Arizona Territories, an authoritarian and brutal commander, General James Carleton, waged war on the Apaches and the Navajos. Both tribes had engaged for generations in raiding the Pueblo and Hispanic peoples of the region to maintain their security and economy. During the Civil War years, Anglo-American farms also became Indian targets. In 1863, the New Mexico Volunteers, commanded in the field by former mountain man Kit Carson, defeated the Mescalero Apaches and forced them onto a reservation at Bosque Redondo in the Pecos River valley.

But the Navajos, who lived in a vast region of canyons and high deserts, resisted. In a "scorched earth" campaign, Carson destroyed the Navajos' livestock, orchards, and crops. On the run, starving and demoralized, the Navajos began to surrender for food in January 1864. Three-quarters of the twelve thousand Navajos were rounded up and forced to march 400 miles (the "Long Walk") to the Bosque Redondo Reservation, suffering malnutrition and death along the way. When General William T. Sherman visited the reservation in 1868, he found the Navajos "sunk into a condition of absolute poverty and despair." Permitted to return to a fraction of their homelands later that year, the Navajos carried with them searing memories of the federal government's ruthless policies of both removal and eradication of Native peoples. The Civil War was thus a harbinger of the more sweeping Indian Wars in the West to follow in the 1870s and 1880s.

13-8i Election of 1864

Back east, war weariness reached a peak in the summer of 1864, when the Democratic Party nominated the popular general George B. McClellan for president and inserted a peace plank into its platform. The plank, written by Vallandigham, called for an armistice and spoke vaguely about preserving the Union. The Democrats made racist appeals to white insecurity, calling Lincoln "Abe the nigger-lover" and "Abe the widow-maker." Lincoln concluded that it was "exceedingly probable that this Administration will not be reelected." No incumbent president had been reelected since 1832, and no nation had ever held a general election in the midst of all-out civil war. Some Republicans worked to dump Lincoln from their ticket in favor of either Salmon P. Chase or John C. Frémont, although little came of either effort. The Republican Party, declaring itself for "unconditional surrender" of the Confederacy and a constitutional amendment abolishing slavery, had to contend with the horrible casualty lists and the battlefield stalemate of the summer of 1864.

The fortunes of war soon changed the electoral situation. With the fall of Atlanta and Union victories in the Shenandoah Valley by early September, Lincoln's prospects rose. Decisive in the election was that eighteen states allowed troops to vote at the front; Lincoln won an extraordinary 78 percent of the soldier vote. In taking 55 percent of the total popular vote, Lincoln's reelection—a referendum on the war and emancipation—had a devastating impact on southern morale. Without such a political outcome in 1864, a Union military victory and a redefined nation might never have been possible.

13-9 1864–1865: The Final Test of Wills

▶ What role did foreign diplomacy play in the direction of the war?

▶ How did Ulysses S. Grant and William T. Sherman institute "total war" in the South in the last year of the war?

▶ What were the human and financial costs of the Civil War?

During the final year of the war, the Confederates could still have won their version of victory if military stalemate and northern antiwar sentiment had forced a negotiated settlement. But events and northern determination prevailed, as Americans endured the bloodiest nightmare in their history.

13-9a Northern Diplomatic Strategy

The North's long-term diplomatic strategy succeeded in 1864. From the outset, the North had pursued one paramount goal: to prevent recognition of the Confederacy by European nations. Foreign recognition would belie Lincoln's claim that the United States was fighting an illegal rebellion and would open the way to the financial and military aid that could ensure Confederate independence. Both England and France stood to benefit from a divided and weakened America. Thus, to achieve their goal, Lincoln and Secretary of State Seward needed to avoid both serious military defeats and controversies with the European powers.

Aware that the textile industry employed one-fifth of the British population directly or indirectly, southerners banked on British recognition of the Confederacy. But at the beginning of the war, British mills had a 50 percent surplus of cotton on hand, and they later found new sources of supply in India, Egypt, and Brazil. And throughout the war, some southern cotton continued to reach Europe, despite the Confederacy's embargo on cotton production, an ill-fated policy aimed at securing British support. The British government flirted with recognition of the Confederacy but awaited battlefield demonstrations of southern success. France, though sympathetic to the South, was unwilling to act independently of Britain. Confederate agents managed to purchase valuable arms and supplies in Europe and obtained loans from European financiers, but they never achieved a diplomatic breakthrough.

More than once, the Union strategy nearly broke down. An acute crisis occurred in 1861 when the overzealous commander of an American frigate stopped the British steamer *Trent* and removed two Confederate ambassadors, James Mason and John Slidell, sailing to Britain. When they were imprisoned in Boston, northerners cheered, but the British interpreted the capture as a violation of freedom of the seas and demanded the prisoners' release. Lincoln and Seward waited until northern public opinion cooled and then released the two southerners. The incident strained U.S.-British relations.

Then the sale to the Confederacy of warships constructed in England sparked vigorous protest from U.S. ambassador Charles Francis Adams. A few English-built ships, notably the *Alabama,* reached open water to serve the South. Over a period of twenty-two months, without entering a southern port (because of the Union blockade), the *Alabama* destroyed or captured more than sixty U.S. ships, leaving a bitter legal legacy to be settled in the postwar period.

13-9b Battlefield Stalemate and a Union Strategy for Victory

On the battlefield, northern victory was far from won in 1864. General Nathaniel Banks's Red River campaign, designed to capture more of Louisiana and Texas, fell apart, and the capture of Mobile Bay in August did not cause the fall of Mobile. Union general William Tecumseh Sherman commented that the North had to "keep the war South until they are not only ruined, exhausted, but humbled in pride and spirit." Sherman soon brought total war to the southern heartland. On the eastern front during the winter of 1863–1864, the two armies in Virginia settled into a stalemate awaiting yet another spring offensive by the North.

Military authorities throughout history have agreed that deep invasion is very risky: the farther an army penetrates enemy territory, the more vulnerable are its own communications and supply lines. Moreover, observed the Prussian expert Karl von Clausewitz, if the invader encounters a "truly national" resistance, his troops will be "everywhere exposed to attacks by an insurgent population." The South's vast size and a determined resistance could yet make a northern victory elusive.

General Grant, by now in command of all the federal armies, decided to test southern will with a strategic innovation of his own: raids on a massive scale. Less tied to tradition and textbook maneuver than most other Union commanders, Grant proposed to use armies to destroy Confederate railroads, thus ruining the enemy's transportation and economy. Abandoning their lines of support, Union troops would live off the land while laying waste all resources useful to the military and to the civilian population of the Confederacy. After General George H. Thomas's troops won the Battle of Chattanooga in November 1863, the heartland of Georgia lay open. Grant entrusted General Sherman with one hundred thousand men for an invasion deep into the South, toward the rail center of Atlanta.

▲ ▶ Both General Grant (left) and General Lee (right) were West Point graduates and had served in the U.S. Army during the War with Mexico. Their bloody battles against each other in 1864 stirred northern revulsion to the war even as they brought its end in sight.

The Civil War in Britain

So engaged was the British public with America's disunion and war that an unemployed weaver, John Ward, frequently trekked many miles from Britain's Low Moor to Clitheroe just to read newspaper accounts of the strife.

Because of the direct reliance of the British textile industry on southern cotton (cut off by the war) as well as the many ideological and familial ties between the two nations, the American war was significant in Britain's economy and domestic politics. The British aristocracy and most cotton mill owners were solidly pro-Confederate and proslavery, whereas a combination of clergymen, shopkeepers, artisans, and radical politicians worked for the causes of Union and emancipation. Most British workers saw their future at stake in a war for slave emancipation. "Freedom" to the huge British working class (who could not vote) meant basic political and civil rights as well as the bread and butter of secure jobs in an industrializing economy, now damaged by a "cotton famine" that threw millhands out of work.

English aristocrats saw Americans as untutored, wayward cousins and took satisfaction in America's troubles. Conservatives believed in the superiority of the British system of government and looked askance at America's leveling tendencies. And some aristocratic British Liberals also saw Americans through their class bias and sympathized with the Confederacy's demand for "order" and independence. English racism also intensified in these years, exemplified by the popularity of minstrelsy and the employment of science in the service of racial theory. Their views on race had also been hardened by their own recent experience in the Indian Rebellion of 1857–1859, a revolt against British control characterized by acts of extreme cruelty on both sides, in which at least 800,000 people (mostly Indians) are thought to have died.

The intensity of the British propaganda war over the American conflict is evident in the methods of their debate: public meetings organized by both sides were huge affairs, with cheering and jeering, competing banners, carts and floats, orators and resolutions. In a press war, the British argued over when rebellion is justified, whether secession was right or legal, whether slavery was at the heart of the conflict, and especially over the democratic image of America itself. This bitter debate about America's trial became a test of reform in Britain: those eager for a broadened franchise and increased democracy were pro-Union, and those who preferred to preserve Britain's class-ridden political system favored the Confederacy.

The nature of the internal British debate was no better symbolized than by the dozens of African Americans who served as pro-Union agents in England. The most popular was William Andrew Jackson, Confederate president Jefferson Davis's former coachman, who had escaped from Richmond in September 1862. Jackson's articulate presence at British public meetings countered pro-Confederate arguments that the war was not about slavery.

In the end, the British government did not recognize the Confederacy and, by 1864, English cotton lords had found new sources of the crop in Egypt and India. But in this link between America and its English roots at its time of greatest travail, we can see that the Civil War was a transformation of international significance.

CRITICAL THINKING

■ How was the debate over the American Civil War in England illustrative of the importance of the United States' economy to the global economy?

The Granger Collection, NYC

◄ Some southern leaders pronounced that cotton was king and would bring Britain to their cause. This British cartoon shows King Cotton brought down in chains by the American eagle, anticipating the cotton famine to follow and the intense debate in Great Britain over the nature and meaning of the American Civil War.

13-9c Fall of Atlanta

Jefferson Davis countered by positioning the army of General Joseph E. Johnston in Sherman's path. Davis hoped that southern resolve would lead to the political defeat of Lincoln and the election of a president who would sue for peace. When General Johnston slowly but steadily fell back toward Atlanta, Davis grew anxious and sought assurances that Atlanta would be held. From a purely military point of view, Johnston maneuvered skillfully. But when Johnston fell silent and continued to retreat, Davis replaced him with the one-legged General John Hood, who knew his job was to fight. "Our all depends on that army at Atlanta," wrote Mary Chesnut. "If that fails us, the game is up."

For southern morale, the game *was* up. Hood attacked but was beaten, and Sherman's army occupied Atlanta on September 2, 1864. The victory buoyed northern spirits and all but ensured Lincoln's reelection. A government clerk in Richmond wrote, "Our fondly-cherished visions of peace have vanished like a mirage of the desert." Davis exhorted southerners to fight on and win new victories before the federal elections, but he had to admit that "two-thirds of our men are absent . . . without leave." In a desperate diversion, Hood's army marched north to cut Sherman's supply lines and force him to withdraw, but Sherman began to march sixty thousand of his marauding men straight to the sea, destroying Confederate resources as he went (see Map 13.5).

13-9d Sherman's March to the Sea

Sherman's army was an unusually formidable force, composed almost entirely of battle-tested veterans and officers who had risen through the ranks from the midwestern states. Before the march began, army doctors weeded out any men who were weak or sick. Weathered, bearded, and tough, the remaining veterans were determined, as one put it, "to Conquer this Rebelien or Die." They believed "the South are to blame for this war" and were ready to make the South pay. Although many harbored racist attitudes, most had come to support emancipation because, as one said, "Slavery stands in the way of putting down the rebellion." Confederate General Johnston later commented, "There has been no such army since the days of Julius Caesar."

As Sherman's men moved across Georgia, they cut a path 50 to 60 miles wide and more than 200 miles long. The totality of the destruction later prompted many historians to deem this the first modern "total war." A Georgia woman described the "Burnt Country" this way: "The fields were trampled down and the road was lined with carcasses of horses, hogs, and cattle that the invaders, unable either to consume or

Map 13.5 Sherman's March to the Sea

The Deep South proved a decisive theater at the end of the war. From Chattanooga, Union forces drove into Georgia, capturing Atlanta. Following the fall of Atlanta, General Sherman embarked on his march of destruction through Georgia to the coast and then northward through the Carolinas.

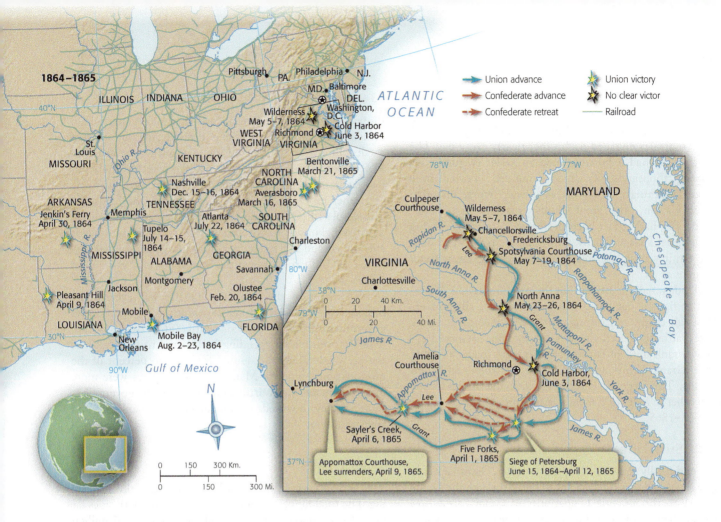

Map 13.6 The War in Virginia

At great cost, Grant hammered away at Lee's army until the weakened southern forces finally surrendered at Appomattox Court House.

to carry with them, had wantonly shot down to starve our people. . . . The stench in some places was unbearable." Such devastation diminished the South's material resources and sapped its will to resist.

After reaching Savannah in December, Sherman marched his armies north into the Carolinas. To his soldiers, South Carolina was "the root of secession." They burned and destroyed as they marched, encountering little resistance. The opposing army of General Johnston was small, but Sherman's men should have been prime targets for guerrilla raids and harassing attacks by local defense units. The absence of both led South Carolina's James Chesnut Jr. (a politician and the husband of Mary Chesnut) to write that his state "was shamefully and unnecessarily lost. . . . We had time, opportunity and means to destroy him. But there was wholly wanting the energy and ability required." Southerners had lost the will to continue the struggle.

Sherman's march drew additional human resources to the Union cause. In Georgia alone, nearly twenty thousand slaves gladly embraced emancipation and followed the marauding Union troops. Others remained on the plantations to await the end of the war because of either an ingrained wariness of whites or negative experiences with federal soldiers. The destruction of food harmed slaves as

well as white rebels, and many blacks lost livestock, crops, and other valuables to their liberators. In fact, the brutality of Sherman's troops shocked some liberated slaves. "I've seen them cut the hams off of a live pig or ox and go off leavin' the animal groanin'," recalled one man. "The master had 'em kilt then, but it was awful."

13-9e Virginia's Bloody Soil

It was awful, too, in Virginia, where the path to victory proved protracted and ghastly. Throughout the spring and summer of 1864, intent on capturing Richmond, Grant hurled his troops at Lee's army and suffered appalling losses: almost eighteen thousand casualties in the Battle of the Wilderness, where skeletons poked out of the shallow graves dug one year before after the Battle of Chancellorsville; more than eight thousand at Spotsylvania; and twelve thousand in the space of a few hours at Cold Harbor (see Map 13.6).

Before the assault at Cold Harbor (which Grant later admitted was a grave mistake), Union troops pinned scraps of paper bearing their names and addresses to their backs, certain they would be mowed down as they rushed Lee's trenches. In four weeks in May and June, Grant lost as many men as were enrolled in Lee's entire army. From early May until July, when Union forces had marched and fought all the way from forests west of Fredericksburg to Petersburg, south of Richmond, which they besieged, the two armies engaged each other nearly every day. The war had reached a horribly modern scale. Wagon trains carrying thousands of Union wounded crawled back toward Washington. "It was as if war," wrote historian Bruce Catton, "the great clumsy machine for maiming people, had at last been perfected. Instead of turning out its grist spasmodically, with long waits between each delivery, it was at last able to produce every day, without any gaps at all."

Undaunted, Grant kept up the pressure, saying, "I propose to fight it out along this line if it takes all summer." Although costly, and testing northern morale to its limits, these battles prepared the way for eventual victory: Lee's army shrank until offensive action was no longer possible, while Grant's army kept replenishing its forces with new recruits. The siege of Petersburg, with the armies facing each other in miles of trenches, lasted throughout the winter of 1864–1865.

13-9f Surrender at Appomattox

The end finally came in the spring of 1865. Grant kept battering Lee, who tried but failed to break through the Union line. With the numerical superiority of Grant's army now greater than two to one, Confederate defeat was inevitable. On April 2, Lee abandoned Richmond and Petersburg. On April 9, hemmed in by Union troops, short of rations, and with fewer than thirty thousand men left, he surrendered at Appomattox Court House. Grant treated his rival with respect and paroled the defeated troops, allowing cavalrymen to keep their horses and take them home. The war was over at last. Within weeks, Confederate forces under Johnston surrendered to Sherman in North Carolina, and Davis, who had fled Richmond but wanted the war to continue, was captured in Georgia. The North rejoiced, and most southerners fell into despair, expecting waves of punishment. In the profound relief and stillness of the surrender field at Appomattox, no one could know the harrowing tasks of healing and justice that lay ahead.

With Lee's surrender, Lincoln knew the Union had been preserved, yet he lived to see but a few days of war's aftermath. On the evening of Good Friday, April 14, he accompanied his wife to Ford's Theatre in Washington to enjoy a popular comedy. There John Wilkes Booth, an embittered southern sympathizer, shot the president in the head at point-blank range. Lincoln died the next day. Twelve days later, troops tracked down and killed Booth. The Union had lost its wartime leader, and millions publicly mourned the martyred chief executive along the route of the funeral train that took his body home to Illinois. Relief at the war's end mingled hauntingly with a renewed sense of loss and anxiety about the future. Millions never forgot where they were and how they felt at the news of Lincoln's assassination.

13-9g Financial Tally

Property damage and financial costs were enormous, though difficult to tally. U.S. loans and taxes during the conflict totaled almost $3 billion, and interest on the war debt was $2.8 billion. The Confederacy borrowed over $2 billion but lost far more in the destruction of homes, crops, livestock, and other property. In southern war zones, the landscape was desolated. Over wide regions, fences and crops were destroyed; houses, barns, and bridges burned; and fields abandoned and left to erode. Union troops had looted factories and put two-thirds of the South's railroad system out of service.

Estimates of the total cost of the war exceed $20 billion—five times the total expenditures of the federal government from its creation until 1861. By 1865, the federal government's spending had soared to twenty times the prewar level and accounted for over 26 percent of the gross national product. Many of these changes were more or less permanent, as wartime measures left the government more deeply involved in manufacturing, banking, and transportation.

13-9h Death Toll and Its Impact

The human costs of the Civil War were especially staggering. The total number of military casualties on both sides far exceeded 1 million—a frightful toll for a nation of 31 million people. Using microdata samples from the 1850, 1860, 1870, and 1880 censuses, a recent study has markedly raised the former official count of 620,000 dead in the Civil War to approximately 750,000. Scholarship also shows that we have never been able to carefully account for civilian casualties in the war, nor for the possibly one in four freedpeople who died in the process of achieving their own freedom. These startling numbers demonstrate that more people died in the Civil War than in all other American wars combined until Vietnam. Not all died on the battlefield: 30,218 northerners died in southern prisons, and 25,976 Confederates died in Union prisons.

The scale and the anonymous nature of death overwhelmed American culture and led to the establishment of national cemeteries, where the large majority of the fallen were buried without identification. This prompted desperate efforts by families to find their loved ones, usually in vain. In a Christian culture believing in the "good death," where the deceased is surrounded by family and a clear narrative of the final hours could be remembered, mass death and dismembered bodies strewn on war-ravaged landscapes violated the values of a religious and romantic age. On the private level, countless Americans, soldiers and family members alike, never psychologically recovered or found true consolation from the war's personal loss. The age's earlier belief that suffering was always purposeful underwent fundamental shock. The desperate urge to memorialize individual soldiers in this war, writes historian Drew Faust, stemmed from "the anguish of wives, parents, siblings, and

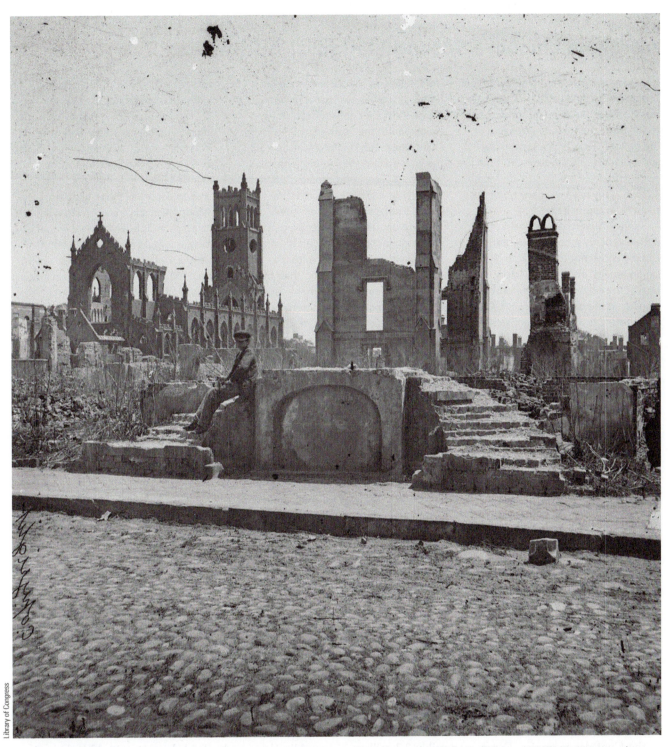

▲ The ruins of Charleston, South Carolina, late spring 1865. The city fell and was evacuated on February 18, 1865. Union gunboats and siege cannons had bombarded Charleston during the final year of the war, leaving much of the beautiful neoclassical architecture of that city, where secession had begun four years earlier, in devastation. An African American regiment accepted the formal surrender of the city.

children who found undocumented, unconfirmed, and unrecognizable loss intolerable." For some, the magnitude of death meant living could never be the same.

These unprecedented losses flowed from fundamental strife over the nature of the Union and the liberty of black people. Both sides saw vital interests in the struggle but lost control of its scope. As Julia Ward Howe wrote in her famous "Battle Hymn of the Republic," they had heard "the trumpet that shall never call retreat." And so the war took its horrifying toll.

Abraham Lincoln's Second Inaugural Address

Historian Don Fehrenbacher wrote that "some of Lincoln's words have acquired transcendent meaning as contributions to the permanent literary treasure of the nation." How is this so with the short oration Lincoln delivered from the north portico of the Capitol on March 4, 1865? Why have so many book titles been drawn from its text?

In a 701-word prose poem at the occasion of his second inauguration, Lincoln chose not to celebrate the Union armies' impending victory, nor his own at the polls. Instead, he probed the tragedy at the heart of the Civil War and interpreted its ultimate meanings. The prosaic first paragraph acknowledges wide understanding of the "progress of our arms" over four years of war. In the second paragraph, Lincoln entwines North and South in a mutual fate, but suggests responsibility for which side "would make war," and which side "would accept war," and leaves it to posterity: "And the war came."

Then, the speech transforms and Lincoln boldly offers a theological-historical explanation of the war that still resonates today in how Americans interpret this crucial turning point in their history. Evenhandedly, but forcefully, Lincoln declares that "all knew . . . somehow" slavery was the "cause" of the conflict. Both sides appealed to the "same God" to favor their cause. But quoting Matthew 18:7, he warned that the "Almighty has his own purposes," and though "offences" will always come from human frailty, "woe to that man by whom the offence cometh!" Wary of judging, but unrestrained, Lincoln called it "strange that any men should dare to ask a just God's assistance in ringing their bread from the sweat of other men's faces." Lincoln did not claim to utterly know God's will, but he imagined slavery as an "offence" that came "in the providence of God," and brought "this mighty scourge of war" as its awful price.

Suddenly, in rhetoric so unusual for presidential inaugurals, Lincoln assumed the prophet's mantle: "Yet if God wills that it [the war] continue, until all the wealth piled by the bond-man's two hundred and fifty years of unrequited toil shall be sunk, and until every drop of blood drawn by the lash, shall be paid by another drawn with the sword, as was said three thousand years ago, so still it must be said 'the judgments of the Lord are true and righteous altogether.'"

Famously, Lincoln ended with a single-sentence paragraph where he declared "malice toward none . . . charity for all" the healing balm for the "nation's wounds." But in that third paragraph—less popular or savored in modern memory—Lincoln transcended time and place and delivered what Frederick Douglass would call a "sacred effort" to explain what the Civil War was really about. Whether Lincoln was the nation's healer or its war-maker who would demand any sacrifice to restore the Union and destroy slavery has always animated the endless study of his personal story. The legacy of the Civil War, and Lincoln's place in it, are forever enmeshed in how we interpret this oratorical masterpiece.

CRITICAL THINKING

- In Lincoln's third paragraph of the address, he asserts that "all knew... somehow" slavery was the "cause" of the conflict, yet in a 2011 CNN poll 42 percent of Americans said that slavery was not the cause of the war. How should we interpret the disparity between how Civil War–era Americans and modern Americans understand the causes of the war?

Summary

The Civil War altered American society forever. The first great legacy of the war in the lives of its survivors was, therefore, death itself. Although precise figures on enlistments are unavailable, it appears that 700,000 to 800,000 men served in the Confederate armies. Far more, possibly 2.3 million, served in the Union armies. All of these men were taken from home, family, and personal goals; their lives, if they survived, were disrupted in ways that were never repaired. During the war, in both North and South, women, too, took on new roles as they struggled to manage the hardships of the home front, to grieve, and to support the war effort.

Industrialization and economic enterprises grew exponentially in tandem with the war. Ordinary citizens found that their futures were increasingly tied to huge organizations. The character and extent of government power, too, changed markedly. Under Republican leadership, the federal government expanded its power not only to preserve the Union but also to extend freedom. A social revolution and government authority emancipated the slaves. A republic desperately divided against itself had survived, but in new constitutional forms yet to take shape during Reconstruction.

It was unclear at the end of the war how or whether the nation would use its power to protect the rights of the former slaves. Secession was dead, but whether Americans would continue to embrace a centralized nationalism remained to be seen. The war ended decisively after tremendous sacrifice, but it left many unanswered questions: How would white southerners, embittered and impoverished, respond to efforts to reconstruct the nation? How would the country care for the maimed, the orphans, the farming women without men to work their land, and all the dead who had to be found and properly buried? What would be the place of black men and women in American life? How would Americans struggle over the memory of this, their most divisive experience in the decades ahead?

In the West, two civil wars had raged: one between Union and Confederate forces and the other resulting in a conquest of southwestern Native peoples by U.S. troops and land-hungry settlers. On the diplomatic front, the Union government had delicately managed to keep Great Britain and other foreign powers out of the war. Dissent flourished in both North and South, playing a crucial role in the ultimate collapse of the Confederacy.

In the Civil War, Americans had undergone an epic of destruction and survival—a transformation like nothing else in their history. White southerners had experienced defeat that few other Americans would ever face. Blacks were moving proudly but anxiously through great hardship from slavery to freedom. White northerners were, by and large, self-conscious victors in a massive war for the nation's existence and for new definitions of freedom. The war, with all of its drama, sacrifice, and social and political change, would leave a compelling memory in American hearts and minds for generations.

Suggestions for Further Reading

Stephen V. Ash, *When the Yankees Came: Conflict and Chaos in the Occupied South* (1995)

Edward L. Ayers, *In the Presence of Mine Enemies: War in the Heart of America, 1859–1863* (2002)

Ira Berlin et al., eds., *Freedom: A Documentary History of Emancipation, 1861–1867,* 3 vols. (1979–1982)

David W. Blight, *Race and Reunion: The Civil War in American Memory* (2001)

Alice Fahs, *The Imagined Civil War: Popular Literature of the North and South* (2001)

Drew G. Faust, *This Republic of Suffering: Death and the American Civil War* (2008)

Gary W. Gallagher, *The Confederate War* (1997)

J. David Hacker, "A Census-Based Count of the Civil War Dead," *Civil War History,* (Dec. 2011).

Chandra Manning, *What This Cruel War Was Over: Soldiers, Slavery, and the Civil War* (2007)

James M. McPherson, *Battle Cry of Freedom: The Civil War Era* (1987)

Philip S. Paludan, *"A People's Contest": The Union and the Civil War* (1989)

Mark R. Wilson, *The Business of Civil War: Military Mobilization and the State, 1861–1865* (2006)

MINDTAP
From Cengage

MindTap® is a fully online personalized learning experience built upon Cengage Learning content. MindTap® combines student learning tools—readings, multimedia, activities, and assessments—into a singular Learning Path that guides students through the course and helps students develop the critical thinking, analysis, and communication skills that are essential to academic and professional success.

Reconstruction: An Unfinished Revolution, 1865–1877

The lower half of the city of Charleston, South Carolina, the seedbed of secession, lay in ruin when most of the white population evacuated on February 18, 1865. A bombardment by Union batteries and gunboats around Charleston harbor had already destroyed many of the lovely, neoclassical townhomes of the low-country planters. Then, as the city was abandoned, fires broke out everywhere, ignited in bales of cotton left in huge stockpiles in public squares. To many observers, the flames were the funeral pyres of a dying civilization.

Among the first Union troops to enter Charleston was the Twenty-first U.S. Colored Regiment, which received the surrender of the city from its mayor. For black Charlestonians, most of whom were former slaves, this was a time of celebration. In symbolic ceremonies, they proclaimed their freedom and announced their rebirth. Whatever the postwar order would bring, the freedpeople of Charleston converted Confederate ruin into a vision of Reconstruction based on Union victory and black liberation.

Still, in Charleston as elsewhere, death demanded attention. During the final year of the war, the Confederates had converted the planters' Race Course, a horse-racing track, and its famed Washington Jockey Club, into a prison. Union soldiers were kept in terrible conditions in the interior of the track, without shelter. The 257 who died there of exposure and disease were buried in a mass grave behind the grandstand. After the fall of the city, Charleston's black people organized to create a proper burial ground for the Union dead. During April,

◀ Photograph of the grandstand and clubhouse of the Washington Jockey Club and Race Course, Charleston, SC, site of Confederate prison and burial ground of more than 260 Union soldiers, as well as the first commemoration of Decoration Day, May 1, 1865. Library of Congress, Prints & Photographs Division [LC-DIG-stereo-1s02451]

Chronology

1865	■ Johnson begins rapid and lenient Reconstruction
	■ White southern governments pass restrictive black codes
	■ Congress refuses to seat southern representatives
	■ Thirteenth Amendment ratified, abolishing slavery
1866	■ Congress passes Civil Rights Act and renewal of Freedmen's Bureau over Johnson's veto
	■ Congress approves Fourteenth Amendment
	■ In *Ex parte Milligan*, the Supreme Court reasserts its influence
1867	■ Congress passes First Reconstruction Act and Tenure of Office Act
	■ Constitutional conventions called in southern states
1868	■ House impeaches and Senate acquits Johnson
	■ Most southern states readmitted to Union under Radical plan
	■ Fourteenth Amendment ratified
	■ Grant elected president
1869	■ Congress approves Fifteenth Amendment (ratified in 1870)
	■ Sharecropping takes hold across a cash-poor southern economy
1871	■ Congress passes second Enforcement Act and Ku Klux Klan Act
	■ Treaty with England settles *Alabama* claims
1872	■ Amnesty Act frees almost all remaining Confederates from restrictions on holding office
	■ Grant reelected
1873	■ Slaughter-House cases limit power of Fourteenth Amendment
	■ Panic of 1873 leads to widespread unemployment and labor strife
1874	■ Democrats win majority in House of Representatives
1875	■ Several Grant appointees indicted for corruption
	■ Congress passes weak Civil Rights Act
	■ Democratic Party increases control of southern states with white supremacy campaigns
1876	■ *U.S. v. Cruikshank* further weakens Fourteenth Amendment
	■ Presidential election disputed
1877	■ Congress elects Hayes president

more than twenty black workmen reinterred the dead in marked graves and built a high fence around the cemetery. On the archway over the cemetery's entrance they painted the inscription "Martyrs of the Race Course."

And then they planned an extraordinary ceremony. On the morning of May 1, 1865, a procession of ten thousand people marched around the planters' Race Course, led by three thousand children carrying armloads of roses and singing "John Brown's Body." The children were followed by black women with baskets of flowers and wreaths, and then by black men. The parade concluded with members

of black and white Union regiments, along with white missionaries and teachers led by James Redpath, the supervisor of freedmen's schools in the region. All who could fit assembled at the gravesite; five black ministers read from scripture, and a black children's choir sang "America," "We'll Rally 'Round the Flag," "The Star-Spangled Banner," and Negro spirituals. When the ceremony ended, the huge crowd retired to the Race Course for speeches, picnics, and military festivities.

Experience an interactive version of this story in MindTap®.

The war was over in Charleston, and "Decoration Day"—now Memorial Day, the day to remember the war dead and decorate their graves with flowers—had been founded by African Americans and their allies. Black people—by their labor, their words, their songs, and their marching feet on the old planters' Race Course—had created an American tradition. In their vision, they were creating the Independence Day of a Second American Revolution.

Reconstruction would bring revolutionary circumstances, but revolutions can also go backward. The Civil War and its aftermath wrought unprecedented changes in American society, law, and politics, but the underlying realities of economic power, racism, and judicial conservatism limited Reconstruction's revolutionary potential. As never before, the nation had to determine the nature of federal-state relations, whether confiscated land could be redistributed, and how to bring justice to both freedpeople and aggrieved white southerners whose property and lives had been devastated. Americans were about to try to redefine citizenship, fundamental civil and political rights, and equality before law against unrelenting opposition. A disunited country faced the harrowing challenge of psychological healing from a bloody and fratricidal war. How they would negotiate the tangled relationship between healing and justice would determine the fate of Reconstruction.

Nowhere was the turmoil of Reconstruction more evident than in national politics. Lincoln's successor, Andrew Johnson, fought bitterly with Congress over the shaping of Reconstruction policies. Although a southerner, Johnson had always been a foe of the South's wealthy planters, and his first acts as president suggested that he would be tough on "traitors." Before the end of 1865, however, Johnson's policies changed direction, and he became the protector of white southern interests.

Johnson imagined a lenient and rapid "restoration" of the South to the Union rather than the fundamental "reconstruction" that Republican congressmen favored. Between 1866 and 1868, the president and the Republican leadership in Congress engaged in a bitter power struggle over how to put the United States back together again. Before the struggle ceased, Congress had impeached the president, enfranchised freedmen, and given them a role in reconstructing the South. The nation also adopted the Fourteenth and Fifteenth Amendments, ushering in equal protection of the law, a definition of birthright citizenship, and universal manhood suffrage into the Constitution.

By 1868–1869, the Ku Klux Klan employed extensive violence and terror to thwart Reconstruction and undermine black freedom. As white Democrats in the South took control of state governments in the 1870s, they encountered little opposition from the North. Moreover, the wartime industrial boom had created new opportunities and priorities. The West, with its seemingly limitless potential and its wars against Native peoples, drew American resources and consciousness like never before. Americans moved in huge numbers and sought new "homes" in the trans-Mississippi West and the homes of Native Americans were displaced or destroyed. Political corruption became a nationwide scandal, and bribery a way of doing business.

Thus, Reconstruction became a revolution eclipsed. The white South's desire to reclaim control of its states and of race relations overwhelmed the national interest in stopping it. But Reconstruction left enduring legacies from which the nation has benefited and with which it has struggled ever since. In every succeeding racial or constitutional reckoning, we often return to Reconstruction as a means of understanding ourselves anew.

- *Should the Reconstruction era be considered the Second American Revolution? By what criteria should we make such a judgment?*

- *What were the origins and meanings of the Fourteenth Amendment in the 1860s? What is its significance today?*

- *Reconstruction is judged to have "ended" in 1877. Over the course of the 1870s, what caused its end?*

14-1 Wartime Reconstruction

▶ **What were the features of Abraham Lincoln's vision for Reconstruction?**

▶ **Why did Abraham Lincoln and Congress differ over Reconstruction policy?**

▶ **How did the creation and operation of the Freedman's Bureau signify a new expansive role for the federal government in society?**

Civil wars leave immense challenges of healing, justice, and physical rebuilding. Anticipating that process, reconstruction of the Union was an issue as early as 1863, well before the war ended. Many key questions loomed on the horizon when and if the North succeeded on the battlefield: How would the nation be restored? How would southern states and leaders be treated—as errant brothers or as traitors? How would a devastated southern economy be revived? What was the constitutional basis for readmission of states to the Union, and where, if anywhere, could American statesmen look for precedence or guidance? As winners of the war, could radical Republicans take their emancipation and human equality agenda abroad and spread it to foreign lands? More specifically, four vexing problems compelled early thinking and would haunt the Reconstruction era throughout. One, who would rule in the South once it was defeated? Two, who would rule in the federal government—Congress or the president? Three, what were the dimensions of black freedom, and what rights under law would the freedmen enjoy? And four, would Reconstruction be a preservation of the old republic or a second Revolution, a reinvention of a new republic?

14-1a Lincoln's 10 Percent Plan

Abraham Lincoln had never been antisouthern, though he had become the leader of an antislavery war. He lost three brothers-in-law, killed in the war on the Confederate side. His worst fear was that the war would collapse at the end into guerrilla warfare across the South, with surviving bands of Confederates carrying on resistance. Lincoln insisted that his generals give lenient terms to southern soldiers once they surrendered. In his Second Inaugural Address, delivered only a month before his assassination, Lincoln promised "malice toward none; with charity for all," as Americans strove to "bind up the nation's wounds."

Lincoln planned early for a swift and moderate Reconstruction process. In his "Proclamation of Amnesty and Reconstruction," issued in December 1863, he proposed to replace majority rule with "loyal rule" as a means of reconstructing southern state governments. He proposed pardons to all ex-Confederates except the highest-ranking military and civilian officers. Then, as soon as 10 percent of the voting population in the 1860 general election in a given state had taken an oath to the United States and established a government, the new state would be recognized. Lincoln did not consult Congress in these plans, and "loyal" assemblies (known as "Lincoln governments") were created in Louisiana, Tennessee, and Arkansas in 1864, states largely occupied by Union troops. These governments were weak and dependent on northern armies for survival.

14-1b Congress and the Wade-Davis Bill

Congress responded with great hostility to Lincoln's moves to readmit southern states in what seemed such a premature manner. Many Radical Republicans, strong proponents of emancipation and of aggressive prosecution of the war against the South, considered the 10 percent plan a "mere mockery" of democracy. Led by Thaddeus Stevens of Pennsylvania in the House and Charles Sumner of Massachusetts

Thirteenth Amendment The constitutional amendment that abolished slavery; passed by Congress in 1865.

in the Senate, congressional Republicans locked horns with Lincoln and proposed a longer and harsher approach to Reconstruction. Stevens advocated a "conquered provinces" theory, arguing that southerners had organized as a foreign nation to make war on the United States and, by secession, had destroyed their status as states. They therefore must be treated as "conquered foreign lands" and returned to the status of "unorganized territories" before any process of readmission could be entertained by Congress.

In July 1864, the Wade-Davis bill, named for its sponsors, Senator Benjamin Wade of Ohio and Congressman Henry W. Davis of Maryland, emerged from Congress with three specific conditions for southern readmission.

1. It demanded a "majority" of white male citizens participate in the creation of a new government.
2. To vote or be a delegate to constitutional conventions, men had to take an "iron-clad" oath (declaring that they had never aided the Confederate war effort).
3. All officers above the rank of lieutenant and all civil officials in the Confederacy would be disfranchised and deemed "not a citizen of the United States."

The Confederate states were to be defined as "conquered enemies," said Davis, and the process of readmission was to be harsh and slow. Lincoln, ever the adroit politician, pocket-vetoed the bill and issued a conciliatory proclamation of his own, announcing that he would not be inflexibly committed to any "one plan" of Reconstruction.

This exchange came during Grant's bloody campaign against Lee in Virginia, when the outcome of the war and Lincoln's reelection were still in doubt. On August 5, Radical Republicans issued the "Wade-Davis Manifesto" to newspapers. An unprecedented attack on a sitting president by members of his own party, it accused Lincoln of usurpation of presidential powers and disgraceful leniency toward an eventually conquered South. What emerged in 1864–1865 was a clear debate and a potential constitutional crisis. Lincoln saw Reconstruction as a means of weakening the Confederacy and winning the war; the Radicals saw it as a longer-term transformation of the political and racial order of the country.

14-1c Thirteenth Amendment

In early 1865, Congress and Lincoln joined in two important measures that recognized slavery's centrality to the war. On January 31, with strong administration backing, Congress passed the **Thirteenth Amendment**, which had two provisions: first, it abolished involuntary servitude everywhere in the United States; second, it declared that Congress shall have the power to enforce this outcome by "appropriate legislation." When the measure passed by 119 to 56, a mere two votes more than the necessary two-thirds, rejoicing broke out in Congress. A Republican recorded in his diary, "Members joined in the shouting and kept it up for some minutes. Some embraced one another, others wept like children. I have felt ever since the vote, as if I were in a new country."

But the Thirteenth Amendment had emerged from a long congressional debate and considerable petitioning and public advocacy. One of the first and most remarkable petitions for a constitutional amendment abolishing slavery was submitted early in 1864 by Elizabeth Cady Stanton, Susan B. Anthony, and the Women's Loyal National League. Women throughout the Union accumulated thousands of signatures, even venturing into staunchly pro-Confederate regions of Kentucky and Missouri to secure supporters. It was a long road from the Emancipation Proclamation to the Thirteenth Amendment—through treacherous constitutional theory about individual "property rights," a bedrock of belief that the sacred document ought never to be altered, and partisan politics. There had not been a Constitutional amendment since 1789, when the Twelfth Amendment established what we today call the Electoral College. But the logic of winning the war by crushing slavery, and of securing a new beginning under law for the nation that so many had died to save, won the day.

14-1d Freedmen's Bureau

Potentially as significant, on March 3, 1865, Congress created the Bureau of Refugees, Freedmen, and Abandoned Lands—the Freedmen's Bureau, an unprecedented agency of social uplift necessitated by the ravages of the war. Americans had never engaged in federal aid to citizens on such a scale. With thousands of refugees, white and black, displaced in the South, the government continued what private freedmen's aid societies had started as early as 1862. In the mere four years of its existence, the Freedmen's Bureau supplied food and medical services, built several thousand schools and some colleges, negotiated several hundred thousand employment contracts between freedpeople and their former masters, and tried to manage confiscated land.

Throughout its existence—it lasted until 1872, when Congress refused to approve renewal legislation—the Bureau remained controversial within the South, where whites generally hated it, and within the federal government, where politicians divided over its constitutionality. Some bureau agents were devoted to freedmen's rights, whereas others were opportunists who exploited the chaos of the postwar South. The war had forced into the open an eternal question of republics: what are the social welfare obligations of the state toward its people, and what do people owe their governments in return? Apart from their conquest and displacement of eastern Native peoples, Americans were relatively inexperienced at the Freedmen's Bureau's task—social reform through military occupation. They were also unaccustomed to the sheer reality that *government* possessed the only resources and institutions capable of confronting the social and economic chaos wrought by the war. Military occupation of significant parts of the South lasted into the late 1860s, but Americans had little experience with this kind of federal power.

14-1e Ruins and Enmity

In 1865, due to the devastation of the war, America was now a land with ruins. Like the countries of Europe, it now seemed an older, more historic landscape. Physically, politically, and spiritually, it had torn itself asunder. Some of its cities lay in rubble, large stretches of the southern countryside were depopulated and defoliated, and thousands of people, white and black, were refugees. Some of this would in time seem romantic to northern travelers in the postwar South.

Thousands of yeoman farmer-soldiers, some paroled by surrenders, walked home too late in the season to plant a crop in a collapsed economy. Many white refugees faced genuine starvation. Of the approximately 18,300,000 rations distributed across the South in the first three years of the Freedmen's Bureau, 5,230,000 went to whites. In early 1866, in a proud agricultural society, the legislature of South Carolina issued $300,000 in state bonds to purchase corn for the destitute.

In October 1865, just after a five-month imprisonment in Boston, former Confederate vice president Alexander H. Stephens rode a slow train southward. In Virginia, he found "the desolation of the country . . . was horrible to behold." When Stephens reached northern Georgia, his native state, his shock ran over: "War has left a terrible impression. . . . Fences gone, fields all a-waste, houses burnt." A northern journalist visiting Richmond that same fall observed a city "mourning for her sins . . . in dust and ashes." The "burnt district" was a "bed of cinders . . . broken and blackened walls, impassable streets deluged with debris." Above all, every northern traveler encountered a wall of hatred among white southerners for their conquerors. An innkeeper in North Carolina told a journalist that Yankees had killed his sons in the war, burned his house, and stolen his slaves. "They left me one inestimable privilege," he said, "to hate 'em. I git up at half-past four in the morning, and sit up 'til twelve at night, to hate 'em."

14-2 The Meanings of Freedom

▶ How did African Americans respond to and explore their new freedom after the war?

▶ What challenges did freedpeople face in obtaining land?

▶ How did education for freedpeople develop after the war?

▶ How did sharecropping affect freedpeople's desire to be economically independent?

Black southerners entered into life after slavery with hope and circumspection. A Texas man recalled his father telling him, even before the war was over, "Our forever was going to be spent living among the Southerners, after they got licked." Freed men and women tried to gain as much as they could from their new circumstances. Often the changes they valued the most were personal—alterations in location, employer, or living arrangements.

14-2a The Feel of Freedom

For America's former slaves, Reconstruction had one paramount meaning: a chance to explore freedom. A southern white woman admitted in her diary that the black people "showed a natural and exultant joy at being free." Former slaves remembered singing far into the night after federal troops, who confirmed rumors of their emancipation, reached their plantations. The slaves on a Texas plantation shouted for joy, their leader proclaiming, "We is free—no more whippings and beatings." A few people gave in to the natural desire to do what had been impossible before. One angry grandmother dropped her hoe and ran to confront her mistress. "I'm free!" she yelled. "Yes, I'm free! Ain't got to work for you no more! You can't put me in your pocket now!" Another man recalled that he and others "started on the move," either to search for family members or just to exercise the human right of mobility.

Many freed men and women reacted more cautiously and shrewdly, taking care to test the boundaries of their new condition. "After the war was over," explained one man, "we was afraid to move. Just like terrapins or turtles after emancipation. Just stick our heads out to see how the land lay." As slaves, they had learned to expect hostility from white people, and they did not presume it would instantly disappear. Life in freedom might still be a matter of what was possible, not what was right. Many freedpeople evaluated potential employers with shrewd caution. "Most all the Negroes that had good owners stayed with 'em, but the others left. Some of 'em come back and some didn't," explained one man. After considerable wandering in search of better circumstances, a majority of blacks eventually settled as agricultural workers back on their former farms or plantations. They often relocated their houses and did their utmost to control the conditions of their labor.

14-2b Reunion of African American Families

Throughout the South, former slaves devoted themselves to reuniting their families, separated during slavery by sale or hardship, and during the war by dislocation and the emancipation process. With only shreds of information to guide them, thousands of freedpeople embarked on odysseys in search of a husband, wife, child, or parent. By relying on the black community for help and information, and by placing ads that continued to appear in black newspapers such as the *Christian Recorder*, a national journal published by the African Methodist Episcopal Church, well into the 1880s, some succeeded in their quest, while others searched in vain.

Husbands and wives who had belonged to different masters established homes together for the first time, and, as they had tried under slavery, parents asserted the right to raise their own children. A mother bristled when her old master claimed a right to whip her children. She informed him that "he warn't goin' to brush none of her chilluns no more." The

freed men and women were too much at risk to act recklessly, but, as one man put it, they were tired of punishment and "sure didn't take no more foolishment off of white folks."

14-2c African Americans' Search for Independence

Many black people wanted to minimize contact with whites because, as Reverend Garrison Frazier told General Sherman in January 1865, "There is a prejudice against us . . . that will take years to get over." To avoid contact with overbearing whites who were used to supervising them, blacks abandoned the slave quarters and fanned out to distant corners of the land they worked. "After the war my stepfather come," recalled Annie Young, "and got my mother and we moved out in the piney woods." Others described moving "across the creek" or building a "saplin house . . . back in the woods." Some rural dwellers established small, all-black settlements that still exist along the back roads of the South.

Even once-privileged slaves desired such independence and social separation. One man turned down his master's offer of the overseer's house and moved instead to a shack in "Freetown." He also declined to let the former owner grind his grain for free because it "make him feel like a free man to pay for things just like anyone else."

14-2d Freedpeople's Desire for Land

In addition to a fair employer, what freed men and women most wanted was the ownership of land. Land represented self-sufficiency and a chance to gain compensation for generations of bondage. General Sherman's special Field Order Number 15, issued in February 1865, set aside 400,000 acres of land in the Sea Islands region for the exclusive settlement of freedpeople. Hope swelled among ex-slaves as forty-acre plots, mules, and "possessary titles" were promised to them. But President Johnson ordered them removed in October and the land returned to its original owners under army enforcement. A northern observer noted that slaves freed in the Sea Islands of South Carolina and Georgia made "plain, straightforward" inquiries as they settled on new land. They wanted to be sure the land "would be theirs after they had improved it." Everywhere, black people young and old thirsted for homes of their own.

But most members of both political parties opposed genuine land redistribution to the freedmen. Even northern reformers who had administered the Sea Islands during the war showed little sympathy for black aspirations. The former Sea Island slaves wanted to establish small, self-sufficient farms. Northern soldiers, officials, and missionaries of both races brought education and aid to the freedmen but also insisted that they grow cotton for the competitive market.

"The Yankees preach nothing but cotton, cotton!" complained one Sea Island black. "We wants land," wrote another, but tax officials "make the lots too big, and cut we out." Indeed, the U.S. government eventually sold thousands of acres in the Sea Islands, 90 percent of which went to wealthy investors from the North. At a protest against evictions from a contraband camp in Virginia in 1866, freedman Bayley Wyatt made black desires and claims clear: "We has a right to the land where we are located. For why? I tell you. Our wives, our children, our husbands, has been sold over and over again to purchase the lands we now locates upon; for that reason we have a divine right to the land."

14-2e Freed Men and Women Embrace Education

Ex-slaves everywhere reached out for education. Black people of all ages hungered for the knowledge in books that had been permitted only to white people. With freedom, they started schools and filled classrooms both day and night. On log seats and dirt floors, freed men and women studied their letters in old almanacs and in discarded dictionaries. Young children brought infants to school with them, and adults attended at night or after "the crops were laid by." Many a teacher had "to make herself heard over three other classes reciting in concert" in a small room. The desire to escape slavery's ignorance was so great that, despite their poverty, many blacks paid tuition, typically $1 or $1.50 a month. These small amounts constituted major portions of a person's agricultural wages and added up to more than $1 million by 1870.

The federal government and northern reformers of both races assisted this pursuit of education. In its brief life, the Freedmen's Bureau founded over four thousand schools, and idealistic men and women from the North established others funded by private philanthropy. The Yankee schoolmarm—dedicated, selfless, and religious—became an agent of progress in many southern communities. Thus did African Americans seek a break from their past through learning. More than 600,000 were enrolled in elementary school by 1877. In a rural agricultural society recovering from wartime devastation, this was a stunning achievement.

Black people and their white allies also saw the need for colleges and universities. The American Missionary Association founded seven colleges, including Fisk University and Atlanta University, between 1866 and 1869. The Freedmen's Bureau helped to establish Howard University in Washington, D.C., and northern religious groups, such as the Methodists, Baptists, and Congregationalists, supported dozens of seminaries and teachers' colleges.

During Reconstruction, African American leaders often were highly educated individuals; many were from the prewar elite of free people of color. Francis Cardozo, who held various offices in South Carolina, had attended universities in Scotland and England. P. B. S. Pinchback, who became lieutenant governor of Louisiana, was the son of a planter who had sent him to school in Cincinnati. Both of the two black senators from Mississippi, Blanche K. Bruce and Hiram Revels, possessed privileged educations. Bruce was the son of a planter who had provided tutoring at home; Revels was the son of free black North Carolinians who had sent him to Knox College in Illinois.

14-2f Growth of Black Churches

Freed from the restrictions and regulations of slavery, African Americans could build their own institutions as they saw fit. The secret churches of slavery came into the open; in countless communities throughout the South, ex-slaves "started a brush arbor." A brush arbor was merely "a sort of . . . shelter with leaves for a roof," but the freed men and women worshipped in it enthusiastically. "Preachin' and shouting sometimes lasted all day," they recalled, for the opportunity to worship together freely meant "glorious times."

Within a few years, independent branches of the Methodist and Baptist denominations had attracted the great majority of black Christians in the South. By 1877, in South Carolina alone, the African Methodist Episcopal (AME) Church had a thousand ministers, 44,000 members, and its own school of theology, while the AME Zion Church had 45,000 members. In the rapid growth of churches, some of which became the wealthiest and most autonomous institutions in black life, the freedpeople demonstrated their most secure claim on freedom.

Photo by Rudolf Eickemeyer. Division of Culture & the Arts, National Museum of American History, Behring Center, Smithsonian Institution.

▲ African Americans of all ages eagerly pursued the opportunity to gain an education in freedom. This young woman in Mt. Meigs, Alabama, is helping her mother learn to read.

◀ Churches became a center of African American life, both social and political, during and after Reconstruction. Churches large and small, like this one in Georgia became the first black-owned institutions for the postfreedom generation.

14-2g Rise of the Sharecropping System

The desire to gain as much independence as possible also shaped the former slaves' economic arrangements. Since most of them lacked money to buy land, they preferred the next best thing: renting the land they worked. But the South had a cash-poor economy with few sources of credit, and few whites would consider renting land to blacks. Most blacks had no means to get cash before the harvest, so other alternatives had to be tried.

Black farmers and white landowners therefore turned to **sharecropping**, a system in which farmers kept part of their crop and gave the rest to the landowner while living on his property. The landlord or a merchant "furnished" food and supplies, such as draft animals and seed, and he received payment from the crop. White landowners and black farmers bargained with one another; sharecroppers would hold out, or move and try to switch employers from one year to another. As the system matured during the 1870s and 1880s, most sharecroppers worked "on halves"—half for the owner and half for themselves.

The sharecropping system, which materialized as early as 1868 in parts of the South, originated as a desirable compromise between former slaves and landowners. It eased landowners' problems with cash and credit, and provided

sharecropping The system of tenant farming that replaced slavery; freedpeople "worked on halves," giving half of their crop to the landowner and taking half to market. The system left most freedpeople mired in debt with no social or geographic mobility.

them a permanent, dependent labor force; blacks accepted it because it gave them freedom from daily supervision. In some districts women could leave field work, or even bargain for themselves to do less physical labor. Instead of working in the hated gangs under a white overseer, as in slavery, they farmed their own plots of land in family groups. But sharecropping later proved to be a disaster. Owners and merchants developed a monopoly of control over the agricultural economy, as sharecroppers found themselves mired in ever-increasing debt.

The fundamental problem, however, was that southern farmers as a whole still concentrated on cotton. In freedom, black women often chose to stay away from the fields and cotton picking to concentrate on domestic chores. Given the diminishing incentives of the system, they placed greater value on independent choices about gender roles and family organization than on reaching higher levels of production. The South did recover its prewar share of British cotton purchases, but cotton prices began a long decline, as world demand fell off.

Thus, southern agriculture slipped deeper and deeper into depression. Black sharecroppers struggled under a growing burden of debt that bound them to landowners and to "furnishing" merchants almost as oppressively as slavery had bound them to their masters. Many white farmers became debtors, too, gradually lost their land, and joined the ranks of sharecroppers. By the end of Reconstruction, over one-third of all southern farms were worked by sharecropping tenants, white and black.

Sharecropping: Enslaved to Debt

Sharecropping became an oppressive system in the postwar South. A new labor structure that began as a compromise between freedpeople who wanted independence and landowners who wanted a stable workforce evolved into a method of working on "halves," where tenants owed endless debts to the furnishing merchants, who owned plantation stores like this one, photographed in Mississippi in 1868. Merchants recorded in ledger books the debts that few sharecroppers were able to repay.

CRITICAL THINKING

- Why did both former slaves and former slave owners initially find sharecropping an agreeable, if difficult, new labor arrangement?
- What were the short- and long-term consequences of the sharecropping system for the freedpeople and for the southern economy?

◀ This Mississippi plantation store, shown in 1868, is a typical example of the new institution of the furnishing merchant and its power over postslavery agriculture in the South.

The Amistad Center of Art & Culture

◀ African Americans stand beside a log cabin home in Savannah, GA, c. 1867–1890.

Library of Congress, Prints & Photographs Division [LC-DIG-ppmsca-39591]

14-3 Johnson's Reconstruction Plan

▶ How did Andrew Johnson's political beliefs and personal background shape his views of former Confederates and freedpeople?

▶ What Reconstruction policies did Johnson enact?

▶ How did Johnson's Reconstruction policies affect freedpeople?

When Reconstruction began under President Andrew Johnson, many expected his policies to be harsh. Throughout his career in Tennessee, he had criticized the wealthy planters and championed the small farmers. When an assassin's bullet thrust Johnson into the presidency, many former slave owners shared the dismay of a North Carolina woman who wrote, "Think of Andy Johnson [as] the president! What will become of us—'the aristocrats of the South' as we are termed?" Northern Radicals also had reason to believe that Johnson would deal sternly with the South. When one of them suggested the exile or execution of ten or twelve leading rebels to set an example, Johnson replied, "How are you going to pick out so small a number? . . . Treason is a crime; and crime must be punished."

14-3a Andrew Johnson of Tennessee

Like his martyred predecessor, Johnson followed a path in antebellum politics from obscurity to power. With no formal education, he became a tailor's apprentice. But from 1829, while in his early twenties, he held nearly every office in Tennessee politics: alderman, state representative, congressman, two terms as governor, and U.S. senator by 1857. Although elected as a southern Democrat, Johnson was the only senator from a seceded state who refused to follow his state out of the Union. Lincoln appointed him war governor of Tennessee in 1862; hence his symbolic place on the ticket in the president's bid for reelection in 1864.

Although a Unionist, Johnson's political beliefs made him an old Jacksonian Democrat. And as they said in the mountainous region of east Tennessee, where Johnson established a reputation as a stump speaker, "Old Andy never went back on his raisin'." Johnson was also an ardent states' rightist. Before the war, he had supported tax-funded public schools and homestead legislation, fashioning himself as a champion of the common man. Although he vehemently opposed secession, Johnson advocated limited government. He shared none of the Radicals' expansive conception of federal power. His philosophy toward Reconstruction may be summed up in the slogan he adopted: "The Constitution as it is, and the Union as it was."

Through most of 1865, Johnson alone controlled Reconstruction policy, for Congress recessed shortly before he became president and did not reconvene until December. In the following eight months, Johnson formed new state governments in the South by using his power to grant pardons. He advanced Lincoln's leniency by extending even easier terms to former Confederates.

14-3b Johnson's Racial Views

Johnson had owned house slaves, although he had never been a planter. He accepted emancipation as a result of the war, but he did not favor black civil and political rights. Johnson believed that black suffrage could never be imposed on a southern state by the federal government, and that set him on a collision course with the Radicals. When it came to race, Johnson was a thoroughgoing white supremacist. He held what one politician called "unconquerable prejudices against the African race." In perhaps the most blatantly racist official statement ever delivered by an American president, Johnson declared in his annual message of 1867 that blacks possessed "less capacity for government than any other race of people. No independent government of any form has ever been successful in their hands; . . . wherever they have been left to their own devices they have shown a constant tendency to relapse into barbarism."

Such racial views had an enduring effect on Johnson's policies. Where whites were concerned, however, Johnson seemed to be pursuing changes in class relations. He proposed rules that would keep the wealthy planter class at least temporarily out of power.

Library of Congress Prints & Photographs Division (LC-B8184-10690)

▲ Combative and inflexible, President Andrew Johnson contributed greatly to the failure of his own Reconstruction program.

14-3c Johnson's Pardon Policy

White southerners were required to swear an oath of loyalty as a condition of gaining amnesty or pardon, but Johnson barred several categories of people from taking the oath: former federal officials, high-ranking Confederate officers, and political leaders or graduates of West Point or Annapolis who joined the Confederacy. To this list, Johnson added another important group: all ex-Confederates whose taxable property was worth more than $20,000. These individuals had to apply personally to the president for pardon and restoration of their political rights. The president, it seemed, meant to take revenge on the old planter elite.

Johnson appointed provisional governors, who began the Reconstruction process by calling state constitutional conventions. The delegates chosen for these conventions had to draft new constitutions that eliminated slavery and invalidated secession. After ratification of these constitutions, new governments could be elected, and the states would be restored to the Union with full congressional representation. But only those southerners who had taken the oath of amnesty and had been eligible to vote on the day the state seceded could participate in this process. Thus unpardoned whites and former slaves were not eligible.

14-3d Presidential Reconstruction

If Johnson intended to strip former aristocrats of their power, he did not hold to his plan. The old white leadership proved resilient and influential; prominent Confederates won elections and turned up in various appointive offices. Then Johnson started pardoning planters and leading rebels. He hired additional clerks to prepare the necessary documents and then began to issue pardons to large categories of people. By September 1865, hundreds were issued in a single day. These pardons, plus the rapid return of planters' abandoned lands, restored the old elite to power and quickly gave Johnson an image as the South's champion.

Why did Johnson allow the planters to regain power? He was determined to achieve a rapid Reconstruction in order to deny the Radicals any opportunity for the more thorough racial and political changes they desired in the South. And Johnson needed southern support in the 1866 elections; hence, he declared Reconstruction complete only eight months after Appomattox. Thus, in December 1865, many Confederate congressmen traveled to Washington to claim seats in the U.S. Congress. Even Alexander Stephens, vice president of the Confederacy, returned to Capitol Hill as a senator-elect from Georgia.

The election of such prominent rebels troubled many northerners. Some of the state conventions were slow to repudiate secession; others admitted only grudgingly that slavery was dead and wrote new laws to show it.

14-3e Black Codes

To define the status of freed men and women and control their labor, some legislatures merely revised large sections of the slave codes by substituting the word *freedmen* for *slaves*.

The new black codes compelled former slaves to carry passes, observe a curfew, live in housing provided by a landowner, and give up hope of entering many desirable occupations. Stiff vagrancy laws and restrictive labor contracts bound freedpeople to plantations, and "anti-enticement" laws punished anyone who tried to lure these workers to other employment. State-supported schools and orphanages excluded blacks entirely.

It seemed to some northerners that the South was intent on returning African Americans to servility and that Johnson's Reconstruction policy held no one responsible for the terrible war. But memories of the war—not yet even a year over—were still raw and would dominate political behavior for several elections to come. Thus, the Republican majority in Congress decided to call a halt to the results of Johnson's plan. On reconvening, the House and Senate considered the credentials of the newly elected southern representatives and decided not to admit them. Instead, they bluntly challenged the president's authority and established a joint committee to study and investigate a new direction for Reconstruction.

14-4 The Congressional Reconstruction Plan

▶ What political divisions existed in Congress?

▶ How did the relationship between the president and Congress evolve in the postwar period?

▶ What was the significance of the Fourteenth and Fifteenth Amendments?

▶ How did Congress re-incorporate former Confederate states into the Union?

Northern congressmen were hardly unified, but they did not doubt their right to shape Reconstruction policy. The Constitution mentioned neither secession nor reunion, but it gave Congress the primary role in the admission of states. Moreover, the Constitution declared that the United States shall guarantee to each state a "republican form of government." This provision, legislators believed, gave them the authority to devise policies for Reconstruction.

They soon faced other grave constitutional questions. What, for example, had rebellion done to the relationship between southern states and the Union? Lincoln had always believed secession impossible—the Confederate states had engaged in an "insurrection" within the Union in his view. Congressmen who favored vigorous Reconstruction measures argued that the war had broken the Union and that the South was subject to the victor's will. Moderate congressmen held that the states had forfeited their rights through rebellion and thus had come under congressional supervision.

14-4a The Radicals

These theories mirrored the diversity of Congress itself. Northern Democrats, weakened by their opposition to the war in its final year, denounced any idea of racial equality and supported Johnson's policies. Conservative Republicans, despite their party loyalty, favored a limited federal role in Reconstruction. The Radical Republicans, led by Thaddeus Stevens, Charles Sumner, and George Julian, wanted to transform the South. Although a minority in their party, they had the advantage of clearly defined goals. They believed it was essential to democratize the South, establish public education, and ensure the rights of the freedpeople. They favored black suffrage, supported some land confiscation and redistribution, and were willing to exclude the South from the Union for several years if necessary to achieve their goals.

Born of the war and its outcome, the Radicals brought a new civic vision to American life; they wanted to create an activist federal government and the beginnings of racial equality. A large group of moderate Republicans, led by Lyman Trumbull, opposed Johnson's leniency but wanted to restrain the Radicals. Trumbull and the moderates were, however, committed to federalizing the enforcement of civil, if not political, rights for the freedmen.

One overwhelming political reality faced all four groups: the 1866 elections. Ironically, Johnson and the Democrats sabotaged the possibility of a conservative coalition. They refused to cooperate with moderate Republicans and insisted that Reconstruction was over, that the new state governments were legitimate, and that southern representatives should be admitted to Congress. Among the Republicans, the Radicals' influence grew in proportion to Johnson's intransigence and outright provocation. It is an old story in American politics: when compromise or coalition fails, more radical visions will fill the void. Sometimes this leads to great social change, but other times to crisis and disaster.

14-4b Congress Versus Johnson

Trying to work with Johnson, Republicans believed a compromise had been reached in the spring of 1866. Under its terms, Johnson would agree to two modifications of his program: extension of the Freedmen's Bureau for another year and passage of a civil rights bill to counteract the black codes. This bill would force southern courts to practice equality under the ultimate scrutiny of the federal judiciary. Its provisions applied to public, not private, acts of discrimination. The Civil Rights Bill of 1866 was the first statutory definition of the rights of American citizens and is still on the books today.

Johnson destroyed the compromise, however, by vetoing both bills (they later became law when Congress overrode the president's veto). Denouncing any change in his program, the president condemned Congress's action and revealed his own racism. Because the Civil Rights Bill defined U.S. citizens as native-born persons who were taxed, Johnson claimed it discriminated against "large numbers of intelligent, worthy, and patriotic

Fourteenth Amendment
Defined U.S. citizens as anyone born or naturalized in the United States, barred states from interfering with citizens' constitutional rights, and stated for the first time that voters must be male.

Library of Congress Prints and Photographs Division [LC-USZ62-63460]

▲ Photograph of Thaddeus Stevens, Republican Congressman and staunch abolitionist from Pennsylvania, and leader of the "radicals" during the creation of Reconstruction policies, 1866–68.

foreigners . . . in favor of the negro." Anticipating arguments used by modern conservatives, the bill, he said, operated "in favor of the colored and against the white race."

All hope of presidential-congressional cooperation was now dead. In 1866, newspapers reported daily violations of black peoples' rights in the South and carried alarming accounts of anti-black violence—notably in Memphis and New Orleans, where police aided brutal mobs in their attacks. In Memphis, forty blacks were killed and twelve schools burned by white mobs, and in New Orleans, the toll was thirty-four African Americans dead and two hundred wounded. Such violence convinced Republicans, and the northern public, that more needed to be done. A new Republican plan took the form of the **Fourteenth Amendment** to the Constitution.

14-4c Fourteenth Amendment

Of the five sections of the Fourteenth Amendment, the first would have the greatest legal significance in later years. Written by John Bingham of Ohio, it conferred citizenship on "all persons born or naturalized in the United States" and prohibited states from abridging their constitutional "privileges and immunities" (see the Appendix for the Constitution and all amendments). It also barred any state from taking a person's life, liberty, or property "without due process of law" and from denying "equal protection of the laws." These resounding phrases have become powerful guarantees of African

Americans' civil rights—indeed, of the rights of all citizens, except for Native Americans, who were not granted citizenship rights until 1924.

Nearly universal agreement emerged among Republicans on the amendment's second and third sections. The fourth declared the Confederate debt null and void, and guaranteed the war debt of the United States. Northerners rejected the notion of paying taxes to reimburse those who had financed a rebellion, and business groups agreed on the necessity of upholding the credit of the U.S. government, an element of the Fourteenth Amendment that was invoked in bitter debates between congressional Republicans and the Obama administration over raising the federal "debt ceiling" in 2011 and again in 2013. The second and third sections barred Confederate leaders from holding state and federal office. Only Congress, by a two-thirds vote of each house, could remove the penalty. The amendment thus guaranteed a degree of punishment for the leaders of the Confederacy.

The second section of the amendment also dealt with representation and embodied the compromises that produced the document. Northerners disagreed about whether black people should have the right to vote. As a citizen of Indiana wrote to a southern relative, "[a]lthough there is a great deal [of] profession among us for the relief of the darkey yet I think much of it is far from being sincere. I guess we want to compel you to do right by them while we are not willing ourselves to do so." Those arched words are indicative not only of how revolutionary Reconstruction had become, but also of how far the public will, North and South, lagged behind the enactments that became new constitutional cornerstones. Many northern states still maintained black disfranchisement laws during Reconstruction.

Emancipation finally ended the three-fifths clause for the purpose of counting blacks, which would increase southern representation. Thus, the postwar South stood to gain power in Congress, and if white southerners did not allow black southerners to vote, former secessionists would derive the political benefit from emancipation. That was more irony than most northerners could bear. So Republicans determined that, if a southern state did not grant black men the vote, their representation would be reduced proportionally. If they did enfranchise black men, their representation would be increased proportionally. This compromise avoided a direct enactment of black suffrage but would deliver future black southern voters to the Republican Party.

The Fourteenth Amendment specified for the first time that voters were "male" and ignored female citizens, black and white. For this reason, it provoked a strong reaction from the women's rights movement. Advocates of women's equality had worked with abolitionists for decades, often subordinating their cause to that of the slaves. During the drafting of the Fourteenth Amendment, however, female activists demanded to be heard. Prominent leaders, such as Elizabeth Cady Stanton and Susan B. Anthony, ended their alliance with abolitionists and fought for women,

while others remained committed to the idea that it was "the Negro's hour." Thus, the amendment infused new life into the women's rights movement and caused considerable strife among old allies.

14-4d The South's and Johnson's Defiance

In 1866, however, the major question in Reconstruction politics was how the public would respond to the congressional initiative. Johnson did his best to block the Fourteenth Amendment in both North and South. Condemning Congress for its refusal to seat southern representatives, the president urged state legislatures in the South to vote against ratification. Every southern legislature, except Tennessee's, rejected the amendment by a wide margin.

To present his case to northerners, Johnson organized a National Union Convention and took to the stump himself. In an age when active personal campaigning was rare for a president, Johnson boarded a special train for a "swing around the circle" that carried his message into the Northeast, the Midwest, and then back to Washington. In city after city, he criticized the Republicans in a ranting, undignified style. Increasingly, audiences rejected his views, hooting and jeering at him. In this whistle-stop tour, Johnson began to hand out American flags with thirty-six rather than twenty-five stars, declaring the Union already restored. At many towns, he likened himself to a "persecuted" Jesus who might now be martyred "upon the cross" for his magnanimity toward the South. And, repeatedly, he labeled the Radicals "traitors" for their efforts to take over Reconstruction.

The elections of 1866 were a resounding victory, though, for Republicans in Congress. Radicals and moderates whom Johnson had denounced won reelection by large margins, and the Republican majority grew to two-thirds of both houses of Congress. The North had spoken clearly: Johnson's official policies of states' rights and white supremacy were prematurely giving the advantage to former rebels and traitors. Thus, Republican congressional leaders won a mandate to pursue their Reconstruction plan.

But Johnson and southern intransigence had brought the plan to an impasse. Nothing could be accomplished as long as the "Johnson governments" existed and the southern electorate remained exclusively white. Republicans resolved to form new state governments in the South and enfranchise the freedmen.

14-4e Reconstruction Acts of 1867–1868

After some embittered debate in which Republicans and the remaining Democrats in Congress argued over the meaning and memory of the Civil War itself, the First Reconstruction Act passed in March 1867. This plan, under which the southern states were actually readmitted to the Union, incorporated only a part of the Radical program. Union generals, commanding small garrisons of troops and charged with supervising elections, assumed control in five military districts in the South (see Map 14.1). Confederate leaders designated in the Fourteenth Amendment were barred from voting until

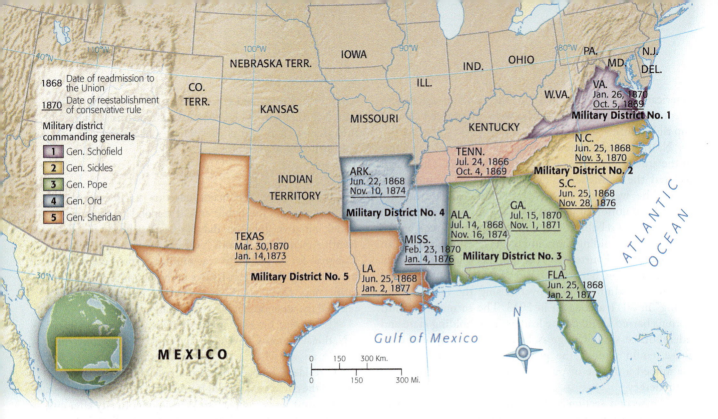

Map 14.1 The Reconstruction Act of 1867

This map shows the five military districts established when Congress passed the Reconstruction Act of 1867. As the dates within each state indicate, conservative Democratic forces quickly regained control of government in four southern states. So-called Radical Reconstruction was curtailed in most of the others as factions within the weakened Republican Party began to cooperate with conservative Democrats.

new state constitutions were ratified. The act guaranteed freedmen the right to vote in elections as well as serve in state constitutional conventions and in subsequent elections. In addition, each southern state was required to ratify the Fourteenth Amendment, to approve its new constitution by majority vote, and to submit it to Congress for acceptance (see Table 14.1).

Thus, African Americans gained an opportunity to fight for a better life through the political process, and ex-Confederates were given what they interpreted as a bitter pill to swallow in order to return to the Union. The Second, Third, and Fourth Reconstruction Acts, passed between March 1867 and March 1868, provided the details of operation for voter registration boards, the adoption of constitutions, and the administration of "good faith" oaths on the part of white southerners.

14-4f Failure of Land Redistribution

In the words of one historian, the Radicals succeeded in "clipping Johnson's wings." But they had hoped Congress could do much more. Thaddeus Stevens, for example, argued that economic opportunity was essential to the freedmen. "If we do not furnish them with homesteads from forfeited and rebel property," Stevens declared, "and hedge them around with protective laws . . . we had better left them in bondage." Stevens therefore drew up a plan for extensive confiscation and redistribution of land, but it was never realized. Some historians see this as the great lost opportunity of Reconstruction.

Racial fears among whites and an American obsession with the sanctity of private property made land redistribution unpopular. Northerners were accustomed to a limited role for government, and the business community staunchly opposed any interference with private-property rights, even for former Confederates. Thus, black farmers were forced to seek work in a hostile environment in which landowners opposed their acquisition of land.

14-4g Constitutional Crisis

Congress's quarrels with Andrew Johnson grew still worse. To restrict Johnson's influence and safeguard its plan, Congress passed a number of controversial laws. First, it limited Johnson's power over the army by requiring the president to issue military orders through the General of the Army, Ulysses S. Grant, who could not be dismissed without the Senate's consent. Then Congress passed the Tenure of Office Act, which gave the Senate power to approve changes in the president's cabinet. Designed to protect Secretary of War Stanton, who sympathized with the Radicals, this law violated the tradition that a president controlled appointments to his own cabinet.

All of these measures, as well as each of the Reconstruction Acts, were passed by a two-thirds override of presidential vetoes. The situation led some to believe that the federal government had reached a stage of "congressional tyranny" and others to conclude that Johnson had become an obstacle to the legitimate will of the people in reconstructing the nation on a just and permanent basis.

Table 14.1 Plans for Reconstruction Compared

	Johnson's Plan	Radicals' Plan	Fourteenth Amendment	Reconstruction Act of 1867
Voting	Whites only; high-ranking Confederate leaders must seek pardons	Give vote to black males	Southern whites may decide but can lose representation if they deny black suffrage	Black men gain vote; whites barred from office by Fourteenth Amendment cannot vote while new state governments are being formed
Office holding	Many prominent Confederates regain power	Only loyal white and black males eligible	Confederate leaders barred until Congress votes amnesty	Fourteenth Amendment in effect
Time out of Union	Brief	Several years; until South is thoroughly democratized	Brief	3–5 years after war
Other change in southern society	Little; gain of power by yeomen not realized; emancipation grudgingly accepted, but no black civil or political rights	Expand education; confiscate land and provide farms for freedmen; expansion of activist federal government	Probably slight, depending on enforcement	Considerable, depending on action of new state governments

Johnson took several belligerent steps of his own. He issued orders to military commanders in the South, limiting their powers and increasing the powers of the civil governments he had created in 1865. Then he removed military officers who were conscientiously enforcing Congress's new law, preferring commanders who allowed disqualified Confederates to vote. Finally, he tried to remove Secretary of War Stanton. With that attempt, the confrontation reached its climax.

14-4h Impeachment of President Johnson

Impeachment is a political procedure provided for in the Constitution as a remedy for crimes or serious abuses of power by presidents, federal judges, and other high government officials. Those impeached (politically indicted) in the House are then tried in the Senate. Historically, this power has generally not been used as a means to investigate and judge the private lives of presidents, although in recent times it was used in this manner in the case of President Bill Clinton.

Twice in 1867, the House Judiciary Committee had considered impeachment of Johnson, rejecting the idea once and then recommending it by only a 5-to-4 vote. That recommendation was decisively defeated by the House. After Johnson tried to remove Stanton, however, a third attempt to impeach the president carried easily in early 1868. The indictment concentrated on his violation of the Tenure of Office Act, though many modern scholars regard his efforts to obstruct enforcement of the Reconstruction Act of 1867 as a far more serious offense.

Johnson's trial in the Senate lasted more than three months. The prosecution, led by Radicals, attempted to prove that Johnson was guilty of "high crimes and misdemeanors."

But they also argued that the trial was a means to judge Johnson's performance, not a judicial determination of guilt or innocence. The Senate ultimately rejected such reasoning, which could have made removal from office a political weapon against any chief executive who disagreed with Congress. Although a majority of senators voted to convict Johnson, the prosecution fell one vote short of the necessary two-thirds majority. Johnson remained in office, politically weakened and with less than a year left in his term. Some Republicans backed away from impeachment because they had their eyes on the 1868 election and did not want to hurt their prospects of regaining the White House.

14-4i Election of 1868

In the 1868 presidential election, Ulysses S. Grant, running as a Republican, defeated Horatio Seymour, a New York Democrat. Grant was not a Radical, but his platform supported **Congressional Reconstruction** and endorsed black suffrage in the South. (Significantly, Republicans stopped short of endorsing black suffrage in the North.) The Democrats, meanwhile, vigorously denounced Reconstruction and preached white supremacy. Indeed, in the 1868 election, the Democrats conducted the most openly racist campaign to that point in American history. Both sides waved the "bloody shirt," accusing each other as the villains of the war's sacrifices. By associating themselves

Impeachment Process to remove a president from office; attempted but failed in the case of Andrew Johnson.

Congressional Reconstruction The process by which the Republican-controlled Congress sought to make the Reconstruction of the ex-Confederate states longer, harsher, and under greater congressional control.

▲ *His First Vote*, 1868, by Thomas Waterman Wood, oil on canvas, invoking the power and significance of black male suffrage during Reconstruction.

His First Vote, 1868, 1868 (oil on panel)/Wood, Thomas Waterman (1823–1903)/CHRISTIE'S IMAGES/Private Collection/Bridgeman Images

with rebellion and with Johnson's repudiated program, the Democrats went down to defeat in all but eight states, though the popular vote was fairly close. Participating in their first presidential election ever on a wide scale, African Americans decisively voted en masse for General Grant.

In office, Grant acted as an administrator of Reconstruction but not as its enthusiastic advocate. He vacillated in his dealings with the southern states, sometimes defending Republican regimes and sometimes currying favor with Democrats. On occasion, Grant called out federal troops to stop violence or enforce acts of Congress. But he never imposed a true military occupation on the South. Rapid demobilization had reduced a federal army of more than 1 million to 57,000 within a year of the surrender at Appomattox. Thereafter, the number of troops in the South continued to fall,

Fifteenth Amendment
Prohibited states from denying the vote to any citizen on account of "race, color, or previous condition of servitude."

until in 1874 there were only 4,000 in the southern states outside Texas. The later legend of "military rule," so important to southern claims of victimization during Reconstruction, was steeped in myth.

14-4j Fifteenth Amendment

In 1869, the Radicals pushed through the **Fifteenth Amendment**, the final major measure in the constitutional revolution of Reconstruction. This measure forbade states to deny the right to vote "on account of race, color, or previous condition of servitude." Such wording did not guarantee the right to vote. It deliberately left states free to restrict suffrage on other grounds so that northern states could continue to deny suffrage to women and certain groups of men—Chinese immigrants, illiterate men, and those too poor to pay poll taxes.

Although several states outside the South refused to ratify, three-fourths of the states approved the measure, and the Fifteenth Amendment became law in 1870. It, too, had been a political compromise, and though African Americans rejoiced all across the land at its enactment, it left open the possibility for states to create countless qualification tests to obstruct voting in the future.

With passage of the Fifteenth Amendment, many Americans, especially supportive northerners, considered Reconstruction essentially completed. "Let us have done with Reconstruction," pleaded the *New York Tribune* in April 1870. "The country is tired and sick of it . . . . Let us have Peace!" But some northerners, like abolitionist Wendell Phillips, worried. "Our day," he warned, "is fast slipping away. Once let public thought float off from the great issue of the war, and it will take . . . more than a generation to bring it back again."

14-5 Politics and Reconstruction in the South

▶ **How did white Southerners resist the end of slavery and Reconstruction?**

▶ **How did Republican governments rule in the South?**

▶ **What was the relationship between African Americans and whites inside and outside of the Republican Party?**

▶ **How did white Southern conservatives seek to discredit Republican governments in the South?**

From the start, Reconstruction encountered the resistance of white southerners. In the black codes and in private attitudes, many whites stubbornly opposed emancipation, and the former planter class proved especially unbending because of its tremendous financial loss in slaves. In 1866, a Georgia newspaper frankly observed that "most of the white citizens believe that the institution of slavery was right, and . . . they will believe that the condition, which comes nearest to slavery, that can now be established will be the best." And for many poor whites who had never owned slaves and yet had sacrificed enormously in the war, destitution, plummeting agricultural prices, disease, and the uncertainties of a growing urban industrialization drove them off land, toward cities, and into hatred of the very idea of black equality.

14-5a White Resistance

Fearing loss of control over their slaves, some planters attempted to postpone freedom by denying or misrepresenting events. Former slaves reported that their owners "didn't tell them it was freedom" or "wouldn't let [them] go." Agents of the Freedmen's Bureau reported that "the old system of slavery [is] working with even more rigor than formerly at a few miles distant from any point where U.S. troops are stationed." To hold onto their workers, some landowners claimed control over black children and used guardianship and apprentice laws to bind black families to the plantation.

Whites also blocked blacks from acquiring land. A few planters divided up plots among their slaves, but most condemned the idea of making blacks landowners. A Georgia woman whose family was known for its support of religious education for slaves was outraged that two property owners planned to "rent their lands to the Negroes!" Such action was, she declared, "injurious to the best interest of the community."

Adamant resistance by whites soon manifested itself in other ways, including violence. In one North Carolina town, a local magistrate clubbed a black man on a public street, and in several states bands of "Regulators" terrorized blacks who displayed any independence. Amid their defeat, many planters believed, as a South Carolinian put it, that blacks "can't be

governed except with the whip." And after President Johnson encouraged the South to resist congressional Reconstruction, many white conservatives worked hard to capture the new state governments.

14-5b Black Voters and the Southern Republican Party

Enthusiastically, black men voted Republican. Most agreed with one man who felt he should "stick to the end with the party that freed me." Illiteracy did not prohibit blacks (or uneducated whites) from making intelligent choices. Although Mississippi's William Henry could read only "a little," he testified that he and his friends had no difficulty selecting the Republican ballot. "We stood around and watched," he explained. "We saw D. Sledge vote; he owned half the county. We knowed he voted Democratic so we voted the other ticket so it would be Republican." Women, who could not vote, encouraged their husbands and sons, and preachers exhorted their congregations to use the franchise. Zeal for voting spread through entire black communities.

Thanks to a large black turnout and the restrictions on prominent Confederates, a new southern Republican Party came to power in the constitutional conventions of 1868–1870. Republican delegates consisted of a sizable contingent of blacks (265 out of the total of just over 1,000 delegates throughout the South), some northerners who had moved to the South, and native southern whites who favored change. The new constitutions drafted by this Republican coalition were more democratic than anything previously adopted in the history of the South. They eliminated property qualifications for voting and holding office, and they turned many appointed offices into elective posts. They provided for public schools and institutions to care for the mentally ill, the blind, the deaf, the destitute, and the orphaned.

The conventions broadened women's rights in property holding and divorce. Usually, the goal was not to make women equal with men but to provide relief to thousands of suffering debtors. In white families left poverty-stricken by the war and weighed down by debt, it was usually the husband who had contracted the debts. Thus, giving women legal control over their own property provided some protection to their families.

14-5c Triumph of Republican Governments

Under these new constitutions, the southern states elected Republican-controlled governments. For the first time, the ranks of state legislators in 1868 included black southerners. Contrary to what white southerners would later claim, the Republican state governments did not disfranchise ex-Confederates as a group. James Lynch, a leading black politician from Mississippi, explained why African Americans shunned the "folly" of disfranchising whites. Unlike northerners who "can leave when it becomes too uncomfortable," landless former slaves "must be in friendly relations with the great body of the whites in the state. Otherwise . . . peace can be maintained only by a standing army." Despised and

▲ Black Southerners attempting to vote are halted by White Leaguers in this engraving by J. H. Wares. The black man doffing his cap holds a "Republican ticket" but it will not get him to the ballot box, guarded by the election judge with a loaded pistol.

lacking material or social power, southern Republicans strove for acceptance, legitimacy, and safe ways to gain a foothold in a depressed economy.

Far from being vindictive toward the race that had enslaved them, most black southerners treated leading rebels with generosity and appealed to white southerners to adopt a spirit of fairness. In this way, the South's Republican Party condemned itself to defeat if white voters would not cooperate. Within a few years, most of the fledgling Republican parties in the southern states would be struggling for survival against violent white hostility. Utter obstruction, the politics of fear, and violence has sometimes worked as a means to power in America. But for a time, some propertied whites accepted congressional Reconstruction as a reality.

14-5d Industrialization and Mill Towns

Reflecting northern ideals and southern necessity, the Reconstruction governments enthusiastically promoted industry. Accordingly, Reconstruction legislatures encouraged investment with loans, subsidies, and short-term exemptions from taxation. The southern railroad system was rebuilt and expanded, and coal and iron mining made possible Birmingham's steel plants. Between 1860 and 1880, the number of manufacturing establishments in the South nearly doubled.

This emphasis on business enterprise, however, produced higher state debts and taxes, drew money away from schools and other programs, and multiplied possibilities for corruption in state legislatures. The alliance between business and government took firm hold, often at the expense of the needs of common farmers and laborers. It also locked Republicans into a conservative strategy and doomed their chances with poorer whites.

Poverty remained the lot of vast numbers of southern whites. On a daily basis during the Reconstruction years, they had to subordinate politics to the struggle for livelihood. The war had caused a massive onetime loss of income-producing wealth, such as livestock, and a steep decline in land values. In many regions, the old planter class still ruled the best land and access to credit or markets.

As many poor whites and blacks found farming less tenable, they moved to cities and new mill towns. Industrialization did not sweep the South as it did the North, but it certainly laid deep roots. Attracting textile mills to southern towns became a competitive crusade. "Next to God," shouted a North Carolina evangelist, "what this town needs is a cotton mill!" In 1860, the South counted some 10,000 mill workers; by 1880, the number grew to 16,741 and, by the end of the century, to 97,559. Thus, poor southerners began the multigenerational journey from farmer to urban wage earner.

14-5e Republicans and Racial Equality

Policies appealing to African American voters rarely went beyond equality before the law. In fact, the whites who controlled the southern Republican Party were reluctant to allow blacks a share of offices proportionate to their electoral strength. Aware of their weakness, black leaders did not push very far for revolutionary economic or social change. In every

The Granger Collection

▲ *The Queen of Industry, or the New South,* cartoon by Thomas Nast, 1882, contrasting the pre-Civil War plantation economy with the more industrialized economy of the 1880s.

southern state, they led efforts to establish public schools, although they did not press for integrated facilities. In 1870, South Carolina passed the first comprehensive school law in the South. By 1875, in a major achievement for a Reconstruction government, 50 percent of black school-age children in that state were enrolled in school, and approximately one-third of the three thousand teachers were black.

Some African American politicians did fight for civil rights and integration. Many were from cities such as New Orleans or Mobile, where large populations of light-skinned free black people had existed before the war. Their experience in such communities had made them sensitive to issues of status, and they spoke out for open and equal public accommodations. Laws requiring equal accommodations won passage, but they often went unenforced.

The vexing questions of land reform and enforcement of racial equality, however, all but overwhelmed the Republican governments. Land reform largely failed because in most states whites were in the majority, and former slave owners controlled the best land and other sources of economic power. Economic progress was uppermost in the minds of most freedpeople. Black southerners needed land, and much land did fall into state hands for nonpayment of taxes. Such land was offered for sale in small lots. But most freedmen had too little cash to bid against investors or speculators. South Carolina established a land commission, but it could help only those with money to buy. Widespread redistribution of land had to arise from Congress, which never supported such action.

14-5f Myth of "Negro Rule"

Within a few years, white hostility to congressional Reconstruction began to dominate. Some conservatives had always wanted to fight Reconstruction through pressure and racist propaganda. They put economic and social pressure on black people: one black Republican reported that "my neighbors will not employ me, nor sell me a farthing's worth of anything." Charging that the South had been turned over to ignorant blacks, conservatives deplored "black domination," which became a rallying cry for a return to white supremacy.

Such attacks were inflammatory propaganda and part of the growing myth of "Negro rule," which would serve as a central theme in battles over the memory of Reconstruction. African Americans participated in politics but hardly dominated or controlled events. They were a majority in only two out of ten state constitutional writing conventions (transplanted northerners were a majority in one). In the state legislatures, only in the lower house in South Carolina did black legislators ever constitute a majority. Sixteen black men won seats in Congress before Reconstruction was over, but none was ever elected governor. Only eighteen served in a high state office, such as lieutenant governor, treasurer, superintendent of education, or secretary of state.

In all, some four hundred black men served in political office during the Reconstruction era, a signal achievement by any standard. Although they never dominated the process, they established a rich tradition of government service and civic activism. Elected officials, such as Robert Smalls in South Carolina, labored tirelessly for cheaper land prices, better health care, access to schools, and the enforcement of civil rights for black people. For too long, the black politicians of Reconstruction were the forgotten heroes of this seedtime of America's long civil rights movement.

14-5g Carpetbaggers and Scalawags

Conservatives also assailed the allies of black Republicans. Their propaganda denounced whites from the North as **"carpetbaggers,"** greedy crooks planning to pour stolen tax revenues into their sturdy luggage made of carpet material. Immigrants from the North, who held the largest share of Republican offices, were all tarred with this rhetorical brush.

In fact, most northerners who settled in the South had come seeking business opportunities, as schoolteachers, or to find a warmer climate; most never entered politics. Those who did enter politics generally wanted to democratize the South and to introduce northern ways, such as industry and public education. Carpetbaggers' ideals were tested by hard times and ostracism by white southerners.

Carpetbaggers' real actions never matched the sensational stereotypes, although by the mid-1870s even some

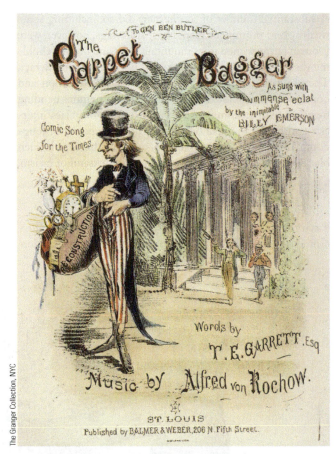

▲ *The Carpetbagger*, American lithograph song sheet music cover, ca. 1869. Emanating from the heyday of anti-carpetbagger propaganda, the figure seems to be part Uncle Sam and part scheming scoundrel with his bagful of Yankee notions, both religious and secular.

northerners who soured on Reconstruction or despaired over southern violence endorsed the images. Thomas Wentworth Higginson, a Union officer and commander of an African American regiment during the Civil War, suggested that any Yankee politician who remained in the South by 1874 was, more likely than not, a "mean man," a "scoundrel," and "like Shakespeare's Shylock." And that same year, the African American editors of the *Christian Recorder* distanced themselves from carpetbaggers. The "corrupt political vampires who rob and cheat and prey upon the prejudices of our people" and "feed upon the political carcass of a prostrate state," the paper insisted, were not black folks' allies. The white southern counterrevolutionaries seemed to be winning the propaganda war.

Conservatives also invented the term **scalawag** to discredit any native white southerner who cooperated with the Republicans.

"carpetbaggers" Derogatory nickname southerners gave to northerners who moved south after the Civil War, perceiving them as greedy opportunists who hoped to cash in on the South's plight.

scalawag Term used by conservative southerners to describe other white southerners who were perceived as aiding or benefiting from Reconstruction.

A substantial number of southerners did so, including some wealthy and prominent men. Most scalawags, however, were yeoman farmers, men from mountain areas and nonslaveholding districts who had been Unionists under the Confederacy. They saw that they could benefit from the education and opportunities promoted by Republicans. Sometimes banding together with freedmen, they pursued common class interests and hoped to make headway against the power of long-dominant planters. In the long run, however, the hope of such black-white coalitions floundered in the quicksand of racism.

14-5h Tax Policy and Corruption as Political Wedges

Taxation was a major problem for the Reconstruction governments. Republicans wanted to repair the war's destruction, stimulate industry, and support such new ventures as public schools. But the Civil War had destroyed much of the South's tax base. One category of valuable property—slaves—had disappeared entirely. And hundreds of thousands of citizens had lost much of the rest of their property—money, livestock, fences, and buildings—to the war. Thus, an increase in taxes (sales, excise, and property) was necessary even to maintain traditional services. Inevitably, Republican tax policies aroused strong opposition.

Corruption was another serious charge leveled against the Republicans. Unfortunately, it was often true. Many carpetbaggers and black politicians engaged in fraudulent schemes, sold their votes, or padded expenses, taking part in what scholars recognize was a nationwide surge of corruption in an age ruled by "spoilsmen." Corruption carried no

▲ Ku Klux Klan "Worse Than Slavery," an 1874 cartoon by Thomas Nast showing "White Leaguers" and the Klan combining in violence against blacks. The Granger Collection New York

party label, but the Democrats successfully pinned the blame on unqualified blacks and greedy carpetbaggers among southern Republicans.

14-5i Ku Klux Klan

All these problems hurt the Republicans, whose leaders also allowed factionalism along racial and class lines to undermine party unity. But in many southern states, the deathblow came through violence. The Ku Klux Klan (its members altered the Greek word for "circle," *kuklos*), a secret veterans' club that began in Tennessee in 1866, spread through the South, and rapidly evolved into a terrorist organization. Violence against African Americans occurred from the first days of Reconstruction but became far more organized and purposeful after 1867. Klansmen sought to frustrate Reconstruction and keep the freedmen in subjection. Nighttime harassment, whippings, beatings, rapes, and murders became common, as terrorism dominated some counties and regions.

Although the Klan tormented black people who stood up for their rights as laborers or individuals, its main purpose was political. Lawless night riders made active Republicans the target of their attacks. Leading white and black Republicans were killed in several states. After freedmen who worked for a South Carolina scalawag started voting, terrorists visited the plantation and, in the words of one victim, "whipped every . . . [black] man they could lay their hands on." Klansmen also attacked Union League clubs—Republican organizations that mobilized the black vote—and schoolteachers who were aiding the freedmen.

Klan violence was not a spontaneous outburst of racism; very specific social forces shaped and directed it. In North Carolina, for example, Alamance and Caswell counties were the sites of the worst Klan violence. Slim Republican majorities there rested on cooperation between black voters and white yeomen, particularly those whose Unionism or discontent with the Confederacy had turned them against local Democratic officials. Together, these black and white Republicans had ousted officials long entrenched in power. The wealthy and powerful men in Alamance and Caswell who had lost their accustomed political control were the Klan's county officers and local chieftains. They organized a deliberate campaign of terror, recruiting members and planning atrocities.

Klan violence injured and ultimately destroyed Republicans across the South. One of every ten black leaders who had been delegates to the 1867–1868 state constitutional conventions was attacked, seven fatally. In one judicial district of North Carolina, the Ku Klux Klan was responsible for twelve murders, over seven hundred beatings, and other acts of violence, including rape and arson. A single attack on Alabama Republicans in the town of Eutaw left four blacks dead and fifty-four wounded. In South Carolina, five hundred masked Klansmen lynched eight black prisoners at the Union County jail, and in nearby York County, the Klan committed at least eleven murders and hundreds of whippings. According to historian Eric Foner, the Klan "made it virtually impossible for Republicans to campaign or vote in large parts of Georgia."

Thus, a combination of difficult fiscal problems, Republican mistakes, racial hostility, and terror brought down the Republican regimes. In most southern states, Radical Reconstruction lasted only a few years (see Map 14.1). The most enduring failure of Reconstruction, however, was not political; it was social and economic.

14-6 Retreat from Reconstruction

▶ **How did the federal government respond to white conservative resistance to Reconstruction?**

▶ **What developments inside and outside of the South contributed to declining support for federal Reconstruction policies?**

▶ **How did relations between various ethnic and racial groups in the West contribute to additional conflict over race in the post-war period?**

▶ **What was the impact of the Supreme Court's rulings, particularly related to the Fourteenth Amendment?**

▶ **How was the disputed election of 1876 resolved?**

During the 1870s, northerners increasingly lost the political will to sustain Reconstruction in the South as a vast economic and social transformation occurred in their own region as well as in the West. Radical Republicans like Albion Tourgée, a former Union soldier who moved to North Carolina and was elected a judge, condemned Congress's timidity. Turning the freedman out on his own without protection, said Tourgée, constituted "cheap philanthropy." Indeed, many African Americans believed that, during Reconstruction, the North "threw all the Negroes on the world without any way of getting along." As the North underwent its own transformations and lost interest in the South's dilemmas, Reconstruction collapsed.

14-6a Political Implications of Klan Terrorism

In one southern state after another, Democrats regained control, and they threatened to defeat Republicans in the North as well. Whites in the old Confederacy referred to this decline of Reconstruction as "southern redemption," and during the 1870s, "redeemer" Democrats claimed to be the saviors of the South from alleged "black domination" and "carpetbag rule." And for one of only a few times in American history, violence and terror emerged as tactics in normal politics.

In 1870 and 1871, the violent campaigns of the Ku Klux Klan forced Congress to pass two **Enforcement Acts** and an anti-Klan law. These laws

Enforcement Acts Laws that sought to protect black voters, made violations of civil and political rights a federal offense, and sought to end Ku Klux Klan violence.

made actions by individuals against the civil and political rights of others a federal criminal offense for the first time. They also provided for election supervisors and permitted martial law and suspension of the writ of habeas corpus to combat murders, beatings, and threats by the Klan. Federal prosecutors used the laws rather selectively. In 1872 and 1873, Mississippi and the Carolinas saw many prosecutions; but in other states where violence flourished, the laws were virtually ignored. Southern juries sometimes refused to convict Klansmen; out of a total of 3,310 cases, only 1,143 ended in convictions. Although many Klansmen (roughly 2,000 in South Carolina alone) fled their state to avoid prosecution, and the Klan officially disbanded, the threat of violence did not end. Paramilitary organizations known as Rifle Clubs and Red Shirts often took the Klan's place.

Klan terrorism openly defied Congress, yet even on this issue there were ominous signs that the North's commitment to racial justice was fading. Some conservative but influential Republicans opposed the anti-Klan laws. Rejecting other Republicans' arguments that the Thirteenth, Fourteenth, and Fifteenth Amendments had made the federal government the protector of the rights of citizens, these dissenters echoed an old Democratic charge that Congress was infringing on states' rights. Senator Lyman Trumbull of Illinois, who had been a key author of the Thirteenth Amendment, declared that the states remained "the depositories of the rights of the individual." If Congress could punish crimes like assault or murder, he asked, "what is the need of the State governments?" For years, Democrats had complained of "centralization and consolidation"; now some Republicans seemed to agree with them. This opposition foreshadowed a more general revolt within Republican ranks in 1872.

14-6b Industrial Expansion and Reconstruction in the North

Both immigration and industrialization surged in the North. Between 1865 and 1873, 3 million immigrants entered the country, most settling in the industrial cities of the North and West. Within only eight years, postwar industrial production increased by 75 percent. For the first time, nonagricultural workers outnumbered farmers, and wage earners outnumbered independent craftsmen. And by 1873, only Britain's industrial output was greater than that of the United States. Government financial policies did much to bring about this rapid growth. Low taxes on investment and high tariffs on manufactured goods aided the growth of a new class of powerful industrialists, especially railroad entrepreneurs.

Railroads became the symbol of and the stimulus for the American age of capital. From 1865 to 1873, 35,000 miles of new track were laid, a total exceeding the entire national rail network of 1860. Railroad building fueled the banking industry and made Wall Street the center of American capitalism. Eastern railroad magnates, such as Thomas Scott of the Pennsylvania Railroad, the largest corporation of its time, created economic empires with the assistance of huge government subsidies of cash and land. Railroad corporations also bought up mining operations, granaries, and lumber companies. In Congress and in every state legislature, big business now employed lobbyists to curry favor with government. Corruption ran rampant; some congressmen and legislators were paid annual retainers by major companies. Indeed, the transcontinental railroads helped Americans imagine how to conquer vast spaces, as well as conceive of time in new ways. The railroads brought modernity to the United States like almost nothing else; but they also taught the nation sordid lessons about the perils of monopoly and corruption, and by the late nineteenth century railroad entrepreneurs were the most hated men in the West. Moreover, in this laissez-faire world without rules, many railroads were overbuilt and thereby endangered the economy.

This soaring capitalist–politician alliance led as well to an intensified struggle between labor and capital. As captains of industry amassed unprecedented fortunes in an age with no income tax, gross economic inequality polarized American society. The workforce, worried a prominent Massachusetts business leader, was in a "transition state . . . living in boarding houses" and becoming a "permanent factory population." In Cincinnati, three large factories employed as many workers as the city's thousands of small shops. In New York or Philadelphia, workers increasingly lived in dark, unhealthy tenement housing. Thousands would list themselves on the census as "common laborer" or "general jobber." Many of the free-labor maxims of the Republican Party were now under great duress. Did the individual work ethic guarantee social mobility in America or erode, under the pressure of profit making, into a world of unsafe factories, child labor, and declining wages? In 1868, the Republicans managed to pass an eight-hour workday bill in Congress that applied to federal workers. The "labor question" now preoccupied northerners far more than the "southern" or the "freedmen" question (see Chapter 16).

Then, the Panic of 1873 ushered in more than five years of economic contraction. Three million people lost their jobs as class attitudes diverged, especially in large cities. Debtors and the unemployed sought easy-money policies to spur economic expansion (workers and farmers desperately needed cash). Businessmen, disturbed by the widespread strikes and industrial violence that accompanied the panic, fiercely defended property rights and demanded "sound money" policies as they sought to crush labor unions. The chasm between farmers and workers on the one hand, and wealthy industrialists on the other, grew ever wider.

14-6c Liberal Republican Revolt

Disenchanted with Reconstruction, a largely northern group calling itself the Liberal Republicans bolted the party in 1872 and nominated Horace Greeley, the famous editor of the

New York Tribune, for president. The Liberal Republicans were a varied group, including foes of corruption and advocates of a lower tariff. Normally such disparate elements would not cooperate with one another, but two popular and widespread attitudes united them: distaste for federal intervention in the South and an elitist desire to let market forces and the "best men" determine policy.

The Democrats also gave their nomination to Greeley in 1872. The combination was not enough to defeat Grant, who won reelection, but it reinforced Grant's desire to avoid confrontation with white southerners. Greeley's campaign for North-South reunion, for "clasping hands across the bloody chasm," was a bit premature to win at the polls but was a harbinger of the future in American politics. Organized Blue-Gray fraternalism (gatherings of Union and Confederate veterans) began as early as 1874. Grant continued to use military force sparingly and in 1875 refused a desperate request from the governor of Mississippi for troops to quell racial and political terrorism in that state.

Dissatisfaction with Grant's administration grew during his second term. Strong-willed but politically naive, Grant made a series of poor appointments. His secretary of war, his private secretary, and officials in the treasury department and navy were involved in bribery or tax-cheating scandals. Instead of exposing the corruption, Grant defended the culprits. In 1874, as Grant's popularity and his party's prestige declined, the Democrats recaptured the House of Representatives, signaling the end of the Radical Republican vision of Reconstruction. "Republican Party Struck by Lightning," read a Buffalo newspaper headline. And "Busted! The Republican Machine Gone to Smash!" said the *Louisville Courier-Journal* gleefully. Of thirty-five states holding legislative elections, twenty-three were won by Democrats.

14-6d General Amnesty

Such a political turnaround in Congress weakened legislative resolve on southern issues. Congress had already lifted the political disabilities of the Fourteenth Amendment from many former Confederates. In 1872, it had adopted a sweeping Amnesty Act, which pardoned most of the remaining rebels and left only five hundred barred from political office holding. In 1875, Congress passed a **Civil Rights Act**, partly as a tribute to the recently deceased Charles Sumner, purporting to guarantee black people equal accommodations in public places, such as inns and theaters, but the bill was watered down and contained no effective provisions for enforcement. (The Supreme Court later struck down this law.)

Democrats regained control of four state governments before 1872 and a total of eight by the end of January 1876 (see Map 14.1). In the North, Democrats successfully stressed the failure and scandals of Reconstruction governments. As opinion shifted, many Republicans sensed that their constituents were tiring of southern issues and the racial legacies of the war. Sectional reconciliation now seemed crucial for commerce. The nation was expanding westward rapidly, and the South was a new frontier for investment.

14-6e The West, Race, and Reconstruction

Nowhere did the new complexity and violence of American race relations play out so vividly as in the West. As the Fourteenth Amendment and other enactments granted to blacks the beginnings of citizenship, other nonwhite peoples faced continued persecution. Across the West, the federal government pursued a policy of containment against Native Americans. In California, where white farmers and ranchers often forced Native peoples into captive labor, some civilians practiced a more violent form of "Indian hunting." By 1880, thirty years of such violence left an estimated 4,500 Californian Native people dead at the hands of white settlers. Some historians have considered this policy a regional genocide.

In Texas and the Southwest, the rhetoric of national expansion still deemed Mexicans and other mixed-race Hispanics to be debased, "lazy," and incapable of self-government. And in California and other states of the Far West, thousands of Chinese immigrants became the victims of brutal violence. Few whites had objected to the Chinese who did the dangerous work of building railroads through the Rocky Mountains. But when the Chinese began to compete for urban, industrial jobs, great conflict emerged. Anti-coolie clubs appeared in California in the 1870s, seeking laws against Chinese labor, fanning the flames of racism, and organizing vigilante attacks on Chinese workers and the factories that employed them. Western politicians sought white votes by pandering to prejudice, and in 1879 the new California constitution denied the vote to Chinese immigrants.

If we view America from coast to coast, and not merely on the North–South axis, the Civil War and Reconstruction years both dismantled racial slavery and fostered a volatile new racial complexity, especially in the West. During the same age when early anthropologists employed elaborate theories of "scientific" racism to determine a hierarchy of racial types, the West was a vast region of racial mixing and conflict. Some African Americans, despite generations of mixture with Native Americans, asserted that they were more like whites than the nomadic, "uncivilized" Native Americans, while others, like the Creek freedmen of Indian Territory, sought Native identities. In Texas, whites, Native peoples, blacks, and Hispanics had mixed for decades, and by the 1870s forced reconsideration in law and custom of who was white and who was not.

During Reconstruction, America was undergoing what one historian has called a reconstruction of the very idea of *race* itself. As it did so, tumbling into some of the darkest years of American race relations, the turbulence of the expanding

Civil Rights Act An act that was designed to desegregate public places, but that lacked enforcement provisions.

◀ Anti-Chinese cartoon, "Every Dog (No Distinction of Color) Has His Day." The imagery here links Native Americans, African Americans, and Chinese immigrants in the same racist and xenophobic fear.

West reinforced the new nationalism and the reconciliation of North and South based on a resurgent white supremacy.

14-6f Foreign Expansion

Following the Civil War, pressure for expansion reemerged, and in 1867 Secretary of State William H. Seward arranged a vast addition of territory to the national domain through the purchase of Alaska from Russia (see Chapter 19). Opponents ridiculed Seward's $7.2 million venture, calling Alaska "Frigidia," "the Polar Bear Garden," and "Walrussia." But Seward convinced important congressmen of Alaska's economic potential, and other lawmakers favored the dawning of friendship with Russia.

Also in 1867, the United States took control of the Midway Islands, a thousand miles northwest of Hawai'i. And in 1870, President Grant tried unsuccessfully to annex the Dominican Republic. Leaders of American foreign policy, including some former abolitionists, believed that the new United States, re-founded by the war and emancipation, should export its values of antislavery and equality to

the world, especially in the Caribbean. This brand of liberal imperialism mixed with the pursuit of commerce and naval coaling stations, animated American expansion for the rest of the century.

Seward and his successor, Hamilton Fish, also resolved troubling Civil War grievances against Great Britain. Through diplomacy they arranged a financial settlement of claims on Britain for damage done by the *Alabama* and other cruisers built in England and sold to the Confederacy. They recognized that sectional reconciliation in Reconstruction America would serve new foreign ambitions.

14-6g Judicial Retreat from Reconstruction

Meanwhile, the Supreme Court played a major part in the northern retreat from Reconstruction. During the Civil War, the Court had been cautious and inactive. Reaction to the *Dred Scott* decision (1857) had been so vehement, and the Union's wartime emergency so great, that the Court had avoided interference with government actions. The justices breathed a collective sigh of relief, for example, when legal

The "Back to Africa" Movement

In the wake of the Civil War, and especially after the despairing end of Reconstruction, some African Americans sought to leave the South for the American West or North, but also to relocate to Africa. Liberia had been founded in the 1820s by the white-led American Colonization Society (ACS), an organization dedicated to relocating blacks "back" in Africa. Some eleven thousand African Americans had emigrated voluntarily to Liberia by 1860, with largely disastrous results. Many died of disease, and others felt disoriented in the strange new land and ultimately returned to the United States.

Reconstruction reinvigorated the emigration impulse, especially in cotton-growing districts where blacks had achieved political power before 1870 but were crushed by violence and intimidation in the following decade. When blacks felt confident in their future, the idea of leaving America fell quiet; but when threatened or under assault, whole black communities dreamed of a place where they could become an independent "race," a "people," or a "nation" as their appeals often announced. Often that dream, more imagined than realized, lay in West Africa. Before the Civil War, most blacks had denounced the ACS for its racism and its hostility to their sense of American birthright. But letters of inquiry flooded into the organization's headquarters after 1875. Wherever blacks felt the reversal of the promise of emancipation the keenest, they formed local groups such as the Liberia Exodus Association of Pinesville, Florida; or the Liberian Exodus Arkansas Colony; and many others.

At emigration conventions, and especially in churches, blacks penned letters to the ACS asking for maps or any information about a new African homeland. Some local organizers would announce eighty or a hundred recruits "widawake for Liberia," although such enthusiasm rarely converted into an Atlantic voyage. The impulse was genuine, however. "We wants to be a People," wrote the leader of a Mississippi emigration committee; "we can't be it heare and find that we ar compel to leve this Cuntry." Henry Adams, a former Louisiana slave, Union soldier, and itinerant emigration organizer, advocated Liberia, but also supported "Kansas fever" with both biblical and natural rights arguments. "God . . . has a place and a land for all his people," he wrote in 1879. "It is not that we think the soil climate or temperature" elsewhere is "more congenial to us—but it is the idea that pervades our breast 'that at last we will be free,' free from oppression, free from tyranny, free from bulldozing, murderous southern whites."

By the 1890s, Henry McNeal Turner, a freeborn former Georgia Reconstruction politician, and now bishop of the African Methodist Episcopal Church, made three trips to Africa and vigorously campaigned through press and pulpit for blacks to "Christianize" and "civilize" Africa. Two shiploads of African Americans sailed to Liberia, although most returned disillusioned or ill. Turner's plan of "Africa for the Africans" was as much a religious vision as an emigration system, but like all such efforts then and since, it reflected the despair of racial conditions in America more than realities in Africa. The numbers do not tell the tale of the depth of the impulse in this link to the world: in 1879–1880, approximately 25,000 southern blacks moved to Kansas, whereas from 1865 to 1900, just under 4,000 emigrated to West Africa.

CRITICAL THINKING

- While there were certainly practical reasons some African Americans did not want to emigrate to West Africa, what other reasons might compel an African American person to prefer to remain in the United States, and perhaps even in the South, despite the unfulfilled promises of freedom and equality?

◄ Departure of African American emigrants to Liberia aboard the *Laurada*, Savannah, Georgia, March 1896. The large crowd bidding farewell to the much smaller group aboard the ship may indicate both the fascination with and the ambivalence about this issue among blacks in the South.

Library of Congress/Getty Images

technicalities prevented them from reviewing the case of Clement Vallandigham, a Democratic opponent of Lincoln's war effort who had been convicted by a military tribunal of aiding the enemy. But in 1866, a similar case, *Ex parte Milligan*, reached the Court.

Lambdin P. Milligan of Indiana had plotted to free Confederate prisoners of war and overthrow state governments. For these acts, a military court sentenced Milligan, a civilian, to death. Milligan challenged the authority of the military tribunal, claiming he had a right to a civil trial. Reasserting its authority, the Supreme Court declared that military trials were illegal when civil courts were open and functioning.

In the 1870s, the Court successfully renewed its challenge to Congress's actions when it narrowed the meaning and effectiveness of the Fourteenth Amendment. The *Slaughter-House* cases (1873) began in 1869, when the Louisiana legislature granted one company a monopoly on the slaughtering of livestock in New Orleans. Rival butchers in the city promptly sued. Their attorney, former Supreme Court Justice John A. Campbell, argued that Louisiana had violated the rights of some of its citizens in favor of others. The Fourteenth Amendment, Campbell contended, had revolutionized the constitutional system by bringing individual rights under federal protection, safeguarding them from state interference.

But in the *Slaughter-House* decision, the Supreme Court dealt a stunning blow to the scope of the Fourteenth Amendment. The Court declared state citizenship and national citizenship separate. National citizenship involved only matters such as the right to travel freely from state to state, and only such narrow rights, held the Court, were protected by the Fourteenth Amendment.

The Supreme Court also concluded that the butchers who sued had not been deprived of their rights or property in violation of the due-process clause of the amendment. Shrinking from a role as "perpetual censor" for civil rights, the Court's majority declared that the framers of the recent amendments had not intended to "destroy" the federal system, in which the states exercised "powers for domestic and local government, including the regulation of civil rights." Thus, the justices severely limited the amendment's potential for securing and protecting the rights of black citizens—its original intent.

The next day, the Court decided *Bradwell v. Illinois*, a case in which Myra Bradwell, a female attorney, had been denied the right to practice law in Illinois because she was a married woman, and hence not considered a free agent. Pointing to the Fourteenth Amendment, Bradwell's attorneys contended the state had unconstitutionally abridged her "privileges and immunities" as a citizen. The Supreme Court rejected her claim, declaring a woman's "paramount destiny . . . to fulfill the noble and benign offices of wife and mother."

In 1876, the Court weakened the Reconstruction-era amendments even further by emasculating the enforcement clause of the Fourteenth Amendment and revealing deficiencies inherent in the Fifteenth Amendment. In *U.S. v. Cruikshank*, the Court overruled the conviction under the 1870 Enforcement Act of Louisiana whites who had attacked a meeting of blacks and conspired to deprive them of their rights. The justices ruled that the Fourteenth Amendment did not give the federal government power to act against these whites, who had murdered possibly as many as one hundred blacks. The duty of protecting citizens' equal rights, the Court said, "rests alone with the States." Such judicial conservatism as well as states' rights doctrine, practiced by justices who had all been appointed by Republican presidents Lincoln and Grant, left a profound imprint down through the next century, blunting the revolutionary potential in the Civil War amendments.

14-6h Disputed Election of 1876 and Compromise of 1877

As the 1876 elections approached, Americans increasingly focused on economic issues. The North was no longer willing to pursue the goals of Reconstruction. The results of a disputed presidential election confirmed this fact. Samuel J. Tilden, the Democratic governor of New York, ran strongly in the South and needed only one more electoral vote to triumph over Rutherford B. Hayes, the Republican nominee. Nineteen electoral votes from Louisiana, South Carolina, and Florida (the only southern states not yet under Democratic rule) were disputed; both Democrats and Republicans claimed to have won in those states despite fraud committed by their opponents (see Map 14.2).

To resolve this unprecedented situation, Congress established a fifteen-member electoral commission. Membership on the commission was to be balanced between Democrats and Republicans. Because the Republicans held the majority in Congress, they prevailed, 8 to 7, on every attempt to count the returns, with commission members voting along strict party lines. Hayes would become president if Congress accepted the commission's findings.

Congressional acceptance was not certain. Democrats controlled the House and could filibuster to block action on the vote. Many citizens worried that the nation would slip once again into civil war, as some southerners vowed, "Tilden or Fight!" The crisis was resolved when Democrats acquiesced in the election of Hayes based on a "deal" cut in a Washington hotel between Hayes's supporters and southerners who wanted federal aid to railroads, internal improvements, federal patronage, and removal of troops from southern states. Northern and southern Democrats simply decided not to contest the election of a Republican who was not going to continue Reconstruction policies in the South. Thus, Hayes became president, inaugurated privately inside the White House to avoid any threat of violence. Southerners relished their promises of economic aid, and Reconstruction was unmistakably over. Tilden had won the popular vote, but

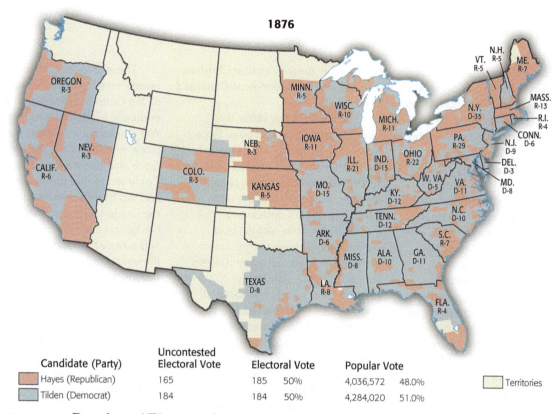

1876

Candidate (Party)	Uncontested Electoral Vote	Electoral Vote		Popular Vote		
Hayes (Republican)	165	185	50%	4,036,572	48.0%	
Tilden (Democrat)	184	184	50%	4,284,020	51.0%	Territories

Map 14.2 Presidential Election of 1876 and the Compromise of 1877

In 1876, a combination of solid southern support and Democratic gains in the North gave Samuel Tilden the majority of popular votes, but Rutherford B. Hayes won the disputed election in the electoral college, after a deal satisfied Democratic wishes for an end to Reconstruction.

narrowly, not winning the Electoral College, the first of four such times in American history when the presidential winner did not win the most votes, a constitutional anomaly that still mystifies much of the world.

Southern Democrats rejoiced, but African Americans grieved over the betrayal of their hopes for equality. The Civil War had brought emancipation, and Reconstruction had guaranteed their rights under law. But events and attitudes in larger white America were foreboding. In a Fourth of July speech in Washington, D.C., in 1875, Frederick Douglass anticipated this predicament. He reflected anxiously on the American centennial to be celebrated the following year. The nation, Douglass feared, would "lift to the sky its million voices in one grand Centennial hosanna of peace and good will to all the white race . . . from gulf to lakes and from sea to sea." Douglass looked back on fifteen years of unparalleled change for his people and worried about the hold of white supremacy on America's historical memory: "If war among the whites brought peace and liberty to the blacks, what will peace among the whites bring?" Douglass's question would echo down through American political culture for decades.

Summary

Reconstruction left a contradictory record. It was an era of tragic aspirations and failures, but also of unprecedented legal, political, and social change. The Union victory brought about an increase in federal power, stronger nationalism, sweeping federal intervention in the southern states, and landmark amendments to the Constitution. It also sparked a revolution in how people would see the role of the state in their lives, often resulting in positive modes of dependence on government heretofore unimagined. But northern commitment to make these changes endure eroded, and the revolution remained unfinished. The mystic sense of promise for new lives and liberties among the freedpeople, demonstrated in that first Decoration Day in Charleston, was tarnished although not dead by 1877.

The North embraced emancipation, black suffrage, and constitutional alterations strengthening the central government. But it did so to defeat the rebellion and secure the peace. As the pressure of these crises declined, Americans, especially in the North, retreated from Reconstruction. The American people and the courts maintained a preference for

The Lost Cause

All major wars and their aftermath compel a struggle over their memory. Sometimes losers prevail over winners in contests to shape historical memory. After the Civil War, white southerners and their northern allies constructed a "Lost Cause" tradition, a potent and racially exclusive version of the war and Reconstruction that persists in American culture today.

The Lost Cause emerged among ex-Confederates as a mourning ritual and a psychological response to the trauma of defeat. But with time it also took root in selective reinterpretations of the war's causes; in southern resistance to Reconstruction; in doctrines of white supremacy; and in a nostalgic popular culture enjoyed and promoted by northerners and southerners alike. Lost Cause advocates—from high-ranking officers to common soldiers writing reminiscences to women leading memorial associations—argued that the war had never been about slavery, that the Confederates had only lost to Yankee numbers and resources, and that the nation should reconcile by equally honoring both southern and northern sacrifice. In the industrial, urban, multiethnic America of the emerging twentieth century, an Old South of benevolent masters and faithful slaves, of Robert E. Lee portrayed as America's truest Christian soldier, provided a sentimentalized road to reunion.

From 1865 to the 1880s, this Confederate legend had been forged by wartime participants determined to vindicate the Confederacy. By the 1890s, however, Lost Cause culture emerged especially with the United Daughters of the Confederacy. Elite southern white women built monuments, lobbied congressmen, delivered lectures, ran essay contests for schoolchildren, and strove to control the content of history textbooks, all in the service of an exalted South. Above all, Lost Causers advocated a story not at all about loss, but about what one historian has called a "victory narrative." This new victory was the nation's triumph over the racial revolution and constitutional transformations of Reconstruction. In his 1881 memoir, Jefferson Davis argued that slavery "was in no wise the cause of the conflict" and that slaves had been "contented with their lot." He also declared the Lost Cause not lost: "Well may we rejoice in the regained possession of self-government. . . . This is the great victory . . . a total noninterference by the Federal government in the domestic affairs of the States."

These stories and images reverberated in the very heartbeat of Jim Crow America, and they endure in modern tastes for Civil War memorabilia, such as the epic *Gone with the Wind*, the 2003 film *Gods and Generals*, and uses of the Confederate flag to oppose civil rights and represent southern identity. And the Confederate state rights tradition has been employed by some states and advocacy groups to suppress the voting rights of certain minority groups, to resist federal environmental policy, national health care reform, and the presidency of Barack Obama. Confederate mythology also inspired a horrendous mass murder by a young white supremacist in the Emanuel AME church in Charleston, South Carolina in June, 2015.

CRITICAL THINKING

- The Lost Cause mythology emerged originally as part of southern whites' mourning for those who died in the war and for the loss of the war. Over time, it transformed the nation's historical memory of the antebellum South, slavery, the war, and Reconstruction, quite literally whitewashing the past. Many modern proponents of the Lost Cause claim that their purpose is "heritage, not hate." Is it possible for the Lost Cause to be solely about heritage?

state authority and a distrust of federal power. The ideology of free labor dictated that property should be respected and that individuals should be self-reliant. Racism endured and transformed into the even more virulent forms of Klan terror and theories of black degeneration. Concern for the human rights of African Americans and other reforms frequently had less appeal than moneymaking in an individualistic, industrializing society.

New challenges began to overwhelm the aims of Reconstruction. How would the country develop its immense resources in an increasingly interconnected national economy? Could farmers, industrial workers, immigrants, and capitalists coexist? Industrialization not only promised prosperity but also wrought increased exploitation of labor. Moreover, industry increased the nation's power and laid the foundation for an enlarged American role in international affairs.

In the wake of the Civil War, Americans faced two profound tasks—the achievement of healing and the dispensing of justice. Both had to occur, but they never developed in historical balance. Making sectional reunion compatible with black freedom and equality overwhelmed the imagination in American political culture, and the nation still faced much of this dilemma more than a century later.

Suggestions for Further Reading

David W. Blight, *Race and Reunion: The Civil War in American Memory* (2001)

Gregory P. Downs, *Declarations of Dependence: The Long Reconstruction of Popular Politics in the South, 1861–1908* (2011)

W. E. B. Du Bois, *Black Reconstruction in America* (1935)

Eric Foner, *Reconstruction: America's Unfinished Revolution, 1863–1877* (1988)

William Gillette, *Retreat from Reconstruction, 1869–1879* (1980)

Gerald Jaynes, *Branches Without Roots: The Genesis of the Black Working Class in the American South, 1862–1882* (1986)

George Rable, *But There Was No Peace* (1984)

Heather Cox Richardson, *West from Appomattox: The Reconstruction of America after the Civil War* (2007)

Elliot West, "Reconstructing Race," *Western Historical Quarterly* (Spring 2003)

Richard White, *Railroaded: The Transcontinentals and the Making of Modern America* (2011)

Richard White, *The Republic for Which It Stands: The United States During Reconstruction and the Gilded Age* (2017)

Declaration of Independence in Congress, July 4, 1776

When, in the course of human events, it becomes necessary for one people to dissolve the political bonds which have connected them with another, and to assume, among the powers of the earth, the separate and equal station to which the laws of nature and of nature's God entitle them, a decent respect to the opinions of mankind requires that they should declare the causes which impel them to the separation.

We hold these truths to be self-evident: That all men are created equal; that they are endowed by their Creator with certain unalienable rights; that among these are life, liberty, and the pursuit of happiness; that, to secure these rights, governments are instituted among men, deriving their just powers from the consent of the governed; that whenever any form of government becomes destructive of these ends, it is the right of the people to alter or to abolish it, and to institute new government, laying its foundation on such principles, and organizing its powers in such form, as to them shall seem most likely to effect their safety and happiness. Prudence, indeed, will dictate that governments long established should not be changed for light and transient causes; and accordingly all experience hath shown that mankind are more disposed to suffer, while evils are sufferable, than to right themselves by abolishing the forms to which they are accustomed. But when a long train of abuses and usurpations, pursuing invariably the same object, evinces a design to reduce them under absolute despotism, it is their right, it is their duty, to throw off such government, and to provide new guards for their future security. Such has been the patient sufferance of these colonies; and such is now the necessity which constrains them to alter their former systems of government. The history of the present King of Great Britain is a history of repeated injuries and usurpations, all having in direct object the establishment of an absolute tyranny over these states. To prove this, let facts be submitted to a candid world.

He has refused his assent to laws, the most wholesome and necessary for the public good.

He has forbidden his governors to pass laws of immediate and pressing importance, unless suspended in their operation till his assent should be obtained; and, when so suspended, he has utterly neglected to attend to them.

He has refused to pass other laws for the accommodation of large districts of people, unless those people would relinquish the right of representation in the legislature, a right inestimable to them, and formidable to tyrants only.

He has called together legislative bodies at places unusual, uncomfortable, and distant from the depository of their public records, for the sole purpose of fatiguing them into compliance with his measures.

He has dissolved representative houses repeatedly, for opposing, with manly firmness, his invasions on the rights of the people.

He has refused for a long time, after such dissolutions, to cause others to be elected; whereby the legislative powers, incapable of annihilation, have returned to the people at large for their exercise; the state remaining, in the mean time, exposed to all the dangers of invasions from without and convulsions within.

He has endeavored to prevent the population of these states; for that purpose obstructing the laws for naturalization of foreigners; refusing to pass others to encourage their migration hither, and raising the conditions of new appropriations of lands.

He has obstructed the administration of justice, by refusing his assent to laws for establishing judiciary powers.

He has made judges dependent on his will alone, for the tenure of their offices, and the amount and payment of their salaries.

He has erected a multitude of new offices, and sent hither swarms of officers to harass our people and eat out their substance.

He has kept among us, in times of peace, standing armies, without the consent of our legislatures.

He has affected to render the military independent of, and superior to, the civil power.

He has combined with others to subject us to a jurisdiction foreign to our constitution, and unacknowledged by our laws, giving his assent to their acts of pretended legislation:

For quartering large bodies of armed troops among us;

For protecting them, by a mock trial, from punishment for any murders which they should commit on the inhabitants of these states;

For cutting off our trade with all parts of the world;

For imposing taxes on us without our consent;

For depriving us, in many cases, of the benefits of trial by jury;

For transporting us beyond seas, to be tried for pretended offenses;

For abolishing the free system of English laws in a neighboring province, establishing therein an arbitrary government, and enlarging its boundaries, so as to render it at once an example and fit instrument for introducing the same absolute rule into these colonies;

For taking away our charters, abolishing our most valuable laws, and altering fundamentally the forms of our governments;

For suspending our own legislatures, and declaring themselves invested with power to legislate for us in all cases whatsoever.

He has abdicated government here, by declaring us out of his protection and waging war against us.

He has plundered our seas, ravaged our coasts, burned our towns, and destroyed the lives of our people.

He is at this time transporting large armies of foreign mercenaries to complete the works of death, desolation, and tyranny already begun with circumstances of cruelty and perfidy scarcely paralleled in the most barbarous ages, and totally unworthy the head of a civilized nation.

He has constrained our fellow-citizens, taken captive on the high seas, to bear arms against their country, to become the executioners of their friends and brethren, or to fall themselves by their hands.

He has excited domestic insurrection among us, and has endeavored to bring on the inhabitants of our frontiers the merciless Indian savages, whose known rule of warfare is an undistinguished destruction of all ages, sexes, and conditions.

In every stage of these oppressions we have petitioned for redress in the most humble terms; our repeated petitions have been answered only by repeated injury. A prince, whose character is thus marked by every act which may define a tyrant, is unfit to be the ruler of a free people.

Nor have we been wanting in our attentions to our British brethren. We have warned them, from time to time, of attempts by their legislature to extend an unwarrantable jurisdiction over us. We have reminded them of the circumstances of our emigration and settlement here. We have appealed to their native justice and magnanimity; and we have conjured them, by the ties of our common kindred, to disavow these usurpations, which would inevitably interrupt our connections and correspondence. They, too, have been deaf to the voice of justice and of consanguinity. We must, therefore, acquiesce in the necessity which denounces our separation, and hold them, as we hold the rest of mankind, enemies in war, in peace friends.

We, therefore, the representatives of the United States of America, in General Congress assembled, appealing to the Supreme Judge of the world for the rectitude of our intentions, do, in the name and by the authority of the good people of these colonies, solemnly publish and declare, that these United Colonies are, and of right ought to be, FREE AND INDEPENDENT STATES; that they are absolved from all allegiance to the British crown, and that all political connection between them and the state of Great Britain is, and ought to be, totally dissolved; and that, as free and independent states, they have full power to levy war, conclude peace, contract alliances, establish commerce, and do all other acts and things which independent states may of right do. And for the support of this declaration, with a firm reliance on the protection of Divine Providence, we mutually pledge to each other our lives, our fortunes, and our sacred honor.

Articles of Confederation

Whereas the Delegates of the United States of America in Congress assembled did on the fifteenth day of November in the Year of our Lord One Thousand Seven Hundred and Seventy seven, and in the Second Year of the Independence of America agree to certain articles of Confederation and perpetual Union between the States of Newhampshire, Massachusetts Bay, Rhode Island and Providence Plantations, Connecticut, New York, New Jersey, Pennsylvania, Delaware, Maryland, Virginia, North Carolina, South Carolina and Georgia in the Words following, viz. "Articles of Confederation and perpetual Union between the states of Newhampshire, Massachusetts Bay, Rhode Island and Providence Plantations, Connecticut, New York, New Jersey, Pennsylvania, Delaware, Maryland, Virginia, North Carolina, South Carolina and Georgia.

Article I The Stile of this confederacy shall be "The United States of America."

Article II Each state retains its sovereignty, freedom and independence, and every Power, Jurisdiction and right, which is not by this confederation expressly delegated to the United States, in Congress assembled.

Article III The said states hereby severally enter into a firm league of friendship with each other, for their common defence, the security of their Liberties, and their mutual and general welfare, binding themselves to assist each other, against all force offered to, or attacks made upon them, or any of them, on account of religion, sovereignty, trade, or any other pretence whatever.

Article IV The better to secure and perpetuate mutual friendship and intercourse among the people of the different states in this union, the free inhabitants of each of these states, paupers, vagabonds and fugitives from Justice excepted, shall be entitled to all privileges and immunities of free citizens in the several states; and the people of each state shall have free ingress and regress to and from any other state, and shall enjoy therein all the privileges of trade and commerce, subject to the same duties, impositions and restrictions as the inhabitants thereof respectively, provided that such restriction shall not extend so far as to prevent the removal of property imported into any state, to any other state of which the Owner is an inhabitant; provided also that no imposition, duties or restriction shall be laid by any state, on the property of the united states, or either of them.

If any Person guilty of, or charged with treason, felony, or other high misdemeanor in any state, shall flee from Justice, and be found in any of the united states, he shall upon demand of the Governor or executive power, of the state from which he fled, be delivered up and removed to the state having jurisdiction of his offence.

Full faith and credit shall be given in each of these states to the records, acts and judicial proceedings of the courts and magistrats of every other state.

Article V For the more convenient management of the general interests of the united states, delegates shall be annually appointed in such manner as the legislature of each state shall direct, to meet in Congress on the first Monday in November, in every year, with a power reserved to each state, to recall its delegates, or any of them, at any time within the year, and to send others in their stead, for the remainder of the Year.

No state shall be represented in Congress by less than two, nor by more than seven Members; and no person shall be capable of being a delegate for more than three years in any term of six years; nor shall any person, being a delegate, be capable of holding any office under the united states, for which he, or another for his benefit receives any salary, fees or emolument of any kind.

Each state shall maintain its own delegates in a meeting of the states, and while they act as members of the committee of the states.

In determining questions in the united states, in Congress assembled, each state shall have one vote.

Freedom of speech and debate in Congress shall not be impeached or questioned in any Court, or place out of Congress, and the members of congress shall be protected in their persons from arrests and imprisonments, during the time of their going to and from, and attendance on congress, except for treason, felony, or breach of the peace.

Article VI No state without the Consent of the united states in congress assembled, shall send any embassy to, or receive any embassy from, or enter into any conference, agreement, or alliance or treaty with any King, prince or state; nor shall any person holding any office of profit or trust under the united states, or any of them, accept of any present, emolument, office or title of any kind whatever from any king, prince or foreign state; nor shall the united states in congress assembled, or any of them, grant any title of nobility.

No two or more states shall enter into any treaty, confederation or alliance whatever between them, without the consent of the united states in congress assembled, specifying accurately the purposes for which the same is to be entered into, and how long it shall continue.

No state shall lay any imposts or duties, which may interfere with any stipulations in treaties, entered into by the united states in congress assembled, with any king, prince or state, in pursuance of any treaties already proposed by congress, to the courts of France and Spain.

No vessels of war shall be kept up in time of peace by any state, except such number only, as shall be deemed necessary by the united states in congress assembled, for the defence of such state, or its trade; nor shall any body of forces be kept up by any state, in time of peace, except such number only, as in the judgment of the united states, in congress assembled, shall be deemed requisite to garrison the forts necessary for the defence of such state; but every state shall always keep up a well regulated and disciplined militia, sufficiently armed and accoutred, and shall provide and constantly have ready for use, in public stores, a due number of field pieces and tents, and a proper quantity of arms, ammunition and camp equipage.

No state shall engage in any war without the consent of the united states in congress assembled, unless such state be actually invaded by enemies, or shall have received certain advice of a resolution being formed by some nation of Indians to invade such state, and the danger is so imminent as not to admit of a delay, till the united states in congress assembled can be consulted: nor shall any state grant commissions to any ships or vessels of war, nor letters of marque or reprisal, except it be after a declaration of war by the united states in congress assembled, and then only against the kingdom or state and the subjects thereof, against which war has been so declared, and under such regulations as shall be established by the united states in congress assembled, unless such state be infested by pirates, in which case vessels of war may be fitted out for that occasion, and kept so long as the danger shall continue, or until the united states in congress assembled shall determine otherwise.

Article VII When land-forces are raised by any state for the common defence, all officers of or under the rank of colonel, shall be appointed by the legislature of each state respectively by whom such forces shall be raised, or in such manner as such state shall direct, and all vacancies shall be filled up by the state which first made the appointment.

Article VIII All charges of war, and all other expences that shall be incurred for the common defence or general welfare, and allowed by the united states in congress assembled, shall be defrayed out of a common treasury, which shall be supplied by the several states, in proportion to the value of all land within each state, granted to or surveyed for any Person, as such land and the buildings and improvements thereon shall be estimated according to such mode as the united states in congress assembled, shall from time to time direct and appoint. The taxes for paying that proportion shall be laid and levied by the authority and direction of the legislatures of the several states within the time agreed upon by the united states in congress assembled.

Article IX The united states in congress assembled, shall have the sole and exclusive right and power of determining on peace and war, except in the cases mentioned in the sixth article—of sending and receiving ambassadors—entering into treaties and alliances, provided that no treaty of commerce shall be made whereby the legislative power of the respective states shall be restrained from imposing such imposts and duties on foreigners, as their own people are subjected to, or from prohibiting the exportation or importation of any species of goods or commodities whatsoever—of establishing rules for deciding in all cases, what captures on land or water shall be legal, and in what manner prizes taken by land or naval forces in the service of the united states shall be divided or appropriated—of granting letters of marque and reprisal in times of peace—appointing courts for the trial of piracies and felonies committed on the high seas and establishing courts for receiving and determining final appeals in all cases of captures, provided that no member of congress shall be appointed a judge of any of the said courts.

The united states in congress assembled shall also be the last resort on appeal in all disputes and differences now subsisting or that hereafter may arise between two or more states concerning boundary, jurisdiction or any other cause whatever; which authority shall always be exercised in the manner following. Whenever the legislative or executive authority or lawful agent of any state in controversy with another shall present a petition to congress, stating the matter in question and praying for a hearing, notice thereof shall be given by order of congress to the legislative or executive authority of the other state in controversy, and a day assigned for the appearance of the parties by their lawful agents, who shall then be directed to appoint by joint consent, commissioners or judges to constitute a court for hearing and determining the matter in question: but if they cannot agree, congress shall name three persons out of each of the united states, and from the list of such persons each party shall alternately strike out one, the petitioners beginning, until the number shall be reduced to thirteen; and from that number not less than seven, nor more than nine names as congress shall direct, shall in the presence of congress be drawn out by lot, and the persons whose names shall be so drawn or any five of them, shall be commissioners or judges, to hear and finally determine the controversy, so always as a major part of the judges who shall hear the cause shall agree in the determination: and if either party shall neglect to attend at the day appointed, without showing reasons, which congress shall judge sufficient, or being present shall refuse to strike, the congress shall proceed to nominate three persons out of each state, and the secretary of congress shall strike in behalf of such party absent or refusing; and the judgment and sentence of the court to be appointed, in the manner before prescribed, shall be final and conclusive; and if any of the parties shall refuse to submit to the authority of such court, or to appear to defend their claim or cause, the court shall nevertheless proceed to pronounce sentence, or judgment, which shall in like manner be final and decisive, the judgment or sentence and other proceedings being in either case transmitted to congress, and lodged among the acts of congress for the security of the parties concerned: provided that every commissioner, before he sits in judgment, shall take an oath to be administered by one of the judges of the supreme or superior court of the state, where the cause shall be tried, "well and truly to hear and determine the matter in question, according to the best of his judgment, without favour, affection or hope of reward:" provided also that no state shall be deprived of territory for the benefit of the united states.

All controversies concerning the private right of soil claimed under different grants of two or more states, whose jurisdictions as they may respect such lands, and the states which passed such grants are adjusted, the said grants or either of them being at the same time claimed to have originated antecedent to such settlement of jurisdiction, shall on the petition of either party to the congress of the united states, be finally determined as near as may be in the same manner as is before prescribed for deciding disputes respecting territorial jurisdiction between different states.

The united states in congress assembled shall also have the sole and exclusive right and power of regulating the alloy and value of coin struck by their own authority, or by that of the respective states—fixing the standard of weights and measures throughout the united states—regulating the trade and managing all affairs with the Indians, not members of any of the states, provided that the legislative right of any state within its own limits be not infringed or violated—establishing and regulating post-offices from one state to another, throughout all the united states, and exacting such postage on the papers passing thro' the same as may be requisite to defray the expences of the said office—appointing all officers of the land forces, in the service of the united states, excepting regimental officers—appointing all the officers of the naval forces, and commissioning all officers whatever in the service of the united states—making rules for the government and regulation of the said land and naval forces, and directing their operations.

The united states in congress assembled shall have authority to appoint a committee, to sit in the recess of congress, to be denominated "A Committee of the States," and to consist of one delegate from each state; and to appoint such other committees and civil officers as may be necessary for managing the general affairs of the united states under their direction—to appoint one of their number to preside, provided that no person be allowed to serve in the office of president more than one year in any term of three years; to ascertain the necessary sums of Money to be raised for the service of the united states, and to appropriate and apply the same for defraying the public expences—to borrow money, or emit bills on the credit of the united states, transmitting every half year to the respective states an account of the sums of money so borrowed or emitted—to build and equip a navy—to agree upon the number of land forces, and to make requisitions from each state for its quota, in proportion to the number of white inhabitants in such state; which requisition shall be binding, and thereupon the legislature of each state shall appoint the regimental officers, raise the men and cloath, arm and equip them in a soldier like manner, at the expence of the united states, and the officers and men so cloathed, armed and equipped shall march to the place appointed, and within the time agreed on by the united states in congress assembled: But if the united states in congress assembled shall, on consideration of circumstances judge proper that any state should not raise men, or should raise a smaller number than its quota, and that any other state should raise a greater number of men than the quota thereof, such extra number shall be raised, officered, cloathed, armed and equipped in the same manner as the quota of such state, unless the legislature of such state shall judge that such extra number cannot be safely spared out of the same, in which case they shall raise, officer, cloath, arm and equip as many of such extra number as they judge can be safely spared. And the officers and men so cloathed, armed and equipped, shall march to the place appointed, and within the time agreed on by the united states in congress assembled.

The united states in congress assembled shall never engage in a war, nor grant letters of marque and reprisal in time of peace, nor enter into any treaties or alliances, nor coin money, nor regulate the value thereof, nor ascertain the sums and expences necessary for the defence and welfare of the united states, or any of them, nor emit bills, nor borrow money on the credit of the united states, nor appropriate money, nor agree upon the number of vessels of war, to be built or purchased, or the number of land or sea forces to be raised, nor appoint a commander in chief of the army or navy, unless nine states assent to the same: nor shall a question on any other point, except for adjourning from day to day be determined, unless by the votes of a majority of the united states in congress assembled.

The congress of the united states shall have power to adjourn to any time within the year, and to any place within the united states, so that no period of adjournment be for a longer duration than the space of six Months, and shall publish the Journal of their proceedings monthly, except such parts thereof relating to treaties, alliances or military operations as in their judgment require secresy; and the yeas and nays of the delegates of each state on any question shall be entered on the Journal, when it is desired by any delegate; and the delegates of a state, or any of them, at his or their request shall be furnished with a transcript of the said Journal, except such parts as are above excepted, to lay before the legislatures of the several states.

Article X The committee of the states, or any nine of them, shall be authorised to execute, in the recess of congress, such of the powers of congress as the united states in congress assembled, by the consent of nine states, shall from time to time think expedient to vest them with; provided that no power be delegated to the said committee, for the exercise of which, by the articles of confederation, the voice of nine states in the congress of the united states assembled is requisite.

Article XI Canada acceding to this confederation, and joining in the measures of the united states, shall be admitted into, and entitled to all the advantages of this union: but no other colony shall be admitted into the same, unless such admission be agreed to by nine states.

Article XII All bills of credit emitted, monies borrowed and debts contracted by, or under the authority of congress, before the assembling of the united states, in pursuance of the present confederation, shall be deemed and considered as a charge against the united states, for payment and satisfaction whereof the said united states, and the public faith are hereby solemnly pledged.

Article XIII Every state shall abide by the determinations of the united states in congress assembled, on all questions which by this confederation are submitted to them. And the Articles of this confederation shall be inviolably observed by every state, and the union shall be perpetual; nor shall any alteration at any time hereafter be made in any of them; unless such alteration be agreed to in a congress of the united states, and be afterwards confirmed by the legislatures of every state.

AND WHEREAS it hath pleased the Great Governor of the World to incline the hearts of the legislatures we respectively represent in congress, to approve of, and to authorize us to ratify the said articles of confederation and perpetual union. Know Ye that we the under-signed delegates, by virtue of the power and authority to us given for that purpose, do by these presents, in the name and in behalf of our respective constituents, fully and entirely ratify and confirm each and every of the said articles of confederation and perpetual union, and all and singular the matters and things therein contained: And we do further solemnly plight and engage the faith of our respective constituents, that they shall abide by the determinations of the united states in congress assembled, on all questions, which by the said confederation are submitted to them. And that the articles thereof shall be inviolably observed by the states we respectively represent, and that the union shall be perpetual. In Witness whereof we have hereunto set our hands in Congress. Done at Philadelphia in the state of Pennsylvania the ninth Day of July in the Year of our Lord one Thousand seven Hundred and Seventy-eight, and in the third year of the independence of America.

Constitution of the United States of America and Amendments*

Preamble

We the people of the United States, in order to form a more perfect union, establish justice, insure domestic tranquillity, provide for the common defense, promote the general welfare, and secure the blessings of liberty to ourselves and our posterity, do ordain and establish this Constitution for the United States of America.

Article I

Section 1 All legislative powers herein granted shall be vested in a Congress of the United States, which shall consist of a Senate and a House of Representatives.

Section 2 The House of Representatives shall be composed of members chosen every second year by the people of the several States, and the electors in each State shall have the qualifications requisite for electors of the most numerous branch of the State Legislature.

No person shall be a Representative who shall not have attained to the age of twenty-five years, and been seven years a citizen of the United States, and who shall not, when elected, be an inhabitant of that State in which he shall be chosen.

Representatives and direct taxes shall be apportioned among the several States which may be included within this Union, according to their respective numbers, *which shall be determined by adding to the whole number of free persons, including those bound to service for a term of years and excluding Indians not taxed, three-fifths of all other persons.* The actual enumeration shall be made within three years after the first meeting of the Congress of the United States, and within every subsequent term of ten years, in such manner as they shall by law direct. The number of Representatives shall not exceed one for every thirty thousand, but each State shall have at least one Representative; *and until such enumeration shall be made, the State of New Hampshire shall be entitled to choose three, Massachusetts eight, Rhode Island and Providence Plantations one, Connecticut five, New York six, New Jersey four, Pennsylvania eight, Delaware one, Maryland six, Virginia ten, North Carolina five, South Carolina five, and Georgia three.*

When vacancies happen in the representation from any State, the Executive authority thereof shall issue writs of election to fill such vacancies.

The House of Representatives shall choose their Speaker and other officers; and shall have the sole power of impeachment.

Section 3 The Senate of the United States shall be composed of two Senators from each State, *chosen by the legislature thereof,* for six years; and each Senator shall have one vote.

Immediately after they shall be assembled in consequence of the first election, they shall be divided as equally as may be into three classes. The seats of the Senators of the first class shall be vacated at the expiration of the second year, of the second class at the expiration of the fourth year, and of the third class at the expiration of the sixth year, so that one-third may be chosen every second year; and if vacancies happen by resignation or otherwise, during the recess of the legislature of any State, the Executive thereof may make temporary appointments until the next meeting of the legislature, which shall then fill such vacancies.

No person shall be a Senator who shall not have attained to the age of thirty years, and been nine years a citizen of the United States, and who shall not, when elected, be an inhabitant of that State for which he shall be chosen.

The Vice-President of the United States shall be President of the Senate, but shall have no vote, unless they be equally divided.

The Senate shall choose their other officers, and also a President *pro tempore,* in the absence of the Vice-President, or when he shall exercise the office of President of the United States.

The Senate shall have the sole power to try all impeachments. When sitting for that purpose, they shall be on oath or affirmation. When the President of the United States is tried, the Chief Justice shall preside: and no person shall be convicted without the concurrence of two-thirds of the members present.

Judgment in cases of impeachment shall not extend further than to removal from the office, and disqualification to hold and enjoy any office of honor, trust or profit under the United States: but the party convicted shall nevertheless be liable and subject to indictment, trial, judgment and punishment, according to law.

Section 4 The times, places and manner of holding elections for Senators and Representatives shall be prescribed in each State by the legislature thereof; but the Congress may at any time by law make or alter such regulations, except as to the places of choosing Senators.

The Congress shall assemble at least once in every year, and such meeting *shall be on the first Monday in December, unless they shall by law appoint a different day.*

Section 5 Each house shall be the judge of the elections, returns and qualifications of its own members, and a majority of each shall constitute a quorum to do business; but a smaller number may adjourn from day to day, and may be authorized to compel the attendance of absent members, in such manner, and under such penalties, as each house may provide.

* Passages no longer in effect are printed in italic type.

Each house may determine the rules of its proceedings, punish its members for disorderly behavior, and with the concurrence of two-thirds, expel a member.

Each house shall keep a journal of its proceedings, and from time to time publish the same, excepting such parts as may in their judgment require secrecy; and the yeas and nays of the members of either house on any question shall, at the desire of one-fifth of those present, be entered on the journal.

Neither house, during the session of Congress, shall, without the consent of the other, adjourn for more than three days, nor to any other place than that in which the two houses shall be sitting.

Section 6 The Senators and Representatives shall receive a compensation for their services, to be ascertained by law and paid out of the treasury of the United States. They shall in all cases except treason, felony and breach of the peace, be privileged from arrest during their attendance at the session of their respective houses, and in going to and returning from the same; and for any speech or debate in either house, they shall not be questioned in any other place.

No Senator or Representative shall, during the time for which he was elected, be appointed to any civil office under the authority of the United States, which shall have been created, or the emoluments whereof shall have been increased, during such time; and no person holding any office under the United States shall be a member of either house during his continuance in office.

Section 7 All bills for raising revenue shall originate in the House of Representatives; but the Senate may propose or concur with amendments as on other bills.

Every bill which shall have passed the House of Representatives and the Senate, shall, before it become a law, be presented to the President of the United States; if he approve he shall sign it, but if not he shall return it with objections to that house in which it originated, who shall enter the objections at large on their journal, and proceed to reconsider it. If after such reconsideration two-thirds of that house shall agree to pass the bill, it shall be sent, together with the objections, to the other house, by which it shall likewise be reconsidered, and, if approved by two-thirds of that house, it shall become a law. But in all such cases the votes of both houses shall be determined by yeas and nays, and the names of the persons voting for and against the bill shall be entered on the journal of each house respectively. If any bill shall not be returned by the President within ten days (Sundays excepted) after it shall have been presented to him, the same shall be a law, in like manner as if he had signed it, unless the Congress by their adjournment prevent its return, in which case it shall not be a law.

Every order, resolution, or vote to which the concurrence of the Senate and House of Representatives may be necessary (except on a question of adjournment) shall be presented to the President of the United States; and before the same shall take effect, shall be approved by him, or being disapproved by him, shall be repassed by two-thirds of the Senate and House of Representatives, according to the rules and limitations prescribed in the case of a bill.

Section 8 The Congress shall have power

To lay and collect taxes, duties, imposts, and excises, to pay the debts and provide for the common defense and general welfare of the United States; but all duties, imposts and excises shall be uniform throughout the United States;

To borrow money on the credit of the United States;

To regulate commerce with foreign nations, and among the several States, and with the Indian tribes;

To establish an uniform rule of naturalization, and uniform laws on the subject of bankruptcies throughout the United States;

To coin money, regulate the value thereof, and of foreign coin, and fix the standard of weights and measures;

To provide for the punishment of counterfeiting the securities and current coin of the United States;

To establish post offices and post roads;

To promote the progress of science and useful arts by securing for limited times to authors and inventors the exclusive right to their respective writings and discoveries;

To constitute tribunals inferior to the Supreme Court;

To define and punish piracies and felonies committed on the high seas and offenses against the law of nations;

To declare war, grant letters of marque and reprisal, and make rules concerning captures on land and water;

To raise and support armies, but no appropriation of money to that use shall be for a longer term than two years;

To provide and maintain a navy;

To make rules for the government and regulation of the land and naval forces;

To provide for calling forth the militia to execute the laws of the Union, suppress insurrections, and repel invasions;

To provide for organizing, arming, and disciplining the militia, and for governing such part of them as may be employed in the service of the United States, reserving to the States respectively the appointment of the officers, and the authority of training the militia according to the discipline prescribed by Congress;

To exercise exclusive legislation in all cases whatsoever, over such district (not exceeding ten miles square) as may, by cession of particular States, and the acceptance of Congress, become the seat of government of the United States, and to exercise like authority over all places purchased by the consent of the legislature of the State, in which the same shall be, for erection of forts, magazines, arsenals, dockyards, and other needful buildings; —and

To make all laws which shall be necessary and proper for carrying into execution the foregoing powers, and all other powers vested by this Constitution in the government of the United States, or in any department or officer thereof.

Section 9 *The migration or importation of such persons as any of the States now existing shall think proper to admit shall not be prohibited by the Congress prior to the year 1808; but a tax or duty may be imposed on such importation, not exceeding $10 for each person.*

The privilege of the writ of habeas corpus shall not be suspended, unless when in cases of rebellion or invasion the public safety may require it.

No bill of attainder or ex post facto law shall be passed.

No capitation, or other direct, tax shall be laid, unless in proportion to the census or enumeration herein before directed to be taken.

No tax or duty shall be laid on articles exported from any State.

No preference shall be given by any regulation of commerce or revenue to the ports of one State over those of another; nor shall vessels bound to, or from, one State, be obliged to enter, clear, or pay duties in another.

No money shall be drawn from the treasury, but in consequence of appropriations made by law; and a regular statement and account of the receipts and expenditures of all public money shall be published from time to time.

No title of nobility shall be granted by the United States: and no person holding any office of profit or trust under them, shall, without the consent of the Congress, accept of any present, emolument, office, or title, of any kind whatever, from any king, prince, or foreign state.

Section 10 No State shall enter into any treaty, alliance, or confederation; grant letters of marque and reprisal; coin money; emit bills of credit; make anything but gold and silver coin a tender in payment of debts; pass any bill of attainder, ex post facto law, or law impairing the obligation of contracts, or grant any title of nobility.

No State shall, without the consent of Congress, lay any imposts or duties on imports or exports, except what may be absolutely necessary for executing its inspection laws: and the net produce of all duties and imposts, laid by any State on imports or exports, shall be for the use of the treasury of the United States; and all such laws shall be subject to the revision and control of the Congress.

No State shall, without the consent of Congress, lay any duty of tonnage, keep troops or ships of war in time of peace, enter into any agreement or compact with another State, or with a foreign power, or engage in war, unless actually invaded, or in such imminent danger as will not admit of delay.

Article II

Section 1 The executive power shall be vested in a President of the United States of America. He shall hold his office during the term of four years, and, together with the Vice-President, chosen for the same term, be elected as follows:

Each State shall appoint, in such manner as the legislature thereof may direct, a number of electors, equal to the whole number of Senators and Representatives to which the State may be entitled in the Congress; but no Senator or Representative, or person holding an office of trust or profit under the United States, shall be appointed an elector.

The electors shall meet in their respective States, and vote by ballot for two persons, of whom one at least shall not be an inhabitant of the same State with themselves. And they shall make a list of all the persons voted for, and of the number of votes for each; which list they shall sign and certify, and transmit sealed to the seat of government of the United States, directed to the President of the Senate. The President of the Senate shall, in the presence of the Senate and House of Representatives, open all the certificates, and the votes shall then be counted. The person having the greatest number of votes shall be the President, if such number be a majority of the whole number of electors appointed; and if there be more than one who have such majority, and have an equal number of votes, then the House of Representatives shall immediately choose by ballot one of them for President; and if no person have a majority, then from the five highest on the list said house shall in like manner choose the President. But in choosing the President the votes shall be taken by States, the representation from each State having one vote; a quorum for this purpose shall consist of a member or members from two-thirds of the States, and a majority of all the States shall be necessary to a choice. In every case, after the choice of the President, the person having the greatest number of votes of the electors shall be the Vice-President. But if there should remain two or more who have equal votes, the Senate shall choose from them by ballot the Vice-President.

The Congress may determine the time of choosing the electors and the day on which they shall give their votes; which day shall be the same throughout the United States.

No person except a natural-born citizen, *or a citizen of the United States at the time of the adoption of this Constitution,* shall be eligible to the office of President; neither shall any person be eligible to that office who shall not have attained to the age of thirty-five years, and been fourteen years a resident within the United States.

In cases of the removal of the President from office or of his death, resignation, or inability to discharge the powers and duties of the said office, the same shall devolve on the Vice-President, and the Congress may by law provide for the case of removal, death, resignation, or inability, both of the President and Vice-President, declaring what officer shall then act as President, and such officer shall act accordingly, until the disability be removed, or a President shall be elected.

The President shall, at stated times, receive for his services a compensation, which shall neither be increased nor diminished during the period for which he shall have been elected, and he shall not receive within that period any other emolument from the United States, or any of them.

Before he enter on the execution of his office, he shall take the following oath or affirmation:—"I do solemnly swear (or affirm) that I will faithfully execute the office of the President of the United States, and will to the best of my ability preserve, protect and defend the Constitution of the United States."

Section 2 The President shall be commander in chief of the army and navy of the United States, and of the militia of the several States, when called into the actual service of the United States; he may require the opinion, in writing, of the principal officer in each of the executive departments, upon any subject relating to the duties of their respective offices, and he shall have power to grant reprieves and pardons for offenses against the United States, except in cases of impeachment.

He shall have power, by and with the advice and consent of the Senate, to make treaties, provided two-thirds of the Senators present concur; and he shall nominate, and by and with the advice and consent of the Senate, shall appoint ambassadors, other public ministers and consuls, judges of the Supreme Court, and all other officers of the United States, whose appointments are not herein otherwise provided for, and which shall be established by law: but Congress may by law vest the appointment of such inferior officers, as they think proper, in the President alone, in the courts of law, or in the heads of departments.

The President shall have power to fill up all vacancies that may happen during the recess of the Senate, by granting commissions which shall expire at the end of their next session.

Section 3 He shall from time to time give to the Congress information of the state of the Union, and recommend to their consideration such measures as he shall judge necessary and expedient; he may, on extraordinary occasions, convene both houses, or either of them, and in case of disagreement between them, with respect to the time of adjournment, he may adjourn them to such time as he shall think proper; he shall receive ambassadors and other public ministers; he shall take care that the laws be faithfully executed, and shall commission all the officers of the United States.

Section 4 The President, Vice-President and all civil officers of the United States shall be removed from office on impeachment for, and on conviction of, treason, bribery, or other high crimes and misdemeanors.

Article III

Section 1 The judicial power of the United States shall be vested in one Supreme Court, and in such inferior courts as the Congress may from time to time ordain and establish. The judges, both of the Supreme and inferior courts, shall hold their offices during good behavior, and shall, at stated times, receive for their services a compensation which shall not be diminished during their continuance in office.

Section 2 The judicial power shall extend to all cases, in law and equity, arising under this Constitution, the laws of the United States, and treaties made, or which shall be made, under their authority;—to all cases affecting ambassadors, other public ministers and consuls;—to all cases of admiralty and maritime jurisdiction;—to controversies to which the United States shall be a party;—to controversies between two or more States;— *between a State and citizens of another State;*—between citizens of different States;—between citizens of the same State claiming lands under grants of different States, and between a State, or the citizens thereof, and foreign states, citizens or subjects.

In all cases affecting ambassadors, other public ministers and consuls, and those in which a State shall be party, the Supreme Court shall have original jurisdiction. In all the other cases before mentioned, the Supreme Court shall have appellate jurisdiction, both as to law and fact, with such exceptions, and under such regulations, as the Congress shall make.

The trial of all crimes, except in cases of impeachment, shall be by jury; and such trial shall be held in the State where said crimes shall have been committed; but when not committed within any State, the trial shall be at such place or places as the Congress may by law have directed.

Section 3 Treason against the United States shall consist only in levying war against them, or in adhering to their enemies, giving them aid and comfort. No person shall be convicted of treason unless on the testimony of two witnesses to the same overt act, or on confession in open court.

The Congress shall have power to declare the punishment of treason, but no attainder of treason shall work corruption of blood, or forfeiture except during the life of the person attainted.

Article IV

Section 1 Full faith and credit shall be given in each State to the public acts, records, and judicial proceedings of every other State. And the Congress may by general laws prescribe the manner in which such acts, records, and proceedings shall be proved, and the effect thereof.

Section 2 The citizens of each State shall be entitled to all privileges and immunities of citizens in the several States.

A person charged in any State with treason, felony, or other crime, who shall flee from justice, and be found in another State, shall on demand of the executive authority of the State from which he fled, be delivered up, to be removed to the State having jurisdiction of the crime.

No person held to service or labor in one State, under the laws thereof, escaping into another, shall, in consequence of any law or regulation therein, be discharged from such service or labor, but shall be delivered up on claim of the party to whom such service or labor may be due.

Section 3 New States may be admitted by the Congress into this Union; but no new State shall be formed or erected within the jurisdiction of any other State; nor any State be formed by the junction of two or more States, or parts of States, without the consent of the legislatures of the States concerned as well as of the Congress.

The Congress shall have power to dispose of and make all needful rules and regulations respecting the territory or other property belonging to the United States; and nothing in this Constitution shall be so construed as to prejudice any claims of the United States, or of any particular State.

Section 4 The United States shall guarantee to every State in this Union a republican form of government, and shall protect each of them against invasion; and on application of the legislature, or of the executive (when the legislature cannot be convened), against domestic violence.

Article V

The Congress, whenever two-thirds of both houses shall deem it necessary, shall propose amendments to this Constitution, or, on the application of the legislatures of two-thirds of the several States, shall call a convention for proposing amendments, which, in either case, shall be valid to all intents and purposes, as part of this Constitution, when ratified by the legislatures of three-fourths of the several States, or by conventions in three-fourths thereof, as the one or the other mode of ratification may be proposed by the Congress; provided *that no amendments which may be made prior to the year one thousand eight hundred and eight shall in any manner affect the first and fourth clauses in the ninth section of the first article;* and that no State, without its consent, shall be deprived of its equal suffrage in the Senate.

Article VI

All debts contracted and engagements entered into, before the adoption of this Constitution, shall be as valid against the United States under this Constitution, as under the Confederation.

This Constitution, and the laws of the United States which shall be made in pursuance thereof; and all treaties made, or which shall be made, under the authority of the United States, shall be the supreme law of the land; and the judges in every State shall be bound thereby, anything in the Constitution or laws of any State to the contrary notwithstanding.

The Senators and Representatives before mentioned, and the members of the several State legislatures, and all executive and judicial officers, both of the United States and of the several States, shall be bound by oath or affirmation to support this Constitution; but no religious test shall ever be required as a qualification to any office or public trust under the United States.

Article VII

The ratification of the conventions of nine States shall be sufficient for the establishment of this Constitution between the States so ratifying the same.

Done in Convention by the unanimous consent of the States present, the seventeenth day of September in the year of our Lord one thousand seven hundred and eighty-seven and of the Independence of the United States of America the twelfth. In witness whereof we have hereunto subscribed our names.

Amendments to the Constitution*

Amendment I

Congress shall make no law respecting an establishment of religion, or prohibiting the free exercise thereof; or abridging the freedom of speech, or of the press; or the right of the people peaceably to assemble, and to petition the government for a redress of grievances.

Amendment II

A well-regulated militia being necessary to the security of a free State, the right of the people to keep and bear arms shall not be infringed.

Amendment III

No soldier shall, in time of peace, be quartered in any house without the consent of the owner, nor in time of war, but in a manner to be prescribed by law.

Amendment IV

The right of the people to be secure in their persons, houses, papers, and effects, against unreasonable searches and seizures, shall not be violated, and no warrants shall issue but upon probable cause, supported by oath or affirmation, and particularly describing the place to be searched, and the persons or things to be seized.

Amendment V

No person shall be held to answer for a capital, or otherwise infamous crime, unless on a presentment or indictment of a grand jury, except in cases arising in the land or naval forces, or in the militia, when in actual service in time of war or public danger; nor shall any person be subject for the same offense to be twice put in jeopardy of life or limb; nor shall be compelled in any criminal case to be a witness against himself, nor be deprived of life, liberty, or property, without due process of law; nor shall private property be taken for public use without just compensation.

Amendment VI

In all criminal prosecutions, the accused shall enjoy the right to a speedy and public trial, by an impartial jury of the State and district wherein the crime shall have been committed,

---

* The first ten Amendments (the Bill of Rights) were adopted in 1791.

which district shall have been previously ascertained by law, and to be informed of the nature and cause of the accusation; to be confronted with the witnesses against him; to have compulsory process for obtaining witnesses in his favor, and to have the assistance of counsel for his defense.

Amendment VII

In suits at common law, where the value in controversy shall exceed twenty dollars, the right of trial by jury shall be preserved, and no fact tried by a jury shall be otherwise reexamined in any court of the United States, than according to the rules of the common law.

Amendment VIII

Excessive bail shall not be required, nor excessive fines imposed, nor cruel and unusual punishments inflicted.

Amendment IX

The enumeration in the Constitution, of certain rights, shall not be construed to deny or disparage others retained by the people.

Amendment X

The powers not delegated to the United States by the Constitution, nor prohibited by it to the States, are reserved to the States respectively, or to the people.

Amendment XI

[Adopted 1798]

The judicial power of the United States shall not be construed to extend to any suit in law or equity, commenced or prosecuted against one of the United States by citizens of another State, or by citizens or subjects of any foreign state.

Amendment XII

[Adopted 1804]

The electors shall meet in their respective States, and vote by ballot for President and Vice-President, one of whom, at least, shall not be an inhabitant of the same State with themselves; they shall name in their ballots the person voted for as President, and in distinct ballots the person voted for as Vice-President, and they shall make distinct lists of all persons voted for as President, and of all persons voted for as Vice-President, and of the number of votes for each, which lists they shall sign and certify, and transmit sealed to the seat of government of the United States, directed to the President of the Senate;—the President of the Senate shall, in the presence of the Senate and House of Representatives, open all the certificates and the votes shall then be counted;—the person having the greatest number of votes for President shall be the President, if such number be a majority of the whole number of electors appointed; and if no person have such majority, then from the persons having the highest numbers not exceeding three on the list of those voted for as President, the House of Representatives shall choose immediately, by ballot, the President. But in choosing the President, the votes shall be taken by States, the representation from each State having one vote; a quorum for this purpose shall consist of a member or members from two-thirds of the States, and a majority of all the States shall be necessary to a choice. And if the House of Representatives shall not choose a President whenever the right of choice shall devolve upon them, before *the fourth day of March* next following, then the Vice-President shall act as President, as in the case of the death or other constitutional disability of the President.

The person having the greatest number of votes as Vice-President shall be the Vice-President, if such number be a majority of the whole number of electors appointed; and if no person have a majority, then from the two highest numbers on the list the Senate shall choose the Vice-President; a quorum for the purpose shall consist of two-thirds of the whole number of Senators, and a majority of the whole number shall be necessary to a choice. But no person constitutionally ineligible to the office of President shall be eligible to that of Vice-President of the United States.

Amendment XIII

[Adopted 1865]

Section 1 Neither slavery nor involuntary servitude, except as a punishment for crime whereof the party shall have been duly convicted, shall exist within the United States, or any place subject to their jurisdiction.

Section 2 Congress shall have power to enforce this article by appropriate legislation.

Amendment XIV

[Adopted 1868]

Section 1 All persons born or naturalized in the United States, and subject to the jurisdiction thereof, are citizens of the United States and of the State wherein they reside. No State shall make or enforce any law which shall abridge the privileges or immunities of citizens of the United States; nor shall any State deprive any person of life, liberty, or property, without due process of law; nor deny to any person within its jurisdiction the equal protection of the laws.

Section 2 Representatives shall be apportioned among the several States according to their respective numbers, counting the whole number of persons in each State, excluding Indians not taxed. But when the right to vote at any election for the choice of Electors for President and Vice-President of the United States, Representatives in Congress, the executive and judicial officers of a State, or the members of the legislature thereof, is denied to any of the male inhabitants of such State, being twenty-one years of age and citizens of the United States, or in any way abridged, except for participation in rebellion, or other crime, the basis of representation therein shall be reduced in the proportion which the number of such male citizens shall bear to the whole number of male citizens twenty-one years of age in such State.

Section 3 No person shall be a Senator or Representative in Congress, or Elector of President and Vice-President, or hold any office, civil or military, under the United States, or under any State, who, having previously taken an oath, as a member of Congress, or as an officer of the United States, or as a member of any State legislature, or as an executive or judicial officer of any State, to support the Constitution of the United States, shall have engaged in insurrection or rebellion against the same, or given aid or comfort to the enemies thereof. Congress may, by a vote of two-thirds of each house, remove such disability.

Section 4 The validity of the public debt of the United States, authorized by law, including debts incurred for payment of pensions and bounties for services in suppressing insurrection or rebellion, shall not be questioned. But neither the United States nor any State shall assume or pay any debt or obligation incurred in aid of insurrection or rebellion against the United States, or any claim for the loss of emancipation of any slave; but all such debts, obligations, and claims shall be held illegal and void.

Section 5 The Congress shall have power to enforce, by appropriate legislation, the provisions of this article.

Amendment XV

[Adopted 1870]

Section 1 The right of citizens of the United States to vote shall not be denied or abridged by the United States or by any State on account of race, color, or previous condition of servitude.

Section 2 The Congress shall have power to enforce this article by appropriate legislation.

Amendment XVI

[Adopted 1913]

The Congress shall have power to lay and collect taxes on incomes, from whatever source derived, without apportionment among the several States, and without regard to any census or enumeration.

Amendment XVII

[Adopted 1913]

Section 1 The Senate of the United States shall be composed of two Senators from each State, elected by the people thereof, for six years; and each Senator shall have one vote. The electors in each State shall have the qualifications requisite for electors of [voters for] the most numerous branch of the State legislatures.

Section 2 When vacancies happen in the representation of any State in the Senate, the executive authority of such State shall issue writs of election to fill such vacancies: Provided, that the Legislature of any State may empower the executive thereof to make temporary appointments until the people fill the vacancies by election as the Legislature may direct.

Section 3 This amendment shall not be so construed as to affect the election or term of any Senator chosen before it becomes valid as part of the Constitution.

Amendment XVIII

[Adopted 1919; Repealed 1933]

Section 1 After one year from the ratification of this article the manufacture, sale, or transportation of intoxicating liquors within, the importation thereof into, or the exportation thereof from the United States and all territory subject to the jurisdiction thereof, for beverage purposes, is hereby prohibited.

Section 2 The Congress and the several States shall have concurrent power to enforce this article by appropriate legislation.

Section 3 This article shall be inoperative unless it shall have been ratified as an amendment to the Constitution by the legislatures of the several States, as provided by the Constitution, within seven years from the date of the submission thereof to the States by the Congress.

Amendment XIX

[Adopted 1920]

Section 1 The right of citizens of the United States to vote shall not be denied or abridged by the United States or by any State on account of sex.

Section 2 The Congress shall have power to enforce this article by appropriate legislation.

Amendment XX

[Adopted 1933]

Section 1 The terms of the President and Vice-President shall end at noon on the 20th day of January, and the terms of Senators and Representatives at noon on the 3rd day of January, of the years in which such terms would have ended if this article had not been ratified; and the terms of their successors shall then begin.

Section 2 The Congress shall assemble at least once in every year, and such meeting shall begin at noon on the 3rd day of January, unless they shall by law appoint a different day.

Section 3 If, at the time fixed for the beginning of the term of the President, the President-elect shall have died, the Vice-President-elect shall become President. If a President shall not have been chosen before the time fixed for the beginning of his term, or if the President-elect shall have failed to qualify, then the Vice-President-elect shall act as President until a President shall have qualified; and the Congress may by law provide for the case wherein neither a President-elect nor a Vice-President-elect shall have qualified, declaring who shall then act as President, or the manner in which one who is to act shall be selected, and such persons shall act accordingly until a President or Vice-President shall have qualified.

Section 4 The Congress may by law provide for the case of the death of any of the persons from whom the House of Representatives may choose a President whenever the right of choice shall have devolved upon them, and for the case of the death of any of the persons from whom the Senate may choose a Vice-President whenever the right of choice shall have devolved upon them.

Section 5 Sections 1 and 2 shall take effect on the 15th day of October following the ratification of this article.

Section 6 This article shall be inoperative unless it shall have been ratified as an amendment to the Constitution by the Legislatures of three-fourths of the several States within seven years from the date of its submission.

Amendment XXI

[Adopted 1933]
Section 1 The eighteenth article of amendment to the Constitution of the United States is hereby repealed.

Section 2 The transportation or importation into any State, Territory, or Possession of the United States for delivery or use therein of intoxicating liquors, in violation of the laws thereof, is hereby prohibited.

Section 3 This article shall be inoperative unless it shall have been ratified as an amendment to the Constitution by conventions in the several States, as provided in the Constitution, within seven years from the date of submission thereof to the States by the Congress.

Amendment XXII

[Adopted 1951]

Section 1 No person shall be elected to the office of President more than twice, and no person who has held the office of President, or acted as President, for more than two years of a term to which some other person was elected President shall be elected to the office of President more than once. But this article shall not apply to any person holding the office of President when this article was proposed by the Congress, and shall not prevent any person who may be holding the office of President, or acting as President, during the term within which this article becomes operative from holding the office of President or acting as President during the remainder of such term.

Section 2 This article shall be inoperative unless it shall have been ratified as an amendment to the Constitution by the legislatures of three-fourths of the several States within seven years from the date of its submission to the States by the Congress.

Amendment XXIII

[Adopted 1961]

Section 1 The District constituting the seat of Government of the United States shall appoint in such manner as the Congress may direct:

A number of electors of President and Vice-President equal to the whole number of Senators and Representatives in Congress to which the District would be entitled if it were a State, but in no event more than the least populous State; they shall be in addition to those appointed by the States, but they shall be considered for the purposes of the election of President and Vice-President, to be electors appointed by a State; and they shall meet in the District and perform such duties as provided by the twelfth article of amendment.

Section 2 The Congress shall have the power to enforce this article by appropriate legislation.

Amendment XXIV

[Adopted 1964]

Section 1 The right of citizens of the United States to vote in any primary or other election for President or Vice-President, for electors for President or Vice-President, or for Senator or Representative in Congress, shall not be denied or abridged by the United States or any State by reason of failure to pay any poll tax or other tax.

Section 2 The Congress shall have the power to enforce this article by appropriate legislation.

Amendment XXV

[Adopted 1967]

Section 1 In case of the removal of the President from office or of his death or resignation, the Vice-President shall become President.

Section 2 Whenever there is a vacancy in the office of the Vice-President, the President shall nominate a Vice-President who shall take office upon confirmation by a majority vote of both Houses of Congress.

Section 3 Whenever the President transmits to the President pro tempore of the Senate and the Speaker of the House of Representatives his written declaration that he is unable to discharge the powers and duties of his office, and until he transmits to them a written declaration to the contrary, such powers and duties shall be discharged by the Vice-President as Acting President.

Section 4 Whenever the Vice-President and a majority of either the principal officers of the executive departments or of such other body as Congress may by law provide, transmit to the President pro tempore of the Senate and the Speaker of the House of Representatives their written declaration that the President is unable to discharge the powers and duties of his office, the Vice-President shall immediately assume the powers and duties of the office as Acting President.

Thereafter, when the President transmits to the President pro tempore of the Senate and the Speaker of the House of Representatives his written declaration that no inability exists, he shall resume the powers and duties of his office unless the Vice-President and a majority of either the principal officers of the executive department[s] or of such other body as Congress may by law provide, transmit within four days to the President pro tempore of the Senate and the Speaker of the House of Representatives their written declaration that the President is unable to discharge the powers and duties of his office. Thereupon Congress shall decide the issue, assembling within forty-eight hours for that purpose if not in session. If the Congress, within twenty-one days after receipt of the latter written declaration, or, if Congress is not in session, within twenty-one days after Congress is required to assemble, determines by two-thirds vote of both Houses that the President is unable to discharge the powers and duties of his office, the Vice-President shall continue to discharge the same as Acting President; otherwise, the President shall resume the powers and duties of his office.

Amendment XXVI
[Adopted 1971]

Section 1 The right of citizens of the United States, who are eighteen years of age or older, to vote shall not be denied or abridged by the United States or by any State on account of age. '

Section 2 The Congress shall have power to enforce this article by appropriate legislation.

Amendment XXVII
[Adopted 1992]

No law, varying the compensation for the services of the Senators and Representatives, shall take effect, until an election of Representatives shall have intervened.

Presidential Elections

Year	Number of States	Candidates	Parties	Popular Vote	% of Popular Vote	Electoral Vote	% Voter Participation[a]
1789	10	**George Washington**	No party			69	
		John Adams	designations			34	
		Other candidates				35	
1792	15	**George Washington**	No party			132	
		John Adams	designations			77	
		George Clinton				50	
		Other candidates				5	
1796	16	**John Adams**	Federalist			71	
		Thomas Jefferson	Democratic-Republican			68	
		Thomas Pinckney	Federalist			59	
		Aaron Burr	Democratic-Republican			30	
		Other candidates				48	
1800	16	**Thomas Jefferson**	Democratic-Republican			73	
		Aaron Burr	Democratic-Republican			73	
		John Adams	Federalist			65	
		Charles C. Pinckney	Federalist			64	
		John Jay	Federalist			1	
1804	17	**Thomas Jefferson**	Democratic-Republican			162	
		Charles C. Pinckney	Federalist			14	
1808	17	**James Madison**	Democratic-Republican			122	
		Charles C. Pinckney	Federalist			47	
		George Clinton	Democratic-Republican			6	
1812	18	**James Madison**	Democratic-Republican			128	
		DeWitt Clinton	Federalist			89	
1816	19	**James Monroe**	Democratic-Republican			183	
		Rufus King	Federalist			34	
1820	24	**James Monroe**	Democratic-Republican			231	
		John Quincy Adams	Independent Republican			1	

Presidential Elections (continued)

Year	Number of States	Candidates	Parties	Popular Vote	% of Popular Vote	Electoral Vote	% Voter Participation[a]
1824	24	**John Quincy Adams**	Democratic-Republican	108,740	30.5	84	26.9
		Andrew Jackson	Democratic-Republican	153,544	43.1	99	
		Henry Clay	Democratic-Republican	47,136	13.2	37	
		William H. Crawford	Democratic-Republican	46,618	13.1	41	
1828	24	**Andrew Jackson**	Democratic	647,286	56.0	178	57.6
		John Quincy Adams	National Republican	508,064	44.0	83	
1832	24	**Andrew Jackson**	Democratic	701,780	54.2	219	55.4
		Henry Clay	National Republican	484,205	37.4	49	
		Other candidates		107,988	8.0	18	
1836	26	**Martin Van Buren**	Democratic	764,176	50.8	170	57.8
		William H. Harrison	Whig	550,816	36.6	73	
		Hugh L. White	Whig	146,107	9.7	26	
1840	26	**William H. Harrison**	Whig	1,274,624	53.1	234	80.2
		Martin Van Buren	Democratic	1,127,781	46.9	60	
1844	26	**James K. Polk**	Democratic	1,338,464	49.6	170	78.9
		Henry Clay	Whig	1,300,097	48.1	105	
		James G. Birney	Liberty	62,300	2.3		
1848	30	**Zachary Taylor**	Whig	1,360,967	47.4	163	72.7
		Lewis Cass	Democratic	1,222,342	42.5	127	
		Martin Van Buren	Free Soil	291,263	10.1		
1852	31	**Franklin Pierce**	Democratic	1,601,117	50.9	254	69.6
		Winfield Scott	Whig	1,385,453	44.1	42	
		John P. Hale	Free Soil	155,825	5.0		
1856	31	**James Buchanan**	Democratic	1,832,955	45.3	174	78.9
		John C. Frémont	Republican	1,339,932	33.1	114	
		Millard Fillmore	American	871,731	21.6		
1860	33	**Abraham Lincoln**	Republican	1,865,593	39.8	180	81.2
		Stephen A. Douglas	Democratic	1,382,713	29.5	12	
		John C. Breckinridge	Democratic	848,356	18.1	72	
		John Bell	Constitutional Union	592,906	12.6	39	

Year	Number of States	Candidates	Parties	Popular Vote	% of Popular Vote	Electoral Vote	% Voter Participation[a]
1864	36	**Abraham Lincoln**	Republican	2,206,938	55.0	212	73.8
		George B. McClellan	Democratic	1,803,787	45.0	21	
1868	37	**Ulysses S. Grant**	Republican	3,013,421	52.7	214	78.1
		Horatio Seymour	Democratic	2,706,829	47.3	80	
1872	37	**Ulysses S. Grant**	Republican	3,596,745	55.6	286	71.3
		Horace Greeley[b]	Democratic	2,843,446	43.9		
1876	38	**Rutherford B. Hayes**	Republican	4,036,572	48.0	185	81.8
		Samuel J. Tilden	Democratic	4,284,020	51.0	184	
1880	38	**James A. Garfield**	Republican	4,453,295	48.5	214	79.4
		Winfield S. Hancock	Democratic	4,414,082	48.1	155	
		James B. Weaver	Greenback-Labor	308,578	3.4		
1884	38	**Grover Cleveland**	Democratic	4,879,507	48.5	219	77.5
		James G. Blaine	Republican	4,850,293	48.2	182	
		Benjamin F. Butler	Greenback-Labor	175,370	1.8		
		John P. St. John	Prohibition	150,369	1.5		
1888	38	**Benjamin Harrison**	Republican	5,447,129	47.9	233	79.3
		Grover Cleveland	Democratic	5,537,857	48.6	168	
		Clinton B. Fisk	Prohibition	249,506	2.2		
		Anson J. Streeter	Union Labor	146,935	1.3		
1892	44	**Grover Cleveland**	Democratic	5,555,426	46.1	277	74.7
		Benjamin Harrison	Republican	5,182,690	43.0	145	
		James B. Weaver	People's	1,029,846	8.5	22	
		John Bidwell	Prohibition	264,133	2.2		
1896	45	**William McKinley**	Republican	7,102,246	51.1	271	79.3
		William J. Bryan	Democratic	6,492,559	47.7	176	
1900	45	**William McKinley**	Republican	7,218,491	51.7	292	73.2
		William J. Bryan	Democratic; Populist	6,356,734	45.5	155	
		John C. Wooley	Prohibition	208,914	1.5		
1904	45	**Theodore Roosevelt**	Republican	7,628,461	57.4	336	65.2
		Alton B. Parker	Democratic	5,084,223	37.6	140	
		Eugene V. Debs	Socialist	402,283	3.0		
		Silas C. Swallow	Prohibition	258,536	1.9		
1908	46	**William H. Taft**	Republican	7,675,320	51.6	321	65.4
		William J. Bryan	Democratic	6,412,294	43.1	162	
		Eugene V. Debs	Socialist	420,793	2.8		
		Eugene W. Chafin	Prohibition	253,840	1.7		

Presidential Elections (continued)

Year	Number of States	Candidates	Parties	Popular Vote	% of Popular Vote	Electoral Vote	% Voter Participation[a]
1912	48	**Woodrow Wilson**	Democratic	6,296,547	41.9	435	58.8
		Theodore Roosevelt	Progressive	4,118,571	27.4	88	
		William H. Taft	Republican	3,486,720	23.2	8	
		Eugene V. Debs	Socialist	900,672	6.0		
		Eugene W. Chafin	Prohibition	206,275	1.4		
1916	48	**Woodrow Wilson**	Democratic	9,127,695	49.4	277	61.6
		Charles E. Hughes	Republican	8,533,507	46.2	254	
		A. L. Benson	Socialist	585,113	3.2		
		J. Frank Hanly	Prohibition	220,506	1.2		
1920	48	**Warren G. Harding**	Republican	16,143,407	60.4	404	49.2
		James M. Cox	Democratic	9,130,328	34.2	127	
		Eugene V. Debs	Socialist	919,799	3.4		
		P. P. Christensen	Farmer-Labor	265,411	1.0		
1924	48	**Calvin Coolidge**	Republican	15,718,211	54.0	382	48.9
		John W. Davis	Democratic	8,385,283	28.8	136	
		Robert M. La Follette	Progressive	4,831,289	16.6	13	
1928	48	**Herbert C. Hoover**	Republican	21,391,993	58.2	444	56.9
		Alfred E. Smith	Democratic	15,016,169	40.9	87	
1932	48	**Franklin D. Roosevelt**	Democratic	22,821,857	57.4	472	56.9
		Herbert C. Hoover	Republican	15,761,841	39.7	59	
		Norman Thomas	Socialist	884,781	2.2		
1936	48	**Franklin D. Roosevelt**	Democratic	27,752,869	60.8	523	61.0
		Alfred M. Landon	Republican	16,674,665	36.5	8	
		William Lemke	Union	882,479	1.9		
1940	48	**Franklin D. Roosevelt**	Democratic	27,307,819	54.8	449	62.5
		Wendell L. Willkie	Republican	22,321,018	44.8	82	
1944	48	**Franklin D. Roosevelt**	Democratic	25,606,585	53.5	432	55.9
		Thomas E. Dewey	Republican	22,014,745	46.0	99	
1948	48	**Harry S Truman**	Democratic	24,179,345	49.6	303	53.0
		Thomas E. Dewey	Republican	21,991,291	45.1	189	
		J. Strom Thurmond	States' Rights	1,176,125	2.4	39	
		Henry A. Wallace	Progressive	1,157,326	2.4		

Year	Number of States	Candidates	Parties	Popular Vote	% of Popular Vote	Electoral Vote	% Voter Participation[a]
1952	48	**Dwight D. Eisenhower**	Republican	33,936,234	55.1	442	63.3
		Adlai E. Stevenson	Democratic	27,314,992	44.4	89	
1956	48	**Dwight D. Eisenhower**	Republican	35,590,472	57.6	457	60.6
		Adlai E. Stevenson	Democratic	26,022,752	42.1	73	
1960	50	**John F. Kennedy**	Democratic	34,226,731	49.7	303	62.8
		Richard M. Nixon	Republican	34,108,157	49.5	219	
1964	50	**Lyndon B. Johnson**	Democratic	43,129,566	61.1	486	61.7
		Barry M. Goldwater	Republican	27,178,188	38.5	52	
1968	50	**Richard M. Nixon**	Republican	33,045,480	43.4	301	60.6
		Hubert H. Humphrey	Democratic	31,850,140	42.7	191	
		George C. Wallace	American Independent	171,422	13.5	46	
1972	50	**Richard M. Nixon**	Republican	47,169,911	60.7	520	55.2
		George S. McGovern	Democratic	29,170,383	37.5	17	
		John G. Schmitz	American	1,099,482	1.4		
1976	50	**James E. Carter**	Democratic	40,830,763	50.1	297	53.5
		Gerald R. Ford	Republican	39,147,793	48.0	240	
1980	50	**Ronald W. Reagan**	Republican	43,904,153	50.7	489	52.6
		James E. Carter	Democratic	35,483,883	41.0	49	
		John B. Anderson	Independent	5,720,060	6.6		
		Ed Clark	Libertarian	921,299	1.1		
1984	50	**Ronald W. Reagan**	Republican	54,455,075	58.8	525	53.3
		Walter F. Mondale	Democratic	37,577,185	40.6	13	
1988	50	**George H. W. Bush**	Republican	48,886,097	53.4	426	50.1
		Michael S. Dukakis	Democratic	41,809,074	45.6	111[c]	
1992	50	**William J. Clinton**	Democratic	44,909,326	43.0	370	55.2
		George H. W. Bush	Republican	39,103,882	37.4	168	
		H. Ross Perot	Independent	19,741,048	18.9		
1996	50	**William J. Clinton**	Democratic	47,402,357	49.2	379	49.1
		Robert J. Dole	Republican	39,196,755	40.7	159	
		H. Ross Perot	Reform	8,085,402	8.4		
		Ralph Nader	Green	684,902	0.7		
2000	50	**George W. Bush**	Republican	50,456,169	47.9	271	51.2
		Albert Gore	Democratic	50,996,116	48.4	266	
		Ralph Nader	Green	2,783,728	2.7		

Presidential Elections (continued)

Year	Number of States	Candidates	Parties	Popular Vote	% of Popular Vote	Electoral Vote	% Voter Participation[a]
2004	50	**George W. Bush**	Republican	62,039,073	50.7	286	55.3
		John F. Kerry	Democratic	59,027,478	48.2	251	
		Ralph Nader	Independent	240,896	0.2		
2008	50	**Barack Obama**	Democratic	69,498,459	53.0	365	61.7
		John McCain	Republican	59,948,283	46.0	173	
		Ralph Nader	Independent	739,165	0.55		
2012	50	**Barack Obama**	Democratic	65,907,213	51.07	332	
		Mitt Romney	Republican	60,931,767	47.21	206	
		Gary Johnson	Independent	1,275,804	0.99		
2016	50	**Donald J. Trump**	Republican	62,984,825	46.1	304	59.7
		Hillary Clinton	Democratic	65,853,516	48.2	227	

Candidates receiving less than 1 percent of the popular vote have been omitted. Thus the percentage of popular vote given for any election year may not total 100 percent.

Before the passage of the Twelfth Amendment in 1804, the electoral college voted for two presidential candidates; the runner-up became vice president.

Before 1824, most presidential electors were chosen by state legislatures, not by popular vote.

[a]Percent of voting-age population casting ballots.

[b]Greeley died shortly after the election; the electors supporting him then divided their votes among minor candidates.

[c]One elector from West Virginia cast her electoral college presidential ballot for Lloyd Bentsen, the Democratic Party's vice-presidential candidate.

Presidents and Vice Presidents

		Office	Term of Service
1st	**George Washington**	President	1789–1797
	John Adams	Vice President	1789–1797
2nd	**John Adams**	President	1797–1801
	Thomas Jefferson	Vice President	1797–1801
3rd	**Thomas Jefferson**	President	1801–1809
	Aaron Burr	Vice President	1801–1805
	George Clinton	Vice President	1805–1809
4th	**James Madison**	President	1809–1817
	George Clinton	Vice President	1809–1813
	Elbridge Gerry	Vice President	1813–1817
5th	**James Monroe**	President	1817–1825
	Daniel Tompkins	Vice President	1817–1825
6th	**John Quincy Adams**	President	1825–1829
	John C. Calhoun	Vice President	1825–1829
7th	**Andrew Jackson**	President	1829–1837
	John C. Calhoun	Vice President	1829–1833
	Martin Van Buren	Vice President	1833–1837
8th	**Martin Van Buren**	President	1837–1841
	Richard M. Johnson	Vice President	1837–1841
9th	**William H. Harrison**	President	1841
	John Tyler	Vice President	1841
10th	**John Tyler**	President	1841–1845
	None	Vice President	
11th	**James K. Polk**	President	1845–1849
	George M. Dallas	Vice President	1845–1849
12th	**Zachary Taylor**	President	1849–1850
	Millard Fillmore	Vice President	1849–1850
13th	**Millard Fillmore**	President	1850–1853
	None	Vice President	
14th	**Franklin Pierce**	President	1853–1857
	William R. King	Vice President	1853–1857
15th	**James Buchanan**	President	1857–1861
	John C. Breckinridge	Vice President	1857–1861
16th	**Abraham Lincoln**	President	1861–1865
	Hannibal Hamlin	Vice President	1861–1865
	Andrew Johnson	Vice President	1865

Presidents and Vice Presidents (continued)

		Office	Term of Service
17th	**Andrew Johnson**	President	1865–1869
	None	Vice President	
18th	**Ulysses S. Grant**	President	1869–1877
	Schuyler Colfax	Vice President	1869–1873
	Henry Wilson	Vice President	1873–1877
19th	**Rutherford B. Hayes**	President	1877–1881
	William A. Wheeler	Vice President	1877–1881
20th	**James A. Garfield**	President	1881
	Chester A. Arthur	Vice President	1881
21st	**Chester A. Arthur**	President	1881–1885
	None	Vice President	
22nd	**Grover Cleveland**	President	1885–1889
	Thomas A. Hendricks	Vice President	1885–1889
23rd	**Benjamin Harrison**	President	1889–1893
	Levi P. Morton	Vice President	1889–1893
24th	**Grover Cleveland**	President	1893–1897
	Adlai E. Stevenson	Vice President	1893–1897
25th	**William McKinley**	President	1897–1901
	Garret A. Hobart	Vice President	1897–1901
	Theodore Roosevelt	Vice President	1901
26th	**Theodore Roosevelt**	President	1901–1909
	Charles Fairbanks	Vice President	1905–1909
27th	**William H. Taft**	President	1909–1913
	James S. Sherman	Vice President	1909–1913
28th	**Woodrow Wilson**	President	1913–1921
	Thomas R. Marshall	Vice President	1913–1921
29th	**Warren G. Harding**	President	1921–1923
	Calvin Coolidge	Vice President	1921–1923
30th	**Calvin Coolidge**	President	1923–1929
	Charles G. Dawes	Vice President	1925–1929
31st	**Herbert C. Hoover**	President	1929–1933
	Charles Curtis	Vice President	1929–1933
32nd	**Franklin D. Roosevelt**	President	1933–1945
	John N. Garner	Vice President	1933–1941
	Henry A. Wallace	Vice President	1941–1945
	Harry S Truman	Vice President	1945

		Office	Term of Service
33rd	**Harry S Truman**	President	1945–1953
	Alben W. Barkley	Vice President	1949–1953
34th	**Dwight D. Eisenhower**	President	1953–1961
	Richard M. Nixon	Vice President	1953–1961
35th	**John F. Kennedy**	President	1961–1963
	Lyndon B. Johnson	Vice President	1961–1963
36th	**Lyndon B. Johnson**	President	1963–1969
	Hubert H. Humphrey	Vice President	1965–1969
37th	**Richard M. Nixon**	President	1969–1974
	Spiro T. Agnew	Vice President	1969–1973
	Gerald R. Ford	Vice President	1973–1974
38th	**Gerald R. Ford**	President	1974–1977
	Nelson A. Rockefeller	Vice President	1974–1977
39th	**James E. Carter**	President	1977–1981
	Walter F. Mondale	Vice President	1977–1981
40th	**Ronald W. Reagan**	President	1981–1989
	George H. W. Bush	Vice President	1981–1989
41st	**George H. W. Bush**	President	1989–1993
	J. Danforth Quayle	Vice President	1989–1993
42nd	**William J. Clinton**	President	1993–2001
	Albert A. Gore	Vice President	1993–2001
43rd	**George W. Bush**	President	2001–2009
	Richard B. Cheney	Vice President	2001–2009
44th	**Barack H. Obama**	President	2009–2017
	Joseph R. Biden	Vice President	2009–2017
45th	**Donald J. Trump**	President	2017–
	Michael R. Pence	Vice President	2017–

Justices of the Supreme Court

	Term of Service	Years of Service	Life Span
John Jay	1789–1795	5	1745–1829
John Rutledge	1789–1791	1	1739–1800
William Cushing	1789–1810	20	1732–1810
James Wilson	1789–1798	8	1742–1798
John Blair	1789–1796	6	1732–1800
Robert H. Harrison	1789–1790	—	1745–1790
James Iredell	1790–1799	9	1751–1799
Thomas Johnson	1791–1793	1	1732–1819
William Paterson	1793–1806	13	1745–1806
*John Rutledge**	1795	—	1739–1800
Samuel Chase	1796–1811	15	1741–1811
Oliver Ellsworth	1796–1800	4	1745–1807
Bushrod Washington	1798–1829	31	1762–1829
Alfred Moore	1799–1804	4	1755–1810
John Marshall	1801–1835	34	1755–1835
William Johnson	1804–1834	30	1771–1834
H. Brockholst Livingston	1806–1823	16	1757–1823
Thomas Todd	1807–1826	18	1765–1826
Joseph Story	1811–1845	33	1779–1845
Gabriel Duval	1811–1835	24	1752–1844
Smith Thompson	1823–1843	20	1768–1843
Robert Trimble	1826–1828	2	1777–1828
John McLean	1829–1861	32	1785–1861
Henry Baldwin	1830–1844	14	1780–1844
James M. Wayne	1835–1867	32	1790–1867
Roger B. Taney	1836–1864	28	1777–1864
Philip P. Barbour	1836–1841	4	1783–1841
John Catron	1837–1865	28	1786–1865
John McKinley	1837–1852	15	1780–1852
Peter V. Daniel	1841–1860	19	1784–1860
Samuel Nelson	1845–1872	27	1792–1873
Levi Woodbury	1845–1851	5	1789–1851
Robert C. Grier	1846–1870	23	1794–1870
Benjamin R. Curtis	1851–1857	6	1809–1874
John A. Campbell	1853–1861	8	1811–1889
Nathan Clifford	1858–1881	23	1803–1881
Noah H. Swayne	1862–1881	18	1804–1884
Samuel F. Miller	1862–1890	28	1816–1890
David Davis	1862–1877	14	1815–1886

	Term of Service	Years of Service	Life Span
Stephen J. Field	1863–1897	34	1816–1899
Salmon P. Chase	1864–1873	8	1808–1873
William Strong	1870–1880	10	1808–1895
Joseph P. Bradley	1870–1892	22	1813–1892
Ward Hunt	1873–1882	9	1810–1886
Morrison R. Waite	1874–1888	14	1816–1888
John M. Harlan	1877–1911	34	1833–1911
William B. Woods	1880–1887	7	1824–1887
Stanley Mathews	1881–1889	7	1824–1889
Horace Gray	1882–1902	20	1828–1902
Samuel Blatchford	1882–1893	11	1820–1893
Lucius Q. C. Lamar	1888–1893	5	1825–1893
Melville W. Fuller	1888–1910	21	1833–1910
David J. Brewer	1890–1910	20	1837–1910
Henry B. Brown	1890–1906	16	1836–1913
George Shiras Jr.	1892–1903	10	1832–1924
Howell E. Jackson	1893–1895	2	1832–1895
Edward D. White	1894–1910	16	1845–1921
Rufus W. Peckham	1895–1909	14	1838–1909
Joseph McKenna	1898–1925	26	1843–1926
Oliver W. Holmes	1902–1932	30	1841–1935
William D. Day	1903–1922	19	1849–1923
William H. Moody	1906–1910	3	1853–1917
Horace H. Lurton	1910–1914	4	1844–1914
Charles E. Hughes	1910–1916	5	1862–1948
Willis Van Devanter	1911–1937	26	1859–1941
Joseph R. Lamar	1911–1916	5	1857–1916
Edward D. White	1910–1921	11	1845–1921
Mahlon Pitney	1912–1922	10	1858–1924
James C. McReynolds	1914–1941	26	1862–1946
Louis D. Brandeis	1916–1939	22	1856–1941
John H. Clarke	1916–1922	6	1857–1945
William H. Taft	1921–1930	8	1857–1930
George Sutherland	1922–1938	15	1862–1942
Pierce Butler	1922–1939	16	1866–1939
Edward T. Sanford	1923–1930	7	1865–1930
Harlan F. Stone	1925–1941	16	1872–1946
Charles E. Hughes	1930–1941	11	1862–1948
Owen J. Roberts	1930–1945	15	1875–1955
Benjamin N. Cardozo	1932–1938	6	1870–1938
Hugo L. Black	1937–1971	34	1886–1971

Justices of the Supreme Court (continued)

	Term of Service	Years of Service	Life Span
Stanley F. Reed	1938–1957	19	1884–1980
Felix Frankfurter	1939–1962	23	1882–1965
William O. Douglas	1939–1975	36	1898–1980
Frank Murphy	1940–1949	9	1890–1949
Harlan F. Stone	1941–1946	5	1872–1946
James F. Byrnes	1941–1942	1	1879–1972
Robert H. Jackson	1941–1954	13	1892–1954
Wiley B. Rutledge	1943–1949	6	1894–1949
Harold H. Burton	1945–1958	13	1888–1964
Fred M. Vinson	1946–1953	7	1890–1953
Tom C. Clark	1949–1967	18	1899–1977
Sherman Minton	1949–1956	7	1890–1965
Earl Warren	1953–1969	16	1891–1974
John Marshall Harlan	1955–1971	16	1899–1971
William J. Brennan Jr.	1956–1990	34	1906–1997
Charles E. Whittaker	1957–1962	5	1901–1973
Potter Stewart	1958–1981	23	1915–1985
Byron R. White	1962–1993	31	1917–
Arthur J. Goldberg	1962–1965	3	1908–1990
Abe Fortas	1965–1969	4	1910–1982
Thurgood Marshall	1967–1991	24	1908–1993
Warren C. Burger	1969–1986	17	1907–1995
Harry A. Blackmun	1970–1994	24	1908–1998
Lewis F. Powell Jr.	1972–1987	15	1907–1998
William H. Rehnquist	1972–2005	33	1924–2005
John P. Stevens III	1975–2010	35	1920–
Sandra Day O'Connor	1981–2006	25	1930–
Antonin Scalia	1986–2016	30	1936–2016
Anthony M. Kennedy	1988–	—	1936–
David H. Souter	1990–2009	19	1939–
Clarence Thomas	1991–	—	1948–
Ruth Bader Ginsburg	1993–	—	1933–
Stephen Breyer	1994–	—	1938–
John G. Roberts	2005–	—	1955–
Samuel A. Alito, Jr.	2006–	—	1950–
Sonia Sotomayor	2009–	—	1954–
Elena Kagan	2010–	—	1960–
Neil Gorsuch	2017–	—	1967–

Note: Chief justices are in italics.

*Appointed and served one term, but not confirmed by the Senate.